To mom
from John
1972
~~Fro~~ Oct. 19,

Old Age

Also by Simone de Beauvoir

Autobiographical
Memoirs of a Dutiful Daughter
The Prime of Life
Force of Circumstance
A Very Easy Death

Other works
The Long March
Brigitte Bardot and the Lolita Syndrome
Djamila Boupacha
Blood of Others
She Came to Stay
America Day by Day
Must we Burn de Sade
The Second Sex
The Mandarins
All Men are Mortal

Old Age

Simone de Beauvoir

Translated by Patrick O'Brian

ANDRÉ DEUTSCH
and
WEIDENFELD AND NICOLSON

First published in Great Britain in 1972 by
André Deutsch Ltd and
George Weidenfeld and Nicolson Ltd
Copyright © Éditions Gallimard, 1970
English translation © 1972 by André Deutsch,
Weidenfeld and Nicolson and
G. P. Putnam's Sons
First published in Paris by
Éditions Gallimard under the title
La Vieillesse

ISBN 0 233 95918 1

Printed in Great Britain by
Cox & Wyman Ltd.,
London, Fakenham and Reading

Contents

Contents

Introduction

When Buddha was still Prince Siddartha he often escaped from the splendid palace in which his father kept him shut up and drove about the surrounding countryside. The first time he went out he saw a tottering, wrinkled, toothless, white-haired man, bowed, mumbling and trembling as he propped himself along on his stick. The sight astonished the prince and the charioteer told him just what it meant to be old. 'It is the world's pity,' cried Siddartha, 'that weak and ignorant beings, drunk with the vanity of youth, do not behold old age! Let us hurry back to the palace. What is the use of pleasures and delights, since I myself am the future dwelling-place of old age?'

Buddha recognized his own fate in the person of a very aged man, because, being born to save humanity, he chose to take upon himself the entirety of the human state. In this he differed from the rest of mankind, for they evade those aspects of it that distress them. And above all they evade old age. The Americans have struck the word death out of their vocabulary – they speak only of 'the dear departed': and in the same way they avoid all reference to great age. It is a forbidden subject in present-day France, too. What a furious outcry I raised when I offended against this taboo at the end of *La Force des choses*! Acknowledging that I was on the threshold of old age was tantamount to saying that old age was lying there in wait for every woman, and that it had already laid hold upon many of them. Great numbers of people, particularly old people, told me, kindly or angrily but always at great length and again and again, that old age simply did not exist! There were some who were less young than others, and that was all it amounted to. Society looks upon old age as a kind of shameful secret that it is unseemly to mention. There is a copious literature dealing with women, with children, and with young people in all their aspects: but apart from specialized works we scarcely ever find any reference whatsoever to the old. A comic-strip artist once had to re-draw a whole series because he had

1

included a pair of grandparents among his characters. 'Cut out the old folks,' he was ordered.* When I say that I am working on a study of old age people generally exclaim, 'What an extraordinary notion! . . . But you aren't old! . . . What a dismal subject.'

And that indeed is the very reason why I am writing this book. I mean to break the conspiracy of silence. Marcuse observes that the consumers' society has replaced a troubled by a clear conscience and that it condemns all feelings of guilt. But its peace of mind has to be disturbed. As far as old people are concerned this society is not only guilty but downright criminal. Sheltering behind the myths of expansion and affluence, it treats the old as outcasts. In France, where twelve per cent of the population are over sixty-five and where the proportion of old people is the highest in the world, they are condemned to poverty, decrepitude, wretchedness and despair. In the United States their lot is no happier. To reconcile this barbarous treatment with the humanist morality they profess to follow, the ruling class adopts the convenient plan of refusing to consider them as real people: if their voices were heard, the hearers would be forced to acknowledge that these were human voices. I shall compel my readers to hear them. I shall describe the position that is allotted to the old and the way in which they live: I shall tell what in fact happens inside their minds and their hearts; and what I say will not be distorted by the myths and the clichés of bourgeois culture.

Then again, society's attitude towards the old is deeply ambivalent. Generally speaking, it does not look upon the aged as belonging to one clearly-defined category. The turning-point of puberty allows the drawing of a line between the adolescent and the adult – a division that is arbitrary only within narrow limits; and at eighteen or perhaps twenty-one youths are admitted to the community of grown men. This advancement is nearly always accompanied by initiation rites. The time at which old age begins is ill-defined; it varies according to the era and the place, and nowhere do we find any initiation ceremonies that confirm the fresh status.† Throughout his life the individual retains the same political rights and duties: civil law makes not the slightest difference between a man of forty and one of a hundred. For the lawyers an aged man is as wholly responsible

* Reported by François Garrigue in *Dernières Nouvelles d'Alsace*, 12 October 1968.
† The feasts with which some societies celebrate people's sixtieth or eightieth birthdays are not of an initiatory character.

for his crimes as a young one, except in pathological cases.* In practice the aged are not looked upon as a class apart, and in any case they would not wish so to be regarded. There are books, periodicals, entertainments, radio and television programmes for children and young people: for the old there are none.† Where all these things are concerned, they are looked upon as forming part of the body of adults less elderly than themselves. Yet on the other hand, when their economic status is decided upon, society appears to think that they belong to an entirely different species: for if all that is needed to feel that one has done one's duty by them is to grant them a wretched pittance, then they have neither the same needs nor the same feelings as other men. Economists and legislators endorse this convenient fallacy when they deplore the burden that the 'non-active' lay upon the shoulders of the active population, just as though the latter were not potential non-actives and as though they were not insuring their own future by seeing to it that the aged are taken care of. For their part, the trades-unionists do not fall into this error: whenever they put forward their claims the question of retirement always plays an important part in them.

The aged do not form a body with any economic strength whatsoever and they have no possible way of enforcing their rights: and it is to the interest of the exploiting class to destroy the solidarity between the workers and the unproductive old so that there is no one at all to protect them. The myths and the clichés put out by bourgeois thought aim at holding up the elderly man as someone who is different, as *another being*. 'Adolescents who last long enough are what life makes old men out of,' observes Proust. They still retain the virtues and the faults of the men they were and still are: and this is something that public opinion chooses to overlook. If old people show the same desires, the same feelings and the same requirements as the young, the world looks upon them with disgust: in them love and jealousy seem revolting or absurd, sexuality repulsive and violence ludicrous. They are required to be a standing example of all the virtues. Above all they are called upon to display serenity: the world asserts that they possess it, and this assertion

* Mornet, the public prosecutor, began his indictment of Pétain by reminding his hearers that the law takes no account of age. In recent years the 'inquiry into personality' that comes before the trial can emphasize the age of the accused: but only as one feature among all the rest.

† *La Bonne Presse* has recently launched a periodical intended for old people. It confines itself to giving information and practical advice.

allows the world to ignore their unhappiness. The purified image of themselves that society offers the aged is that of the white-haired and venerable Sage, rich in experience, planing high above the common state of mankind: if they vary from this, then they fall below it. The counterpart of the first image is that of the old fool in his dotage, a laughing-stock for children. In any case, either by their virtue or by their degradation they stand outside humanity. The world, therefore, need feel no scruple in refusing them the minimum of support which is considered necessary for living like a human being.

We carry this ostracism so far that we even reach the point of turning it against ourselves: for in the old person that we must become, we refuse to recognize ourselves. 'Of all realities [old age] is perhaps that of which we retain a purely abstract notion longest in our lives,' says Proust with great accuracy. All men are mortal: they reflect upon this fact. A great many of them become old: almost none ever foresees this state before it is upon him. Nothing should be more expected than old age: nothing is more unforeseen. When young people, particularly girls, are asked about their future, they set the utmost limit of life at sixty. Some say, 'I shan't get that far: I'll die first.' Others even go so far as to say 'I'll kill myself first.' The adult behaves as though he will never grow old. Working men are often amazed, stupefied when the day of their retirement comes. Its date was fixed well beforehand; they knew it; they ought to have been ready for it. In fact, unless they have been thoroughly indoctrinated politically, this knowledge remains entirely outside their ken.

When the time comes nearer, and even when the day is at hand, people usually prefer old age to death. And yet at a distance it is death that we see with a clearer eye. It forms part of what is immediately possible for us: at every period of our lives its threat is there: there are times when we come very close to it and often enough it terrifies us. Whereas no one ever becomes old in a single instant: unlike Buddha, when we are young or in our prime we do not think of ourselves as already being the dwelling-place of our own future old age. Age is removed from us by an extent of time so great that it merges with eternity: such a remote future seems unreal. Then again the dead are *nothing*. This nothingness can bring about a metaphysical vertigo, but in a way it is comforting – it raises no problems. 'I shall no longer exist.' In a disappearance of this kind

4

I retain my identity.* Thinking of myself as an old person when I
am twenty or forty means thinking of myself as someone else, as
another than myself. Every metamorphosis has something frightening about it. When I was a little girl I was amazed and indeed deeply
distressed when I realized that one day I should turn into a grown-up.
But when one is young the real advantages of the adult status usually
counterbalance the wish to remain oneself, unchanged. Whereas old
age looms ahead like a calamity: even among those who are thought
well preserved, age brings with it a very obvious physical decline.
For of all species, mankind is that in which the alterations caused by
advancing years are the most striking. Animals grow thin; they
become weaker: they do not undergo a total change. We do. It
wounds one's heart to see a lovely young woman and then next to
her her reflection in the mirror of the years to come – her mother.
Lévi-Strauss says that the Nambikwara Indians have a single word
that means 'young and beautiful' and another that means 'old and
ugly'. When we look at the image of our own future provided by
the old we do not believe it: an absurd inner voice whispers that
that will never happen to us – when *that* happens it will no longer
be ourselves that it happens to. Until the moment it is upon us old
age is something that only affects other people. So it is understandable that society should manage to prevent us from seeing our
own kind, our fellow-men, when we look at the old.

We must stop cheating: the whole meaning of our life is in question
in the future that is waiting for us. If we do not know what we are
going to be, we cannot know what we are: let us recognize ourselves
in this old man or in that old woman. It must be done if we are to
take upon ourselves the entirety of our human state. And when it
is done we will no longer acquiesce in the misery of the last age;
we will no longer be indifferent, because we shall feel concerned, as
indeed we are. This misery vehemently indicts the system of exploitation in which we live. The old person who can no longer provide for
himself is always a burden. But in those societies where there is
some degree of equality – within a rural community, for example,
or among certain primitive nations – the middle-aged man is aware,
in spite of himself, that his state tomorrow will be the same as that
which he allots to the old today. That is the meaning of Grimm's
tale, versions of which are to be found in every countryside. A

---

* This identity is all the more strongly guaranteed to those who believe they have an
immortal soul.

5

peasant makes his old father eat out of a small wooden trough, apart from the rest of the family: one day he finds his son fitting little boards together. 'It's for you when you are old,' says the child. Straight away the grandfather is given back his place at the family table. The active members of the community work out compromises between their long-term and their immediate interests. Imperative necessity compels some primitive tribes to kill their aged relatives, even though they themselves have to suffer the same fate later on. In less extreme cases selfishness is moderated by foresight and by family affection. In the capitalist world, long-term interests no longer have any influence: the ruling class that determines the fate of the masses has no fear of sharing that fate. As for humanitarian feelings, they do not enter into account at all, in spite of the flood of hypo-critical words. The economy is founded upon profit; and in actual fact the entire civilization is ruled by profit. The human working stock is of interest only in so far as it is profitable. When it is no longer profitable it is tossed aside. At a congress a little while ago, Dr Leach, a Cambridge anthropologist, said, in effect, 'In a changing world, where machines have a very short run of life, men must not be used too long. Everyone over fifty-five should be scrapped.'*

The word 'scrap' expresses his meaning admirably. We are told that retirement is the time of freedom and leisure: poets have sung 'the delights of reaching port'.† These are shameless lies. Society inflicts so wretched a standard of living upon the vast majority of old people that it is almost tautological to say 'old and poor': again, most exceedingly poor people are old. Leisure does not open up new possibilities for the retired man; just when he is at last set free from compulsion and restraint, the means of making use of his liberty are taken from him. He is condemned to stagnate in boredom and loneliness, a mere throw-out. The fact that for the last fifteen or twenty years of his life a man should be no more than a reject, a piece of scrap, reveals the failure of our civilization: if we were to look upon the old as human beings, with a human life behind them, and not as so many walking corpses, this obvious truth would move us profoundly. Those who condemn the maiming, crippling system in which we live should expose this scandal. It is by concen-trating one's efforts upon the fate of the most unfortunate, the worst-used of all, that one can successfully shake a society to its

* This was written in December 1968.
† Racan's phrase.

foundations. In order to destroy the caste system, Ghandi tackled the status of the pariahs: in order to destroy the feudal family, Communist China liberated the women. Insisting that men should remain men during the last years of their life would imply a total upheaval of our society. The result cannot possibly be obtained by a few limited reforms that leave the system intact: for it is the exploitation of the workers, the pulverization of society, and the utter poverty of a culture confined to the privileged, educated few that leads to this kind of dehumanized old age. And it is this old age that makes it clear that everything has to be reconsidered, recast from the very beginning. That is why the whole problem is so carefully passed over in silence: and that is why this silence has to be shattered. I call upon my readers to help me in doing so.

Preface

Hitherto I have spoken of old age as though that expression stood for a clearly defined reality. In fact, as far as our own species is concerned old age is by no means easy to define. It is a biological phenomenon – the elderly man's organism displays certain particularities. It brings with it psychological consequences – certain forms of behaviour are rightly looked upon as being characteristic of old age. And like all human situations it has an existential dimension – it changes the individual's relationship with time and therefore his relationship with the world and with his own history. Then again man never lives in a state of nature: in his old age, as at every other period of his life, his status is imposed upon him by the society to which he belongs. What so complicates the whole problem is the close interdependence of all these points of view. Nowadays we know that it is pointless to study the physiological and the psychological aspects separately, for each governs the other; and as we shall see, this relationship is especially clear in old age – the chosen realm of psychosomatic disturbance. Yet what is termed the individual's psychic or spiritual life can only be understood in the light of his existential situation: this situation, therefore, also affects his physical organism. And the converse applies, for he experiences his relationship with time differently according to whether his body is more or less impaired.

Lastly, society takes into account the aged man's personal make-up – his decrepitude or his experience, for example – when it allots him his role and his position: and conversely. The individual is conditioned by society's theoretical and practical attitude towards him. An analytical description of the various aspects of old age is therefore not enough: each reacts upon all the others and is at the same time affected by them, and it is in the undefined flow of this circular process that old age must be understood.

That is why a study of old age must try to be exhaustive. Since my essential aim is to show the fate of the old in our present-day society, it may seem surprising that I should devote so many pages

9

to the place they occupy in what are called primitive communities and to that which they have occupied at various periods in the history of mankind. But although old age, considered as a biological fate, is a reality that goes beyond history, it is nevertheless true that this fate is experienced in a way that varies according to the social context: and conversely, the meaning or the lack of meaning that old age takes on in any given society puts that whole society to the test, since it is this that reveals the meaning or the lack of meaning of the entirety of the life leading to that old age. In order to judge our own society we have to compare the solutions it has chosen with those adopted by others through space and time. This comparison will allow us to distinguish that which is inescapable in the state of the aged; to see how far and at what cost these hardships can be eased; and hence to gauge the responsibility of the system in which we live with respect to these hardships.

Every human situation can be viewed from without – seen from the point of view of an outsider – or from within, in so far as the subject assumes and at the same time transcends it. For the outsider, the aged man is the object of a certain knowledge: the aged man himself experiences his condition at first hand – he has an immediate, living comprehension of it. In the first part of this book I shall adopt the first viewpoint: I shall examine what biology, anthropology, history and contemporary sociology have to tell us about old age. In the second I shall do my best to describe the way in which the aged man inwardly apprehends his relationship with his body, with time and with the outside world. Neither of these two inquiries will enable us to define old age *per se*: on the contrary, we shall find that it takes on a great many different aspects, no one of them being a function of the others. Both today and throughout history, the class-struggle governs the manner in which old age takes hold of a man: there is a great gulf between the aged slave and the aged patrician, between the wretchedly pensioned ex-worker and an Onassis. There are still other reasons for the differences between aged individuals, such as health, family, and so on: but here we have two classes of old people, the one extremely numerous, the other reduced to a small minority; and these two classes are brought into being by the conflict between the exploiters and the exploited. Any statement that claims to deal with old age as a whole must be challenged, for it tends to hide this chasm.

10

One question arises at the very outset. Old age is not a mere statistical fact; it is the prolongation and the last stage of a certain process. What does this process consist of? In other words, what does growing old mean? The notion is bound up with that of change. Yet the life of the foetus, of the new-born baby and of the child is one of continuous change. Must we therefore say, as some have said, that our life is a gradual death? Certainly not. A paradox of this kind disregards the basic truth of life – life is an unstable system in which balance is continually lost and continually recovered: it is inertia that is synonymous with death. Change is the law of life. And it is a particular kind of change that distinguishes ageing – an irreversible, unfavourable change; a decline. The American gerontologist Lansing suggests this definition: 'a process of unfavourable, progressive change, usually correlated with the passage of time, becoming apparent after maturity, and terminating invariably in death of the individual'.

But here we run into a difficulty straight away: what is the meaning of the word *unfavourable*? It implies a value judgement. Advance or retreat can exist only in relation to some given goal. From the moment she skied less well than her younger competitors, Marielle Goitschel was obliged to look upon herself as old – old on the plane of sport. It is within the context of life as a whole that the hierarchy of the different ages is established, and here the criteria are far less certain. We should have to know what the aim of human life was before we could tell what changes lead it nearer to the goal or farther from it.

The question is simple if all we take into account is a man's physical being, his organism. Every organism tends to go on living. To do so it has to recover its equilibrium every time it is upset; it has to defend itself from outside attack; and it must take the widest and strongest possible grip on the world. In this context the words *favourable*, *neutral* and *harmful* have a clear meaning. From birth until the age of eighteen or twenty the organism's development tends to increase its chances of survival: it grows stronger and more resistant; its resources and its possibilities increase. The individual's physical abilities, taken as a whole, reach their peak at about twenty. During the first twenty years, therefore, the sum of the changes in the organism is for the good.

There are certain alterations that lead neither to physical improvement nor to deterioration; they are neutral changes – the degeneration of the thymus in early childhood, for example, and that of the

11

cerebral neurons, whose number is very far in excess of the individual's requirements.

Some unfavourable changes occur very early. The margin of visual accommodation diminishes from the age of ten. Even before adolescence the power of hearing very high sounds does the same. At twelve a certain form of unstructured memory grows weaker. Kinsey states that in men sexual potency declines after sixteen. These very restricted losses do not prevent development throughout childhood and adolescence from following a rising curve.

After twenty, and above all after thirty, there begins a retrograde alteration in the organs. Should we, from this time on, speak of ageing? No. With mankind the body itself is not in a purely natural state; it can compensate for loss, deterioration and failure by various adjustments and automatic responses, by practical and intellectual knowledge. The word ageing does not apply so long as these deficiencies occur only now and then and so long as they are easily mitigated. When they assume considerable proportions and become incurable, then the body grows fragile and more or less decrepit: at this point it is possible to state unequivocally that it is declining.

The question becomes far more complex if we consider every side of the individual as a whole. A man begins to go down after he has reached his highest point: but where is this to be placed? Although each depends upon the other, the physical and the mental aspects do not follow a strictly parallel development. An individual may have suffered important mental impairment before his physical decline begins; or, on the contrary, it is possible that during this decline he may make important intellectual acquisitions. To which are we to attribute the greater value? Everyone will give a different answer; and his answer will show which he rates highest, physical or intellectual abilities or a happy balance between the two. It is by choices of this kind that individuals and societies establish their hierarchy of ages: and there is not a single one of these that is universally accepted.

The child surpasses the adult by the wealth of its possibilities, the vast range of its acquisitions and its emotional freshness: are we therefore to suppose that as the child grows older it deteriorates? It seems that to a certain degree this was Freud's opinion. 'Think of the saddening contrast that we find between a healthy child's radiating intelligence and the intellectual feebleness of the average adult,' he wrote. This is an idea that Montherlant has often treated at some length. 'When the genius of childhood goes out, it goes out for ever. People always say that from a worm there comes a butter-fly: with mankind, it is the butterfly that turns into the worm,' says Ferrante in *La Reine morte*.

Both of them had private reasons – very different in either case – for putting a great value upon childhood. Their opinion is not widely shared. In itself the word *maturity* shows that the world in general sets a greater worth upon the fully-grown adult than it does upon the child or the young man: the man in his prime has acquired knowledge, experience and abilities. Generally speaking, scientists, philosophers and writers consider that the individual reaches his highest point of development in the middle of his life.* Some look upon old age itself as the most desirable period: they believe that it brings experience, wisdom and peace. According to them human life experiences no falling-off.

A clear statement of what constitutes advance or retreat for man implies the knowledge of a certain goal: but there is no given *a priori* end, existing in the absolute. Every society creates its own values: and it is in the social context that the word *decline* takes on an exact meaning.

This discussion bears out what I said earlier – old age can only be understood as a whole: it is not solely a biological, but also a cultural fact.

---

* According to Hippocrates, it is reached at fifty-six. Aristotle thought that the body attained perfection at thirty-five and the soul at fifty. Dante was of the opinion that old age began to be felt at forty-five. Modern industrial societies usually retire their workers at sixty-five. I shall use the words *old*, *elderly* and *aged* for people of sixty-five and over. When I speak of others I shall state their exact age.

PART ONE

Old age seen from without

1

Old age and biology

As we have just seen, the notion of decline has, on the biological plane, a straightforward meaning; the organism declines when its chances of continuing to live are reduced. At all periods men have been aware of the inevitability of this change, and we know that they have searched for the causes of it since ancient times. The answer has depended upon the idea of life formed by medicine taken as a whole.

In Egypt and among all the nations of antiquity medicine and magic were intermingled. In ancient Greece medicine formed part of religious metaphysics or philosophy in earlier days, and it was not until Hippocrates that it stood on its own feet, becoming a science and an art, raising itself up by experiment and rational argument. Hippocrates took over Pythagoras's theory of the four humours: blood, phlegm, choler and black choler; illness is caused by their balance being upset; so is old age – a state whose beginning he set at fifty-six. He was the first to compare the stages of human life to nature's four seasons, and old age to winter. In several of his books, and especially in his *Aphorisms*, he collected exact observations on the aged. (They need less food than the young. They suffer from respiratory troubles, catarrhs that bring on fits of coughing, painful urination, pains in their joints, kidney diseases, vertigo, apoplexy, cachexy, generalized itching and drowsiness; they expel water from their intestines, eyes and nostrils; they often have cataract; their sight and hearing are poor.) He advises moderation in all fields, but he also says that they should not give up their occupations.

Hippocrates was followed by comparatively mediocre successors. Aristotle's opinions were those that had the greatest influence – opinions that were based upon speculation rather than upon

17

experiment. For him the necessary condition of life was the body's inward heat, and he likened growing old to the loss of this heat. Rome inherited the notions by which the Greeks had explained physical phenomena – temperaments, humours, crasis and pneuma. Medical knowledge in the Rome of Marcus Aurelius was no more advanced than it had been in Periclean Athens.

It was in the second century that Galen wrote his all-embracing synthesis of classical medicine. He looked upon old age as something lying between illness and health. It was not exactly a pathological condition: yet on the other hand all the old man's physiological functions were reduced and weakened. He explained this state of affairs by reconciling the theory of humours with that of inner heat. The heat derived its sustenance from the humours, and it died away when the body became dehydrated and the humours evaporated. In his *Gerocomica* he gave advice on health that continued to be respected in Europe until the nineteenth century. He maintained that according to the principle *contraria contrariis* the aged body ought to be warmed and moistened, that the old should take hot baths and drink wine, and, furthermore, that they should be active. He gave lavish and highly detailed advice upon the diet of the aged. He held up the example of the aged physician Antiochus, who still went to see his patients at eighty and who took part in the political assemblies, and of Telephos, the old grammarian, who preserved his health until he was close on a hundred.

For centuries after this, medicine merely paraphrased Galen's work. He was an authoritarian writer, convinced of his own infallibility; and at a time when people preferred belief to argument he carried the day. And, above all, he lived at a period and in a world in which the monotheism from the East was asserting itself against paganism. His theories were stamped with religiosity. He believed in the existence of a single God. He looked upon the body as the material instrument of the soul. The Fathers of the Church adopted his opinions, and so did the Jews and the Islamized Arabs. And this is why medicine made virtually no progress whatsoever throughout the whole of the Middle Ages, with the consequence that old age remained very poorly understood. Nevertheless, in the eleventh century Avicenna – he too was one of Galen's disciples – made some interesting observations on the chronic diseases and the mental troubles of the aged.

The Schoolmen loved comparing life to a flame that is fed by the

18

oil in a lamp: it was a mystical image, for in the Middle Ages the soul was often represented by a flame. On the earthly plane, the physicians were very much more concerned with prevention than with cure. The school of Salerno, where Western medicine was born and elaborated, concentrated its efforts upon the working out of 'regimens of health and long life'. A copious literature grew up with this as its theme. In the thirteenth century Roger Bacon, who looked upon age as a disease,* wrote a treatise on the hygiene of old age for Clement vi; and in this book he attached much importance to alchemy. Nevertheless he was the first to have the idea of correcting poor sight by magnifying lenses. (They were being made in Italy a little after his death in 1300. False teeth were already in use among the Estruscans: in the Middle Ages teeth were obtained from the bodies of animals or young people.) Until the end of the fifteenth century all the works on old age dealt merely with hygiene. The school of Montpellier, in its turn, drew up various regimens of health. In Italy, at the end of the fifteenth century there occurred a renaissance in science comparable with the renaissance in the arts. The physician Zerbi's *Gerontocomia* was the first monograph devoted to the pathology of old age: but he discovered nothing new.

One branch of medicine made extraordinary progress at the beginning of the Renaissance, and this was anatomy. For a thousand years men had been forbidden to dissect the human body: at the end of the fifteenth century it became possible to do so, more or less openly. It is noteworthy, but not surprising, that the founder of modern anatomy was Leonardo da Vinci: as a painter he was passionately concerned with the representation of the human body, and he longed for an exact knowledge of it. 'For my part,' he wrote, 'I have dissected more than ten cadavers, in order to acquire a full, true knowledge of the human body.' By the end of his life he had in fact dissected more than thirty, among them some of old men. He drew a great many old men's bodies and faces; and from first-hand observation he also sketched their arteries and intestines. (He made notes upon the anatomical changes that he discovered, too; but these notes were only found very much later.)

With the great master Vesalius anatomy continued to advance. But the other disciplines made no progress. Science was still steeped in metaphysics. Humanism struggled against tradition but could not manage to break free from it. In the sixteenth century Paracelsus, in

* He agreed with the opinion that Terence had expressed in classical times.

his zeal for modernity, wrote his book in German rather than in Latin. He did have certain new and striking intuitions, but they were drowned in his muddle-headed theories. According to him, man was a 'chemical compound', and old age was caused by auto-intoxication.

Up until this time the works devoted to old age were concerned only with preventive hygiene: they contained only a few scattered remarks about diagnosis and treatment. A Venetian physician, David Pomis, was the first to deal with these problems in a clear and orderly method. Some of his descriptions of senile diseases are very precise and thorough, particularly that of high blood pressure.

The seventeenth century produced many works on old age, but they are devoid of interest. In the eighteenth Galen still had his followers, among them Gerard Van Swieten. He looked upon old age as a kind of incurable disease: he made game of remedies based on alchemy or astrology: and he wrote exact descriptions of the anatomical changes brought about by the process of ageing. Meanwhile the rise of the bourgeoisie and its support of rationalism and mechanicalism brought a new school of thought into being – that of iatrophysics. Borelli and Baglivi introduced La Mettrie's ideas into medicine: the body was a machine, a combination of cylinders, spindles, wheels. The lungs were bellows. The iatrophysicists therefore took over the mechanistic theories of classical antiquity,* holding that the organism deteriorated just as a machine wears out when it has been used too long.† This view had its supporters as late as the nineteenth century, and indeed it was then that it enjoyed its greatest popularity. But the notion of 'wear' always remained very indefinite. Stahl, on the other hand, initiated the theory known as vitalism: according to this there is in man a vital principle, an entity; the weakening of this principle brings about old age and its disappearance, death.

There was a great deal of pointless wrangling between the upholders of tradition and the supporters of the new systems. Medicine was going through a time of serious difficulty as far as theory was concerned: it was no longer satisfied with the old pathology based upon the humours, and it had not yet discovered any new foundations. It was in a blind alley. Yet it did advance empirically. There were more and more post-mortems, anatomy made great strides,

---

* Those of Democritus and Epicurus, among others.
† The comparison is wholly mistaken: far from wearing out, the organs maintain themselves in good condition as they function: if they stop working they atrophy.

and this was favourable for the study of old age. In Russia, Fischer, the head of the health service, broke with Galen and produced a systematic description of the senile degeneration of the organs. In spite of its inadequacies, his work marked the beginning of an era. The Italian Morgani's huge book, appearing in 1761, was also of great importance. For the first time it established a correlation between clinical symptoms and the observations made during post-mortems: it had a section devoted to old age.

Between 1790 and 1800 there were published three books on the subject that anticipated the discoveries of the nineteenth and twentieth centuries. The American physician Rush brought out a great physiological and clinical study, based on his own experience. The German Hufeland also gathered a large number of valuable observations, and his treatise was exceedingly popular. He was a vitalist: he supposed every organism to be endowed with a certain vital energy that became exhausted in the course of time. The most important of these books was Seiler's, published in 1799; it was entirely concerned with the anatomy of the aged, and it was based upon post-mortems. It was not a particularly original work, but for many years it was one of the most valued working tools, being used until the middle of the nineteenth century.

When the nineteenth century began, the Montpellier physicians were still supporting the theory of vitalism.* Nevertheless, medicine was beginning to profit from the advances in physiology and all the experimental sciences. The studies of old age became exact and systematic. In 1817 Rostan investigated the asthma of the aged, and he discovered its relationship with a cerebral disturbance. In 1840 Prus wrote the first systematic treatise on the diseases of old age.

It was after about 1850 that geriatrics really came into existence, although it did not yet bear that name. In France it was encouraged by the setting up of huge institutions in which a great many old people were brought together. The Salpetrière was the largest in Europe, holding eight thousand patients, two or three thousand of whom were old people. There were also a great many at Bicêtre, and it therefore became an easy matter to accumulate clinical observations about them. The Salpetrière may be looked upon as the nucleus of the first geriatric establishment. It was here that Charcot gave his famous

* The theory of humours was given up, but it continued to exist upon the mythical plane. In a very well-known lecture, Faraday compared old age and death with a candle-flame that flickers and goes out. The figure still retains its life even now.

lectures upon old age – lectures that were published with very great success in 1886. At this period there were published numbers of stereotyped, commonplace works on hygiene; but on the whole preventive medicine was giving way to the idea of treatment – from now onwards the doctors were concerned with curing the old. All the more so because there were continually increasing numbers of them, first in France and then in other countries: more and more patients appeared, suffering from the degenerative diseases that are characteristic of old age. Pennock had written a book in 1847, well before Charcot, and so in 1852 had Réveillé-Parise; both studied the pulse and breathing rates among the aged. Between 1857 and 1860 Geist brought out a valuable synthesis of the geriatric literature that had appeared in Germany, France and England.

Towards the end of the nineteenth century and in the twentieth, research increased considerably. In 1895 Boy-Tessier, in 1908 Rauzier, and in 1912 Pic and Bamamour published important general surveys in France, while in 1908 very important works were brought out in Germany by Bürger and in America by Minot and Metchnikoff, and these were followed in 1915 by the zoologist Child. A few scientists still hoped, as their predecessors in earlier times had done, to explain the process of ageing by a single cause. At the end of the nineteenth century there were some who maintained that it was owing to the degeneration of the sexual glands. At the age of seventy-two, Brown-Séquard, a professor at the Collège de France, injected himself with extract of guinea-pigs' and dogs' testicles; but with no lasting result. Voronoff, also a professor at the Collège de France, thought of grafting the glands of monkeys upon elderly men: a failure. As for Metchnikoff, he adopted a modern version of the view that senility was caused by auto-intoxication. At the beginning of the twentieth century Cazalis asserted that a man was as old as his arteries – a formula that had an immense success. In his opinion atherosclerosis was the determining factor in ageing. The most widely-spread notion was that it arose from a lowering of the metabolism.

It is the American Nascher who is held to be the father of geriatrics. Born in Vienna (an important centre for the study of old age), he went to New York as a child and there he studied medicine. When he was visiting an institution with a group of students he heard an old woman tell the professor about various complaints that she was suffering from. The professor explained to her that her disease was her great age. 'What can be done about it?' asked Nascher. 'Nothing.' Nascher was so struck by this reply that he devoted himself to the study of ageing. When he was back in Vienna he went to see an old people's home: he was astonished by the length of time they lived and by their good health. 'It is because we treat our old patients in the same way as paediatricians treat children,' said his colleague. It was this that induced him to set up a special branch of medicine, one that he christened geriatrics. He published his first proposals in 1909; in 1912 he founded the Society of Geriatry in New York; and in 1914 he brought out a new book on the problem. He had difficulty in finding a publisher – the subject was thought uninteresting.

Of recent years, side by side with geriatrics another science has developed, the science that is now called gerontology: it does not inquire into the pathology of old age but into the ageing process itself. At the beginning of this century, biological research on old age was a mere by-product of other work: scientists investigating the life of plants and animals were interested in the alterations they underwent as they grew older; but this interest was of a secondary character. Many specialized works were devoted to childhood and adolescence: old age was not studied for its own sake, largely because of the taboos that I have mentioned.* It was a disagreeable subject. Almost the only considerable work upon it between 1914 and 1930 was that of Carrel, whose ideas were widely known in France. He went back to the notion that old age was a form of auto-intoxication caused by the products of cellular metabolism.

After this period the position changed. In the United States the number of aged persons had doubled between 1900 and 1930, and it doubled again between 1930 and 1950: the industrialization of society brought about the concentration of great numbers of old people in the towns and this caused serious problems. The many inquiries that were launched in an attempt at finding a solution focused attention upon the aged, and this led to a desire to know more about them. From 1930 onwards research on biology, psychology and sociology increased; and this also applied to other countries. A national congress on senescence was held in Kiev in 1938, and in the same year Bastaï and Pogliatti published their great general survey in France, while the first specialized periodical began publication in Germany. In 1939 a group of English scientists and

* The American gerontologist Birren observes that research on old age may cause a feeling of discomfort. But today, he says, science takes no notice of this.

medical men decided to found an international club for research on old age. In the United States Cowdry brought out his monumental work *Problems of Ageing.*

Work slowed down during the war. But as soon as it was over research began again. In 1945 a gerontological society was formed in the United States; in 1946 a second periodical devoted to old age began to appear, and this was followed by similar publications in many other countries. In England Lord Nuffield set up the handsomely endowed Nuffield Foundation: it began to study geriatrics and to inquire into the condition of the aged in Great Britain. In France these studies, encouraged by Léon Binet, took on fresh vigour. An international gerontological association was founded at Liège in 1950, and it held a congress there in the same year, followed by others at Saint Louis (Missouri) in 1951, London in 1954, and by many more in subsequent years. Research associations came into being in a great number of countries. By 1954 a bibliographical index on gerontology drawn up in the United States gave nineteen thousand references. According to Dr Destrem this figure should now be multiplied by two. As far as France is concerned, 1958 saw the foundation of the *Société française de gérontologie*; and in the same year the *Centre d'études et de recherches gérontologiques* was set up, with Professor Bourlière at its head. Important works appeared – the treatise of Grailly and Destrem in 1953, and that of Binet and Bourlière in 1955. In 1954 the *Revue française de gérontologie* was founded. And lastly a special social hygiene commission was set up in Paris to deal with the problems of old age. In the States, the University of Chicago produced three works in 1959 and 1960 that constitute positive epitomes of our knowledge of old age from the individual and the social points of view in America and Western Europe.

Gerontology has developed on three planes – the biological, the psychological and the social. In all these fields it remains faithful to the same positivist bias: it is not a question of explaining why the phenomena occur but rather of giving a synthetic description, as exact as possible, of their manifestations.

Modern medicine no longer claims that biological ageing has a given cause; it looks upon it as something that is inherent in the life-process, forming part of it in the same way as birth, growth, reproduction, and death. Dr Escoffier-Lambiotte, referring to McCay's experiments on rats,* made this striking observation: 'So it appears that ageing and subsequent death are not related to a certain level of expenditure of energy, a given number of heart-beats, but that they occur when a set programme of growth and ripening reaches its end.' In other words, ageing is not a mere mechanical contingency, something non-essential; it seems that from the very beginning every organism contains its own old age, the inevitable consequence of its full completion,† and in this it resembles death which, as Rilke puts it, 'each man bears within himself, just as a fruit enfolds its stone'.

The general opinion is now that ageing is a process that is common to all living beings. Until recently it was thought that the cells themselves were immortal and that it was only the associations of cells, their combined forms, that came apart with the passage of the years. Carrel maintained this point of view, and he thought he had proved it. But recent experiments have shown that the cells too change with time. According to the American biologist Orgel age brings about failures in the system that normally provides an exactly determined programming of the production of cell protein. But then again, biochemical research is still in its early stages.

The physiological characteristic of ageing in man is what Dr Destrem calls 'an unfavourable transformation of the tissues'. The quantity of metabolically active tissues diminishes while that of the metabolically inert increases – these are the interstitial and fibro-sclerous tissues, and they undergo dehydration and fatty degeneration. There is a pronounced lessening in the ability to initiate cellular regeneration. The advance of interstitial tissue in relation to the higher tissues is particularly striking in the main organs and there is a marked weakening of certain functions, which deteriorate continuously until death. Biochemical phenomena occur: there is an increase in sodium, chlorine and calcium; a decrease in potash, magnesium, phosphorus and protein-synthesis.†

The individual's appearance changes, and this change allows his

* McCay showed that rats whose growth was retarded in youth by a 'calory-restriction in their food' lived far longer than rats that were fed normally. The life of one of these under-nourished rats was almost twice as long as the average for the control-group.

† Of course, accidents and abnormalities of every kind may bring life to an end before the completion of the programme, above all among human beings: as far as man is concerned, it would be pointless to study his biological fate in isolation, since he never lives in a state of nature and since the community in which he lives governs his development.

age to be estimated to within a few years. The hair whitens and grows sparse: the reason for this is unknown, and the mechanical process by which the capillary bulb loses its pigment has not been discovered. The hair whitens, yet at the same time it makes its appearance in new places – on the chins of old women, for instance. As a consequence of dehydration and of the loss of elasticity in the underlying dermal tissues the skin becomes wrinkled. The teeth drop out. In August 1957 it was reckoned that there were 21·6 million toothless people in the United States, or thirteen per cent of the population. The loss of teeth brings about a shortening of the lower part of the face, so that the nose, lengthened vertically by the atrophy of its elastic tissues, comes nearer to the chin. The growth of skin in the aged causes a thickening of the eyelids, while at the same time hollows appear beneath the eyes. The upper lip becomes thinner: the lobe of the ear increases in size. There are changes in the skeleton, too. With the compression of the spinal discs the vertebrae come closer together; the spine is bowed. Between forty-five and eighty-five men's chest measurements diminish by ten centimetres and women's by fifteen. The shoulders become less wide, the pelvis broader: the thorax tends to assume a sagittal shape, particularly in the case of women. Muscular atrophy and the sclerosis of the joints cause difficulties in working and movement. The skeleton suffers from osteoporosis: the dense part of the bone becomes spongy and fragile, and this is why a fracture of the head of the femur, which supports the body's weight, is a common accident.

The heart does not change much, but its functioning deteriorates: it progressively loses its powers of adaptation, and its owner has to reduce his activities in order to take care of it. The circulatory system is affected: atherosclerosis is not the cause of ageing, but it is one of its most invariable characteristics. We do not know exactly what brings it about – some attribute it to disturbed hormones, others to over-high blood-pressure; but the usual opinion is that the chief cause is an imperfect metabolism of lipids. The consequences of atherosclerosis vary. Sometimes the brain is affected. In any event, the cerebral circulation is diminished. The veins lose their elasticity, the heart's output declines, the circulation becomes slower and the blood-pressure rises. Yet it should be pointed out that although high blood-pressure is very dangerous in middle age, old people put up with it very well. The brain's consumption of oxygen diminishes. The thoracic cage becomes more rigid, and the respiratory capacity,

26

which is five litres at twenty-five, drops to three at the age of eighty-five. Muscular strength declines. The motor nerves do not convey stimuli so fast, and the reactions are slower. The kidneys, liver and digestive glands degenerate. The sense organs are affected. The power of visual accommodation diminishes. Presbyopia is an almost universal phenomenon among the old; and as the sight becomes less keen so its power of differentiation declines. This applies to the hearing as well, and it often goes as far as positive deafness. Touch, taste and smell are all less sensitive than they were.

The involution of the ductless glands is one of the most usual and the most obvious consequences of ageing: it is accompanied by an involution of the sexual organs. Certain precise facts have recently been established on this subject.* There is no special anomaly in the spermatozoa of the aged man: theoretically the fertilization of the ovule by his sperm remains indefinitely possible. There is no general law upon the cessation of spermatogenesis, only specific cases. Nevertheless, erection is two or three times slower than in youth. (The morning erections that occur even at a very advanced age are not of a sexual nature.) Erection can be preserved for a long period without ejaculation, this control being due both to experience in coitus and to a diminution in the sexual response. The detumescence after orgasm is exceedingly rapid, and the old man is unmoved by fresh stimuli for a far longer period than the young.

With young men ejaculation takes place in two stages: first the expulsion of the seminal fluid into the prostatic urethra and then its movement through the urethra to the urethral meatus and so to the exterior: in the first stage the subject feels that the ejaculation must inevitably occur. Generally speaking, the aged man feels nothing of the kind. In his case the process is reduced to a single stage and he often has the impression of a seeping rather than of an expulsion. The possibilities of erection and of ejaculation diminish and even disappear with age. But impotence does not always bring about the extinction of the libido.

In women, the reproductive function is suddenly interrupted at a comparatively early age. This phenomenon is unique in the ageing process, which in every other respect is a continuous development; and it takes place at about fifty with the menopause – the abrupt termination of the ovarian cycle and of menstruation. The ovaries

* Particularly by Masters and Johnson in *Sexual Reactions* (1966).

harden, and the woman can no longer be made pregnant. The sexual steroids* vanish and the sexual organs degenerate.

There is a widely-held belief that old people sleep badly. In fact, according to an inquiry carried out in the French institutions in 1959, they sleep for more than seven hours a night. Yet dysomnia is observed among some of them. They find it difficult to go to sleep, or they wake up early, or their sleep is interspersed with short waking periods: the reasons for these anomalies may be physiological, biological or psychological. After the age of eighty, almost all doze during the day.

The organic involution of the aged, taken as a whole, brings with it a 'fatigability' that spares none: physical effort is possible for the aged only within strict limits. The old resist infection better than the young, but their impoverished organisms have little defence against the attacks of the outside world – the degeneration of the organs reduces the margin of safety that allows resistance. Some physicians go so far as to look upon old age as virtually the same as a disease: this was the view expressed recently† by the well-known Romanian geriatrician Dr Aslan in an interview that she gave in Italy. I cannot agree with this assimilation of the two: disease is contingent, whereas ageing is the law of life itself. Yet the phrase 'old and frail' is almost a tautology. 'Growing old, that summary of infirmity,' wrote Péguy. Dr Johnson said, 'My diseases are an asthma and a dropsy, and what is less curable, seventy-five years.' Speaking to an old woman who was wearing spectacles, a physician asked, 'What is your trouble, Madame? Long sight or short?' 'My trouble is old age, Doctor.'

There is a mutual relationship between old age and disease: disease hastens ageing and age renders the old person more subject to pathological disturbances, especially to those degenerative processes that are characteristic of it. It is most unusual to come across what might be called 'old age in the pure state'. Old people are overtaken by a chronic polypathology.

If we take a hundred old people who are sick and a hundred young, it will be found that the proportion of those who see doctors or buy medicines is far higher in the second group. On the other hand, the old amount to only about twelve per cent of the population: yet they represent a third of those admitted to hospital in France and

* Products of the ductless glands.
† Written in October 1969.

28

half of the patients in the wards at any given time, since they stay longer than the rest. In America they amounted to no more than a twelfth part of the population in 1955, yet they occupied a fifth of the hospital beds. In the same year an inquiry carried out in California showed that the number of medical consultations increased with age. They were fifty per cent more frequent for old women than for old men. It is also the women who form the majority in the hospitals. They live longer than men, but throughout the course of their lives they are more often ill.* Taking the United States as a whole, the number of chronic sick is on the average four times greater among the old than among the others. Inquiries made in Australia and Holland have given similar results.

The old suffer chiefly from 'ill-defined discomfort' and rheumatism. One set of American statistics shows the main diseases of the aged as arthritis, various forms of rheumatism, and heart diseases. Another gives heart diseases, arthritis, rheumatism, nephritis, high blood-pressure, and atherosclerosis. Still another gives disturbed coordination, rheumatism, respiratory, digestive and nervous diseases. Dr Vignat, studying hospitalized old people at Lyons, found that they suffered, in decreasing order, from cardio-vascular, respiratory and mental diseases, tabes, vascular and neurological diseases, cancer,† disturbances of the locomotor apparatus and digestive troubles. Old age being the most favourable of all fields for psychosomatic disorders, organic diseases are also closely related to psychological factors.

To tell the truth, in many cases it is often impossible to separate the two sets of causes. Take accidents, for example – and accidents are comparatively frequent among old people. They are the result of certain forms of behaviour that bring intellectual faculties such as attention and perception into play, and of emotional attitudes such as indifference, self-neglect and lack of will-power. But on the other hand they are also largely to be explained by disturbed orientation, giddiness, muscular stiffness and the fragility of the bones. It

---

* In the United States the National Health Survey found that during the year 1957–8 people of between forty-five and sixty-four had been disabled by illness for an average of twenty-five days; those of over sixty-five for fifty days; and those above seventy-five for seventy-two days.

† Cancer has no relation to age as such. Although it usually appears between fifty and eighty, this is because of the manner in which the cancerigenic agents work. The number of deaths caused by cancer is high because modern medicine can successfully deal with a great many other diseases but has not yet managed to overcome this one.

is therefore proper that they should be mentioned here. In the group examined by the National Health Survey, thirty-three per cent of the men and twenty-three per cent of the women had had an accident causing one day or more of disability in the course of the year. Out of a hundred thousand persons aged between forty-five and fifty-five there was an average of fifty-two accidents a year: for those over seventy-five the average rose to 338. These accidents are above all falls at home, sometimes leading to death. The old are often victims of traffic-accidents, too, since it is hard for them to move and their sight is poor. Many stop going out.

Some inquiries provide optimistic information on the health of the aged: but we have to know the exact meaning that the investigators give to their words. According to the report that Sheldon brought out in the United States in 1948, only twenty-nine per cent of the 471 persons of over sixty were found to be below normal. There were many people in their eighties in this group: 2·5 per cent of them were bedridden; 8·5 per cent confined to their homes; twenty-two per cent went no farther than the immediate neighbourhood; forty-six per cent were completely normal and 24·5 per cent were unusually vigorous. Very well. But what norm was Sheldon basing himself upon? Was it that which he would have applied to a man in his forties? Surely not. More exact information is provided by an inquiry conducted in Sheffield in 1955: out of 476 people over sixty-one, 54·9 per cent of the women and 71·2 per cent of the men were still fully active. Similar results were obtained in Holland in 1954 and 1957. Activity does indeed imply a certain degree of health: but there are many reasons, both psychological and social, that may induce people to remain active even when they are in a very bad physical condition.

One point that arises from all these findings is that there are great differences between individuals of the same age. Chronological and biological ages do not always coincide – far from it; and physical appearance tells more about the number of years we have lived than physiological examination. The years do not weigh with the same burden upon all shoulders. Ageing, says the American gerontologist Howell, 'is not a simple slope which everyone slides down at the same speed. It is a flight of irregular stairs down which some journey more quickly than others.'* There is one disease, known as

* 'For certain people the measure of time itself may move faster or more slow,' says Proust.

progeria, which causes all the patient's organs to age prematurely.*
On 12 January 1968 a child of ten died at Chatham hospital in
Canada, and this child had all the outward appearance of a woman
of ninety. One of her brothers had died of the same disease at the
age of eleven. Dr Dénard-Toulet told me of a woman of forty-five
who died as a consequence of the senile degeneration of her organs.
Apart from these very unusual cases, there are many factors that
increase or diminish the speed of the decline – health, heredity,
environment, emotion, former habits, and the standard of living. It
takes on different forms, according to what functions deteriorate
first. Sometimes it is a continuous process; at others a subject who
up until that time seemed to be just about his age or even less will
suddenly 'turn old'. It is not the organs that abruptly lose their
powers in the case of illness, stress, bereavement or serious misfortune: it is the build-up which hid their deficiencies that falls to
pieces. The individual's body had in fact undergone the decay, the
involution of age, but he had successfully dealt with the situation
by conscious or unconscious compensatory reactions; all at once he
can no longer make use of these forms of defence and his latent
old age becomes apparent. The spiritual or psychological collapse
has physical repercussions, and it may even lead to death. I have
been told of a very well preserved woman of sixty-three who bravely
put up with the violent pain for which she was being treated. A
house-physician having stupidly told her that she would never get
well, she immediately aged by twenty years and her pain grew worse.
An important setback, such as the loss of a law-suit, can turn a man
of sixty into an aged person, both physically and mentally.

Yet on the other hand, if there is no sudden shock of this kind
and if he retains his health, the subject may go on compensating for
his lost powers to a very considerable age. Thanks to long technical
experience and to a precise knowledge of their own bodies, some
players keep their form for years and years. The international
footballer Ted Meredith was still selected at the age of fifty-two.
At sixty-three Eugène Lenormand gave swimming exhibitions; and
Borotra was world tennis champion when he was fifty-six.

In former times there was often a glaring contrast between a
man's mental and his physical evolution – a divorce lamented by

---

* The existence of this disease suggests that of an unknown but clearly-defined
agent that causes senescence. If this could be discovered, perhaps it would be possible
to stop its action or at least to slow it down considerably.

31

Montesquieu. 'Oh, the unhappy state of man! Scarcely has the mind reached full ripeness before the body begins to fall away.' In his diary Delacroix observes, 'The strange disharmony between the spiritual strength brought by age and the bodily weakness that also comes with it has always struck me; and to me it seems a contradiction in the laws of nature.'

Medical progress has changed this. The body is protected against a great many kinds of infirmity and disease, and it holds out longer. Generally speaking, so long as the mind retains its strength and balance, the subject can be kept in good physical health: it is when the intellectual, spiritual side is badly shaken that the body deteriorates. And the converse applies: if the individual undergoes severe physiological damage his mental powers are impaired. In any event, they suffer from the alterations of the body. Messages are sent less rapidly and they are distorted by the poor quality of the receiving centres. The functioning of the brain is less flexible: as we have seen, its consumption of oxygen is reduced, and the blood's oxygen-content brings about a reduction in immediate memory and in retention; it causes a slowing-down of the conceptual processes, irregularity in simple mental operations, and very strong emotional reactions such as euphoria or depression. Senescence can be looked upon as an example of that 'generalized amputation' that Goldstein refers to, speaking of post-traumatic damage to the brain. In this case too there is a loss of brain-cells. As there are a very great many of them the subject can easily deal with the situation, so long as an extreme effort is not required of him. But if his life has violent ups and downs, then there is the risk of disaster. Intellectual effort tires him in any case: his capacity for work and for concentration declines, at least from the age of seventy onwards.

When they carry out research on the psychology of old age, the gerontologists use the same methods that they employ when they are concerned with its physiology. They study their subjects from the outside, and they base their work primarily upon psychometry. This seems to me the most questionable of methods of inquiry. The person submitted to a test is in an artificial situation, and the results that are obtained are merely academic, quite different from the practical, living reality. The truth of the matter is that a man's intellectual reactions depend upon the entirety of his situation: it is common knowledge that disturbed family life can make a child who has hitherto been well advanced seem stupid. When I deal with the psychology of the old later in this book, I shall look upon it as a complete entity, tying it in with the biological, existential and social context, according to the principle of circularity that I have already mentioned. For the moment, since I should like to give my readers a clear notion of the work the gerontologists have done so far, I must speak of their methods and of the results they think they have established.

In 1917 the American army wanted to determine the mental level of its officer-candidates: for this purpose the first intelligence tests were invented. Later there was more work in this field. In 1927 Willoughby took over certain tests that had been used in the American army and tried them on a group of families living in the neighbourhood of Standford University. In 1925–6 Jones and Conrad tested 1,191 subjects in New England and published the collected results. Research went on in America, Germany and England. In 1955 Suzanne Pacaud, working in France, studied the reactions of four thousand railway employees aged between twenty and fifty-five, and of apprentices from twelve and a half to fifteen and a half. Recently at Sainte-Périne, Professor Bourlière has perfected a battery of tests that probe the intellectual faculties. The subject is asked to note the mistakes in a series of drawings for example, or to show the quickest way out of a maze, to complete unfinished drawings, to collect or separate like and unlike, to underline synonyms, to state the shades of meaning that differentiate them, to manipulate associated groups of letters and figures (code test), to reproduce geometrical figures from memory, to react to a signal, to reply 'true' or 'false' to statements about behaviour or personality, and to make mirror-drawings. It is found that the immediate memory is scarcely affected; but the concrete memory (that which has to do with thoroughly known data) diminishes between the ages of thirty and fifty, and the logical memory does the same. The side of memory that shows the greatest change for the worse is that which has to do with the formation of new associations – the learning of a language, for example. It must be added that there are very important differences according to the cultural level of the subjects. Memory tests carried out on three thousand persons at Groningen showed that memory decreased in every case with great age, but less among intellectual than among manual workers, less among former specialized craftsmen than among labourers, and less among those who were still working than among the retired.

As for the motor reactions, it is at the age of twenty-five that they are quickest and most exact: their speed and precision begin to diminish at thirty-five and to decline even more after forty-five. The speed of mental operations increases up to fifteen, remains stable from fifteen to thirty-five, and then diminishes. The subject of over sixty reacts badly to intelligence tests when he has only a limited time; but if, on the contrary, he has all the time he wants he may do as well as the man in his prime or even better. Old people find it very hard to adapt themselves to new situations: it is easy for them to reorganize things they are familiar with, but they resist change. They have to make a very great effort to acquire what is known as a set – an attitude, a habit of mind – for they are wholly dominated by the mental patterns adopted earlier and they lack flexibility. Once they have adopted the set they are most reluctant to let it go. Even when they are faced with problems to which the set no longer has the least reference, they still cling to it. This means that their possibilities of learning are very much reduced. All powers such as observation, abstraction and synthesis, integration, and structuration, in which adaptation is a necessary part, diminish after thirty-five, particularly if they are not exercised. Mental arithmetic is found to be less perfect; so is the organization of space and logical reasoning. The results of the tests bearing on vocabulary are contradictory: with uneducated people it grows poorer after sixty, but with those of a high intellectual standard it retains its level and may even become richer. Generally speaking, thoroughly acquired knowledge, vocabulary, and the immediate or delayed recall of words and figures scarcely deteriorates at all. To put it shortly, the individual possesses a fluid, adaptable potentiality that does age, and a set, crystallized part of his mind, made up of acquired mechanisms, that does not.

One important consequence arises from these tests and statistics taken as a whole – the higher the subject's intellectual level, the slower and less marked is the decline of his powers. If he keeps on using his memory and intelligence he can preserve them unharmed. I shall come back to this point, which can only be explained by the existence of a connexion between the individual's memory and intelligence on the one hand and his involvement with awareness of life, and on the other his outside interests, attitudes and plans. For the moment let us merely say that there are some very old people who prove more effectual than the young. Indeed, there is a great

34

deal of intellectual work performed without any relation to age. Professional skill, technical ability, sound judgement and organization can compensate for the weakening of memory and of resistance to fatigue, and for the difficulties of adaptation. Many old people remain active and clear-minded to the very end of their days.

Yet the old man's psychological structure is fragile, being linked to his physical organism and resembling it: the old are more liable to mental disease than the young.* According to a report published by the United States National Institute of Mental Health out of a hundred thousand subjects belonging to the same age-group, the number of mentally sick is 2·3 under fifteen years of age, 76·3 between twenty-five and thirty-four, 93 between thirty-five and fifty-four, and 236·1 among the aged. Out of seven million people in Sweden there are nine thousand cases of senile dementia in the strict meaning of the word. In the United States the number of mentally sick taken as a whole quadrupled between 1904 and 1950, whereas the number of old people admitted to psychiatric hospitals increased nine-fold: this is partly because they are less reluctant to turn to them for help. In Sweden there has been no change for the last twenty-five years.

Nowadays the old are less at a disadvantage than they used to be: fewer are bedridden. Indeed, it sometimes happens that when several age-groups are compared, the older seem to show the reverse of a decline; for in order to live so long there had in the first place to be a remarkable potentiality for health. Nevertheless, as a general rule every individual does begin to go downhill after a certain point. The words 'a fine old age', 'a green old age', mean that the elderly person has found a physical and mental balance, and not that his physical being, his memory and his possibilities of psychomotor adaptation are those of a young man. No man who lives long can escape old age: it is an unavoidable and irreversible phenomenon.

Old age invariably ends in death. But rarely does it cause death without the intervention of some pathological factor. Schopenhauer asserts that he knew some exceedingly aged people who died without any precise reason. Professor Delore tells of a woman aged a hundred who came to the hospital on foot and there asked for a bed to die in, because she felt so very tired. She did die the next day and the post-mortem showed no organic trouble of any sort. But

* I shall return to this subject later, when I have looked into the state of the aged as a whole.

35

this case is almost the only one of its kind. The deaths that are called 'natural', as opposed to those caused by accidents, are in fact brought about by some organic deterioration.

Man lives longer than the other mammals. I have come across only one properly documented case of a life exceeding one hundred and five years: this was Antoine-Jean Giovanni, who was a hundred and eight and who lived in the village of Grossa.* It is believed, but with no certainty, that heredity plays a direct or an indirect part in longevity: many other factors are concerned, the most important being sex – in all animal species the female lives longer than the male. In France women live upon the average seven years longer than men. Then come the factors of growth, nourishment and environment, and of economic conditions.

All these have a very important influence upon the ageing process, as the gerontologists have established by a great many inquiries. That which was carried out in Sheffield, and which I have mentioned, showed that health was closely related to the standard of living. Professor Bourlière's team, studying peasants and fishermen in Brittany, came to the same conclusion. It is often said that the country has more healthy old people than the towns: in fact all the subjects questioned were far less fit than well-to-do Parisians of the same age.†

The part played by economic factors shows the limits of gerontology in so far as that discipline defines individual senescence in biological terms. Its conclusions are of the very highest interest, and old age cannot possibly be understood without reference to them. But they cannot tell the whole story. They amount to no more

* This was reported in *France-Soir* at the beginning of 1969. A.-J. Giovanni was born on 1 August 1860 at Zicavo in Corsica and he had spent his whole life at Grossa. See Appendix I, 'The hundred-year-olds', p. 544.

† Research carried out in Marseilles by Professor Desanti in 1969 on seventeen thousand persons covered by social insurance shows that the various groups of workers do not age in the same manner. From his results we may list the different callings in an increasing order of wear and tear:
Primary, secondary and technical school teachers
higher executives
executives of the middle rank
auxiliary medical staff and social workers
office and municipal clerical staff
drivers, travelling salesmen, the unemployed
heads of firms
domestic staff
foremen, craftsmen, specialized workers
labourers.

than a brief academic passage in the study of old age. A man's ageing and his decline always takes place inside some given society: it is intimately related to the character of that society and to the place that the individual in question occupies within it. In itself the economic factor cannot be isolated from the social, political and ideological superstructures that contain it: from an absolute point of view the standard of living is also an abstract notion, no more – with the same resources a man will be considered wealthy in a poor community and poor in a rich one. In order to understand the meaning and the reality of old age we are therefore obliged to look into the place that has been allotted to the elderly and the image that has been formed of them, in different times and different places. As I have already said, the value of this comparison lies in the fact that it will allow us if not to reply then at least to have some notion of the answer to the fundamental question 'what is there that is inescapable in the state and condition of the old?' Let us begin our inquiry with those societies that are termed 'primitive', or devoid of history.

2

The ethnological data

However brutish it may be, there is no human community that does not possess a certain culture; the work man performs by means of tools he has made constitutes an activity upon which is based at least the first beginnings of a social organization. So do not let us try to imagine what a *natural* old age would be for him. On the other hand we can see what happens among the animals; although here again the word nature can cause discussion. In many species (and the higher they are in the evolutionary scale the more this applies) the old, experienced animals are much respected: they pass on the knowledge they have acquired in the course of their lives. The rank that each occupies in the group is in direct relationship to the number of its years. The zoologists provide us with a number of interesting observations upon this point. If a young jackdaw shows fear, the others take no notice of it; but if an old male bird gives the alarm they all fly away. It is the old and experienced jackdaws that teach the others to recognize their enemies. The team working with the zoologist Yerkes taught a young chimpanzee how to get bananas by working a complicated apparatus: not a single one of its fellow-apes attempted to copy it. The same course of instruction was given to an old chimpanzee, one who was therefore of superior rank: all the others watched and copied it. It is their principle to imitate only companions of higher standing.

It is particularly interesting to see what happens among the creatures nearest to us, the anthropoid apes. In all bands the old male has a dominating position in relation to the females and the young. Sometimes a whole group of males rule the band and share the females among themselves; sometimes there is only one leader and he agrees to the sharing. In both these cases the old males arouse no aggressiveness or enmity, and they die a natural death. But it may also happen that the oldest male monopolize the females, so that the younger apes can only come to them secretly, running the risk of severe punishment. The old leader, still vigorous at fifty, defends the females and the little apes when they are attacked by wild beasts. As the young males grow older and stronger they rise up against him. They keep watch on him. He grows weaker. His teeth – his most formidable weapon – break and decay. When the young feel that the moment has come, either because the old leader has been exhausted in some fight with a predator or because his fate is on him, the eldest suddenly attacks. Often he kills him or gives him a mortal wound. But even if he is only slightly injured the old leader knows that he is beaten, and he is afraid. He leaves the community and goes to live alone, while his attacker takes over the band. The vanquished ape finds it hard to feed himself, and he pines away. At this point he is often the prey of wild beasts. Or he catches some mortal disease: or he grows too weak to look after himself and dies of hunger. When the younger males get rid of him he is still robust. And he is not a burden upon the community, on the one hand because he is still active and on the other because the band may be looked upon as an affluent society – seeing that it moves easily about in a rich landscape the question of food-shortage does not arise. The reason why the old male is ill-used (as his successor will be later on) is that he monopolized the females and ruled the young tyrannically. The old females are never killed in any circumstances: the band looks after them.

We shall see that in human communities, as in those of many other species, experience and accumulated knowledge constitute an asset for the aged person. We shall also see that the aged person is often expelled, more or less violently, from the community. Yet in this case the tragedy of old age does not take place upon the sexual but upon the economic plane. The old man is not the individual who can no longer fight, as he is among the apes, but the one who can no longer work and who has become a useless mouth to feed. His condition never depends upon the biological facts alone: cultural factors come into play. For the ape that monopolizes the females old age is an absolute evil that puts him at the mercy of his fellows and prevents him from withstanding outside attack. It brings with it either a violent death or a pining away in solitude; whereas in human societies old age, that natural curse, is an integral part of a civilization that always has something of the character of an antiphysis, however slight, and that is therefore capable of altering the meaning of old age to a very great extent. Thus in certain societies we find the old men monopolizing the women at a time when they, the men, have lost their physical strength; and this they are able to do because their high standing protects them from violence.

Yet whatever the context may be, the biological facts remain. For every individual age brings with it a dreaded decline. It is in complete conflict with the manly or womanly ideal cherished by the young and the fully-grown. The immediate, natural attitude is to reject it, in so far as it is summed up by the words decrepitude, ugliness and ill-health. Old age in others also causes an instant repulsion. This primitive reaction remains alive even when custom represses it; and in this we see the origin of a conflict that we shall find exemplified again and again.

It is the tendency of every society to live, and to go on living: it extols the strength and the fecundity that are so closely linked with youth and it dreads the worn-out sterility, the decrepitude of age. This is one of the many conclusions that arise from Frazer's work. There are many communities, he says, in which the chief is revered as the incarnation of the divinity, a divinity that will dwell in the body of his successor after his death: but if the incarnate god were weakened by age it could no longer protect the community efficiently, so the chief must be killed before the decline begins. This is how Frazer explains the putting to death of the priest of Nemi in ancient times and the killings that were still to be seen at the beginning of this century among the Shilluks of the White Nile: at the first sign of illness, weakness or falling-off the chief was destroyed.* In the same

---

* Evans Pritchard disputes Frazer's interpretation. He says that the nation was divided into two regions, the north and the south: each had a royal family and the king was chosen alternately from the one and then the other. The ruler was the incarnation of the great ancestor in whom the interests of both parts of the nation were combined. The notion of regicide, on the contrary, is a manifestation of the breaking up of the community – of its fragmentation. It means that if some disaster falls upon the country it will be put down to a lessening of the king's power and that a prince belonging to the other branch will be incited to rise up against him. And indeed rebellions do take place when some misfortune occurs, and then the king dies a violent death. The kingship embodies a conflict between the office and the person, a conflict that is solved by the traditional killing of the king. This explanation is more complex than Frazer's, but it does not contradict it. The loss of power is not directly connected with ageing, though ageing may be put forward as a justification for the revolt, the continual possibility of which is an essential part of the social organization. Nevertheless, in both theories a negative quality is assigned to old age.

way the Chitumé, the high priest in the Congo, was put to death as soon as his health seemed to be impaired: if he were to die naturally, all his strength exhausted, the god would expire with him and the world would at once be annihilated. The king of Calicut was killed in the same way. Struck down at the height of his powers, the chief handed on a vigorous soul to his successor.

According to Frazer similar beliefs lead elderly men in the Fiji Islands and many other places to kill themselves of their own free will: they are of the opinion that they will live on with the age they had when they left this world, so they do not wait for the decrepitude which would then be their lot for all eternity.

These customs should be compared with that of the 'burial alive' which is stated by a number of writers to be practised by the Dinka.* There are some old men, such as the rain-makers and the experts with the fishing-spear, who play so important a part in the life of the community that they are looked upon as the guardians of its existence: as soon as they show signs of weakness they are buried alive, amidst ceremonies in which they voluntarily take part. It is supposed that if they were to let out their last breath naturally rather than keeping it inside their bodies, then the life of the community would expire with them. The death-feasts, on the contrary, are a kind of rebirth for the whole tribe, a rejuvenation of the vital principle.

The passing of time brings about wear and decay: this persuasion is apparent in the myths and rites of regeneration that play so important a part in all repetitive societies – the nations of antiquity, the primitive tribes and even the more advanced rural communities. The essential mark of these societies is that in them technology makes no progress: there the passage of time is not looked upon as something that brings the future closer but rather as something that thrusts youth back into the past. And this youth must be recovered. In many mythologies it is held that the reason why nature and the human race have the strength to live and to go on living indefinitely is that at some given moment their youth was given back to them – the old world was wiped out and the present world rose up. That was what the Babylonians believed: a flood overwhelmed mankind, and the world that emerged from the water was re-peopled. We find the same myth again in the Bible. Noah is a new Adam, the animals

* A people numbering about nine hundred thousand and living in the Southern Sudan.

in the ark those of Eden beginning all over again, and the rainbow a sign of the starting of a new age. The peoples now dwelling around the Pacific believe that the world was flooded because of a ritual error: each community traces its origin from a legendary being who is said to have escaped from the catastrophe. The fertilization of their souls by the periodic overflowing of the Nile suggested to the Egyptians the idea of a continual regeneration: for them Osiris, the god of vegetation, died every year at harvest-time, to be born again with the springing of the new seed, full of the green vigour of a youth perpetually renewed.*

There were and there still are many rites whose purpose is to wipe out the time that has passed in the course of a given cycle: once this is done, a life freed from the weight of years can begin again. Among the Babylonians the poem of the Creation was read during the new year ceremonies. The Hittites re-enacted the battle between the serpent and the god Teshup, and the victory that allowed the god to set the world in order and to rule it. In many places there are feasts at the end of the old year – feasts in which it is abolished, done away with. It is burnt in effigy; fires are put out and others are lit; ritual orgies bring back the primeval chaos. The Saturnalia, the rejoicings in which all social rank and order is overturned, also imply the rejection of the established state of things – society and the whole world dissolve, and they are then recreated in all their pristine freshness. There are feasts of this kind throughout the year as well as at its beginning; and those of spring endow that season with the significance of a cosmic rejuvenation. A ruler's accession is often looked upon as starting a new age. When the Emperor of China came to the throne he established a new calendar: the old order vanished and a new was born. It is this idea of regeneration that explains one of the Shinto customs of Japan: at stated intervals the temples have to be entirely rebuilt and their furnishings and decoration completely renewed. The great temple of Isé in particular, the very centre of the religion, is rebuilt every twenty years: this was done for the first time by the Empress Jito (686–9), and since then the temple and the great bridge that leads to it and to the fourteen subsidiary temples have been put up again fifty-nine times. These

* In their dreams of a golden age when the human race escaped from death, the Bambara suppose that life in those days was a continual return from old age to childhood. The old men climbed a sacred tree and there opened their veins; they came down again, emptied of their blood. The young people plucked out their hair and beat them. They lost consciousness and became seven-year-old children once more.

Shinto temples are a positive manifestation of the blood-tie between the individual and the world as a whole: their rebuilding prevents time from weakening this bond. Still more significant are those ceremonies described by Frazer in which communities symbolically expel old age from their midst. In Italy, France and Spain, on the fourth Sunday in Lent, there was the 'sawing of the old woman', in which the people went through the motions of cutting a real old woman in two. The last of these feigned executions took place at Padua in 1747. In other cases little images representing old men were actually burnt.

So on the plane of myth, therefore, the repetitive societies were afraid that nature and their institutions might be worn out by time, and they protected themselves against this attrition. For them it was not a question of going forward towards a new future, but of preserving an honoured past upon which the present was modelled – of preserving it unharmed by a continuous ritual reanimation.

The problem is completely different when the community has genuine people, flesh and blood individuals, to deal with: it has to establish a real relationship with them. Old age is hateful: it is driven out. But when, as is usually the case, the aged person does not represent the ageing of the whole group, there is no *a priori* reason for doing away with him. His status will be settled empirically, according to the circumstances. Age makes him unproductive, and he represents a burden. But as I have said, in certain societies when the grown man determines the lot of the old, he at the same time chooses his own future: he therefore takes his own long-term interests into consideration. It may also happen that there are very powerful emotional bonds between him and his old parents. Then again, years bring the aged man qualifications that may make him very useful. The primitive human community is more complex than animal societies, and it has still greater need of a knowledge that can only be handed down by oral tradition. If, because of his memory, the aged man is the holder and the guardian of knowledge and of the recollected past, then he is respected. What is more, he already has one foot in the world of the dead: this marks him out for the role of intercessor between this world and the next, as well as giving him formidable powers. These factors have a direct bearing upon his status. It should be observed, by the way, that among primitive peoples it is most unusual to reach the age of sixty-five – rarely do three per cent of the population live so long. Generally speaking, those of fifty are looked upon as being old or even very old. In this chapter I shall use the words elderly, old, and very aged for those who are thought to be so by the community in which they live and who, for the most part, are in fact biologically old.

In order to study their condition I shall base myself upon the work of the ethnologists. My principal source has been the *Human Relation Area Files* which the *Laboratoire d'anthropologie sociale* kindly produced for me. The information is sometimes very old and sometimes incomplete or of uncertain value, so here we must advance with caution. There are but few observers who, in describing a given community, adopt that community's values. They see it and judge it by the criteria of their own civilization, never supposing that anyone could of set purpose deviate from its standards and customs. And there are few who make an organized synthesis of their observations on the subject of old age – it is not one that interests them very much, either: they provide data that are sometimes unintelligible or even contradictory. I shall try to relate the data we have on the state of the aged to the structure of the society as a whole. I know that samples run the risk of being arbitrary, but then statistics are no less so – they give no light at all; whereas it is possible to hope to bring meaningful relationships into evidence by the use of contrast and comparison.

Because of the circumstances in which they live primitive peoples are either hunters and gatherers of food, or cattle-raisers, or peasants: the two first classes are nomadic and the third is settled. There are also semi-nomads, cattle-raisers who have various places where they stay and agricultural societies that clear different parts of the forest in succession. I shall arrange them according to the nature of their occupations and their environment, not according to their geographical position – there are more similarities between the gatherers of Australia and Africa than there are between the African gatherers and the African peasants.

There is often a very important gap between the myths a society creates and the customs it actually follows. This is particularly striking when we consider the part played by the old in primitive societies. In their myths many of the poorest of them all glorify old age. The Eskimo have many legends in which an old man is miraculously saved and a terrible punishment falls upon those who had conspired to get rid of him. In other tales old people are powerful magicians, discoverers, healers. Primitive nations often represent the gods as ancient men, full of wisdom and vigour. The Eskimo goddess Nerwik is a very old woman who lives under the sea with the spirits of the dead: sometimes she will refuse to protect the seal-hunters until a shaman comes to comb her hair. In other parts of the world it is an old woman who controls the winds. The Hopi believe that the crafts were invented by an ancient spider-woman. There are great numbers of examples. But as we shall see, these fables have no influence whatsoever upon practice.

Extreme poverty leads to improvidence: the present is all-important, and the future is sacrificed to it. Where the climate is severe, the environment harsh and the resources inadequate, human old age often resembles that of the animals. This was so among the Yakuts, who led a semi-nomadic life in north-eastern Siberia: they raised cattle and horses; their winters were appallingly cold, their summers torrid. Most of them suffered from hunger all their lives long.

In this rudimentary civilization it was impossible for knowledge and experience to be of any value. Religion scarcely existed. There was magic, however, and shamanism was widely practised.* The shaman was usually revealed and initiated at quite an early age: but the powers he acquired did not diminish with the passage of time. The aged shamans were the only old people to be respected. The family was patriarchal. The father owned the herds. He had absolute authority over his children and exercised it; he could sell them or kill them, and it was quite usual to get rid of daughters. If a son insulted his father or disobeyed him, the father disinherited him. So long as he retained his strength, the father ruled the family tyrannically. As soon as he weakened, his sons took his possessions from him by force and let him more or less perish. They had been ill-treated in their childhood and they had not the slightest pity for their old parents. When a Yakut was blamed for his cruel behaviour towards his old mother he replied, 'Let her cry! Let her go hungry!

---

* The border between magic and religion is somewhat imprecise. Both claim to be in control of supernatural forces. According to Mauss religion never makes use of them except for the good of the community: magic often possesses a social dimension, but it may also divert these supernatural powers for the benefit of the person who can command them, and sometimes it does so with evil intentions. Lévi-Strauss says that religion is a humanization of the laws of nature, and magic a naturalization of human actions: here we have two components, always appearing together, the only variation being in their relative proportions. All magic contains at least a trace of religion. The supernatural exists for mankind only in so far as men believe they have supernatural powers and at the same time attribute their superhuman powers to nature.

She made me cry often enough, and she grudged me my food. She used to beat me for no reason at all.' Trostchansky lived in exile for twenty years among the Yakuts, and he says that the old were either expelled from their homes and reduced to beggary or turned into slaves by their sons, who beat them and compelled them to work very hard. Another observer, Sieroshevski, writes, 'Even in well-to-do houses I have seen living skeletons, wrinkled, half-naked or completely naked beings who hid in the corners, only emerging when there were no strangers there to come nearer to the fire and fight with the children for the remaining scraps of food.' It was still worse for more distant relatives. 'They let us perish slowly of cold and hunger in a corner, dying not like men but like brute-beasts.' To escape from this hideous fate they would often ask their sons to stab them to the heart. Extreme shortage of food, a low cultural level and the hatred of parents bred by patriarchal harshness – everything conspired against the old.

A similar state of affairs was to be found among the Ainu before they were influenced by Japanese civilization. Their society too was very primitive: the climate was extremely cold and their food – raw fish, for the most part – insufficient. They slept on the ground, possessed few tools, hunted bears and fished. The old people's experience was of little use to them. Their religion was a gross animism – no temples, no worship: all they did was to honour the gods by setting up willow-branches, which were called *inao* and which were looked upon as sacred. They knew a few songs, but they had neither set feasts nor ceremonies. Their main and indeed almost their only amusement was getting drunk. There were therefore no traditions for the old to hand down. Then again the mothers neglected their children, and after puberty the children no longer showed the least attachment to them. When the parents grew old, they in their turn were neglected. Throughout their lives the women were treated as outcasts: they worked hard; they were not allowed to take part in prayer; and their fate grew harsher with the years. Landor* describes his visit to a hut in 1893:

As I came nearer I discovered a mass of white hair and two talons not unlike slender human feet with long hooked claws; a few fish-bones were scattered on the ground and filth was piled up there in the corner: the stench was horrible. I heard the sound of breathing beneath this

* *Alone with the Hairy Ainu.* Batchelor's book is more indulgent than Landor's, but it draws much the same picture.

mass of hair. I touched it, parting the hair; and with a groan two thin bony arms reached up towards me and grasped my hand . . . she was no more than skin and bone, and her long hair and nails made her a horrifying sight. . . . She was almost blind, deaf and dumb: she seemed to be suffering from a rheumatism that had stiffened her arms and legs; she had leprous patches. It was horrible, revolting and humiliating to look at her. She was neither misused nor yet taken care of by the village or by her son, who lived in the same hut; but she was something that had been thrown away, and that was how they treated her. Now and then they tossed her a fish.

When poverty reaches the extreme point, it is a deciding factor – it stifles feeling. The Siriono, who live in the Bolivian forest, never kill their new-born babies, although many of them are club-footed: they love their children, and their children love them in return. But this semi-nomadic tribe is always hungry. They live in a savage state, almost naked, without ornaments or tools; they sleep in hammocks and make bows, but they have no canoes and they move from place to place on foot. They no longer even know how to make fire, but carry it about with them. They have no domestic animals. During the rainy season the lie up in dusty huts: they do cultivate a few plants, but it is chiefly wild fruit and vegetables that they eat. In the dry season they hunt and fish. They have no myths and no witchcraft; they can neither count nor measure time. They have no social or political organization, and no one deals out justice. They quarrel violently and incessantly over food: each struggles for his own life. This existence is so arduous that their strength begins to go at the age of thirty: when they are forty they are worn out. The children then neglect their parents: they overlook them when the food is being shared out. The old people walk slowly, and they hinder the tribal movements. Holmberg says that the day before one of these expeditions he noticed an old woman who was lying sick in a hammock – too ill to speak. 'I asked the chief of the village what they were going to do about her; he told me to ask her husband, who said that they were going to let her die there. . . . The next day the whole of the village left without even saying goodbye to her. . . . Three weeks later . . . I found the hammock again, with the remains of the sick woman.'

The Fang are less poverty-stricken than the Siriono: they are a people who number about 127,000, and they inhabit the upper reaches of the Gaboon, most of them living in insecurity. They have been more or less converted to the religious and cultural ideas of the whites, and they are in a transitional phase between the customs that they have lost and that no longer suit their way of life and a modern ethic that has not yet been worked out.

For many years they made their living by means of warlike and economic conquest: the elders had the political power, but it was a council of young men who directed the expeditions. These raids called for a degree of mobility that hindered the setting-up of a graduated organization, a hierarchy, so even now they form a society in which the chiefs are continually changing. They are scattered among several villages, and these villages often move. Today the Fang are mainly concerned with hunting and fishing. There is also a settled peasantry among them, growing cocoa for the most part and enjoying a certain prosperity. In all these communities it is the richest members that are the most respected. Their religion, now largely destroyed by Christianity, was based upon an ancestor-worship in which an essential part was the ancestral skulls. These were kept in a basket: the possession of the basket conferred power, and it was obtained either by consanguinity or by strength of character and intellectual talent; age was an advantage, always providing that it was not too advanced, but not such an advantage as talent.

The head of the family is the eldest of the active adults. The old parents live with him, and they retain a certain moral authority so long as they remain 'real men' and 'real women'. The women never enjoy much authority at any time, however; they are mere instruments of production and reproduction. When they are old, those who are looked upon as witches are feared – a state of affairs that may be dangerous for them. They begin to age early, that is to say as soon as they can no longer bear children; whereas a man reaches his peak when he has grandchildren living under his roof – this happens when he is about fifty. Later, when their strength declines, the elders lose all their standing. The Fang look upon human life as a curve that rises from childhood to maturity; then it goes down to the lowest level, rising again after death. Wealth and magical knowledge may counterbalance the decline of old age. But generally speaking the old men are thrust out of public life; they lead a marginal existence and no one has the least consideration for them. If they become decrepit they are so despised that after their death their skulls are not used in the religious ceremonies. If they have no

48

children life is very hard for them. Even among the Fang who have been converted to Christianity they are very unhappy and neglected, particularly the widows. In former times they were abandoned in the forest during migrations. Even now, when a village moves, as it often does, they are left behind in a state of utter destitution. They accept their fate, and it is said that they will even joke about it. Some say that they are 'tired of life' and have themselves burned alive. Sometimes it is their heirs who get rid of them.

The Thonga are not nomads: they are Bantu who have settled in the arid country on the east coast of South Africa. The population is scattered. The land belongs to the chief, who distributes it among the members of the community: each man has the absolute disposal of the fruits of the work he does himself or has done by his wives – a great many tasks are ritually reserved for women. The Thonga grow maize, fruit and vegetables, and they raise cattle and goats. They hunt and fish. They carve wood a little and make some pottery. Their folklore includes dances and songs. They have times of plenty, but there are also famines caused by floods or by swarms of locusts. They eat their meals communally. First the husbands are served, then the children, and then the women: as a general rule the sick and the aged are given a share. The old are little respected. They have no economic resources, and they inspire almost no affection. Between the ages of three and fourteen the children live with their grandparents, who let them grow up as well as they can on their own; they are always hungry and they are much given to pilfering; the boys' initiation ceremony is a very severe trial indeed. After this the young of both sexes live together in a hut that is set aside for them. There are few links between them and their parents and they feel resentment against the generation that brought them up so carelessly. When they are fully grown their behaviour towards old people is coarse and rude. The children, who are obliged to live with their grandparents, do not like them: they make game of the old people and eat their share of the food. The Thonga have almost no cultural or social tradition whatsoever: the memory of the elders is of no value. Their religion is rudimentary. It is the elder brother who makes the family's sacrifices to the ancestors: sometimes these ancestors reveal themselves in dreams. They are asked questions by means of divinatory bones. In some ceremonies the old women dance and sing, often in an obscene manner. They are no longer subject to certain taboos; only they and the girls under the age of puberty may eat the flesh of the sacrificial buck. Both the old women and the little girls escape the curse laid upon their sex, but for all that they do not belong to the community of men. Because of this curious position, the old woman no longer has to fear certain supernatural perils: it is to her that the people turn when the village or the fighting-men's weapons have to be purified. But when she can no longer work on the land – and she perseveres until her strength quite leaves her – she becomes a burden, and her decrepitude is despised. The aged men often officiate in the ceremonies. This is not enough to give them any standing. The most respected among the Thonga are the fattest, the strongest and the richest: in order to grow rich a man will marry several wives, since it is chiefly they that do the work. The husband then has abundance of food; he provides feasts for his children, he entertains strangers, he is admired and respected, and he has a great deal of influence. But when a man's wives have died, and when he is wrinkled, dried up, weak and poor, then he is no more than a drop-out, a burden unwillingly borne. There are few whose children display much affectionate care for them. On the whole the state of the old people is wretched, and they repine. When a village moves it leaves them behind. In times of war great numbers of them die: when the others fly, panic-stricken, the old hide themselves in the woods, where they are either found and cut to pieces by the enemy or they perish of hunger.

Yet most societies do not let their old people die like mere animals.* Their death is surrounded by ceremony, and the others ask or pretend to ask for their consent. This was what used to happen† among the Koryak, for example, a North Siberian people who lived in an environment as harsh as that of the Yakuts. Their only resource was the herds of reindeer with which they travelled across the steppes; their winters were extremely severe, and the long marches exhausted the older people. It was unusual to find one who wanted to outlive his strength. The old were killed, just as the incurables were killed. This seemed so natural to the Koryak that they would cheerfully boast of their skill, pointing out the places where the thrust of a spear or a knife was fatal. The killing took place in

* In his survey published in 1945, *The Role of the Aged in Primitive Society*, Simmons states that out of thirty-nine tribes studied from this point of view the habit of neglecting and abandoning the old was usual in eighteen, not only among the nomadic but also among the settled communities.

† We are very poorly informed about the present condition of the peoples living in Siberia.

the presence of the whole community, after long and complex ceremonies.

Among the Chukchee, a Siberian tribe that was in contact with white traders, those who lived on their fishing found it extremely hard to get enough to eat. They used to kill deformed children at birth, as well as those who looked as though they might be difficult to rear. Some few elders managed to carry on trade and to amass a little capital: they were respected. The others were a burden, and they were led such a life that it was easy to persuade them to prefer death. A great feast was given in their honour, a feast in which they took part: the assembly ate seal-meat, drank whisky, sang and beat upon a drum. The condemned man's son or his younger brother slipped behind him and strangled him with a seal-bone.

Among the Hopi, the Creek and the Crow Indians, and the Bushmen of South Africa, it was customary to lead the aged person to a hut specially built for the purpose away from the village and there to abandon him, leaving a little food and water. The Eskimo, whose resources are meagre and most uncertain, persuade the old to go and lie in the snow and wait for death; or they forget them on an ice-floe when the tribe is out fishing; or they shut them into an igloo, where they die of cold. It was usual for the Amassalik Eskimo in Greenland to kill themselves when they felt that they were a burden on the community. One evening they would make a kind of public confession, and then two or three days later they would get into their kayak, paddle away from the land and never reappear.* Paul-Emile Victor tells of a sick man who was unable to get into his kayak; he asked to be thrown into the sea, death by drowning being the quickest way to the other world. His children did as he asked, but he floated, being buoyed up by his clothes. A daughter who loved him much called out tenderly, 'Father, push your head under. The road will be shorter.'

Many societies respect the old so long as they are clear-minded and robust, but get rid of them when they become senile and infirm. This is the case with the Hottentots, who lead a semi-nomadic life in Africa. Each family owns its hut and its herds, and the links between the members are very close. The words 'grandfather' and 'grandmother' are used as terms of friendship, quite apart from any family tie: their sagas and tales show the respect they have for the aged. The Hottentots grow old early – they are aged at fifty. By this time

* According to R. Gessain.

they can no longer work and they are taken care of. Their knowledge and experience are valuable to the community. The council asks their opinion and takes notice of what they say. Their age protects them against the supernatural powers, and this allows them to play a remarkable and very important part in social life. Above all, they preside over the rites of passage from one state to another. The individual who happens to be in a transitional situation, because of convalescence or a recent widowhood, for example, no longer belongs to any set group: he is in danger and he is dangerous – he is *inau*. Only those who have gone through all the ages of life, and who are beyond good and evil may come near him unharmed and bring him back into the community. But even so, they have to belong to the same category as the *inau* – the widower looks after the widower, and someone who has recovered from a serious illness takes care of the convalescent. All old people are qualified for the initiation of the adolescent boys. Thus it is thanks to the aged that society maintains its cohesion: yet this does not prevent them from being neglected once the loss of their faculties renders them useless. Indeed, at least up to the beginning of the last century* their sons used to ask for the right to get rid of them, and it was always granted. The sons would provide a feast for the village, and all the people would come to say goodbye to the old man: he was hoisted on to the back of an ox and escorted to a remote hut. There he was left, with a little food. He either died of hunger or he was killed by wild beasts. This was chiefly a custom of the poor, but the rich sometimes followed it too, because old people, and particularly old women, were believed to have magical powers, and they were afraid of them.

The northern Ojibway, who live near Lake Winnipeg, are now deeply influenced by white civilization. But at the beginning of the century they still retained their former ways, and there was a striking contrast between the status of the still-vigorous elderly men and those who were broken by age. These Indians live in a region where the winters are cold, but the climate is healthy and the soil rich, producing rice, vegetables and fruit. The families gather in camps of from fifty to two hundred people in the summer, and in the winter they scatter in small groups to hunt the animals whose furs they sell. The children are very well treated: they are not weaned until they are three or four, and the mothers take them about wherever they go. They are given a great deal of affection; they are never punished;

* The accounts that refer to this custom all date from before 1900.

they live in complete freedom. In this society, generally speaking, no one ever persecutes anyone else. The sick are patiently looked after. The Ojibways' careful avoidance of giving offence to their neighbours arises partly from mistrust – they are afraid of witch-craft. The chief aim of religion is protection against spells and the furthering of private interests.

The grandparents usually live with the parents and advise them. It is a grandparent who gives the new-born child its name. They have what might be termed a playful relationship with their grand-children: the grandfathers treat their grandsons as equals and the grandmothers do the same with their granddaughters: they tease one another and do one another kindnesses. This does not prevent the children from respecting them: the young are taught to honour all old people. The old men form part of the council to which the adults belong, and the middle-aged men behave deferentially towards the elders. This respect is, to a certain extent, merely a question of outward forms and words. Nevertheless, some tribes have a 'great medicine society' that studies plants, some of which are supposed to bring health and long life. The young men are brought into this society and initiated by the elders, who are thought to possess great magical powers and to be potentially dangerous. They sometimes officiate as priests. It is from their ranks that the 'criers' are chosen – the men who announce the next day's working programme in the evening, and who give advice. Length of years is admired, so long as it is accompanied by good health. The Ojibway believe that longevity is acquired by virtue and the use of herbs.

When very great age and decrepitude come upon a man there are striking differences in his treatment according to the families; but it often happens that the old are neglected and that the young steal the food meant for them. It is thought that they have lost their magical powers, and they are no longer feared. They used sometimes to be abandoned in a distant hut or on an uninhabited island. If some relative wanted to go to their help he was made game of and stopped. Generally speaking the old preferred being solemnly put to death. There was a feast; they smoked the pipe of peace, sang a death-song and danced; and while the father was still singing the son would kill him with a tomahawk.

The ethnologists are much inclined to say that the old find it easy to resign themselves to being put to death – it is the custom, and their children could not do otherwise; perhaps they themselves had killed their own parents in earlier days; they feel honoured by the feast that goes on around them. How far is this hopeful view justified? It is hard to tell. There is very little evidence upon this subject. I have come across two documents, however. The first is the beautiful Japanese novel *Narayama*, in which Fukasawa, basing himself upon facts, relates the death of an old woman. Until quite recently there were remote parts of Japan where the villages were so poor that in order to survive the people had to sacrifice the aged: they were carried up to what were called the 'mountains of death' and there they were abandoned.

At the beginning of the book, O'Rin, a woman nearly seventy years old, of outstanding piety and abnegation, and much beloved by her son Tappei, hears the Narayama* song in the street: this song says that when three years have passed one is three years older, and its intention is to make the old people understand that the time for the 'pilgrimage' is coming near. The day before the Feast of the Dead those who must 'go to the mountain' invite the villagers who have already taken their parents up: this is the only great feast of the year – they eat white rice, the most valued food, and they drink rice-wine. O'Rin determines to celebrate the feast this very year. She has made all her preparations, and what is more her son is about to marry again: there will be a woman to look after the house. She is still strong, she can work, and she has all her teeth; this indeed is a source of anxiety for her, for in a village that is so near starvation it is disgraceful still to be able to eat every kind of food at her age. One of her grandsons has made up a song in which he mocks her, calling her the old woman with thirty-two teeth, and all the children hum it. She manages to break two with a stone, but the mockery does not stop. The eldest of her grandsons marries: now that there are two young women in the house she feels useless and she thinks about the pilgrimage more and more. Her son and her daughter-in-law weep when she tells them of her decision. The feast takes place. She hopes that it will snow up there, for snow would mean that she will be welcomed in the next world. At dawn she sets herself upon a plank and Tappei carries it on his shoulders. In the customary way they steal silently out of the village, no longer exchanging so much as a word. They climb the mountain. As they get near the top

* This is the name of the mountain where the old people are abandoned – the pine-tree mountain.

they see dead bodies and skeletons beneath the rocks. Watchful crows are flying about. The top itself is covered with bones. The son puts the old woman down on the ground: under a rock she spreads a mat that she has brought with her, sets a bowl of rice upon it, and sits down. She does not utter a word, but she makes violent gestures to send her son away. He goes, weeping. While he is making his way down the mountain the snow begins to fall. He comes back to tell his mother. It is snowing on the mountain-top as well; she is quite covered with white flakes and she is chanting a prayer. He calls out, 'It is snowing: the omen is good.' Once again she waves him away and he goes. He loves his mother dearly, but his filial love has evolved within the frame of reference provided by the society he belongs to, and since necessity has dictated this custom, it is by carrying O'Rin to the top of the mountain that he proves himself to be an affectionate, dutiful son.

In contrast to this death, which obeys tradition and which is blessed by the gods, the novel tells of the last days of Matayan: he is an old man – more than seventy – but he does not get ready to leave for the mountain. Yet his son wants to be rid of him. On the day of the Narayama feast he ties the old man up with a straw rope. The father bites through it, thus severing his relationship with his son, the community and the gods, and he runs away. But his son catches him. The next day, as Tappei is coming down, he sees the old man on the edge of a cliff, tied hand and foot: the son throws him into the abyss as though he were an old sack, and the crows swoop down into the valley. It is an ignominious death. The son has behaved criminally, but the father deserved his fate because he tried to escape from the divinely ordained custom.

Do the sacrificed elders often have Matayan's reaction of dread and rebellion or not? We should like to know. The fact that Fukasawa gives him so important a place in his novel must mean that his attitude is not exceptional but representative. Maybe it is O'Rin's edifying submission that is the exception.

There is a striking piece of evidence to prove that the old have often cursed their unhappy fate: this is the epic of the Narte, which came into being a very long time ago among the Ossets and which was handed down orally to the Tcherkesse. It has passages* that describe the anguish of the old men with execution hanging over them. The Narte were the mythical ancestors of the Ossets, who

* Given by Dumézil in *Mythes et épopée*.

endowed them with their own ways and customs. According to this epic, the Narte were divided into three families, living at different levels on a mountain. Those above were warriors and those at the bottom were 'wealthy people'. Half-way up there were the Alaegatae: they were known for their intelligence and they held the highest offices. All the Narte assembled in the Alaegataes' part of the mountain for the discussion of matters of general concern and for the feasts of a religious nature. During the feast the old men belonging to the three families who had been chosen by the 'council for the killing of the aged' were put to death. They were either poisoned or knocked on the head. The elder Pliny and Pomponius Mela say that among the Scythians, who were related to the northern Ossets, the killing of the old was usual. If the *satietas vitae* did not persuade them to leap into the sea from the top of a certain rock, then they were thrown over forcibly. The Narte epic describes a similar case of voluntary death. 'Urizmaeg had grown old. He had become the laughing-stock of the young Narte, who spat on him and wiped their dirty arrows on his clothes. . . . He determined to die. He cut his horse's throat, had a sack made from its hide and put himself into it: he was thrown into the sea.' But generally the old who were killed did not die willingly: they suffered the common fate that was based upon religion and the law. The elders were respected and they played an important part in the community; but when they reached a very great age, the poem says that the Narte 'tied them into a cradle like little children and sang the cradle-song to send them to sleep'.

The daughter-in-law to the father-in-law:

> Sleep, sleep, my princely father,
> Sleep, my little father . . .
> Little father, if thou dost not sleep,
> I shall have thee taken to the Aleg.

The daughter-in-law to the mother-in-law:

> Sleep, sleep, princess,
> My princess mother, sleep.
> If thou dost not sleep, old mother,
> I shall have thee taken to the Aleg.

The old woman:

> Do not have me taken to the Aleg, golden princess!
> For there they kill the old . . .

In another scene there is a dialogue between an old man and his wife.

The wife:

> The cruel, wicked daughter-in-law!
> Oh that they do not take thee to the Aleg!
> Those who are taken to the Aleg
> Are flung into the valley from the mountain-top.

The husband:

> Shut your mouth, woman!
> If they have not thought of taking me thou wilt make them
>   think of it.
> It is said that what is often repeated happens.
> Oh, if only I had been able to get away from thee for good!

To the men who appear with the very intention of taking him away:

> Give me to the wild beasts: their jaws will devour me.

Another scene relates the last quarrel between two old married people.

The head of the council for the killing of the aged asked, 'Which is the older of you two?' 'It is the old woman, of course, that is the older,' said the man between his teeth. At this the little old woman could bear it no longer and burst out, tossing in the cradle so as to break the thongs, 'Ah! God has struck me! Is it possible for a man to speak as thou hast spoken? Now it is the time for killing he says I am the older. . . . If you do not believe me, look at our teeth: mine have not yet dropped out – he has lost his twice, three times . . .' When the council looked at their teeth it was decided that the husband was the older. They took him away, muttering and complaining; they made him drink beer and they threw him into the valley.

The Ossets of today respect the old, and they have changed certain episodes in the poem. The killings of the old people are represented as guilty conspiracies and not as the carrying out of ancestral custom. A young hero arrives in the middle of the feast and he saves the ancient man.

There are very poor tribes in which the old people are not done away with: when one compares them with the examples I have just cited, it is interesting to see how this difference arises. Unlike those of the coast, the inland Chukchees respect the old. Like the Koryak, they move over the northern steppes with their herds of reindeer; their life is so hard that they age early, but the weakness that age brings with it is not accompanied by a collapse of status. The family bond is very close. It is the father who rules and who owns the herds and he remains their owner until he dies. Why does custom grant him this economic power? Clearly because in one way or another the community as a whole finds that it is to its interest – either because the younger adults dislike the idea of seeing themselves dispossessed one day, or because they see this state of affairs as the guarantee of a social stability that they think desirable. An important fact is that the aged man often plays a most significant part as far as marriage-portions are concerned, and it may be so in this case: the possession of herds, or of land, means that it is his duty to distribute them among his sons and sons-in-law according to custom. He is not so much the owner as the intermediary between the legal inheritors of his wealth. There is therefore no question of this wealth being snatched from him by any one of them, as sometimes occurs among such primitive tribes as the Yakuts. However this may be, the possessions that the old man retains confer great standing upon him. It may happen that he continues to govern the camp even when he is almost senile: it is he who decides upon the migrations and upon the location of the summer camp. When they move from one camp to another, the old men sit in the sledges with the rest; if there is not enough snow, the young men carry them on their backs. Bogoras tells how one of these elders used to go to the Wolverene river every spring to buy implements from the shopkeepers in the arctic villages. He did his buying very badly, bringing back table-knives instead of hunting-knives. The young men laughed good-naturedly, saying, 'The old fool. But then after all, he's old.' Bogoras also speaks of a man in his sixties who limped along on crutches but who nevertheless remained the master of the herds and the household. He went to the fair every year and spent nearly all his money on spirits. Yet this did not lower his standing.

The Yaghan,* a people who number about three thousand and who live on the coasts of Tierra del Fuego, are among the most primitive of all known tribes – no axes, fish-hooks, cooking utensils or pots.

---

* I speak of them in the present tense, but they have now vanished. These observations date from the end of the last century.

They lay up no stores of food* and they therefore have to live from day to day; they have no games, no ceremonies, no real religion – only a vague belief in a supreme being and in the power of shamans. Still, they do possess dogs and canoes. They live a nomadic life on the water, hunting and fishing. They are vigorous and healthy, but their existence is precarious in the extreme; they are nearly always hungry, and they spend all their time in the search for food. They are divided into conjugal families that come together at times of inactivity; in these camps, however, there is no form of government by any superior authority whatsoever. There is no one who acts as a judge. They have a great many children, whom they adore and for whom they live; the grandparents, too, are devoted to their grandchildren. Babies are killed only if the mother has been left by her husband or if the new-born child is misshapen or abnormal: it happens very seldom. The boys and girls are very well treated; they are deeply attached to their parents, and when they are in camp they always want to live in their parents' hut. This love persists when the parents are very old, and all the aged people are respected. Food is shared between the whole community, and the old are served first; they are also given the best place in the hut. They are never left alone; one of their children is always there to take care of them. They are never made game of. Their opinion is valued. If they are intelligent and upright they have great moral influence. Some aged widows are the heads of families, and they are strictly obeyed. The old people's experience is useful to the community: they know how to find food and carry out the household tasks. It is they who hand on the unwritten law and cause it to be respected. They give a good example, and if the occasion arises they correct and even punish those who behave badly.

Their status forms part of a harmonious whole. The Yaghan are singularly well adapted to their harsh environment. They like the company of their fellows, visit one another, help one another, and gladly welcome strangers. For them the struggle for life is hard, but it is devoid of selfish bitterness. They may carry out euthanasia to shorten the sufferings of a dying man. But his condition has to be hopeless and everybody has to agree.

The observers who describe the customs of the Yaghan give no

---

* The storing of food implies that quite a high degree of civilization has already been reached. The community can then think of aims other than mere subsistence. As we shall see, the Incas had huge granaries.

explanation for their idyllic nature. But the fact is that their case is not unique. The fate of the old is happy among the Aleuts, too, in spite of their precarious living-conditions. No doubt the reason for this is the value set upon their experience, and even more the mutual love that binds parents and children. The Aleuts are sturdy, well-built Mongols, and they live in the Aleutian Islands. They move about in canoes, and fishing is their livelihood: they eat whale-meat and fermented fish-heads. They store no reserves of food, and although they have little they are wasteful with what they have. They are tough and resistant, and they can go without eating for days on end. They share their food with the whole community. They live in little huts. They work slowly, but they are skilful and tireless. Their memories are good: they can copy Russian craftsmen and play chess. Some observers have said that they are lazy: in fact they do not have the same values as commercial societies – they do not want to accumulate possessions. They respect the rich because of the technical skill that has earned them their wealth, but they do not admire them for their possessions. Yet the women have very costly jewels, and sometimes the Aleuts make great expeditions to search for rock-crystal and other precious minerals. They give feasts, with dances, plays and a great deal to eat. They have little in the way of religion, but they believe in the power of shamans. Infanticide is very rare with them. They are devoted to children: the little Aleuts are given everything of the best – everything is done for them. A man may kill himself from despair after the loss of a son or a nephew. And the reverse is true: the children are deeply attached to their parents and do their best to make their last years comfortable; it is a disgrace to abandon them; they have to be helped and everything must be shared with them; if necessary the children must sacrifice themselves for their parents. They are especially devoted to their mothers, even if the old women are quite broken by age. If the Aleut treats his parents well and if he attends to their advice he will be rewarded: his fishing will be good and he will live to be old. Living to be old means providing the later generations with a great example. The very old men teach the young: every village used to have one or two elders who instructed the children; they were listened to respectfully, even if they wandered in their speech. They are responsible for seeing to the calendar (they move the matchstick that points to the day of the month). The old women take care of the sick; they are trusted and believed in. Considering it as a whole, we find a happy balance between the economy and filial love. Nature provides enough for the parents to be able to feed their children and to have time to look after them; and in their turn the children see to it that the old parents lack for nothing.

The societies that we have examined hitherto possess nothing but rudimentary techniques: in these communities religion and even magic are comparatively unimportant. When economic life calls for more complex knowledge and when the struggle against nature is less ferocious, thus allowing some degree of detachment, then magic and religion evolve. When this happens, the part played by the aged man assumes many other aspects, and he may acquire very important powers. The most typical example is that of the Aranda, who, before the coming of the missionaries, had established a positive geronto-cracy. The Aranda are hunters and gatherers of food who live almost naked in the Australian forests. Generally speaking, although they may pass through difficult periods, they have enough to eat. Each family consists of a man, one or two wives, the children, and the dogs: many sets of families are united in totem-groups. They practise infanticide when the mother cannot bring up the baby because she is still feeding another; twins are put to death;* and a small child may be killed to feed an older one that is not thriving (the mother some-times shares in the feast). But the children that are kept are treated very well. The mothers are generous: they never refuse to suckle a child and weaning takes place very late. The children are given great freedom, and they are already quite old by the time they are com-pelled to observe the sexual taboos. Yet their initiation is extremely painful. The most respected members of the community are the grey-heads. The 'half-dead', too far gone to lead a clear-minded, active life, are well fed, cared for and looked after;† but they no longer have any influence, whereas those who are only going grey are of the very first importance. Their practical experience is essential for the welfare of the group; and indeed hunters and gatherers have to know a very great many things – what can be eaten and what cannot, how yams can be found, how to detect underground water, and how to treat certain kinds of food so that their harmful properties are removed.

* It is a widely-spread custom to kill both twins or at least one of them – a frightening anomaly.

† Yet since hunting and the gathering of food require perpetual movement from place to place they are abandoned when they become too much of a burden.

The necessary observation and manual skills can only be acquired by long practice. And if, in addition to all this, the older men also know the sacred traditions, the tribal songs, myths, customs and ceremonies, then they have immense authority. Among primitive peoples knowledge and magic are inseparable: a science of the nature of things allows objects to be made use of both according to the rational laws of cause and effect and according to their magical affinities; then again, techniques are indissolubly bound to the magic rites without which they would be useless. The 'greying men's' knowledge coincides with the possession of magic powers: both the one and the other increase with age. These men reach their highest point when they become *yenkon*, on the verge of decrepitude. They are able to inflict disease upon whole vast groups of individuals, and they are dreaded. They are no longer required to observe the taboos concerning food.* In a way it may be said that they are in fact raised above the human state and that they have become immune to the supernatural dangers that threaten it. Those things that are forbidden to the ordinary man, both for his own sake and for the sake of the community, are forbidden to them no longer. Their exceptional state marks them out for a religious role. The man whom age has already brought close to the other world is the best mediator between this and the next. It is the old people who direct the Aranda's religious life – a life that underlies the whole of their social existence. It is they who own the sacred objects that are used during the ceremonies. They alone have the right to touch the *churinga*, the holy stones that are the symbols both of the mythical ancestors and of the totems. These *churinga* are the more prized the older they are, for they bring the living community closer to the heroes of ancient times. The old people conduct the ceremonies at which the *churinga* are exposed. They are treated with the utmost deference, and during these feasts the young speak to the old only if they are spoken to. The old people must teach their descendants: they hand on the songs and myths to the next generation, but they keep certain secrets to themselves.†
The initiation rites subject the young to them; and the young fear the old. Again, the young have to submit to severe restrictions in the matter of food to the advantage of the old. In some tribes the young give them their blood to strengthen them: it is taken from a vein in

* This feature is to be seen in a great number of societies.
† To punish the young men who work for the whites they will not teach them, which means that many traditions have been lost.

the arm or from the back of the hand or from under the nails; and it is either sprinkled on the aged men or they drink it. The old are given presents of food because of their knowledge of the ceremonies or for their ritual activities and their chants. Their wealth and standing mark them out to be the leaders of the community. Theoretically it is the oldest that govern. But if their powers diminish they retain no more than a nominal power and a younger man is quietly put into their place. He asks the advice of the men of his own age. Even in those tribes which have hereditary chiefs, and in which the leader may therefore be a young man, it is the elders who are the real governors. They settle disputes; they decide upon the new camping places; they organize the feasts. Nothing can be done without their consent. Until not long ago they profited by this authority to monopolize the women, insisting that all the girls should be kept for them. The motive was less sexual than economic and social. The girls had to marry as soon as they reached the age of puberty and the boys had to wait for their initiation. And above all it was to the interest of an old man and his old wife to have a young woman to feed them. The aged woman would say, 'The poor old man must have a young wife who will go and find honey and water for him.' The young people found it impossible to marry.

Techniques, magic and religion make up the essence of primitive societies' culture. These three fields are very closely linked, magic being related both to techniques and to religion. The last two are beneficial to the community: magic is ambivalent. Among the Aranda, the 'greying man' triumphs in all three. He is of great value as the possessor of knowledge and as the man who is fitted for religious functions. Because of his magic powers he inspires both respect and awe.

A similar pattern is to be found among the Zande of the Sudan, but here magic predominates, and the aged man bases his domination primarily upon his supernatural powers. These people dwell in the savannah, living by hunting, fishing, gathering and growing food – maize, manioc, sweet potatoes and bananas. There is plenty of game. Their craftsmanship is reasonably well-developed. They believe in a god called Mbori. But most of the time their minds are taken up with witchcraft. They believe that each person has a power called *mangu*: this is a substance that is related to the liver and that grows with the years. The aged Zande, like the aged Aranda, possess useful knowledge; what is more, they are the most powerful of sorcerers – they have fewer scruples about using spells than the others because, being nearer to death, they fear the danger of reprisals less. The result is that they have the running of the community in their hands. They are asked to bless the hunting expeditions, which would surely fail if the witch-doctors put a curse upon them; and their goodwill is bought by presents of game when the hunting has been successful. In former times the son was rigidly subjected to his father. The elders took advantage of this state of affairs to monopolize the women; and they did so to such an extent that it was difficult for a young man to marry. Contact with the whites has changed things somewhat, as far as this is concerned.

White influence is no doubt also responsible for differences of belief between the young and the older generations. The old invariably attribute all deaths to witchcraft; when a man dies at a great age they think that he has used up all the time that was allowed him on earth and that only a very weak *mangu* was needed to kill him. Sometimes the death is attributed to God. 'Mbori has carried him off,' they say. Existence is likened to a stick that Mbori eats away little by little: when he reaches the end life stops, but not without the intervention of a witch-doctor – an act that the family tries to revenge. But the younger people associate death with decrepitude. Speaking of the dead man they say, 'He has eaten his share.' They believe in witchcraft, but an old man's death seems natural to them, something that does not call for any drama. They will express this cynical opinion in private, while at the same time they carry out their public duties with regard to the dead.

Magic is of considerable importance among the Indians of the Grand Chaco, the Chorati, Mataco and Toba. These are semi-nomadic tribes who live off the abundant fruits that grow in the forest and by raising ostriches. They are content with little and they store no food because they trust in the morrow – they will not go short. The chief is an elderly man who is chosen by the oldest fathers of families when his predecessor dies: his authority is more nominal than real, and his influence arises primarily from the sacredness that age confers upon him. These Indians live without difficulty and they have the leisure to devote a great deal of their time to their religious life – a life that is governed by the elders. These men are no longer required to obey the alimentary taboos. They are feared because of their magic powers, for they are able to cast spells upon their enemies. It is thought that after their death they become evil spirits; and when these Indians say that they have seen evil spirits they always describe them as having the form of aged men. They believe that their malignant capacities increase with age; and when an aged man becomes decrepit he is killed with an arrow in the heart and his corpse is burnt. As we see in the tales of zombies, it seems that this complete destruction of the body serves to prevent its changing into a ghost.

The connexion between knowledge and magic is strikingly obvious among the Navajo, and here it provides some old men with great authority. The Navajo have a complex society with a highly developed culture that has been influenced by the white civilization, with which they are in continual contact.* The Navajo inhabit an immense territory in the north-west of Arizona; it is an arid country, but it is made fertile by irrigation and by abundant rains. They possess horses and cattle and two or three places of settlement where they gather according to the season. Theirs is an affluent society. They eat bread, meat and tinned food that they buy from the whites. They have beautiful clothes decorated with silver and turquoises: they work silver, they weave and they paint. Among them the arts of the imagination, poetry, song and dance, are highly developed. The Navajo family is matrilinear and the women are respected. Their herds are sometimes more numerous than their husbands'. Close and affectionate relationships are usual between grandparents and grandchildren, and the mother's parents in particular share in the bringing-up of the little ones. Sometimes, after the age of nine or ten, the children live with their grandparents and help them. The grandson has a 'playful relationship' with his grandfather. They challenge one another to races, and the winner gets a saddle. It is often the child who suggests competitions, such as rolling in the snow or jumping a ditch and he will make kindly fun of his grandfather.† The grandparents treat the little ones extremely well. Yet often the tasks the children have to do arouse their resentment.

This civilized and well-to-do society looks after all its weaker members, the sick and the unadapted. It is most attentive to the old, even when they are in senile decay. If, as sometimes happens, an old person whose mind is wandering rambles away from his home, he is fetched back. Yet do not the Navajo compensate for the repressions

* They sell objects produced by their craftsmen to the whites and buy manufactured goods, etc., from them.

† Roheim looks upon this custom as a way of diverting the aggression that a son usually feels for his father towards the grandfather.

caused by the respect they are required to display? The young and the middle-aged men make fun of the dodderers: they do so secretly from fear of the old men's vengeance. For indeed age raises the elderly from the earthly to the sacred plane and they, particularly the men, are credited with great supernatural powers. In a case brought against 222 sorcerers, it appeared that thirty-eight of them were women, all old, and 184 men, of whom 122 were aged. All the old are feared. No one would dare refuse an aged man hospitality, however inconvenient it might be. But many of them have no influence whatsoever, and they belong only to the fringe of the community. The Navajo have little respect for an ignorant old man. Those who are esteemed above all are the singers who can preserve and hand on the traditions – the tales, myths, rites, ceremonies, dances and formulae. They are looked upon as sacred beings possessed of enormous powers. Thanks to their memory they ensure the community's continuity throughout the ages. But what is more the chants are also magical incantations: they are literally capable of causing rain or fine weather, of curing illness and of foretelling the future. These chants are the personal property of the man who knows them, and if he teaches them to the young they give him presents, such as horses or sums of money. These men also receive gifts when they make use of their knowledge for a private person, a group or a community.

It is in his old age that a singer has his greatest reputation. Aged singers, therefore, are doubly powerful – powerful both because of their years and because of their knowledge. They are the wealthiest members of the community. They stand at the very top of the social pyramid.

After his death, the old man becomes a dangerous ghost: it is a belief common to all primitive peoples that the dead live on in the shape of spectres that are more or less to be dreaded. But whereas the Grand Chaco Indians hold that the older the man the more his malignance after death is to be feared, the Navajo have an opposite belief – one strongly emphasized by all observers. If a person dies when he has 'exhausted his life', that is to say painlessly and in a state of senile decay in which he can no longer walk or do anything without help, then this is a piece of great good fortune for him and for his family: nothing more is to be wished for, since he will not then turn into a ghost. He will be reincarnated and he will live again, growing once more old enough to be born afresh, and so on endlessly. Neither his last moments nor his funeral are accompanied by the usual rites, which are intended to protect the family and the community against his spirit. His relatives themselves see to his burial just as though it were some ordinary household task and they do not observe the usual mourning. This suggests that as the Navajo see it – and other primitive people certainly share this view – the ghost's malignance arises from resentment: he has died unwillingly, earlier than he wanted, and he takes his revenge; his aggression is directed primarily against his own family – the Navajo never see any spirits who are unrelated to them. If a man goes peacefully, because he has had his time, then he will have nothing to feel revengeful about. Among the Navajo the death of a baby aged less than a month is not at all worrying either: the child has not had enough real life to turn into a ghost.

The Jivaro too are a prosperous society: they live by gardening, hunting and fishing, in the tropical forest at the foot of the Andes. The men hunt, the women work the land; there is plenty of game, the ground is fertile, and they never lack for food. They weave cloth and make fine-looking pots. They have no political life; the families are scattered; they are very fond of their children and only the abnormal are done away with. The elderly men are respected. It is thanks to their experience that the knowledge of animals and plants and also of pharmacology has been able to evolve. They hand on the myths and the songs. In addition to this wisdom, they also possess supernatural powers that continually grow, even when the men themselves are decrepit. It is the oldest members of the family that give the children their names: it is they who make the new-born baby an integral part of the household. The old interpret the young men's dreams and carry out their initiation; they teach them the use of narcotics and tobacco. It is the old men and women – although they are not priests – who direct the ceremonies and the religious celebrations. War is the Jivaros' favourite pastime, and the leader of the expedition is usually a man of considerable age. It may happen that the old warriors bring home female prisoners chosen from the tribes of the enemy; they go to bed with them, but the girls often deceive them with younger men; then there is a fight sometimes leading to death. The Jivaro also fear the posthumous vengeance of the aged. If they have been badly used they will be born again in the shape of some dangerous animal such as a jaguar or an anaconda, and they will come back to punish those who mistreated them.

The Lele are a tribe who live in forest and savannah country near

67

the Congo, and until about 1930 their elderly men had important rights and privileges. The tribe was far less wealthy than the neighbouring Bushong, who lived in similar conditions on agriculture, hunting, fishing and weaving cloth. The Lele's earth is a little poorer and their dry season a little longer, but these variations are not enough to explain the difference in the standard of living, which arises solely from the social context. The ethnologists who studied them at the beginning of the century state that the Lele work less and with more primitive techniques; they do not aim at personal success, partly because they are afraid of jealousy but even more because it is not accumulated wealth that confers standing but rather age. The division of labour means that they can undertake only a small number of tasks; but they are polygamous – they monopolize the women, who work for them. Their sons-in-law are also required to do them service. The young men are allowed only one wife among many: in exchange for garments made of woven cloth an aged man will give one of his daughters to the youths of his village, and this young generation in its entirety thus becomes his son-in-law. There is no friendly cooperation between the age-groups. The young may not compete with the old: the aged man has the monopoly of his trade, whether he is a smith, a beater upon a drum or a wood-carver. At a given point he teaches his craft to some young man, who from that time on has the monopoly, while the old man retires.

The old occupy no high political office, but they do possess religious powers that provide them with great privileges. In order to retain them, the old men take the utmost care to remain necessary to the community. They keep the secrets of the rites, ceremonies and medicines; they are the only ones within their own clan who have a full knowledge of the debts between the various members of it and of the marriage-bargains; and this knowledge is essential to the smooth running of affairs. Yet they in their turn need the young men, for it is the young men alone who have the bodily strength required for hunting and fishing and acting as porters for the Europeans; and when the young men feel that they are being too harshly treated they threaten to go away. The old punish unruly youths by refusing them wives and excluding them from the religious ceremonies. There is a certain balance, however, in spite of this conflict. The young know that in the end the old will die and that they will inherit their widows and attain the privileges of great age. It was just as though the Lele gave up their prestige, their general standing, in order to create a kind of social insurance to take care of their old age. By about 1949 the position had changed a great deal: the young had become Christian and they were protected by the missionaries and the government. They married Christian girls and worked for the Europeans. Age-classes had almost ceased to exist.

The aged men of the Tiv derive their privileges from their cultural contribution. The Tiv are Bantu who live in Nigeria: they farm, raise stock in a small way, hunt, collect food, weave cloth and make pots. They bring up their children in the utmost liberty; and the grown children work with their parents. The children are also very close to their grandparents, who often hand on their religious and magical knowledge to them. The Tiv look upon maturity as the highest state: the adult has warmth – heat is his natural prerogative – whereas the bodies of the old people and the children are cold. Very aged men are said to be 'finishing their bodies'. (Yet the Tiv associate neither senile impotence nor desiccation with old age: they put the one down to spells and the other to disease.) Officially all the old are respected, but an elderly man has no real influence unless he possesses knowledge and ability. If he does not, the Tiv give him no position, no post of any kind: he is fed, he is treated politely, but he counts for nothing. The Tiv family structure is patriarchal: the head of the family is the oldest man belonging to it, always providing that he possesses the necessary qualifications. The chief of the community is also the oldest man, subject to the same conditions: otherwise he has a title, but not the least genuine authority. The old men who are looked upon as sages and who lead the people are those whose judgement is clear and sound, who know the tribal genealogies and titles, and who can speak well. They 'understand the nature of things', and they have magic powers. They watch over and protect the earth's fertility. Every form of social activity – war and peace, treaties, inheritance, law-suits – has to do with magic and is therefore within their scope.* They heal the sick; they judge in case of disagreement; they maintain the social structure. Since they are close to the forebears of the tribe they play a great part in religious life, and they act as oracles. The Tiv worship sacred stones, and it is the old women who cook the food that is provided for these objects, while the aged of both sexes lead the religious ceremonies. When the old lose their strength and their powers they withdraw from social life, retaining

* Here magic displays that collective aspect that Mauss attributes to it. The individual is not suspected of making a wrong use of it for his own advantage.

no more than an honorary role or perhaps none whatsoever. It may happen that some keep their religious functions. In the case of an aged man's growing weary of life, he calls his relative together and shares his fetishes among them before killing himself.

The Kikuyu elders also base their authority upon the respect of the younger people for their wisdom. The Kikuyu are Bantu who live at the foot of Mount Kenya and upon its slopes: they numbered more than a million in 1948 and they were in very frequent contact with modern civilization – they were enslaved by the European farmers. They make their livelihood from agriculture and stock-raising. The key of their civilization is the tribal system, and this is founded upon the family group: the Kikuyu work together within the 'extended family'. They attach very great importance to age-groups, which include all the men circumcised during the same year. The eldest of these groups has precedence over all the rest. There are close links between grandparents and grandchildren, and symbolically they belong to the same age-group. The grandmother calls her grandson 'husband' and the grandfather calls his granddaughter 'wife'. Children honour their parents and a father's or a mother's curse is the most terrible disaster that can happen – a disaster that no purification can do away with. When they are old the parents are looked after and taken care of. A childless old man is helped by his neighbour's children, whom he looks upon as his own. The Kikuyus' military organization is in the hands of the young men. The elders rule over public business. One generation governs for twenty or thirty years and then, during a ceremony called *itwika*, it abdicates in favour of the next. A generation, therefore, includes all the age-groups between two *itwika*. When all a man's children have been circumcised and his wife is beyond childbearing, he no longer directs public affairs; but he does step up to the highest social rank, becoming a member of the supreme council. This council has high religious functions. Those who join it are obliged to undergo an initiation.* They then have the right to sacrifice to the gods and the ancestral spirits; it is they who wipe out ritual impurities and who curse evil-doers – their curse is dreaded. They settle the dates for circumcision and the *itwika*. They act as judges, because they are thought to be

* This initiation is not a 'rite of passage' similar to those which all adolescents undergo in any given community. It is a course of instruction reserved for the chosen few. In order to attain it and to become a member of the supreme council, a man must have reached a certain stage of development in his life. This initiation does not merely confirm the change of age as such.

free from passion and to be capable of impartial decisions. There is also a council of old women that watches over morals and punishes the young when they do wrong – a council possessed of magic powers. Aged men and women play an essential part in the initiation ceremonies. The elders are looked upon as pious beings, holy men, serene and detached from the world. Their influence depends upon their abilities and upon their wealth. Generally speaking, they are regarded as being wise. The Kikuyu have a saying, 'An old goat does not spit without a reason', and again, 'Old people do not tell lies.' The old women are much respected when they have no teeth left; they are thought to be 'filled with intelligence', and their bodies are buried with great ceremony instead of being left to the hyenas.

Old people often acquire a high, privileged status because of their memories. This is the case among the Miao, who live in the high forest and bush country in China and Thailand. At one time the Miao began to evolve a high degree of civilization, but their development was checked, no doubt by wars. The family is patriarchal, and the son does not leave his father's roof until he is thirty. Theoretically the head of the house has the right of life and death over all its members, but in fact the relationship between father and son is very good, each taking the other's advice. The Miao run to large families, and the grandparents look after the grandchildren. Women, children and old people are very well treated. If, having outlived his descendants, an old person is quite by himself, he will seek the protection of the head of an important family; he is always accepted, even though he is a burden. The Miao think that the souls of the dead live in the house and guard it, and that they are reincarnated in the new-born. It is the old who hand on the traditions, and the respect in which they are held is chiefly based upon the ability to do so; their memory of the ancient myths can provide them with a very high standing. They are the community's guides and counsellors. Political decisions are carried out by the young, and their agreement is therefore necessary; but in general they bow to the wishes of the elders.

The role of memory is even more striking among the Mende, a people whose political organization is rooted in the distant past. The Mende are Moslems, living in Sierra Leone, and in 1931 there were about 572,000 of them.* The family is patriarchal, several generations living under the same roof. The head of the family is the oldest

* There are no doubt a million today.

male member; he is served before anyone else at table, and he begins by sharing the food with those of his own generation. There are two markedly distinct classes. The higher is made up of the descendants of the hunters and warriors who first settled in the country, and it includes the chiefs and their families: the oldest of these are called the 'great men'. The lower is made up of newcomers and the descendants of slaves. The upper class owns the land; and land is left by the father to his eldest son. The people of the lower class are mere tenants. The owner has a right to the services of the whole household, and those who live under his roof do the farm work, grow rice, make palm-oil, hunt and fish. The owner weaves garments for them. Each group has an elderly person as its chief, not necessarily the oldest, but the most influential: the chief may be a woman if her husband is dead and if she has an outstanding personality. When the chief becomes senile a deputy is appointed. It is memory alone that makes it possible to state whether a person belongs to one class or the other. A man who aims at becoming a chief must know the country's history, the genealogies of the Mende, the lives of their first founders and of their descendants; and this knowledge is necessarily passed on to them by their ancestors. It is they, the old people, who possess the traditions, and the Mende's political organization is therefore based upon them. Then again, the Mende live in close intimacy with the spirits of their immediate forebears, the two preceding generations. They are called the grandfathers and they are thought to take part in the life of the family. Seeing that the elders are closer to them than the rest of the household they act as mediators. It is the oldest member of the family who leads their worship, and the closest attention is paid to whatever he has to say on any religious question. He has a great deal of influence in every field of life.

The old play a less important part among those nations that are sufficiently advanced not to believe in magic and to think oral tradition of no great consequence. This we find among the Lepcha of the Himalayas: they know how to read and they practise lamaism; they work in the tea-plantations, grow maize, rice and millet; they raise cattle and they hunt. As far as food and drink is concerned, their standard of living is very high. The Lepcha family is patriarchal; the children are happy and they love their parents. Within the family, age is honoured. As an expression of respect, people are moved back one generation, parents-in-law being called grandfather and grandmother, while elder brothers and sisters are addressed as father and mother. To call someone old is to honour him. Children take the utmost care of their aged parents. An old person with many living descendants has a very happy lot; the younger members of the family delight in his health and his well-being – he is looked upon as a kind of talisman, and he is brought presents in the hope that the giver may acquire his virtues. But if he has neither children nor the strength to work, then he is a mere reject; if he is fortunate he may be treated civilly, but he is looked upon as a curse. This attitude is the same for both sexes. G. Gorer, who spent some time among the Lepcha, says that an old man was pointed out to him; this old man was very pious, but he was despised because he did not know how to read; he had no children, and he was covered with sores. Everybody made game of him, saying that he would be better dead. 'Why don't you die while the Europeans are here, so they can watch your burial?' The only asset the old possess in this society is their children's love; in themselves, they are not of the slightest value.

We have already come across many examples in which the old are either at the summit or at the very bottom of the social scale, their position depending upon their abilities and their possessions. A striking instance of discrimination based upon wealth is provided by the Thai. These are Buddhists who live on the frontier between Yunnan and Burma. They divide human existence into four periods, and the passage from each to the next is marked by a religious service called the Pai. In order to reach the fourth stage a man, once he has brought up his children, must celebrate the Great Pai; this is a long ceremony, accompanied by songs, dances, games, processions and sacrifices, and it lasts at least three days. It costs a very great deal of money. Only the rich can afford it. If they are wealthy enough they will celebrate it not once but several times; and this increases their standing. Length of years is not in itself enough to bring higher social prestige; but a man who has ruined himself by holding the Great Pai twelve times enjoys the utmost respect. His title of Paga confers no political or economic power whatsoever, but by the ritual scattering of his entire fortune he sets himself at the very top of the social pyramid.

There are some prosperous and well-balanced societies in which age is neither a falling away nor yet a source of honour. We shall see this in the three following and remarkably varied examples.

The twenty-five thousand Cuna live on the Atlantic coast and the

islands of Panama; the climate is mild, although the villages are
sometimes swept by tidal waves. They move about the virgin forest
in canoes. They have excellent constitutions, and many of them live
to be a hundred. They dwell in villages, working in groups: the
women keep house and work in the fields, the men fish, hunt and cut
trees; their harvests of maize, bananas and coconuts are abundant
and they sell their produce. The women look after the money, which,
among other things, allows the men to buy motorboats: the women
and children wear handsome clothes and the men dress in the European style. They are all very careful of their appearance; they often
have baths; their houses and streets are remarkably clean. They have
a fairly advanced culture – songs, a system of arithmetic, two esoteric
languages reserved for the chiefs and the shamans, and a primitive
form of writing. Their religion amounts to no more than paying
honour to the gods and spirits connected with physical health. The
shamans and the medicine-men protect the people from disease. Cuna
families are conjugal and they are grouped in a matrilocal community
with the husband of the eldest sister at its head. They have many
children. Thanks to their health, old and even very old people continue to lead an active life; the old women are responsible for the
house and it is they who look after the coconut trade. For their part
the old men are the experts in religious matters, but this does not give
them any special standing. Unless it is accompanied by intelligence
and experience, age confers no particular status. The head of the
family is usually old, and he is obeyed if he is a capable man. The
first thing that is required of a village chief, who presides over the
meetings, is that he should have learning: age is a factor, but only
to a certain degree. Generally speaking, the old live the same kind
of life as their juniors: they give rise to no special problems.

The Incas had a history. In a single century they conquered and
lost an empire. Yet theirs was a repetitive civilization and it was based
upon oral tradition. It is one of those that we know best of all the
archaic civilizations; and it is interesting to see the place that it
allotted to the old.

The Incas had a savage, ferocious way of life, but their techniques
and their social organization were remarkably highly developed. The
men spent a great deal of their time making war, and they treated
their prisoners brutally. They were skilful farmers: they knew how
to terrace their mountain slopes and to use guano as a fertilizer; they
grew potatoes, maize, cereals and a very wide variety of plants; they

successfully domesticated the llama and the alpaca, keeping great herds of them; they stored corn in enormous granaries. They mined gold, silver, lead and mercury. They carried out vast schemes for canals, reservoirs and dams. Six great highways traversed their country, and they threw rope suspension-bridges across the rivers. They built splendid towns, palaces and temples. The crafts, including those of the gold and silversmiths, were highly developed, and the Incas had an active economic life, with fairs at which the peasants exchanged their produce. The land was divided into three sections, one being dedicated to the Sun, the second to the Inca as his own property, and the third to the upper classes, who had their land worked by the peasants.

The most remarkable thing about this civilization is that it was one of full employment. From the age of five everyone was required to make himself useful. The men were divided into ten classes and the women into ten more: nine were age-categories and the tenth was made up of all who were sick, crippled, or unable to look after themselves. Each class had its duties, and it was obliged to serve the community to the best of its powers. The most highly respected category was that of the warriors, the men of from twenty-five to fifty. They were in the service of the king and the great lords: some were sent into the mines. They married when they were about thirty-five, and the women when they were about thirty-three. Until the age of twenty-five they had to obey and help their parents, and to work for the caciques. From nine onwards the girls, great and small, worked in the house, wove cloth and guarded the herds.

Age did not do away with the obligation to work. After they were fifty the men were exempt from military service and all very laborious tasks, but they had to work in the chief's house and in the fields. They retained their authority within the family. The women over fifty wove cloth for the community or took service in rich women's houses as caretakers, cooks, etc. From eighty onwards the men were deaf and hardly able to do more than eat and sleep; but for all that they were made to be useful. They made ropes and carpets, looked after houses, raised rabbits and ducks, picked up leaves and straw: the old women wove and span, looked after houses, helped bring up children and went on working for the rich, supervising the young servant-girls. If they had fields of their own they lacked for nothing: if they did not, they were given alms. The men, too: they received food and clothing and their goats were looked after; if they were ill, they were taken care of. Generally speaking, elderly men were feared, honoured and obeyed. They could give advice, instruction and a good example; they could extol right conduct and help in the service of the god. They guarded the younger married women. They had the right to beat unruly boys and girls.

The inhabitants of Bali cannot be looked upon as primitive people: they have had a high degree of civilization for hundreds of years. Because of the remoteness of the island this civilization has been preserved from all outside influence. The Dutch ruled it by means of the Balinese aristocracy, which exploited the rural population but which did not change their social structure nor their way of life. In the country this archaic culture has lived on until our time, handed down by oral tradition, for the Balinese can neither read nor write. We may therefore set this culture among those of the societies that have no history.

The Balinese grow rice and they have perfected the management of this crop to a degree unknown to any other nation whatsoever. They have excellent cattle, and pigs and poultry. The island has great quantities of fruit, vegetables and other produce. They sell all these things at their big, frequently-held markets. The villages are well-built and very carefully looked after. Craftsmanship is highly developed; so is music, poetry, dancing and the theatre. The people respect the aristocracy, and the aristocracy do not interfere with them. For practical purposes each village is a little republic. It is governed by an assembly to which all the married men who own a house or a piece of land must belong. The chiefs are usually elected, but sometimes descent plays a part. They are the earthly representatives of the authority of the gods: they supervise the land, the houses, social life as a whole. The bonds between the individual and the community are very close, and the greatest punishment that can be inflicted upon a member is expulsion. They are hospitable and remarkably polite to one another. The Balinese are intelligent, and they have fine bodies: they are exceedingly aware of them and their movements are studied and full of grace. They adapt themselves with pliant goodwill to the parts they are required to play – child, adolescent, woman, adult, and elderly person.

The children are petted and cherished by their parents and grandparents. Age is respected, although it brings no magical powers with it. Every man's rank in the assembly rises with the years. Every month the elders of the village meet and share a banquet with their gods. These gods are close to men and often come to see them. The Balinese have a syncretic religion, borrowed from India, China and Java – a religion that is impregnated with animism. They worship the sun, the moon, water and all sources of fertility. Rice is the centre of one form of worship. They believe in the existence of ghosts that have malignant powers over the living.

In Bali it is said that once upon a time the people of a remote mountain village used to sacrifice and eat their old men. A day came when there was not a single old man left, and the traditions were lost. They wanted to build a great house for the meetings of the assembly, but when they came to look at the tree-trunks that had been cut for that purpose no one could tell the top from the bottom: if the timber were placed the wrong way up, it would set off a series of disasters. A young man said that if they promised never to eat the old men any more, he would be able to find a solution. They promised. He brought his grandfather, whom he had hidden; and the old man taught the community to tell top from bottom.

The inhabitants of the village assert that no such custom ever existed. However that may be, old men are respected throughout the country: this is largely because, having led favourable lives, they escape the degradation of age. They retain their health for a great while; they are neither bent nor awkward; they keep the physical poise and control that they acquired when they were young. Women of sixty and even more still have an elegant shape and the strength needed to carry heavy pots of water on their heads, or baskets with forty or fifty pounds of fruit in them. They do not stop working, unless they are very seriously disabled: they think that idleness would imperil their bodily and mental health and that they might be attacked by supernatural powers. Indeed, the older the women become the busier they are; some are to be seen governing an entire household at the age of more than sixty, and doing most of the tasks themselves. The elderly men work little: they talk and chew betel. But they have many duties – they direct the village assembly, practise medicine, tell tales, and teach the young poetry and art. And they also often take the ducks out into the fields. They play an important part in the religious ceremonies. There are some very old men and women who are excellent dancers. They go into trances and speak as oracles. The old have a very important role – both male and female, for the distinction between the sexes disappears with age. Their opinion is asked on every subject. When they grow very old and decrepit they are called grandfather or grandmother. When they have lost all their teeth they are looked upon as being close to little children, and it is believed that they will soon be reincarnated in the form of a new-born baby. They then lose their influence, but they are still well fed and looked after. Even when he is feeble and doddering an old man may be the priest in a temple; but he has a younger assistant, and his function becomes honorary.

It does not seem that the old inspire fear. Yet in magic plays Ranga, the witch who eats children, is shown as a huge old woman with drooping breasts and a mat of white hair that comes down to her feet. An old actor takes the part: because of his age he escapes the evil spirit of the witch he represents.

The materials at my disposal have not allowed me to isolate one factor that the ethnologists consider of very great importance in relation to the state of the aged: this is the factor of social organization. Some communities are wandering hordes, or bands – lightly-structured groups. But when clans or tribes settle on a given territory (which implies becoming an agricultural society) they often find it necessary to make an exact definition of their various lines of descent in order to determine rights of inheritance, marriage-exchanges and the relationships between individuals. The genealogy, the line of descent, leads back to the ancestor; it is the ancestor who authenticates it; and it is indeed an extension of that ancestor. The forebears are not flung back into the past; the community – family, clan or tribe – to which the land belongs includes the dead as well as the living; and its rights are mystically based upon the rights of the dead, for the community looks upon itself as their heirs. It is sometimes thought that the ancestor is reincarnated in a new-born child descended from him, so that the new generations bring back the old to life. Not all societies of this kind practise ancestor-worship, but most do. The ancestor is a benevolent spirit that dwells in his descendants' house; or at least he is one that is favourable to them if he is worshipped as he ought to be. It is an aged man who must direct the ceremonies and sacrifices by which the ancestor is honoured. He is closer to the ancestor than the young; he will soon become an ancestor in his turn; and he is endowed with a sacred character. He is the incarnation of his stock, and it is because of him that right relationships can be established with other stocks: he is the symbol of order and its architect. In societies of this kind, therefore, there is a clearly-defined image of the old man, and he has an officially-acknowledged status. Whereas in nomadic hordes and bands – as in our modern industrial societies – his status is merely fortuitous. It varies within the group and from one group to another.

Clearly we must take care not to over-simplify when we consider the condition of the old in primitive societies. It is not true that the 'coconut-palm is shaken' in all parts of the world; nor is it right to paint an idyllic picture of their lot, which is explained by the factors that we have mentioned in the course of these examples – factors whose significance and relationship we must now elucidate.

It is perfectly evident that an old person has a greater chance of survival in wealthy societies than in poor, and among settled rather than among nomadic people. The only problem that arises for settled communities is that of maintenance; for the nomads there is also the more difficult question of transport. Even if they live tolerably well, they do so only at the cost of perpetual movement: the old cannot follow, and they are left behind. In agricultural societies the same comparative plenty would be enough to feed them. Yet the economic situation is not wholly decisive: generally speaking it is a question of a choice made by the community, a choice that may be influenced by various circumstances. It is a fact that in spite of the harshness of their life the inland Chukchee do manage to take their old people with them when they move from place to place. On the other hand there are some agricultural societies, and not the most poverty-stricken of them either, that watch unmoved while their old people die of hunger.

It might be supposed that in the poorest societies magic and religion would step in to protect the old. But this is not so. For the very reason that they live in a state of continual emergency these communities do not develop anything but the most rudimentary religious culture. With them magic is not a 'knowledge of the nature of things' but a mere collection of rude, uncouth formulas, the property of the shamans. The old shamans are respected, but age in itself confers no magic power. It may happen that a religion exists, but that it does no more than confirm a custom imposed by necessity, giving it a sacred character; a single impulse allows the community to set up the customs needed for survival and to provide them with an ideological justification. We have seen an instance of this among the

Narte; and in *Narayama* O'Rin supposes that she is obeying the wishes of the gods.

A surer protection is that which their children's love provides for the old parents. Roheim has emphasized the connexion between the happiness of the earliest days and that of the last. We know how important early treatment is to the subsequent development of a child's personality. If a child is kept short of food, protection and loving kindness he will grow up full of resentment, fear, and even hatred; as a grown man his relations with others will be aggressive – he will neglect his old parents when they are no longer able to look after themselves. On the other hand, if the parents feed their children well and cherish them, the result is cheerful, open, kindly beings in whom altruistic feelings develop: the children will be fond of their parents, acknowledging their duty towards them and performing it. I have looked into many more examples than I have quoted, and among them all I have come across only one in which happy children turn into adults who are cruel to their fathers and mothers – the Ojibway. Whereas the Yakut and the Ainu, who are badly treated as children, neglect the old most brutally, the Yaghan and the Aleut, who live in almost the same conditions but among whom the child is king, honour their old people. Yet the aged are often the victims of a vicious circle: extreme poverty obliges the adults to feed their children badly and to neglect them. It must also be observed that filial affection takes the form dictated by custom and religion – a son may show his respect and affection for his parents by the most meticulous performance of the ceremonies in which they are put to death.

The old might hope to carry on with their lives if they retained enough strength to work. But when they have been badly fed, badly looked after and are worn out with labour, they soon grow decrepit; and here again we have a vicious circle that is often disastrous for them.

Rarely do we find poor communities in which an old person has possessions that allow him to look after himself. Among the hunters and collectors property does not exist: they do not even store food. Among the pastoral and agricultural societies property is often collective: the individual possesses no more than the product of his own or his wives' labour; if he outlives them or if they become infirm and he can no longer work himself – or if he is forbidden by custom to perform tasks reserved for women – then he is wholly destitute.

Sometimes the head of the family is the master of his herds or his land; but when his strength wanes his heirs take them from him by force or even do away with him to inherit the sooner. We have seen only two instances where old men remain the masters of their possessions – the inland Chukchee and the very few coast Chukchee who have traded with the whites.

We may infer that the most usual choice of communities with inadequate resources, whether they are agricultural or nomadic, is to sacrifice the old.

The truth as to the way in which the aged undergo their fate is unknown. Reporters and sociologists like to say that they die cheerfully: I have shown literary evidence that throws doubt on this.

When a society has a certain margin of security, there seems on the face of it to be a reasonable supposition that it will maintain its aged people: it is in the adults' interest to look to their own future. Instead of forming a vicious circle, the sequence of events moves in a favourable direction: well-treated children will treat their parents well; proper food and attention to health will protect the individual from premature decay. Culture evolves, and because of it old people may acquire great influence. Magic then grows into a system of thought which comes close to being a science.

Primitive peoples acknowledge a 'magic vocation' in certain individuals who are set apart by some particular characteristic – law-breakers, cripples, etc. Old age also sets men apart, so that they form a distinct category. But it is above all by their memory that the old make themselves necessary in this field; the Balinese legend that I have mentioned makes this eminently clear – deprived of tradition, the community would be unable to carry on its activities. These activities are concerned not only with techniques, which the adults might rediscover; they must also obey ritual requirements which are not apparent in the immediately present aspect of things but which are imposed by the past, and which are known only to the elders. It is always possible to build with tree-trunks: but if they are not erected in a particular way, which is not self-evident in practice, disaster will be the result. Arrows cannot possibly be shot with any real success if the archer does not know the incantations that will direct them to their target. It is the old who have the secret and they are careful how they let it go: we have seen how the Lele elders take their precautions so that the tribe will have need of them: they pass on their knowledge only late in life.

The old man is necessary: he is also dangerous, because he may turn his magic knowledge to his own advantage. There is still another cause for his ambivalence – seeing that he is close to death he is also close to the supernatural world. As to this aspect, primitive thought wavers. Death, except in the case of very young children, never seems natural to them. Even at a great age, it is the result of a spell.* Yet they are perfectly well aware that the aged man is soon going to die: so much so that there are some who call him an 'almost dead'. He is already slipping away from the human state – he is virtually a ghost, a ghost with provisional exemption, and the other spirits have no power over him. The relationship with the dead ancestor is felt to be ambivalent: in many societies he is a forebear who wishes his descendants well. In all he is a spirit, and as such he is dreaded. Almost everywhere it is ghosts who are held responsible for any misfortune that happens to the individual and the tribe. Their afterlife is dubious: after a shorter or a longer time they vanish – nothing is left of them. But as long as they do survive, there must be an attempt at conciliating them by rites and sacrifices; or at least the living must be protected from them. In all circumstances in which the spirits are threatening, such as the passage from one group to another or from one age to another, or impurity caused by a ritual offence, it is only the aged man who can deal with their menace. He has moved from the earthly to the sacred world; and this means that he has powers similar to those possessed by the ghost that he himself will be in a little while.

It is thus that the aged man inspires fear at the same time as respect. In those societies in which magic is nearer to sorcery than to a science and in which spirits are very much dreaded, fear predominates over respect. This allows old men to reach high positions and even to tyrannize over the young. Yet there is not the same attitude towards the 'greying head' as there is towards the very ancient man. Sometimes great length of years inspires admiration. It proves that the old man has succeeded in living his life wisely, and he then becomes an example. He must have been endowed with uncommon magical virtues to have withstood so many natural and supernatural trials. Nevertheless, when decrepitude makes its appearance, many think that this virtue weakens along with the other powers, and fear no longer protects the aged man. Others, on the contrary, feel that the magic power grows steadily with the years. Here again, two

* Except when, as among the Navajo, a very old man has 'exhausted his life'.

attitudes are possible. The dread that the living old man or the potential ghost inspires may mean that he is treated with respect even in extreme decrepitude. Or else this increase of power, making him continually more dangerous both now and in the future, is hurriedly stopped: he is killed and his body is wholly done away with. In the Polynesian Trobriand Islands and in some remote parts of Japan the adults used to eat the old men once they had reached a certain age; they thus absorbed the victims' wisdom and at the same time prevented them from becoming sorcerers and then over-powerful wizards.

In his role as priest or servant of the gods there is no ambivalence about the old man. Here his part is of the very greatest positive importance. And here again it is thanks to his memory that he is fitted for it. The ceremonies, rites, dances and chants that are required for proper worship all come through him. He does teach them to others, but his knowledge marks him out particularly as a right person to perform himself. He is also fitted for this because of the reason that we have already mentioned – he is the intercessor between the earthly and the supernatural world.

As the custodian of the traditions, the intercessor, and the protector against the supernatural powers, the aged man ensures the cohesion of the community throughout time and in the present. It is often he who is entrusted with making the new-born baby an integral part of the group by choosing a name for it. And if the community has a complex political organization it may also happen that he is the man who sees to its functioning – his memory alone retains the genealogies that allow the placing of each individual or each family in its proper order.

Generally speaking, the services, taken as a whole, that the old are enabled to render because of their knowledge of the traditions, mean that they have not only respect but also material prosperity. They are rewarded with presents. The gifts that they receive from those whom they initiate into their secrets are of particular importance – they are the surest source of private wealth, a source that exists only in societies that are sufficiently well-to-do to have an advanced culture. And it is available only to men of great repute.

But in still more highly developed societies the influence of the old men diminishes. These communities believe less in spirits and less even in magic: they are no longer afraid of the 'almost dead'. Here the aged men's standing is based upon their positive cultural contribution, which loses much of its value in those societies in which technique breaks away from magic, and even more in those which can write.

When a community is in a state of harmonious balance it provides the old with a decent position by entrusting them with work suitable for their strength. But it does not grant them privileges.

Old age does not have the same meaning nor the same consequences for men and for women. For the women it presents one particular advantage: after the menopause the woman is no longer a being with a sex. Her state now corresponds to that of the little girl before puberty; and like the little girl she is not subject to certain alimentary taboos. Those things that were forbidden to her because of her monthly impurity no longer weigh upon her life; she may take part in the dances, she may drink, smoke and sit down next to the men. The factors that favour the old men come into play for her too, providing her with certain advantages. In matrilinear societies, above all, the aged women play a very important cultural, religious, social and political part. In others their experience has a certain worth. Supernatural powers are attributed to them, and these may give them standing, though they may also turn against them. Generally speaking their status remains inferior to that of the men. They are more neglected: they are abandoned more readily.

In many societies the aged men and women are in close relationship with the children. There is an analogy between the helplessness of the baby and that of the very old person: this is made particularly clear in the Narte epic, where it is said that the old men were strapped into cradles. The baby has scarcely emerged from the shadows: the ancient is about to plunge into them. For the Navajo both the child that has barely come into existence and the very old man who is hardly still alive die without resentment and do not turn into ghosts. From the practical point of view both are useless mouths that have to be fed – burdens. Very poor tribes, and especially very poor nomadic tribes, practise both infanticide and the killing of the aged. Sometimes we find the second without the first. But not the contrary, for the child, representing the future, has priority over the old man, who is mere waste. Both are parasites, and sometimes in the case of extreme poverty, this leads to rivalry between them: the children steal the old people's share of food. But if they have high standing, then thanks to rigid alimentary taboos the old monopolize a large share of the food. Grandchildren and grandparents are often closely associated. They belong symbolically to the same age-group: the aged see to the bringing up of the little ones, and the grandchildren render them services. Hope for the future lies with the child: the old man, rooted in the past, is the custodian of knowledge; he must educate his heirs, who will ensure his own survival by means of ancestor-worship or by begetting women through whom he will be reborn. It is this connexion that binds the society's unity throughout time. In practical terms, the old person, being freed from the labour of the adults, has time to look after the young; and in their turn they have the leisure to provide their grandparents with the services they need. This exchange of kindness is accompanied by a playful relationship; both the very young and the very old, because of their physical inadequacy and because they are marginal members of the community, free from many social obligations, are removed from the serious life of the adults; they joke and laugh together, challenging one another to games.

Among primitive peoples the aged man is truly the Other, with the ambivalence that that word implies. In masculine myths the woman, the Other, appears as an idol and as a sex-object at one and the same time. Similarly, for other reasons and in another manner, the old man in those societies is both a sub-man and a superman. He is decrepit and useless: but he is also the intercessor, the magician, the priest – below or beyond the human state, and often both together.

As it happens in all societies, these attitudes are experienced in a way that is both contingent and particular for each case. The fate of the aged depends largely upon their abilities and the standing and wealth that these abilities have provided them with: the fate of the privileged is not the same as that of the ordinary people. There is also differentiation according to the group and the family. Theory and practice do not always agree; the old may be mocked in private and at the same time treated with outward respect. And the contrary is often to be seen – old age is honoured in words and at the same time allowed to wither away in physical neglect.

The most important fact to emphasize is that the status of the old man is never *won* but always *granted*. In *The Second Sex* I showed that, where women derive great standing from their magic powers, they owe it in fact to the men. This is equally true for the aged in relation to the adults. Their authority is based upon the dread or the respect they inspire: the moment the adults break free from this, the aged have no power left whatsoever. This has happened frequently enough when there has been contact with whites. The aged Zande and Aranda no longer monopolize the women. Some young men – the African Lao, for example – leave the villages where they maintained their old parents and go to find jobs in the towns. The young Lele have thrown off the yoke of the aged by becoming Christian and working for Europeans.

Where the authority of the old is still strong, the reason is that the community as a whole wishes to maintain its traditions by means of them. It is the community, according to its potentialities and its interests, that determines the fate of the old: and the old are subject to this determination even when they think themselves the strongest.*

Brief though it may be, this survey is enough to show the degree to which the condition of the aged depends upon the social context. The old man is subject to a biological fate that has one inevitable economic consequence – he becomes unproductive. But his degradation is faster or slower according to the community's resources: in some decrepitude begins at forty, in others at eighty. Then again, when a society is comparatively well-to-do it is able to make various choices: the outlook of an aged man who is thought of as a useless burden is very unlike that of one who is a part of a society whose members have chosen to sacrifice their wealth up to a certain point in order to make sure of their own old age. It is not only his material position that is in question, but also the value that is accorded to him: he may be well treated and despised, or well treated and honoured or dreaded. This status depends upon the aims the country sets itself. As I have pointed out, the word decline has no meaning except in relation to a given end – movement towards or farther from a goal. If a community is merely trying to subsist from day to day, a member who becomes a useless mouth that has to be fed is in decline. But if this community, mystically linked to its forebears, desires to live on spiritually, then it looks upon the ancient man, who belongs both to the past and to the after-world, as its embodiment. In this case even the utmost possible degree of physical decay may be looked upon as the highest point of life. Most often this

---

* Simmons seems to contradict this, but in fact he does not. What he shows is that once a status has been laid down, there are some old men who succeed in profiting by it better than others: they work furiously, they find ways of making themselves useful, etc. But the status itself is always established by the community as a whole.

acme is placed at the 'greying age', and decrepitude is regarded as a falling away: but not always.

It is the meaning that men attribute to their life, it is their entire system of values that define the meaning and the value of old age. The reverse applies: by the way in which a society behaves towards its old people it uncovers the naked, and often carefully hidden, truth about its real principles and aims.

The practical solutions adopted by primitive peoples to deal with the problems set by their old people are very varied: the old are killed; they are left to die; they are given a bare minimum to support life; a decent end is provided for them; or they are revered and cherished. As we shall see, what are called civilized nations apply the same methods: killing alone is forbidden, unless it is disguised.

3

Old age in historical societies

It is not easy to study the condition of old people throughout the ages. The written evidence that we have very rarely mentions them: they are included in the general category of adults. In mythology, in literature and in representative art we do obtain a certain picture of old age: this picture varies according to the century and to the place. But how real a vision do we get? It is difficult to say. The picture is blurred, uncertain and contradictory. It is important to realize that the expression 'old age' has two very different meanings throughout the various pieces of evidence that we possess. It is either a certain social category which has greater or lesser value according to circumstances. Or for each person it is one particular fate: his own. The first point of view is that of the lawgivers and moralists; the second that of the poets; and for the most part they are radically opposed. Lawgivers and poets always belong to the privileged classes, which is one of the reasons why their words have no great value. They never say anything but part-truths and very often they lie. The poets are the more sincere, however, since they express themselves more spontaneously. The ideologists produce conceptions of old age that fit in with the interests of their class.

Another statement must be made at once: it is impossible to write a history of old age. History implies a certain circularity. The cause which produces a given effect is in its turn influenced by this same effect. The unity throughout time which thus evolves has some kind of meaning. At a pinch, we could speak of a history of women, since they have been the symbol and the locus for certain male conflicts: between their own family and their husband's, for example. In the human adventure they have never been a primary cause; but they have at least been a pretext and an incentive; the evolution of their status has followed a capricious but meaningful line. The aged, considered as social categories, have never influenced the progress of the world.* So long as the aged man retains some efficiency he remains an integral part of the community and he is not distinguished from it – he is an elderly adult male. When he loses his powers he takes on the appearance of *another*; he then becomes, and to a far more radical extent than a woman, a mere object. She is necessary to society whereas he is of no worth at all. He cannot be used in barter, nor for reproductive purposes, nor as a producer: he is no longer anything but a burden. As we have just seen his is a *granted* status, and it is therefore never subject to any sort of development. It has been said that the Negro problem is a white problem; and that of women, a masculine problem: yet women are struggling for equality and the blacks are fighting against oppression; the aged have no weapons whatsoever, and their problem belongs strictly to the active adults. It is the adults who decide, according to their own interests, practical and ideological, the role that can most suitably be given to the aged.

Even in more complex societies than those we have looked into this role may be important, the middle-aged men seeking the support of the older generation against the unruly young. The aged refuse to be dispossessed of the power that has been given them, and if there is an attempt at taking it from them, they will make use of it to preserve their authority. We find the echo of these struggles throughout the chronicles, the various mythologies and literatures. In the end the old are inevitably defeated, because they amount to no more than a helpless minority, drawing their strength only from the majority, which makes use of them.

Although the problem of old age is one of power, it arises only within the body of the ruling classes. Until the nineteenth century there was never any mention of the 'aged poor'; there were not many of them, for longevity was only possible among the privileged classes; the aged poor represented nothing whatsoever. History, like literature, passes them over in total silence. Old age is revealed, and then only to a certain degree, within the privileged classes alone.

Another fact is staringly obvious at first glance: what we have here is a man's problem. As a personal experience, old age is as much a woman's concern as a man's – even more so, indeed, since women live longer. But when there is speculation upon the subject, it is considered primarily in terms of men. In the first place because

* In particular cases, of course, women and old men have played active roles.

it is they who express themselves in laws, books and legends, but even more because the struggle for power concerns only the stronger sex. Among the apes, the young wrest it from the old male; he alone is killed, not the aged females.

The societies that have a history are ruled by the men: the women, both young and old, may perfectly well lay claim to authority in private, but in public life their status is always the same – that of perpetual minors. The masculine state, on the contrary, changes with the passage of time: the young man becomes an adult, a citizen, and the adult an old man. The men form age-groups whose natural limits are vague, though society may set precise bounds to them, as it does today by laying down the age for retirement. The movement from one group to the next may amount to a promotion or to a fall.

Both ethnology and biology show that the positive contribution of the aged to the community is their memory and their experience, which, as far as repetitive work is concerned, increases their performance and their judgement. What they lack is health and strength: they also lack the power of adapting themselves to new things and situations and obviously, therefore, inventive ability. On the face of it, then, we may presume that strongly organized and repetitive societies will look to the aged for support. In divided societies and in troubled or revolutionary times, the young will take command. The part that elderly men play in private family life will be a reflection of that which is allowed them by the state. When we look into the condition of the old throughout the ages we shall find that this pattern is borne out.

In the following pages I shall confine myself to a study of Western societies. Yet there must be one exception – China, because of the uniquely privileged position that it provided for its old men.

In no country was civilization so static for so many hundreds of years as it was in China; nor so strongly hierarchical, either. It was a hydraulic civilization, requiring a centralized and authoritarian rule: because of the geographic and economic conditions the people were concerned not with development but with survival: the administration limited itself to preserving that which had always existed. It was made up of literati whose position and responsibilities increased with the years: the most senior were automatically at the top. This lofty position was reflected in family life. When Confucius laid down his strict system of relations between inferior and superior, he modelled the microcosm that was to be the basis of the community upon the community itself; and this microcosm was the family. The entire household owed obedience to the oldest man. His moral prerogatives met with no practical dispute, for China's intensive agriculture called more for experience than for strength. This way of life provided the family with no questions or contradictory element, for the wife owed obedience to her husband and she had no appeal against him. The father had the right of life and death over his children, and he often did away with daughters at their birth; or he would sell them later as slaves. The son had to obey his father, and the younger brother the elder. Young people were married by parental authority, without ever having met one another, and they remained under the rule of the bridegroom's elders. The patriarch's authority did not lessen with age. Even the bitterly oppressed women profited from the rise in status that came with the years: an old woman had a much higher standing than the young of either sex, and she controlled the bringing up of her grandchildren, usually treating them with great severity. And her daughters-in-law paid for the harshness which she had experienced from her own mother-in-law. Respect reached out beyond the limits of the family to embrace all elderly persons, and they would often pretend to be older than they were in order to have a right to deference. His fiftieth birthday was an important date in a man's life. Yet after seventy they laid down their official positions in order to prepare themselves for death. Although they preserved their authority, they would leave the running of the household to their eldest son. The old man was honoured as an ancestor, an ancestor who would presently be worshipped. The young submitted to the old man's authority either with resignation or with despair (as we see in Chinese literature, particularly the ancient operas), for the young had no way of escaping from it except by suicide, which was particularly frequent among the young married women. Confucius provided a moral justification for this system by putting old age and the possession of wisdom on the same footing. 'At fifteen, I applied myself to the study of wisdom; at thirty I grew stronger in it; at forty I no longer had doubts; at sixty there was nothing on earth that could shake me; at seventy I could follow the dictates of my heart without disobeying the moral law.'

There were not, in fact, many very old men, for circumstances were not favourable to longevity. In Taoism old age was taken as a virtue in itself. Lao Tzu's teaching sets the age of sixty as the moment at which a man may free himself from his body by ecstatic experience and become a holy being. In Chinese neo-Taoism man's supreme aim is the quest for the 'long life'. All the fathers of Taoism speak of this. It amounted to something like a national discipline. Asceticism and ecstasy could lead to a holiness that would protect the adept from death itself. Holiness was the art of not dying, the absolute possession of life. Old age was therefore life in its very highest form. It was supposed that if life lasted long enough it would culminate in apotheosis. Chuang Tzu calls ancient beliefs to mind when he says that 'tired of the world after a thousand years of life, the superior men raise themselves to the rank of spirits.'

Sometimes, in Chinese literature, young people may deplore the oppression of which they are the victims; but never is old age cried out against as a curse. In the West, on the other hand, the first known text that speaks of old age draws a gloomy picture: it is to be seen in Egypt, and it was written by Ptah-hotep, a philosopher and poet, in 2500 B.C.

How hard and painful are the last days of an aged man! He grows weaker every day; his eyes become dim, his ears deaf; his strength fades; his heart knows peace no longer; his mouth falls silent and he speaks no word. The power of his mind lessens and today he cannot remember what yesterday was like. All his bones hurt. Those things which not long ago were done with pleasure are painful now; and taste vanishes. Old age is the worst of misfortunes that can afflict a man. His nose is blocked, and he can smell nothing any more.

We shall find this unhappy list of the infirmities of old age repeated century after century, and it is important to emphasize the permanence of this theme. Although the meaning and the value attached to old age vary in different societies, old age nevertheless remains a fact that runs throughout all history, arousing a certain number of identical reactions. Physically it is without any question a decline, and for that reason most men have dreaded it. Even as early as the Egyptians they cherished the hope that they might defeat it. There is a papyrus that reads, 'The beginning of the book on the way of changing an old man into a young one'. It advises the eating of fresh glands taken from young animals. And we find this dream of rejuvenation again and again, lasting until our own days.

The Jewish nation is known for the respect with which it surrounded old age. How much is myth and how much reality in the accounts that were brought together from the ninth century onwards to form the Bible? It is hard to say. They derive their inspiration both from ancient oral traditions and the then present situation. At that time the Hebrews had settled in Palestine; the nomads had become farmers, and the old, tribal, patriarchal civilization had been transformed. Social classes had come into being: the rich were at the same time the judges, the holders of administrative authority, the masters of commerce, and the money-lenders. The writers of the holy books were homesick for the past and they projected the values they wanted their contemporaries to accept back into the past. Although among the Jews we find echoes of a very ancient matrilinear descent, these authors describe a patriarchal society in which the great ancestors, to whom they attribute fabulous longevity, were the chosen of God and his mouthpieces. They looked upon great age as the supreme reward of virtue. 'Ye shall harken diligently unto my commandments,' says God in Deuteronomy, 'that your days may be multiplied, and the days of your children, in the land which the Lord sware unto your fathers to give them, as the days of heaven upon the earth.' 'The fear of the Lord prolongeth days: but the years of the wicked shall be shortened,' we find in the Proverbs. 'The hoary head is a crown of glory, if it be found in the way of righteousness,' we read elsewhere in the same book. Blessed by God, old age commands obedience and respect. 'Thou shalt rise up before the hoary head, and honour the face of the old man,' says Leviticus. The Commandments require children to honour their father and mother. If a son refuses to obey his father and all attempts to make him yield are in vain, then, says Deuteronomy, the father must take him before the elders of the town: 'And all the men of his city shall stone him with stones, that he die.' We should like to know whether such punishments were really carried out. One thing is sure, and that is that the fact of laying them down means that the submission of the children must have been less absolute than it was in China: the Jewish society was far less rigorously organized, and it left more room for individualism. In this society the elder had a political role. According to the Book of Numbers, Yahweh said to Moses, 'Gather unto me seventy men of the elders of Israel, whom thou knowest to be the elders of the people, and officers over them . . . and they shall bear the burden of the people with thee, that thou bear it not thyself alone.' We do not know whether such a council really existed. The Bible also tells how Rehoboam was punished for not having listened to the elders who advised generous treatment for Israel – the oppressed tribes that broke away from the house of David. No doubt all these traditions were brought forward to support and strengthen custom. In Palestine, as in all advanced agricultural societies, the elders undoubtedly played an important part in public life; and so long as he retained some physical and spiritual strength the oldest man in the family ruled it. Speaking of the days of Antiochus the Great (223–181 B.C.), Josephus refers to a Gerusia whose president was the High Priest and whose most influential members were the priestly aristocrats – this was the Sanhedrim. It seems that this body did not make its appearance until the later centuries. It was made up of seventy members: the princes of the priests (former High Priests), the representatives of the twenty-four priestly classes of scribes, of the doctors of the Law, and of the elders of the people. It was the supreme court. It enacted the laws and stepped in where relationships with the occupying Romans were concerned. It supervised all that had to do with religion, that is to say virtually everything. The elders therefore had an important part to play. But it was thought that the perfect judge should be neither too young nor too old.

There is only one incident in the Bible that associates not virtue with old age but vice: it is to be found in a late work, written between 167 and 164 B.C. – the Book of Daniel.* It is the well-known story of Susannah and the two elders. These men, who were judges and who were respected by the master of the house, fell in love with the beauty of his wife. One afternoon they hid in the garden to watch her taking a bath. She refused them her favours and in revenge they said they had seen her lying with a young man. They were believed and Susannah was condemned to death. But Daniel, still a youth, saved her by questioning the two judges separately – their evidence was contradictory, and it was they who were sentenced to death.† Perhaps at that period there was a feeling of resentment against the aged men, some of whom made an ill use of their wealth, their high office, and the respect with which they were treated.

Ecclesiastes, an enigmatic book certainly made up from different

* This episode is suppressed in the Protestant Bible, no doubt because of the immense respect with which the Puritans surrounded old men.
† Book of Daniel, ch. XIII.

sources and of disputed date, contrasts with the rest of Jewish thought. In it we find a striking instance of that opposition which I have mentioned between society's official attitude towards old age and the spontaneous reactions that it arouses in the poets. Ecclesiastes reckons old age among man's misfortunes, and the description of decay, if we read it according to the interpretation of the Jewish exegetist Maurice Jastrow, is bitterly cruel.

Remember now they Creator in the days of thy youth, while the evil days come not, nor the years draw nigh, when thou shalt say, I have no pleasure in them; while the sun, or the light, or the moon, or the stars, be not darkened, nor the clouds return after the rain [diminution of sight, extinction of intellectual powers] in the day when the keepers of the house [the arms] shall tremble, and the strong men [the legs] shall bow themselves, and the grinders [the teeth] cease because they are few, and those that look out of the windows [the eyes] be darkened, and the doors shall be shut in the streets [digestive and urinary difficulties], when the sound of the grinding is low [deafness], and he shall rise up at the voice of the bird [poor sleep, early wakening], and all the daughters of musick shall be brought low [difficulties in speech]; also when they shall be afraid of that which is high [breathlessness in going up stairs or slopes], and fears shall be in the way, and the almond tree shall flourish [white hairs], and the grasshopper shall be a burden [fading of sexual power]. . . . Or ever the silver cord be loosed [bending of the spinal column], or the golden bowl be broken, or the pitcher be broken at the fountain, or the wheel be broken at the cistern [malfunction of the liver and kidneys] . . .

As to the position of the aged among the other nations of antiquity, we have very little information indeed. In this poverty we cannot overlook mythology, although what is to be gathered from customs, way of life and fable is extremely vague. Most mythologies deal with old age from the point of view of the conflict between the generations. The earliest of all civilizations that we know is that of Sumer and Akkad. Here we learn that at the very beginning there first existed Apsu, the god of the water, and Tiamet, the goddess of the sea. From their union was born Mummu (the surging of the waves), and then Lahmu and Iahamu, who, marrying, begot Anshar, the sky, and Kishar, the earth. These begot Anu, Bel-Marduk, Ea and other gods of the earth and the lower regions. The turbulence of these young deities disturbed the peace of old Apsu, who complained to Tiamet: they conspired to wipe out their descendants.

But Ea seized upon Apsu and Mummu. Tiamet then gave birth to huge serpents and a large number of monsters, placing them under the orders of Quingu, one of the gods she had persuaded to join her. The other gods appointed Marduk to be their king; he challenged Tiamet to battle and killed her.* After this he set the world in order and created mankind. We find a similar series of events among the Phoenicians, recorded by the Ras-Shamas tablets. Philon of Byblos, writing at the end of the first century after Christ, hands on an echo of these beliefs. He tells how Cronus mutilated his father Epigeios, who then took the name of Uranus.

This pattern matches that which we find in many other religions: at the beginning of the world there exists a Uranian god, a solitary principle who remains distant, abstract, with no relationship to mankind – a god unworshipped by men. The sacred principle then descends to a plurality of concrete gods who are in direct connexion with the world and whom men worship by means of sacrifices, prayers and ceremonies. But it is significant that this shift, this devolution, should assume the appearance of a lineal descent, the ancestor being thrust back far from the world ruled by his descendants.

Nor did the Greeks look upon Uranus as a simple abstract entity: for them he was the great procreator, but also an unnatural and destructive father. Here we have a conflict between the generations that ends in the triumph of the young. This mythology was influenced by that of the Phoenicians: it would be valuable to know what reality it corresponds with. Greek literature and history often echo the conflict between the young and the old, the sons and the fathers. Did it exist at the time when the myths took shape? Are we to suppose that the old men had a high position that was subsequently wrenched from them? Or did the young, who possessed the real power, take it back, embellishing it with myths that justified their own superiority? The evidence that would allow us to choose between these two hypotheses does not exist. We must limit ourselves to examining the data at our disposal, both in the realm of fact and that of mythology.

According to Hesiod, before all there was Chaos; then came Gaea and Eros. Gaea 'gave birth to a being of her own size, who could cover her entirely, Uranus'. From their embraces was born the

* This killing no doubt symbolizes the change from a matriarchal to a patriarchal society.

second generation, that of the Uranids, which included (1) the Titans and Titanids, numbering twelve; (2) the three Cyclopes; and (3) the three Hecatoncheirae, with a hundred arms and fifty heads apiece. Gaea hated Uranus because of his inexhaustible fertility, and Uranus hated his children. As soon as they were born he hid them in Gaea's bosom, that is to say, he buried them in the earth. The outraged Gaea created a hard cutting metal, steel, made a sickle from it and ordered her sons to castrate their father. Only Cronus obeyed, and with the sickle he gelded Uranus. We see, then, that the Greeks described the great ancestor, Uranus, as a chaotic begetter, a hateful and tyrannical sovereign. Cronus wrested the power from Uranus and then married his own sister Rhea. They had many children. But Cronus, perhaps because he had castrated his father himself and therefore distrusted them, hated his children and ate them. Rhea hid her last-born, Zeus, and instead of the child she gave Cronus a large stone wrapped in cloth. When he had grown up Zeus attacked his father. He made him disgorge the swallowed children; he declared war on his father and on his father's brothers, the Titans. In this war he was helped by the Hundred-handers. After a hideous battle, the Titanomachy, the Titans were overcome.

Meanwhile Gaea had been impregnated by the blood of the mutilated Uranus and had given birth to the Giants. These half-brothers of Cronus, belonging to his generation, attacked Zeus. Pindar was the first to recount this Gigantomachy, from which Zeus emerged as the conqueror. He also defeated Typhoeus.

There are many variants of these mythological events. What is interesting is the general idea behind them: as they grow old the ancient gods become more and more unbearable, and this ends by causing a revolt that dethrones them. From that time on almost all the gods who rule over the world are young. The only exceptions are Charon, the ferryman of Hades, whom the Greeks saw as a hideous or at least a sour-tempered, gloomy old man; and a few marine deities such as Nereus, 'the old man of the sea', son of Pontus and Gaea, a quiet and kindly being; his brother Phorcys, whom Homer calls 'the old man who commands the waves'; Proteus, 'the old man of the sea', the son of Uranus and Tethys. We might also mention the Gnaeae, horrible old women who had only one eye and one tooth between the three of them and who passed them from hand to hand.

The occasional myths in which old people appear provide us with

97

a few other clues to the attitude of the ancient Greeks towards old age. The legend of Philemon and Baucis tells of an old couple: their open-handed hospitality and their conjugal fidelity earn them a long, happy old age and a metamorphosis that perpetuates their love. It is their virtues that are rewarded, and here longevity represents a victory over death – an uncertain victory, however, since it needs a miracle on the part of Zeus to save them from it for ever. The myth of Tiresias establishes a connexion – one that we often meet with later – between age, blindness and inner light. Tiresias, blinded by the anger of Hera, was granted the gift of prophecy by Zeus as a compensation; he gave infallible answers to all questions. This too was how the Greeks pictured Homer, old and blind: the poet, like the prophet, is all the more inspired in that the outer world exists less for him. The legends with the greatest meaning are those of Tithonus and of Aeson. The first shows that the Greeks thought physical decay a curse worse than death itself. Aurora, his wife, asked that he should be made immortal, but she forgot to ask that eternal youth should come with his immortality. She fed him with ambrosia, but in vain: he fell into decrepitude. Lonely and wretched, he withered and dried to such an extent that the gods, taking pity on him, changed him into a cicada. The tale of Aeson, who was made young again at the point of death by the spells of Medea, his daughter-in-law, expresses the old dream of everlasting youth. It is the counterpart of the legend of Tithonus – immortality is nothing without youth, but on the other hand the perpetuation of youth would be man's supreme happiness. The Greeks had many Fountains of Youth, the most famous being that of Carathos, near Nauplia.

What in fact was the state of the aged in archaic Greece? Although deformed or unwelcome children were done away with in fairly recent times, and not only in Sparta, we have no right to suppose that the Greeks ever got rid of their old people. Semantics seem to show that in remote antiquity the notion of honour was attached to that of old age. *Gera, geron*: the words that mean great age also mean the privilege of age, the rights of seniority, representative position. Jeanmaire, studying the remains of archaic Greek civilization in his *Kouroi et Kourètes*, comes to the same conclusion – the ancient institutions connected the idea of honour with that of age. In the heroic times the head of the city, the king, was helped by a council of elders; but according to Homer they had no more than a consultative role. Sometimes the king entrusted them with the task of giving justice: they did not always do it well, and their mistakes were the cause of natural disasters.

Nevertheless we find in Homer that old age was associated with wisdom: it was embodied in Nestor, the supreme counsellor – the passage of time had given him experience, eloquence and authority. Yet he is shown as being in physical decline. And it was not Nestor who obtained the victory for the Greeks. Only a man in the prime of life could discover a ruse more efficient than all the traditional tactics. Ulysses far outweighs both Nestor and his own father, Laertes, who resigns the crown to him. In the same way Hector eclipses Priam. We may infer that so long as Greece was feudal, the old men had more honour than real power. It needed the physical energy of Ulysses to expel the suitors whom Laertes, in his weakness, was obliged to put up with. As we shall see when we deal with the Middle Ages, if property is not guaranteed by stable institutions but has to be earnt and defended by force of arms, the old are pushed back into the shadows: the system is based upon the young, and it is they who hold the reality of power. Again, Homer makes game of the Trojan demogerontes, speaking of 'the accursed threshold of old age', and in a hymn attributed to him, Aphrodite says, 'The gods too detest old age.'

In the seventh century B.C. the colonization of a new world brought about an economic revolution. Landed property was no longer the sole source of wealth, for now there was industry, trade and finance. The aristocracy changed in character. The class below it, that of the demiurges – craftsmen and independent workers – grew richer. The city was dominated by a plutocracy. Kingship was done away with or limited to a mere honour. The city was small and it had few inhabitants – some five to ten thousand citizens, with the addition of the slaves and the metics who had no political rights. Its constitution assumed different forms, which changed progressively as the rich became richer and the poor poorer, and as the class-struggle grew fiercer. Whether it was an oligarchy, a tyranny or a democracy, at its head there was always a council. It is most significant that in the oligarchies (which, since a minority of wealthy men wanted to keep the power, were necessarily authoritarian and conservative) the council was always a gerusia. Its members joined it late in life and went on belonging to it until they died. This was the case at Ephesus and Crotona, in Crete, at Cnidus and many other places.

Ellis had ninety gerontes; Corinth eighty. The oligarchies prevented the young from reaching important public positions, dreading their ambition and spirit of enterprise: the elders' aim was the preservation of the established order.

In a great many of the ancient cities, therefore, age was a qualification. But age as a personal experience was not appreciated at all, as we see in the poets.

Burckhart observes that among the Greeks 'old age occupies a quite exceptional place in the lamentations upon man's earthly life'. Mimnermus, a priest at Colophon in the voluptuous and hedonistic Iona of about 630 B.C. expresses the feelings of his fellow-citizens: he celebrates pleasure in its various forms, youth and love; and he hates old age. 'What kind of life, what kind of delight can there be without the golden Aphrodite?' He pities Tithonus: 'Unhappy man! It was a deathless misery that the gods inflicted upon him.' Again and again he repeats that he would rather die than grow old. 'Like the leaves that bring on the time of flowers beneath the sun, for a fleeting moment we rejoice in the bloom of our youth; and presently there are the dark Fates at our side, the one bringing wearisome old age and the other death. The fruit of youth rots early; it barely lasts as long as the light of day. And once it is over, life is worse than death. When the time of youth is past, he who once was beautiful arouses pity, even in his children and his friends.' And again, 'When youth vanishes, it is better to die than to live. For many, many unhappinesses seize upon man's soul – the destruction of his home, poverty, the death of children, sickness, want of strength; there is no man to whom Zeus does not send an abundance of misfortunes.' Again, 'Once painful age has come, making a man ugly and of no use, evil cares no longer leave his heart and the warmth of the sun brings him no comfort. Children dislike him and women despise him. Thus has Zeus sent old age, filled with pain.' He hoped he would not live to be old. 'Oh that I may meet Fate and death when I am sixty, without disease and without sorrow.'

In Archilochus, the priest of Thasos, we find a theme that was to be used again and again in the ensuing ages: the discarded lover* tells his mistress of her coming decay. 'Already thy skin is withering, and sad old age draws furrows through it.' Theognis of Megara cries out, 'Unhappy Theognis! Unhappiness! Oh youth! Oh age

---

* He had sung the beauty of Neobule, the daughter of an important citizen: he wanted to marry her, but her father was against the match.

that ruins everything! The one comes near, the other turns away.'
Like Mimnermus, Anacreon – also from Iona – celebrated love,
pleasure, wine and women in the sixth century: to grow old was to
lose everything that made life delightful. Sadly he describes his own
reflection looking back at him from the mirror – faded hair, grey
temples, long teeth – and he laments his coming death. Pindar's
optimism seems far more academic. He was an opportunist all his
life long. When the battle of Salamis was to be fought, he, a Theban,
was all in favour of collaboration; subsequently he wrote poems
about his country's liberation. He was rich and well known and he
had the highest possible opinion of himself; his line was to arouse
envy rather than pity. He declared that for him old age was a source
of calm contentment: he thanked the gods for having granted him
fame and wealth.

As we have seen, the ideologies that look upon old age as a social
category are in direct opposition to the attitude of the poets when
they are faced with what is for them a personal experience, an
adventure. Thus Solon will have nothing to do with Mimnermus'
sorrowful idea of age. He replies that it would be a very good thing
to live to be eighty. 'I do not stop learning as I grow older and older.'
His values were, of course, quite different. Pleasures and sensual
delight meant little to him. His problems were political. He claimed
to be the arbiter between the Eupatrids and the Thetes: in fact he
favoured the aristocracy. Like all conservatives, he wished to gain
the support of the elders and to give them an important role in the
constitution of the city.

Among the privileged classes, the state of the aged is bound up with
the regime of property. When property is no longer based upon
strength but is institutionalized and firmly guaranteed by law, the
character of the owner becomes non-essential and irrelevant – he is
identified with his property and it is respected in his person. It is
not his individual abilities that matter, but his rights; and so age,
weakness or even decrepitude are of little consequence. Since wealth
usually increases with the years, it is therefore no longer the young
who stand at the top of the scale but the older men. This was the case
in the Greek cities once they had endowed themselves with strong,
unchanging institutions. For the Eupatrids the interests of property
merged with those of old age.

We know that Sparta honoured old age. The military caste (who called themselves 'the equals' or 'peers', although there were great inequalities of fortune between them) were maintained by a great number of non-citizens, helots and perioeci. Sparta was a huge camp, in which, until they were sixty, the adults lived as though they were in barracks: both men and women were subjected to a pitiless discipline. The men of sixty and over were freed from military service, and they were as one might say foredoomed to maintain the system they had experienced: the whole exploiting caste, and particularly the great landowners, was interested in the preservation of the status quo. It was natural that this oppressive, oligarchic and motionless society should entrust a great share of the power to those citizens who were at the same time the oldest and the richest: it was from them that the twenty-eight members of the gerusia were chosen. They met at the request of the ephors, five younger magistrates, who thus exercised a certain control over them; but nevertheless the power was in their hands. The old men who had the bringing up of the young carefully taught them respect for age.

In Athens the laws of Solon gave all the power to the old: the Areopagus, which governed public affairs, was made up of former archons. So long as the regime remained aristocratic and conservative, the older generation held on to its privileges. It lost them when Cleisthenes established the democracy. But it resisted: in Thuycides and Isocrates we find the echoes of a conflict between the generations. The old people did retain some power. When children were accused of bad conduct towards their parents, such as assault, or lack of proper care, the judges who were to try the case had to be over sixty. This age was also required of the exegetes, who were entrusted with the interpretation of the law. Then again, some old people of either sex were admitted to have supernatural powers. Sometimes they appeared in dreams, revealing truths or giving valuable advice. Sometimes dreams or oracular statements were submitted to them and they interpreted the meaning. Still, their authority was much diminished, and in private life they were shown little respect. Xenophon complains of this: 'When will the Athenians respect their elders, as the Lacedemonians do? The Athenians, who begin by despising the old in the person of their fathers.' According to Cicero's account in *De Senectute*, an old Athenian once came late to the public games, and his fellow-citizens refused him a seat; the Lacedemonian deputies stood and made him sit down. Seeing this, the assembly applauded. One of the Spartans then observed, 'It appears that the Athenians know what ought to be done, but do not choose to do it.' And indeed this attitude seems very strange. What has literature to say on the subject?

Tragedy is not an exact reflection of a way of life; for aesthetic reasons all its protagonists are endowed with a superhuman dimension, and it concedes nobility and lofty dignity to the old. Yet their grief speaks with more sincere a voice than the praise that is conventionally addressed to them.

> We, bankrupt old bones,
> left here by the expedition,
> we stay here, our sticks
> guiding our childish strength;
> for when the heart's young sap
> starts to flow, it is as though it were worn out:
> no room for Ares there. What is an old man?
> His foliage withers
> He goes on three legs and
> no firmer than a child
> he wanders like a dream at noon

says the coryphaeus in the *Agamemnon* of Aeschylus. In *The Persians* the old men speak of their white beards with anguish.

'When a man is old,' says Sophocles, 'the light of his reason goes out, action becomes useless and he has unmeaning cares.' Yet Sophocles himself showed that loftiness of soul might go along with this distress, and he showed it splendidly. When he was eighty-nine, in *Oedipus at Colonus*, he describes Oedipus near the very end of his life, a wanderer, wretched and blind.

> Have pity on the poor ghost of Oedipus
> For this old body is no longer he.

> My body no longer has the strength to walk without
> someone to lead it.

He still retains passion and anger, hatred for his sons and a warm, loving tenderness for his daughters:

> Even dying
> I shall not be too unhappy if you are by me.

Yet on the mere earthly plane he is no more than a shadow of himself. What he does not know is that he has become a sacred figure: this is how the audience saw him as soon as he came on to

103

the stage, and the beauty of the tragedy lies in the contrast between Oedipus' seeming degradation and the supernatural character that, without his knowledge, the gods have conferred upon him. The country that takes him in gains the favour of the gods for his sake: he is a saviour and he dies in apotheosis. Thus Sophocles throws magnificent light upon the ambivalence of great age: it is a source of misfortunes and it seems most pitiful; yet for the Greeks in certain particular cases it assumes an aspect of sacredness.

Euripides had a pessimistic view of life and he saw old age in dark and gloomy colours. In the *Alcestis* Admetus bitterly reproaches his father for not agreeing to die instead of him. He cries out angrily, 'Old people always say they long for death – their age crushes them – they have lived too long. All words! As soon as death comes near, not a single one wants to go, and age stops being a burden.'

In the *Hecuba* the old queen calls the other captives to support her.

> Come, daughters, take the old woman out before the house.
> . . . Come hold me, carry me, help me, prop my weakened body.
> And I, leaning my hand on the crutch of your elbow bent
> shall totter my slow steps.

In the *Trojan Women* she curses her powerless state; she cries out 'Useless hornet!' to herself. But like Oedipus she too takes on a sacred character. The failure of her body and her misfortunes do but set off her superhuman greatness.

In the *Ion* the old slave grieves because he finds it hard to walk, and in the *Phoenissae* Jocasta goes with trembling steps. Yet it is through her mouth that Euripides defends old age.

> Not all is contemptible in age,
> Eteocles my son; experience has something to say indeed,
> wiser than the young men's words.

She does in fact give good advice: it is not followed.

But in Euripides it is the pessimistic view of old age that prevails. One chorus groans, 'As for us, we old men are no more than a flock, a semblance; we wander like the figures in a dream; we have no wits left, however intelligent we may think ourselves.'

In tragedy, the old man is a subject: he is shown as he exists for himself. When, fifty years after Euripides, Aristophanes brought the comedy into full flower, it seized upon the old man as an object. The Athenian audience continued to be stirred by the grandeur of Oedipus and Hecuba, but it laughed heartily at the sight of ridiculous old men.

In his comedies, Aristophanes put forward his political and moral views: at that time Athens was ruled by Cleon, a demagogue who fought against the influence of the upper classes and who carried out a war-mongering policy. Aristophanes respected the aristocracy and loved the old traditions; he loathed Cleon and all the innovations he had brought into the city – party spirit, denunciations, trials, war, and also philosophy. Old age played only a secondary role in the plots of his comedies, which were directed against the sins and follies of the age, and therefore his attitude towards his elderly characters varies.

As a conservative he claims respect for them. In the *Acharnians* he takes the side of the old against the young, though without hiding their decay: they should be treated justly because of the services they have rendered to the republic. He puts these words into their mouth:

We, the elders, the forefathers, have a right to complain of our fellow-citizens. You have not given us the rewards and the treatment worthy of our deeds in the sea battles; far from it; we suffer a wretched fate. You drag us, at our age, before the courts; you allow new-fledged young orators to make fun of us, now that we are no good any more, with our deafness and our trembling speech. . . . Old and in our dotage, we stand before the stone table and we see nothing but the shadow of justice.

They speak indignantly and at length about the way the young lawyers harass them and make them fall into traps.

Yet in other plays Aristophanes does not hesitate to make game of them; for him age is a comic resource. In *The Clouds* it is an old man who begs Socrates for a knowledge of the unfair reasoning that will allow him to get rid of his creditors. The audience laugh at the Sophists, but they also laugh at this pupil, too senile to learn anything at all. The old man sends his son to learn instead; the youth profits by Socrates' lessons and beats his father, proving to him that he is right in doing so. Aristophanes was the first to treat this theme of the old man mocked and beaten, a theme so hackneyed in after times.

In *The Wasps* Aristophanes attacks an institution that he looked upon as a curse – the trial. The regime regarded wealthy or powerful citizens as suspects and brought innumerable cases against them. The judges were taken from the general body of citizens. Cleon had increased the sum they received each time they judged to three oboli. This did not interest the well-to-do Athenians and they refused to sit. The heliasts were therefore people of modest condition and their judgements reflected the spirit of the lower classes. Aristophanes agreed with the upper classes in hating them: he wanted the state to stop feeding these thousands of useless judges, who are often old men, the younger being kept away by their work.

So it is old men with no means that Cleon, at the beginning of the play, urges to condemn Laches, whom he accuses of embezzlement and venality: there is in fact a community of interests between the demagogue and the judges. Old Philocleon* is not among them, because his son Bdelycleon,† has shut him up to prevent his coming. But he escapes and utters a long eulogy upon the courts, which is in fact a satire. His son counter-attacks and wins over the old heliasts. Not his father, however, who absolutely insists upon coming to judge. The son shuts him up again and makes him judge at a trial in which the accused is a dog. Then he tries to divert him. He is richer than his father, and takes him to banquets; the old man gets drunk, makes a spectacle of himself, talks nonsense, beats his slaves, brings home a stark naked flute-dancer and pets her obscenely. And he spends the night in ridiculous dances. It is the young man who stands for common sense in the play: the heliasts are discredited as mere tools of Cleon.

It is much the same in the *Lysistrata*, a play against war. Aristophanes wanted Athens to make peace with Lacedemonia, whereas Cleon carried on with the fighting. In the play all the women of the city have shut themselves up in the citadel in order to stop the war. The old men adopt Cleon's views and try to recapture the citadel. Their war-mongering attitude makes them odious and what is more they cover themselves with ridicule: their impotent fumblings provoke bitter mockery from the young women. Aristophanes also caricatures them in the *Plutus*.

Why did the audience clap? The greater part of it was made up of small men owning their own land who lived in the neighbourhood of Athens and who liked seeing the townsmen ridiculed. They too were hostile to Cleon's demagogy. The old Athenians, traditionally

---

* The name means he who loves Cleon.
† The name means he who hates Cleon.

106

respectable men with a certain authority, were in their eyes guilty of collaboration with their enemy, enabling him to win his court cases and supporting his policy of conquest. We should observe that on two occasions the old man appears in the role of the ridiculous father: no doubt sons, compelled to unwilling obedience by the head of the family, delighted in seeing the old man mocked.

Aristophanes also lashes the wantonness of the old: here again is a theme that was to be tirelessly exploited throughout the later ages, especially in the comic theatre. Why does the adult find this particular characteristic so very repugnant? Is it because the old man is still capable of making love or because he is not? In the first case he appears as a rival, made dangerous by his wealth and standing; and then again he wounds the adults in their narcissism, which is almost always an important element in love, even venal love – the sexual act, divorced from youth, vigour and charm, is brought down to the level of a mere animal function, and the woman who consents to it diminishes the value of her younger partner's embraces. But it is above all the lecherous and impotent elder who disgusts men in the prime of life: he is the incarnation of the spectre that haunts the most virile of them. Psychoanalysts are of the opinion that the castration-complex is never entirely resolved: for the mature man the sight of aged impotence brings to life the threat that had frightened him so when he was a little boy. In other words it might be said that the male adult is never free from anxiety about his sexual vigour; he hates to think that the day will come when he still has desires and yet no power to assuage them. In the old man he hates his own future state; he rejects it by means of laughter – he can easily convince himself that he will never be like the grotesque figure moving about on the stage.

There are few old women in Aristophanes, and those few are somewhat flat: we find the occasional bawd and, in the *Ecclesiazusae*, three old women who quarrel for the favours of a handsome youth.

Menander, who succeeded Aristophanes in the favour of the public a hundred years later, was no gentler to the old. In his opinion it was better not to reach too great an age. 'The man who stays too long dies disgusted; his old age is painful and tedious; he is poor and in need. Whichever way he turns he sees enemies; people conspire against him. He did not go when he should have gone; he has not died a good death.'*

* Fragments.

107

Menander too finds it saddening that an old man should lay claim to a sexual life. 'There can be no more unhappy being than an ancient lover, unless it is another ancient lover. How is it possible that a man who tries to rejoice in what is leaving him – and time is the cause of its going – how is it possible that he should not be wretched?'

To Menander – and this theme too was often taken up again – old age seems a baleful force that attacks men from outside. 'Old age, enemy of mankind, it is you that destroys the beauty of every shape; you change the splendour of limbs into heaviness, speed into languor.'

'A long life is a painful thing. O burdensome old age! You have nothing good to offer mortals, but you are lavish with pain and disease. And yet we all hope to reach you and we do our very best to succeed.'

In the comedies of Menander that have come down to us, either in fragments of the original or through Terence, we find many old men. In the *Samia* the author raised the questions of the generations. The 'positive hero' is Demeas, an affectionate, open-handed old man who loves his son and watches sadly while the youth destroys the illusions he had nourished about him. But he remains serene in the midst of his disappointments. Niceratos, on the other hand, is one of a whole family of ill-natured, miserly and coarse old men. There is a pair of similar characters in Terence's *Heautontimorumenos*, which he took from Menander and expanded. The ancient Pataicos in the *Perikeiromene* is like Demeas; he is a wise, kind, moderate, sensitive man. On the other hand, Craton in the *Theophorumene* is a gloomy creature, and in the *Epitrepontes* Smicrines is a grasping, rough and thoroughly disagreeable old brute. Menander carried the character of the ludicrous, unbearable ancient (which was later to become so exceedingly popular), much further than Aristophanes. But his ideas had light and shade, and he thought that great age might also be accompanied by wisdom and kindness.

Plato and Aristotle both thought deeply about old age; and they came to opposite conclusions. Plato's concept is closely linked to his political preferences. When he wrote the *Republic*, experience had disgusted him with oligarchy and with tyranny, and he was a severe critic of the Athenian democracy's men, political ways and public spirit – he thought it anarchic, and for this he blamed egalitarianism, which did not take enough account of abilities. He had a high opinion of the Spartan 'temocracy', but he very much regretted that Sparta should choose not the wisest men as magistrates but rather those who had been formed by war. According to him, the ideal city was that which ensured men's happiness; but happiness was virtue, and virtue sprang from knowledge of the truth. Only the men who had come out of the cave and who had gazed at the ideas were therefore fitted to rule. They were capable of doing so only after an education that must begin at adolescence and which would bear its full harvest at the age of fifty. From that time onwards the philosopher possessed the truth and he then became a guardian of the city. The rule of 'the talents' desired by Plato is therefore at the same time a gerontocracy. His philosophy allowed him to discount the physical decline of the individual entirely. Indeed, according to him, a man's truth dwells in his immortal soul, which is allied to the ideas: the body is a mere illusion. At first Plato saw the union of the body with the soul as an impediment, no more; later he came to think that the soul might profitably make use of the body, but that it had no need of it. The physical decay brought about by age did not affect the soul; indeed, if the body's appetites and vigour decreased, this gave the soul a greater freedom. Plato, who was still young when he wrote the *Republic*, puts a eulogy of old age into the mouth of Cephalus: 'As age blunts one's enjoyment of physical pleasures, one's desire for the things of the intelligence and one's delight in them increase accordingly.' And Socrates adds that a man learns by being in the company of the old. It is true, observes Cephalus, that when they come together most of them are full of regret for the pleasures of youth and speak bitterly of their relatives' insults and ill-treatment. Yet he recalls that Sophocles, speaking of love, said, 'It was with the utmost relief that I escaped from it – it was as though I had escaped from slavery under a ferocious master.' Cephalus approves of these words. 'Old age . . . arouses in us an immense feeling of peace and liberation.' The spiritualistic concept expressed here is in total contradiction with the opinion of the satirical writers on the sexuality of old men: according to the first view libido vanishes together with sexual vigour, and thanks to this harmony the aged man achieves a serenity forbidden to those who are still a prey to their instincts. In spite of innumerable contradictions this idea has lived on until our days because of the comfort that it brings – it allows us to thrust the disagreeable and disturbing image of the lustful old man aside.

The value of old age having been established, Plato concludes,

'The older must cor.mand, the young obey.' Yet to the criterion of age he does add that of worth. In his *Republic* the correctors, who supervise all the magistrates, are between fifty and seventy-five. The nomophylebres, who play a very important part, are between fifty and seventy. Men over sixty no longer share in the songs and heavy drinking at the banquets. But they preside over them, preventing excesses; they make speeches on moral subjects and these inspire song.

When he was eighty Plato returned to the question in the *Laws* and dealt with it at length; in several places he dwells on children's duty to their old parents. They must speak to them respectfully and put their wealth and their persons at their disposal. Dead ancestors were worshipped: the future ancestor was already sacred. 'It is impossible for us to possess any object of worship more deserving of respect than a father or a grandfather, a mother or a grandmother bowed down with old age.'

Aristotle's philosophy brought him to a very different set of conclusions. For him the soul is not pure intellect; it is in necessary relationship with the body and even the brutes possess one; man exists only by the union of the two. The soul is the body's mould, and the diseases and misfortunes that affect the body affect the individual as a whole. The body must remain intact for old age to be happy. 'A beautiful old age is one which may have its inherent slowness but without any infirmity. The whole depends not only upon the physical advantages the person may have, but also upon chance,' he says in the *Rhetoric*. In the *Ethics* he admits that the wise man is capable of bearing all vicissitudes with greatness of soul. Yet physical and external wellbeing is necessary for the good of the soul. He thinks man advances until he is fifty. One has to reach a certain age in order to possess phrenosis, that prudent wisdom which allows a man to behave rightly, and in order to have accumulated experience, a knowledge that cannot be communicated because it is not abstract – that has to be lived. But later the body's decline drags the whole person down with it. In the *Rhetoric* Aristotle describes youth in the most glowing colours – warm, passionate, magnanimous – whereas age seems to him its opposite in every respect. 'Because they have lived many years, because they have often been deceived, because they have made mistakes, and because human activities are usually bad, they have confidence in nothing and all their efforts are quite obviously far beneath what they ought to be.' They are reserved,

110

fearful and hesitant. Then again, 'They are ill-natured, since after all it is ill-natured to suppose that everything is getting worse. They always expect things to turn out badly, because of their distrustful attitude; and they are distrustful because of their experience of life.' They are as lukewarm in their love as they are in their hatred. They are selfish, timid, cold. They are shameless: they despise public opinion. 'They live more upon memory than upon hope.' They are garrulous; they go over the past again and again. Their anger breaks out suddenly, but it has no strength. They have the appearance of moderation because they no longer have desires but only interests, and it is for their interests that they live, not for beauty. They are open to pity, but only out of weakness, not magnanimity. They are sorry for themselves: they no longer know how to laugh.

What is particularly interesting about this description, which is based not upon an *a priori* theory but upon far-reaching and apposite observation, is the notion that experience is not a factor of progress but of degradation. An old man is one who has spent the whole of a long life getting things wrong, and this cannot make him superior to younger people who have not piled up as many mistakes as he has.

In the *Politics* Aristotle therefore criticizes the Spartan gerusia. 'Lifelong sovereign power to make important decisions is a very questionable institution; for like the body the intelligence has its old age, and the education the gerontes have received is not of such a kind that the legislator himself should be without some suspicion of their virtue.' He accuses them of frequently allowing themselves to be corrupted and of being harmful to the public interest. In his opinion old men should belong to the priesthood, where they would be asked for no more than wise advice and upright decisions.

His view of old age led Aristotle to remove the elderly from power; for he looked upon them as beings on the wane. Furthermore, his political theory, which was very unlike Plato's, did not put intellectuals, but a police force, at the head of the city: the ideal would be for all the citizens to be men of exalted virtue and for each to rule and to be ruled in turn. But this was a mere dream of impossible perfection that could never be realized. If facts are to be taken into account, the best constitution, says Aristotle, would be one that reconciles democracy with a large proportion of oligarchy. The qualification for the exercise of power would be the military worth, the military virtue of a middle class: it would be that class that has the duty of maintaining order. But soldiers are young or in the prime of life; the police of a city would not be recruited from among the old. It was both for psychological reasons and because of his social concepts that Aristotle dismissed the aged from the government.

The gloomy attitude of the Greeks towards old age is to be found again in Plutarch in the first century after Christ. He had personal experience of it, since he died at the age of eighty. He was a philosopher, a moralist, and, towards the end of his life, a very pious man – he was a priest at Delphi; and he was a representative of what has been called middle Platonism. But as far as old age is concerned he is nearer to Aristotle's severity than Plato's optimism. He likens it to a sad autumn.* 'Now it seems that autumn is like the year growing old as it finishes its round of seasons. For moisture has not yet come and the warmth has gone or has grown weaker, and – a sign of coldness and drought – it makes bodies liable to disease. Is it necessary, then, that the soul should sympathize with the body's disposition, and that once the spirits are heavy and clogged, that the power of divination should grow dull, clouding like a mirror all dimmed with breath?'

This pessimism carries on with Lucian in the second century of our era.† In an epigram he addresses an elderly woman: 'You may dye your locks, but you can never dye your years; you will never make the wrinkles vanish from your cheeks.... Never will white lead or vermilion turn Hecuba into Helen.' In the *Dialogues of the Dead* he, like Euripides, speaks of his amazement at the obstinacy with which old men cling to life. Two or three times he paints a cruel portrait of them: 'A broken-down old man, only three teeth left, hardly alive, who leans on four slaves to get along, whose nose never stops running and whose eyes are filled with rheum, indifferent to any kind of delight, a living grave, the laughing-stock of the young.'

Once again the unhappy, half-dead, doddering old man arouses neither pity nor horror, but laughter. We have seen why.

Greek pictures and sculpture are in agreement with literature. The vases of the fifth and the later centuries show Hercules fighting old age, represented by a wizened dwarf or a thin, wrinkled, almost bald figure. Or sometimes by a very tall, bearded, long-haired man on his

---

* This is strange, since for the ancients the fall was the season of abundance – *pomifer autumnus.*

† Lucian belonged to the ancient world. He was a satirical, irreligious sceptic, and he knew Christianity only to make fun of it.

knees before Hercules, begging for mercy. In the fourth century Demetrios carved a Lysimachus in the form of a hideous old woman.

As we see in the history of Rome, there is a close relationship between the state of the old and the stability of society. It is probable that the ancient Romans used to get rid of their old people by drowning them, since it was usual to speak of sending them *ad pontem*, and the senators were called *depontani*. It seems that in Rome, as in almost all societies, there was a radical contrast between the lot of the old who were members of the privileged class and those belonging to the masses. However, in later days, although the new-born were still exposed according to the pleasure of the *pater familias*, there was no longer any question of touching the life of the aged. I have already mentioned the respect paid them as proprietors once private property was guaranteed by the law. This was the case as soon as the Roman institutions were firmly established. Property assumed various forms. A Roman patrician's wealth was primarily his land; but he would also possess houses built for letting and sometimes shares in the great financial companies that farmed the taxes and public works. The *equites* made up a financial aristocracy; they lent money at usurious rates of interest. And lastly trade was a source of wealth. In all these fields, a citizen's fortune was ordinarily greater by the end of a life devoted to administering and increasing it than it had been at the beginning. Among the wealthy there were many aged men, and their property was one of the sources of their prestige.

It was they who were the chief holders of power: the Senate was composed of rich landed proprietors who had reached the end of their career as magistrates. Until the second century B.C. the Republic was powerful, coherent, and conservative; order reigned, and wealth brought important privileges. It was ruled by an oligarchy which favoured the old, the conservative tendencies of both being in agreement with one another. The Senate had enormous prerogatives. It directed the whole of Roman diplomacy. It controlled the great military commands: every leader had at his side lieutenants chosen by the Senate from among its own members. It administered the finances. It was the Senate that judged important crimes such as treason and abuse of trust. The high offices were reached only at a fairly advanced age: the 'round of honours' was carefully arranged and it was impossible to make a spectacular, very rapid career. Then again, the old men's votes counted for more than those of the other citizens. In Rome the electoral division was the century, and the centuries of the *seniores* had as much weight as those of the *juniores*, although they contained fewer individuals; the legal majority therefore did not correspond with the numerical majority, and the elderly men had an advantage.

This political situation was founded upon an ideology rooted in an essentially rural economy. The peasant distrusted novelty, and for the Romans the prime virtue was *lastingness*. The *mos majorum* (ancestral custom) had the force of law, and it assumed belief in the ancient wisdom. The ancestors remained present in the family: their *manes* came back from the lower regions on certain days and they had to be appeased by sacrifices. They must be obeyed by showing respect for tradition. Permanence was ensured by *pietas*; and pietas with regard to his country, the magistrates, and especially his father, was required of every citizen.

Here is a problem for historians: in the course of the centuries this traditionalistic society which seemed doomed to stagnation nevertheless conquered the world. The fighting men did not form a caste; they had no privileges: yet under the direction of the Senate Roman imperialism never ceased to expand. Why?

The historians' answers are hesitant. Towards the end of the Republic conquest had brought into being the physical and moral conditions for an anarchy that urged still further conquest: but how did this machinery begin to work? Some put forward the greed of a peasant lower class; a longing for security; Roman pride and vanity; the desire for wealth; private ambition. What is certain is that military expansion put itself at the service of economic expansion. Rome, collecting booty and war indemnities and exacting tribute, grew far richer. Another striking factor is the nature of the conquest: it was slow, indeed very slow compared with Alexander's. Except at the end of the Republic it was not carried out by men whose social and political role was very extraordinary: the generals, even the glorious generals, remained the simple servants of Rome. The collective task, directed by the Senate – that is to say by elderly men – went on methodically, continuously, never upsetting the permanence of the established order: for many centuries it did not disturb it at all.

The privileged status of the old men asserted itself within the family. The power of the *pater familias* was almost limitless. He had the same rights over persons as he had over things: he could kill, mutilate or sell. This power came to an end only with death or with the *capitis deminutio*, which very occasionally removed the citizen from civil life. A son who struck his father was held to be a *monstrum*; he no longer belonged to human society; he was declared *sacer* – that is to say, he was rejected from the world by being put to death. If a young man wanted to marry, not only was his father's consent required but even his grandfather's, supposing his grandfather to be still alive: this proves that the patriarch kept his authority to the very end.

In spite of the father's theoretical powers, it became rarer and rarer for him to sell his son as a slave, and it appears that custom and public opinion limited the exercise of his authority. The Roman matron had a great deal of influence* in the home, and this division of power must have been an advantage to the children. What literature has to tell us about Roman customs is somewhat equivocal; but if the old men had been as powerful as and respected as they were in China, it is scarcely conceivable that Plautus could have mocked them on the stage with so much applause. The Atellans had taken over the character of the ridiculous ancient from the Greeks, and he appeared under the names of Casnar and Pappus. In Plautus he plays a role of the first importance. He always appears as a father whose miserliness hinders his son's pleasures, a father who is as lustful as a character out of Aristophanes and who competes with the young man as a rival. He makes use of his wealth and of ignoble tricks to steal the woman the young man loves – for example, he buys her and gives her in marriage to a slave who is supposed to yield his place on the wedding night. But his plots always fail, thanks to another sharp-witted slave who comes to the son's rescue; he is unmasked, and his wife – invariably old and shrewish – covers him with bitter reproaches. He is the laughing-stock of the household and the whole neighbourhood. This is the theme of the *Asinaria*, in which the shameless senator Demenetes is humiliated by his wife, despised by his slaves, disowned by his son and flouted by a whore. In the *Casina*, Stalinon sprinkles himself with scent to make himself agreeable to a girl beloved by his son; he hopes to find her in bed, but a man is put into it in her place. It is the theme of the *Mercator*, too. In the

* Being a member both of her father's and her husband's clan, she could appeal to either. From the day she received her dowry from her father she was wholly independent economically. Being there in the house and directing the slaves' work, she had a great deal to do with the bringing up of the children.

Bacchides two old men try to win their sons away from loose women, but in the end it is they who are debauched.

Even when the old men are good-natured and agreeable, their age is enough for them to be objects of mockery: the two in the *Epidicus* are neither vicious nor wicked, yet the humour of the play lies in their being cheated of money by a cunning slave. In the *Curculio* the audience laughed at the sight of the worthy Theoropides being duped by a slave who is all in favour of the debaucheries of the son of the house.

Plautus created many sympathetic old-man characters. In spite of his sordid avarice, Euclion in the *Aulularia* turns out in the end to be a loving and generous father; and a friend of his of the same age, a well-bred and agreeable old man, marries his daughter without a dowry. The old men brought on to the stage in the *Pseodolus*, the *Rudens*, the *Trinummus* and the *Poenulus* are cheerful, intelligent and kindly. The best old man is the one in the *Miles Gloriosus*. The thoroughly unpleasant character is the soldier, a man in the prime of life; Periplectomenes, on the contrary, is wise, merry, witty, kind to the young; he is himself young at heart and he understands the art of living. He helps the heroine's lover to protect her against the boastful soldier. In a pleasant self-portrait, he points out the faults that the old should guard against: 'At table, I do not prate about public affairs, deafening one and all; during the meal I never slip my hand under the dress of a woman who does not belong to me; I never snatch dishes from my neighbours or hurry to get at the wine first; drink never makes me quarrelsome in the middle of a feast.' He is the only character in Plautus who was never married: he congratulates himself on having neither wife nor child. One old man alone, a character in the *Menaechmi*, complains of his age: 'Worthless goods, these vile back-bending worthless years! What pains and weariness they bring!'

Old women do not appear much: the shrewish wives and the old whores who are also bawds, more or less, hardly count. It is above all the *pater familias* that Plautus deals with. No doubt the young men felt his power and resented it bitterly: it was he who held the purse-strings and who controlled their lives. It amused them to see him caricatured, and at the same time they got rid of their repressions. Perhaps the young and middle-aged men also found it hard to be ruled by the old: Demenetes in the *Asinaria* is not only a father but also an old senator. Yet Plautus does contrast lovable old men with his lewd and ridiculous tyrants; age is in itself respectable, and a man proves that he is unworthy of this respect if he abuses his authority to satisfy his vices. Plautus does not take the young men's side unreservedly: they are often scheming, debauched and selfish.

Terence, more cultured and more refined, handles the problem of the conflict between the generations with more thought and with more light and shade. In the *Andria*, which is based upon Menander, the old men characters are sympathetic, but not very lively. They have much more depth in the *Heautontimorumenos*. The two heroes, both over sixty, are wealthy and authoritarian. The violent, passionate Menedemes is against the marriage of his son, who has gone off to enlist in the army in Asia. Out of remorse, his unhappy father turns himself into a heautontimorumenos, a 'self-punisher', undertaking exhausting labours. Chremes, who is also on bad terms with his son, is a false philosopher, with fine words always ready in his mouth;* he persecutes his wife, a better person than her husband; and he is tricked by his slaves. Chremes' son, who is not much good either, complains, 'What unjust judges for young men fathers are! They want us to be grey beards from childhood up.' Menedemes' love for his son, and the open-handed magnanimity engendered by it does not lessen right through the play, even when he is worried about the young man's behaviour and mistakenly believes that he has ruined him.

There is a similar pair in the *Adelphoe*. Demea has two sons and he entrusts one to his unmarried brother Micion. Micion is full of kindness and indulgence; he loves young people and understands them. His adopted son therefore adores him – he is loved by everyone. Demea is as hard to others as he is to himself; he bullies his son, who rebels against him. In the end Demea understands and becomes a reformed character. 'I too long for my children to love me.' In the *Phormio*, Demiphon, the hero's father, is an authoritarian, a violent-tempered man. He makes the most appalling scenes when he finds that his son has married in his absence, and tries to force him to break with his wife.

Terence is more didactic than Plautus, and he tells fathers how to behave if they want to make their sons and themselves happy. His intention is less to ridicule the old than to warn them. From his plays

---

* It was he who said, 'I am a man and nothing to do with mankind is foreign to me.' But he said it in reply to a neighbour, who was astonished at his impertinent curiosity about his private concerns.

we may infer that young men found it hard to put up with their authority – an authority that was, furthermore, restrained by public opinion.

It is striking to see how the privileges of the old diminished and then collapsed altogether with the decay of the oligarchic system. From the time of the Gracchi onwards there was no longer any stable governmental majority but only majorities formed by coalitions. The failure of the agrarian* and Italian† reforms condemned the republican regime to death. The Roman conquests finally brought about a political and social decomposition. During this troubled era the Senate gradually lost its powers; they passed into the hands of the soldiers, that is to say of young men. The magistrates broke free from the council's authority; and once personal power was established, the Senate's influence went into a steady decline. The emperor, a young man, ruled virtually without any reference to the Senate. Its political and administrative functions were taken away: under Gallienus, in about A.D. 271, it also lost its financial privileges. At the same time the power of the *pater familias* was restrained. Rights over persons were no longer on the same footing as those over things, and the exercise of the right of life and death over a slave was looked upon as homicide. The aged or sick slave whose master left him without support was automatically liberated.

It is in this context that we must read Cicero's *De Senectute*. Cicero was sixty-three and a senator when he wrote his defence of old age in order to prove that the diminished authority of the Senate ought to be strengthened. At the time he wrote it, the nobles and the wealthy men no longer believed in anything but their pleasures and their ambitions; but in public they professed respect for the accepted values. It was upon these values that Cicero based himself. In particular he looked for support to the distorted version of stoicism that had made its way into Rome since the beginning of the Senate's decline. The senators had turned it into a conservative ideology: the world is harmony; everything that is natural is good; each element should be satisfied with the place allotted to it in the general design; the status quo must be respected and the privileged should be left in possession of their privileges. We find echoes of these convenient notions in *De Senectute*.

* Which would have distributed land among the body of Roman citizens.
† Which would have distributed land to the Italians by making them citizens.

'It is impossible for old age to be borne in extreme poverty, even by a wise man,' admits Cicero. But very poor men were not senators, and it was senators that he was talking about. Cicero wishes to prove that far from rendering them unsuitable, age increased their abilities. In order to do so, he supposes that Cato the Elder is speaking – Cato, who was in full possession of his faculties at eighty. Cato concedes that old age has a bad reputation but this is because of prejudices that he will try to do away with.

They say old age produces nothing. That is untrue. 'Old age is far from being deprived of good council, authority and wise maturity; on the contrary, it has these qualities in the highest degree,' and it is by means of them that great things are accomplished. 'States have always been ruined by young men, saved and restored by old.' Cato denies that aged men show any falling off. 'The old man keeps all his mental powers so long as he neither gives up using them nor adding to them.' Cicero quotes Sophocles, Homer, Hesiod, Simonides, Isocrates, Gorgias, Pythagoras, Democritus, Plato and many others in support of this statement. He refutes Caecilius' words,* 'What I find most lamentable about old age is that one feels that now one is repulsive to the young.'

Second, the old are said to lack strength. But what is physical strength? Nothing. Milo, weeping over his arms and saying 'Alas, they are already dead', awakens nothing but contempt. 'I shall always think a man who gives an example of wisdom and virtue happy, however slow and feeble he may be.' Cato states that at eighty and more he still remains fit and well. There are some old men who are in poor health; but the same applies to the young. 'That senile decay which is commonly called second childhood is not to be seen in all old men, but only in those whose mind is naturally weak.'

Cicero then takes over the commonplace set forth in the *Republic*: the aged man is said to enjoy few pleasures; this means that he is preserved from the passions and the vices, and what higher privilege can there be? To compensate for his blessed impotence, Cato offers him the pleasures of the table, of conversation, study, literature and farming. Plausibly he asserts that 'when a man is deprived of something that he does not want, the deprivation is not very painful'. Whereas in fact we may feel the mutilation that kills desire far more

---

* Caecilius, who wrote comedies and who died in 166 B.C., also said, 'Old age, I swear that even if you brought no other woe your mere coming would be woe enough.'

119

keenly than being disappointed of a pleasure. The loss of a sense is far more saddening than not always being able to satisfy it.

Forgetting Aristotle's very sensible words, he also states that the faults attributed to old age do not come from the weight of years but from the character: in the *Adelphoe* one of the old men is delightful and the other is odious. From this he draws the edifying conclusion that old age is happy and agreeable when it comes at the end of a virtuous life.

Finally, he goes so far as to produce this wonderfully strange argument: death strikes the young just as much as it does the old, the proof being that there are very few old men. In any case, there is nothing terrible about death. 'Everything that is natural must be considered good.' This conclusion, which is based upon stoicism, might have relieved him from the task of writing his books, since old age is quite as natural as death.

A hundred years later, in his *Letters to Lucilius*, Seneca maintained the same ideas as Cicero (though at nothing like so great a length) and for much the same reasons. He was one of the richest men of his time. Claudius banished him; Messalina brought him back and made him Nero's tutor; when Nero came to the throne Seneca made use of his influence to strengthen the authority of the Senate against that of Agrippina. He shared in the distribution of Britannicus' fortune, became consul and did everything possible to advance his political aims. He was an accomplice in the murder of Agrippina. When he was about sixty-two he asked permission to retire: Nero refused. Seneca represented the Senate at the emperor's court, and for Nero he was a guarantee. He stayed, acting as a hostage;* but he was not so active and he spent most of the time shut up at home. It was then, at the age of sixty-one, that he wrote these *Letters*. He was a Stoic, but his stoicism was of that aberrant kind that I have described. This self-seeking optimism and his political attitude, his support of the Senate, determined what he had to say upon the subject of old age. Old age, like everything natural, was good, and it brought with it no falling away. 'Let us welcome old age and cherish it; if we know how to make the most of it, it is full of comforts. Fruit has its best flavour only when it is fully ripe. Gliding down the slope of the years with a motion that is not yet in any way abrupt or sudden is an exquisite time of life. . . . One might say that no longer feeling the need for pleasure takes the place of pleasure

* Until he was implicated in Piso's plot and condemned to death.

itself' (Letter 12). And in Letter 20, 'The soul, no longer having any great commerce with the body, burgeons and comes into full flower.'

We have seen the motives underlying the praise of Solon, Plato, Cicero and Seneca – eulogies of old age that the privileged have smugly repeated throughout the centuries, claiming to find truth in them. The learned man's objective point of view is very different. The Elder Pliny feels that he is stating established facts when he launches straight into the subject and says, 'The shortness of life is undoubtedly nature's greatest blessing. The senses grow dull, the limbs stiff; sight, hearing, legs, teeth and even the organs of digestion move towards death faster than we.'

The poets too were much more sincere than the moralists, because they did not expect to gain anything from their poetry. Cicero was dead and Seneca not yet born when Horace and Ovid wrote. When they were still young they regarded age not as a universal state but as a personal experience; it filled them with a bitterness that they expressed in their verse. Horace returns to a theme dear to the Ionian poets: like them he celebrated wine and women and pleasure, and for him everything that makes life delightful vanishes with old age: he speaks of it as peevish, sour-tempered. 'Sad age comes,' he writes. 'Farewell to laughing, happy love and easy sleep.' He describes the round of the seasons, from cheerful spring to the frigid winter,* and he ends, 'The swiftly-moving seasons at least find their rebirth in the heavens; as for us, once we have gone down to where the pious Aeneas, Tullus and Ancus lie, we are dust and ashes, no more.'

Ovid is among those who see time and old age as a destructive power. 'Time, O great destroyer, and envious old age, together you bring all things to ruin; and as your slowly gnawing teeth devour them all at last, a gradual death.'

No one has described the ugliness of age more ferociously than Juvenal. In his tenth satire he warns men against incautious prayers: wishing to live for a long time is one of them.

What a train of woes – and such woes – comes with a prolonged old age. To begin with, this deformed, hideous, unrecognizable face; this vile leather instead of skin; these pendulous cheeks; these wrinkles like those around the mouth of an old she-ape as she sits scratching in the shady Thabarcan woods. . . . Old men are all the same; their voices tremble, so do their limbs; no hair left on their shining scalps; they run

---

* His source is Hippocrates: the idea has been used incessantly, hackneyed without a pause until today.

at the nose like little children. To chew his bread, the poor ancient has
nothing but toothless gums. He is such a burden to his wife, his children
and himself that he would disgust a Cossus, that fisher for legacies. His
deadened palate no longer allows him to take pleasure in wine and food
as once he did. As for love, he has forgotten it long since. . . . Among
old men, one has a shoulder that hurts him, another his back, another
his leg. Here is one who has gone quite blind, and he envies those who
have one eye left. . . . The ancient no longer has his wits. A perpetual
train of losses, incessant mourning and old age dressed in black, surrounded by everlasting sadness – that is the price of a long life.

Physical decay, infirmity, mutilation: there is no compensation
in this picture of the miseries of old age. Juvenal ends with an idea
that no one had yet expressed: growing old means seeing the death
of those we love; it means condemnation to mourning and sadness.*
The Latin poets cried out against the ugliness of the aged woman
with particular vehemence. In the *Epodes* Horace describes a dis-
gustingly amorous old woman; and he is no kinder to the witch
Canidia. The old woman looks horrible. 'Your teeth are black.
Antiquity ploughs furrows in your ancient forehead ... your breasts
are as flaccid as the dugs of a mare.' She smells. 'What a sweat, what
a reek enwraps every part of her flabby limbs.' Ovid, in the *Tristia*,
speaks of the future appearance of the beloved† with a cruelty
touched with sadness; he says to Perilla, 'The years will wear these
charming features; this forehead, time-withered, will be crossed with
wrinkles; this beauty will become the prey of the pitiless old age
which is creeping up silently, step by step. They will say, she *was*
beautiful. And you will be utterly wretched; you will say your
mirror lies.' He draws a harsher picture of the sorceress Dipsas, an
old bawd who 'dirties shamefaced love' with her spells. Acanthis,
the object of Propertius' insults, was another revolting old bawd:
'Her bones can be counted through her skin: bloody spittle shows
in the hollows between her teeth.' Martial's *Epigrams* deal very
roughly with all old people, but particularly with the women.
'Vetusilta, three hundred consuls you have seen, and you have only
three hairs left and four teeth.' 'Thais smells worse than a fuller's
pot, worse than an amphora spoilt by rotting brine.' Since, as men
see it, a woman's purpose in life is to be an erotic object, when she

* These lines inspired Victor Hugo. The idea has occurred spontaneously to many
writers.
† We have already met this theme among the Greek poets.

grows old and ugly she loses the place allotted to her in society: she becomes a *monstrum* that excites revulsion and even dread. Just as we see in certain primitive nations, she takes on a supernatural character when she falls outside the human state: she is a witch, a dangerously powerful sorceress.

Yet in spite of these outbursts, the usual butt of satire is old men, old men who possess wealth and authority. A reading of the Greek and Latin authors confirms what I put forward at the beginning of this chapter: their works make no mention of old men who are devoid of social importance.* What matters is the power held by the older generation. The middle-aged men's attitude towards this generation is ambiguous; they look to it for support in order to maintain a state of affairs advantageous to their class, and in the person of the wealthy old man they respect the holy rights of property; but at the same time they envy him the status that they themselves confer upon him by their institutions, and in daily life they hate the individuals who benefit from it.

In Greece, the tragedy clothed the old with an almost supernatural halo: this was not so in Rome. The comic authors and the satirical poets, both Greek and Latin, cried out against the contrast between the economic and political privileges of the old and their physical decay: they, and the public with them, were indignant that these wrecks of humanity should be granted the right to sit in council, to judge, govern public affairs and rule over the whole family: in the *Plutus* the ancients who go to the assembly to decide the fate of the republic are almost incapable of walking.

It was above all the young who thought it unjust that senile decay should not have any disqualifying social consequences. Plautus' audience clapped when pleasant old men were deceived by their sons. Caecilius states that the young men loathed the old. Lucian says that they are 'the laughing-stock of youth'. It was certainly with envy, hatred and resentment that the young suffered their authority. Juvenal's ferocity is explicable only if he was the mouthpiece of public opinion. Cicero calls the generally-held ideas on old age 'prejudices', but he admits that most people hate it. Old age is ridiculous for the comic authors and their public; for the poets it is a

---

* In the *Ion* there is an old slave: but he brought up the heroine, Creusa, who looked upon him as her father. It is he who embodies the continuity of the house. He is Creusa's confidential friend, her adviser, the man who carries out her plans. He is a relative being, drawing his importance from the princess to whom he is devoted. He has no personal existence.

destroying power whose stroke they dread. The moralists who defend it do so for political reasons. Aristotle, whose interests were not at stake, paints a gloomy picture.

Two facts marked the end of the ancient world: the barbarian invasion and the triumph of Christianity. What was the state of the aged among the barbarians? There is little evidence. In their mythologies we once more find the idea of a battle between the generations in which the young are the victors: Scandinavia provides an instance of this. According to the Icelandic poems and sagas, at the world's beginning there was a mass of ice. From this ice was born a giant called Ymir; while he was sleeping another giant and a giantess appeared under his left armpit. The ice also gave birth to a cow which, licking the frozen blocks, produced a live being, Buri, who had a son named Bor; Bor married Bestia, the daughter of the pair begotten by Ymir, and they had three offspring, the gods Odin, Vili and Vie. These gods killed Ymir, and all the giants were drowned in his blood, except for Bergelmir, who escaped together with his wife. The gods created the world and ruled it.

The Teutonic mythology, with its twilight of the gods, also asserts the superiority of youth. After they had ruled over the world for a great while, the powerful Odin and all the ancient gods came into conflict with the new gods and there was a great battle. The new gods won; all the others were killed and the world was utterly destroyed. Waters swallowed the land. Then the earth came to life again; a new sun appeared, the child of the old one. The land rose from the flood. A few people who had managed to survive begot a new mankind. Even for the gods there comes a moment when time's attrition forces them to give way to others. For the Slavs the handing over of power was peaceful, the Sun and the Fire succeeded their father Svarog, the first god, the Sky, without any fighting.

History, properly so called, tells us little about the nations conquered by Rome or about the invading barbarians. Caesar says that the Gauls killed the sick and the old people who wanted to die. Procopius says the same of the Herulae. Most of the barbarians were conquering warrior hordes who lived for fighting and nothing else; and what Ammien-Marcellin says of the Alans no doubt applies to the rest: 'Death from old age or an accident was a shameful, contemptible thing that they loaded with the most hideous insults.' In societies of this kind there can have been few old men, and those few would have been despised. It is reasonable to suppose that their life remained difficult even when the warlike hordes had settled down on the land. Among the Teutons the family was very tightly knit, which implies that the 'useless mouths' were taken care of. But we have exact figures showing that with age the individual underwent a loss of value: this was the scale of blood-money that had to be paid if a free-man were killed. In the sixth century the Visigothic law required:

> Sixty gold sous for a child from the age of one
> A hundred and fifty for a boy from fifteen to twenty
> Three hundred for a man from twenty to fifty
> Two hundred for a man from fifty to sixty-five
> One hundred for a man over sixty-five
> Two hundred and fifty for a woman from fifteen to forty
> Two hundred for a woman from forty to sixty.

In Burgundian law the price was three hundred gold sous between twenty and fifty, two hundred between fifty and sixty-five, and a hundred and fifty over sixty-five. The Salic law required the same price for all men whatever their age.

The other event that marked the end of the ancient world was the triumph of Christianity. It settled firmly within the Roman empire; it spread among the barbarians; it became the ideology of the Western world. Did it succeed in making customs gentler, and in particular did it improve the lot of the aged? It seems doubtful. Christianity succeeded in spreading only at the cost of abandoning its original idea of brotherhood and mutual aid. By the third century worldliness was already rampant among the Christians. The new religion had almost no influence upon manners and customs. In 374 it did cause infanticide to be forbidden in Rome, but it did not go so far as to prevent babies being exposed; nor did it forbid slavery. Christianity succeeded in spreading among the various nations and in being adopted by them only by adopting their customs in its turn; and of these the Teutonic were particularly contaminating. The heads of the church sanctioned a retreat from spirituality; and the adoration of the saints brought heathen superstitions back to life.

Christianity, degraded in practice by the customs of the people it had converted, became the ideological heir of the thought of the ancient world. The church had begun by opposing it: primitive

Christianity, turning towards the lowest, least cultured classes, had nothing to do with Graeco-Roman classicism. But from the third century onwards the church took over the ancient culture, though at the same time shattering and deforming it. As we have seen, the classical world, with a few exceptions, took a very dark, melancholy view of old age. We find this echoed in the works of that great compiler, Saint Isidore of Seville.* According to *Le Grand Propriétaire de toutes choses*, an encyclopedia based on the works of the writers of the Lower Empire that was published in 1556, Saint Isidore divided life into seven ages (by analogy with the days of the week). Youth lasted from thirty-five to forty-five or fifty. Then came *senecte*. 'After this there follows old age, which according to some lasts until seventy while according to others death is its only end. Old age, says Isidore, is so called because when they reach it people grow smaller; for old people's wits are not as good as they were, and in their old age they dote.'

On one point the church made a positive contribution. From the fourth century onwards it built asylums and hospitals. In Rome and Alexandria it saw to the maintenance of the orphans and the sick. It looked upon alms-giving as a duty and continually stressed its importance. The old no doubt benefited from this charity, but they are never specifically mentioned.

The period that the English call the Dark Ages was a time of destruction and confusion. 'We see nothing but emptied towns, monasteries thrown down or burnt, fields laid waste. . . . Everywhere the strong oppress the weak, and men are like the fishes of the sea, devouring one another promiscuously,' declared the bishops of the province of Rheims in 909. The ninth and tenth centuries ring with lamentations. Material life was much harder than it had been in the ancient world. Techniques had fallen off and the castes had deteriorated; the towns had many fewer people; life had become rural and the middle classes had disappeared. Work on the land was very arduous, and an elderly man could not take part in it. At this period it does not appear that religion can have been a help to him, either. In theory the church continued the tradition of the Commandments, which required men to honour their parents; but in fact the cult of the family had no place in an age whose ideal was ascetic and unworldly. Christ had said that his disciples were to leave their father and mother to follow him. A minority of Christians fled from

* Born at Carthagena in 560, died in 636.

126

the world; they practised celibacy, hiding in the wastes or shutting themselves up in monasteries. The others went along with the times; and for these times religion was made up only of outward gestures: both clergy and laymen atoned for their irregular lives by prayer. People believed in the power of the devil and in witchcraft; they respected sexual and alimentary taboos based upon superstition. Secular and even ecclesiastical courts made use of the ordeal in their judgements.

During the Lower Empire and the early middle ages, old men were almost entirely shut out of public life: it was the young who ruled the world. Society, divided, threatened, disturbed and warlike, was governed much more by the fortune of battle than by settled institutions: there was little room for the man rich in experience. In the seventh century the Visigoths chose Khindaswintz as their king at the age of seventy-nine, and he restored the prestige of the crown. Charlemagne ruled until he was seventy-two. These, as far as I know, are the only exceptions. At this time even the popes were, for the most part, young men. Gregory I, the first real head of the universal church, was elected in 590 at fifty, and he died at sixty-four: he was comparatively aged. But up until the eighth century the popes were young Romans of good family, intended for the church because they were orphans and had no money. Later, when the popes possessed material wealth and great power, the nobles coveted the papal throne. In the ninth and tenth centuries they forced leaders upon the church who were usually young men and who were deposed shortly after their election. The average reign did not amount to three years. For sixty years, during the period that was called the Pornocracy, it was women who controlled the papacy. Sometimes very aged cardinals were chosen, but John XII was elected at sixteen, Benedict IX at twelve and Gregory V at twenty-three. But whether they were young or old, they were mere puppets in the hands of a powerful aristocracy.

Thanks to a fortunate expansion of the economy towards the year 1000, civilization emerged from the darkness. Feudal society, whose origins go back to the eighth century with the appearance of vassalage, began to be organized. Here again the elderly man had but an unimportant role. The holding of a fief required that the vassal should be capable of defending it by the sword. He owed his lord armed service: he had to possess 'weapons and horses, and unless he is held back by old age he must join the host and take part in the ridings, the trials and the courts'.* The bond of vassalage lasted until death and it was not broken when age took away the knight's powers: but age did mean that the knight was pushed to one side. Fiefs began to be hereditary in France as early as the tenth century, and it was the son, knighted in due time, who defended the land and did service to the lord. It was he too who avenged the honour of the family by force of arms, if necessary. Society looked upon itself as being divided into three orders, those who prayed, those who fought, and those who worked: it placed the sword above work and even above prayer; the active warrior, the man in the prime of life, filled the forefront of the stage.

The literature of the period confirms this: the heroes of the *chansons de geste* are grown men or even sometimes youths. In the courtly romances the idea of ageing does not appear at all. The heroes are immensely long-lived, and their years do not weigh upon them in the least: in *La Mort d'Arthur* the king is over a hundred, while Lancelot, Guenièvre and Gauvain are between sixty and eighty – they behave as though they were in the flower of their age in every respect. It is the same today in thrillers and comic strips: age is purely theoretical. The heroes' adventures are lasting enough and numerous enough to take up a hundred years, yet they remain set for ever in unchanging youth.

The literature of the early middle ages is not interested in old men. We come across only one important exception – Charlemagne. During his lifetime those about him had laboured to build up a Charlemagne legend, particularly Alcuin and Angilbert. Alcuin compares him to a lion and shows him being acclaimed by the land, the sea, the birds, all the animals, and even the stars. He likens this prince, 'such as has not been seen since the world began', to John the Baptist, the Forerunner. Angilbert describes him going off to war 'his head covered with a golden helmet and his body with glittering armour, mounted on a great horse and towering a full head above his companions'. Charlemagne adopted the name of David, and he identified himself with that king. Even the dry *Annales* relate a great many marvels about him. As soon as he was dead the Christian sense of wonder seized upon him. The Germans made him a saint. In France, as the Carolingian decadence grew worse and worse, his image by contrast – and also as propaganda – was more and more idealized. Seventy years after his death the monk of Saint

* The Customs of Catalonia.

Gall wrote his biography in a series of edifying and naïve episodes. A Spoleto text of 897 speaks of him as 'the terrible, the awe-inspiring Charles'. His eyes darted such flashes that in his presence people fainted away. His penetration was such that he solved all riddles. Yet the same text also describes him as a wag, loving to play jokes on those around him: and its description of his wild laughter, his blowing out of his nostrils and rubbing his ears, and the grimaces that accompany his words and deeds gives him a caricatural aspect.

In the tenth century a great many accounts were written in the monasteries, showing him perpetually making war on the unbelievers. In *La Geste du roi* of the eleventh century (and in a great number of other cycles), he appears as a splendid old man with a flowing white beard, and he is surrounded with an almost religious veneration. One *Vie de Charlemagne* describes him as tall and powerful, white-haired and white-bearded, with shining eyes: he lives two hundred years. Yet there is another and an opposing image, one that expresses the antimonarchic attitude of the barons. In the *Pèlerinage à Jérusalem* of the twelfth century the emperor is a 'covetous' and 'doting' old man. In other poems the hero is a great vassal and Charles (several Carolingian kings were merged in his person) is unjust, weak and capricious, the tool of his flatterers; in the end he is punished.

In the eleventh century the handing over of power by an aged, enfeebled father to his son inspired the first part of the Spanish legends that were later written down and called the *Romancero del Cid*. The oldest manuscript version dates from the end of the fifteenth century, but the tradition goes back to the time of the Cid, a minor noble who served Sancho II and then Alfonso VI. In 1081 Alfonso disgraced and banished him, whereupon the Cid became a sort of condottiere, conquered the region of Valencia for himself and stopped a second invasion by the Moors, thus saving Spain. The *Romancero* begins by telling of don Diego Lainez, who is heartbroken at the dishonour that has fallen on his family: in a quarrel over a hare with Count Lozano, the king's chief counsellor and the best of his captains, the count insulted him grossly. Honour calls for revenge. 'Knowing that he lacks strength to take his vengeance and that he is too old to wield the sword, he cannot sleep by night and food has no savour for him.' There is only one single remedy – that one of his four sons should wipe out the insult. He calls them in one after the other and grips their right hand in his. 'Wounded honour gives his chilled blood strength in spite of the years and white hair', and he grips so hard that the three elder brothers groan. 'That is enough.' The youngest son, Ruy Diaz de Bivar, starts angrily. 'If you were not my father!' he cries in a threatening tone. With tears of joy the old man entrusts him with the vengeance. The Cid challenges the count and cuts off his head. By this feat he supersedes his father, who himself hands over his power, saying, 'Sit here, at the upper end of the table, for he who carries such a head* shall be the head of my house.'

This tale, which was immensely popular, illustrates the relationships between the nobles, old and young, in feudal society. The good knight was a 'big-boned, stout-limbed athlete' with a 'well-cut' body and vigorous appetites, one who loved war, hunting and tournaments. The qualities glorified in the *Chansons de geste* are courage and generosity. The hero they admire is the one who gives himself without sparing – he spends his blood for his lord. He defends widows and orphans, he comes to the rescue of the weak, he challenges his rivals. He also flings his fortune out of the window. A chronicler tells of a curious competition in waste: one knight has a ploughed field sown with silver pieces; in vainglorious rivalry another has thirty of his horses burnt alive. Glorifying these values, heroism and splendid lavishness, meant glorifying youth; for they could never find their embodiment in old men with chilled blood and stiffened muscles.

Even among the common people, the harshness of medieval civilization removed the old from active life. In those days the merchants were 'dusty-footed men', travelling in caravans 'sword on the saddle' and exposed to many dangers. It could be said of many burgesses that they were 'mighty men of arms'. Physical decline therefore compelled the aged man to withdraw.

In the countryside, if the father insisted upon maintaining his authority, the young would rise up against him. Quarrels were frequent, and the son often left the family home. But in most European countries and particularly in England, the son took the father's place at the head of the family. Once he had reached a certain age and was too feeble to work the land, he yielded his position to the eldest son, who, after receiving this heritage would marry. His wife took her mother-in-law's place and the old pair moved into the room

* The severed head of the count.

that was traditionally kept for them; in Ireland it was called the western chamber. The dispossessed father was often badly treated by his heirs. The legend of King Lear was very popular in medieval England because it illustrated a story well known in everyday life; and we find echoes of this situation in the German tales collected by the brothers Grimm. As for the aged who had no family or whose family could not maintain them, they were helped by the lord or the monastery; the monks had infirmaries for the sick and the poor. In the towns the guilds looked after those of their members who could no longer work. The guild's chief function was to do away with competition; yet it was often a religious fraternity as well, coming to the help of the needy in case of illness or death. But generally speaking this help was quite inadequate. The old were reduced to beggary; and seeing that there was no better solution at hand, begging was more readily tolerated at this period than at any other.

The condition of old people, then, was most unfortunate, from the highest level of society to the lowest. Among the nobles physical strength was of the first importance, just as it was among the peasants: there was no room for the weak. The young people formed an age-group of considerable importance. The youths underwent an apprenticeship and an initiation: for the young noble it was when he was dubbed a knight. The young peasants had to pass various trials during their rural ceremonies – leaping over the fire on Midsummer Eve, for example. The class of old people as such did not exist.

In the harsh conditions with which this society had to struggle, it could not afford itself the indulgence of worrying about the fate of children: it was concerned with the young who had survived the illnesses of childhood and who represented the future, not with the very small children, most of whom were doomed to an early death. Besides, it might be said that childhood hardly existed. As soon as they had left their mother's apron-strings children were treated as small adults, either starting their apprenticeship as fighting men or being put to work the land. *Enfances* are often mentioned in the *chansons de geste*; but this should not be misunderstood – what is meant is the first exploits of a very young boy who is nevertheless already a small-sized man. Until the thirteenth or fourteenth century (when the bourgeoisie appeared), only the adult was taken into consideration.

During this period the world continued to be run by young men.

With the exception of the twelfth-century Barbarossa, who ruled until he was sixty-eight, the head of the Holy Roman Empire was always a man in the prime of life. Gregory VII won back the independence of the papacy in 1073, and at this time too the popes were generally young; their struggle against the Empire required vigour, courage and determination. Some old men are found among them, and Celestine III began his pontificate at eighty-five: but Innocent III was elected when he was thirty-seven.

Venice alone stands out as an exception. The doge was old. First a subject and then a vassal of Byzantium, its 'very humble duke' had seen his authority increase: at first he was elected by the people, but then his office became hereditary, and until the beginning of the eleventh century his power was tyrannical. But there were conflicts between the doge and the aristocracy, and sometimes they were bloody. The aristocracy grew more and more powerful, acquiring great wealth by the accumulation of inherited money and by trade; and it tried to lessen the authority of the doge to the advantage of a patrician republic. The law of 1031 did away with the hereditary regime; the doge was elected not by the people but by the nobility, and he was obliged to take an oath that bound him to them. As early as the middle of the twelfth century he could no longer decide upon peace, declare war, or conclude a treaty without the consent of the Council of Forty. He no longer administered the finances, nor chose the judges and public officers. He might on occasion lead military operations and command the fleet: at the end of the twelfth century the blind Dandolo, elected doge at the age of eighty-four, won the greatest fame by his successful attack upon Constantinople.*
But he was only the servant of the patricians. Later the office became purely decorative; the doge had sonorous titles and a magnificent costume; his function was to represent the republic splendidly, particularly in the presence of foreign ambassadors. But he had no power whatsoever. He was no more than 'the first, the most supervised and the most obedient of the servants of the republic'. Nobody was more fitting than an old man for this office; weakened by age, the prisoner of long-established habits, he could renounce all initiative and put up with the outward show of importance more easily than a young man. Then again, in a society where wealth is safeguarded by law, age may confer additional prestige upon its

* When he was ninety-six he refused the throne of the Eastern Empire, and he died, still doge, at the age of ninety-seven.

possessor: this was so in Venice, which honoured old age for the very reason that it was convenient to set an old man in the most honourable of all positions. Age did not prevent Marino Faliero from conspiring against the aristocracy in 1354.* But generally speaking the system worked, and the doges were the amenable servants of the patricians. Apart from Andrea Dandolo, in the fourteenth century, who was elected at the age of thirty-six, they were all old men. They did not rule.

The superiority of youth and especially the transference of power from the father to the son (as we see in the legend of the Cid), had a deep influence upon Christianity, the ideology that dominated the middle ages. From the first ages of the church, for the ordinary people if not for the theologians, the central figure of the new religion was Christ. The Trinity was too hard a concept: they turned to the figures of the Father and the Son and to the relationship between the two – the second dethroned the first. During the apostolic period, Christianity was above all the religion of the Saviour: the Father was not forgotten, but it was primarily Christ that the Christians invoked. The church was 'the body of Christ'. It was his flesh and blood that were present in the eucharist; it was by means of them that the people took Communion. The mass and the sacraments derived their whole meaning from him. His teaching was the basis of morality. It is he whom the symbolic paintings in the catacombs show: in them he is the Good Shepherd, Orpheus in the underworld, a lamb, a phoenix, a fish – the Greek for fish being an acrostic of the name Jesus. He was also drawn as a fairhaired beardless man; and in the churches he was symbolized by a mystic winepress or a mill, a vine, a bunch of grapes, a lion, an eagle or a unicorn.

This supremacy of the Son over the Father grows steadily stronger from the eleventh century onwards. It is he who is carved on the tympana of the churches. In the twelfth century he is shown in his glory, the King of Kings. In the thirteenth he becomes more human, being represented as the Child Jesus and above all as Christ crucified, wearing the crown of thorns. Artists painted pictures of every episode in his life. Yet he died in the flower of his age. So the ageless Eternal is henceforward shown as an ancient man; he is imagined as being like those patriarchs in whom, since he delegated his powers

* He was seventy-six. His head was cut off.

to them, he must have recognized his own image. He is more or less thrust back into the past, to the world's beginning and to the distant heavens. He becomes the Lord, the 'Master of the heavenly fortress', as remote as the feudal lord in his castle. He is often to be seen in the illuminated Bibles and in the pictures of simple piety. He always has a white beard. But the less naïve artists did not presume to paint him until very late, and then only occasionally.* Generally speaking they limit themselves to showing a white beard appearing through the clouds and a hand that at once blesses and threatens. There are some sculptures of the Trinity: in these God is shown as a bearded ancient, supporting his son. The result of all these carved or painted images is to clarify the evolution that, in popular iconography dethroned the Father ever more thoroughly in favour of the Son.†

What has the literature of the twelfth and thirteenth centuries to tell us about old age? Precious little. These centuries, like those immediately before them, took scarcely any interest in the subject. The attitude of the learned, as far as they mention it at all, remains negative. Hugues of Orleans, a forerunner of the Goliards, those wandering scholars whose verse celebrated wine and love, wrote a poem in about 1150, when he was sixty: having spoken of the pleasures of life he laments his own decline.

> Dives eram et dilectus
> Inter pares praeelectus
> Modo curvat me senectus
> Et aetati sum confectus.

Le Grand Propriétaire de toutes choses, reminding the fifteenth century of the ideas that had been current in the Middle Ages, tells

---

* As far as my knowledge goes, Masaccio did so, in Florence: Michelangelo, on the ceiling of the Sistine chapel, endowed him (as he did his Moses) both with a white beard and, he being the all-powerful Creator, with the muscles of an athlete. He was also painted by Titian, Tintoretto, an artist of the Ferrara school, by Lippo Lippi (in Rome), and by Cranach in his Garden of Eden: he is a bearded old man, still upright and vigorous. Raphael painted him appearing to Moses in the burning bush. Cosimo Rosselli and two or three others show glimpses of him in the clouds, giving Moses the Tables of the Law.

† It is interesting to observe that in the East, the saviour of mankind, Buddha, passes through all the stages of life and that it is in the last that he reaches the highest point of perfection: he died at eighty. In the West, the Saviour accomplishes his mission between thirty and thirty-three, the age at which he dies. We have seen how in ancient mythology the old gods were also supplanted by their sons, men in the prime of life.

us, 'The last part of old age is called *senies* in Latin, and in French it has no other name than old age. Old age is full of coughs and phlegm and filth, until the time it returns to the dust and the ashes whence it was taken.'

Philippe de Novare, writing in 1265, speaks of the 'four stages of man's life', each of which is made up of two periods of ten years. 'The life of the old is but pain and labour,' he says, concluding that after the age of eighty death is all that can be wished for. The middle ages loved to discover analogies between the various realms, and the 'four stages' were compared to the four elements and the four seasons. And in the calendars meant for the people, the months were related to the periods of a man's life. A poem, written in the thirteenth century and often printed in the fourteenth and fifteenth centuries, provides notes for the calendar:

> Du mois qui vient après septembre
> qu'on appelle mois d'octembre
> qu'il a LX ans et non plus.
> Lors devient vieillard et chenu
> Et a donc lui doit souvenir
> Que le temps le mène à mourir.*

As I have said, Christianity did not reach far down into the depths of people's way of thought, which kept its pagan roots and which expressed itself in folklore. The brothers Grimm collected the essence of German folklore, and here we occasionally see the aged man as one who is full of experience and who knows secrets of the greatest value. But most of the time he is a pitiful creature.

One tale written down by the Grimms puts forward a singular interpretation of the stages of life. God had set thirty years as the age for man and all the animals. The ass, the dog and the monkey, thinking so long a life too wearisome, begged him to reduce it by eighteen, twelve and ten years. The man was not so wise as the animals – the lack of sense in this allegedly sensible being is one of the favourite themes in folklore – and he did not understand that long life had to be paid for with decrepitude. He asked for his to be longer and he was given the ass's eighteen years, the dog's twelve and the monkey's ten. 'So man has seventy years of life. The first thirty are his own, and they pass by quickly. . . . Then come the ass's eighteen, and

* From the month after September, which is called October, he is sixty and no more. Then he becomes old and hoary, and so he must remember that time is leading him towards his death.

135

during these he has to carry countless burdens on his back; it is he who brings corn to the mill to feed others. . . . Then come the twelve of the dog, and all this time he does little but growl and drag himself from one corner to another, for he has no teeth left to bite with. . . . When these have gone, all he has left for the end is the monkey's ten. He no longer has his right wits; he grows rather strange, doing things that make children laugh at him.' So if man's old age is longer and more unpleasant than that of the beasts, it is he who is answerable for it; he condemned himself to it by his own foolish greed.

In these tales the old woman – the mere fact of her being a woman makes her suspect – is always a baleful creature. If ever she does good it is because her body is really no more than a disguise – she puts it off and appears as a fairy, glowing with youth and beauty. Real old women are ogresses and wicked, dangerous witches, as they were in the Latin poets. The misogyny of the middle ages is expressed in all the old woman characters to be met with in their literature – the literature of the fabliaux, particularly in *La Male Femme qui conchia la prude femme* and the Old Woman in the *Roman de la Rose*. As we have seen, it was old women who were symbolically expelled or killed in the small towns and the countryside to rid society of old age. In the Roussillon Lent was symbolized by the *patorra*, a figure of an old woman with seven feet (the seven weeks of Lent), that was burnt on Easter Day.

Then again it should be pointed out that both very old men and very old women were extremely rare. They were hardly ever to be met with among the ordinary people. For the peasants, under the conditions in which they lived, thirty was already a considerable age. A thirteenth-century fabliau, praising the merits of a youth-giving spring, says, 'Then there will no longer be any old white-haired men, nor yet any grey and hoary old women, even if they have reached the age of thirty.'

The medieval world, like the world of classical antiquity, cherished the dream of a victory over old age; it was obsessed by the idea of rejuvenation. The *Alexandrécite*, a medieval romance whose hero is Alexandeo, describes a magic lake which makes those who plunge into it young again, and in *Le Livre des merveilles* Jean de Mandeville tells the story of a fountain of youth hidden in the Indian jungle. But the legend was handed on chiefly by oral tradition, never being a central theme in any of the written tales. It takes the form of a rejuvenating talisman – a fruit, a wine-skin full of air, or the elixir of long life. Generally it is found in association with the legend of the Island of Life, the Isle of Avalon where no one ever dies or grows old. In the *Perce-forest* the main characters are carried to the Isle of Avalon when they are in the flower of youth and they remain young for two or three generations. Later they come back to die in the realm of Brittany. As soon as they touch land they take on the ordinary look of ancient people who have lived as long as they.

The iconography of the middle ages has more to say on the subject of old age – as indeed it has on many other subjects – than the literature; for it spoke far more understandably to a still illiterate mankind. As we have seen, the dethronement of God the Father by the Son is pre-eminently clear in painting and sculpture. They often show old people: the sculptors produced statues of bearded ancients for church porches – the elders of the Apocalypse,* prophets or venerable saints. In religious pictures, hermits and anchorites are often shown as emaciated, long-bearded, very aged men. The theme of the stages of man's life appears for the first time in an eighth-century Arabian fresco; it occurs again on the twelfth-century capitals in the Parma baptistry, which show old age as a farm labourer resting beside his mattock. In the Palace of the Doges (where of course old age was honoured) and at Padua, in the Ere-metani fresco, old age takes the form of a bearded scholar, sitting at his desk by the fire. But the popular image that the middle ages created and that has prevailed throughout the following centuries is less serene; it is that of Old Father Time, winged and terribly thin, carrying a scythe in his hand. The conjunction of the two notions would seem self-evident, since old age is the result of the accumula-tion of years; yet in his *Essais d'iconologie* Erwin Panofsky shows that the relationship has not always existed. In the ancient world, time was represented by two series of images. The first emphasize its fleeting nature. They show Kairos, Chance, the turning-point in the life of a person or of mankind, and they take the form of a figure running fast away or of something in a state of uneasy equilibrium that must soon change, such as the Wheel of Fortune – a symbol with

* In the Apocalypse, Christ is surrounded by twenty-four elders in white robes, wearing golden crowns. They are thought to correspond to the twenty-four signs of the zodiac, represented in Babylon by twenty-four old men, for they, presiding over the twenty-four hours of the day, were the incarnation of time. The sculptors, taking their inspiration from illuminated manuscripts of the Apocalypse, often carved these elders. They were taken to be wise counsellors.

which it merged from the eleventh century on. The second series emphasizes its productive character: time is Aion, the creative principle, infinite fertility. Time passes; but as it passes so it creates. The ancients stressed time's ambivalence: at Olympia the Pythagorean Paron, hearing a eulogy upon time, 'time, in which we learn and in which we remember', protested: he asked whether it was not in time, within time, that forgetfulness came into being, and he proclaimed it the king of ignorance. As we have seen, the poets spoke of its devastating power. Greek poetry often refers to 'grey-haired time'. Yet the representational art of the ancient world never shows Time in a form that evokes either decline or destruction.

Plutarch was the first to point out the interaction of *Chronos* and *Kronos*, the first being the Greek for time and the second the name of the most formidable of the gods. According to him, Kronos, who ate his children, *meant* time; and the neo-Platonists accepted this conjunction, although in doing so they provided an optimistic interpretation of time. As they saw it, Kronos was the *nous*, cosmic thought, 'the father of all things', 'the wise builder'. Kronos was always shown with a sickle in his hand: in those days it was always looked upon as an agricultural instrument, a symbol of fertility.

In the middle ages this image was overturned; for now time was looked upon as a cause of decay. For the middle ages, the macrocosm too passed through six stages of life,* comparable to the days of the week, just as man, the microcosm, did. The last stage was that of decrepitude, and that was the stage the world was thought to have reached. The idea is to be found both in popular writers such as Honorius Augustodunensis and in Saint Thomas Aquinas. *Mundus senescit*: that was what primitive Christianity thought when it was confronted with the miseries and afflictions of the lower Empire; and it handed on this concept to its heirs. It finds expression at the beginning of the eleventh century *Vie de saint Alexis*:

> Bon fut le siècle, n'aura plus tel valeur;
> Vieux est et frêle, tout s'en va déclinant,
> S'est empiré, le bien plus n'y fait on.†

In the feudalized version of the twelfth century it reads:

* Sometimes seven stages are distinguished, sometimes four.
† The world was good; it will never be as good again. It is old and feeble; everything is going down, getting worse; and good is no longer done in our time.

138

Bon fut le siècle au temps des anciens
Et si changé perdu a sa valeur
Ne sera plus tel que nos aïeux
. . . Frêle est la vie, ne durera longtemps.*

The same idea is treated at greater length in the thirteenth-century version:

La fin est proche par le mien escient.†

In the twelfth century Otho of Frersing wrote in his *Chronicle*, 'We see the world failing and, as it were, breathing out the last sigh of extreme old age.' The miniatures in the *Liber Floridus*‡ of the same period show the successful spread of this idea. Indeed, Saint Norbert thought that his own generation would see the end of the world.

In the thirteenth century Hugues de Saint-Victor wrote, 'The end of the world is coming and the sequence of events has already reached the farthest points of the earth.' The world was shrinking as it grew old; even the men were stunted. In the same century Guiot de Provins observed that they were no more than dwarfs and children. We find this notion among the Goliards, and the *Carmina Burana* treats it at length: 'Youth no longer wants to learn anything at all; knowledge is in decay; the whole world is upside down; the blind lead the blind. . . . Everything has strayed from its right path.' Dante makes Cacciaguida, his ancestor, deplore the decadence of towns and families. The world was growing smaller, like a cloak round which 'Time paces with his scissors'. Few were they who saw any gain in this ageing. Bernard of Chartres did say, 'We are dwarfs perched on the shoulders of giants, yet we see farther than they.' But almost no one shared his optimism. There was nothing encouraging about what the middle ages saw in the distance: for many it was the reign of Antichrist. This vision, first seen in the Apocalypse, was perfected in the eighth century by a monk named Pierre, then by Adson in the tenth, and in the eleventh by Albuin, who transplanted the prophecies of the fourth-century Tiburtine sibyl to the Western world. The religious plays made it familiar to everyone. An opposing figure came into being, that of the 'righteous king', of

* The world was good in our forefathers' days, and now it is changed so that it has lost its worth. Never again will it be as they knew it. . . . Life is frail: it will not last long.
† By my certain knowledge, the end is near.
‡ A muddled compilation that we owe to Lambert, a canon of Saint-Omer.

an earthly Messiah who would inaugurate a millennium of happiness. But this belief was not widely spread: the medievals were convinced that because of original sin, mankind was doomed to an unhappiness that could only get worse with time. Filled with this discouraging idea, those who governed society limited themselves to ruling from day to day, without looking forward to any clear political future. No one expected that history would bring any improvement. The hopes of the middle ages were outside time: man had to free himself from earthly life and look to his salvation. Time was dragging the world to its downfall, and soon it would drag it to its end.

It is this context that explains how, under the influence of the astrologers, the name of Saturn, the Latin for Kronos, was attributed to the slowest planet, the most remote of all; it was thought to be cold and dry, and it was associated with poverty, senility and death. In astrological works it was usually represented by a gloomy, sickly old man holding a scythe, a pick, a spade or a staff, and leaning on a crutch, the sign of decrepitude. He either has a wooden leg or he is castrated. (A reminder of the mythological account in which Zeus emasculates him.) Medieval iconography made use of him to deal at greater length with the theme of the castrated man and the eaten child. Saturn being the most malignant of the planets, the pictures of him are revolting. But then again, from the eleventh century onwards Death is shown holding a scythe.* Time, in that it is the enemy of life, is allied to death: and Kronos was identified with Chronos. So it was natural enough that in illustrating Petrarch (for whom time was a destructive force), the artist should have borrowed the image of Saturn to evoke Time: he has wings, he is holding an hour-glass, and he is decrepit. This was the image that was to prevail from that period onwards. In the 'triumphs of death' that appear in such numbers during the fifteenth century Death is a skeleton carrying a scythe and an hour-glass. Time too has a scythe, and this scythe is no longer a symbol of fertility – it cuts lives off just as the Parcae used to cut off the thread of days.

Life was still precarious towards the end of the middle ages and longevity was rare. When Charles v died in 1380 at the age of forty-two he had the reputation of a wise old man. Yet society was evolving. A revival of urban life began in the thirteenth century and

* In the Uta Gospels. He also has one in the Gumpert Bible, which is earlier than 1195.

140

it was even stronger in the fourteenth. The church no longer condemned the quest for profit so severely; finally it was even legitimized,
and commercial pursuits were honoured. In Venice and Pisa it was
the nobles themselves who took to business. Elsewhere the aristocracy
usually remained outside the mercantile world: trade would have
meant a loss of standing. But the bourgeoisie throve, and the great
merchants and bankers acquired titles by buying land and by
marriage: a new nobility came into being, and with it the development
of a body of urban patricians. From now on property was based
upon contracts, not upon physical strength; and now there first
appeared the traditional type of shopkeeper who dreads physical
violence. Both goods and money could be accumulated. In the well-
to-do classes this change altered the condition of the aged, for by
piling up wealth they might become powerful.

During this period there were two currents of ideological opinion,
existing side by side; the one was religious and spiritual, the other
pessimistic and materialist. It was from within the first that Dante
dealt with old age in the *Convivio*. He compares the line of human
life to a curve rising from the earth to a culminating point in the
sky and then coming down again. He places the zenith at the age of
thirty-five. Then slowly man declines. From forty-five to seventy is
the time of old age. After that it is extreme old age. If this end is
wise, it is peaceful. Dante likens the old, old man to a mariner who
gently lowers his sail on seeing land and who slowly comes into
harbour. Man's truth being in the world beyond, he must with an
untroubled mind accept the end of an existence that has been no
more than a short voyage.

Reaching harbour peacefully: that, in the opinion of the clergy
and the pious souls, should be the chief preoccupation of the aged:
the last stage was looked upon as being essentially the time in which
a man should prepare himself for death. There was an outpouring of
artes moriendi. Gerson wrote 'short instructions for an aged man on
how he should prepare himself for death'. He advises him – no
doubt because he has lost his sight – to take someone into his house
to read him devotional books that will turn his mind from the
things of this world. Similar books were published all over Europe,
very large numbers appearing in Germany from 1400 onwards. They
also advise the old man how to make his will: if he possesses any
wealth it is fitting that he should leave some of it to monasteries or
hospitals.

For the convinced Christian, therefore, old age was the time for ensuring his salvation. But its worth was not particularly enhanced. To an ever-increasing degree during the fourteenth and fifteenth centuries it was Christ who monopolized the devotion of the faithful: the fourteenth was a tragic century, with wars, plagues, famines and the disasters of over-population. In the midst of the trials that were tearing it apart, the West set all its trust in the Redeemer. From that time on, he hardly ever appeared as the King of Kings: it was as the Saviour that he was exalted. The Father and the Holy Ghost were eclipsed. The mass was no longer a sacrifice addressed to God the Father, but a representation of Calvary. The Host was adored, the relics of the Passion venerated. Crucifixes were produced in far greater numbers, and this period saw the beginnings of the cult of the Holy Face and of the practice of making the Stations of the Cross. We find many paintings and sculptures of the Agony in the Garden, with Christ waiting for his crucifixion in lonely anguish. At the same time the devotion to Mary increased. The Annunciation was rediscovered at the beginning of the fifteenth century and it inspired an extraordinary number of pictures and statues. A whole iconography was devoted to the theme of the childhood of Christ and to that of the Holy Family, which up until then had scarcely been treated at all. The effect of all these evocations of Jesus's life was to sanctify childhood, adolescence and above all maturity. Old age was forgotten.

Then again, a profane literature evolved in the courts of the nobles and among the urban patricians – a satirical and realistic literature that mocked society and everything in it – wives and their husbands, monks, merchants, the common people. It did not take much account of the aged. Yet, like Plautus in former times, the Italian Boccaccio and the English Chaucer did make game of rich old men who made use of their wealth to procure themselves handsome wives.

In Boccaccio's story,* a very elderly Pisan judge marries the young and beautiful Bartolomea. He only just manages to do his duty on their wedding-night. In the morning he is so exhausted that he tries to find ways of evading it: every day he shows his wife the calendar and points out that it is the feast of some great saint, in whose honour they ought to abstain. He scarcely has conjugal relations with her as often as once a month. One day when they have gone sailing she is carried off by a corsair, who proves the

---

* This was taken over by La Fontaine in his *Contes*. It is the only one in which an old man appears.

warmth of his ardour every day without troubling about the calendar. The husband finds her again: she refuses to go back to him. He dies of it and the whole city laughs heartily.

In *The Canterbury Tales*, Chaucer tells of the misfortunes of an old knight, January, whose money allows him to marry the lovely twenty-year-old May. On their wedding afternoon he drinks electuaries that enable him to be active all night long.

> Thus laboureth he til that the day gan dawe;
> And than he taketh a sop in fyn claree,
> And upright in his bed than sitteth he,
> And after that he sang ful loude and clere,
> And kiste his wyf, and made wantoun chere.
> He was al coltish, ful of ragerye,
> And ful of jargon as a flekked pye.
> The slakke skin aboute his nekke shaketh,
> Whyl that he sang; so chaunteth he and craketh.
> But god wot what that May thoughte in hir herte,
> When she him saugh up sitting in his sherte,
> In his night-cappe, and with his nekke lene;
> She preyseth nat his pleying worth a bene.

Shortly after she deceives him with a young and handsome squire in ludicrous circumstances. As I have said, the old man's sexuality disgusts, whatever he does. Boccaccio laughs at his impotence: Chaucer makes him artificially virile, but the old man's absurdity and ugliness turn physical love into a revolting performance. Side by side with this realistic pessimism, the middle ages seem to have had a kind of idealistic pessimism too. I see a sign of this in the increasing importance of Belisarius in the fourteenth and fifteenth centuries – a figure that later became exceedingly popular.* After a glorious life in which he had won Italy back from the Goths and had refused the Western Empire, the great general, the saviour of Byzantium, fell into disgrace; in 562 he was implicated in a plot against Justinian, who was then eighty; he was confined to his palace and his goods were confiscated. He was tried in 563. Theophanus used contemporary documents in his late eighth-century *Chronographia*, and according to him Belisarius' innocence was proved; he was set free and his property was restored to him. It was later, in the

---

* The theme of Belisarius was often used in the sixteenth century. Rotrou wrote a tragedy upon it and Marmontel a famous book. It provided countless allusions and comparisons as well as many pictures.

eleventh century, that the anonymous author of the *Antiquities of Constantinople* (a work crammed with errors), made a quick reference to Belisarius' having been blinded and reduced to beggary. Tretzes, a thirteenth-century grammarian famous for his erudition who lived in Constantinople, acknowledged that many historians denied this version, but nevertheless he adopted it. He described Belisarius, old and blind, a beggar at the palace gate, saying, 'Give Belisarius an obolus.' The punishment of blinding was usual in Byzantium; but there is nothing to show that it was inflicted upon Belisarius. Why did the story become so widely accepted?

We might ask in the first place how it came to be so generally known that all the Renaissance compilers took it over for their own books. It should not be forgotten that this happened to all legends in the middle ages; in spite of the difficulty of travelling, people did move about to a remarkable extent, and merchants and pilgrims carried tales, true or false, from one end of the world to the other, and the itinerant story-tellers gathered them up. Then again there was perpetual communication between the learned: and the knowledge of the learned should not be partitioned off from popular tradition – there was an osmosis between the two. Lastly, many people knew how to read in the thirteenth and fourteenth centuries. Any striking event, real or mythical, became quickly and widely known.

A more interesting question is, why was the legend so successful? The reason is no doubt that the middle ages gave every sombre vision an eager welcome. Now Belisarius was a perfect example of the wretchedness of very old age – the passive suffering of infirmity and dependence, and above all the downfall to which he was condemned by the hard-hearted ingratitude of men. And then this tragedy was edifying from the religious point of view: a man raised to the heights of glory and then thrown down into abject misery illustrated the scriptural 'vanity of vanities': on this earth, nothing was sure; man must set his trust in God alone.

There was a mythic link between old age and blindness in the middle ages, just as there had been in the ancient world. Blindness symbolized the exile to which their over-long life condemned the aged: they were cut off from the rest of mankind. This loneliness increased them in stature and made them spiritually clear-sighted. What is more, the myth had firm roots in reality: no one then knew how to operate for cataract and many old men were blind in fact.

The pessimism of the earlier ages continued in fifteenth-century France. It was still thought that the world was on the wane. Gerson likened it to an old man wandering in his mind, beset by illusions and wild imaginings of every kind. Eustache Deschamps to an ancient in his second childhood:

> Or est laches, chétis et molz
> Vieulx, convoiteux et mal parlant:
> Je ne vois que foles et folz . . .
> La fin s'approche en vérité . . .
> Tout va mal . . .*

The idea of death was more present than ever; the 'dances of death' multiplied and became more and more macabre. Artists painted corpses and carrion in all their full ugliness; preachers contrasted them with the misleading graces of youth, man being merely a corpse under suspended sentence and beauty an illusion. Odin de Cluny described the ignominy hidden within our bodies with a vehemence few have ever reached: the body itself he termed 'a sack of excrement'. Others reminded their readers that the body was doomed to decrepitude, and they pitilessly described the wretchedness of this state. In these instances the old man was looked upon not as Another but as the Same; but he was described only from the outside, and the sole intention was to disqualify youth and beauty. There were some poets who cheerfully took over these clichés. Eustache Deschamps saw old age as nothing but misfortune, unhappiness and reasons for disgust, deterioration of the soul and the body, ridicule and ugliness. For him it began at thirty for women and at fifty for men: at sixty all that was left was to die. Olivier de La Marche was in agreement with his times when he took up the hackneyed theme and addressed his dismal prophecies to a beautiful girl:

> Ces doux regards, ces yeux faiz pour plaisance,
> Pensez-y bien, ils perdront leur clarté . . .
> Vostre beauté changera en laydure
> Vostre santé en maladie obscure . . .†

---

* Now those we see are indolent, sickly and weak, old, covetous and babbling. . . . Mad men and mad women are all I see. . . . In truth, the end is coming near. . . . Everything is out of joint.

† These sweet looks, these eyes made for delight, will lose their brilliance: think of that, I say. . . . Your beauty will change into ugliness, your health into obscure disease.

The aged woman continued to be an object of disgust and mockery. On the south tower of Bayeux cathedral there is a contemporary inscription concerning Isabelle de Douvres, and its author laments that a hundred old women were not buried instead of one:

> Quarte dies paschale erat
> Que jacet hic vetule venimus exequias
> Leticie diem magis amisisse dolemus
> quam centum tales si caderunt vetule.

When Villon deplored the ravages committed by old age on a woman's body in *Les Regrets de la belle heaulmière* he was writing in the same tradition. But however many may have written before him, he wipes them all from one's memory; for he shows in the full force of its truth everything that bad literature hides under empty words.

Villon loved the female body. '*Corps féminin qui tant est tendre.*' In the *Testament* he revolts at the idea that it may rot beneath the ground; he would like to see it 'rise living up to heaven'. And when he too tells a beautiful woman who does not care for him of her coming decline, it is with sadness that he does so:

> Ung temps viendra qui fera dessecher
> Jaunir, flestrir votre épanouie fluer.
> . . . Vieil je serai, vous laide et sans couleur.*

A tender compassion tempers the harshness of the description in the famous *Regrets de la belle heaulmière*, also. He had dearly loved his mother: 'A woman I am, unhappy now and old.' Perhaps it was for that reason that instead of looking coldly and from the outside at the decrepit woman the beautiful armouress† was to become, he left it to her to speak. No doubt he also understood that falling away is piercingly sad only if the subject is aware of it.

> Quand je me regarde toute nue
> Et je me vois si très changée
> Pauvre, sèche, mègre, menue
> Je suis presque toute enragée.‡

Most writers who spoke about the aged did not even take the

---

* A time will come that will dry, yellow and wither your full-blown flower. . . . I shall be old, you ugly and without colour.

† Heaulmière: some say that this meant a whore (trs.).

‡ When I look at myself quite naked and I see that I am so very changed, poor, dry, meagre, thin, I go almost out of my mind.

trouble to look at them closely, but Villon's picture is strikingly exact:

> Oreilles pendantes, moussues,
> Le vis pali mort et déteint
> Menton froncé, lèvres peaussues
> C'est d'humaine beauté l'issue.*

This is not an allegory; it is a precise individual portrait, yet it is one that has reference to all of us. The whole human condition, the whole of man's estate, is called into question in the person of this decayed old woman. Old age is not reserved for others: it is lying in wait for us, just as it lay in wait for the beautiful young woman whose regrets Villon foretold: it is our fate. And it is because he was so fully aware of this that Villon's poem has such an extraordinarily far-reaching ring.

In the sixteenth century civilization in the countryside was still repetitive and conservative, but in the Italian cities an early form of capitalism continued to evolve, and it made its appearance in other towns; they too saw the development of business, industrial undertakings and finance. This new prosperity allowed a vast cultural flowering that ran through the sciences, literature, the arts and techniques – an evolution in which many very different currents were to be seen. The Renaissance carried on the traditions of the middle ages. It still lived with the obsession of the Antichrist and the Last Judgement.† Yet it tried to establish a new and harmonious idea of man. Humanism, in its rediscovery of the ancient world, tried to make a syncretic bond between the classical values and the Gospels – an attempt at integrating the love of life and of beauty with Christianity. Erasmus in particular set himself to this task; and his contribution was a 'civil and moral' doctrine.

He devoted one of his *Colloquies* to the aged, and in it he describes an exemplary old man: at sixty-six no wrinkles, no white hairs, no spectacles, and his complexion is ruddy; the others, who have lived debauched or rakish lives, might be his father. In Italy a Venetian nobleman, Cornaro, took up the theme 'a wise life leads to a fine old age'. In his *Sure and Certain Method of Attaining a Long and*

---

* Drooping, mossy ears, dead, pale, colourless face, puckered chin and leather lips – this is the last end of human beauty.

† In Germany there was an 'Antichrist play'; and lives of the Antichrist were written. Preachers foretold his coming. It was he who inspired Signorelli's frescoes at Orvieto.

Healthful Life, he offers himself as an example. In fact, both these books are primarily concerned with praising virtue and with claiming that it finds its reward in the health and serenity of the virtuous man's last years.

As far as old age itself was concerned, Renaissance literature was no kinder than that of the foregoing centuries. The middle ages despised the tattered rag of the human body, and thought it particularly revolting among the aged. The Renaissance exalted physical beauty, praising female excellence to the skies. By contrast, the ugliness of the aged seemed even more detestable, and never has that of old women been more savagely decried. The misogyny of the middle ages carried on into the sixteenth century, and the influence of the ancient world, particularly of Horace, was of the greatest importance. Petrarch's followers had gone to absurd lengths, and reaction produced a satirical and mocking poetry. These reasons combine to explain why the theme of the old woman was handled so often, as well as the manner in which it was treated.

The writers who made use of it were deeply influenced by Rojas' *Celestina,* a play that he wrote in 1492, describing the Spanish society of his day. This was the first time that an old woman had appeared as the main heroine; in the traditional way she was of course a bawd, but a bawd of dimensions quite unlike those of any characters who had yet been produced. She was a former whore who had stayed in the trade because she liked it, a self-seeking, lewd, and intriguing old woman, and something of a witch as well – the leading, most active character in the play. In her are summed up all the vices that had been attributed to old women since classical times, and in spite of all her shrewdness she ends by being severely punished. The French theatre turned to this source of inspiration, but with less striking results: we find old bawds and prostitutes in Jodelle, Odet de Turnèbe and Larivey.

The anti-feminist prejudice against old women is quite obvious in Erasmus. It was natural that he, as a moralist, should reprove those who were so indecent as still to think of love. But the gratuitous savagery of his descriptions is surprising in a humanist. He speaks of 'these broken-down women, these walking corpses, stinking bodies surrounded by the reek of the charnel-house that nevertheless still cry, "There is nothing so sweet as life". Sometimes they display their flaccid, disgusting breasts and sometimes they try to stimulate their lovers' vigour with quavering yelps.' Among all these clichés

148

there is one new theme to be noted – the contrast between the hideous being, the old woman seen from outside, and the pleasure she still has in living. Erasmus holds it against her, although in those times it was usual to praise those men in whom age did not put out the love of life.*

We find the same disgust in Marot, confronted by an old woman who wants to be loved:

> . . . Veux-tu, vieille ridée, entendre
> Pourquoi je ne te puis aimer?†

And he tells her at length. He speaks of her 'ugly dugs' and paints a revolting picture of her body. He also describes a witch who is a 'hideous old woman'. The same disgust in Desportes, in his *Le Mépris d'une dame devenue vieille*:

> Avec tes apas dégoutants
> . . . Tu penses éveiller mes esprits.‡

They cheerfully humiliate the old woman by comparing her with a girl. D'Aubigné contrasts a dreadful old woman's 'lousy wig' with his sweetheart's beautiful hair.

Why did Du Bellay turn to these themes in his *L'Antérotique de la vieille et de la jeune*? He had just published *L'Olive*, a poem glorifying woman and love, which took its inspiration from Petrarch and which had been remarkably successful. It was surprising that he should then have written this violent diatribe against an aged woman:

> Vois, ô vieille immonde
> Vieille déshonneur de ce monde
> Celle qui (si bien m'en souvient)
> Sur l'an quinzième à peine vient. §

The first reason is of a literary nature: he was angry at the Petrarchism that he himself had cultivated and that was then rampant in France; and he reacted against it. He had lived in Italy, and there he had no doubt read the invectives that the Italian poets often directed against old duennas – they had influenced him. Perhaps he had

---

* This is the theme of Beckett's *Ah! les beaux jours*, but taken from a completely different point of view.

† Wrinkled old woman, do you want to hear why I cannot love you?

‡ With your repulsive charms . . . you think you can arouse my desire.

§ Look, oh you foul old woman, ancient dishonour of the world, look at this girl, who (if I remember right) is hardly yet fifteen.

had reasons for disliking one for not helping him in some amorous affair. For the poets duennas were ambiguous, disagreeable characters: sometimes the men reproached them for playing the bawd, sometimes for hindering their love.

The old woman was chiefly attacked for having once been a whore. She is filthy if she still looks for love, and she is a hypocrite if she has taken to extreme piety. Du Bellay also wrote a cruel and realistic poem about an old Roman courtesan. She tells her life, the waning of her charms, her poverty and illness:

> Dame vieillesse
> Ne m'a laissé que la gravelle aux reins
> La goutte aux pieds et les galles aux mains.*

Nevertheless, he angrily cries

> Tu es sorcière et maquerelle
> Tu es hypocrite et bigote.†

Does this inveteracy of the poets against former whores arise from a sexual resentment? It seems not unlikely. At all events, it must be pointed out that the amorous old person, male or female, aroused disgust. But when men were concerned literature attacked the wealthy who bought pleasure by means of their gold; with women, on the contrary, it set about those of the lowest possible kind, those who sold themselves. The resentment caused by the first is easily understood: the ill-feeling whose object is an ancient whore has murkier sources. No doubt it is to be explained by some frustration.

As it was in the ancient world and in folklore, the old woman and the witch were often looked upon as one: Rabelais describes the sibyl of Panzoust as an old woman 'ill-looking, ill-dressed, ill-fed, toothless, rheumy, bent, running at the nose, creeping along'.

And lastly the old woman looks like death. Sigonio‡ writes

> Respirante momie
> Dont on connaît l'anatomie
> Au travers d'un cuir transparent.§

And

---

* Dame old age has left me no more than gravel in my kidneys, gout in my feet and swellings on my hands.
† You are a witch and a bawd, a hypocrite and a bigot.
‡ Classical scholar, born at Modena.
§ Breathing mummy, whose anatomy can be seen through the transparent hide.

> Portrait vif de la mort, portrait mort de la vie
> Charogne sans couleurs, dépouille du tombeau
> Carcasse déterrée, atteinte d'un corbeau . . .*

Any other tone of voice is rare in the sixteenth century; yet side by side with an ode in which he explains how shameful it is to love an aged woman, Pierre Le Loyer wrote another, a tender description of feminine old age

> La vieillesse à la pomme ressemble
> Qui est douce et salubre ensemble . . .†

An apple is all the better the more wrinkled it is, and the same applies to an old woman. François Hulot contrasts the 'vile toothless wretched old woman' and the 'honourable old lady'

> dont la grâce et la forme
> A la beauté des jeunes se conforme
> . . . En vérité vieille de grand value
> Que pour sa grâce et vertu on salue.‡

Here it was a matter of distinguishing between the aged lady of quality and the base herd of old women branded by their evil ways or their poverty. There was only one writer who came wholeheartedly to the defence of elderly women, and this was Brantôme in his *Vie des dames galantes*. He thought it natural that they should continue to indulge in the pleasures of love; and he asserted that some remained beautiful and that they were loved when they were over seventy.

While the poets loaded the aged woman with opprobrium, the comic theatre turned the aged man to ridicule. As we saw in Aristophanes and Plautus, the comic theatre refused the old man the status of subject, presenting him as the Other, a mere object, one from which the spectators dissociate themselves entirely by means of laughter. By bringing ludicrous old men on to the stage and giving them important roles, the *commedia dell'arte* carried on a tradition that had persisted right through the Lower Empire and the middle ages. In the third century of our era, Julius Pollux, in his *Onomatiscon*, drew up a list of the various masks used in comedy and tragedy.

---

* Living portrait of death, dead portrait of life, colourless carrion, remnants from the grave, disinterred, crow-eaten carcass.

† Old age is like an apple that is both sweet and sound.

‡ . . . whose grace and shape matches the beauty of the young. . . . Indeed an old lady of great worth, to whom we bow for her grace and her virtue.

151

There were two of very old grandfathers: 'The first is the older; his head is entirely shaved, he has very soft eyebrows, a long beard, thin cheeks, his eyes cast down, white skin, a cheerful expression. The second is thinner; he has a sadder, more anxious look; he is rather pale; a long beard, red hair, crushed ears.' Pollux puts a second pair in another category: 'The principal old man has a crown of hair round his head, a Roman nose and a long face; his right-hand eyebrow is raised. The other has a long fan-shaped beard and a crown of hair round his head; his beard is thick. He does not raise his eyebrows; his eyes are sluggish.'

Pollux mentioned three old-women masks: the fat, kindly old woman; the she-wolf – that is to say, the old bawd – with a snub nose and two molars to each jaw; and the concubine who is trying to get herself married.

The *commedia dell'arte* had two old-man characters, Pantaloon and the Doctor. The first is the more important. He is a retired merchant, sometimes rich, and sometimes poor, either the father of a family or an old bachelor, but always very grasping, like Euclion in the *Aulularia*. In addition, he is always amorous. An illustration of 1577 shows him as a tall lean old man with a pointed beard and a huge erect phallus: this last feature was part of Pantaloon's usual costume. At the same time he is lousy, rheumy, and afflicted with the gout. He tries to corrupt the young women he fancies with gold. He is deceived by his children and maid-servants, cuckolded by his wife if he has one, and tricked by his strumpets. He thinks himself very wise, tries to give advice, makes turgid speeches and attempts to meddle with state affairs; he is so irritating that they beat him to make him be quiet. According to the illustrations, the actors set off his senile outbursts with extraordinary feats of agility. The character had different names in the different parts of Italy, being called Pancrace, Cassandre or Zanobio. In France he was Gaultier-Garguille and Jacquemin-Jadot.

The other old man, the Doctor, is a fat pedantic old fool, a member of all the academies. The aged man is no longer only the person who monopolized wealth but also one who claims to be the repository of wisdom. This only makes him the more ridiculous, because the Doctor is in fact an ignorant fellow; he commits the most appalling blunders, perpetually mangling Greek and Latin tags. He is also called Baloardo, the clod. He is Pantaloon's friend, and like Pantaloon he is both miserly and goatish. Everybody makes game of him.

There is only one old-woman character, the bawd. The respectable old woman who has lost her charms without acquiring power is neither an object nor a subject – she is nothing. The wives are neither young nor old, and they play no more than a relative part, that of their old husband's companion and the witness or censor of his follies. When the courtesan grows old, having made her fortune and become independent, she makes use of her experience to pursue her own ends – to become richer. She is a person in her own right, a subject. Yet she is not particularly interesting because she is little more than a minor character, a stereotyped figure.

The elderly men are also very conventional. The *commedia dell'arte* does not really tell us much about the manners of the time; in its not very varied plots it confines itself to the use of the different 'masks' that it inherited from tradition – masks whose role was already fixed beforehand.

There was not much more invention in Machiavelli's *Clizia*, which he wrote at the beginning of the sixteenth century and in which he does little but copy Plautus. Nicomaro is seventy and he has few teeth left. He is in love with Clizia and decides to marry her to his servant, who will pass her on. He makes himself ready for his wedding-night by taking an electuary called satyricon. In the end he is fleeced, and he repents. Once again the theme is the contrast between the wise behaviour suitable to the old and the sexual desires that still disturb their peace. His wife describes the ideal man he was before he became infatuated with Clizia and she laments the change: 'In those days he was respectable, serious and reserved. He spent his time honourably; he got up early, went to mass and saw to what was needed for the day, then he attended to whatever business there might be ... after dinner he talked to his son, giving him wise advice. His regular life was an example to everyone in the house. ... But since he has lost his head over this wench his business is neglected, his estate goes to ruin, and his trade is falling off; he is always shouting without knowing why. ... If you speak to him he either does not answer at all or his reply makes no sense.'

And in one of the *canzone* that occur at intervals during the play it is said, 'Just as love is lovely in a youthful heart, so it is revolting in a man who has seen the flower of his life fade. ... So, you amorous old men, the best thing for you to do is to leave gallantry to hot-blooded youth.'

Ruzzante's plays were far more original in their inspiration: his was a drama of struggle. We know little about Angelo Beolco, who played the part of Ruzzante in his own plays and who was known by that name. He was the natural son of a Paduan physician and he was brought up in his father's house; later he was the friend and protégé of the wealthy patrician Cornaro; and in his *Orazioni* he eagerly took up the defence of the peasants, the poor and the oppressed. His sympathy for them shows in everything that he wrote. He did not bring stereotyped masks on to the stage: even the character of Ruzzante varies a great deal. The *Pastorale* is rather conventional. The old shepherd Milesio is in love with a nymph and he laments his folly. When she rejects him he goes out of his mind to such a degree that he is thought to be dead: 'Oh unhappy lover, where has this brought you? See where you lie, preposterous old age!'

But generally speaking Ruzzante turned to the manners and the speech of the people of his own time, particularly of the peasants. He himself was young, and he set about those old men whose wealth allowed them to oppress the poor. In *La Vachère*, an imitation of the *Asinaria*, old Placidio does no harm to anyone and he is therefore drawn with some kindliness; he is like Demenetes, but he has good qualities – he loves his son, and when he is cheated and discomfited his wife forgives him. On the other hand, the hero of the *Aconitaire*, a successful money-making eighty-year-old Venetian, is mercilessly abused.* He is shameless, rakish, absurd and weighed down with infirmities; although he is grasping he is even more lecherous, and he tries to buy the courtesan Doralia whatever the price. He is so vain that he thinks she loves him. His own servant deceives him.

In the *Deuxième dialogue rustique* Ruzzante carried the caricature of the amorous old man much further: no other writer has described him with such hideous realism. This old man has seduced Bilora's young wife, who agrees to live with him from interested motives, because he is very rich. But she complains, 'He is half rotten. He coughs all night like a sick sheep. He never goes to sleep; he is always trying to get hold of me, he kisses me all over . . .' 'His breath stinks worse than a dunghill, that is certain,' replies Bilora. 'He smells of death a hundred miles off, and he has so much shit in his arse that it has to get out the other end, isn't that right?' In the end Bilora

---

* Ruzzante was a friend of the patrician Cornaro: it was surely not by mere chance that he made game of a man just come to wealth – a *nouveau riche*.

takes his wife back, having according to the comic tradition beaten the old man.

In the *Piovana* Ruzzante expresses his disgust for old age through Tura, an old man: 'Youth is like a lovely tree in flower where all the birds perch to sing, while old age is like a lean dog with flies swarming all over it and biting its ears.'

'Everything to do with old age is wide open to misfortune. . . . Old age is indeed a pond into which all the foul waters run and which has no outlet but death. Would you like to put a curse on anyone? Then say to him, "May you live to be old". '

Why did the sixteenth century attack the aged with such ferocity? The father was far from possessing the authority of the Roman *pater familias*; and indeed it was not the father that was mocked, but the rich old man who set himself up as a rival to the young. The literature of this period was no more interested in old men of the lower classes than that of the earlier centuries. Furthermore, it must be pointed out that the nobles and the patricians were not attacked: it was conceded that they held their power and their wealth by divine right. The established social hierarchy was not disputed. The person who aroused ill-feeling and rancour was the *nouveau riche*, the bourgeois whose personal attempt at rising had succeeded. If his business throve, he would be the possessor of considerable wealth during the last years of his life: in the eyes of a middle-aged man working for a mere living or of the often penniless young, this heaping-up would look like injustice. It provoked envy and hatred; his success was put down to avarice. The scandal became unbearable if the old men used their gold to buy young wives, for then the young men felt sexually frustrated. The reaction was to take revenge, to try to make them disgusted with their 'vices' either by caricaturing them savagely or by laughing at the caricatures: the writers and the audience banded together against them. This is the explanation for the multiplicity of Pantaloon's appearances in various forms, and for their success.

Side by side with these works that present the aged, both men and women, as mere objects, we find a few that make them an integral part of humanity. For example, there is a dancing-song quoted by Jacques Yver in *Le Printemps*: it advises the young to make the most of their golden days, because old age is lying in wait for them, and it will bring nothing but sadness and regret:

Chagrin et jalousie
Aiment le poil grison
La douce frenaisie
N'a si rude prison.

Ha jeunesse trop folle
Qui attent désormais
Car l'aage qui s'en vosle
Ne retourne jamais.

Puis le feu devient cendre
Où se couve un regret . . .*

In *L'Esté* Poissenot likens old age to autumn, as Plutarch had done before him; an autumn not of ripe fruitfulness but of sterility. And it is as such a season that it is part of the fate he anticipates for himself:

If we look attentively at the whole of the time nature has allotted man in this human life, we shall see that just as the trees in full green leaf and the spring-time fields all spangled with their flowers please the spectator's eyes far more than when ripeness has gradually taken away and undone this ornament, the fruits beginning to lose that bloom which set them off and the many-coloured meadows to fade, so in the same way I presume to assert that no man of good sense will be so much his own enemy as not to admit, that the season that imbues us with a vigour full of eager cheerfulness and a brisk aptitude for all undertakings is not far more delightful than any other.

Old age has an important place in Ronsard. He too, under the influence of the classics and his own time, described the decay of elderly whores with repulsion. His Catin is an 'image with the gold worn off' whose teeth are 'black in ulcered gums'; she has 'rheumy eyes and a running nose'. He often used the theme of the fleeting nature of youth, with a future of melancholy and ugliness lying in wait for it.

Cueillez, cueillez votre jeunesse!
Comme à cette fleur la vieillesse
Fera ternir votre beauté.†

But he also spoke of his own old age in a personal, deeply touching

* Sorrow and envy love grey hairs; the sweet madness knows no harsher prison. Oh it would be far too foolish for youth to wait now, for the age which is flying will never come back. Then the fire turns to ashes in which there glows a regret . . .

† Gather, gather your youthful days! For old age will dull your beauty like a flower's.

tone. It was towards the end of his life that he reached the height of his fame and wrote his finest work. Nevertheless he rebelled against the weight of the years. He had suffered from it prematurely. As a young man he was handsome, charming, and a good horseman. At thirty-eight he had an illness that he confused with the ravages of time; he looked like a toothless, white-haired old man, he complained of having a bad digestion, a bad circulation, sleeplessness and bouts of fever:

> Ma douce jeunesse est passée
> Ma première force est cassée
> J'ai la dent noire et le chef blanc
> Mes nerfs sont dissous, et mes veines,
> Tant j'ai le corps froid, ne sont pleines
> Que d'une eau rousse au lieu de sang.*

He never got over it, particularly since he still retained his desire for physical activity and love. Arthritis and gout kept him from sport; he became irritable and unsociable, under the influence, as he supposed, of 'inimical Saturn', the sign under which he was born and which made him 'grim, suspicious, sad and melancholy'.

He thought he was cursed by the stars. After a youth in which he had believed in the triumph of humanism, he had seen the ruin of his hopes – France was ravaged by civil war, and when he was forty-eight the massacre of St Bartholomew took place. He was deeply sincere when he wrote

> Le vrai trésor de l'homme est la verte jeunesse.
> Le reste de nos ans ne sont que des hivers.†

Agrippa d'Aubigné was no less convinced when he held up the pleasures of old age for admiration; he too likens it to winter, but his winter is a season for calm leisure rather than one of frigid sterility.‡ He had led an active, full, adventurous life; he had been to the wars, he had been wounded and imprisoned, he had taken towns and been forced to yield them up again; he had suffered extreme fatigues and bitter disappointments. He had loved his first

---

* My sweet youth is gone, my first strength broken; my teeth are black and my head is white, my muscles have melted away, and so cold is my body that my veins are filled with no more than a reddish water instead of blood.

† Man's true treasure is his green youth. The rest of our years are but so many winters.

‡ In *Les Tragiques* he had written the famous line 'An autumn rose is more lovely than any other'.

wife and lost her. When he was seventy he still wanted to fight in the Protestant ranks in the defence of La Rochelle. They refused his help and he retired to his château of Crest with his beloved new wife Renée Burlamachi. She was a highly-cultivated woman of fifty, passionately attached to him. This life as a learned country gentleman, having distinguished foreigners to stay, was very agreeable to him. He saw the winter of his life as a peaceful harbour, and he wrote poems in praise of it.

> Voici moins de plaisirs mais aussi moins de peines;
> Le rossignol se tait, se taisent les sirènes.
> Nous ne voyons cueillir ni les fruits, ni les fleurs.
> L'espérance n'est plus, bien souvent tromperesse.
> L'hiver jouit de tout; bienheureuse vieillesse
> La saison de l'usage et non plus des labeurs.*

Neither Ronsard's sincerity nor d'Aubigné's meant that they would have nothing to do with clichés. There was only one writer in this century who set them rigorously aside, and that was Montaigne. Using his own experience, he examined old age as though no one before him had ever spoken of it; and here, in this direct, hard look at a reality that most people did their best to disguise, is the secret of his profundity. The ancient world caricatured old men while at the same time it praised old age. Montaigne refused either to make fun of it or to glorify it. He wanted to disentangle the truth. For himself, he thought that age had not enriched him. He brought forward his own evidence in opposition to Plato's and Cicero's moralizing optimism and in opposition to the claim of the old to wisdom. He was a little over thirty-five when he looked back at the period of his life before thirty and wrote, 'For my part, I think it certain that since that age both my mind and my body have rather lessened than grown and rather gone back than forward. It may be that with those who use time well knowledge and experience increase with life; but liveliness, firmness, quickness and other qualities far more part of ourselves, more important and essential, fade and grow weaker.'

Again, 'Since then I have grown older for a great length of time, but not an inch wiser am I, I am sure. Myself at this moment and

* There are fewer pleasures here but also fewer pains; the nightingale falls silent, and the sirens too. We see the gathering neither of fruits nor flowers. Hope, that deceives so often, is no more. Winter enjoys everything; happy, happy old age, the time of enjoyment, no longer that of toil.

myself then are certainly two different beings; but which the better? I cannot tell. Being old would be very well if we moved on only towards improvement. But it is with a drunkard's step that we advance, staggering, giddy, with no set direction; or like straws that the wind turns according to its own mere motion.'

In the later third book, Montaigne still preferred his youth to the period that he already looked upon as old age. He felt that he had only moved backwards, that he had not advanced.

In any event, I hate this incidental repentance that age brings with it. That man who once said he was grateful to the years for having taken sensual delights away from him had an opinion quite unlike mine: I could never thank impotence for the kindness it does me. . . . In old age our appetites are rare, and afterwards deep satiety comes upon us; here I see nothing of conscience at work. Affliction and weakness impart a rheumy, faint-hearted virtue. I who stir my reason briskly and attentively, find that it is the very same that I had in my more licentious days, except perhaps in so far as it has weakened and deteriorated in growing older. I think it none the braver, just because I see it unable to fight. I do not find it considers anything now that it did not consider then; nor has it any new lights.

. . . I should be grudging and ashamed if the wretchedness and misfortune of my decrepitude were rightly to set itself above my good, healthy, eager, vigorous years, and if men were to judge me not by where I have been but by where I am no longer. . . . In the same way, my wisdom may well be of the same size in both the one time and the other; but it was far prompter to do, more supple, green, gay, natural than it is at present, stale, sullen, painful . . .

Our humours are hard to please; present things disgust us; and this we call wisdom. But the truth is that we do not so much leave our vices as change them; and in my opinion for the worse. . . . Never a soul is to be seen, or very few, who in growing old does not take on a sour and mouldy smell. A man moves towards his full and his decline as an entity, a whole.

I find it wonderful that Montaigne, tossing traditional and comforting clichés overboard, refuses to accept any kind of mutilation as an advance, or to look upon the mere accumulation of years as an enrichment. But in Montaigne there is a curious paradox that may have escaped him but that is strikingly obvious to the reader: the *Essais* become richer and richer, more and more intimate, original and profound as the author of the book advances in age. He would never have been capable of writing these fine, biting, disillusioned pages upon old age when he was thirty. It was when he felt that his powers had declined that he was at his greatest. But no doubt he would never have attained this greatness but for the severity with which he treated himself. All self-satisfaction dulls: the ageing Montaigne was able to preserve himself from it. The reason why he advanced is that his attitude towards the world and towards himself became more and more critical; and the reader is in the difficult position of agreeing with the criticism while at the same time he observes the advance.

The contribution of Renaissance iconography to our understanding of the period's ideas on old age is very uncertain. There are some pictures that convey popular notions, just as there were in the middle ages. But there is also a sophisticated painting in which the artists express themselves personally: how far were they influenced by their times?

In the pictures meant for the people the comparison of the different ages with months or seasons of the year had become commonplace. A calendar of the time illustrates the months with scenes of family life. In November the father is old and sick. In December he is on his death-bed. Other prints show the 'steps of age' in a fashion that lasted until the nineteenth century: in these life is represented as a climb followed by a descent. We see a double staircase that ends in a landing. On this landing there is a man or a married couple aged fifty; on the left there is a cradle at ground-level, then, climbing in succession towards the landing, a child, an adolescent, a young man and a middle-aged man; on the right men of sixty, seventy, eighty and ninety go down step by step; at the foot of the stairs, on the same level as the baby, there is the bed-ridden centenarian. The people are dressed in the clothes of their time. Under the staircase stands Death, holding his scythe. An odd thing about this representation of life is that even now it is very unusual for people to reach the age of a hundred and that it was even rarer then. These pictures were not in fact concerned with human life as it was in its contingent reality but with establishing a kind of archetype. Their pessimism had its source in Christianity: man, doomed to a sad decline, must above all look to his salvation, even in the time of his prosperity.*

* This is confirmed by the texts that accompany the pictures. In an early seventeenth-century example the title, *The Great Staircase of the World*, is right at the top, and on

Some painters also worked on the theme of the different stages of life. They usually showed these stages by a group of three – a youth, an adult and an aged man. Titian did this in his *Concert*, where the old man is bald and bearded; but he seems still to be full of life.*

Another popular theme was that of the Fountain of Youth. It was the subject of many prints in the fifteenth century: in one of them we see old women diving into a pool; they emerge rejuvenated and instantly fall into the arms of handsome young men. The myth was still so lively in the sixteenth century that Ponce de Leon went off to search for the fountain in 1512 – an expedition that led to his discovery of Florida. Many engravings and paintings treat similar themes. There is the younger Cranach's well-known picture, for example: in the middle we see an immense pool with naked bodies swimming in it; on the left old people are being brought to the edge of the water in little carts or on men's shoulders; they come out on the right, delighted; and both men and women dance and play in the meadows.

In Renaissance painting there are many portraits of old people. They vary greatly in character according to the circumstances. At that time wealthy and highly respected old men were proud of their years. In Italy many renewed the classical tradition and had portrait-busts, showing them as they would like to be seen, by Rossellino or Mino de Fiesole. The popes had themselves painted by Raphael or Titian, and the Venetian doges and nobles by Tintoretto: in their portraits they have fine white beards and an air of peaceful calmness. The old people in the pictures that took their inspiration from the ancient world or the Bible were often idealized. But the painters were also quite ready to take subjects in which the aged do not appear in a very edifying light – Noah overtaken in wine, for example, the grotesque and inebriated Silenus, or Lot and his daughters. Dürer, among others, used the last theme; so did Guercino, Tintoretto and Lucas van Leyden, who treated it in a particularly licentious manner – he often showed old men in ridiculous attitudes. Lewd old men are frequently to be seen in the many pictures of Susannah taking her bath. There were many painters who also denounced the ugliness

* A century later we see the same in one of Van Dyck's pictures.

_____

either side there are two panels that read, 'Oh what a beaten track this staircase is; mortal fate walks upon it all the time', and on the other side, 'For the evil-doer life is a slope leading down to Hell. And for the good it is a way up to Heaven'. There are two cherubs attending the old woman on her death-bed.

of old age. In Dürer's *Christ among the Doctors* we see two fairly good-looking old men and one who is quite horrible. In Van Reymer Swaete's *Two Taxgatherers* the more hideous is a very ancient man. Ghirlandaio carried realism to the point of cruelty in his famous *Old Man and Grandchild*.*

We also find the theme of the 'ugly old woman' among the painters. Giorgione's fine *Col Tempo* shows a time-ravaged woman. The ugliness is often exaggerated into caricature: Baldung painted flesh-less, withered, horrible witches who might have escaped from the poems of Sigogno or Marot. Erasmus' friend Quentin Matsys pro-duced what a contemporary called 'monstrous bloated senile faces of old men and women'. The best known is *The Ugly Duchess*; she is grotesquely bedizened, she wears a hideously low dress, and her face is bestial. Wengel Hollar painted the same character in his *King and Queen of Tunis*; the man is not handsome, but he is in no way remarkable; the woman is a replica of *The Ugly Duchess*.

Very great artists form their times rather than bear witness to them. Frans Hals, then very aged and at the height of his powers, followed no conventional ideas in his splendid *Regenten* groups, particularly that of the women; he neither glorified nor denigrated old age: he tried to seize the truth of the faces that he drew. This was also the case with da Vinci, and Rembrandt, in whose works old people have a very important place. Da Vinci carried his examina-tion of their features to the point of caricature, as he did for people of all ages, but he endowed some of the old he painted with great beauty. Rembrandt painted aged men when he was no more than thirty; and one of his last works was the wonderful *Blind Homer*. He was not interested in contemporary notions: he was attempting to reproduce his own vision.

As it moves away from popular representation and becomes a body of individual creations, iconography loses a great deal of its value as evidence; from this point of view its interest lessens just as that of writing increases. I shall rarely have occasion to refer to it again.

We see that from ancient Egypt to the Renaissance the theme of old age was almost always handled in a stereotyped manner – we find the same comparisons and the same adjectives. It is the winter of

* A cruelty even more striking since the portrait was painted not from a living face but after the model's death.

life. White hair and white beards call snow and ice to mind; to the coldness of white is opposed not only red's fire and ardour but also green, the colour of the plants, of spring and of youth. These clichés persisted partly because the old person does in fact follow his unchangeable biological destiny; but also because, not being an active element in history, the old person was of no interest – no one took the trouble to study him as he really was. Indeed, there was the tacit commandment that society should pass him over in silence. Literature, whether it glorified or disparaged old age, always buried it under a heap of preconceived ideas, hiding it instead of making it apparent. In relation to youth and maturity it was looked upon as a kind of foil or set-off: the old person was not true man, man himself, but rather man's further boundary; he was on the periphery of the human state; he was not acknowledged and no observer acknowledged himself in him.*

At the beginning of the seventeenth century there was one most striking exception. In writing *King Lear*, Shakespeare chose his aged hero as the summary and embodiment of man and his fate. Why and how?

In the sonnets Shakespeare had cried out passionately against the ravages of time. He likened human life to the passing of the year or of a day; or to both. Old age was an unhappy waning.

> That time of year thou mayst in me behold
> When yellow leaves, or none, or few, do hang
> Upon those boughs that shake against the cold,
> Bare ruin'd choirs, where late the sweet birds sang.
> In me thou see'st the twilight of such day
> As after sunset fadeth in the west;
> Which by and by black night doth take away . . .
>
> For never-resting time leads summer on
> To hideous winter, and confounds him there;
> Sap check'd with frost, and lusty leaves quite gone,
> Beauty o'ersnow'd and bareness every where . . .
>
> Then let not winter's ragged hand deface
> In thee thy summer, ere thou be distill'd . . .
>
> Lo! in the orient when the gracious light
> Lifts up his burning head, each under eye

* Except for Villon, Montaigne and a very few others.

Doth homage to his new-appearing sight,
Serving with looks his sacred majesty . . .
But when from highmost pitch, with weary car,
Like feeble age, he reeleth from the day,
The eyes, 'fore duteous, now converted are
From his low tract, and look another way . . .

And time that gave now doth his gift confound.
Time doth transfix the flourish set on youth
And delves the parallels in beauty's brow,
Feeds on the rareties of nature's truth,
And nothing stands but for his scythe to mow:
     And yet to times in hope my verse shall stand,
     Praising thy worth, despite his cruel hand.

. . . confounding age's cruel knife . . .

When I have seen by Time's fell hand defac'd
The rich-proud cost of outworn buried age.

In spite of their heartfelt bitterness, these passages do apply the classic stereotypes to old age: it is winter, the twilight in which all the wealth of youth is buried; the only way of fighting against it is by winning immortality with one's genius.

Shakespeare cast a cold eye upon the old: in Romeo and Juliet* he said that many old men looked already dead, pale, slow, heavy and as dull as lead. And he described it cruelly in *As You Like It*:

          . . . the lean and slipper'd pantaloon,
          With spectacles on nose and pouch on side,
          His youthful hose well sav'd, a world too wide
          For his shrunk shank; and his big manly voice,
          Turning again toward childish treble, pipes
          And whistles in his sound. Last scene of all,
          That ends this strange eventful history,
          In second childishness and mere oblivion,
          Sans teeth, sans eyes, sans taste, sans everything.†

In the tragedies he gave some old people nobility of character – John of Gaunt in *Richard II*, for example, or the extraordinary Queen Margaret in *Richard III*. But these are only secondary roles,

---

* Written in favour of the young against the adults of all ages.
† Written in about 1599.

representing the older generation in comparison with the hero in the prime of life.

King Lear is the only great work, apart from *Oedipus at Colonus*, in which the hero is an old man: here old age is not thought of as the limit of the human state but as its truth – it is the basis for an understanding of man and his earthly pilgrimage.*

The legend, very ancient in its origin, is part of Anglo-Saxon folklore. I have explained why the medieval English way of life made it so very popular. Shakespeare no doubt took it from a chronicle play called *Leir* that was performed in 1594. He borrowed the parallel plot of Gloucester and his two sons from the story of the King of Paphlagonia in Sidney's *Arcadia*. But going far beyond these anecdotes he used the old man's tragedy to express all the absurd horror of our existence. Lear is not mad at the beginning of the play: but in him old age itself looks like insanity. He is unadapted to reality and he foolishly decides to share out his kingdom among his daughters; he is weak-minded enough to require them to make verbal declarations, so that he may measure their affection. Being a king he is used to the most outrageous flattery; he is easily deceived by it and he believes in his two elder daughters' fine words. But Cordelia will not take part in the senile game, and the narrow, obstinate, domineering old man is furious with her. The two hypocritical daughters judge him with a cruel lucidity. '. . . We must look to receive from his age, not alone the imperfections of long-engraffed condition, but, withal the unruly waywardness that infirm and choleric years bring with them,' says Goneril.

In the same way, Gloucester's blindness, his foolishness in letting himself be persuaded that his loving son Edgar is a villain and in trusting the false Edmond, confirms that Shakespeare saw not wisdom in very old age but wandering of the mind. Lear is condemned, by the wickedness of his daughters, to stray about, like the wandering Oedipus, in the midst of a hostile landscape: the old man is a being set apart, an exile. Gloucester, whose eyes are put out, is also symbolic of that absence which is the fate of old age, as are Homer, Oedipus and Belisarius. But it is above all Lear, with his wits gone and everything lost, who is the incarnation of man's tragic abandonment. At the beginning of the play he is like all those Shakespearean heroes who are urged on by some rooted passion – jealousy, ambition

---

* The fifteenth-century preachers did make old age an integral part of the human state, but only in order to debase that state and never taking the aged man as a subject.

or resentment – to mad and disastrous resolutions. Shakespeare draws him from outside as harshly as he draws Macbeth or Othello; but when his destitution and his appalling distress have shown Lear the truth of his state, Shakespeare projects himself into the king and speaks through his mouth. 'Is man no more than this? ... unaccommodated man is no more but such a poor, bare, forked animal as thou art. Off, off, you lendings! Come; unbutton here,' cries Lear, tearing off his clothes. He wishes to destroy the old order that made man the slave of wealth and honours, hiding his humanity from him; he has caught sight of a new order in which the individual would start again from the very beginning, in the nakedness of childhood. But it is too late. He is sinking into a madness, momentarily lit by flashes of truth: these blinding revelations can be of no use to him: they raise him above himself, but he no longer has the time to match his life to them. The ancient world and the middle ages looked upon madmen as having a certain sacred, prophetic quality; and as old age frequently verged upon madness, it often combined in itself the two traditional and contradictory images of the venerable sage and the old lunatic. The raving yet inspired Lear is an example of this. The moment in which he reaches sublimity is also that of his total collapse as a person. At last his mind clears and Cordelia is given back to him: but it is her corpse that he folds in his arms. And for Lear himself there is no way out but death. Kott* was right when he compared the play to *Fin de partie*. In that it shows us the meaninglessness of our futile suffering, it is the tragedy of old age. If this bewildered impotence is the end of life, then in this light the whole of existence is seen to be a miserable experience, a wretched adventure. Many people have asked what reasons Shakespeare can have had for writing *King Lear*, that is to say for incarnating humanity in an aged man. Perhaps he was moved to do so by the tragic lot of the aged in the English towns and countryside – the fate to which they had been reduced. When the manorial system broke down under the Tudors and unemployment played havoc in the towns, beggary spread everywhere, although – except under Edward VI – it was forbidden. It is not impossible that the wretchedness of these old, bewildered, penniless, destitute wanderers may have been the inspiration for the aged king. But it should also be pointed out that Shakespeare's hero, unlike Corneille's or Racine's, is not a man who is in the active pursuit of some end

* In *Shakespeare, Our Contemporary*.

that would give his life a meaning. He is moved by blind passions that turn his life into 'a tale told by an idiot, full of sound and fury, signifying nothing'. If we adopt the old man's outlook upon humanity, the outlook of one cut off from the future and reduced to the mere passiveness of his immediate being, then this absurdity blazes out with an extraordinary brilliance. It is natural that Shakespeare, having exhibited man as the slave of ambition, jealousy, or resentment, should have seen fit to show him overwhelmed by the fatality of old age. People absorbed in their undertakings will not acknowledge the dark side of our ambivalent condition: *King Lear* has, generally speaking, been the least well received and the least understood of all the great Shakespearean plays.

In the seventeenth century the young retained the reality of power. The only exception among the rulers was Louis XIV who, in his old age and manipulated by the elderly Madame de Maintenon, still played an active part in the government. After the Council of Trent the popes too were usually old. The church had become stabilized, and from that time onwards the Holy See was identified with the church against the decentralizing forces. It increased its influence by means of the religious orders, particularly the Jesuits, of the theologians and the system of nuncios, whose work was now made easier by the regular posts. The counter-Reformation endowed the popes with a very high standing, and they were required to lead austere lives; age helped in giving them holiness, a sacred character, and it was presumed that it would also help them to practise virtue. Then again the conservatism of the old was in their favour. There was a danger that a young, forty-year-old pope might set about new, undesirable undertakings; whereas it was supposed, sometimes mistakenly, that a pope elected at seventy or seventy-five would retain the character for which he had deliberately been chosen and would not stray off the beaten path. Of the twelve successive pontiffs who reigned after the council, two were elected at fifty-three and fifty-five, three at sixty, two at sixty-four, four at seventy and one at seventy-seven. Later, the popes and the members of the Sacred College were almost always very elderly.

In France the seventeenth century was exceedingly hard on the aged. Society was authoritarian and absolutist. The adults who ruled it allowed the children and the aged – people who did not belong to the same category as themselves – no place at all. The average length

167

of life was from twenty to twenty-five years. Half the children died before they were a year old, and most adults between thirty and forty. Exhausting labour, under-nourishment and bad hygiene meant that people wore out very early. A peasant women of thirty was a bent, wrinkled old woman. Even kings, nobles and burgesses died at between forty-eight and fifty-six. Public life began at seventeen or eighteen and promotion started early. Men in their forties were looked upon as old fogies. Their contemporaries thought it quite impossible that Madame de La Fayette and La Rochefoucauld should have gone to bed together because she was thirty-six and he fifty.* There was no longer any place in society for a fifty-year-old. It was too tiring to follow the court as it travelled, moving from town to town, and to take part in sport. The man of fifty retired to his estate in the country or took holy orders. It was the wealthy man, the landowner, the leader and the dignitary who was respected: not age in itself. Some particular individuals might acquire value from their memory and experience: 'An old gentleman who has lived at court, who has great good sense and a sound memory, is a most precious treasure,' said La Bruyère. But old age as such earned no consideration.

Among the peasants and craftsmen the system of maintaining the old at home continued. The church came to the help of the very poor. But life was so harsh, with its famines, the exploitation of the peasants by nobles and of the workers by the big employers, that its help was quite inadequate.

The condition of the children was, like that of the aged, very hard indeed. During the Renaissance society had taken an interest in them and had tried to preserve them from the corruption of the adult world; but now life was too rough for much care to be devoted to them. In the seventeenth century children were kept apart from the community as a whole and they were brought up with great severity. Pages and schoolboys were whipped without distinction of class until the age of twenty: the young were brought down to the lowest level of the population. Literature took no notice of them whatsoever. La Fontaine observed, 'This is an age without pity.' La Bruyère drew

* Yet Ninon de Lenclos had lovers until she was fifty-five (not, as legend would have it, until she was eighty). The Duc de Bouillon was sixty-six when his son Turenne was born, in 1611. Monsieur de Senneterre was eighty when he married in 1654, and the Maréchal d'Estrées ninety-six when he did the same in about 1633: both of them had young brides. When she was seventy, Madame de Maintenon complained to her confessor that she still very often had to lie with the old king.

children as little monsters, ending, 'They cannot bear to suffer wrong yet they love to do it.' Bossuet went so far as to say, 'Childhood is a brutish life.' Not a single other writer makes any reference to children. As they grew up they were still subject to their father's authority: in the middle ages they had escaped from it at fourteen. In the sixteenth and seventeenth centuries the age of majority was fixed at twenty-one. From 1557 onwards a son had to have his father's consent to marry; before, he had been able to do so when he chose. In the seventeenth century a father had the right to disinherit his son in favour of a third party: up until that time it had been impossible.

At the beginning of the seventeenth century the tradition of misogyny still inspired invective directed against old women. It was especially violent in the Spanish poet and novelist Quevedo. This aristocratic Catholic satirist* painted mankind as a world of grotesque objects; all his characters are lifeless puppets, sometimes monstrous in their inhuman beauty (though this is exceedingly rare), and very often monstrous in their ugliness. Quevedo took a pleasure in describing their physical decline, a degradation that brought them down below the beasts. Women were one of the objects of his disgust. If they were young then for him they were 'appetizing devils', and even if they were beautiful he did not spare them: as he saw it, there was something revolting in femininity itself. As for ugly women, he likened them to death. But it was the old women who obsessed his mind. He overwhelmed them with years: 'She is six thousand years older than the pyramids, and units of a thousand apiece would be needed to count her age from one end to the other.' She is hideous, wrinkled, loathsome, with her 'unpaved' mouth, holes instead of molars and a nose that touches her chin; her breath stinks; she is a bag of bones, death in person. The furrows on her forehead are the 'ruts made by time in its passage, its footsteps'. Yet – and this is a theme that recurs again and again in Quevedo – she will persist, against all the evidence, in her claim that she is young. 'You warble with your great-grandmother's chops and you call your skirts swaddling-clothes.' He is particularly severe on witches, housekeepers and above all duennas, who for him are the quintessence of old age. 'Her nose is in conversation with her chin, and they are so close

---

* Everyone knows how Spanish Catholicism delighted in repulsive colours when it described the state of mankind: in Quevedo we find the same inspiration as that which lay behind certain pictures of corpses being eaten by worms.

together that they form pincers.' These duennas were meant to protect the girls under their charge, but in fact they corrupted them. For two centuries after Quevedo Spanish literature was to exploit this theme of the duenna-bawd.

In France at the beginning of the century there grew up a literature on the fringes of classicism that delighted in the grotesque and the ludicrous, taking pleasure in the evocation of ugliness. It is particularly striking in Saint-Amant, for whom an old woman was 'a living image of death'. He thought it droll to pile the weight of years on her back: 'In former days you nursed Melusina's grandfather.'* And he too described an aged whore:

> Perrette à la mine de plâtre
> De qui la gueule sent plus fort
> Que ne fait quelque vieil emplâtre.†

In his very successful *Marette* Mathurin Regnier also described an old bawd turned bigot. In addition to this he drew three portraits of hideously emaciated old women. Théophile de Viau's old woman is stout and thickset, but this is no advantage to her:

> Le menton, qui pend sous un autre,
> Dessus le sein flac vous descend;
> Ce sein sur le ventre vous pend
> Et dessus les genoux le ventre.‡

It is clear that a no less conventional anti-rhetoric had succeeded the rhetoric of the Petrarchian school – an anti-rhetoric that died away during the first half of the century. Only one single poet defended old age in women, and this was Maynard. He too makes an incidental reference to a horrible old woman who breathes out 'from her toothless mouth a reek so foul that it makes cats sneeze',§ but he wrote a fine poem, the *Ode à une belle vieille*, in which he celebrates the charm of old age. He assured his beloved that she is as dear to him with her grey hair as she was in the days when it was golden:

* Cf. Martial. And Sigogno, 'You speak like someone older than Amadis.'
† Plaster-faced Perrette whose maw smells worse than some old poultice.
‡ Your double chin hangs lower than your flabby breast, your bosom droops upon your belly, and your belly below your knees.
§ From classical times until the sixteenth and seventeenth centuries, we see the persistence of this cliché about old people, particularly women, smelling unpleasant. It has even less to do with reality since those concerned belong to the well-to-do class – a mere continual repetition of the same old rhetorical cant.

La beauté qui te suit depuis ton premier âge
Au déclin de tes jours ne veut pas te laisser.*

This was a completely new note in literature; and it was one that had almost no later echoes.

Old age in men was less open to sarcasm. Yet Rotrou's description of a fifty-year-old in *La Sœur* is hardly very kind:

Il n'est dans la nature homme qui ne le juge
Du siècle de Saturne ou du temps du Déluge.
Des trois pieds dont il marche il en a deux goutteux
Qui jusqu'à chaque pas trébuchent de vieillesse
Et qu'il faut retenir ou relever sans cesse.†

But for all that, the literature of the time allowed aged people a far greater value than did the earlier centuries. In Don Diègue and Horace, Corneille created most impressive characters who were old men.

It was contemporary events that inspired him to turn back to this subject, to the theme treated by the *Romancero* and later by Guilhem de Castro. In Corneille's time the state was still incomplete. An individualistic and feudal ethos lived on. The bonds between lord and vassal had not been broken and the great men still had vast numbers of followers under their protection; the families that served them looked upon their duty towards their lord as more important than their obedience to the king. What Corneille wished to see was a balance between the crown and the aristocracy; he wanted to reconcile respect for the law – and the king was the embodiment of the law – with the ancient values of generosity and knightly prowess. Just as in the *Romancero* and Guilhem de Castro it is a conflict between the generations that sets off the drama; and in Corneille's *Le Cid* this conflict has a double aspect. The Count, a man in the prime of life, contrasts his present ability with Don Diègue's now abolished past. 'Although you were once a valiant man, that is what I am today.' It is noteworthy that he does not take Don Diègue's former exploits into account at all: he has not the least respect for age. What Don Diègue cannot bear is the idea that the past has vanished and that the present is all-important:

* The beauty that has followed you from childhood will not leave you in the waning of your days.

† No man on earth does not suppose him to belong to Saturn's age or the time of the Flood. Two of the three legs he walks on are gouty, and at every step they stumble with old age and they are always having to be supported or picked up.

N'ai-je donc tant vécu que pour cette infamie?
Et me suis-je blanchi dans les travaux guerriers
Que pour voir *en un jour* flétrir tant de lauriers?*

Age should be the crown of true and life-long service; but there is the danger that because of the physical weakness it brings with it, age may destroy all its own former glory. His only resource is his son, for in so far as the son too is the symbol of the family, he is identical with the father. In spite of the pause of the Stanzas, Rodrigue at once confirms this identification: he will revenge his father's honour, his ancestor's and his own. But although he instantly bows to the feudal morality, of which his father is the mouthpiece, he speaks roughly to Don Diègue the individual. 'His name? These needless words waste our time.' We find no deference for old age in itself either in the adult or in the young man. Rodrigue, avenging his father, supplants him. He, Rodrigue, is the conqueror of the Moors, the upholder of the realm.

The king proclaims it:

> Rodrigue maintenant est notre unique appui
> Le soutien de Castille et la terreur du More.†

But although he has lost his status as an 'active' man, Don Diègue nevertheless plays a very important part. He is a wise counsellor to his son: it is he who persuades Rodrigue not to abandon himself to despair and who sends him to fight the Moors in order to win back the king's favour. It is he who urges the king to pause to think again before punishing Rodrigue, and this gives the Cid time to cover himself with glory. In the end Rodrigue and Chimène, having done their duty towards their lineage, come to pay their obedience to the king. Corneille gives an imaginary reality to his dream of the nobility and the crown being reconciled through the intercession of an aged aristocrat.

The aged Horace is also invested with this role of intercessor. He is the guardian of the Roman order, just as Don Diègue is that of the feudal. The great difference is that in Horace's order there is no room for individualism; at the beginning of the play the transfer of power has taken place without the least conflict, in conformity with settled custom; there is nothing humiliating for the father in standing

---

* Have I then lived solely for this dishonour? And have I grown white in waging war merely to see so many laurels blasted in a single day?

† Rodrigue is now our sole support, Castille's prop and the terror of the Moor.

aside from the fight while his sons go to risk their lives. He calmly accepts that the meaning and the honour of his life should no longer be in his own hands but in those of his descendants. Yet if his sons were to betray Rome he would suffer both for the city and for himself – he feels himself personally involved. And in fact there is no gap between Rome and himself: he is the incarnation of the Roman values, and this gives him an almost sacred character. It is his virtually supernatural status that allows him to succeed in his plea that his son should not be punished for the murder of Camille: the justice that he calls for is absolute justice, and the earthly law-givers bow before it.

Corneille not only granted – at least in theory – that the aged man should have an important place in the community, but he also claimed the right to love for the ageing individual; and on this point, as we have seen, the century was in two minds. Corneille was over fifty, a very considerable age for his day, when he fell in love with Mademoiselle Du Parc. He wrote her several very well-known poems:

> Je sais mes cheveux gris, je sais que les années
> Laissent peu de mérite aux âmes les mieux nées
> . . . Que si dans mes beaux jours je parus supportable
> J'ai trop longtemps aimé pour être encore aimable
> Et que d'un front ridé les replis jaunissants
> Mêlent un triste charme aux plus dignes encens.*

And

> Marquise si mon visage
> A quelques traits un peu vieux
> Souvenez-vous qu'à mon âge
> Vous ne vaudrez guère mieux.
>
> Le temps aux plus belles choses
> Se plaît à faire un affront
> Et saura faner vos roses
> Comme il a ridé mon front . . .
>
> Chez cette race nouvelle
> Où j'aurai quelque crédit
> Vous ne passerez pour belle
> Qu'autant que je l'aurai dit.†

* I know I am grey, I know that the years leave me little worth even for the best-born minds . . . that although in my prime I seemed bearable, I have loved too long to be lovable still, and that a forehead wrinkled with yellowing lines adds a dubious charm to the finest praise.

† Marquise, although my face has features that are somewhat old, remember at my

There are these lines too, published after the death of Mademoiselle
Du Parc:

> Je suis vieux, belle Isis, c'est un mal incurable;
> De jour en jour il croît, d'heure en heure il accable;
> La mort seule en guérit; mais si de jour en jour
> Il me rend plus mal propre à grossir votre cour
> Je tire enfin ce fruit de ma décrépitude
> Que je vous vois sans trouble et sans inquiétude.*

In the character of Sertorius he describes the torments of an old
man in love. He speaks of the worn state of his hero's body and of
the grey hair that crowns 'a forehead wrinkled with yellowing lines'.†
He is a fearful, trembling lover:

> A mon âge, il sied si mal d'aimer
> Que je le cache même à qui m'a su charmer.‡

When he was sixty-six, Corneille analysed the feelings of an aged,
love-stricken man in *Pulchérie*. Martian, like Sertorius, blames
himself for experiencing them:

> L'amour en mes pareils n'est jamais excusable
> Pour peu qu'on s'examine, on s'en tient méprisable;
> On s'en hait; et ce mal qu'on n'ose découvrir
> Fait encore plus de peine à cacher qu'à souffrir.
>
> Pour ne prétendre rien on n'est pas moins jaloux
> . . . Que le moindre retour à nos jeunes années
> Jette alors d'amertume en nos âmes gênées!
> . . . Le souvenir en tue et on ne l'envisage
> Qu'avec, il faut le dire, une espèce de rage
> . . . Mon âme, de feu nonchalamment saisie
> Ne l'a point reconnu que par ma jalousie.

---

* I am old, fair Isis, and it is an incurable disease; it increases day by day, from
hour to hour it crushes me; death is the only cure. But although day by day it makes
me more unfitting to swell your court, at least I draw this profit from my decrepitude,
that I can see you with a calm, untroubled mind.
 † This line is exactly the same as one in Mademoiselle Du Parc's poem.
 ‡ It is so indecent for my age to love that I hide it even from her who has charmed
me.

---

age yours will not be much better. Time delights in insulting the loveliest things, and
as it has ploughed my forehead, so it will make your roses fade. . . . For this new
generation yet to come, with whom I shall have some credit, you will be thought beautiful only in so far as I have said you were.

... Quel supplice d'aimer un objet adorable
Et de tant de rivaux se voir le moins aimable.*

Martian, loyal and discreet, hides his love from the empress and urges her to marry another. In the end it is she who suggests marriage – a marriage not to be consummated. Many old gentlemen recognize themselves in this character, which, according to Fontenelle, was Corneille's own self-portrait. The Maréchal de Gramont congratulated the poet; never before had a lover who was old been brought on to the stage; he was glad that Corneille had done so, and if it was true that he, Gramont, had acted as his model then he congratulated himself too. Corneille's tenderness for the old is to be explained by his optimistic conception of society: in spite of his origins he was an anti-bourgeois and he admired what he hoped to be the lasting alliance between the state and the nobility.†

A similar point of view is to be found in Saint-Evremond, who admired Corneille and shared many of his ideas. Towards the end of his life he was an exile in London, having been banished after a fierce attack upon Mazarin, and there he lived a peaceful old age, reading, writing, and above all enjoying conversation, which he ranked the highest of pleasures. He was a follower of Montaigne, and like him he thought that age did not bring wisdom. 'I have lost all inclination to vice without knowing whether I owe this change to the weakness of an outworn body or to the moderation of a mind that has grown wiser than it was before. At my age it is hard to tell whether the passions one no longer feels are extinguished or overcome.' Like Epicurus, he had always held that the essence of happiness lay in not being unhappy: as his health was good, he enjoyed this ataraxy, and it sufficed him. Yet he did feel that old age had its causes for sadness. He had a long and affectionate correspondence with Ninon de Lenclos; he told her that he had very little hope of

* Love in men like me can never be forgiven; a slight self-examination makes one despise oneself for such feelings. One hates oneself for them; and this disease that one dares not avow, is even harder to conceal than it is to suffer. . . . Although one makes no claims, one is no less jealous. . . . How the least return of youth sends bitterness into our tortured hearts! The memory of it kills, and cannot indeed be thought of without a kind of fury. . . . My heart, thoughtlessly set ablaze, became aware of it only through my jealousy. . . . What a torment to love a lovely object, and to know that, among so many rivals, one is the least likely to be loved.

† At about the same period Racine wrote *Mithridate*. The old king wants to force marriage upon the woman he loves but who does not love him. But Racine deals with him much more as a despot than as an aged man, and he gives us no information at all about the feelings of the time on the question that we are concerned with here.

ever seeing her again and that this grieved him deeply. 'What I find the most saddening at my age is that hope is lost, that sweetest of passions, which contributes most to making life agreeable.' Friendship had always meant a great deal to him, and he hardly made any distinction between it and love: according to him, love should be ruled by one's mind, that is to say, based upon esteem; if this were so it did not become a passion and it caused no suffering. It is a feeling that a man may be proud of, even at a very advanced age. He asserted that an old man had the right to love, always provided that like Martian he made no claim to any love in return. At the age of eighty he loved the Duchesse de Mazarin dearly, and she was an excellent friend to him. When she died, he fell in love with the Marquise de La Perrine, but with the same discretion. 'You are mistaken in being astonished that old people can still love,' he wrote, 'for the absurdity lies not in allowing one's heart to be touched, but in the ridiculous claim that one can still be pleasing. . . . The greatest of pleasures that remain for old men is living; and nothing makes them more certain of their life than loving. . . . *I love therefore I exist* is a most lively inference that reminds one of the desires of youth, sometimes even to the point of imagining that one is still young.' In his essay on friendship he approved of the late marriages of Monsieur de Senneterre and the Maréchal d'Estrées. Solomon himself was their example, he said. Indeed, he thought men more inclined to love in their later years than they were before. In 1663* he wrote, 'We hardly begin to age before a secret self-disgust forming within us begins to make us disagreeable to ourselves. After this our hearts, emptied of self-love, are easily filled with that love which is inspired by others.' According to Saint-Evremond, then, the ageing man is wounded in his narcissism – a new and interesting thought – and is therefore defenceless against another's charm.†

Clearly the image of the old man was becoming more subtle than it had been before. He remains a man and no human feelings are forbidden to him. The love that Corneille and Saint-Evremond spoke of was platonic: it was therefore allowed by those laws of love that had been more or less exactly formulated in the ruelles‡ to

* He was then forty-nine.
† We shall discuss this idea later.
‡ A bedroom, where ladies of fashion, in the seventeenth and eighteenth centuries, especially in France . . . held a morning reception for persons of distinction (OED).

distinguish between aristocrat and bourgeois. It was touching in the Princesse de Clèves, a married woman of whom faithfulness was required, so why should it be shocking in an elderly man? And the feeling of the age was even more indulgent, for although some blamed them, others congratulated men of eighty for marrying again.

With Molière we go right back to convention: old age is a theme that he treats without the least originality, following the classical and Italian writers. From them he took over the character of the distrustful but foolish old man, grasping but credulous, bullying but cowardly. He is a laughing-stock, but far from realizing this he makes extravagant claims for himself. Molière is more severe to age than Terence or even Plautus. There is only one pleasant old man in all his plays. In the *Ecole des maris*, which is based on the *Adelphoe*, Sganarelle is a jealous and tyrannical old fogy – he is no doubt in his forties; but his brother Ariste, twenty years older than Sganarelle, is generous, wise, and careful of his person though exempt from vanity. He renders himself amiable to the woman he wants to marry, whereas Sganarelle is tricked by Isabelle whom he persecutes. In passing, it might be as well to point out a common mistake: it is not true that all Molière's old fogys are men of forty. Arnolphe is indeed forty-three. But in *Le Marriage forcé* Sganarelle, who absurdly desires the love of a girl and who is punished for doing so, is fifty-three. Géronte, in the *Fourberies*, is very old. Harpagon is over sixty: he is even more disagreeable than the hero of the *Aulularia*; he not only loves his purse, but he is also a tyrannical father and a ridiculous lover. Did the conflict between fathers and sons that we see in Molière correspond to a reality? Since it is more a question of imitation than invention we can scarcely look upon his plays as evidence for the feeling of his age upon this subject.

In an attempt at dealing with the terrible poverty that was ravaging England at the end of her reign, Elizabeth created the Poor Law in about 1603: the government became responsible for the paupers, operating through the parishes and taxing their inhabitants to raise the necessary funds. Those who were held to be capable of labour were exploited in workhouses;* the children were put out to farmers or craftsmen; the crippled and the old were placed in asylums. The

---

* The word did not appear until 1652, but the thing came into existence with the Poor Law.

labour in the workhouses was exceedingly hard. And the parishes helped only their own paupers; it took no care of newcomers, still less of the then very numerous vagabonds.

During the first forty years of the seventeenth century various charitable institutions tried to alleviate this harshness, and alms-houses and hospitals were founded. At that time religion preached respect for poverty, and it insisted that the rich should give charity. But the seizing of power by the Puritans caused an ideological revolution as far as this was concerned. The Puritans were small landowners, craftsmen, and above all merchants. The merchants had struggled against the crown-granted monopolies that strangled them; they called for the freedom of trade and they believed that only a republic could bring it about. Whereas France, with its efficient bureaucracy, had managed to associate the middle classes with the government without any upheaval, in England, where the administration was incapable, conflict broke out between the oppressed bourgeoisie and the crown – a conflict in which the crown was defeated. The middle classes decided to build up the economy, for in this respect England was at a very much lower level than Holland. Puritanism made an effort to adapt Christianity to an industrial and commercial society dominated by the spirit of competition. Its chief care was to emphasize the precept 'He that works not shall not eat.' All the preachers dwelt upon the duty of labour, because in the opinion of the bourgeois it was idleness and drink that held back progress. 'There is no worse state than that of the idle man,' wrote Elizabeth Jocelyne in 1632. 'God looks upon him as a useless drone, incapable of serving him; and the world condemns him for his destitution.' The loftiest religious and moral virtues lay in the carrying on of successful business. The best way of praying was working; work was a kind of sacrament and profit was a mark of divine election. The poor were accused of improvidence and idleness, vices that were not to be encouraged. Begging was condemned as immoral. Loans on interest took the place of alms-giving.

The aged poor suffered from this. In the middle classes, on the other hand, it set a new value upon old age. As we have seen, in the middle ages the family as such was not idealized: it *was* among the bourgeoisie from whom the Puritans were recruited. The grandfather was the symbol and embodiment of the family, and he was respected. In the sixteenth century parents were already insisting upon strict obedience from their children; their marriages were arranged by parental authority, and it might happen that a boy of five would be married to a girl of three. The Elizabethan theatre showed young people struggling for freedom of choice in marriage. Among the Puritans of this period the authoritarian principle was asserted more specifically and more severely than ever. In 1606 the Anglican convention adopted the ideas of Bodin, a Frenchman whose book had recently been translated and in whose opinion fathers should have the right of life and death over their children. The king ought to be a father to his subjects, said the Puritans, and the head of a family should have sovereign power over it. There were a great many sermons on the government of the household and the authority that should belong to the aged. The aged, being set free from passions – at least, that was the theory – were able to practise the asceticism that the Puritans set up as a pattern for life, and to practise it naturally, as it were: they were an example to follow. And since all forms of success were a mark of the divine blessing, old age showed as a guarantee of virtue. For all these reasons, the old were venerated among the Puritans. When they were in power they tried to force their morality upon the whole country. They closed the theatres, which they looked upon as sinks of iniquity.

The Restoration reacted violently against the Puritans. It was a great event when the theatres opened again under King Charles II and for the first time the women's parts were played by actresses. For thirty years the dramatic authors and the audiences who applauded them belonged to a very limited group of gentlemen. These aristocrats trampled upon the middle-class values that the Puritans had glorified. Their hard, cynical plays made game of virtue in all its forms. They were particularly violent against old age.

In the Elizabethan plays the young people struggled for their liberty, but the old were described with a mixture of sympathy and irony. At the end of the seventeenth century there was an abundant production of comedies dealing with the conflict between the generations. One of the most significant was Congreve's *Love for Love*. There are two lovers, Valentine and Angelica; he has a father and she an uncle, and both are very disagreeable, ridiculous old men. Foresight is 'an illiterate old fellow, peevish and positive, superstitious, and pretending to understand astrology and palmistry', and he utters pedantical prophecies all the time. His young wife deceives him. His niece tells him plainly just what she thinks of him and turns him to ridicule. As for Sampson, he is an unnatural parent:

179

in order to punish Valentine for his spendthrift ways he tries to force him to give up his inheritance to his younger brother Ben, a sailor who has just come home: Valentine's debts will be paid only on this condition. Valentine is obliged to give way, because his debts are pressing and he has to get rid of them if he wants to marry Angelica. Nevertheless, he insults his father in the course of a violent scene, reproaching him for his avarice and hard-heartedness. The father addresses him with unbelievable arrogance. 'Why, sirrah, mayn't I do what I please? Are you not my slave? Did I not beget you? . . . Did you come a volunteer into the world? Or did I, with the lawful authority of a parent, press you into the service?' As a final stroke he wants to marry Angelica himself. She pretends to accept and manages things so that the father pays his son's debts without Valentine's having to give up his inheritance. Then she laughs in Sampson's face and says, 'I always loved your son, and hated your unforgiving nature. . . . You have not more faults than he has virtues; and 'tis hardly more pleasure to me, that I can make him and myself happy, than that I can punish you.' Valentine echoes this: he rejoices loudly in his father's discomfiture. This pattern is to be found in a great many other plays. The young man, whose superiority has become more and more evident during the first four acts, triumphs in the fifth. The traditional hostility for 'dreary old age' reached a violence that had not been known up until that time. Sons and daughters proclaim open rebellion. They deny all the moral and social values imposed by the Puritans.

In the eighteenth century improved hygiene caused an increase and a rejuvenation of the population throughout Europe. An inquiry carried out at Villeneuve-de-Rivière in the Comminges shows that after 1745 the death-rate among the young, which had been from fifteen to twenty a year, fell to three or four. At the same time the improvement in material conditions favoured longevity. Before 1749 it was rare to meet with men of eighty, but now they, and even centenarians, increased in number. Yet this advance was scarcely felt outside the privileged classes. In 1754 an English writer, speaking of French peasants, observed, 'They are a kind of men that begin to decay before the age of forty, for want of a nourishment in proportion to their labour.' In 1793 an Englishman travelling in Europe wrote, 'In spite of the diseases caused by their over-indulgence at the table, by their lack of exercise and by vice, they [the rich] live

180

ten years longer than men of a lower station, who are worn out before their time by work, poverty and fatigue, and whose penniless state prevents them from providing themselves with the necessities of life.' Even when those who were exploited did manage to live on to an advanced age, their years condemned them to beggary. Societies for mutual aid appeared in central Europe as early as the fourteenth century. In France they had an uneasy, clandestine existence. Together with all trade associations, they were forbidden by the Le Chapelier law. In any case they did not dispose of adequate means, and the old person who was not kept by his family could count only on the help that the church might give him.

In England these associations, under the name of friendly societies, increased in scope and number. In the second half of the eighteenth century the current of 'feeling', of 'sentiment', that influenced the whole of European thought stirred public opinion on the question of poverty. It was understood that responsibility lay with society, not with the pauper himself. The law of 1782 gave the parishes the power to combine in unions for the collection and the spending of the poor-rate. The state seemed to acknowledge that every man had a right to live.* This was what the magistrates asserted when they met at Speenhamland in 1785: if a man could not earn his living by his labour, society must provide for him. Public assistance was recast on this basis, and the wretched condition of the sick, the crippled and the old was somewhat alleviated. Then again there was an increase in workers' associations formed to struggle against the employers, but also for mutual insurance against unemployment and sickness.

In the privileged classes, the elderly profited from the general softening of the way of life. In its material aspect, thanks to technical progress, life became more comfortable and less wearing, both in France and the whole of Europe: travelling, for example, was no longer such an arduous undertaking. The more complex social life called for intelligence, experience, and less physical exertion – the Maréchal de Saxe won the battle of Fontenoy in spite of his gout. The time of active life grew longer. Men in their sixties took part in social gatherings; they went to the theatre and attended the salons. If they had a good memory people appreciated their acquaintance and their conversation, as they had done in the seventeenth century.

* Yet at this period the State did not prevent the appalling exploitation of children in factories and workshops.

The young listened to Fontenelle at ninety and more with utter astonishment. When he said, 'I was at Madame de La Fayette's, and I saw Madame de Sévigné come in', it gave them a wonderful feeling of speaking to a ghost. Society was not unduly surprised at the sight of elderly men marrying very much younger wives, as it happened with Marmontel. The rising middle class provided itself with an ideology that set a greater value on old age.

In England more than anywhere else, technical progress brought about an expansion of industry, finance and trade. The new class, rich and powerful, became proudly self-aware and worked out an ethic that suited it. As early as the end of the seventeenth century London saw the rapid growth of the societies, gatherings and coffee-houses – there were more than three thousand – in which innumerable conversations gave the new man his shape. It may be said that Steele and Addison were his godfathers. The *Tatler* and still more the *Spectator* set themselves to recasting the man of yesterday and creating a hitherto unknown species: he found his particular expression in the person of the merchant; the merchant was the friend of the human race, the century's adventurer and hero – but a peaceful hero, the walking-stick replacing the sword. He hated ostentation. He was plain and unpretentious and he looked for usefulness rather than show. He disliked fashionable gatherings and led a very quiet life, preferably in the country. He placed moral above artistic considerations. The theatre showed this alteration in a very striking manner. At the end of the seventeenth century a moral crusade had begun against the clique that controlled it. By this time the austerity of the Puritans was no more than a distant memory and no one felt the need to oppose it, but in the end the licence of the fashionable authors scandalized public opinion. A clergyman who was also a journalist and a pamphleteer wrote a scurrilous attack upon them that had considerable success. This did not prevent Congreve from having a very much greater success with his *Way of the World* two years later. But after that he fell silent. The theatre became moral and sentimental, displaying devoted old retainers and fathers and sons who loved one another. All the characters were sympathetic.*

These tendencies spread to France. Here the new man was the *philosophe*, and the ethics he professed were the secular, humanitarian doctrines of which Diderot was the most influential proponent. In fact the eighteenth century in France was dark, unquiet, torn by the

* Cf. among others Steele's *The Conscious Lovers*, acted in 1722.

conflicts and disorders that ended in the Revolution; its literature described man in harsh and even malignant terms – the Abbé Prévost, Marivaux, Laclos, Sade. But for all that the bourgeoisie professed optimism; it made a tender, feeling defence of Man, of whom it imagined itself to be the most perfect expression – human nature was good, all men were brothers, each should respect the freedom and the opinions of his neighbour. Love your neighbour as yourself out of love for yourself became the basic moral precept. And the idea of the neighbour expanded. The eighteenth century explored time and space: it was no longer the realm of the civilized adult alone. Society turned with interest to the 'savages'. Rousseau reminded the adult of the child he had been, and the man recognized himself in the child. Mothers nursed their own babies. There was strong feeling against the whip as early as the beginning of the century, and it was abolished in 1767. Children were of much greater importance in the family. The adults recognized themselves in the old people that they were to become. The elderly man indeed took on a particular significance, being the symbol of the family's unity and permanence: because of inheritance, the family allowed the accumulation of wealth; it was both the basis of capitalism and the field in which bourgeois individualism came into full flower. In his old age the head of the family remained in control of his property and he enjoyed high economic standing. The respect that he inspired took on a sentimental form, for this indeed was the age of 'feeling', and truth was sought with the heart. Virtue was praised to the skies; moral tales, 'humane tracts', abounded. The weaker members, the grandfather and the little child, were objects of tender emotion. Marmontel touched the hearts of his contemporaries with tales of his country childhood – the good old grandmothers 'still with us at eighty, sitting by the fireside, drinking their little glass of wine and remembering the old times'. Greuze aroused tender emotions with his pictures of old men. Voltaire's old age increased the blaze of his glory: he was called the Patriarch of Ferney. From July 1789 to July 1790 old people had the place of honour at all the celebrations of the Federation, and it was they who presided over them.* During

* Michelet says, 'At the great Rouen Federation, at which the National Guards of sixty towns appeared, an old knight of Malta aged eighty-five was fetched from as far away as Les Andelys to preside over the assembly. At Saint-Andéol two ancients of ninety-three and ninety-four were given the honour of taking the oath before everybody else. . . . Everywhere an old man sat in the first place, before all others, high above the crowd.'

those of 10 August 1793 the banners of the eighty-six *départements* were carried by eighty-six old men.

All this feeling did have some practical consequences. *Bienfaisance*, beneficence, was encouraged: the word had been invented by the Abbé de Saint-Pierre in order to replace the religious notion of charity with a secular idea. A mass of writing was devoted to the question of mendicity. The newspapers provided special columns for instances of beneficence and of humanitarian actions. In 1788 the list of beneficent societies filled two fat volumes of *La Bienveillance française*. It was the women above all who made the collections and distributed the aid. S. Mercier described them comforting the distress of 'octogenarians, the blind from birth, women in their confinement, etc.'. In 1786 the *Société philanthropique* congratulated itself on having helped more than 814 unfortunate people, the aged, those born blind and women in childbirth.

The practice of philanthropy was in fact primarily a means of ensuring one's own happiness. The theme of making others happy in order to be happy oneself was handled again and again with wearisome reiteration. Ensuring his own happiness was one of the bourgeois' chief preoccupations: he thought it could be obtained by virtue, by a modest competence, and by the cultivation of the bonds of the family and of friendship. Happiness was essentially looked upon as rest. Extremes were to be feared; none but gentle passions to be felt. That is to say, old age was seen as a happy and even as an exemplary period: it was liberated from violent passions, it was calm, it was wise. The absence of desire was worth more than the enjoyment of wealth and possessions. A well-balanced life ended in ataraxy and euphoria.

This was the opinion of Buffon, among others. 'Every day that I rise from my bed in good health, have I not as full and immediate an enjoyment of the day as you? If I match my desires, my impulses and my appetites to the promptings of wise nature alone, am I not as wise as you, and more happy? And does not the retrospect of the past, the sadness of foolish old men, provide me on the contrary with the delights of memory, charming pictures and precious images that are certainly worth as much as those objects that you take pleasure in?'

Considerations of this kind left d'Alembert sceptical. 'These eulogies of friendship and old age are quite unnecessary for youth and love,' he wrote. Diderot observed, 'Old age is honoured, but it is not loved.' Yet in his work there are lovable old men, the first of them being his own father. Rétif de La Bretonne's *La Vie de mon père* had an immense success with the public. In his kindly, affectionate description of the 'venerable ancient' he held up the virtues and delights of the united family for praise just at the period when it was beginning to fall apart – a time, too, when most French people still retained a longing for it. He also spoke of the pleasures of country life; and just then the middle classes were rediscovering its charm. In the 'feeling' style then in fashion he spoke of his father's deathbed, with all the elders of the village present – 'the sick man's room was filled with weeping old men.'

We see the image of the aged man beginning to evolve in the French theatre at the end of the seventeenth century and during the eighteenth. In *Le Triple Mariage* Destouches shows us the grasping and authoritarian Oronte who prefers his wealth to his children and who tries to force them into merely profitable marriages. In *L'Ingrat* and *L'Obstacle imprévu* the father is tyrannical and unbearable. But in *L'Irrésolu* Pyrante adores his son and yields to all his whims. In Madame de Graffigny's *Cénie* Dorimard is a delightful old man, quite devoted to the nephews he has brought up; he is somewhat authoritative and a little too sure of himself, and this leads him to make mistakes; but his good qualities far outweigh his faults, and after the happy ending one of the characters says, 'Although extreme kindness is sometimes deceived, it is nevertheless the highest of virtues.'

The concept of old age that we see in Beaumarchais' plays is finely shaded, and sometimes it is surprising. He was only thirty-five when he brought out his unsuccessful *Eugénie*. Baron Hartley, the girl's father, has the leading part, and Beaumarchais, describing this old Welsh gentleman, says,* 'The baron always looks and behaves like what he is, a straightforward, plain-living man; but the moment he is stirred by a strong emotion he becomes extremely fiery and passionate, and true, glowing, unexpected words and actions fly from the blaze.' This was certainly the first time that an elderly man was ever endowed with an inner passion whose explosions astonished his household. In the first draft the father was a Breton gentleman, 'devoted to hunting, a man of an abrupt and very unreasonable character'. This picture was much closer to the series of traditional old men we see in the comedies. There is nothing to show why

* In his *Essai sur le théâtre sérieux*.

Beaumarchais transformed him. But his sympathy for elderly men appeared again in *Les Deux Amis*, which was acted three years later. Here the most sympathetic character is the *philosophe* father, a man of feeling: he is wise, altruistic and generous, and he saves the situation. In *Le Barbier de Séville*, so new in tone, Beaumarchais nevertheless returned to the stereotype of the aged lover: Bartholo is very like Molière's old fogies.* He has almost no part in *Le Mariage de Figaro*, a play in which there are no other old men, either. At the end of his life Beaumarchais adopted the soothing, moralizing view of old age that pleased the times, as we see in his completely unsuccessful *La Mère coupable*, which was acted in 1792. Referring to Count Almaviva in the preface, he said, 'Does *La Mère coupable* and the picture of his old age persuade you, as it persuades us, that any man who is not born horribly wicked always turns out good in the end, when the age of passions fades away and above all when he has tasted the happiness, the sweet delights, of being a father?' In the play the count says, 'Oh, my children! There comes an age when right-thinking people forgive themselves for their errors and former weaknesses, and so behave that a gentle, affectionate attachment takes the place of the stormy passions that once divided them.'

In 1799 a certain Billy wrote a play about the Abbé de l'Epée as he was at the age of sixty-six and whom he described in his preface as having 'an insight that nothing could escape . . . goodness and a brilliant mind . . . gentle, unaffected piety . . . a great understanding of nature'. Such were the characteristics of the elderly man of whom the moralists dreamed.

The countless melodramas of the early nineteenth century adopted this line. In these the aged men play only secondary parts, but they are stately and touching. Sometimes they make mistakes but they atone for them by the nobility of their hearts. Thus, in Lamartelière's *Robert, chef des brigands*, Robert's father commits the error of preferring another son; this son shuts him up in a tower and Robert saves him. The old man is shown as a martyr with a heart full of splendid sentiments. In *La Femme aux deux maris*, which Pixérécourt wrote in 1801, the blind and aged Werner is the embodiment of the loftiest virtues: his unbending sense of honour makes him hard and authoritarian, and he has cursed his daughter, whom he believes to be guilty, without hearing her defence. He remains obstinately set

* Although he is much sharper and harder to deceive, which makes the plot more interesting.

against her, but when at last he learns the truth he forgives her and everybody around him weeps with emotion. One of the heroes ends by saying, 'A father who forgives is the most perfect image of the Deity.' In 1821 Pixérécourt treated the same subject again in his *Valentine*. Alberto is blind too, and he treats his daughter harshly: finally they are reconciled. He is unselfish and fearless; he reaches sublimity and compels admiration.

A new theme made its appearance, that of the devoted old retainer. The feudal relationship between lord and vassal implied the complete surrender of the inferior: the rising middle classes longed to revive a bond of this kind for its own advantage. In *Misanthropie et repentir*, which was adapted from Kotzebue, the aged Tobie's noble serenity and calm resignation wring tears from the other characters. He is very old and poor, but he manages to find a humble happiness in the mere fact of living. In Cagniez' *L'Illustre Aveugle*, of 1806, one of the chief characters is the aged Oberto, who is passionately attached to the young blind prince; he is brave, extremely dignified, the incarnation of all the virtues.

There are numbers of devoted old retainers in Pixérécourt's work. The lack of quality in these inferior productions makes them all the more significant: they answered the requirements of the public and therefore reflected their fantasies. The public revered the old within their own class, and outside it they admired them in so far as they were the embodiment of an unconditional devotion to a higher caste. The aged poor had made their timid entry into literature. They were of interest not in themselves but in their feudal relationship with a master, the custodian of their truth.*

A parallel development was to be seen in the Italian theatre. As we have seen, in the sixteenth century Pantaloon was an odious, goatish old man. By the end of the seventeenth he had changed. Speaking of him in 1699, Perruci said, 'He is a decrepit old man who tries to feign youthfulness.' But in 1728 Riccoboni describes him as 'a good father of a family, a very honourable man, exceedingly tender of his word and severe with his children'. He is 'outwardly rough'. He is not miserly but only very economical; yet in spite of his qualities he is still duped.

The alteration was particularly striking in Goldoni. The reason was that in Venice too – and it was Venetian manners that he

* This was the case with the old slave in the *Ion* of Euripides.

described – the bourgeoisie had risen in status, and middle-class values had been placed on a pinnacle. Since the sixteenth century the city's maritime supremacy, faced with the competition of the Turkish empire, Spain and Ragusa, had declined. Venice had turned itself into a great industrial port, manufacturing woollens. But the nobles thought this kind of work degrading; they bought estates on the mainland and turned away from business. In the eighteenth century the aristocracy still retained political power, but its continuing existence was solely owing to the wealth that the mercantile class accumulated in the city. The ideal man was the honest, sparing, industrious merchant: these virtues were more useful to the city, to his family and to himself than titles of nobility. The nobles led meaningless, dissipated lives: it was the merchant who was the incarnation of common sense and straightforward honesty. The essential basis of his moral code lay in the family relationship. Such was the conviction of the middle class to which Goldoni belonged.

Pantaloon was traditionally a merchant. Goldoni's early pieces, imitating the *commedia dell'arte*, showed a conventional figure. In the far more personal *Les Rabat-joie* the aged man is still most unsympathetic: here Goldoni brought four versions of Pantaloon on to the stage, four misanthropic, tyrannical, miserly, selfish, obstinate old men; they have out-of-date ideas and they hate the young; they oppress their families; they prevent the women and children from going out, amusing themselves or buying clothes. One of them wants to marry his daughter to the son of another, but both refuse to allow the young people to see one another before the wedding-day. But thanks to the complicity of their mothers they succeed in doing so.

In the course of his career Goldoni became more and more concerned with describing Venetian society as he saw it, and his Pantaloon came closer to the ideal merchant. Furthermore, he was not aged but neither young nor old, a man who had taken good care of his fortune and had lived his life intelligently – a man capable of giving wise advice, and one whom Goldoni often used as his own mouthpiece. In one of his most successful plays, *Le Bourru bienfaisant*, he treated the character of the father with some little irony but also with the greatest esteem. Géronte is brusque, domineering and difficult; he pays no attention to anyone; and without asking her opinion he decides to marry his niece Angelica to an old friend of his. But he is open-handed; he maintains his servant's family generously. He agrees to pay his nephew's debts. And in the end he comes to understand that he must let Angelica do as she likes with her own heart and he allows her to marry the young man she loves.

We see how the image of the rich old merchant had evolved since Chaucer. In his day and throughout the following centuries, the merchant's wealth was a cause for envy: he was thought to be unfairly privileged, and revenge took the form of mockery. It was only in the eighteenth century that a more developed understanding of economics allowed society to see the nature of the services he rendered to the community as a whole. Once his role was understood, utilitarianism (and the Puritans were the first to profess it) led to his being endowed with every deserving quality. He was even more respected when he was very old: his prosperity was a warrant for his wisdom and his virtues.

The writers of the eighteenth century were no less influenced than other men by their times. But since this influence was all in favour of individualism, novelty and the profusion of ideas, we find many strikingly original authors. Among these we must number Swift, to whom we owe the cruellest portrait of old age that was ever drawn. He was fifty-five, and he had reached a difficult period of his life – the end of his relationship with Vanessa – when he wrote the third part of *Gulliver's Travels*. In the fourth, which was written earlier, he had ferociously satirized humanity in general in the guise of Yahoos. 'I hate and detest the animal called man,' he said a little later, in a letter to Pope. He had a profound disgust for women, and a few years after this he wrote his well-known poem *The Lady's Dressing-Room* on the theme 'Celia shits'. Old age, in so far as it was at least theoretically looked upon as the noblest, most perfected aspect of the human state, could not but arouse his fury. He was himself quite old; he was ill; and as it turned out his old age was in fact a disastrous physical and mental decay – it seemed that he had some premonition of it. He would never have described his immortals, who were in reality merely very aged people, in such precise detail if he had not been haunted by terrifying forebodings of his own future. It was certainly not by mere chance that in his last years he was himself changed into a horrible Struldbrug.

When Gulliver learns that certain Luggnaggians are born with a mark on their foreheads showing that they are to be immortal he is struck with inexpressible delight: he supposes them to be happily free from the apprehension of death, full of learning, wealthy, conversing among themselves upon lofty questions; if he were one

189

of them, he says, he would struggle against corruption and he would try to carry out great schemes of research and discovery. The Luggnaggian tells him that everywhere else in the world the aged retain their appetite for life, but that in Luggnagg they do not, since they have the fate that awaits them before their eyes; and 'that the system of living contrived by me was unreasonable and unjust; because it supposed a perpetuity of youth, health, and vigour . . . that the question therefore was not, whether a man would chuse to be always in the prime of youth, attended with prosperity and health; but how he would pass a perpetual life under all the usual disadvantages, which old age brings along with it'. In fact, when they were about thirty the Struldbrugs began to be melancholy and dejected and this increased upon them until they were eighty. Then 'they had not only all the follies and infirmities of other old men, but many more, which arose from the dreadful prospect of never dying. They were not only opinionative, peevish, covetous, morose, vain, talkative; but incapable of friendship, and dead to all natural affection, which never descended below their grandchildren. Envy and impotent desires are their prevailing passions. But those objects, against which their envy seems principally directed, are the vices of the younger sort, and the deaths of the old. . . . They have no remembrance of any thing, but what they learned and observed in their youth and middle age, and even that is very imperfect. . . . The least miserable among them appear to be those, who turn to dotage, and intirely lose their memories; these meet with more pity and assistance, because they want many bad qualities, which abound in others.' At eighty they are looked upon as dead in law; and if the Struldbrug has married another the marriage is dissolved. They have a small pittance to keep them. At ninety they lose their teeth and hair; they have no distinction of taste. 'In talking they forget the common appellation of things. . . . For the same reason they can never amuse themselves with reading, because their memory will not serve to carry them from the beginning of a sentence to the end. . . . The language of this country being always upon the flux, the Struldbrugs no longer understand it, and thus they lie under the disadvantage of living like foreigners in their own country.'

This last idea was completely new. Formerly, and especially in the middle ages, time's motion had been circular, and the aged man's decline took place in an unchanging world. In the eighteenth century the middle classes believed in progress; it was this that led Swift to

think that the old person repeats his experience and stands motionless in a changing, perpetually rejuvenated world. The aged man,
unable to evolve with the rest of the world, stays behind, solitary,
shut in, deprived of everything that is moving away from him.* Old
age is not only decrepitude but also as it was soon going to be for
Swift – the loneliness of exile.

To be an undying old man: that was the unhappy fate for which
Mimnermus, the Ionian poet, pitied Tithon. Men have never wished
for it. On the other hand, as I have said, they have dreamed of the
Fountain of Youth. One of the themes in Goethe's *Faust* is rejuvenation. This is an idea that never appeared in any of the ancient Faust
legends nor in Marlowe's play. Faust was a scholar turned magician
who lost his soul because of his thirst for learning. Goethe's play is
primarily the drama of knowledge and of the bounds of the human
state. But the notion of old age also plays a great part in it. The aged
Faust no longer derives happiness from learning – no pride any more,
no exaltation: it is still there, open to him, but he is the victim of his
own limits, his own finitude. The desire to know is dead in him; he
no longer has any reason for living. To find it again, the love,
delights and enthusiasms that belong to youth would have to be
reborn in all their first freshness: he wagers that if Mephistopheles
gives him back his youth he will not let himself be so deceived by
pleasures that he will want to halt the course of time; but this
challenge has a meaning only if he is capable of enjoying them. It is
clear, therefore, that Goethe looked upon old age as something
remote, frigid and disappointing. He was only twenty-five when he
began *Faust* and forty-eight when he finished it in 1807. But although
he had no personal experience of being really old, he was already fully
aware of the limited nature of mankind. He had always wanted to be
able to change his skin, like a snake; and the reason for this was that
sometimes he was ill at ease in it and that it seemed to him worn out.
The question was not so much being young as the possibility of
rejuvenation: escaping from his limitations, reliving life like an
adventure, not allowing it to end in a blind alley.

In the nineteenth century Europe was transformed: and the great
changes that took place had a considerable effect upon the state of

* In one of her letters Ninon de Lenclos had spoken of the isolation of an old man
in a century no longer his own. The theme was often handled in later times, particularly by Chateaubriand. I shall have a good deal to say on it. But this was the first time
that it was treated publicly and with great emphasis.

the aged and upon society's idea of old age. The first thing to point out is that all countries experienced an extraordinary rise in population: the Europe of 1800 had 187 million inhabitants; this rose to 266 million in 1850 and 300 million in 1870. The consequence was that at least in certain classes the number of old people increased. This growth, together with scientific progress, led to the myths about old age being replaced by real knowledge; and this knowledge made it possible for medical science to care for and heal the elderly. From now onwards there were too many old people for literature to pass them over in silence: in France, England and Russia novelists were doing their utmost to draw a complete picture of society, and this led them to describe not only the aged of the privileged classes but also those of the lower – people who, apart from a few unimportant exceptions, had never been written about at all.

This was very far from meaning that the world had become a much better place for the aged taken as a whole. On the contrary, we shall see that many of them were the victims of the economic evolution that took place in the course of the century.

Three closely linked phenomena accompanied the growth of population in all countries: industrial revolution; a movement away from the countryside and a consequent urban increase; and the appearance and development of the new class, the proletariat.

In England the depopulation of the countryside had begun with the enclosures, which reduced a great number of peasants to destitution. At the beginning of the nineteenth century one side-effect of the poor-laws was a lowering of the incomes of the farmers and the agricultural workers, a lowering that forced them off the land. The coming of free trade in 1846 meant that industrial and commercial England had finally triumphed over agricultural England.

In France there had been an important flight from the land at the end of the eighteenth century, raising the urban population from a tenth of the total to a fifth, or about five and a half million people. The peasants' sons moved chiefly into the small towns, where they became shopkeepers, employees or civil servants, thus rising socially. At the beginning of the nineteenth century, on the other hand, this movement came to a halt: between 1800 and 1851 the urban population did rise by three and a half million, but because of the total increase in numbers, only twenty-five per cent of the French lived in towns. Thanks to a decrease in taxes the total amount of money at the peasants' disposal grew larger, but this increase was offset by the simultaneous growth of the population. Between 1840 and 1850 the countryside could no longer feed those who lived upon it, and more and more people left the land between 1850 and 1865. During the years that followed, the concentration of urban industry caused the withering away of rural industry, an important source of supplementary income for the peasants. Technical progress made it harder for the poor to work the land; they could not stand up against the competition of the capitalist methods introduced by the middle-class owners. What is more, after 1880 the improvement in communications allowed America to export wheat to France; in the resulting serious economic crisis the flight from the land continued. By 1881 a third of the population was concentrated in the towns. As the century drew to its end it was industry that offered openings for the peasants' sons: they came to swell the ranks of the proletariat.

These changes were disastrous for the old. Neither in France nor in England had their condition been so cruelly hard as it was in the second half of the nineteenth century. Labour was not protected: men, women and children were pitilessly exploited. As they grew old, the workers were unable to keep up with the rhythm. The industrial revolution was carried through at the cost of an unbelievable wastage of human material. Between 1880 and 1900 Taylorism wrought havoc in the United States: all the workers died before their time. In every country, those who managed to survive were reduced to extreme poverty when their age deprived them of their jobs. After the Bourbon restoration mutual insurance societies were tolerated in France, and in 1835 they were officially recognized: in 1850 and 1852 they were once more placed under strict supervision. The Third Republic gave them complete freedom by the law of 1 April 1898. But even in the best of conditions their means were always insufficient when it was a question of guaranteeing a risk as heavy as old age. This also applied to the friendly societies in England. 'Produce savings rather than children,' said J. B. Say. This advice, addressed to workers, was a mockery. England and France saw an immense increase in the number of aged tramps and beggars, destitute old people.

In the French countryside maintenance at home was still the rule. If the elder who governed the household was physically strong enough or rich enough to retain the control of his land, that is to say if he could go on working or could hire labourers, then he also retained his authority over his children. The patriarchal family continued to exist in the country, and the authority of the old man who ruled it might be tyrannical. But this was only to be met with among the well-to-do peasants, and there were few of these. Agriculture was still archaic in 1815, and its subsequent progress was slow; the yield was so small that the peasants could hardly make a living. When they were old they no longer had the strength to go on working the land and they had not saved the money needed to pay for outside labour. They were at their children's mercy. The children lived on the edge of destitution and they had nothing to spare for the feeding of useless mouths. Sometimes they got rid of them by abandoning them in institutions – alms-houses or asylums. In 1804 the head of the Hospice de Montrichard* said indignantly, 'The old people are required to bring everything they may possess to the institution and leave it there when they die; yet when these unnatural children bring their old parents they strip them before leaving them in the wards, taking away even their very last garments.' Generally speaking the children kept their parents at home; but the situation that the middle ages illustrated with the tale of Lear had persisted throughout the centuries – the father, no longer able to work his land himself, gave it over to his children, who would very often starve and ill-treat him. In his *Mémoire sur les paysans de l'Aveyron et du Tarn*, Rouvellat de Cussac wrote, 'There is nothing more usual than sons and daughters forgetting all their duties towards the authors of their being, once the parents are aged. If the parents have been so imprudent as to give their property without any written reservation or otherwise than by a revokable will, then they run the risk of finding themselves despised and often that of wanting the necessaries of life.'

This theme is to be found in many novels that were certainly founded upon reality. In Theuriet's *Eusèbe Lombard,* which was written in 1885, the sister, after the father's death, accuses her elder brother of having confined the old man. 'The reason why he came to us was that you fed him on rotten potatoes.' 'Well, you let him die on a bed of straw in midwinter.' In *Autour du clocher,* a novel that Fèvre and Desprez based upon their observations of the peasants of Rouvres, old father Bonhoure is treated very roughly by his children. 'And so he lived on aimlessly, maltreated, insulted, fed on bad potatoes like the pigs.' In the end he hangs himself. In Maizeroy's *L'Aveugle* the nephews force their old uncle to go out begging. 'When he came back with an empty bag he was violently insulted and

* Abbé C. Labreuille, *Etude historique de Montrichard.*

abused, and all of them, even the smallest, mocked him savagely, taking away his bowl and playing a thousand ugly tricks on him.' One day he dies on the road. In *Le Père Amable* Maupassant describes the melancholy, silent existence of a deaf, half-crippled widower with his son. Against Amable's wishes the son remarries: his wife has had a child by another man. For the old man life becomes sadder and sadder, more and more reduced. The son dies. The wife does not behave badly to her father-in-law, but she marries again. Upon this he hangs himself.

The law did its best to protect the aged against their descendants' harshness and neglect. In the place of an actual, de facto state of affairs it set up a legal situation. A father who dispossessed himself by a distribution of his property *inter vivos* received in exchange a life annuity whose amount was settled in the presence of a notary: if his children refused to pay it to him he could bring an action against them. Unhappily he often paid dearly for the protection that the law thus provided. Before this it had been to his children's general, undefined interest to spend as little as possible on him: now their interest was exact and measurable: the pension that they were compelled to pay him made it wholly and immediately real. They therefore had a powerful motive for bringing about his disappearance, since this was the easiest way of escaping from the severity of a legal obligation. No one can possibly tell in what century the murder of old parents, by violence or by privation, was proportionately most common. Most of these killings remain buried in the silence of the countryside; but the fact that in the nineteenth century public opinion was uneasily aware of them proves that they must have been frequent. Did this publicity mean that people were more concerned with the fate of the aged peasants? Or did it mean that the murders were increasing in number and that they were committed with less caution? There is no evidence upon which we can base a decision.

What is certain is that many people spoke out about the dangers that lay in wait for the aged, dispossessed father. Bonnemère, in his *Histoire des paysans* (1874), said 'He carries the wretchedness of his last days with him from cottage to cottage, unwelcome, ill-received, a burden to everybody and to himself, a stranger in his children's house. At last he dies. . . . But it is as well for him to make haste, for greed is there, and greed nerves the arm of the hidden parricide.' Bonnemère states that an old man might well be buried before he was really dead – a frequent occurrence. 'Under thatched roofs coma is called by the name of death, because, as Monsieur Dupuis* observes, there are not always two bedrooms and the heirs are eager to take his place.' Bonnemère quotes four cases of parricide for 1855 alone.† These crimes were so usual, and, in spite of the darkness surrounding them, so well known, that there was no hesitation in referring to them in the official inquiry into agriculture carried out between 1866 and 1870 and summarized by Paul Turot in 1877. Turot, speaking in the name of the government, advised the older generation not to share out their property during their lifetime. He strongly emphasized the wretched fate awaiting aged parents after their dispossession, referring to 'the crimes that are committed to hasten death, crimes to which the obligations contracted in consequence of the distribution are an incitement, indeed a kind of encouragement. Once the father of a family has given away his property he is deprived of all authority. His status becomes that of a despised being, repulsed by his children, rejected from their homes, sent from one to another with a life annuity that is often unpaid or a lodging place that is often not provided for him.'

In an article in *Le Temps* of 5 August 1885 Cherville stressed the unhappy lot of old parents who were continually harassed, kept short of food, and sent out to beg. A grandfather would often be attached to his grandson, but 'as he grows older the child withdraws from him' and behaves like the others. Cherville pointed out that there was a great temptation to hasten the end of the aged parents, who always cost too much.

Zola dealt with one of these dark tragedies in *La Terre*: he had done a great deal of serious research in order to write it. The novel has been compared to *King Lear*,‡ and indeed Zola referred to the

---

* *Dictionnaire de la conversation*, under Inhumations.

† In the Maine-et-Loire a peasant named Guyomard murdered his mother-in-law, who had surrendered her property to him and to whom he paid twenty francs a year and twelve bushels of rye. (*Le Constitutionel*, 12 February 1855.)

At Gensac, near Libourne, a man of sixty murdered his eighty-year-old mother, stabbing her twice in the throat, to set himself free from an annuity. (*La Presse*, 22 March 1855.)

In a side-lane of La Ferté-sous-Jouarre one night a farmer beat out the brains of his father-in-law, to whom he paid an annuity of eight hundred francs. A girl who heard the shrieks denounced him and he confessed. (*La Presse*, 29 July 1855.)

Near Nemours Pierre Besson, a peasant, beat his father to death because some clauses in his will favoured a younger brother.

I will mention still another, which caused a great stir in 1886. At Luneau in the Loir-et-Cher a couple named Thomas burnt the wife's mother alive.

‡ Particularly by Legouis in *Revue de littérature comparée*, 1957. The great difference is that old Fouan is not an embodiment of the human state.

play in his notes. Shakespeare and Zola, with hundreds of years lying between them, were in fact describing analogous situations. At the beginning of the novel the aged Fouan and his children meet before the notary; he intends to share out his property between them, no longer having the strength to cultivate it; the children wrangle bitterly over the annuity their father asks for. 'The old couple's life was spread out, ransacked, turned in every direction, their needs discussed one by one. The weight of bread, vegetables, meat. . . . When people no longer worked, they ought to learn how to put up with less.' A figure is settled. At first the old man goes on living in his own house with his wife. The children pay him only a small part of the agreed annuity. This causes a shocking scene between the father and his younger son Buteau: the mother dies of it. The old man is persuaded to sell the house and go to live with his daughter; her mean persecution makes his life miserable. Like Lear, he goes to each of his children in turn: he is very unhappy. A few wretched years pass by. Buteau induces the old man to come to his house in the hope of stealing his little fortune, and he treats him savagely. During a scene the father raises his hand in a threatening gesture that once used to terrify his son; but this time Buteau seizes it, shakes his father and flings him into a chair. Like an old gorilla vanquished by the young, the father feels that he is finally and completely beaten: with the loss of his physical strength he has lost all his authority. Even the protection of the law is not strong enough to defend him against direct, unqualified violence. Buteau succeeds in stealing his savings. The conflict between father and son becomes so acute that one night – like Lear again – the old man escapes and wanders about in a storm until daybreak. Because he witnessed a crime committed by his son and daughter-in-law, and even more because they can no longer bear having to keep him, they smother him by setting fire to his straw mattress, making it look like an accident. The doctor does not look into it too closely and gives a burial certificate.

Zola made use of the fact mentioned in *Le Temps* – the relationship of the grandfather and his grandson. For a while his affection for the child, an affection that seems to be returned, is some comfort to old Fouan in his unhappiness. But the day comes when he goes to fetch his grandchild from school; the child refuses to come and joins the other boys in making fun of him.

Because the nineteenth century sheds at least some light on the fate of exploited old people, the contrast with that of the privileged classes is more striking than at any other period. The aged poor, with worn-out workers reduced to destitution and homeless, wandering elderly peasants treated like animals, were at the very bottom of the social scale. But at the very top we find the aged belonging to the upper classes: the antithesis is so enormous that one might almost be looking at two different species. The economic and social changes that had been so disastrous for the first had worked to the advantage of the second.

At the beginning of the nineteenth century the return of the royalists at the Restoration set up a positive gerontocracy. The émigrés bought land, often their own former estates: by 1830 half the great holdings had been reconstituted. There were not a great many landowning nobles, but they had large numbers of followers among the middle classes. These aristocrats, clustered round the king, caused a suffrage based on property-qualification to be adopted – landed property – and this gave them complete political control. There were ninety thousand electors: that is to say, out of a hundred Frenchmen who were of age, only one had a vote. And the number of citizens who could be elected amounted to about eight thousand. Since the returned royalists were very elderly, the country was in a position that might be termed pathological. Fazy, a pamphleteer, denounced it in 1829. 'France has been cut down to some seven or eight thousand men who can be elected, asthmatic, gouty, paralytic beings with weakened powers who have no wish for anything but peace and quiet.' He strongly criticized 'the strange law that requires only old men to be the nation's representatives'. After 1830 this privilege of age continued in the House of Peers: talking to Guizot in 1835, Talleyrand said, 'I went to the House of Peers yesterday. There were only six of us . . . and we were all over eighty.'

Meanwhile the upper middle class, exploiting the workers and a good many of the peasants and lending money on interest, was growing wealthy. By means of its economic superiority, it tore political power from the hands of the landowning aristocracy. Under Louis-Philippe it was the manufacturers, the bankers and the big businessmen who governed, together with the top civil servants, lawyers and teachers. Since it had needed time for them to accumulate their fortunes, most of them were elderly. Here again, we may speak of a gerontocracy. Charles Dupin asserted that half the electors were over fifty-five. According to him, the fifty-four thousand liberal electors had twenty-eight million citizens behind them, and the forty-six thousand right-wing electors three million elderly men. The figures are approximate, but the general idea is correct. It was a question of a plutocracy, and the majority of wealthy men were old. Firms were family undertakings, and the head of the firm was usually the eldest member of the family. Profit, increased by investment, had taken the place of rent and interest as the prime mover of the economy. The members of the family-cell were closely bound by their common interests, and the grandfather was the symbol of the unit.

After 1845 it was banking and industry that held political power. This was the final stage of the industrial revolution, with railways, textiles, metallurgy, mines, sugar factories and so on coming into full action. The part played by the banks continually increased in importance. In this active, changing world, the most respected figure was that of the entrepreneur, and initiative was the most necessary quality: bolder than his father, the son would persuade him to install the latest machines in the factory and to try the most modern techniques. Then again, joint-stock companies took the place of family capitalism. The elderly man lost his economic prestige. Universal suffrage took his political supremacy from him. Yet nevertheless in 1871 the National Assembly was largely made up of aged country members: there were four hundred royalists against two hundred republicans and fifty deputies with no clear affiliation. It was the first group that contained by far the greatest number of old men.

Generally speaking, in France and throughout the western world, the conflict between the generations vanished as far as the bourgeoisie was concerned: a kind of balance had come into being. Young and old asserted their solidarity in the face of the 'dangerous' classes. In the lower bourgeoisie it would often happen that the son held a higher social position than his father, and in these cases the father was proud of his success: this rise from generation to generation took all the bite from animosity. What is more, the new society required collaboration between the young and the old. Because of its complexity, experience and accumulated knowledge were necessary for its life and progress: in many fields seniority was a qualification. Young men compelled recognition by their dash and their inventive powers; but they often found it useful to shelter behind the reassuring figure of an elderly partner, ostensible head of the concern, a figurehead who left the real running of the firm to his more active associates.

The reason why an elderly man seemed to be a sound guarantor was that the middle-class ideology of the time set a high value on age. In France, as in Victorian England, the virtues that were extolled were those that the Puritans had honoured: strict morality went hand in hand with economic success, and since profits had to be ploughed back, austerity was of the first importance. Long tradition held up the aged man as one who was by his nature devoid of appetites and who was therefore naturally ascetic: and then the economic theory that looked upon the accumulation of capital as the universal remedy reached out – mistakenly – into the realm of psychology, holding that accumulation was always good – accumulating years meant making a profit, acquiring the value called experience, a value before which the nineteenth-century middle class bowed its respectful head. The associationalist empiricism which was then regarded as the supreme truth confirmed these ideas: the older a man grew the greater number of associations of ideas he had and the greater became his knowledge and wisdom. It was therefore at the end of his life that in the ordinary course of events an individual reached his highest point.

In the towns the family was no longer patriarchal. From the end of the eighteenth century onwards the great increase in the number of jobs and the broadening of social life allowed young couples to set up house for themselves. But the idea of the larger family remained dear to the middle class, and their veneration for the grandfather was a figurative perpetuation of it. Even when modern capitalism reached its full development and the grandfather's influence declined, public opinion still required his relatives to treat him with a great show of respect and to see to it that his last days were spent in comfort.

The transformation of the family changed the relationship between grandparents and grandchildren. An alliance took the place of the former antagonism; and the grandfather, no longer being the head of the family, became the children's abettor over their parents' heads, while for their part the children found in him an amused and indulgent companion.*

The social importance allotted to the old angered a certain

* As we have seen, the relationship between grandparents and grandchildren, in different forms, is of great importance in many primitive communities.

number of adult writers. Lamennais made a violent attack upon the very elderly: when he was thirty-six he wrote, 'I have never seen an old man whose age had not weakened his mind and I have seen very few who were sincerely persuaded that this was so.' And again, 'What is an old man in this world? A tomb that moves. The crowd opens: a few come nearer to read the epitaph.'* Dickens strongly protested against the usual coupling of old age and childhood. Speaking of old age he wrote, 'We call it a state of childhood, but it is a poor, hollow simulacrum of it, as death is a simulacrum of sleep. Where in the eyes of a senile man is the light and the vivacity that laugh in the eyes of a child? . . . Put a child and a man who has fallen into his dotage side by side and blush at that emptiness which libels the happy beginning of our life by giving its name to this horrible and convulsive imitation.'

Voices like these were very rare. Those writers who, from very different points of view, concerned themselves with old age, put forward more or less finely-shaded defences of it; they, like the essayists of the earlier centuries, were interested in old age only in so far as it affected their own class. I shall quote the most important examples.

Chapter 6 of the *Aphorisms on Wisdom in Life* is entitled *Concerning the difference between ages,* and here Schopenhauer brings the light of his philosophy to bear on the various periods of existence. He did, of course, profess a total pessimism: mankind's only chance is to eradicate the will to live, and by no longer reproducing itself to move bodily into the void. The time when the individual's will is the strongest, that is to say in his youth, is the very time when he is furthest from wisdom. The child is a privileged being because he is contemplative: he has an aesthetic attitude that keeps the world at a distance: he sees objects *sub specie aeternitatis* and has an intuition of their essence. That is why childhood is so bitterly regretted in after life: childhood is happy because it is representation and not will. The young man, on the contrary, is eager for life: he pursues happiness, and he does not find it because the fact of pursuing it means that it is already lost. If he is intelligent he gradually comes to understand that happiness is illusory whereas suffering is real, and his only desire is to be free from it. Youth is intellectually fertile:

---

* Lamennais had a sour and gloomy view of mankind's condition as a whole. At the age of thirty-six he was going through a period of depression. Perhaps he also had a lasting grudge against some particular old people: he was much given to resentment.

knowledge and invention belong to it. Intellectual powers reach their height at thirty-five. But for all this man lives in error and illusion: his sexual instincts maintain a state of harmless insanity in him.

After forty he grows melancholy because although he gives up neither his passions nor his ambition, he begins to be disillusioned; he now sees death at the end of his road, whereas formerly he took no notice of it. The happiest time of life are the years that come before decrepitude, always provided that one is in good health and that one has enough money to compensate for the strength that is now lacking: 'poverty in old age is a very great misfortune.' If these two conditions are granted, old age 'may be a very tolerable period of life'. Time begins to pass very quickly, and for this reason a man is no longer conscious of boredom. The passions fall silent, the blood runs cooler; set free from his sexual instincts, the individual rediscovers his reason. Then 'we become more or less convinced of the emptiness, the utter void, of everything upon earth'. The discovery of this truth gives us an intellectual calmness that is 'the condition and the essence of happiness'. 'The young man believes that in this world he could overcome God knows what extraordinary things if only he knew where to find them: the old man is imbued with the words of Ecclesiastes *all is vanity*, and now he knows very well that all nuts are hollow, however well gilded they may be. It is only at an advanced age that a man comes wholly to Horace's *nil admirari*, that is to say to a strong and heart-felt conviction of the vanity of all things and of the emptiness of all the pomp of this world. No more vain imaginings! He is entirely disillusioned.' Because of this clarity of mind, a man's true worth is of more value to him in his very old age than at any other time. Yet most people turn into automata; their ways become fixed and their actions are repetitive; when this is so then old age is no more than the *caput mortuum* of life. Decrepitude is beneficent because it helps men to bear death. After ninety, instead of dying of some disease, people often merely fade away.

Clearly the high value that Schopenhauer sets upon old age is a direct consequence of his pessimism. He concedes that the disillusionment which is its essence does suffuse it with 'a certain gloomy tinge'. But its merit lies in the fact that the will to live almost entirely disappears: there is a return to the contemplative attitude of childhood. If life is unhappiness and if death is preferable to it, then this half-death of old age is better than the time of illusions. Schopenhauer's appreciation is entirely negative: 'The burden of life is in fact lighter in old age than it is in youth.'

Madame Swetchine* made some very wise and accurate observations on old age. She emphasized the contrast between its dignity and the low estimation in which it is held. 'The old man is the high priest of time past, which does not prevent him from being a seer for time yet to come.' Yet 'it is an astonishishing thing that old age arouses not horror, but contempt'. She very truly says, 'Nothing creates more contradictions in men's minds than old age: it is a spectre that youth does not believe in, a bugbear for men in their prime, nevertheless . . . all hope to reach it and they compromise with its disadvantages as far as ever they can.'

Again, 'Youth does not pay old age the honour of looking upon it as a necessary evil, of accepting it as death is accepted: youth almost goes so far as to promise itself escape from age and takes pride in not wishing to prolong its life at the cost of so much ignominy.'

She admits that on the human plane it is a terrible affliction and she describes it with horror: but because of its cruelty old age allows a closer approach to God. 'If we consider man in a state of nature, then youth is the true and perhaps the only good period. . . . Religion works in a direction diametrically opposed to nature.' 'As far as the outside world is concerned, old age is certainly a kind of blindness. . . . God is the inheritor of all the wishes it no longer makes, of all the impulses that it suppresses, and he opens the inner world to it, wider and still wider.' She was sorry that Christ had not sanctified this stage of life by living through it.

Both Schopenhauer and Madame Swetchine made an effort to reflect upon old age from an original standpoint. But the old clichés were hard to kill, and they are to be found again in Emerson's brief essay on the subject. Emerson belonged to the American middle class; his ideology was strongly conformist; and towards the end of his life he carried the optimism that he had always professed to extremes – much shaken by the Civil War, he preferred to lay down his arms and to take no notice of the terrible period of Reconstruction. He had persuaded himself that he was living in the best of worlds and the best of times. When age had weakened him and his

---

* She was a Russian convert to Catholicism, and she lived in Paris. Montalambert, Lacordaire and Dupanloup often attended her salon. The end of her life was very distressing – bereavements and terrible physical suffering. Falloux gathered her remarks on old age into a kind of essay.

powers had declined, he praised the value and the pleasures of the last stage of life. Like Cicero, he admits that 'the popular belief is that old age is not discreditable, but exceedingly disadvantageous', and he uses every possible argument to prove the contrary. He calls to mind famous old men in history, though it must be added that he did not trouble to find out whether their last days were happy, since he lumps together the Cid, Dandolo, Michelangelo, Galileo, etc. The aged man is happy, he says, in the first place because he has escaped from many dangers, and he rejoices in his escape. He no longer has anything to fear: his life is there behind him, and nothing can take it away. This means that Emerson was satisfied with his position and his celebrity: we see nothing that allows him to generalize. Thanks to this, he goes on, success no longer has any meaning. He no longer has to strain for achievement. A man may descend below his own level without danger. The third argument reproduces the second: the man has shown what he is worth; he has given his measure; now he has a right to rest on his past. No more doubt; no more uneasiness. Here Emerson's optimism has an odd resemblance to Schopenhauer's pessimism: when a man is old, he no longer acts or even thinks; he stops living, and this is a deliverance that brings peace with it. Finally, Emerson puts forward the statement that the aged man has acquired experience, thus supporting the notion that the mere piling up of years begets knowledge – a notion dear to the bourgeoisie.

In Germany Jacob Grimm gave a celebrated lecture on old age in 1880; he ended thus: 'I think I have brought forward proofs to support the view that old age does not merely represent a decline of manly vigour but that it bears its own powers within itself and that these powers develop according to their own laws and conditions. It is the period of a tranquillity and a peace that did not exist before; and particular effects must correspond to this particular state.'

Here he was basing himself upon the organicism that was then in favour – each age had its own particular organization, its own specific quality; the aged man was not an older, devirilized adult; his condition was not to be described in negative terms, in terms of lacking or of deprivation, but positively, as a different balance in the individual and in his relationship with the world.

In no writer's work has old age been so important or so highly glorified as in that of Victor Hugo. Why? One would have to know his life in its most intimate details to be able to tell. What is certain is that it was one of his favourite subjects for imagination. When he was still young he saw the poet as a magus, a prophet reigning in clouds of glory: now by tradition it was great age that conferred high standing and supreme authority. He must have had a pre-monition that his own old age would be the time when he would most perfectly fulfil his destiny. He delighted in antitheses, and one of those which he most readily used was the contrast between an old, worn-out body and a noble, lofty soul – and old age is one of the embodiments of this antithesis. Thus, when he was still under forty, he took up the legend of the return of Barbarossa in his play *Les Burgraves*, bringing terrible and awe-inspiring ancients on to the stage: age, breaking them physically, exalted their sombre magnific-ence. In order to summon them up, Hugo turned to the ordinary clichés. He emphasized the isolation of old age, its remoteness from the world. The ancient Job 'keeps apart . . . for months on end he does not speak a word'. Hidden in a cave, Barbarossa is deep in the silence of sleep '. . . He slept with a fierce and an astonishing sleep'. The beard is a symbol of longevity: 'His beard, once golden and now snow-white, turned three times round the stone table.' Later, in *La Légende des siècles*, he drew epic portraits of old age. The greatest of these heroes is Eviradnus: he has a stainless life behind him, a succession of splendid feats, and age does not affect him.

> Il rit des ans . . .
> Tout vieux qu'il est, il est de la grande tribu
> Le moins fier des oiseaux n'est pas l'aigle barbu.
> Qu'importe l'âge! Il lutte. Il vient de Palestine,
> Il n'est point las. Les ans s'archarnent; il s'obstine.*

These lines seem to foretell the future: Hugo, the fighter, flings down an early challenge to the years and shows himself the victor in the struggle. Single-handed, Eviradnus kills the Emperor of Germany and the King of Poland, who both fight him together. Under the cover of the legend Hugo endows the old man with the qualities of youth – he gives him a giant's strength. And he is as gracious as he is strong: when Mahaud, whom the villains have drugged to rob her, wakes up, he kisses her hand, saying, 'Madame, did you sleep well?'

In *Les Misérables*, which Hugo finished between fifty and sixty,

* He mocks at the years. Old he may be, but he is of the splendid race – the bearded eagle is not the least proud of birds. What does age matter! He fights. He has come from Palestine, not weary in the least. The years beset him fiercely: he stands fast.

Marius' grandfather is a man who has been very hard to his family all his life long. But when he believes his grandson is dead, he discovers the magnitude of his love. He hears of his recovery with a joy that transfigures him. 'When grace combines with wrinkles it is adorable. There is an indescribable light of dawn about intensely happy old age.' He agrees to the marriage of Marius with Cosette. By this time Jean Valjean is old too: at the age of eighty he is still tragic and sublime, as he has been all his life. As indomitable as Eviradnus, he retains strength enough to carry the inanimate Marius through the Paris sewers on his back. His moral strength is even more extraordinary, because he feels it is his duty to confess to Marius that he is a former convict, and he gradually withdraws from the life of Cosette, the one woman he has loved. His death is an apotheosis, for he dies surrounded by the love of the young couple, Marius having recognized him as the man who saved his life.

When Hugo was fifty-seven and on the verge of old age, he sublimated it magnificently in *Booz endormi*:

> Sa barbe était d'argent comme un ruisseau d'avril . . .
> Car le jeune homme est beau, mais le vieillard est grand
> . . . Et l'on voit de la flamme aux yeux des jeunes gens,
> Mais dans l'oeil du vieillard on voit de la lumière.*

Here it is spiritual qualities – nobility of mind and light – that mark the patriarch, who is made young by the comparison of his beard with an April stream. He has retained sexual attraction, too, since Ruth lies 'bare-bosomed' at his feet in the hope of awakening his desire.

L'Art d'être grand-père is even more of a hymn to old age than it is to childhood, an old age that Hugo glorifies through his own image, as we shall see later. But he also deals with that bond of intimacy between grandfather and grandchildren which found a favourable environment in the society of the time. In *Les Misérables* he had already spoken in moving terms of the union between the aged Jean Valjean and the child Cosette: 'When you are old, you feel like a grandfather to all small children.' In his well-known *Jeanne était au pain sec* he emphasizes the mutual nature of the understanding between the grand-daughter and her grandfather, leagued against the severity of the grown-ups. In status they are both

* His beard was silvery like an April stream. . . . For the young man is handsome, but the old superb. . . . And fire is seen in the eyes of the young, but it is light that we see in the old man's eyes.

on the fringe of society. But he feels that the bond which unites them is deeper than this. For the Greek tragedians a child and an aged man were alike because both were powerless: among many primitive peoples the connexion is carried much further – a single age-class includes both the child, who has scarcely emerged from the other world, and the ancient, who will soon return to it. Both are in a state of transition that frees them from certain taboos. Hugo expresses a similar idea in different terms. He was boasting when he claimed to 'have invented the child'; the discovery had taken place in the eighteenth century, and children had an important place in nineteenth-century literature and art. But no earlier writer had ever so well displayed the affinities between childhood and old age. According to Hugo, there is a spiritual communion between the child, still below man's estate, and the aged person, who rises above it. Grown-up ethics and mean-minded reason do not suit them; in their simplicity and their wisdom they are both close to the mysteries of the world, close to God:

> Jeanne parle, elle dit des choses qu'elle ignore.
> . . . Dieu, le bon vieux grand-père, écoute émerveillé.*

When he is with the little girl, the old man rediscovers his own childhood. In speaking of Marius' grandfather Hugo referred to the 'dawn' of a very happy old age. He also says, 'Yes, becoming a grandfather means stepping back into the dawn.'

As we have seen, the old peasants' only comfort was often their grandchildren, up until the time the little ones began to ape the adults. Hugo's success in L'Art d'être grand-père lay in his ability to give the value and depth of a myth to a social fact.

The public found this alliance of the old man and the child very touching. Dickens's Old Curiosity Shop had an immense success. In this book he makes Little Nell and her grandfather wander through England, a pair linked by the deepest affection. Misfortune has weakened the old man's mind; he ruins himself gambling; he steals from Nell in order to gamble again and he considers committing a burglary: but he touches the reader in spite of his vagaries because of his love for Nell and because of hers for him. When she dies he spends his days at her grave, and it is there that he dies in his turn. A similar pair is to be found in Hector Malot's Sans famille, which was

---

* Jeanne talks: she says things whose significance she does not understand. . . . God, the good old grandfather, listens, filled with wonder.

also exceedingly popular: a foundling, stolen from society at the threshold of life, shares the wandering existence of Vitalis, once a famous singer but now an outcast, banished from society and on the threshold of death.

Nineteenth-century literature as a whole saw old age in a far more realistic light. It dealt with aged people belonging to the upper classes – nobles, wealthy bourgeois, landowners and manufacturers – but it was also concerned with those of the exploited classes. The feudal lord-retainer bond was still dear to the bourgeoisie: in *Madame Bovary* and *Un cœur simple* Flaubert spoke of servants whose life had been nothing but one long course of self-sacrifice. But generally speaking the old people were looked upon as the subjects of their own stories. In Balzac, Zola, Dickens and the Russian novelists we scarcely ever come across any aged workers, because in fact the proletariat scarcely ever reached old age. But as we have seen, there are many old peasant characters. And the novelists also studied the effects of age in the various social categories – soldiers, employees, shopkeepers, etc. I shall make use of the abundant evidence they provide when I come to deal with old age as a personal experience. It is a question that many aged nineteenth-century writers touched upon; they spoke of their own old age, and Chateaubriand's moved him to write some of his finest pages. Being admitted to their confidence in this way helps us to understand just how elderly people feel their state.

In the twentieth century the urbanization of society continued, and one of its consequences was the disappearance of the patriarchal family. Yet it lived on for a considerable time in some parts of the French countryside. Chamson described one in *Le Crime des justes*.

Arnal, a universally respected old man commonly known as the Councillor, the very type of the righteous man, rules a large and prosperous farm in the Cévennes. He is the absolute master of his household. One of his grand-daughters, a mentally-retarded girl, gets herself with child by one of her brothers: the righteous man orders the family to kill and bury the new-born baby: they do so. Families of this kind no longer exist in France, but they are still to be found in some other countries – not long ago occurrences like that recounted by Chamson took place in rural Yugoslavia. In southern Italy, Sicily and the south of Greece a father may put his daughter to death over a question of honour. The law forbids it, but custom does not. In Corsica and Sardinia sons obey their aged father.

Because of a slight improvement in the peasants' position and of the fact that technological civilization has more or less done away with their isolation, crippled and helpless old people are certainly far less often abandoned or killed than they were in the nineteenth century. Yet in these same Mediterranean regions where the patriarchal father is most powerful it may still happen that he is helped to die when he has lost his strength. It may be, as it is among certain primitive peoples, that the descendants whom he has ruled tyrannically feel a vindictive relief in getting rid of him. But the regions in question are also those which are exceptionally poor – they are regions in which an extra mouth to be fed is a heavy burden. These are exceptional cases: on the other hand, it is quite usual in France that a son, tired of submitting to parental authority, leaves home to go and work in a town.*

Taken as a whole, the advance of industrialization has led to a progressive dissolution of the family unit. The marked ageing of the population that has been observed these last fifty years in the industrial countries has forced the community to take the place of the family. Society has adopted a policy with regard to old age that we shall examine later in this book.

In the ruling classes the balance that came into being in the nineteenth century has been maintained, both experience and inventive powers being needed. Almost all the great new and violent political movements have been led by young men – the Russian revolution, Italian fascism, nazism, the Chinese and the Cuban revolutions, the Algerian war of independence. In conservative societies elderly men have held important positions. Their function has often been merely that of a representative figure, as in the case of the presidents of the republic in France.† But a certain number of

---

* In one of his *Bloc-Notes* in the autumn of 1969, Mauriac spoke of the harshness of the aged peasants' life. 'I remember an old tenant in one of our farms whose children made him work to the utmost limits of his strength, and when he was quite incapable of going on, and was forced to stop, they grudged him the bread he ate . . . and that he had not earned. Lamenting, he agreed with their reproaches, and he longed for death.'

† Jules Grévy retired at eighty, in 1887; René Coty resigned at seventy-seven, in 1958; Paul Doumer was assassinated when he was seventy-five, in 1932; Fallières finished his term of office when he was seventy-two, in 1913. MacMahon retired at seventy-one, in 1879.

elderly men have played an active part: among others there was
Thiers, who was seventy-six when he left office in 1873. Clemenceau
was seventy-seven when he took power in 1917. Churchill was eighty-
one and Adenauer eighty-seven when they retired. Other men, such
as Stalin, Mao Tse-tung and Ho Chi Minh have grown old in power
in those countries where revolution had triumphed. At present the
rulers of the developing countries are usually young: the Emperor
Haile Selassie is an exception; he is only one year younger than de
Gaulle. In the rest they are often aged – de Gaulle, Franco, Tito,
Salazar.* But they are helped by younger men: in France the average
age of ministers is not very high. In 1968 that of the deputies was
fifty-five and of the senators sixty-three. Within the political parties,
as within the nations, there is a sharing of power between the old and
the middle-aged man: generally speaking the young have little
influence.

A striking fact, and one that I shall deal with at length later,
though it must be mentioned here, is that the standing of old age has
been markedly lowered since the notion of experience has been
discredited. Modern technocratic society thinks that knowledge
does not accumulate with the years, but grows out of date. Age
brings disqualification with it: age is not an advantage. It is the
values associated with youth that are esteemed.

Because of the mass of documentary evidence that we have on the
present state of the aged, that provided by literature is only of minor
interest; and in any case it does not amount to much. Proust, whose
essential subject is the adventure of time lost and time recovered, has
a great deal to say about old age and he says it very well; but he is an
exception. In *Les Faux-monnayeurs* Gide makes the old La Pérouse
say, 'Why do books have so little to say about old people? I believe it
is because the old can no longer write them and because when one is
young one does not bother with the old. An elderly man – he no
longer interests anyone at all.' It is true that if an old man is dealt
with in his subjective aspect he is not a good hero for a novel; he is
finished, set, with no hope, no development to be looked for; as far
as he is concerned it is all over and death already dwells within, so
nothing that can happen to him is of any importance. Then again, a
novelist can identify himself with a man younger than himself
because he has already passed through that age; but he only knows
aged people from the outside. He therefore usually gives them only

* Written in 1968.

minor parts, and his portraits of them are often sketchy or conventional. The twentieth century has inherited the clichés of those that went before it. On the social, psychological and biological planes the notion of ageing has grown richer with the course of time; yet the stereotypes go on and on. It does not matter if they are contradictory: they are so worn that people repeat them and nobody minds – nobody pays any attention. Old age is an autumn, filled with ripe fruit: it is also a barren winter, and we hear of its coldness, snow and frost. It has the sweet gentleness of a lovely evening. But it is also associated with the dark sadness of twilight. The image of 'the dear old man' lives quite happily with that of the 'cross-grained ancient'. There is one myth that has grown remarkably in our days: it is that of the detachment peculiar to old age. Montherlant, who has always affected a scornfully remote attitude towards things and people, attributes this detachment to the king in *La Reine Morte*, an aged man whom the author in his commentary describes as 'gradually separating himself from the human state'. He sees nobility of character in Ferrante's clear-minded indifference. 'As far as I am concerned, everything is repetition, reiteration, a return to the same old theme. I spend my days rebeginning what I have already done and not rebeginning it so well. The things I have succeeded in and the things I have failed in all taste the same to me now. And men too, they all seem to me far too much alike. . . . One after another things leave me behind, abandon me.'

'The bow of my mind is unstrung. Reading what I have written I ask, "Who did this?" Those things I did understand, I understand no longer. And what I had learnt I have forgotten. I am dying, and it seems to me that everything is still to do and that I am at the same stage as I was when I was twenty.'

'I also have to try to make people believe I still have some feelings, whereas I no longer have any left. The world touches me so lightly that I am hardly aware of it.'

'At my age you lose the desire to concern yourself with other people. Now there is nothing but a vast "What do I care?" that for me overspreads the whole world.'

The chief character in Vailland's novel *La Loi* is a man of seventy-two – Don Cesare, a wealthy and respected landowner. He reads a great deal, collects antiques, and is writing the history of an ancient Greek city that existed in the part of Italy where he lives. He has splendid health; he is still the best shot in the neighbourhood and a tireless hunter of girls – he has had almost all the village maiden-heads and he lives surrounded by women, one of whom shares his bed. But he has long since learnt to *dissociate* himself. Tormenting his heirs no longer amuses him because he knows that human servility has no bounds. His life seems to be the same as it has always been. He goes to bed with Elvire, but he does not speak to her and he caresses her only occasionally. He shoots, but 'his eye does not even light up'. He talks, but 'his words sound in an unresponding world'. He still gazes at his antiques, but he no longer takes notes. He is devoid of love, devoid of hatred, devoid of desire; and he feels that he is like the unemployed who stand doing nothing all day long in the village square. It would seem that although Vailland was still young he was beginning to feel this 'dissociation' that he takes to be a mark of an individual's 'quality', and to feel it personally.

I must speak of the very particular part played by old age in what has been called the theatre of the absurd. In Ionescu's *Les Chaises* we see an old couple imprisoned in their blown-up, delirious memories of a past that they do their best to bring back to life. They give a party to which nobody comes; they welcome invisible guests, giving them chairs, moving about among them, bumping into them; and all the time more and more chairs come on to the stage. It is the very reality that their wandering minds call up – the brilliant soirées and fashionable gatherings – which is shown to be absurd. And when in the end they jump out of the window they do so because in losing all meaning their life makes it clear to them that it never had one.

In Beckett we find a similar indictment of life by the pitiful degradation of its end. The old pair in *End Game* who, speaking from one dustbin to another, conjure up past happiness and love amount to a condemnation of all love and all happiness. In *Krapp's Last Tape* and *Happy Days* the theme is the crumbling of memory and therefore of the whole of the life behind us; and Beckett deals with it cruelly. The recollections come in no sequence; they are maimed, spoilt, and as it were foreign. It is as though nothing had ever really happened, and out of this emptiness there emerges the present, which is no more than a senile, aimless being. The most ludicrous aspect of it all is that throughout this wreckage there is a clinging to the myth which says that old age means learning, going forward, an advance. In fact growing old means 'sliding down gently into eternal life, remembering . . . the whole of this wretched unhappiness . . . as though . . . it had never happened'.*

In his novel *Molloy* the hero is already elderly at the beginning of the book, and he sinks lower and lower; his other leg stiffens and he loses half his toes; at first, in spite of these difficulties, he can still just get about on a bicycle. Then he can no longer manage it and he drags himself along on crutches; in the end all he can do is to crawl. His chief occupation, during this gradual dissolution, is the summoning up of his memories; but they crumble, they are vague, amorphous, cloudy, and no doubt untrue. Life is only the recollection that we have of it; and recollection is nothing. This nothing takes up a space in time; time passes, although it goes nowhere; we are in perpetual movement, yet in this journey that has no goal we remain stationary. Looking at it in the light of old age we discover this truth about life, which, fundamentally, is no more than an old age hidden under so much tinsel. In Ionescu and Beckett old age does not appear as the further boundary of the human state, but, as in *King Lear*, it is that state itself at last exposed. They are not interested in the old men for themselves: they only make use of them to express their concept of mankind.

As we said at the beginning, in this chapter we have not given a general outline of the history of old age: all we have done is to describe the attitudes of historic societies towards old people and the relevant images that they have worked out for themselves. All known civilizations are marked by the contrast between an exploiting class and the classes of the exploited. The words old age cover two profoundly different kinds of reality according to whether they are applied to the one or to the other. What distorts our view of the whole is the fact that the evidence, the opinions and the books concerning the last stage of life have always been a reflection of the state of the upper classes: it is the upper classes alone that speak, and until the nineteenth century they spoke only of themselves. Our brief summary will therefore begin with a review of the situation of these privileged old people.

They belonged to an unproductive minority, and their fate depended upon the interests of the active majority. When the majority wished to avoid lawless rivalry between its members and to maintain the established order they found it convenient to choose

* *Tous ceux qui tombent*. The points of suspension are the author's.

men of a different kind to act as intermediaries, adjudicators or representative figures, men upon whose authority all could agree; and the aged obviously fulfilled these conditions.* Sometimes they had real power, sometimes they played the part that, in certain mathematical operations, is played by imaginary numbers – they are necessary for the working out of the problem, but once the answer has been reached they are eliminated. Old age was powerful in the stratified and repetitive China, in Sparta, in the Greek oligarchies, and in Rome up until the second century before Christ. It played no political part whatsoever in the periods of change, expansion or revolution. In times when property was institutionalized the ruling class respected those who owned property in so far as they were identified with that property; age was not a disqualification; and when aged men, having accumulated real estate, goods or money in the course of their lives, had become wealthy, they had great weight in public and private life.

The aim of the ruling class's ideology was to justify its behaviour. When it was ruled or influenced by old men it attributed value to great age. Some philosophers and writers linked the notion of age with that of virtue and extolled the experience that it brought. Old age was held up as the end of life in both senses of the word – its termination and its supreme completion. Any man who had accumulated years upon years of life was the living man in the highest sense of the word; he represented as it were a quintessence of being. Old age for its own sake was therefore to be honoured. Age was a qualification for certain dignities and titles. The meaning of those jubilees that were so often celebrated, particularly in Germany, was a homage to old age: the seventieth or eightieth birthdays of a musician or a philosopher were occasions for solemn rejoicings.

Yet even when a sense of right social order compelled the younger generations to acknowledge political or economic authority in the elder, they often found it irksome to submit. The young were conscious of a physical decline that they feared for themselves, and they were hostile to the old, attacking them with ridicule.† Against the myth of the old man enriched by the number of his years was set up that of the shrunken ancient, dried and shrivelled, like Tithon or

* They often have this function of intermediary or adjudicator among primitive peoples.

† This ambivalence has also been seen in some primitive communities.

the Tiburtine sibyl. Emptied of his pith, he was a diminished, mutilated being.

On the other hand, although no one ever spoke of the state of the exploited aged, it had a profound influence upon the ideas of the privileged. We have nothing but an occasional vague glimpse of it. It seems that from the middle ages up to the eighteenth century there were very few of these old people: in the country and in the towns, the workers died young. Those who survived were dependent on families usually too poor to keep them; they turned to public charity and to that of the great houses and monasteries. At certain times even these resources were closed to them; and their fate was particularly harsh at the period when Puritan capitalism was coming into existence in England and during the industrial revolution of the nineteenth century. Society never exploited them directly, inasmuch as they possessed no labour-power to sell, but nevertheless they were the victims of exploitation. In their youth and maturity, the ruling class never granted them more than was necessary to keep alive, and once they were worn out with work it abandoned them, leaving them empty-handed. They were useless and in the way; their fate was like that of the aged in primitive communities. Their prime dependence was upon their own people. Some families, moved by affection or the force of public opinion, took real care of them or at least treated them decently. But more often they were neglected: they were abandoned in an institution, pushed out of the house or even secretly put to death.

The ruling class watched these tragedies unmoved: its efforts at helping the aged poor were always derisory. From the nineteenth century onwards the numbers of the aged poor became very great and the ruling class was unable to pass them over in silence. In order to justify its brutal indifference it was forced to undervalue them. Far more than the conflict between the generations, it was the class struggle that gave the notion of old age its ambivalence.

4

Old age in present-day society

It is common knowledge that the condition of old people today is scandalous. Before examining it in detail, we must try to understand how it comes about that society puts up with it so easily. As a general rule society shuts its eyes to all abuses, scandals and tragedies, so long as these do not upset its balance; and it worries no more about the fate of the children in state orphanages, or of juvenile delinquents, or of the handicapped, than it does about that of the aged. In the last case, however, this indifference does on the face of it seem more astonishing, since every single member of the community must know that his future is in question; and almost all of them have close personal relationships with some old people. How can their attitude be explained? It is the ruling class that imposes their status upon the old, but the active population as a whole connives at it. In private life children and grandchildren rarely do much to make their elders' lot any pleasanter. Let us see, then, what the general attitude of adults and young people is towards the older generation.

A society is a whole made up of individual parts. Its members are separate, but they are united by the need for reciprocal relationships. The individuals understand one another, not inasmuch as they are all men in the abstract, but by means of the variety of their praxis. 'The basis of comprehension is a fundamental association in all under-takings: all ends, as soon as they are announced, emerge from the organic whole composed of all possible human ends.'* Reciprocity, says Sartre, implies (1) that the Other should be the means of a tran-scendent end; (2) that I should acknowledge him as a praxis at the same time that I integrate him as an object in my project as a whole; (3) that I recognize his motion towards his ends in the movement by means of which I project myself towards mine; (4) that I see myself

* Sartre, *Critique de la raison dialectique.*

as an object and as an instrument of those ends through the very act which constitutes him an objective instrument for my ends. In this relationship each steals one aspect of the real from the other and thereby shows him his boundaries: the intellectual knows himself as such when he is faced with a manual worker.

The essential requirement of reciprocity is, that basing myself upon my own teleological dimension I should apprehend the other man's. When, in pathological cases of depersonalization, the patient no longer has any connexion with his own ends, he sees men as the representatives of a species to which he does not belong. The opposite occurs in the case of the adult–old man–adult relationship. Apart from some exceptions, the old man no longer *does* anything. He is defined by an *exis*, not by a *praxis*: a being, not a doing. Time is carrying him towards an end – death – which is not *his* and which is not postulated or laid down by any project. This is why he looks to active members of the community like one of a 'different species', one in whom they do not recognize themselves. As I have said, old age arouses a biological repugnance: from a kind of self-defence one thrusts it from oneself; but this shutting out, this rejection is possible only because in this case the basic association in all undertakings does not apply.

Up to a certain point this state of the aged person is analogous to that of the child, with whom the adult does not establish any reciprocal relationship either. It is not mere chance that makes families speak of a child who is 'extraordinary for his age' and also of an old man who is 'extraordinary for his age': the extraordinariness lies in their behaving like human beings when they are either not yet or no longer men. We have seen that in many primitive communities they belong to the same age-class, and that throughout history the general attitude of the adults has been much the same towards both. But since the child is a potential active member, society ensures its own future by investing in him, whereas in its eyes the aged person is no more than a corpse under suspended sentence.

The idea of non-reciprocity is not adequate for a positive definition of the relationship between the adult and the aged. This depends upon the relationship between children and parents, and above all – since we live in a male world and since old age is primarily a male problem – upon the relationship maintained with their father by means of their mother.

According to Freud a characteristic feature of this relationship is its ambivalence.* The son respects his father, admires him, would like to identify himself with him and even take his place: this last wish gives rise to hatred and fear. The heroes of myth always rise up against their father and end by killing him. In real life the killing is symbolical. The father-image is stripped of its glamour, and when this is done the son can be reconciled with him. But the reconciliation is complete only when the son has in fact taken the father's place. Thus, says Freud, in Christianity there was a reconciliation that ended with the dethronement of the Father, Christ having become the Person of the greatest importance. Where the antagonism exists, it is not mutual; it is active in the son, taking the form of aggression and resentment, but generally speaking it does not appear in the father. This aggressive sexual resentment undoubtedly provides the framework for the development of the one-way relationship of the young with the old. (When resentment of the young by the old occurs it is no more than a secondary reaction.) The father is killed by being depreciated; but for this to be brought about, old age as such has to be discredited as well.

The characteristic mark of the adult's attitude towards the old is its duplicity. Up to a certain point the adult bows to the official ethic of respect for the aged that has, as we have seen, asserted itself during the recent centuries. But it is in the adult's interest to treat the aged man as an inferior being and to convince him of his decline. He does his best to make his father aware of his deficiencies and blunders so that the old man will hand over the running of his affairs, give up advising him and submit to a passive role. Although the pressure of public opinion forces the son to help his old parents, he means to rule them as he sees fit; and so the more he considers them incapable of managing for themselves the fewer scruples he will feel.

It is in an underhand, sly manner that the adult tyrannizes over the dependent old man. He dares not give him orders openly, for he has no right to his obedience: avoiding a frontal attack, he manipulates him. Naturally, he always says he is acting in the old man's own interest. The whole family abets him. The old man's resistance is worn down; he is overwhelmed with paralysing attentions; they treat him with ironic kindness, talking in childishly simple terms and even exchanging knowing winks over his head; they let slip wounding observations. If persuasion and artifice fail to make him yield, they do not hesitate to use lies or a bold, decisive stroke. For example,

* *Totem and Taboo* and *Moses and Monotheism.*

they will induce him to go to a rest-home, 'just to try it', and then abandon him there. The wife and the boy who are dependent on the adult can defend themselves better than the old man: the wife renders service – bed-service and the housework – and the boy will grow into a man capable of calling the adult to account; the old man will do nothing but travel downwards to decrepitude and death. He is a mere object, useless and in the way: all they want is to be able to treat him as a negligible quantity.

The interests at stake in this struggle are not solely of a practical nature: they also have a moral aspect – there is a desire that the aged should conform to the image that society has formed of them. They are required to dress themselves in a certain way and to respect outward appearances. More than in any other, it is in the sexual aspect of life that this repression makes itself felt. When the old Prince Sokolski thinks of marrying again in *The Adolescent* his family mounts guard over him; they do so out of interested motives but also because they are utterly shocked by the idea. They threaten to put him into a madhouse; in the end they keep him shut up at home: he dies of it. I have known similar tragedies in middle-class families of this century.

Daughters often feel resentment with regard to their mothers, and their attitude is much the same as that of sons to their father. The least ambivalent affection is that of a daughter for her father and of a son for his mother. They are capable of great self-sacrifice for a beloved parent who has grown old. But if they are married, the influence of the spouse often limits their generosity.

Where there is no personal connexion, adults feel a contempt not unmixed with disgust for the aged: throughout the centuries, as we have seen, comic authors have exploited this feeling. Since the younger man looks upon the ancient as a caricature of himself, he makes fun of him, so as to break the connecting bonds by means of laughter. Sadism sometimes comes into this mockery. I was taken aback in New York, when I went to the well-known show in the Bowery, where horrible old women in their eighties sing and dance, lifting up their skirts. The audience roared with laughter: what exactly was the meaning of all this mirth?

Nowadays the adults take quite another kind of interest in the aged: they have become objects of exploitation. In the United States more than anywhere else, but also in France, there are greatly increasing numbers of nursing-homes, rest-homes, residences, villages and even towns where elderly people who have the means are made to pay as much as possible for an often inadequate comfort and care.*

In extreme cases the old lose whatever they do: they are the victims of the contradictions inherent in their status. In the death-camps they were the first to be chosen for slaughter; seeing that they had no power to work they were given no chance of any kind. Yet in Vietnam the Americans 'question' them as ferociously as they do the adults, for they are as capable of giving information as the rest.

The relationship of young men and adolescents with the aged is less a reflection of the relationship with their father than of that with the grandfather: since the last century, mutual affection is often found between grandfathers and grandsons. The old people, in revolt against the adults, seem to the young fellow-victims of oppression: they feel a solidarity with them. In January 1968 it was the young who launched an indignant campaign in favour of the aged in Czechoslovakia. The gerontophilia that is found in certain young women is explained by a fixation upon the grandfather-image. (It does not exist in young men: except for pathological cases, they do not seek for their grandmother as a sexual partner, though they often do for their mother.) Yet where the grandparents are a burden for the family, the young think it unfair to have to undergo self-sacrifice to prolong their lives. In the cruel and charming Spanish film *El Cochecito* the girl waits impatiently for her grandfather's death: she wants his bedroom. This resentment often extends to all old people. The young are jealous of their economic or social privileges, and they think it would be as well if they were put on the shelf. They are less hypocritical than the adults and they express their hostile feelings more openly.

Many children love their grandparents;†and children are taught to respect the aged. Yet if they belong to the lower classes the child often tends to make fun of them, taking his revenge upon the whole oppressive adult world in the person of this weakened, peculiar and degraded grown-up. I remember at La Grillère how my cousins, imitated by my sister and me, used to make game of their old governesses; our butts were socially inferior, so the grown-ups watched us indulgently, without reproof. Vian was not so far from the truth when he spoke about an old people's fair in *L'Arrache-cœur*: here

* See Appendix II, p. 546.
† See Violette Leduc's love for her grandmother Fidéline in *La Bâtarde*. I shall refer to the relationship between grandchildren and grandparents again, and at greater length.

the aged and poor were sold at auction, and parents bought them for their children as something to have fun with.

'The least debatable of all the phenomena of our day, the surest in its progress, the easiest to foresee far ahead and perhaps the most pregnant with consequences is the ageing of the population,' says Sauvy.

The expectation of life at birth has continually increased since classical times: it was eighteen years under the Romans and twenty-five in the seventeenth century. At that period the average son was fourteen when his father died. (Presently he will be fifty-five or sixty.) Out of a hundred children, twenty-five died before they were one year old, twenty-five more before twenty, and twenty-five between twenty and forty-five. Only about ten reached the age of sixty. An eighty-year-old – whom legend would change into a centenarian – was an extraordinary exception: he was looked upon as an oracle, and his community displayed him with pride. In the eighteenth century the expectation of life in France was thirty years. For long centuries the proportion of individuals of over sixty varied very little: it was about 8·8 per cent. The ageing of the population began in France at the end of the eighteenth century, and a little later the same phenomenon was observed in some other countries. In 1851 there were ten per cent of persons aged more than sixty: there are now about eighteen per cent, or nine million four hundred thousand, of whom half live in the country. That is to say, since the eighteenth century the proportion of old people in the population has doubled. In October 1969 there were 6,300,000 persons aged over sixty-five in France, or more than twelve per cent of the population, about three fifths of them being women.* According to a report drawn up in September 1967, between 1930 and 1962 the proportion of individuals over sixty-five increased from 7·6 per cent to 10·6 per cent in the six Common Market countries, and from 7·8 per cent to 11·5 per cent in the bloc formed by the Scandinavian countries, Great Britain and Ireland. In the United States there are sixteen million people over sixty-five: this amounts to nine per cent of the population, whereas the proportion was 2·5 per cent in 1850 and 4·1 per cent in 1900. The proportion of octogenarians has doubled in France since the beginning of the century: there are now a million of them, two-thirds being women. The forecast is that this ageing will become more pronounced

* An earlier census showed two million men and 3·3 million women over sixty-five.

221

until 1980, when the number of individuals aged over sixty will amount to nineteen per cent of the population and those over sixty-five to fourteen per cent. It is thought that in 1980 the situation will become stable, for the birth-rate has risen since 1946. If the case of East Germany, where for the last twenty years large-scale emigration has partially drained the country of its younger people is not taken into account, the ageing of the population is most marked in France and Sweden. Everywhere we find the same causes – a lowering of infant mortality and a lowering of the birth-rate. In a single century infant mortality has dropped from forty per cent to 2·2 per cent. It is this fact that has raised the expectation of life to sixty-eight for men and seventy-five for women in France and to seventy-one for men and seventy-seven for women in the United States. In reality, a man who has reached adult years does not have a very much greater stretch of life before him than his ancestors: a fifty-year-old Frenchman could look forward to eighteen more years in 1805, whereas now he can reckon on twenty-two. The ageing of the population does not therefore mean that the limit of life has been thrust back very far, but rather that the proportion of elderly people is much greater. This alteration has been to the disadvantage of the proportion of the young, for that of the adults has remained more or less steady: it has all taken place, says Sauvy, as though the population had swung about a central pivot, the young being replaced by the old. This phenomenon is seen in almost all Western countries, and it is accompanied by an absolute increase in the number of inhabitants (except in Ireland, where the population has dropped).

The under-developed countries, on the contrary, have young populations. In many of them the infant mortality rate is still very high, and even in those where it has dropped, under-nourishment, inadequate medical care, and the material conditions of life in general all militate against longevity. In some of these countries half the population is under eighteen. In India there are 3·6 per cent of aged people, about 2·45 in Brazil, and 1·46 in Togoland.

In the capitalist democracies, the ageing of the population has raised new difficulties. It is 'the Mount Everest of the present-day social problems', said a British minister of health, Iain Macleod. Not only are there many more aged people than there were, but they no longer spontaneously integrate with the community: society is compelled to decide upon their status, and the decision can only be taken at governmental level. Old age has become the object of a policy.

222

Indeed, in the society of former times, made up primarily of peasants and craftsmen, livelihood and life coincided precisely: the worker lived in the place where he worked, and productive and domestic work merged into one another. For the highly-skilled craftsmen, ability increased with experience and therefore with the years. In those callings where ability declined with age there was a division of labour within the craft that allowed the work to be adapted to each man's powers. When the aged man became completely incapable of work he lived with his family, and the family saw to his maintenance. His fate was not always enviable, as we have seen. But the community did not have to worry about him.

In our day, the worker lives in one place and works in another, solely as an individual. The family has nothing to do with his productive work. The family amounts to no more than one or two couples of adults, burdened with children still unable to earn their living: with their scanty resources they cannot undertake to maintain their old parents. Yet the worker is condemned to idleness much earlier than he was formerly: his specialized task remains the same throughout the whole of his life, and it is not adapted to the capabilities of all ages.

As I have already said, at the end of the nineteenth century the aged worker in being dismissed from his job was tragically abandoned to his own devices. Society found itself compelled to take the problem in hand. It did so without resistance.

In the beginning pensions were thought of as rewards. As early as 1796 Tom Paine suggested that rewards in this form should be given to workers aged fifty. In Belgium and Holland pensions were granted to public employees in 1844. In nineteenth-century France, too, soldiers and civil servants were the first to have pensions; the Second Empire subsequently extended them to miners, seamen, arsenal workers and railwaymen. It was thought that in these dangerous callings pensions were a proper reward for many years of loyal service, and their allocation became organized and usual, so long as the two conditions of a long period of work and a given age were fulfilled.

At the end of the nineteenth century Germany experienced a rapid progress of capitalism and an important industrial expansion; at the same time socialist agitation grew stronger and more general. Bismarck saw that to counteract it the proletariat would have to be assured a minimum of security. Between 1883 and 1889 he set up a system of social insurance that was completed and extended between 1890 and 1910. It was primarily intended to cover the risk of accidents at work, but it also protected the wage-earners against the incapacity of old age. Contributions were required both from the employers and the workers, with the possibility of a state subsidy. Systems of this kind were subsequently brought into operation in Luxembourg, Romania, Sweden, Austria, Hungary and Norway. There was also another conception of retirement, one in which the protection of the workers was financed by funds arising from taxation. This was the system that was adopted in Denmark in 1891 and in New Zealand in 1898; in the United Kingdom it made a beginning in 1908 and it was fully established there in 1925. In France the law of 5 April 1910 dealing with the retirement of peasants and workers was only partially applied – the courts dared not compel either the wage-earners or the employers to pay their contributions. The law of 5 April 1928, modified by that of 30 April 1930, was the first serious attempt at ensuring retirement for the aged workers. It was a hybrid system of capitalization and apportionment. In 1933, when the ILO adopted the thirty-fifth to fortieth conventions on the retirement of the aged, there were already twenty-eight countries, including six outside Europe, that had already set up pension schemes. A French law of 14 May 1941 granted the worst-paid workers a special allowance; and the ordinance of 19 October 1945 set up old-age insurance.

To begin with pensions were given to wage-earners in commercial and industrial undertakings: they should have been extended to the population as a whole, but the opposition of the non-wage-earning middle classes wrecked the plan. In 1956 a *Fonds national de solidarité* was brought into being, and at present eighty per cent of the people in France draw retirement pensions. In 1964, out of the hundred and twelve states who were members of the ILO, sixty-eight had retirement schemes. Generally speaking, a national system of social security is too burdensome for a developing country. Ireland has no social insurance but only public assistance.

The state sets the age at which a worker has the right to a retirement pension; this is also the age at which public and private employers dismiss their workers, and it is therefore that at which the individual passes from the active to the inactive category. When is this change to take place? What total must the contributions have reached? To decide upon this, society has to take two factors into account: its own interests and those of the pensioners.

Of the capitalist countries, there are three that look upon it as an imperative duty to ensure decent conditions for all citizens; these are Denmark, Norway and Sweden. They are sparsely inhabited; their political life goes on without violent disagreements; and in the midst of a liberal capitalistic system there has grown up a kind of socialism. In order to guarantee the fullest possible protection for all, big incomes are heavily taxed and luxury goods pay high duties. The aged profit by these arrangements, particularly in Sweden, where twelve per cent of the population are elderly and where their average age of seventy-six is the highest in Europe. The first laws on old age date only from 1930, but now the insurance system covers the entire population, and it is continually being improved. Whatever his resources, every citizen draws a pension from the set retiring age of sixty-seven. The basic minimum is 4,595 Swedish crowns* for a single person and 7,150 for a couple. In 1960 a system of supplementary pensions came into force: the retired person draws two-thirds of his average annual wage, calculated according to the fifteen best-paid years of his life. Civil servants and regular soldiers retire at sixty-five. Some other people stop work at the same age, covering themselves for two years by private insurance. But as work is adapted to the various ages, never calling for undue exertion, they usually prefer to stay at their jobs until the end. The position is much the same in Norway, where the age-limit is seventy, and in Denmark, where it is from sixty-five to sixty-seven for men and from sixty to sixty-two for women.

It is completely different in the other capitalist countries. Almost their only consideration is in the interests of the economy, that is to say of capital, and not those of the individual people. The retired are removed from the labour-market early; they constitute a burden, and it is one that the profit-based societies take upon themselves in a mean-minded spirit. Allowing workers to go on as long as they can and then assuring them of a decent existence is one right solution. Retiring them early and guaranteeing them a satisfactory standard of living is another. But the bourgeois democracies, in taking from the workers the possibility of working, condemn the greater part of them to poverty. Their policy with regard to old age is scandalous, particularly in France. Just after the war the government set itself to raise the birth-rate, and a large proportion of the budget was devoted to family allowances: the aged were sacrificed. The authorities were

* One Swedish crown = 1s 8d (1970).

sufficiently aware of this to set up a commission to inquire into the problems of old age on 8 April 1960; the commission, presided over by Monsieur Laroque, produced its report; and nothing whatsoever was done.

The retiring-age for both sexes is sixty-five in Belgium, West Germany, Luxemburg and Holland; in Austria, the United Kingdom and Greece it is sixty-five for men and sixty for women. The limit is usually lower for miners: and this often applies to the army, the police, civil aviation, transport and primary education. In France the age is fifty-five for the police and the primary-school teachers, who may delay their retirement until sixty if they wish: it is sixty for a great many state employees, particularly for those in education, and sixty-five for some others – those who work in the Seine prefecture, for example. The regulations of many private firms fix the age of retirement at sixty-five: a very few (three per cent as against ninety-seven per cent) prefer sixty. Sometimes there is no rule, and the employees leave at about sixty-five.

Some systems proceed on the assumption that old age is the equivalent of a disability and the pension of assistance granted to the needy: the beneficiary is forbidden to undertake paid work of any kind. In Belgium, up until 1968, the pensioner was only allowed to do sixty hours of paid work a month: he may now do ninety. Other countries feel that it is the duty of society to look after the aged workers. Pension and work may be combined without any restrictions in France, Germany, Luxemburg, Holland and Switzerland. When they can, the retired take advantage of this state of affairs. An inquiry carried out in France in July 1946 by the *Institut national d'études démographiques* and covering 2,500 persons found that twenty-nine per cent of them worked an average of twenty-five hours a week, sometimes at jobs related to their former calling: schoolteachers gave lessons, and a tax-inspector worked as a private financial adviser. It has been calculated that at present more than a third of the people over sixty and a quarter of those over sixty-five do some kind of work to make both ends meet, particularly the women, who go out charring. They are paid less than the union rate.

The last fifty years have seen a general diminution in the aged labour-force. Between 1931 and 1951, a period during which the proportion of old people was increasing everywhere, the numbers of aged workers dropped. In France, one of the countries with the highest proportion, the percentage of workers in the aged population fell from 59·4 to 36·1; in Italy, from 72 to 33; and in Switzerland from 62·5 to 50·7. It is true that at present the number of people in their seventies and eighties is higher than it was. But even if we look at the sixty-five to sixty-nine age-group we see a drop in the proportion of workers. Active old men are found among land-workers, heads of firms, small employers, craftsmen and independent workers; and women in agriculture, domestic and health services, and commerce. But in industry age brings with it a loss of value for the executives and office-staff as well as for the workers.

Employers dislike the idea of taking on elderly people: a glance at the Situations Vacant pages of a newspaper will make this perfectly obvious. In almost all countries the stated age limit is from forty to forty-five. In America, twenty-three states have laws that forbid all discrimination on account of age; but the employers give semi-official instructions to the agencies, and these instructions are taken into account. According to an inquiry carried out in New York in 1953, ninety-four agencies regarded the aged seeker for work as their worst enemy: 'He talks too much, nothing suits him, he is set in his ways, he lacks discipline and self-control.' According to another, which covered eight important American cities in 1963, one-fifth of the employment agencies fixed the age-limit at thirty-five and one-third at forty-five. In Belgium and Austria there are public labour-exchanges that will find jobs only for those under forty. In the United Kingdom fifty per cent of the requests that the agencies receive from employers lay down that the candidate must be under forty. In France research workers looking into forty-one thousand offers found that thirty per cent were directed at people under forty, forty per cent at those between twenty and twenty-nine, and thirty per cent at those between fifty and sixty-five. Ninety-seven per cent of the advertisements in American papers set forty as the limit. Another inquiry states that eighty-eight per cent of the advertisements in France require the applicant to be under forty; and in Belgium the same is found in eighty per cent. This discrimination is almost universally observed, even in times of full employment. Of course, when two firms combine or when for some reason there is a reduction of staff, it is the engineers, executives and office-workers of over forty who are dismissed. The bigger and the more streamlined the firm, and the faster its rhythm of work, then the greater its eagerness to get rid of the aged. Factories in the country keep their workers longer than those in the industrial part of a town. Elderly women suffer even more from this discrimination than men, although their expectation of life is greater. This, it may be added, is no new phenomenon. In 1900 a woman of forty-five or a man of fifty had the greatest difficulty in finding a job. In 1930, both in New York and the States in general, between twenty-five and forty per cent of firms only took on workers below a given age: in 1948, thirty-nine per cent were doing the same. The fact is very general.

A consequence of this is that many elderly people are out of work long before they retire. In critical times, when the total number of unemployed rises, the proportion of aged unemployed drops; it increases in periods of full employment, the residual unemployment falling upon old workers. And once they are out of a job they cannot find another. A 1955 report of the ILO states that the average age of those who had been unemployed for twenty-four months was over fifty. There is no necessary connexion between the extent of the unemployment and the capacities of the workers. Labourers and specialized workers are the most affected, but highly-skilled jobs are also done away with by the modernization of plant; the young men monopolize the office-work, leaving the laborious and unhealthy tasks for the old, who are compelled to lower their demands with regard to pay and the nature and conditions of work. Often enough they cannot bring themselves to it straight away, and when they do agree they are economically, socially and spiritually weakened.

What are the reasons that the employers bring forward? Are they sound? Many inquiries have tried to find the answer to these questions.

In France, Fernand Boverat studied two hundred and fifty firms employing a total of sixty-eight thousand seven hundred workers. The majority of the employers said that age brought about a decline in muscular strength, hearing and sight; a majority also spoke of a diminution in dexterity and in resistance to fatigue, cold, heat, dampness, noise and vibration. According to another inquiry carried out by the IFOP in 1961, employers were of the opinion that a worker began 'to age' at fifty; he lost much of his efficiency because he could no longer adapt himself to new situations; he had less strength and he was slower. These failings were not counterbalanced by his experience, qualifications and his conscientiousness, in all of which, however, he was superior to the young men. Women's capabilities declined faster than men's. The time of ageing varied according to the calling: miners aged sooner than any, at forty-six or forty-seven, and book-keepers later, at about sixty. Elderly executives had less drive than the young. In all callings, the older workers lacked interest in novelty and routine was bad for their output.

English inquiries find that after the age of fifty workers have the same output and fewer accidents. But after sixty-five, twenty-five per cent of the men (and after sixty, forty per cent of the women) suffer from pathological conditions that affect their mobility, half of them being caused by cardio-vascular diseases. A recent investigation in Great Britain showed that eighty-five per cent of the retired people of sixty-five or over who were examined were in fact incapable of carrying on with their work, even though they might say they could.

A seminar held at Heidelberg in December 1966 came to much the same conclusions. One speaker said that the proportion of older workers who could no longer produce the same output or carry out the same work as before had recently increased.

But this point has often been denied. There is no very great difference between the powers of a man of sixty and another of fifty. Muscular strength reaches its maximum at twenty-seven: at sixty it has diminished by 16·5 per cent – that is to say, by no more than seven per cent in comparison with men of between forty-eight and fifty-two. Speed in manual skills changes little between fifteen and fifty. Between sixty and sixty-nine the time needed for carrying out an operation of this kind increases by fifteen per cent.

It is true that these are academic figures: they refer only to healthy subjects, and age often brings with it pathological disturbances. It is more interesting to look at the results of inquiries covering clearly-defined groups of individuals. In one such inquiry in 1951, medical men examined five thousand industrial wage-earners in Norway, and they were of the opinion that 82·6 per cent of those from sixty to sixty-four were fit for full-time normal work, 7·3 per cent for light work, 2·3 per cent for part-time work, and that 7·7 per cent should have retired. The respective proportions for those between sixty-five and sixty-nine were 81·5 per cent, 7·7 per cent, 2·1 per cent and 8·7 per cent; and for those over seventy, 80·7 per cent, 4·1 per cent, 2·8 per cent and 12·4 per cent. In Sweden, manual workers and office-staff carry on satisfactorily until the age of sixty-seven. Medical research in Birmingham showed that total disability resulting from chronic disease or infirmity amounted to only twenty per cent at the age of seventy and to ten per cent at sixty-five.

According to the very important work done at the Nuffield

Foundation in England, the deficiencies of old age are very largely compensated for and overcome up until very late in life. A good example of this is provided by the Yorkshire textile mills: the folding and the setting-up of the threads is work calling for great exactness, but many elderly women do it perfectly well in spite of their poor eyesight – their skill is in their fingertips.

A gerontologist gave me the following account: bus-drivers were submitted to sight tests; there were some whose visual accommodation was so inadequate that in theory it made them incapable of dealing with the glare of headlights at night. Yet when they were observed on the road, it was found that many of them drove in the dark as well as those whom the laboratory had passed as fit for night driving, or even better. They had their own methods of avoiding dazzle and of finding where they were on the road. Their shortcomings were cancelled out by skill, experience and a way of coping with their deficiencies – of tricking them, as it were. That is why laboratory results should not always be trusted. It is only in the field work that valid comparisons are to be found.

An English report of 1947 which covered 11,154 workers over sixty-five, established that except in very arduous trades such as mining there was little difference in output between workers of fifty and those of fifty-nine, or between those of sixty and those of sixty-nine. Efficiency remained very high. At the London gerontological congress of 1954, Patterson, comparing sixty-year-olds with younger workers, said, 'Their output is about the same in quantity, and the quality of their work is higher. Seventy would be a better retiring-age than sixty.' What is more, an inquiry dealing with eighteen thousand office-workers showed that far from increasing, absenteeism diminished with age.

The Nuffield Foundation, studying fifteen thousand elderly workers, found that during the last war fifty-nine per cent of them had carried on with their earlier occupations and that they worked as well as they had before the age of sixty-five. According to the Foundation, aged workers are at a disadvantage when their job requires continual change of motion, when it calls for strength, and when time is strictly measured, as it is in chain-production. Those tasks that demand knowledge and care and that also leave a certain margin of time are suitable for them. The quality of their output is widely acknowledged in industry. They are far more conscientious in their work. The gains and the losses with age are reckoned to be these:

INCREASE	DECREASE
pleasure in work, steadiness of rhythm, punctuality, method, close and watchful attention, willingness, discipline, prudence, patience, conscientiousness.	sight and hearing, manual strength and precision, physical resistance and suppleness, speed of rhythm, memory, imagination, creativity, adaptability, general attentiveness, diligence, energy, initiative, drive, sociability.

It is generally admitted that old people find it hard to learn new forms of work. In 1950 an English inquiry showed that they were very good at doing the tasks they were accustomed to, even if these tasks were arduous, but that they adapted poorly to change.

But this point too is open to discussion. During the war Canada, the United States and England used great numbers of elderly workers in their factories: many found themselves confronted with work that was completely new to them, and yet they carried it out perfectly well. Many experts think that they are capable of acquiring new skills. Trams were replaced by buses in south London in 1953, and the drivers had to change over: ninety-three per cent of those between fifty-six and sixty managed to do so, only taking between one and four weeks more than the younger men, while forty-four per cent made the change in three weeks, like the others. Sixty-three per cent of those between sixty-one and sixty-seven succeeded. The elderly Yorkshire women I mentioned before easily acquired the rapid reflexes needed for sewing by machine.

Yet old people do have certain disadvantages to overcome during the learning period. Their nervousness and anxiety bring about failure of memory, and this grows worse when they are in competition with the young. When he thought he was the only one being examined, a man of seventy-two managed tests as well as a man of thirty-five: when he knew he had a younger rival, his inferiority complex caused him to fail. Out of dread of making mistakes old people grow set in a negative attitude. They have a tendency to persevere in their errors, and the set notions that they have already acquired have a paralysing effect. Workers who have a knowledge of electricity find it harder than former miners to follow lectures on electronics: they are worried by the comparison of electric current with the flow of water. The aged are also often wanting in interest and curiosity. As we have seen, they find it hard to acquire new 'sets', new attitudes of mind. At the beginning their decisions are slower than those of the young and their reaction-time is therefore longer. But they often overcome these difficulties. Repetition is to their advantage: in a factory they will go on performing the movements they have learnt all day long and in the end they will do so automatically. Here again we must not trust too much to laboratory results: they are not always applicable to everyday work.

Some of the failings of old age can easily be mitigated: sometimes a worker can be readapted to his task simply by being provided with spectacles or a seat that will allow him to work sitting down rather than standing up. But there are very few firms that will do this. A worker generally has his job changed at the first sign of weakening. He is appointed door-keeper, overseer, checker, book-keeper, store-man, or he issues the tools. He is in fact reduced in rank. He earns less. It affects him in his pay and in his mind. What is more, mechanization has reduced the number of these jobs, and the old worker is often condemned to unemployment.

All these inquiries and the example of the Scandinavian countries prove that the idleness forced upon the aged is not something that necessarily happens in the course of nature but that it is the consequence of a deliberate social choice. Technical progress disqualifies the aged worker, and the training that he had forty years before is usually inadequate, though a suitable retraining might improve it. Then again, illness and fatigue make him long for rest: but these are not the direct consequences of ageing. If he had taken care of his strength, a man of sixty-five could easily perform tasks that are too hard for one who has been overworked. We can conceive a society that would require less effort and fewer working hours during their middle years, so that they would not be fit for the scrap-heap at the age of sixty or sixty-five: this is to some degree the case in Norway and Sweden. But in our society, which thinks only of profit, the employers of course prefer an intensive exploitation of the wage-earners: when they are worn out they are tossed aside and others are taken on, the employers leaving it to the state to provide the rejects with charity.

This whole discussion would be pointless if the retired worker drew a comfortable pension. If this were the case we should merely be glad that he was given the right to a rest as early in life as possible. But since he is in fact condemned to poverty, his dismissal looks more like a denial of the right to work. Far from taking a rest, he is often compelled, as we have seen, to take on unpleasant and ill-paid jobs.

As to the proper age for retirement, there are many opinions that can be defended, and we shall compare them later. But an important increase in pensions is essential.

When we look into the way these pensions are distributed at present the first thing that strikes us is its injustice. For there are special systems that were retained in 1945; there are complementary systems in operation parallel with the general rule. In a lecture on 7 December 1966, Monsieur Laroque said, 'The inequalities between the present systems are shocking: some provide perfectly adequate pensions whereas others are very small, while at the same time there is no rational justification for these differences. The reasons for their existence are primarily historical. But it is very hard to put this right, since it is economically impossible to raise all the rates to the level of the highest, and it is psychologically impossible to ask the generous systems to reduce their terms.'

The following table will give an idea of the system's complexity.

THE RESOURCES OF THE AGED

A person of sixty may be looked after either by
the *Sécurité sociale* if he has established rights,
or by the public organizations (*département*,* town hall) if he has no social security rights.

The *Sécurité sociale* may provide
1 an old-age pension
2 an 'aged wage-earner's allowance'
3 an annuity
4 a supplementary allowance
5 a widow's or widower's pension
6 a 'mother of a family' allowance.

Old-age pension
The condition for obtaining this is to have contributed to the *Sécurité sociale* for thirty years: in this case the full pension is drawn. It may be obtained after fifteen years of contribution, but the payment is in proportion to the contributions made. It may only be drawn after the sixtieth birthday. It is usually applied for at the age of sixty-five, since the rate increases by four per cent a year after the sixtieth birthday.

Examples: 20 per cent pension at 60
24 per cent   61
28 per cent   62

* Roughly the equivalent of the county (trs.).

233

32 per cent	63
36 per cent	64
40 per cent	65, etc.

Amount of the pension
This depends on
1 the length of the period of insurance
2 the average yearly pay
3 the age at which the application is made.

Average yearly pay
This is reckoned by the pay that appears from the contributions paid during the ten preceding years.
either at the age of sixty
or at the date of the request for the pension.

The size of the pension therefore depends upon the applicant's age.

The rate of the pension varies according to the pay that was subject to contribution.

Retirement and other pensions are adjusted on 1 April every year, the adjustment being related to the rise in wages.

Maximum annual rate, 5,472 francs:* this is a forty per cent pension at the age of sixty-five. There is no upper limit for private resources.

The aged worker's allowance
Conditions:
1 to have reached the age of sixty-five, or of sixty in the case of incapacity for work
2 to be French or the subject of a country that has signed an agreement with France
3 to reside in French territory or in a state formerly under French suzerainty or a French overseas possession
4 to produce evidence of having worked for twenty-five years during one's life
5 to have contributed to social insurance if these years of work occurred after 31 December 1944.

'Mothers of families' allowance
Conditions:
1 To have reached the age of sixty-five, or of sixty in the case of incapacity for work
2 to be French or the subject of a country that has signed an agreement with France
3 to reside in French territory

* The franc was worth about 1s 6d in 1969 (trs.).

234

4 to have brought up five children of French nationality for at least nine years.

Note: in the case of the aged workers' and the mothers of families' allowances the contributions are insufficient, and therefore an upper limit for private resources is applied.

Maximum private resources for a couple: 5,400 francs a year; for a single person, 3,600 francs a year (including the allowance).

Supplementary allowance: Fonds national de solidarité

These are paid in the case of the two allowances mentioned above. The annual rate is eight hundred francs. The maxima and minima remain the same. The upper limit cannot be exceeded.

As far as medical care and hospitalization are concerned, the aged, whether they have retirement or other pensions or allowances, are taken in charge by the *Sécurité sociale*. The amount paid by the *Sécurité sociale* varies from seventy per cent to eighty per cent and a hundred per cent, according to the length and the seriousness of the disease. The *ticket modérateur** remains the responsibility of the insured person. The *Fonds d'action sociale* of the *Sécurité* may be applied to through the *Service social* for reimbursement of the *ticket modérateur*, and in case of need for the provision of help in cash as well.

Sécurité sociale annuities

Conditions:

1 to be sixty-five years of age
2 to have paid contributions for five years or less than fifteen
3 if payments have been made for less than five years the applicant can only claim repayment of his contributions.

Amount of the annuity: about ten per cent of half the contributions paid.

Note: at present there are old people who cannot claim a pension, an allowance or an annuity, either because they have worked without contributing to the *Sécurité sociale*, or because they have worked only periodically, or because they are widows with no right to a reversionary pension, or because they have brought up several children and have therefore been unable to work. The essential fact is that they have not acquired social insurance rights.

In these cases, therefore, application is made to the public services, which are:

1 the *départements*
2 the town halls
3 the *Assistance publique*

* The sum that is not paid by the *Sécurité sociale*.

4 specialized charities
5 private charities.

Special old-age allowance: this is paid by the *Caisse des Dépôts et Consignations.*
Conditions:
    1 not to come under the *Sécurité sociale*
    2 not to exceed a certain limit of private resources
    3 to own no property
    4 to be in receipt of no maintenance allowance for children.
Rate of the special allowance: 1,300 francs a year.
Upper limit of resources (including the special allowance): 3,600 francs a year for a single person, 5,400 francs a year for a couple.

This income being so small, the *Bureaux d'Aide sociale* provide additional help in the form of:
    1 grant for rent* (half the main rent)
    2 heating grant (from 150 to 180 francs a year)
    3 monthly grant in cash (from 50 to 150 francs)
    4 coupons for gas and electricity, food parcels, old people's meals, reductions on transport. Sponsorship by private charitable organizations
    5 free medical assistance.

*Increase of retirement and other pensions, and 'third person allowances',†
granted either* by the *Sécurité* or the *départements.*
Conditions:
    1 to have reached the age of sixty-five, or, in the case of acknowledged incapacity for work, of sixty
    2 to be unable to carry out the ordinary activities of life alone (various infirmities).
This increase is paid whatever the amount of the pension or allowance.
Annual rate: 6,700 francs.
This increase is granted for the beneficiary's lifetime only.
Medical assistance in this case is a hundred per cent.

Complementary retirement pensions
These are paid at the age of sixty-five.

    * This is granted only if the lodging is unfurnished and the rent less than two hundred francs.
    † If a very sick pensioner is in need of continual care the service concerned pays a pension to the person – whether a member of his family or not – who looks after him. This is the 'third person' in relation to the pair formed by the sick man and the organization that provides his pension.

Conditions:
   to have worked for ten years in the same sector (commerce, industry, the professions).
In these cases the employer is associated with his sector's retirement fund. (Contributions paid by the employer and the worker.)
The complementary pension may be paid at the age of sixty in the event of incapacity for work.
A widow may draw the complementary pension at the age of fifty.
The rate of the complementary pension varies according to the total of the contributions paid.

Executives' retirement pension
   1 paid at sixty-five or, in the event of incapacity, at sixty.
   2 the conditions are the same as for the complementary pension.
The *Service social* is not concerned with this class of elderly persons. The income is relatively comfortable, since it includes the *Sécurité sociale*'s old-age pension as well as the executive's pension.

There are two points that should be emphasized: the retired person of sixty-five draws only forty per cent of his pay; and the pension is calculated according to what he received during the last ten years, which is not always the period of his highest earnings. It would be proper to refer to the highest or at least to the average pay. If the employer demotes the worker on the pretext of readapting him, his pension is thereby reduced – a flagrant injustice. Again, the upward adjustment of pensions is far from equalling the rise in the cost of living, since it amounts to no more than ten per cent a year. Whereas the guaranteed minimum industrial wage is 567·61 francs a month for a forty-hour week, the amount granted to the aged is less than half that: the latest decree published in the *Journal officiel** raised the minimum income of the aged to 225 francs a month, or 7·30 francs a day: a million of them have this sum and no more – two and a half times less than the keep of a common-law prisoner. One and a half million live on less than 320 francs a month. In other words, about half the aged population is reduced to beggary. Old people who live alone are the most wretchedly unhappy. There are very many more widows than widowers, and they amount to between seventy and eighty per cent of the *économiquement faibles*, the people with inadequate resources, with whom the social assistance services have to deal. Research carried out by the *Caisse interprofessionelle*

* Written at the end of 1969.

237

paritaire des Alpes on 6,234 retired people between fifty* and ninety-four showed an average monthly income of 280 francs for a single person and 380 for a couple, some of the pensioners doing light work. For one-fifth of them the sum dropped to two hundred francs. Fifteen per cent did not even buy a paper, because it was too dear.

Children very rarely help their parents: two-thirds of the old people receive no assistance from them at all. Sometimes the parents bring them before the courts to obtain maintenance: but even if they win, the sum awarded is often unpaid. Aged parents suffer all the more from this refusal since official assistance is withheld if it is thought that their children are in a position to maintain them. This again is a scandal: the officials do not take into account what the children do in fact give but rather what they could provide.

A typical case is that which was reported in *Le Journal du dimanche* for 17 November 1968 under the heading 'Alone in Paris at the age of seventy-five with 317 francs a month'.† Madame R. had been a waitress and dish-washer in various restaurants. She had stopped work at the age of sixty-eight because it was too hard for her. Her former employers had not entered her name with the social insurance and she found herself with a retirement pension of 180 francs a quarter. Her savings allowed her to hold out for four years. Then, rendered desperate by having to live on sixty francs a month, she spoke to a neighbour on a bench in the Place des Vosges, and this woman advised her to see a social assistant. The assistant obtained 870 francs a quarter for her, by means of pension adjustments, and eighty francs as a grant for rent. She lives in the attic of a house in the Marais – three storeys of handsome staircase, then two half-floors of steep, narrow steps. No gas or electricity in her tiny room: she lights and heats the room with paraffin. The tap is at the back of a niche that is reached by a step: for a person who is not very fit it is an acrobatic feat to get down it carrying a bucket. The lavatories are at the other end of the house: she has to go down a half-floor, go up another and then climb fifteen more steep steps. 'It is a nightmare for me,' said Madame R. 'Sometimes in winter, when I am not very steady on my feet, I stay there leaning against the wall, wondering whether I shall ever manage to get down again.' Every quarter she pays 150 francs rent. 'That's the main thing, because my neighbours want to get my room back and they're trying to make me go to the

* The retirement pension can be taken early if there is incapacity for work.
† An inquiry carried out by Annie Coudray.

238

institution. But I'd rather die.' This leaves her 240 francs a month, or eight francs a day. She scarcely heats the room at all: in winter she stays late in bed and she spends her days in shops or churches. Sometimes she goes to the cinema – to one of those that have a cheap matinée before one o'clock – and she sits on for two or three showings: she goes by underground and comes back on foot. She spends almost nothing on clothes: every spring she has a ten-year-old overcoat cleaned. She has had two 'grants' of shoes and one for a skirt. She buys three pairs of lisle thread stockings a year, at 9·90 francs a pair. She eats very little: three two-franc steaks, three or four francsworth of gruyère cheese and five pounds of potatoes a week. She often dines off an apple with a little sugar and butter. She drinks three and a half pints of wine a month and about a pound of coffee a week. She has two nephews whom she helped when they were children. But they have settled in the provinces and she never sees them. Almost every Sunday she has lunch with a friend. She takes a little cake, and the friend – who has a real cooker and can make dishes that Madame R. could not possibly make on her paraffin stove – gives her what is left over to warm up the next day. She is not bored, she says. She walks about a great deal; she reads the headlines at the newspaper stand, and neighbours give her yesterday's paper. When she can she goes to ceremonies in Paris: she was at Charles Munch's funeral, but she did not like to go in because of her old coat. The darkest side of her life is the question of housing. Friends had promised to keep her a two-roomed flat with a kitchen in their house at Mantes. She dreamt of it. But they died and their children let the little place to other tenants.

Now that we have considered this particular case, the following figures, drawn up by a social assistant in 1967, will have more meaning.

EXAMPLES OF RESOURCES AND LIVING CONDITIONS

medical assistance undertaken by the *Sécurité sociale* or the *Assistance publique*

Age	marital status	amount of pension	housing	rent	social assistance
63. Very sick	single	260 francs a month	One room and kitchen. No conveniences. W.C. in the yard	70 francs a month	100 francs a month. Daily average 9·06 francs

239

Age	marital status	amount of pension	housing	rent	social assistance
76. Serious heart disease	widow	210 francs a month	One room and kitchen. Conveniences	90 francs a month	120 francs a month. Daily average 8 francs
82. Worked until the age of 77	single	230 francs a month	One hotel room since 1930	80 francs a month	150 francs a month. Daily average 10 francs
78. Mentally deficient	single	180 francs a month	One room in a hotel kept by Algerians	100 francs a month	150 francs a month. Daily average 7·66 francs
Husband 73, wife 74	husband incurably ill	two pensions 460 francs a month	Two rooms and kitchen	90 francs a month	100 francs a month. Daily average 7·83 francs each
Husband 70, wife 69. Three children	wife hemiplegiac	690 francs a month	Two rooms. Conveniences	200 francs a month	children's allowance 150 francs a month. Daily average for each person 10·66 francs
72. Domestic servant for 50 years	single	280 francs a month	One room and kitchen; W.C. Evicted, then rehoused	130 francs a month	60 francs rent aid; 100 francs social aid. Daily average 11·33 francs
82	war widow 1914–18	320 francs a month	Two rooms. No conveniences	100 francs a month	90 francs a month. Daily average 10 francs
64. Incurable bone disease	single	160 francs a month	One room, storage space, kitchen	60 francs a month	150 francs a month. Daily average 8·33 francs
70. A son of 40, mentally incurable	single	mother 210 francs a month. Son 180 francs a month. Total 390 francs	Two rooms. Fair conveniences	80 francs a month	150 francs a month. Daily average 7·66 francs each

240

An income of seven to ten francs a day to cover food, clothing and heating means being condemned to under-nourishment, to cold, and to all the diseases that they bring with them; it means being driven to unworthy, humiliating courses – when a market is over and the street-sweepers are busy, neat, cleanly-dressed old women may be seen searching through the leavings and filling their baskets. This is particularly striking at Nice, where there are a great many elderly people: a flight of little old women swoops on the half-rotted fruit and vegetables. Research on old people living alone in Marseilles and Saint-Etienne showed that ten per cent of the men and nineteen per cent of the women were 'near starvation'. Professor Bourlière states that several thousand old people die of hunger in the region of Paris every year. And every winter the papers report cases of those who have died of cold.

Those who survive suffer not only from a cruel and biting poverty but also from the precariousness of their position. Their budget is continually thrown out of balance, and this forces them to turn to the social services again and again. The organizations to which they appeal for help are unsympathetic and often submit them to humiliating investigations. The old people are required to fill in masses of complicated forms in which they lose their way.

In a programme on old age by Eliane Victor* a hidden camera recorded interviews between old women and social assistants. The assistants did their best for them. But it was extremely painful to see the old women getting lost among their papers, vainly searching their memories, making desperate attempts at understanding the position. Even more painful was their humility, their crushed, beseeching attitude. The old people have the feeling that they are begging, and many cannot bring themselves to it. Although the price is the same for both, only twenty per cent of the aged who depend on an assistance organization go for medical treatment, whereas forty per cent of those with social insurance do so: this means that they refuse the principle of assistance. In any case, help from time to time is merely palliative, and they live in perpetual anxiety about the days to come.

The position is much the same in Belgium, England, West Germany and Italy. A hypocritical sense of decency forbids a capitalist society to get rid of its 'useless mouths'. But it allows them only just enough to keep them this side of death. 'It is too much to die on and not enough to live on,' said one pensioner sadly. And another, 'When

* 'Grow old in the sun.'

you're no longer up to being a worker, you're only good enough to be a corpse.'

The position of the executives and people at the managerial level is less disagreeable, but it is still not satisfactory. There is one highly privileged class among them – the engineers, top administrators, higher civil servants and professional men, some of whom earn twenty-five times as much as a manual worker. But there are also the middle-range executives, the lower civil servants and the technicians, whose incomes are far more modest – the women are particularly badly paid. These people are in constant danger of dismissal and unemployment. For most of them retiring means a loss of status and a much lower standard of living. According to *Les Cadres retraités vus par eux-mêmes*, a book that appeared in 1964, eighty per cent stated that their income was adequate, though for seventy-seven per cent it was only 'just adequate': no more than two per cent claimed that they had money to spare. For nineteen per cent the material position was precarious, and this applied above all to the women – one widow in six had no more than 250 francs a month and fifty-eight per cent had less than five hundred francs. Taken as a whole, eight per cent of retired executives had less than 250 francs a month, thirty-two per cent between 250 and five hundred, thirty-two per cent between five hundred and a thousand, and twenty-five per cent more than a thousand. (Some did not reply.) For half, their pension was the whole of their income, and for twenty-six per cent it amounted to more than half. They would all have liked to draw two-thirds more or even twice as much. At all ages from sixty-five to seventy-five one in two would have preferred to go on working. Yet two-thirds said that they had adapted themselves: only one-third, made up chiefly of the poor and those who were unwell, found it hard to put up with their new way of life. Twenty per cent had returned to some kind of work: for fifty-two per cent this was to increase their income and for sixteen per cent it was a distraction, an occupation; for twenty-six per cent the two reasons were combined. Of those who did not work any more, eighty-three preferred to rest. None had any desire to go into a home for elderly people: they wanted to stay in their own place.

There is one category that stands retirement badly – the foremen. For them it means a serious loss of income; they cannot get used to leisure; and they look for additional work with an almost obsessional eagerness. But it is very hard for them to readapt themselves.

. . . . . .

In order to increase profit, capitalism tries to increase productivity whatever it may cost; and as the goods produced become more and more abundant, so the system insists upon an even greater output. The old workers are unable to keep up with the rhythm required of them. They are thrown out of work and society treats them as pariahs. This becomes staringly obvious if we look at the most prosperous of these societies and one that claims to be a welfare civilization – the United States.

In 1870, seventy per cent of the aged had paid employment; at present only three million, or twenty per cent of the aged population, receive wages. Of these two million are men and one million women. Generally speaking their pay is low. It is already difficult for them to find jobs between the ages of forty-five and sixty-five. They can only keep going by means of retirement pensions, and these are very parsimoniously doled out.

For a long while public assistance in the United States operated in the same way as in England. Old people who were still healthy were boarded out with the family that asked the least amount of money for their maintenance: the infirm were taken to the county institution that was simultaneously hospital, lunatic asylum, orphanage and home for the old and sick. It was not thought that the aged who were incapable of work had any rights; they were looked upon as idlers, failures, rejects. The responsibility for keeping them lay primarily with their families.

A great many workers in California in 1850 were pioneers who had come from the east and who had no families: brotherhoods were formed, and these succeeded in obtaining state subsidies for the aged. Beginning in 1883, the State of California made grants to those counties that maintained old people's homes and then to those which gave out relief. The system was done away with in 1895 because of abuses, and after that California financed state institutions only.

At the end of the nineteenth century statistics showed how many poor were to be found among the aged population, and public opinion began to stir. In 1915 Alaska passed a law authorizing the state to grant relief of $12.50 a month to certain persons aged sixty-five and more. Similar laws were passed in other states.

In 1927 California authorized the department of social welfare to carry out an inquiry in the state: it was found that only two per cent of the population aged sixty-five and over received any kind of aid. That same year the Fraternal Order of Eagles, which had always been concerned with helping the aged, made a great effort to win acceptance for the idea that the federal government was responsible for old people; and they were supported by other less well-known bodies. But what with individualism, liberalism and a dread of all 'socialism', a great part of public opinion was opposed to this. The Eagles' plan was nevertheless studied in twenty-four states. In 1929 California adopted a law that extended relief to all needy old people. By 1930 thirteen other states had followed its example. By 1934, thirty states had some kind of an assistance programme, but only ten took over the whole responsibility for relief: aid was hard to get and it was quite inadequate. Some philanthropists, trade unions and churches had also begun to build old people's homes. In the great depression of the thirties the position of the aged became tragic: they were thrown out of work; it was not in the power of the states to maintain them; many had seen their savings vanish, and they were evicted from their homes. This distress brought the Social Security Act into existence, and it authorized federal grants to those states which provided programmes of aid to the aged. The plans of the various states continued to function, and a second principle came into operation – that of insurance. But very few profited from it, and what they received was wretchedly small.

By 1943, 23·4 per cent of the aged received aid, but only 3·4 per cent received retirement pensions. The lowness of their standard of living remained most painfully obvious. At this period the agencies designed to help them were in full development. Yet in 1951 the immense majority of the aged population had incomes far below the subsistence level and they received no private assistance of any kind. More and more meetings were held for the study of the problems of old age. Between 1950 and 1958 the number of those who benefited from social security increased, so that from affecting only three-quarters of the aged population it reached nine-tenths: the pensions were also raised. Yet according to Steiner's and Dorfman's research in 1957, the incomes of twenty-five per cent of the couples, thirty-three per cent of the single men and fifty per cent of the single women over sixty-five did not reach subsistence level.

'Poverty among the aged remains one of our most persistent and difficult problems,' writes Margaret S. Gordon. Today, out of sixteen million old people there are more than eight million who are very poor. A man who retires at sixty-five, having paid the highest contribution, draws $162 a month for himself and his wife; if he is alone, then it is $108.50. In 1958 the Bureau of the Census statistics showed that sixty per cent of the people over sixty-five had incomes of less than $1,000 a year, which is twenty per cent lower than the 'subsistence budget' in those cities where living was cheapest and forty per cent lower in those where it was dearest. The help given by children or friends scarcely amounts to ten per cent of the income, and the only elderly people to benefit by it are those who have a comparatively stable position. Those who live alone (and they are mostly women, for as in France there are many more widows than widowers) are the most unfortunate. A quarter of them live on less than $580 a year – only a trifle more than the Agriculture Department's lowest budget for food alone. (And they have to clothe, house and warm themselves.)

In his book *The Other America* M. Harrington shows that the millions of old people who live in poverty are the victims of a 'downward spiral'. Poor people are ill more often than others because they live in unhealthy slums, feed themselves badly and can hardly afford any heating; but they are too poor to take care of themselves, so their illnesses grow worse, preventing them from working and making their poverty even more acute: they are ashamed of their destitute condition, and they stay at home, avoiding all social contact: they do not want their neighbours to know that they live on public assistance, so they deprive themselves of the little services and the minimum of treatment that those services might give them, and they end up by being bed-ridden. One witness, testifying before a senatorial commission set up to inquire into old age, stated that these outcasts of society were the victims 'of a threefold set of causes – bad health, poverty and solitude'. Some of them 'join the ranks of poverty' after an ordinary life in which their work was properly rewarded. Their abilities diminish as they grow older; they can no longer find jobs because their techniques are out of date – even in the countryside mechanization has brought about the elimination of the elderly. For those who have earned a reasonable amount retirement means a sudden violent drop in income. But most of the very poor have always been poor. They came from the country when they were young and they have not thriven in the cities. Then again, social security does not cover farm labourers. The mass of these very poor people – the retired with inadequate incomes or workers with no retirement pension – have to turn to the assistance agencies. There are some states, such as Mississippi, which are very poor and in which the aid granted is trifling. Everywhere the officials are hostile to the applicants:

half the requests are rejected. The applicants are required to produce papers that most of them do not possess; they are often only half literate and some can scarcely speak English; the forms and the set-up of the assistance office terrify them. This impersonal, powerless bureaucracy humiliates them and at the same time it does nothing for them. The Welfare State works the wrong way round. Protection, guarantees and assistance go to the powerful and well-organized, not to the weak. It is those most in need of medical care that get the least. Their condition is made even worse by their loneliness. The young slum-dwellers get out into the streets and form gangs: the old stay shut in. In a country where the distances and the rhythm of life make it difficult for them to meet and where they communicate chiefly by telephone, five million have none. Dr Linden, of the Philadelphia public health department, writes, 'Among the factors that contribute most to the development of our elderly fellow-citizens' emotional problems, we must place the social ostracism to which they are subject, the shrinking of their circle of friends, their intense loneliness, the reduction and loss of human respect, and their feeling of self-disgust.'

Only an affluent society can have so many old people, says Harrington: but it refuses them the fruits of abundance. It grants them 'mere survival' and nothing more.

Because of the disappearance of the family unit, the urbanization of society, and the wretchedly low incomes of the aged, housing them is now an urgent and very difficult problem. England is urbanized to eighty per cent, Germany to seventy per cent, the United States to sixty-five per cent, Japan and Canada to sixty per cent, and France to fifty-eight per cent. The patriarchal family has survived in Japan because of the strength of traditions in that country; in West Germany many parents live with their children because of the housing-shortage. In the United States 25·9 per cent of the elderly men live with their children, 22·6 per cent as head of the family, 3·3 per cent in their children's houses. In France twenty-four per cent of the old people live with their children, particularly in the country – it is only there that four generations may sometimes be seen under the same roof. This solution has its advantages. It is cheap; it ensures contact between the generations; it provides young couples with their parents' help. But there are serious disadvantages too. Where it is the father who owns the house and land – and this is very often the case

246

in France at present – he refuses to adopt modern ways, and the children find it difficult to put up with his authority. In his study of the village of Plodemet,* Morin emphasizes the clash between the generations: 'A bitter conflict divides the young adults and the fathers with whom they live and work.' A twenty-eight-year-old tiler said, 'We'd like to modernize, but we always come up against the old men.' Until he is thirty or thirty-five the son waits for the father to hand over, and for ten years on end he is consumed with impatience. The old men grow irritated: referring to the young, they say 'They talk about things nobody has ever heard of; they want to go over our heads.'

A great many young men leave the country for the towns, with the result that there are rural hamlets and even whole villages with nothing but old people, who work the land according to out-of-date methods and who suffer from their isolation. If, on the other hand, the father or mother live in their children's home there is the risk that they may be badly treated or neglected. In any event, they suffer from their status as dependants; they feel that the rest of the family exploits or oppresses them. This also works in the other direction – their being in the house is bad for the young couple's relationship: many divorces arise from this living together. Some peasant societies prefer the formula of 'intimacy at a distance': in the country parts of Switzerland, Germany and Austria, the aged couple leave the family dwelling for a 'small house', which is close to the large one but independent of it. A similar custom is to be found in some regions of France. When he is about sixty the father hands the property over to his sons and goes to live in a house in the village. He retains his interest in the land, he helps in the work and gives advice. An inquiry made at Vienne in 1962, covering a thousand old people, showed that they preferred this 'intimacy at a distance' to living all in one household and to isolation.

The problem has another aspect in the towns; and in France it is a very distressing aspect, because of the widespread housing-shortage, of the worn-out state of the buildings as a whole, and because of the slow rate of construction. Most of what is built consists of great blocks in which the rent is beyond the reach of those with very, very small incomes: they have a rent-allowance if they live in an unfurnished place that does not cost more than 190 francs a month, but if the owners do not want an aged tenant they have only to set the

* *Commune en France. La Métamorphose de Plodemet.*

monthly rent at 200 francs, and the old applicant, who will then get no allowance, cannot afford it.* This practice is general at Nice, among other towns, because very great numbers of old people retire there. A sociologist has said that everywhere the aged 'are doomed to the slums'. According to IFOP surveys, most retired people stay in their old home, in spite of their dreams of a little house in the south. Sixty-eight per cent of the couples have at least two rooms and a kitchen; but these are in old, dilapidated, and sometimes insanitary buildings without water or central heating. An inquiry carried out in 1968 by the CNRO,† which has 1,800,000 members and 340,000 recipients of allowances, showed that only 15·5 per cent of retired building-trade workers had water, gas, electricity, a shower and an indoor lavatory all at the same time. Thirty-four per cent of the aged lived in the attics of old buildings without lifts and they had to climb from four to six storeys. Sometimes the flat had become too big with the departure of the children and it was difficult to keep up. In most instances old people lived in dwellings that were not suited to their powers: the lack of water, central heating and lift meant extreme fatigue for weakened bodies. One aged person out of two owned his dwelling: this figure includes those who live in the country, which explains the high rate. One-third were tenants and the rest were either housed for nothing or they shared with others.

The problem of housing is bound up with that of loneliness. In the United States two-thirds of the aged men live with their wives; 16·2 live alone; and 3·5 per cent in homes for the retired. In France thirty-five per cent of the aged live with their spouses; thirty per cent live alone (most of these are women); and nine per cent live with friends, a brother or a sister. According to a 1968 report on retired building and public works employees, forty-three per cent have relatives in the neighbourhood; twenty-three per cent have relatives close at hand; twenty-five per cent relatives at a distance; and nine per cent are quite alone. The frequency of contact is in direct relation to the distance.

But these figures throw little light on the real importance of the bonds of family or friendship: research on this question has given results that are sometimes contradictory and often doubtful. In Milan, ten per cent of the men questioned and thirteen per cent of

---

* The injustice and absurdity of this rule is evident. If the rent is 190 francs an aged tenant may receive an allowance of 95 francs: he has only 95 francs to pay. If the rent is 200 francs, then 200 francs is the sum he must find.

† *Caisse nationale des Retraites ouvrières.*

the women said that they were 'very lonely'; twenty per cent of the men and twenty-two per cent of the women were 'sometimes lonely': the feeling of loneliness grew with age. In California fifty-seven per cent of those who did not live with a spouse and sixteen per cent of those who did answered 'very lonely'.

These inquiries have been particularly frequent in England. The researches of Townsend, Young and Willmot, J. M. Mogey, and E. Bott show that the family, in the very broad sense, plays a most important part as a unit for social relationships and mutual aid, especially the maternal family, whose nucleus is the grandmother, her daughters and granddaughters. The men are more inclined to visit the pub or to go out with friends. 'Men have friends; women have relations.' Townsend's investigations in the Bethnal Green district of the East End of London, in 1957, were particularly important. Of the old people he questioned, five per cent said they were 'very lonely', twenty-five per cent 'sometimes lonely', and seventy per cent 'not lonely'. According to him, few aged people were really cut off; some had as many as thirteen relatives living in the neighbourhood: and an important point was that there were always one or two children living within less than a mile of their parents. In Bethnal Green the grandparents, particularly the grandmothers, took great care of their grandchildren: they saw them to school, took them for walks, looked after them, gave them their meals. Three-quarters of the people questioned saw at least one helpful relative every day. Sheldon (the medical director of the Royal Hospital) found that one-fifth of the aged suffered from loneliness to a heartbreaking degree, especially the widowers – far more than the widows. Of those who lived alone, almost a third had relatives less than half a mile away: forty per cent said they were happy because of their good relations with their children. But these results are to be treated with caution. Another investigator, an American, observed that ninety-two per cent of the aged said that they were loved and respected by their children; but only sixty-three per cent said that children loved and respected their parents as a rule. It seems that self-deception or pride comes into many of these replies: a person does not wish to say that he is lonely or neglected. Then again, it has been observed that contact with relatives does not improve the morale of the under-privileged, the very poor. For those who are in easy circumstances, friends count more than their family. Brothers, sisters, cousins and so on in the fairly close neighbourhood do not help the old person in his life. Almost nobody counts apart from the spouse and the children: and even then a couple may suffer from shared loneliness. These are some of the results of an inquiry recently carried out in the 13th *arrondissement* of Paris by Dr Balier and L.-H. Sébillotte. Couples shut themselves away in their own homes more rigidly than single people, widowers or the unmarried. The bond between the couple is often jealous, hypersensitive and tyrannical, and it means that they live in a vacuum that they themselves have created. A 1968 survey* of a crowded Paris *arrondissement* showed that one aged person out of three no longer had any social contacts, never had a letter,† never received or paid a visit, and no longer knew anybody.

There have been plans for protecting the aged physically and spiritually against discomfort and loneliness by building residences in which they would live in groups. Here we find a very striking contrast between the northern and the southern countries of Europe. In Italy and France almost nothing has been done. In the last few years the CNRO, in France, has put up some of these residences: they are near big towns so that the people who live in them will not feel out of their element, and they are very intelligently laid out, whether they are of the horizontal type, the semi-horizontal (a maximum of four storeys), or the vertical (eight storeys or more). The first was opened in December 1964; it is in the neighbourhood of Bordeaux, and it houses about a hundred persons, healthy or partially infirm. Since then five or six more have been built, each taking an average of a hundred and twenty. The retired people like these residences, and their only complaint is that they are left with no more than ten per cent of their money, the rest being taken up by rent and upkeep. But from the point of view of the numbers concerned, the results are still trifling. Switzerland and West Germany have done rather more for housing their old people; Holland and England have accomplished a great deal. In about 1920 a village for the aged was built in the suburbs of London: this is Whiteley Village. The Committee for the Welfare of the Aged has built others in London, at Hackney and in other places. In 1940 nearly all the English slums were inhabited by old people: a great many have been rehoused in new dwellings constructed specially for them.

It is the Scandinavian countries that have made the greatest effort. Copenhagen has the well-known 'old people's town', which was built

---

* See *France-Soir*, 8 November 1968.
† Apart from official post.

in 1919 and modernized in 1950: it has 1,600 beds and it has long been considered a striking success. In 1940 the few Swedish slum-dwellings were occupied by old people: all have been rehoused, and there are very well-laid-out complexes for the aged. Since 1947 Sweden has built 1,350 homes for the retired and they house 45,000 persons. Elderly people also have the advantage of another kind of special housing: these are flats reserved for pensioners in ordinary blocks. Some old people are given 'supplementary communal grants' that help them to pay the rather high rent of flats of the usual kind.

In 1950, President Truman drew the problems of old age to the attention of the American public, and he set up a commission, eight hundred strong, to examine them. Nothing much came of all this. The aged are often brought together in kinds of ghettoes – this is the case in Saint Louis, for example: old houses are cut up into furnished rooms or very small flats and the old people are crowded into them. A few associations, such as the Fossils, the Octogenarians, the Merry Widows, the Young at Fifty, etc., have been formed by old people and they have organized retirement homes; but their average price for board and lodging is $150 a month. Some collective housing projects have been carried out with government loans, and these are designed to make either no profit or very little: others have been built by private enterprise. Their prices are far beyond the reach of the majority of retired people: at Isabella House, one of the best known of residences, the lowest rent is $75 a month.

The success of the Victoria Plaza should be mentioned, although unhappily it is an exception.* A big modern block was erected and badly-housed old people were resettled in it: there were 352 applicants and 204 were chosen. Nearly sixty per cent of them were living alone; the others had a spouse, relatives or friends; many were in slum-dwellings. They were shown the building before they were transferred, and they thought it wonderful. At the end of a year most of them still thought it wonderful. There is a club with a library and various kinds of games, and ninety per cent of them use it. They pay $28 a month, which is usually rather more than their former rent; but considering the space and the comfort they enjoy they think it reasonably cheap. Their whole life has been transformed. They do feel their lack of money more, because instead of neglecting themselves and their homes they now buy clothes and furniture; but they are delighted at having leisure and so many ways of filling it. They join groups and

* Described in Carp's *Future for the Aged*.

they make new friends, which does not prevent them from keeping up with their old acquaintances or frequently telephoning their family. They think their health is better than it was and they speak of themselves as being 'middle-aged', whereas their contemporaries who have stayed in their old homes speak of themselves as elderly or old. Their physical and emotional lives have blossomed out, and almost all of them consider themselves happy. From this experiment and some others it appears that the habitat has an extremely important influence on the old person's general state. How lamentable, then, that it should usually be so wretched.

A question that is much discussed at present is whether it is good for old people to live exclusively among their contemporaries. A great deal of the success of the Victoria Plaza arises from the fact that it lies in the heart of a town and that its residents are not cut off from their families. In the United States there are several 'Sun Cities', inhabited solely by elderly people with a high standard of living. Those who organize and run these communities say that the members are very happy to live with their own kind. But these are highly profitable enterprises, and the organizers have every interest in crying up their wares. Calvin Trillin wrote a series of articles about one of these communities for the *New Yorker* in 1964, and he seemed very sceptical about the 'happiness' that was supposed to prevail. The people who live there have bought their houses, investing a great deal of money and burning their bridges behind them: they are forced to stay, and most make the best of it; but that does not mean that they would do so again if they had the choice.

A plan much recommended at present is the setting up of *béguinages* like those at Bruges, made up of small independent houses in the middle of the town, so that the old people would be near their children. An even better plan would be the creation of dwellings combined with a centre – private dwellings but with certain common facilities, the whole forming part of a large complex inhabited by people of all ages.

When old people can no longer manage for themselves, physically and economically, their only resource is the *hospice** – the institution. In most countries it is utterly inhuman – no more than a place to wait

* There is no exact modern English equivalent of *hospice*: 'poor-house' would have done fifty years ago, but it has the wrong sound now, so in this particular context I am using the word institution which, though imprecise, has much the same ring for English ears (trs.).

for the end, a 'deathbed', a 'last halt', as someone said in a recent programme on the Salpêtrière.

In France 1·45 per cent of the aged live in institutions. On the average they are between seventy-three and seventy-eight. Two per cent live in retired people's homes. An inquiry has shown that seventy-four per cent of the aged are extremely unwilling to go into an institution: fifteen per cent tolerate the idea because they are infirm. There are 275,000 beds, and at present there are between 150,000 and 200,000 who would like to be admitted and for whom there is no room. Four main reasons induce the aged to apply for a place. First, the inadequacy of their means. Three-quarters of those in the big institutions depend upon public assistance; pensioners prefer the small private establishments. Second, the impossibility of finding somewhere to live or the fatigue of maintaining the home they possess. Third, family reasons: the children refuse to take responsibility for the old person or they decide to get rid of the responsibility. During the programme (January 1968) on the 'last halt' of the Salpêtrière, the director indignantly stated that families would often come and leave an old relative in order to go off for their holidays and would then forget to come back for him. And lastly some old people are in need of medical care. They usually go into their departmental institution, some as paupers and others paying part of their pension. There are also the 'rolling stones' who continually change from one institution to another: between whiles they wander about and drink. Some establishments will not take in the sick aged: others accept sick people, even when they are young.

According to a survey made by M. Delore in one institution in 1952, the number of women was twice that of the men. Out of a hundred women there were seventy-four widows, twenty-two spinsters and four married women. Sixty-five were mentally and physically fit; thirty-five were infirm or senile. Before coming in, eighty had lived alone in one or two rooms, in a concierge's lodge or in the attics. Twenty-one of these dwellings were slums, particularly the lodges. The women received between eight thousand and fifteen thousand francs a month.* The twenty-four concierges undertook light work. A cupboard in the lodge belonging to one of them was found to contain sixty-five pounds of sugar, together with rice, macaroni, etc. In another woman's room 200,000 francs were hidden in various places. They were on good terms with their children, with distant relatives,

* These are 1952 francs.

with friends and neighbours. Forty-five of the widows had children, and thirty-two were on good terms with them. In thirty per cent of the cases, the admission ticket was marked 'general decay' or 'social deficiency'.

At present no homes for the retired may be built with more than eighty beds, and they have to be in separate rooms intended for single persons or couples. During the last few years a certain number of establishments complying with these rules have been erected: in all they contain 35,000 beds. This does not amount to much, and the situation remains deplorable.

In a recent report the minister of public health denounced 'the extreme poverty of the French *hospices*'; and all the evidence is in agreement. They are today, as they were in former times, very much like reception-centres for tramps. Monsieur Laroque made this admission: 'In the past an institution was a place for gathering the infirm, the bedridden and the healthy aged together with the one idea of giving them some slight degree of shelter, often in shocking promiscuity and with a minimum of food: everyone knew the formula. Unhappily, this same formula is still being widely used.' In 1960, the minister of health wrote, 'There are but few *hospices* and retired people's homes in which the sanitary services are what they should be. In many of them it is not an exaggeration to speak of a downright medical abandonment.' In the same year the ministry's central inspectorate reported, 'Supervision and medical treatment are quite inadequate in most of the *hospices* and public homes for the retired. In these the bedridden aged end their lives amidst what appears to be a general indifference. Their situation is all the more unacceptable since nowadays the motor re-education of hemiplegiacs gives satisfactory results and confinement to bed can be avoided in the majority of cases.'

In France there is a deplorable confusion between *hospice* and *hôpital* – between institution (in this particular sense) and hospital. The majority of institutions take in the infirm and the sick whatever their age. Out of the 275,000 beds intended for the aged (twenty-five per cent belong to the private sector), seventeen per cent are occupied by young people with motor and other troubles. 25·12 per cent are occupied by the bedridden.

The reverse applies. As well as the grandfathers left at the hospital and never taken away again, many old people come to the emergency reception centre with a letter from their doctor saying, 'Monsieur (or

Madame) X is in urgent need of admission because he (or she) is living alone and he (or she) is old.' The hospital never sends them away. At the Salpêtrière and Bicêtre there are some who have been waiting for death for twenty-four years in the fifty-bed 'decay-wards'.* At the Saint-Antoine hospital there are three 'clearing' wards in which old people wait for others to die and so liberate their beds in the new hospitals that have been opened outside Paris: they are well laid out, but beds cost fifty-one francs a day. At least 16,000 beds are needed to provide space for the acutely ill.

About 178,000 hospital or institution beds are housed in buildings a hundred years old. These are often former hospitals, castles, barracks or prisons that are in no way suited to their new functions. They have a great many staircases and quite often no lift, so that some old people cannot leave their floor. Dormitories were condemned in 1958, but in fact the great majority of beds are still so arranged; and in these beds the sick and the bedridden lie all day long. Often there is no screen between the beds, no private bed-table, no private locker: the old person does not possess an inch of space he can call his own. The sexes are separated: old couples are pitilessly divided, and it is not unusual for husband and wife to be put into different institutions. (In the spring of 1967 a couple in their eighties drowned themselves together in the Seine because they had been separated.) If the institution has any separate rooms they are generally reserved for those who can pay for their keep. The time comes when they can no longer do so, and they are moved from their room to the dormitory – still another step down into degradation. Because of the age of the buildings, the rooms are usually very gloomy. The dining-hall is commonly furnished with long tables and benches, and only too often it also acts as the general living-room: when there is a separate one, it is too small and badly fitted up. It is often cold, too, the place either having no central heating or a system that does not warm the whole institution. The laundries and kitchens usually have more modern equipment; but the food is the same for everybody and no attention whatsoever is paid to the diets that might be desirable in particular cases. The plumbing is inadequate: in most of these establishments there are no baths, but only showers, and these the

* In an article in *France-Soir* in April 1968, Madeleine Franck wrote, 'These revolting wards are being done away with. Only a few remain at the Salpêtrière. And at the Bicêtre *hôpital-hospice* the director, Monsieur Musière, has succeeded in abolishing 500 out of the 1,300 "rubbish-beds", as he calls them.'

255

inmates take once a week or even once a month. The 'medical abandonment' is scandalous. A doctor for 350 patients is the usual figure: but it may happen that one solitary doctor is in charge of 965 inmates. The medical expenditure in these institutions amounts to 2·7 per cent of their budget, although there are a very great many serious pathological conditions among the inmates.

It is understandable, then, that in these conditions an old person should look upon going into an institution as a tragedy. Women feel the psychological shock with particular force, they being even more attached to their homes than men. They display anxiety and they are seized with fits of trembling. Many of them gradually become resigned. Occasionally, it seems, being put into an institution gives an old person back his taste for life: he feels less cut off, he makes friends, and out of a sort of competition he neglects himself less than before. But this is very rare.

Figures drawn up by Dr Pequignot – and many sources confirm them – show that of the healthy old people admitted to an institution

8 per cent die in the first week
28·7 per cent die in the first month
45 per cent die in the first six months
54·4 per cent die in the first year
64·4 per cent die in the first two years.

In other words, more than half the old people die within a year of their admission. It is not only the living conditions in an institution that are responsible: with the aged, any kind of uprooting may cause death. It is rather the fate of those that survive that should be deplored. In a great number of cases this fate may be summed up in a few words – abandonment, segregation, decay, dementia, death.

In the first place the inmate suffers from the restraint to which he is subjected. The rules are very strict, the routine hard and unbending: everyone gets up early and goes to bed early. The inmate is cut off from his past and his surroundings; he is often dressed in a uniform; he loses all his personality, becoming a mere number. Generally speaking, visits are allowed every day, and his family comes to see him from time to time – though rarely, and in some cases not at all. The institution is often hard to reach; friends and relations can only go on Sundays, and they are put off by the time that the journey takes. A striking instance is the *Maison départementale* at Nanterre. By underground and bus it takes two hours to get there from the middle of Paris. A great deal of affection is needed if people are to sacrifice the little spare time they have; and the old person therefore finds that he is left to himself. In an interview on television, the head of a large retired people's home at Nice stated that only two per cent of the inmates received visits. Generally speaking the residents may not go out when they choose: at Nanterre they are only allowed one afternoon a week. The inmate does not know what to do with his day. Sometimes he will undertake some small job inside the institution so as to make a little money, and a few of the women are employed in the linen-room or the kitchens. But the old people's hearts are not in the work. Most of them are of a low intellectual level; they do not read much and they scarcely listen to the radio at all. When there is a television set, it tires their eyes. Even cards do not amuse them: their interest-level falls to zero and they stay there doing nothing all day long. Indeed, after breakfast they will go back to bed and spend almost all their time there, slowly turning over the same old thoughts about sickness and death. According to Professor Bourlière, the only activity that can interest a community of old people is manual work. In London there is a workshop attached to an institution where the old men make things such as crutches and so on for the use of the infirm members of the community: this gives them the feeling of being useful. Some few provincial institutions in the country have kitchen-gardens, and some inmates take a pleasure in working them. But these cases are rare. An old man in an institution, doing nothing, reduced to the state of an object, falls rapidly into senile decay. On the day he is allowed out he has little more than one amusement – drinking. Many inmates who are not given to drink when they are admitted turn into alcoholics within the first month of their stay. The pocket-money they are allowed* and what they make by odd jobs is often entirely devoted to drink. The regulations stipulate that there must be at least two hundred yards between the gate of the institution and the nearest place where drink is sold: at Nanterre it is forbidden to supply the old people with any alcoholic drink other than wine – but wine is enough. In summer the Nanterre streets near the institution are filled with old people of both sexes, lying on the ground, sitting, leaning against the wall, clasping bottles of wine to their bosoms and dead drunk already. Their weakened frames cannot stand up to these drinking-bouts, and they go back to the institution staggering, shouting and vomiting: this promiscuity is extremely painful for those inmates who like cleanliness and peace. Wine

* Twenty-five francs a month.

stimulates wild notions of grandeur – the momentary compensation for their wretchedness. It also sets free their sexuality: in their drunken state they often form couples, hetero- or homosexual, and they do what they can to satisfy their desires.

Most of the inmates find communal life very hard to bear: they are unhappy, anxious, turned in upon themselves, and they are herded together without any social life being arranged for them. Their touchiness, their demanding and often paranoid tendencies lead to frequent antagonistic reactions – to situations of conflict. All the pathological processes to which old age is subject are accelerated by life in an institution.

This life has been very well described by Jacoba Van Velde in *La Grande Salle*, a novel that must surely be the result of careful personal observation.* The author shows a Dutch institution for women through the eyes of a new inmate. The 'new girl', brought in by a daughter who loves her but who can no longer look after her, is seized with horror at the idea that she will never have a moment to herself again. 'I have always hated having people look at me,' she says to herself. 'Being stared at was always a torment to me.' From now on all the actions of her life, including dying, are to be carried out before witnesses, often unkind or at least critical. 'Never alone – it's dreadful. Always surrounded by people!' says the inmate of another home for the retired as they talk together. 'And they treat you as though all old people fell into second childhood. They talk to you as though you were one or two years old – a baby.' The old woman suffers from the material discomforts and vexations, but even more from this denial of all privacy in life, from this compulsory metamorphosis from human being to mere object.

I was unable to visit Nanterre because I was refused admittance; but I have seen over an *Assistance publique* institution. It is very well situated, right in the heart of Paris, and it houses about two hundred men and women. It is surrounded by a large garden full of trees and flowers; I went there on a fine autumn day, and the sun was pouring into all the rooms. Everything, floor, walls and curtains, was meticulously clean. I met conscientious doctors, young kindly and dedicated nurses. Yet although I already knew a great deal about the question I shall not easily forget the horror of that experience: I saw human beings reduced to a state of total abjection.

* *Un plat de porc aux bananes vertes*, by Simone and André Schwartz-Bart, deals with the same subject, but it has far less value as evidence.

A few privileged inmates who could pay the considerable price of their maintenance lived in private rooms, and a few others in wards with four or five beds. But by far the greater number were herded in dormitories. Each inmate had a bed, a bedside table, an armchair and a little locker at the foot of the bed. The space between the beds was about the width of two bedside tables, and it was there that the inmates spent the whole of their day: they did not even have a refectory (except for one men's dormitory, which had a dining-room at the end). Their meals were served on a little table next to the bed. There was no living-room, apart from a little place so uncomfortable that no one ever went there, not even to see their visitors. By a strange anomaly that no one could explain to me, the healthy inmates lived on the ground floor, the partially-infirm on the first floor, and the bedridden on the second. The last were incapable of managing for themselves; they were fed and cleaned like babies. But there was nothing peaceful about this decay: the faces of the old women I saw were convulsed with horror and despair, fixed in a kind of half-witted terror. Maybe nothing more could be done for them. The staringly obvious scandal was the first floor. Among the partially infirm, many could move about from one end of the dormitory to the other; they might have gone out; but they could not get down the stairs, and as there was no lift they were literally imprisoned. So even the garden was forbidden them. What made their position even worse was that in the same dormitory there were old men no longer in control of their bodies who spent their days sitting on commodes; these old men were in the same room as the others, who were therefore condemned to live in a stinking atmosphere. The ground floor was less stifling and evil-smelling; but it wrung my heart to see the utter listlessness bred by life in an institution. This inertia went so far, particularly among the men, that as the doctor told me, many of them were incontinent in their beds, although they were not infirm: society had taken over responsibility for them, he explained, so they abandoned themselves entirely to it, carrying their passiveness to the furthest point. (I suppose they were also living their situation in a state of resentment, and that they were taking their revenge.) All day long they stayed sitting there on their chairs, doing nothing. I did see one man lying on his bed and knitting, and two others sitting on a bed and playing cards. But that was all. I was told that one inmate in twenty read the paper. A few listened to the radio a little. They had fallen into such a state of torpor that even if amusements were offered, they refused them: a free excursion by bus to the surroundings of Paris was suggested to about forty women. Only two accepted. Their only diversion was quarrelling: the women, particularly, were given to gossiping over trifles, to wrangling, to forming cliques and alliances, and to renouncing them. Among the men there were some aggressive and even violent characters. As at Nanterre and everywhere else, they drank heavily as soon as they could. They spent what was left of their pensions after the payment for their board on red wine. There was no difficulty about this, for the district is full of cafés and wine-shops. In summer they were to be seen on the benches of a nearby avenue, clasping bottles. The women drank too. When they came back in the evening, more or less drunk, they squabbled with the others.

Every Wednesday the applicants for admission undergo a medical examination: they are accepted only if they are reasonably fit. (When later they become infirm they are kept.)* The doctor told me that it was terribly moving to see their distress when they were admitted. They knew that they were leaving the world of the living, that they were going into a place where they could look forward to nothing but death. When they had got over the anguish of the change, the women ended up by adapting themselves to it a little better than the men. The men remained cut off, solitary. And they had an intense awareness of their degradation. One of the medical staff said to me, 'To begin with I used to ask them what they had done before: they would tell me they had been ticket-collectors or labourers, and burst into tears – they had been working in those days, they had been men. . . . I understood what they meant. I no longer ask any questions.' Many of the inmates had no family left: the others had between one and four visits a month.

There was a striking contrast between the women housed in dormitories and those who had a room to themselves. I saw four of these: they were neat and tidy, they read or knitted, and they joked with the doctor. In one fairly spacious five-bed ward they seemed almost merry: one of the women, a former beauty-specialist, was violently made-up, although she only had one tooth left. In a large room with three beds, a smiling, carefully-dressed woman had arranged her own corner with two low tables and a positive garden

---

* There were many blind and deaf people. One woman was both blind and deaf, wholly imprisoned within herself. There is an infirmary: but when the case is serious, the patient is taken to hospital.

on the window-sill. The mere fact of having a little space and homeliness seemed capable of transforming their lives.

What I thought monstrous was the state of spiritual dereliction in which the authorities left all these people. If there had been rooms in which they could come together, or if there had been amusements with somebody in charge to look after them, they would not have slid down the slope that changed them into mere organisms with such horrifying speed. A nurse told me that in fact next year measures were to be taken to raise the standing of the institution, to organize living-rooms, etc. Only the price of staying would then be much higher. The tragic side of it for the present inmates was that they would be moved to the outskirts of Paris, to Ivry or Nanterre.

The situation is no better in the United States. Sociologists have observed that the institutions and retired people's homes have scarcely made any advance in the last centuries. In 1952 the commission on the nation's health requirements stated, 'The health services for old people are totally inadequate, both in quality and in quantity, wherever they are.' On 10 July 1965 the new Medicare legislation came out, many of its sections being devoted to the aged. The doctors as a whole were deeply disturbed by this intervention on the part of the state. They looked upon Dr Spock, the well-known paediatrician, as a traitor for having agreed to collaborate with the government to such a degree. The reason for their dislike of Medicare seems to be that same individualism and liberalism which made the adoption of earlier social security measures so difficult in the United States.*

In the immense majority of cases, being suddenly flung from the active into the inactive category, being classed as old, and undergoing a frightening drop in income and standard of living is a tragedy that has serious psychological and spiritual consequences. It is men who feel the effect most. Women live longer, and it is the very aged solitary women who make up the most underprivileged stratum of the population; yet generally speaking the elderly woman adapts herself to her state better than her husband. She is the person who runs the home, and in this her position is the same as that of the peasants and crafts-men of former times – for her too, work and life merge into one another. No decree from without suddenly cuts her activity short. It

* See Appendix 2.

does grow less from the time her grown-up children leave the home, and this crisis, which often happens quite early in life, often disturbs her very badly; but still she does not see herself thrown into total idleness, and her role of grandmother brings her fresh possibilities. The number of women of sixty to sixty-five who work outside their own homes is not very great. Apart from some exceptions, most women commit much less of themselves to their calling than men; and because of the number of young women who do not work, retirement does not automatically class them in a certain age-group. And they have a part to play in their homes and families that allows them to remain active and to retain their identity. It is they who have the household responsibilities and who keep up the active relationships with the family, above all with the children and grandchildren. At this juncture the wife assumes a greater consequence than her husband, and she often derives a feeling of revenge from her superiority. Some will do their utmost to humiliate the man in his manhood. Elderly people are aware of this alteration in the roles. A drawing used by the TAT (Thematic Apperception Test) shows two men, one young and one old, and two women, also one young and one old: when those who undergo the test are young, their interpretation of the picture gives the old woman no important role; when they are elderly they see the old man as a submissive being in the background, dominated by his wife, and at the same time they see her as the ruling partner, the embodiment of the law. This interpretation reflects the normal evolution of the average couple.

Retirement brings a radical break into a man's life; he is entirely cut off from his past and he has to adapt himself to a new status. This status does bring certain advantages such as rest and leisure, but also serious disadvantages – it makes him poorer and it disqualifies him.

Hemingway said that the worst death for anyone was the loss of what formed the centre of his life and made him what he really was. Retirement was the most loathsome word in the language. Whether we chose it or whether we were compelled by fate, retiring, giving up one's calling – the calling that made us what we were – was the same as going down to the grave.

As everyone knows, he killed himself: he had other reasons too, no doubt, but still he did so just when he felt he could no longer go on writing. When the work has been chosen freely and when it amounts to fulfilling of oneself, then indeed giving it up is the same as a kind of death. When it has not been a matter of choice, when it has been an obligation, then being freed from it is a release. But in fact work almost always has a double aspect: it is a bondage, a wearisome drudgery; but it is also a source of interest, a steadying element, a factor that helps to integrate the worker with society. Retirement reflects this ambivalence, and it may be looked upon either as a prolonged holiday or as a rejection, a being thrown on to the scrap-heap.

The choice between these two points of view and the way in which they will blend depend on many factors. And the first of these is the individual's health. Industrial organizations and government authorities have fixed the age for retirement by a general rule. Yet as we have seen, biological age is far from coinciding with chronological age: a tired, worn-out worker will not have the same reactions as one who retires in full physical and mental strength. The teachers who are allowed to retire either earlier or later usually make their decision according to the state of their health. They consult a doctor, and his diagnosis has an influence upon their choice.

In 1680 Saint-Evremond wrote, 'Nothing is more usual than the sight of old people who yearn for retirement: and nothing is so rare than those who have retired and do not regret it.' The first part of his remark is true for many people, but not for all. The image of the 'miraculous retirement' that will at last allow so many old dreams to be realized is very widespread; but on the other hand there is also an image of the 'disastrous retirement'. Because they regard it with dread, many workers avoid thinking of it at all. A recent inquiry among building-trade workers showed that one year before retiring eighty-five per cent knew absolutely nothing about what their income would be. The CNRO offered to send them a folder containing the necessary information: of those aged sixty-four, ninety-five per cent asked for it; of those aged sixty, forty per cent; and below that age almost nobody. Retirement therefore drops upon the worker like a sudden blow from an axe. 'I never thought about stopping work: I supposed I'd be dead first, I was so tired,' said one storekeeper. 'I thought I'd never give up at all: it was my eyesight that let me down,' said a maid-servant. 'I woke up one morning and found I was retired,' said an English worker. Another, 'At half past seven on Tuesday evening I was still working: the next morning I woke up, and I no longer had anything to do.' According to Moore's 1951 inquiry among United States teachers, forty-one per cent were waiting impatiently for retirement, fifty-nine per cent were indifferent or negative. Another American inquiry among garment-industry workers showed that fifty per cent wanted to retire, but more because they felt they could not go on than for any other reason. Other American research on manual workers showed that only a quarter, or at the most a half, looked forward cheerfully to the idea of stopping work.

Recently ninety-five teachers in the Seine were questioned two months before their retirement. They were asked whether they were afraid that from then onwards they would have the feeling of ageing faster; fifty-five per cent answered *yes*; they took a gloomy view of the future. Some others replied *no* in such an abrupt manner that they too seemed to dread retirement. Many of them said, 'When that happens I shall begin to realize my age.' They loved their profession, and contact with the children kept them young. They were afraid of boredom and of falling into a rut; they felt they were 'being tossed aside'. It seemed to them that when they were socially useless there would be no point in living. They dreaded the isolation. The older they were, the more intense their feeling of ageing. The most affected in this group were the single women. But in some cases the existence of a spouse increased the anxiety, producing a fear that he or she would find the position hard to bear. Children were no help in facing the future unless they lived with the person who was about to retire: in that case, however, the person was not afraid of growing old. The men of sixty who had grandchildren felt older than those who had none. Some teachers said with apparent sincerity that on the contrary being able to rest would make them feel younger: they meant to go and live in the country and to take an interest in a great many things. Some said that they did not mind either way about growing old and left it at that. Many of the women questioned worked, although they were married, from a sense of vocation, and out of a refusal to accept the traditional state of women: they hated the idea of being rejected from their life as teachers.

There was also much variation in the attitudes of those who had already retired. It is worth noting that the state of mind in which retirement is faced has a direct relationship to the manner in which it is experienced. Of those who were asked how they had looked forward to retirement and what they now thought of it, twenty-nine per cent found it more agreeable than they had expected and thirty-one per cent less agreeable. Fifty-one per cent of the first had looked forward to it as something pleasant; sixty-six per cent of those who now found it irksome had dreaded it. The pessimistic frame of mind was usually strengthened and made more pronounced; and the same applied to the optimists.

Generally speaking the worker stops working because he is obliged to do so, either because his employer has dismissed him, or for reasons of health and infirmity. He has not really wished for his new condition.* Sometimes he has prepared himself for it by making plans. And he starts by carrying them out. If he has lived in a town he settles in the country. He travels. But this does not always help him to adapt himself: sometimes the plans themselves have ossified, and when they come to be realized they have lost their savour.

Then again, the retired worker often finds that in changing his way of life he has made a serious mistake. Many building-workers in the Paris region, for example, go back to the villages where they were born when they retire: after a little while they are bored and they come back to Paris. Numbers of retired people leave their homes in order to be nearer their children: the children do not pay much attention to them, and they find that they have given up their life-long habits for nothing. Or they go to the Mediterranean coast, and there they find that the climate is bad for their rheumatism. They also discover that rents are too high, which condemns them to the institution. They know nobody and they suffer from loneliness. Even if the plans were sound in the first place, once they have been carried out the old people find themselves with nothing to do: they have merely postponed the time at which they must adapt themselves. There are very few who can make plans for a real pattern of living. For the rest the 'guillotine', the sudden break of retirement, is an ordeal, and some find recovery very hard.† Research at Prairie City in America shows that people who go on working have a much higher tonus than the retired; and although they have less spare time, their recreations and social activities are far richer.

For this reason and even more out of need for money, many retired people try to find paid work; only a minority succeed, and they do not derive the same satisfaction from this work as they did from their former calling. It is very rare that their leisure allows the

* In 1955 Tréanton's inquiries among 264 persons showed that forty-seven per cent had stopped work because of their health, twenty-two per cent had been dismissed and only four per cent had voluntarily retired. (Some did not reply.)

† In his book *Les Délices du port* Dénuzière tells of a retired station-master who went on to the platform every day and sadly watched the trains go by. After six months of this he died.

development of a vocation that had necessarily been stifled up until that time. The opposite is usually the case, and people put up with jobs of a lower quality and with lower pay, than those they had worked at before. This kind of work brings little consolation.

The retired, snatched from their working environment, have to change their ways and their pattern of living. Most elderly people have a feeling that their value has declined, and this is far worse in the retired. Not only do they in fact have less money than before, but what they do receive is no longer money they have earned. If they have a strong political formation they look upon their pension as a right they have acquired by their work. But many see it as something not unlike a charity. They feel that no longer earning their living is a loss of caste. A man defines his identity by his calling and his pay: by retiring he loses this identity. A former mechanic is a mechanic no longer – he is nothing. 'The role of the retired person,' says Burgess, 'is no longer to possess one.' It therefore means losing one's place in society, one's dignity and almost one's reality. In addition to this, the retired do not know what to do with their leisure, and they grow bored. 'Indeed, the change from activity to retirement is a critical time for office workers,' says Balzac in *Les Petits Bourgeois*. 'Among the retired, those who cannot find new occupations to take the place of those they have left, or do not know how to do so, alter strangely: some die; others take to fishing, a diversion that resembles their office work in its emptiness.'

According to an inquiry carried out in Brussels by the *Office d'identification*, eighty-seven per cent of retired people would like to work, at least from time to time. According to another carried out in Paris, two thirds complained of boredom: 'I can't bear it any more: I'm bored.' An assistant retired from a big store said, 'I go back to see the people I worked with. I try to get back into the atmosphere that was my life for forty years – I can't do without it.' Broadly speaking, the manual workers expressed regret more often than the office staff and the like.

Tréanton found that of the 264 persons he questioned one year after they had retired, 42·5 per cent were discontented, 28·5 per cent were contented, and 16 per cent were glad to rest but found their income insufficient. The contentment was found chiefly among the white-collar workers, because they had a better standard of living. Idleness was disagreeable, but the primary cause for discontent was poverty: that was why it was above all the manual workers who were sorry they had stopped work, although they were less attached to their calling than the others.

Another inquiry provided somewhat different results. A group of recently-retired elderly men were asked whether they thought of working. Half said yes; but only sixteen per cent wanted the retiring age to be raised. In another group of retired people who were questioned about their financial position, one out of two stated that he did not find it satisfactory; yet thirty-nine per cent were against raising the age for retirement: it was particularly the white-collar workers who disliked the idea – the manual workers were not so much opposed to it, and a quarter of them would have agreed to retiring five years later, so long as they had fifty per cent more. One third of a group of building-workers questioned in 1968 had asked for their employment to be terminated before they were sixty-five. (Yet eight per cent went on working after that age without drawing their pensions.) 82·5 per cent of the men wanted the retiring-age to be fixed at sixty. They were all against the idea of paid work after retirement. They hoped to retire because of their state of health.

The contradictions, or at least the uncertainties, in the replies obtained from the various groups arise from the twofold require-ments of the worker – to rest and to live decently. He is compelled to sacrifice either the one or the other. The manual workers are happy not to have to labour any more, but they are worried by the questions of money, health and housing. They suffer more than the white-collar workers from the isolation that their drop in income condemns them to: 'Once I have no money, who do you suppose will bother with me? ... When you are down and out, you don't find people any more. ... I don't want anybody to stand me a drink, because I can't pay my round. ... When I'm asked, I always find some reason for refusing, because I know I can't do anything in return.' Tréanton collected a great number of remarks of this kind.

Boredom and a feeling of loss of value: these same features were apparent in the research carried out by the Nuffield Foundation in the East End of London. A retired man of seventy who still did some odd jobs said sadly, 'I've not yet reached the point of sitting in the corner and watching other people work, but I dare say I'll come to it.' Another in the same situation said, 'I'd like to work until I'm a hundred. Work fills a gap, when you're old. There was a day when I looked forward to the time when I could rest, but now I'm glad to work – it fills a gap.' In Townsend's survey of men retired four years before, one of them complained, 'I don't like just sitting here. I wish my leg would let me go back to work.' Another said, 'I've had enough of it. There's nothing to fill my time. My wife runs the house. If I do anything, she says it's done all wrong.' One woman spoke of the day her husband was pensioned off: 'That was a day to remember! He cried, and the children cried too.' And the husband went on, 'I didn't know what to do any more. It was like when you're put in chokey in the army. I just sit staring at these four walls, that's all. Before, I used to go out with my mates on Saturday evening, or with my sons-in-law. I can't do that any more. I'm like a pauper. I haven't got a pound-note in my pocket, not now, and I couldn't stand my round. Life's not worth living, once you're retired.' One continually recurring leitmotif is, 'What I give my wife doesn't amount to anything. . . . I give her less than nothing – I'm ashamed.' The retired man no longer has enough money to maintain the household; he is dependent on his wife and children; he feels that he is useless, lessened; he hangs about, trying to do little things to help his wife, but she generally finds him a nuisance and packs him off. One wife said to the researchers, 'It's murder, having him in the house. He worries about what you're doing – and he's always asking questions.' Another, 'Once they've stopped working, there's nothing to be done for them in places like this. It's not as though there was a garden. The minute they give up, they're done for. I don't want him about the place.'

Women usually dread the day of their husband's retirement: the standard of living will drop and there will be money-worries; he will be under-foot all the time; there will be more work to do in the house. It is only in very comfortably-off circles that some few women are pleased at the idea of seeing more of their husbands. Generally speaking, the husband feels that he is in the way. He is humiliated before his wife, and often before his sons too, they being better adapted than he to modern life and having a higher status. From one day to the next, domestic tyrants may become so timid that they no longer cut a slice of bread without asking permission. Others sink into hypochondria.

What is the effect of this situation upon health? Opinions vary. Most French gerontologists think it exceedingly bad: they say that during the first year of retirement the death-rate is far higher than at any other time. The American gerontologists, set in a facile optimism, reply that this is the case only where the retirement has been voluntary – it is bad health that causes the retirement and not the other way about: in fit people obligatory retirement has no bad effect upon their health; indeed, its effect is often good, since it provides the individual with rest and sleep. Yet everybody acknowledges the connexion between state of mind and state of body; and in America too it is admitted that elderly men's morale drops year by year, and most markedly between sixty-five and sixty-nine, just after retirement, particularly if their economic status is unsatisfactory. This must necessarily have an effect upon their physical condition.

The anxieties provoked by retirement sometimes end in a lasting state of depression. According to Dr Blajan-Marcus these depressions are made up of many superimposed factors – the retirement which is experienced as a period of mourning and exile has a background of badly-resolved bereavements in the past, of dependence upon parents, of depressive temperament and no doubt glandular and circulatory disturbance, although these are hard to detect. In other words, the shock of retirement is quite overwhelming for those whose past has left a certain mark upon them. Retirement revives the sorrow of parting, the feeling of abandonment, solitude and uselessness that is caused by the loss of some beloved person.

Listlessness is disastrous from every point of view, and to protect himself against it the elderly person must retain some activities: whatever they are, they will improve his functions as a whole. Professor Bourlière studied a group of a hundred and two aged bicyclists: their intellectual level was very much higher than the average for people of their age. F. Clément and H. Cendron questioned forty-three remarkably well-preserved Burgundians in their eighties: their inquiry showed that the old men's health was connected with their activity. Their average age was eighty-six. Thirty-four per cent continued with their former callings, working full time. Forty per cent worked with their children or at secondary occupations. Twenty-six per cent no longer did any paid work, but they read, worked in their gardens, etc. Sixty-one per cent had never found their work tiring. They all had normal social lives. The average age of the most active group was eighty-seven: the group with an average age of eighty-three was somewhat less so. The first still had many physical activities – riding a bicycle, walking, shooting. In the second group twenty-five per cent never read at any time, not even the newspaper: the others kept themselves up to date. Of the old men taken as a whole, eighteen per cent preferred reading to anything else, and fourteen per cent shooting. Only seven per cent had no amusements.

It is therefore very important for elderly people to find something to do. American research shows that between forty and sixty per cent of them have hobbies: between the ages of fifty and seventy they spend more time on them than before, but after that they lose interest. Not much is known about how people of over seventy spend their time. On the whole they have lost their pleasure in occupations that call for skill and dash; they have lost their taste for reading and writing, and above all for varying their activities. Morgan made a survey of 381 Americans over seventy in 1937, and this showed that for 32·9 per cent their chief occupation was household tasks; for 31·5 per cent games and intellectual amusements; for 13·6 walking and seeing friends: 9·6 merely sat in the sun or looked out of the window; 8·1 per cent liked gardening and looking after domestic animals; and 4·3 per cent did odd jobs for which they were paid.

The higher the person's intellectual level, the richer and more varied his occupations remain. But retired manual workers spend much of their time doing nothing. Among elderly people there is a high percentage of complete inactivity; and in this respect too we may speak of a 'downward spiral' – inactivity causes an apathy that in its turn destroys all desire for activity. Carrel observed that excessive leisure was even more dangerous for old people than for young – the more they had, the less they were able to fill it. Boredom took away their desire for amusement. Professor Bourlière, replying to the remark, 'Still, they could at least play cards', said, 'When they might do something but do not do it – that is the very moment when you can be sure they may be said to be really bored.' The statement is sound, both for life inside institutions and out.

In his novel *Late Call*, Angus Wilson deals with a woman's difficulties in adapting herself to a life of retirement. She is sixty-five; she has run a hotel; and she is very active. She goes to live with her children, who as she knows do not need her. 'At the idea that her new life would consist of nothing but blank pages she had a moment of something like panic.' She would like to be useful, but she cannot manage to work the electrical equipment in the kitchen. Her clumsiness makes her anxious, and her anxiety makes it difficult for her to learn. Her son behaves towards her in the usual adult manner; he is kind and polite, but his impatience often shows through and he speaks sharply. She is given little to do, and the barrenness of the years to come frightens her. She does not succeed in sharing her children's life, and indeed she makes little attempt at doing so, because she feels herself an alien, someone peripheral. She is overcome by gloom; she scarcely takes any interest in the television or in reading. She sleeps during the day, goes to bed without any dinner, takes dreary, mechanical walks, oppressed by a kind of torpor. Then something happens that gives her the feeling of being useful and her morale rises; as soon as she recovers some pleasure in life many things begin to interest her again, particularly her son's work, which she had not appreciated before. She decides not to live as a parasite any longer and moves to a village for old people. In spite of this timidly optimistic conclusion, what strikes one about the novel is that it describes a dead-end situation.

In order to protect the inactive against loneliness and boredom, England, Sweden and above all the United States encourage them to join associations. Some of these bring together men of all ages; others, in the United States, have been formed especially for the old, either by themselves or by younger people. Amusements are organized for them – games, excursions, plays, etc. There are also 'day-centres', a formula that has no equivalent in France: the first were opened during the last war, and there are now forty in New York. In these the retired people of a given district can meet, which allows them both to have a social life and to engage in certain activities – they do useful work, they play music or listen to it, they are taken on excursions, and discussions are organized for them. Churches and trades unions have set up centres of the same kind. The people who have joined clubs or who go to the centres feel that they are happier than others; but it is also because they are happier that they like going. We always come back to the same vicious circle – an extreme degree of material or intellectual poverty does away with the means of alleviating it. The higher the standard of living, the greater the individual's participation in social life. The participation always declines with age. Half the people questioned in various inquiries have stated that their social activity began to slow down from the age of fifty; only one per cent said that it had increased. At Orlando half the elderly people did not belong to any kind of association; at Palm Beach this applied to two-thirds. The only way of dealing with the cheerless inertia of old age is by a radical alteration of the circumstances. This is shown by the Victoria Plaza experiment: before they were moved there, most of its future inmates spent a great deal of

271

time dozing, sitting and doing nothing. As soon as they were re-housed in a way that suited them and made part of a community they began to read, to watch the television and to take part in social activities. But successful experiences of this kind affect only a minute number of people.

I should mention an experiment carried out in France over the last three years: at Grenoble the *Office grenoblois des personnes âgrées* (OGPA) has set up twenty-three leisure-time clubs run by two paid professional leaders and about fifty volunteers. They have about two thousand members, 1,500 of them being regular in their attendance; and cultural, manual and physical activities are organized for them – men and women of over eighty follow classes in gymnastics. The organization has also opened a centre to prepare its members for retirement. This is a worthwhile undertaking; but here again only a very small minority profits from it. The situation of the majority is summed up by the slogan or device suggested by a similar club recently formed in the thirteenth arrondissement in Paris: 'There is spare time in retirement, but there is also boredom.'

'Retirement, combined with the falling apart of the family unit, renders the state of the aged person lonely, useless and gloomy,' says a French sociologist. This indeed is how we see the world as it is made for the aged in the capitalist countries (apart from Scandinavia), and especially in France: but the two causes that are to blame produce their disastrous effects only because of the context in which they exist. The fate of the aged would be less horrible if the amount of money devoted to them were not so ludicrously inadequate. The pensioner who can no longer even have a drink with his friends, who has no place of his own, no scrap of garden to cultivate, nor even the money to buy himself a paper, does not suffer so much from excess of leisure as from the impossibility of using it and from his loss of caste. A decent pension and decent housing would spare him the humiliation that undermines his strength, and they would allow him at least a minimum of social life.

Yet even the well-to-do old people suffer from their uselessness. The paradox of our time is that the aged enjoy better health than they used to and that they remain 'young' longer: this makes their idle-ness all the harder for them to bear. All gerontologists agree that living the last twenty years of one's life in a state of physical fitness but without any useful activity is psychologically and sociologically impossible. Those who live on must be given some reason for living:

mere survival is worse than death. 'You can't be retired and live,' said a former mechanic when he was asked to explain what he had done – without any apparent reason he had fired a gun at a policeman, wounding him badly.*

A gradual retirement would certainly be less hurtful than the 'sudden chop'. This is proved by the fact that unless they are struck by a sudden illness, independent workers so arrange their lives that they have more and more spare time, but still go on working, at least for short spells. It has been suggested that for wage-earners too the withdrawal should be carried out by stages: for example, jobs would be divided into several categories according to the effort required, and the worker would move gradually down from the hardest to the easiest. Or his hours of work would be reduced. Apart from those who are seriously ill or incapacitated, these solutions would satisfy the majority, since most people cannot bear complete inactivity. The only trouble is that these solutions would call for a radical alteration of society. In the first place the pension would have to be based on the highest figure earned, for it is only upon this condition that a worker could accept a less tiring but lower-paid job towards the end of his life. And then there would have to be no threat of unemployment hanging over the young and middle aged.

There are few more controversial questions in France today than that of the retirement age. The gerontologists are strongly opposed to elderly people being condemned to an idleness that hastens their decline. But the unionists are against any raising of the retirement age; indeed, they want it to be lowered. Their first argument is that elderly workers are in need of rest. They certainly feel that excessive leisure may be dangerous; but working conditions being what they are, they think that lengthening the worker's active life is more dangerous still. In *Le Monde* in 1967 Dr Escoffier-Lambiotte spoke of an inquiry into the condition of Parisian workers: this showed that their physical and intellectual state was not nearly so good as that of the average Parisian. A random sample of 102 craftsmen was taken from the pay-roll of a big car-works: in those under fifty-five blood-pressure was higher than the average, heart-rhythm faster, muscular weakness more marked, cardio-vascular disturbances more frequent and difficulties with sleeping more usual. A precocious lowering of their intellectual powers was also remarked. In modern societies, jobs are less arduous than they used to be in so much as they

* At Phoenix, Arizona, at the beginning of 1964.

273

call for less muscular effort; but the faster rhythm of work combines with the extreme subdivision of labour to increase their wearing effect. As I have said, this decline is not a natural consequence of ageing but rather of the conditions of work: nevertheless, until these conditions have been changed, the aged worker's right to rest must be defended.

Then again, the unionists say that in a profit-based economy the creation of a cheap reserve of labour would be entirely wrong: it would be grossly exploited by the employers and it would make the workers' struggle far less effective. These are decisive arguments. In its present state, society insists upon an odious choice: either millions of young people must be sacrificed, or millions of old ones must be abandoned to a wretched, aimless half-existence. Everyone agrees that the first solution is bad, so all that remains is the second. It is not only the hospitals and institutions that are 'waiting-rooms for death' for the aged: it is society as a whole.

What is so heart-breaking about the replies of old people who are asked whether they would rather go on working or retire is that the reasons they bring forward are always negative. If they would rather go on, it is out of fear of poverty; if they would rather stop, it is in order to look after their health; but in neither case do they look forward to that particular way of life with any kind of pleasure. They do not see either work or leisure as a form of self-fulfilment; neither the one nor the other is freely chosen.

In his *Le Socialisme difficile* Gorz clearly shows that the counterpart of enforced work – of work that has not been freely chosen – is 'passive consumption'. The 'molecular individual' is master neither in his work nor in his consumption. But old age is non-work; it is mere consumption: and the 'passive leisure' of a whole lifetime can end only in the great 'passive leisure' of retirement – a half-life that amounts to no more than a waiting for death.

The tragedy of old age is tantamount to a fundamental condemnation of a whole mutilating system of life that provides the immense majority of those who make part of it with no reason for living. Labour and weariness hide this void: it becomes apparent as soon as they have retired. It is far more serious than boredom. Once the worker has grown old he no longer has any place on earth because in fact he was never given one. No place: but he had no time to realize it. When he does discover the truth he falls into a kind of bewildered despair.

Compared with this reality all 'praises of old age' look like mere intellectual elucubrations for the sole use of those who used to be called the eupatrids, the highly-privileged. For hundreds of years they were the only people writers troubled about. Cicero and Schopenhauer might acknowledge that being old and poor was an intolerable state even for a wise man; but they did so only in a passing phrase and then went straight on to congratulate themselves on the fact that old age set men free from their passions. In our days we know that 'old and poor' is almost a tautology. Although it may do away with passions, old age makes needs all the worse because of its inability to satisfy them: old people feel hunger and they feel cold: they die of them. It is the void alone that sets them free from their bodies, and until then their bodies have a cruel existence in the form of suffering and frustration. In no other aspect of life does the indecency of the culture we have inherited show itself more nakedly.

For a certain number of old people their condition is so unbearable that they prefer death to the 'torment of living'. Old age is by far the most usual time for suicide. Durkheim was the first to draw up statistics showing that the percentage of suicides increases from forty to eighty years of age. The following figures show the number of suicides in France between 1889 and 1891 for every million of population, divided according to age-group, sex and marital status:

	MEN			WOMEN		
	single	married	widowed	single	married	widowed
40–50	975	340	721	171	106	168
50–60	1,434	520	979	204	151	199
60–70	1,768	635	1,166	189	158	257
70–80	1,983	704	1,288	206	209	248
over 80	1,571	770	1,154	176	110	240

It will be seen that the number of suicides is far higher for men than for women. Statistics established in the other centuries agree with Durkheim's figures. So they do with those drawn up later by Halbwachs and with those produced by the *Revue lyonnaise de médecine* in 1957.

Recent statistics show that in France suicides committed by old people account for three-quarters of voluntary deaths. We find fifty-one suicides for every hundred thousand persons up to the age

275

of fifty-five: a hundred and fifty-eight after fifty-five. A 1960 report of the World Health Organization states that the highest rate of male suicides occurs at seventy and later, in Great Britain, France, Italy, Belgium, Holland, Portugal, Spain, Switzerland and Australia. The maximum rate for women comes ten years earlier, and it is far lower. In Canada, in the United States as far as the Afro-Americans are concerned, and in Norway and Sweden, the highest rate occurs between sixty and sixty-nine. Among the elderly, suicide is a more frequent cause of death than pulmonary tuberculosis, although that is a disease which claims many victims. Taking the world as a whole, suicide has diminished since the First World War (in the United States there are proportionately a third fewer); but this reduction is scarcely noticeable among those of over sixty. In the States, according to S. de Grazia, twenty-two out of every hundred thousand people in their forties kill themselves: this figure rises with age, and at eighty it reaches 697 in a hundred thousand. Some old people kill themselves after neurotic depressions that have not yielded to treatment; but most of these suicides are the normal reaction to a hopeless, irreversible situation that is found to be unbearable. In his *Suicide in Old Age* (1941) Gruhle states that psychosis is rarely the cause of old people's suicides. These are explained by social and psychological factors – physical and mental decline, solitude, idleness, inadaptation, incurable disease. According to him their suicide is never the outcome of a single depressive episode but rather of a whole lifetime's history.

One of the hopeless, dreadful aspects of the condition of the aged is their powerlessness to change it. The two and a half million old and needy people in France are scattered all over the country; they do not possess the least cohesion since they no longer play an active part in the nation's economic life, nor have they any means of bringing pressure to bear. There is a concentration of old people in Nice, where they amount to twenty-five per cent of the population and where their votes matter in elections. But they do not know one another and as usual they carry out no joint action. The notion of social change frightens them – they always fear the worst. They vote for the conservative candidates. In the United States old people do sometimes have a certain political power: when they retire they often move to Florida or California, and in some places (particularly St Petersburg in Florida) there are very large numbers of them, amount-

276

ing to a considerable proportion of the voters. Then again, in the context of American political life, it has been possible to set up new politico-economic organizations in which the aged have real influence. But these observations apply only to the privileged. The poor do not move to Florida and they possess no political influence: they are weak, crushed and powerless.*

* For the state of the aged in the socialist countries, see Appendix III, p. 555.

Hitherto we have looked at the aged man as an object, an object from the scientific, historic and social point of view: we have described him from the outside. But he is also a subject, one who has an intimate, inward knowledge of his state and who reacts to it. Let us try to understand how he experiences his old age – how he actually lives it. The difficulty is that one can adopt neither a nominalist nor a conceptual view of age. It is just something that happens to people who become old, and this plurality of experiences cannot possibly be confined in a concept or even in a notion. But at least we can compare them with one another; we can try to isolate the constants and to find the reasons for the differences. One of the drawbacks of this process is that the main source of my examples is the writing of the privileged few who, as we have seen, were almost the only people to have the means and the leisure to record their evidence. Yet generally speaking their information does have a significance that goes beyond their own particular cases.

I shall make use of these data without troubling about their chronological order. The great number of clichés and set phrases about old age that we have come across show that it is a reality which runs clean through history. To be sure, the state of the aged has not been the same in all places and at all times; but rising through this diversity there are constants that make it possible for me to compare various pieces of evidence independently of date.

The most serious difficulty is the way the various factors that define the old person's state influence one another, as I have pointed out: none has its real meaning except in its relationship with the others. Any kind of isolation is arbitrary. These chapters, in which I shall examine what happens to the individual's relationship with his body and his image during his last years, to his relationship with time, history and his own praxis, and to his relationship with others and the outside world, each in turn, must be read from the viewpoint of a final synthesis.

PART TWO

The Being-in-the-world

5

The discovery and assumption of old age; the body's experience

Die early or grow old: there is no other alternative. And yet, as Goethe said, 'Age takes hold of us by surprise.' For himself each man is the sole, unique subject, and we are often astonished when the common fate becomes our own – when we are struck by sickness, a shattered relationship, or bereavement. I remember my own stupefaction when I was seriously ill for the first time in my life and I said to myself, 'This woman they are carrying on a stretcher is me.' Nevertheless, we accept fortuitous accidents readily enough, making them part of our history, because they affect us as unique beings: but old age is the general fate, and when it seizes upon our own personal life we are dumbfounded. 'Why, what has happened?' writes Aragon. 'It is life that has happened; and I am old.' The fact that the passage of universal time should have brought about a private, personal metamorphosis is something that takes us completely aback. When I was only forty I still could not believe it when I stood there in front of the looking-glass and said to myself, 'I am forty.' Children and adolescents are of some particular age. The mass of prohibitions and duties to which they are subjected and the behaviour of others towards them do not allow them to forget it. When we are grown up we hardly think about our age any more: we feel that the notion does not apply to us; for it is one which assumes that we look back towards the past and draw a line under the total, whereas in fact we are reaching out towards the future, gliding on imperceptibly from day to day, from year to year. Old age is particularly difficult to assume because we have always regarded it as something alien, a foreign species: 'Can I have become a different being while I still remain myself?'

'False dilemma,' people have said to me. 'So long as you feel young, you are young.' This shows a complete misunderstanding of the complex truth of old age: for the outsider it is a dialectic relationship between my being as he defines it objectively and the awareness of myself that I acquire by means of him. Within me it is the Other – that is to say the person I am for the outsider – who is old: and that Other is myself. In most cases, for the rest of the world our being is as many-sided as the rest of the world itself. Any observation made about us may be challenged on the basis of some differing opinion. But in this particular instance no challenge is permissible: the words 'a sixty-year-old' interpret the same fact for everybody. They correspond to biological phenomena that may be detected by examination. Yet our private, inward experience does not tell us the number of our years; no fresh perception comes into being to show us the decline of age. This is one of the characteristics that distinguish growing old from disease. Illness warns us of its presence and the organism defends itself, sometimes in a way that is more harmful than the initial stimulus: the existence of the disease is more evident to the subject who undergoes it than to those around him, who often do not appreciate its importance. Old age is more apparent to others than to the subject himself: it is a new state of biological equilibrium, and if the ageing individual adapts himself to it smoothly he does not notice the change. Habit and compensatory attitudes mean that psychomotor shortcomings can be alleviated for a long while.

Even if the body does send us signals, they are ambiguous. There is a temptation to confuse some curable disease with irreversible old age. Trotsky lived only for working and fighting, and he dreaded growing old: he was filled with anxiety when he remembered Turgenev's remark, one that Lenin often quoted – 'Do you know the worst of all vices? It is being over fifty-five.' And in 1933, when he was exactly fifty-five himself, he wrote a letter to his wife, complaining of tiredness, lack of sleep, a failing memory; it seemed to him that his strength was going, and it worried him. 'Can this be age that has come for good, or is it no more than a temporary, though sudden, decline that I shall recover from? We shall see.' Sadly he called the past to mind: 'I have a painful longing for your old photograph, the picture that shows us both when we were so young.' He did get better and he took up all his activities again.

The reverse applies: the discomforts caused by age may sometimes be scarcely noticed or mentioned. They are taken for superficial and curable disorders. One must already be fully aware of one's age before it can be detected in one's body. And even then, the body does not always help us to a full inward realization of our condition. We know that this rheumatism, for example, or that arthritis, are caused by old age; yet we fail to see that they represent a new status. We remain what we were, with the rheumatism as something additional.

Opinions vary on elderly people's ideas about their health; and these variations are important. According to the Laroque report, 'More than half the people over sixty think of themselves as being in bad or very bad health. This impression does not always correspond with the facts, in so far as – apart from cases of obvious disease – it is primarily the interpretation of a reflex of fear on being faced with the process and the symptoms of ageing.' An inquiry carried out in England by Tunbridge and Sheffield in 1956 reached opposite conclusions: the team questioned old people about their health, and the research-workers were of the opinion that only twenty-six per cent of the men were fit, although sixty-four per cent believed themselves to be in perfect health. Twenty-three per cent of the women were healthy, whereas forty-eight per cent supposed themselves to be so. The inquiry decided that generally speaking the very old person was under-nourished, that his respiratory, motor and intellectual organs were unsound; but that he did not realize it.

This idea seems to be confirmed by a fact that I have already mentioned – aged invalids see their doctors far less often and take far less medicine than younger people who are ill. They were brought up in a society that paid less attention to health than is usual today: but this is not an adequate explanation, since in many other ways they move with the times. Professor A. Ciusa, working at the Bucharest Geriatrics Institute, observes that elderly people do not usually take advantage of their right to medical care, and he offers two reasons for this: '1: They do not realize just when their condition becomes pathological: even serious disturbances seem to them a natural consequence of their age. 2: They have adopted a passive attitude of renunciation: this is far more usual than the opposite attitude of exasperation with the worries of their state, and it arises from a feeling of uselessness.'

All in all, there is truth in the idea of Galen, who placed old age half-way between illness and health. What is so disconcerting about old age is that normally it is an abnormal condition. As Canghilem says, 'It is normal, that is to say it is in accordance with the biological laws of ageing, that the progressive diminution of the margins of safety should bring about a lowering of the threshold of resistance to attack from the environment. What is normal for an old man would be reckoned deficient in the same person in his middle years.' When elderly people say that they are ill – even when they are not – they are emphasizing this anomaly: they are adopting the point of view of a man who is still young, and who would be worried by being rather deaf and dim-sighted, by feeling poorly from time to time and by tiring easily. When they say that they are satisfied with their health and when they will not look after themselves, then they are settling down into old age – they realize what is the matter. Their attitude depends upon how they choose to regard age in general. They know that elderly people are looked upon as an inferior species. So many of them take any allusion to their age as an insult: they want to regard themselves as young come what may, and they would rather think of themselves as unwell than old. Others find it convenient to speak of themselves as elderly, even before the time has really come – age provides alibis; it allows them to lower their standards; and it is less tiring to let oneself go than to fight. Others, although they do not accept age willingly, still think it better than frightening diseases that would force them to take certain steps.

A research-worker who questioned the inmates of a CNRO* home summed up his impressions thus: 'It is the body as a whole, its organs and functions, that do not work properly . . . old age expresses itself by physical difficulties and discomforts of this kind and by the slowing down of all functions. This reality is at the heart of daily life; yet on the other hand it is habitual now, and it is no longer shocking. They speak of it in a detached, remote and judicial manner. . . . That is how things are, but we know what it is all about . . . we are old – it is not worth going to see the doctor.' As far as health is concerned, old age, that normal abnormality, seems to be experienced with a mixture of indifference and uneasiness. The notion of disease is exorcized by calling upon age: that of age by summoning up disease. And by means of this alternation it becomes possible to believe neither in the one nor the other.

The aspect of our face and body provides us with more certain evidence: what a contrast with ourselves at twenty! Only this change goes on all the time, so continuously that we scarcely notice it.

* *Caisse nationale des Retraites ouvrières.*

Madame de Sévigné expressed it very prettily: on 27 January 1687 she wrote.

Providence leads us so kindly through all these different stages of our life that we hardly feel them at all. The slope runs gently down; it is imperceptible – the hand on the dial whose movement we do not see. If at the age of twenty we were given the position of the eldest member of our family and if we were taken to a mirror and shown the face that we should have or do have at sixty, comparing it with that at twenty, we should be utterly taken aback and it would frighten us. But it is day by day that we go forward; today we are as we were yesterday and tomorrow we shall be like ourselves today. So we go on without being aware of it, and this is one of the miracles of that Providence which I so love.*

A sudden alteration can destroy this tranquillity. When she was sixty Lou Andreas Salomé† lost her hair after an illness: up until then she had felt 'ageless', but now she confessed that she was 'on the wrong side of the ladder'. But unless there is some accident of this kind, we must already have some cause for uneasiness before we stand and study the reflection offered us by the looking-glass.

As for intellectual falling-off, if the sufferer's requirements and abilities have both declined at the same time, he is incapable of detecting it. The seventy-two-year old La Fontaine thought he was perfectly fit mentally and physically, when he wrote to Maucroix on 26 October 1693: 'I am still in good health and my appetite and strength are quite out of the ordinary. Five or six days ago I walked to Bois-le-Vicomte, having eaten almost nothing; and it is a good sixteen miles from here.' Yet in June of the same year Ninon de Lenclos wrote to Saint-Evremond, 'They tell me you long for La Fontaine in England. He does not give much pleasure in Paris: his mind is sadly weakened.' Perhaps it was because he suspected this that he boasted to Maucroix of his youthfulness: but he had also

* When Diderot was still young he expressed the same idea in *Le Rêve de d'Alembert*. 'If you had passed in a flash from youth to old age, you would have been thrown into this world as you were at the very moment of your birth! You would no longer have been the same person either for yourself or for others – others who would never have been themselves for you. . . . How could you have told that that dull-eyed man, creeping painfully along with a stick, even more unlike himself inside than out, was the same as he who but yesterday walked so easily, who could pick up heavy burdens, and who could plunge into deepest meditations or the sweetest and most strenuous of exercises?'

† Nietzsche, Rilke and many others loved this remarkable woman. She was Freud's friend and disciple, and he valued her contributions to psychoanalysis.

chosen not to realize it. In this field too, the signals assume their full significance only in a given context.

Since it is the Other within us who is old, it is natural that the revelation of our age should come to us from outside – from others. We do not accept it willingly. 'It comes as a shock to a man, the first time he hears himself called old,' observed Oliver Wendel Holmes. When I was fifty I gave a start when an American student told me that one of his friends had said, 'So Simone de Beauvoir is an old woman, then!' Long tradition has loaded the word with pejorative connotations; it has the ring of an insult. So when one is called old a frequent reaction is anger. Madame de Sévigné was cut to the quick when she read the words 'You are old' in a letter from Madame de La Fayette, who was trying to persuade her to come back to Paris. She complained of them when she wrote to her daughter on 30 November 1689:

> For up until now I feel no decline that obliges me to remember it. Yet I do often reflect and work things out in my mind, and I think life's conditions are somewhat harsh. It appears to me that in spite of myself I have been dragged to this inevitable point where old age must be undergone: I see it there before me; I have reached it; and I should at least like so to arrange matters that I do not move on, that I do not travel farther along this path of the infirmities, pains, losses of memory and the disfigurement. Their attack is at hand, and I hear a voice that says, 'You must go along, whatever you may say; or if indeed you will not, then you must die', which is an extremity from which nature recoils. However, that is the fate of all who go on a little too far.

When Casanova was sixty-eight a correspondent called him a 'venerable old man', and he replied very sharply, 'I have not yet reached that wretched age at which one can no longer make any claim to life.'

I have known many women whose age has been revealed to them by the same kind of unpleasant experience that happened to Marie Dormoy: she told Léautaud how a man, deceived by her youthful shape, followed her in the street; as he overtook her he saw her face, and instead of accosting her he hurried on.

We see those who are close to us *sub specie aeternitatis*, and the discovery of their ageing is also a painful blow. The reader will remember what a shock it was for Proust when he walked casually into a room and suddenly saw a very old woman instead of his grandmother, who was ageless as far as he was concerned. Before the war one of Sartre's friends who was travelling with us came into the hotel dining-room and said, 'I've just met your friend Pagniez: there's an old lady with him.' We were utterly taken aback; we had never thought that Madame Lemaire was an old lady – it was Madame Lemaire. An alien eye had transformed her into another being. I had a foreboding that time would play curious tricks on me too. The surprise is even more painful when it is a question of people of the same age as ourselves. Everyone has had this experience: you meet someone you scarcely recognize, someone who looks at you with puzzled eyes, and you say to yourself, 'How he has changed! And how I must have changed too!' Léautaud, coming back from a funeral on 25 February 1945, wrote that the most ghastly part of it was 'seeing people one knows but has not seen for five or six years – people one has not seen growing older day by day (although in that case you scarcely notice it) so that one is confronted with an ageing of five or six years all at once. What a sight! And what a sight one must be oneself!' And then again how astonishing some photographs can be! It is really hard for me to persuade myself that this triumphant girl, this golf champion, was not my school-fellow at the Cours Désir, rather than the white-haired old lady beside her, her mother, who was in fact my contemporary, and whose championship and dashing air impressed me so.

There is everything to be said for re-reading the long passage in *Le Temps retrouvé* in which Proust tells how he went back to the Princesse de Guermantes' salon after many years' absence.

'At first I could not understand why I found some difficulty in recognizing the master of the house and the guests, and why everyone there was "made up" – a make-up that usually included powder and that altered them entirely. The prince . . . had provided himself with a white beard and as it were with leaden soles which dragged at his feet, so that he seemed to be playing the part of one of the Ages of Life.' The narrator often finds it hard to make what he actually sees agree with his recollections: when he sees Bloch, for example, it is difficult for him to make his 'sickly, prating' old man's look coincide with the youthful high spirits of his adolescent years. 'A name was mentioned to me, and I was dumbfounded at the thought that it applied both to the blonde waltzing girl I had once known and to the stout, white-haired lady now walking heavily by just in front of me.' Some people's faces had remained more or less unaltered, but 'at first it seemed that their feet were hurting them, and it was only later I understood that age had shod them with lead'. Still others 'were not old men but exceedingly faded youths of eighteen'. Proust had the feeling that he 'was attending a fancy-dress party, that he was seeing puppets swimming in the insubstantial colours of the years, puppets that were the outward expression of time'. It was that which struck him most – time was as it were visible to the naked eye. 'For me the completely new aspect of such a being as Monsieur d'Argencourt was a striking revelation of the date, the year, which is usually no more than an abstraction. ... One feels that one has obeyed the same law as these creatures who have undergone so strange an alteration. .... The transformations that all these people had suffered made me aware of the time that had passed for them; this had never happened to me before, and I was overwhelmed by the revelation that time had passed for me too.' What is more, Madame de Guermantes calls him 'My old friend'. Someone says to him, 'You, who are an old Parisian.' In the course of the evening he convinces himself of his age: 'We did not see our own appearance, our own age; but each, like a facing mirror, saw the other's.'

One day, when I was in Rome, I was present when the change took place in the other direction: a tall, sixty-year-old American woman was sitting at the terrace of the café where I happened to be. She was talking to a friend, and suddenly she laughed, a burst of laughter, a young woman's laughter – it transfigured her and moved me back twenty years in time, to California, where I had known her. In this case too, the abrupt contraction of time revealed to me its shattering power with painful clarity. I am used to seeing the present-day faces of well-known people of my own age on the screen or in magazines: when I see their forgotten freshness in old papers or films I shudder.

Whether we like it or not, in the end we submit to the outsider's point of view. When he was seventy, Jouhandeau scolded himself: 'For half a century I have persisted in being twenty years of age. The time has come to relinquish this unjust claim.' But this 'relinquishment' is not so easy. A kind of intellectual stumbling-block is in the way. We must assume a reality that is certainly ourselves although it reaches us from the outside and although we cannot grasp it. There is an insoluble contradiction between the obvious clarity of the inward feeling that guarantees our unchanging quality and the objective certainty of our transformation. All we can do is to waver from the one to the other, never managing to hold them both firmly together.

The reason for this is that old age belongs to that category which Sartre* calls the unrealizables. Since they stand for the reverse of our situation their number is infinite. It is impossible for us to experience what we are for others in the for-itself mode: the unrealizable is 'my being seen from without which bounds all my choices and which constitutes their reverse aspect'. A Frenchwoman, a writer, a person of sixty: this is my situation as I *live* it. But in the surrounding world this situation exists as an objective form, one that escapes me. However, the unrealizable only reveals itself as such in the light of a project that aims at its realization. A Frenchwoman in France: there is nothing that urges me to ponder over the meaning that this description may possess: in a foreign or a hostile country my nationality would exist for me and I should be required to adopt some given attitude towards it – I should have to claim it, conceal it, forget it, etc. In our society the elderly person is pointed out as such by custom, by the behaviour of others and by the vocabulary itself: he is required to take this reality upon himself. There is an infinite number of ways of doing so: but not one of them will allow me myself to coincide with the reality that I assume. Old age is something beyond my life, outside it – something of which I cannot have any full inward experience. Speaking more broadly, my ego is a transcendent object that does not dwell in my consciousness and that can only be viewed from a distance.

This viewing is effected by means of an image: we try to picture what we are through the vision that others have of us. The image itself is not provided in the consciousness: it is a cluster of rays of intentionality directed through an analogon towards a missing object. It is generic, contradictory and vague. Yet there are times when it suffices to assure us of our identity – this is the case with children if they feel themselves loved. They are satisfied with this reflection of themselves, a reflection that they perceive by means of the words and behaviour of those near to them; they adapt to it and they take it over for themselves. At the threshold of adolescence the image falls to pieces: the blunders and the clumsiness of the awkward age arise from the fact that one cannot tell what to replace it with straight away. A similar hesitation and uncertainty appears at the threshold of old age. In both cases the psychiatrists speak of an 'identification crisis'. But there are great differences. The adolescent realizes that he is going through a period of transition: his body is

* *L'Etre et le Néant.*

changing, and it torments him. The aged person comes to feel that he is old by means of others, and without having experienced important changes;* his inner being does not accept the label that has been stuck to him – he no longer knows who he is. In *La Mise à mort* Aragon symbolizes this want of knowledge and the distress, the confusion that it begets: the hero no longer sees his reflection in the glass – he is no longer capable of seeing himself.

The underlying reason for this asymmetry must be looked for in the unconscious mind of the subjects in question. As Freud says, the unconscious does not distinguish between the true and the false; it is a structured set or body of desires; it is not reflexive. But it may or may not hinder reflection. It does not impede the transition from adolescence to manhood. The fully-grown man's sexuality is in fact foreshadowed in that of the youth and even of the child. Generally speaking, the grown man's status seems to them desirable because it will allow them to satisfy their desires. The boy has fantasies of virility and the little girl dreams of her coming womanhood. They look forward cheerfully to this future in their games and in the stories they tell one another. The adult, on the contrary, associates great age with fantasies of castration. And as the psychoanalyst Martin Grotjhan emphatically states, our unconscious mind knows nothing of old age: it clings to the illusion of perpetual youth. When this illusion is shattered, in many cases it causes a narcissistic traumatism that gives rise to a depressive psychosis.

We see the explanation for the 'surprise', the incredulity and the profound indignation that the revelation of his age so often provokes in the elderly man. Among the unrealizables that surround us, this is the one that we are the most urgently required to realize, and it is the one that consciously and unconsciously we are the most reluctant to assume. It is this fact that allows us to understand the old person's attitudes towards his state – attitudes that are often at first glance disconcerting.

It is because age is not experienced in the for-itself mode and because we do not have the same lucid knowledge of it that we have of the cogito that we can say we are old quite early in life or think ourselves young to the very end. These choices are evidence of our general relationship with the world. The young Baudelaire was expressing his disgust of it when he wrote, 'I have more memories

* Women do have the physical experience of the menopause; but it takes place well before old age.

than if I were a thousand years old.' Because of his position with regard to his family, living always seemed an exhausting undertaking to Flaubert: from childhood on, he called himself 'old'. When he was fifty-four and his niece's husband was threatened with bankruptcy, he was afraid that Croisset would be sold – it filled him with despair. 'I cannot bear it! I am at the end of my tether. Stifled tears choke me, and I am on the very edge of the precipice. What breaks my heart, my poor dear Caro, is your ruin. Your present and future ruin. It is not amusing to come down in the world.' This was a question of an economic fall; it distressed him bitterly and humiliated him. Straight away he added to it the idea of a biological fall, caused by age. 'Life is not amusing, and I am beginning a dismal, gloomy old age.' Croisset was saved, but Flaubert was dependent on his nephew, with whom he was on bad terms, and he still dreaded ruin: he could no longer work, he was ill, he cried, he trembled. 'I look upon myself as a dead man.' 'I should like to die as soon as possible, because I am done for, finished, emptied, and older than if I were a hundred.' He went on, 'At my age there is no beginning again: you come to an end, or rather you fall to pieces.' He did manage to write again. But he went on feeling overwhelmed by age and he died prematurely.

People who are worn out by their calling and their life say that they are old although their behaviour is not that of an aged person. Professor Bourlière's team examined a group of 107 school teachers – fifty-two women and fifty-five men – aged a little under fifty-five: forty per cent seemed younger than they were and only three per cent older. The psychometric performances were outstanding. They were extremely active, intellectually and socially. Yet their physical resistance was below the average; they complained of nervous fatigue; they had a pessimistic view of themselves and they thought of themselves as old. The teacher's profession is in fact very trying. These subjects were overworked and tense, and they rightly felt worn out: and the idea of wear brings with it that of old age.

Usually the subject profits by the distance that separates the in-itself from the for-itself in order to claim that everlasting youth their unconscious longs for. In 1954, in America, Tuckmann's and Lorge's team questioned 1,032 people of various ages to find whether they felt young or old. Only a very small number of those about sixty said they were old: after eighty, fifty-three per cent called themselves old, thirty-six per cent middle-aged and eleven per cent young. Replying recently to the same question, most of the inmates of a CNRO old people's home said, 'I don't feel old at all. . . . I never think about old age. . . . I never go to see the doctor. . . . I'm still twenty.' In this context it is not enough to speak of psychological blindness or perceptual defence, as some psychologists do. It has still to be shown that a blindness of this kind is possible. It is possible, because all unrealizables tend to provoke the assertion, 'As far as I am concerned it is not the same thing.' When one is faced with people of the same age as oneself, one is tempted to say 'I belong to a different category', because one sees them only from the outside and does not credit them with the same feelings that are possessed by that unique being which each man is for himself. One of the women in the CNRO home said, 'I don't feel at all old; sometimes I help the grannies, and then I say to myself, "But you're a granny too." ' (*Mais toi aussi, tu es une mémé.*) Confronted with the other old women, her immediate reaction was to think of herself as ageless: it required an effort of reflection for her to liken her situation to theirs. It is significant that at this moment of awareness she spoke to herself as *tu*: it was the Other within her that she was addressing, the Other that existed for the rest but of whom she herself had no immediate knowledge.

For a man who is sure of himself, who is contented with his lot and who is on good terms with those around him, age remains theoretical. That is what Saint-John Perse meant when he said in one of his last poems, 'Old age, you lied. . . . The time measured out by the year is in no way the measure of our days.' Gide, who kept his physical and mental powers intact, wrote on 19 June 1930, 'I have to make a great effort to convince myself that I am at present as old as those who seemed to me so ancient when I was young.'

There is nothing that obliges us in our hearts to recognize ourselves in the frightening image that others provide us with. That is why it is possible to reject that image verbally and to refuse it by means of our behaviour, the refusal itself being a form of assumption.* This is a usual choice with some women who have staked everything on their femininity and for whom age means being entirely

---

* In certain pathological instances this refusal goes so far as to pervert memory and perception. This was so with Professor Delay's patient Noémie. At the age of sixty-four, believing what she said, she stated, 'I am a little girl: I am eight.' Or ten or sometimes sixteen. To the objection, 'But your hair is white' she replied 'Some people go white very early.' She thought she had been carried back to her childhood and she experienced episodes of her former life as though she were there. This is the phenomenon of ecmnesia.

294

out of the running. They try to deceive the rest of the world by means of their clothes, make-up and behaviour; but above all they make a hysterical attempt at convincing themselves that they are not affected by the universal law. They cling to the idea that 'this only happens to other people' and that for them, who are not 'other people' it is 'not the same thing'.

Anyone who takes pride in his clear-sightedness rejects this illusion, but it perpetually comes to life again and it must be perpetually fought against. Madame de Sévigné bears witness to this struggle in her letters. When she was still young she spoke of 'hideous old age'. Later she was deeply distressed at the sight of other people's decline. On 15 April 1685 she wrote, 'Oh, my dear, how humiliating it is to have to bear with the dregs of one's mind and body; how much it is to be wished – how much pleasanter it would be to leave behind us a memory worth preserving than to maim and spoil it by all the wretchedness that old age and infirmity bring us! I should love those countries where they kill their old relations out of kindness, if only they could be reconciled with Christianity.'

Five years later she knew she was no longer young, but she was obliged to be firm with herself before she was wholly convinced of it. Having delighted in a walk on a charming spring day, she wrote on 20 April 1690, 'What a pity it is that nothing should remain to me of all that lovely youth I enjoyed so fully,

> Mais hélas! quand l'âge nous glace
> Nos beaux jours ne reviennent jamais!*

'It is sad, but sometimes I feel like boxing my own ears so as to mortify my imagination, which is still crammed with those nonsensical trifles and pleasures that must be given up, although they are said to be innocent.'

And on 26 April, 'There is nothing yet that warns me of the number of my years, and so I am sometimes surprised by my health; I have got over innumerable little troubles that used to plague me; not only do I go forward as slowly as a tortoise, but I am almost ready to believe that I advance backwards like a crayfish; however, I try hard not to be taken in by these deceitful appearances.'

In his diary Gide often speaks of this alternation between inner conviction and objective knowledge. In March 1935 he wrote, 'If I did not keep telling myself my age over and over again, I am sure I

---

* But alas, when age freezes us, our happy, youthful days never come back again.

should scarcely be aware of it. Nevertheless, even by repeating "I am over sixty-five" like a lesson to be learnt by heart I can hardly persuade myself of it: all I manage to do is to convince myself of this – that the space in which my desires and my delights, my powers and my will can still hope to spread out is very narrow. They have never been more exacting.'

On 17 January 1943, 'I scarcely feel my age, and although every hour of the day I tell myself "My poor old fellow, you are seventy-three and more", I cannot really persuade myself of it.'

So long as the inner feeling of youth remains alive, it is the objective truth of age that seems fallacious: one has the impression of having put on a borrowed mask. Juliette Drouet wrote to Hugo, assuring him that her love would stand the proof of time, 'The setting has changed and I have put on the disguise of old age.' Gide uses the words *role* and *costume*. On 6 March 1941 he wrote, 'My heart has remained so young that I have the continual feeling of playing a part, the part of the seventy-year-old that I certainly am; and the infirmities and weaknesses that remind me of my age act like a prompter, reminding me of my lines when I tend to stray. Then, like the good actor I should like to be, I go back into my role, and I pride myself on playing it well.

'But it would be much more natural for me to abandon myself to the coming spring: only I feel that I no longer have the costume that it calls for.'

Was it true that he was consciously playing the character that society required of him? Or was it out of horror of old age that he looked upon his behaviour as a seventy-year-old in the light of an act? At all events, this passage once more emphasizes the unrealizable nature of old age.

Speaking of disguises, costume and role is one way of escaping from the problem. In order to resolve the 'identification crisis' we must unreservedly accept a new image of ourselves. There are cases where the grown man has already built up a hideous or a triumphant image of his old age in advance – Swift, when he described his Struldbrugs; Hugo, with his Burgraves, Eviradnus and Booz. When the time comes, they take it over, or at least they make use of it. But most people are caught unawares, and in order to recapture a picture of themselves they are forced to use another's eyes – how does he see me? I ask this question of my looking-glass. The reply is vague: each man sees us in his own way and it is certain that our own vision does not coincide with any one of theirs. They all agree in stating that our face is that of an elderly person; but for those who see us after a lapse of years it has changed, it has changed for the worse; for those near to us it is still our face – the sameness outweighs the deterioration; and for outsiders it is the ordinary face of a person of sixty, or of seventy. And what is it for us? We interpret our reflection, cheerfully, angrily, or with indifference, according to our general attitude towards old age. Voltaire was on such good terms with his that he let Pigalle sculpture him naked. He did not like any of the portraits that had been made of him up until then, and at first he was against the idea of another bust. He wrote to Madame Necker, 'They say Monsieur Pigalle is to come and model my face; but, Madame, in the first place I should have to have a face to model – one can scarcely even guess where it is. My eyes have sunk three inches and my cheeks are old parchment, badly stuck to bones that have nothing to hold on to. The few teeth I had have gone. . . . Never has a poor man been sculptured in such a state.' Yet in the end he agreed. Although he was an unflinching critic of his own appearance, he came to terms with it because he came to terms with his state as a whole.

I have never come across one single woman, either in life or in books, who has looked upon her own old age cheerfully. In the same way no one ever speaks of 'a beautiful old woman': the most one might say would be 'a charming old woman'.* Some 'handsome old men' may be admired, but the male is not a quarry; neither bloom, gentleness nor grace are required of him, but rather the strength and intelligence of the conquering subject: white hair and wrinkles are not in conflict with this manly ideal. Michelangelo's Moses or Hugo's sleeping Booz allow flattering self-identifications. Sartre's grandfather, as he described him in *Les Mots*, likened himself to that powerful, wise and patriarchal figure. He had always been very pleased with himself, and he enjoyed splendid health. He delighted in his role of the respected master, the beloved grandfather, the charming old man. Sartre says that he continually gave the impression of posing for an unseen photographer – that is to say, that he was playing parts meant to make other believe in an image that he arrogated to himself.

The most amusing example of narcissism in an old man is that

---

* The poetic theme 'To a beautiful old lady', which was often used in various centuries and various countries, applied to a former beauty who had ceased to be so on growing old. I know only one exception, Maynard's *Ode à une belle vieille*. Cf. p. 171.

which Léautaud provides in his *Journal*: I will return to it later, in connexion with his sexuality.

Jouhandeau at eighty, although he felt that his decline was at hand, looked at his body with a tolerably indulgent eye. In his *Réflexions sur la vieillesse et la morte* he wrote, 'I am not yet a repulsive object, to be sure. Indeed, I am still comparatively young in spite of my age, because I am slim, I might even say svelte; but there is no doubt that in my body I have felt that flaw, that hint of withering which is the sign of ageing, and piously I am beginning to bury it. I shall no longer be able to look at myself without sadness. Already I see the bandages of the embalmer seizing upon my person, and they hide me from myself out of a kind of respect.'

The ageing Yeats wavered between two contrary attitudes in his relationship to himself. At the height of his fame – at fifty-seven he had just received the Nobel prize – he was filled with bitterness about old age; he could only see with one eye and he was afraid of becoming deaf, but above all it was the very fact of growing old that exasperated him. 'Being old makes me tired and furious; I am everything that I was and indeed more, but an enemy has bound and twisted me so that although I can make plans and think better than ever, I can no longer carry out what I plan and think.' Yet he was still capable of writing very fine poems. In many of them he breathes out his anger against old age: 'What shall I do with this nonsense, oh my heart, my troubled heart/ This caricature, this decrepitude tied to me as to the tail of a dog?' What infuriated him was the accidental, casual aspect of this inescapable old age; he too tripped over the odious stumbling-block of this unrealizable reality – he was the same person, but he was being forced to suffer revolting usage. In one of his last poems he speaks of the woman he had once loved and he describes the couple they would make now – two old scarecrows in horrible contrast with the picture of their youth. It is so dreadful a sight that if a woman could see her child as it would be at sixty, she would give up motherhood. Yet he took pleasure in playing the part of the absurd old man. He astonished the Irish Academy by making a speech in which he announced that he was going to change into a butterfly 'and fly, and fly, and fly'. He described himself as a 'sixty-year-old smiling public man'; later he assumed the character of a 'wild old wicked man'.

If an elderly man hates his age, he is revolted by his own image. Chateaubriand, whose political influence had gone and whose fame

298

was declining, detested his old age. 'Old age is a shipwreck,' he said. An artist wanted to paint his portrait: Chateaubriand replied arrogantly, 'At my age, there is no longer life enough in a man's face for anyone to presume to entrust the ruins to canvas.' Wagner had a horror of growing old. Catching sight of himself in a shop window, he cried angrily, 'I do not recognize myself in that grey-head: can I possibly be sixty-eight?' He was persuaded that his genius set him outside space and time, and it appeared to him an outrage to see himself defined, fixed and summed up in his reflection. Gide felt young at seventy, but later he had difficulty in coming to terms with his old age. When he was eighty he wrote in *Ainsi soit-il*, 'Oh, come now, I really must not meet myself in a mirror – these eyes with bags under them, these hollow cheeks, this lifeless look. I am hideous and it depresses me terribly.' Valéry, when Léautaud spoke of 'how horrible it was to grow old', replied, 'Don't talk to me about it: I never look at myself in a mirror, except to shave.' In fact the age-marked faces of both Valéry and Gide remained handsome. The alteration that they saw in the mirror was, in their eyes, evidence of their age; and it was their age that they hated. In the same way, when Aragon wrote, 'And with horror I see the copper-coloured blotches of old age appear upon my hands' it was not the blotches themselves that revolted him, but the age they proclaimed.

Ronsard spoke of his disgust at his withered body. As we have seen, he had always loathed old age. A year before his death – he was only sixty, but in his days that was a great age – he was ill and he suffered from insomnia. He complained of it in many sonnets. In one of them he says

> Je n'ai plus que des os, un squelette je semble
> Décharné, dénervé, démusclé, dépoulpé
> Que le trait de la mort sans pardon a frappé.
> Je n'ose voir mes bras de peur que je ne tremble.*

The cruellest self-description that an aged man ever made was Michelangelo's. He was overwhelmed with cares and bodily pain. Bitterly he wrote, 'My long-drawn-out labours have broken, undermined and dismembered me, and the inn to which I am travelling, the inn at whose common table I shall eat and drink, is death. . . . I cage

* I have nothing left but bones; I look like a skeleton deprived of flesh, sinew, muscle and marrow, struck with the mark of unforgiving death. I dare not look at my arms for fear I should tremble.

a buzzing wasp in a leathery bag full of bones and sinews, and I have three balls of cobbler's wax in a tube. My face is a scarecrow's. I am like those rags they hang out in times of drought and that frighten away the birds. A spider runs about in one of my ears and in the other a cricket chirps all night. Weighed down by my catarrh I can neither sleep nor snore.'

In a sonnet he also said

> Once our eyes were whole,
> Reflecting the light in either of their mirrors.
> Now they are empty, fogged and dark.
> That is what time brings with it.

And in a letter to Vasari, 'My face has something frightening about it.' In the self-portrait that he left – Saint Bartholomew in the Last Judgement fresco – his face resembles a funeral mask, sombre, almost haunted, ravaged by a sorrow he can scarcely endure.

It is interesting to reflect upon the self-portraits of aged painters: by means of their faces they express their relationship with their own life and the world at the moment when they strike the balance in their accounts.

Leonardo da Vinci, at sixty, made of his face an extraordinary allegory of old age: the torrent of beard and hair and the bushy eyebrows show an undamaged and even impetuous vitality; the features are chiselled by experience and knowledge – they are those of a man who has reached the highest point of his intellectual powers and who stands beyond gaiety and sadness; he is disillusioned, on the edge of bitterness yet without letting himself fall into it. Rembrandt, who recorded his different faces on canvas throughout his life, left us a kind of testament in his last portrait of himself. He had reached the summit of his art and he knew it; behind him lay a lifetime's work of which he had every right to be proud; he had done what he wanted to do – he had won; but he was aware of the proportion of failure that is implicit in all success, and looking in the mirror he seems to be saying to the man reflected there, 'What then?' Tintoretto painted himself in 1588, when he was over seventy. Sartre has analysed this picture in an unpublished essay. Tintoretto, he says, makes us understand that he is in despair. On the canvas he has fixed for ever 'an ancient, exhausted amazement, frozen like his life, hardened like his arteries. ... In this picture he gives himself the loneliness of a corpse. ... He pleads guilty: if he did not, would he have this haunted look of an aged murderer? He is saying to himself,

"I, who am a great painter, the greatest of my century, what have I done with painting?" Yet what a look of resentment! In the moment of confessing he accuses. Whom? Mankind, surely. . . . You feel you can hear him endlessly repeating "I do not understand." ' Yet 'there is still something about him that compels us to keep our distance – the austere pride of his despair'. Titian's self-portrait, which he painted at the age of eighty or ninety (according to which date one accepts for his birth), has something rather conventional in the grave serenity of its expression.

I know only one old man's self-portrait that is downright cheerful: it is that which Monet painted as a present for Clemenceau. Although at one time his sight dimmed and he could no longer see colours with precision, he never stopped painting: his memory compensated for the failure of his eyes. Later his sight came back entirely and in his very old age he produced his most astonishing masterpieces. He did reach the point of doubting the value of his work; but that was a secondary question – his delight in painting outweighed it. He was endowed with a surprising capacity for work; he had very good health; he was surrounded with affection; he loved life: and this was how he painted himself, in what might be called the exuberance of old age – upright, merry, with a fine clear complexion, an abundant beard, his eyes full of life and gaiety.

Goya's self-portrait, painted at the age of seventy, must be mentioned. He denied his age. He painted himself with the features of a man of fifty.

Whether we have recovered a more or less convincing, more or less satisfactory image of ourselves or not, we are obliged to *live* this old age that we are incapable of *realizing*. And in the first place we have to live it, to experience it, in our bodies. It is not our body that makes us aware of old age; but once we know that it inhabits our body, it worries us. Old people's indifference with regard to their health is more apparent than real; if we look more closely into the matter, we find that they are anxious. This anxiety is strikingly obvious in their reactions to Rorschach tests. Generally speaking, great numbers of those subjected to these tests see bodily images in the blots of ink: but among elderly people anatomical interpretations are very unusual and very meagre. The interpretations have a morbid character – for example, the images are those of lungs or stomachs seen by X-ray. Old people frequently have a distorting view of the blots, seeing skeletons, monsters or hideous faces. Sometimes this anxiety goes as far as hypochondria. The retired man often transfers the attention no longer required by his work to his body. He complains of his aches and pains to hide from himself the fact that he is suffering from a loss of standing. For many, illness acts as an excuse for the inferiority to which they are now doomed. It can also justify their self-centredness – henceforward their body requires all their care. But these forms of behaviour are based upon a very real and intense anxiety.

In some aged writers we find an open confession of this state of mind. In his *Journal* for 10 June 1892, Edmond de Goncourt speaks of 'the frightened years, the anxious days when a mere scratch or something a little out of order straight away makes us think of death'. We know we do not resist outside attack so well, and we feel vulnerable. 'The unpleasant side of being a certain age,' says Léautaud in his *Journal*, 'is that the least indisposition makes one wonder what disaster is going to strike us.' The deteriorations observed are saddening in themselves; and they foretell others of a more final nature. 'It is attrition, ruin, the downward slope that can only grow steeper,' says Léautaud in another place. It is perhaps this which is most piercingly sad about growing old – this feeling of irreversibility. With disease, there is at least a chance of getting well or of halting its progress. Incapacity caused by an accident is what it is and no more. The degeneration caused by senescence is irreparable and we know that year by year it is going to increase.

This deterioration is inevitable: no man escapes from it. But there are many factors that decide whether it shall be fast or slow, partial or entire, and whether it will have a greater or a lesser influence upon our life as a whole. For those fortunate people who position allows them a margin of freedom, it largely depends upon the way the subject attempts to govern his fate.*

Very often the burden of the body counts for less than the attitude that is adopted towards it. Claudel, pledged to optimism, wrote in

---

* It may happen that no choice is allowed. The subject may be the victim of a stroke or of a gradual physical degeneration that ends in decrepitude. This was how Rodin ended at the age of seventy-seven. His health began to decline when he was sixty-seven: he went through periods of prostration. His first stroke, at seventy-two, left him gloomy, ill-tempered and mentally weakened. After the second he was senile; he no longer knew where he was and he did not recognize Rose Beuret, who had lived with him all his life. Cases of this kind belong to the field of geriatrics and teach us nothing from the point of view of inward experience.

his *Journal*, 'Eighty years old! No eyes left, no ears, no teeth, no legs, no wind! And when all is said and done, how astonishingly well one does without them!' A man like Voltaire, overwhelmed with ailments, one to whom his body has been a burden all his life and who has said that he is on the point of death from his youth, may deal with the situation better than others. At seventy and more Voltaire referred to himself as 'the sick old man', and then as 'the sick octogenarian'. Here it was the outsider's point of view of himself that he adopted, and not without a certain pleasure in his role: when it was his own *I* that was speaking he said he was accustomed to his state: 'It is eighty-one years now that I have suffered and that I have seen so much suffering and death around me.' 'The heart does not grow old, but it is sad to dwell among ruins,' he wrote. And again he said 'I undergo all the calamities connected with decrepitude.' But he was wealthy, famous and revered; he was busier than ever, passionately concerned with what he was writing, and he accepted his condition with serenity. 'It is true that I am rather deaf, rather blind and rather crippled; and that all this is capped by three or four atrocious infirmities: but nothing deprives me of hope.'

Others, on the contrary, make their infirmities worse out of resentment. 'It is a torment to preserve one's intellectual being intact, imprisoned in a worn-out physical shell,' wrote Chateaubriand. This complaint echoes Voltaire's; but Voltaire had the good fortune to live in full harmony with his time and even to embody it, and this predisposed him to a vital optimism. Chateaubriand had fallen from his pedestal; he was alone in a century that was taking less and less notice of him; and he brooded over his grievances. Although he had been able to work on his *Mémoires d'outre-tombe* as late as 1841, and to revise and correct them in 1847 a year before his death, he let his body fall to pieces.

Gribouillisme is the psychiatrists' name for the attitude that consists of plunging into old age because of the horror that it inspires. The subject exaggerates: because he is rather lame he goes through the motions of paralysis; because he is rather deaf, he stops listening altogether. The functions that are no longer exercised degenerate, and by playing the cripple, the subject becomes one. It is a widely-spread reaction since many old people are justifiably resentful and demanding because they have lost hope. They take their revenge upon the outside world by exaggerating their infirmity: as we have seen, this often occurs in institutions – since they have been abandoned,

303

they abandon themselves and refuse to make the slightest effort. As this tendency is not checked – no one looks after them – many end up by being bedridden.

For those who do not choose to go under, being old means fighting against age. That is the harsh new aspect of their condition: living can no longer be taken for granted. At forty, a healthy man is biologically free to do what he likes. He can push himself to the utmost limits of his strength – he knows he will soon regain it. The danger of sickness or accident does not frighten him overmuch – except in extremely serious cases he will get well and return to his former state. The aged man is obliged to take care of himself: excessive effort might cause heart-failure; an illness would leave him permanently weakened; he would never, or only very slowly, recover from an accident, since his wounds take a long time to heal. Fighting is forbidden to him: he is sure to get the worst of it and he would only make himself ridiculous by starting any violence. He can no longer run fast enough to take part in any political manifestations, and he would be a burden to his younger companions. Mental and physical work, exercise and even amusements tire him. The elderly man often suffers from exactly located or generalized pains that take away all his pleasure in life. Colette was tortured by her rheumatism. An admirer congratulated her upon her fame and her apparent happiness; she replied, 'Yes, my dear, but age is there.' 'But apart from age?' 'Still more age.' During the last years of her life my mother suffered cruelly from arthritis, in spite of the ten tablets of aspirin she took every day. Sartre's mother was so tortured by rheumatism that she almost lost any desire to live. Even if the elderly person bears his ailments with resignation, they come between him and the world: they are the price he pays for most of the things he does. So he can no longer yield to a sudden desire or follow his whims: he ponders on the consequences and he finds that he is forced to make a choice. If he goes for a walk to take advantage of a fine day, his feet will hurt him when he comes home; if he has a bath, his arthritis will torment him. He often needs help to walk or to wash, dress and so on; he hesitates to ask for it, preferring to do without. The level of inimicality in things rises: stairs are harder to climb, distances longer to travel, streets more dangerous to cross, parcels heavier to carry. The world is filled with traps; it bristles with threats. The old person may no longer stroll casually about in it. Every moment difficulties arise, and any mistake is severely punished. He needs artificial assistance to carry out his natural functions – false teeth, spectacles, hearing aids, walking-sticks. 'This is old age, too – all this arsenal of spectacles on my desk,' wrote Léautaud. The sad part of it is that most old people are too poor to be able to afford good spectacles or hearing aids – these are very expensive – and they are therefore condemned to half-blindness and total deafness. Shut in upon themselves, they fall into an inanition that diverts them from their struggle against their decline. A partial failure often brings about a renunciation that is followed by a rapid and general collapse.

When an old person is rich enough to have different possibilities open to him, the way in which he reacts to the disagreeable aspects of age will depend upon the choices he made in earlier life. Those who have always chosen mediocrity will not find it very hard to husband their strength and to live at a lower rate. I knew one old man who was perfectly adapted to his age: he was my paternal grandfather. He was selfish and superficial, and there was not much difference between the futile activities of his middle age and the inactivity of his later years. He did not over-exert himself; he had no worries because he did not much care about anything; his health remained excellent. Gradually his walks grew shorter, and he would doze more often over the *Courrier du Centre*. Right up until his death he had what is called 'a fine old age'.

Only a certain emotional and intellectual poverty can make this dreary state of balance acceptable. There are some people who pass their whole lives preparing themselves for it and who regard it as their highest peak. Cornaro, the sixteenth-century Venetian noble, was one of these. When he was eighty-five he enjoyed splendid health, and he held himself up as an example to posterity in a book he wrote at that period, the *Sure and Certain Method of Attaining a Long and Healthful Life*. He dwells upon the moderation with which he enjoyed pleasures, on the prudent manner in which he arranged his day, and above all on the frugality of his diet – for more than half a century he ate no more than twelve ounces of solid food a day and drank only fourteen ounces of wine. He describes himself as being surrounded with friends, children and grandchildren, hearing and seeing perfectly well, reading, writing, riding, hunting and travelling. 'I think my present age, although it is very advanced, the pleasantest and the finest of my life. I would not exchange my age and my life for the most flourishing youthfulness.' In his opinion this was his reward for having been moderate in his use of the world's goods.

In fact he was less deserving than he said he was, for circumstances had been very kind to him. He had an immense fortune, and he lived in a splendid house in the middle of a great spreading garden. He went on to reach almost a hundred, and one of his nieces states that he remained healthy and even vigorous to the end.

In all these prudent, moderate, balanced aspects, Fontenelle also lived his life in such a way as to have a successful old age: he died when he was nearly a hundred, murmuring, 'I feel nothing but a certain difficulty in being.' He was born a weakly creature, and out of care of his health 'he spared himself any kind of emotion with scrupulous care', as one of his biographers put it. He had a reputation for being unfeeling; Madame du Tencin once said to him, pointing to his heart, 'It's only brain you have there – just more brains.' He was intelligent, brilliant, and passionately devoted to science; and he was only twenty-nine when he wrote *Les Entretiens sur la pluralité des mondes,* the book that made him famous and that was followed by many more. He discovered nothing, confining himself to popularizing the science of his time; but this he did very skilfully. He was elected to the *Académie française* and to the *Académie des sciences.* Everything interested him, and everything is touched upon in his books. He did not hestitate to take sides: he defended the Moderns against the Ancients, and he attacked religion. But he always kept a cool head and he avoided any kind of over-exertion. He reached old age in excellent health and he found himself very much at his ease there. According to him, the happiest age was that 'between sixty and eighty; by this time a man's reputation is made. He no longer has any ambition or desires; he enjoys what he has sown. It is the age of harvest-home.' When he was eighty-two, says Madame Geoffrin, he was still an astonishing conversationalist. Yet at eighty-eight he grew deaf and at ninety-four his sight became very dim. The hosts with whom he passed his evenings found him something of a bore.

Swift was the victim of a physiological misfortune (after his death he was found to have water on the brain), of the position of Ireland, and of his gloomy attitude towards mankind. He had always been ambitious and he was very keen on money; his career and his modest fortune left him unsatisfied. He minded gossip very much, and was very apt to feel persecuted – all the more so since he was sometimes persecuted in fact. In spite of the self-vindications that he wrote, he did not like himself. For all these reasons he loathed his fellow-men: he displayed this hatred by describing first the Yahoos and then the

Struldbrugs, through whom he painted hideous pictures of old age. When it seized upon him he struggled furiously. He lost Stella when he was fifty-nine, and by this time he was already seriously undermined – his hearing was bad and he had fits of giddiness. 'I am still very ill, shaken and deaf . . . and I should be perfectly happy if God were to choose to call me to him.' Having solicited the Whigs, then the Tories and then the Whigs again, he hoped that Queen Caroline would give him an important post in England; but he fell into disgrace and returned from London to Dublin for good. He disliked Dublin more than ever, 'the dirtiest place in Europe'. Confronted with the poverty and filth of Ireland, he alternated between sorrow and rage. When he was sixty-one, he wrote his bitterest pamphlet, the 'modest proposal' for dealing with the children of the Irish poor. His disgust with the world and with life was so violent that he had to express it in writing with ever greater urgency – it was no doubt for this reason that he struggled so furiously against the decline of his powers. He forced himself to take exercise to overcome his deafness and vertigo, going for long walks and rides: when it rained, he ran madly up and down the stairs. At this period his horror of the human body expressed itself in scatalogical verse. Although he was surrounded by mature women and found young ones attractive, he became more and more of a misogynist. He was eaten up by resentment. In a note he stated that after Queen Anne's death 'the highest posts in the Church were allotted to the most unlearned, the fanatics were caressed, and Ireland was completely ruined and reduced to slavery while a few ministers accumulated millions'. His health fell to pieces. On 3 April 1733, when he was sixty-five, he wrote, 'My old giddiness has made me so ill all this last month that I am in Deally's hands, and I take medicine every day. I stagger in the darkness. Nevertheless I struggle against it, and I ride at least three times a week. To this list of my infirmities I shall only add that I have lost half my memory and all my powers of invention.' And on 9 October 1733, 'My spirits are very low.' His only consolation was the writing of ever more virulent pamphlets: indeed, it would seem that this was the reason why he so obstinately clung to life – he could not bear to stop hating and expressing his hatred at the top of his voice. He drew up a pamphlet on a 'home for incurables' in which there were to be shut up incurable fools, incurable rakes, incurable shrews and incurables of many other kinds – in short, half the nation, including himself. Perhaps this pamphlet was the outcome of personal anxiety:

307

perhaps he was afraid of going mad. He did at all events feel a kinship with lunatics, since he left all his property to a Dublin asylum. All his friends were dead; he wrote to Pope, 'You are the only one left to me now – be so kind as to outlive me.' The younger Sheridan described him in these words: 'His memory was much weakened and the decline of his other faculties manifest; his temper was unstable, fretful, gloomy, and given to sudden outbursts.' His avarice had grown worse. He was very far removed from a thoughtless optimism like La Fontaine's, and he was perfectly aware of his intellectual decadence. When his friends celebrated his seventieth birthday he said bitterly, 'I am no more than a shadow of myself.' He was tormented by gout. He could not bear feeling that his powers were diminishing; he brooded over his grievances and he suspected that everyone was against him. England's policy towards Ireland still disgusted him. He was in a state of permanent anger. When London debased the Irish gold coinage he hoisted a black flag on St Patrick's Cathedral. In 1742 he had a scuffle with one of his canons, and at this time a commission stated that 'he was no longer sound in his mind or his memory'. He dragged on for another three years.

Whitman, who was a friend and contemporary of Emerson, drew upon a vitalistic optimism in his poems. He celebrated life in all its forms. He glorified old age when he was himself in the prime of life. In *Leaves of Grass* we find

TO OLD AGE

I see in you the estuary that enlarges and spreads itself grandly as it pours in the great sea.*

And in another poem

Youth, large, lusty, loving – youth full of grace, force, fascination,
Do you know that Old Age may come after you with equal grace, force, fascination?
Day full-blown and splendid – day of the immense sun, action, ambition, laughter,
The Night follows close with millions of suns, and sleep and restoring darkness.

He was shattered by a stroke when he was fifty-four, and this man, overflowing with energy, who so passionately loved nature, found himself clamped to an invalid chair, half paralysed. His courage was

* Cf. Ruzzante, ' . . . Old age is indeed a pond into which all the foul waters run and which has no outlet but death . . .'

such that he bore the trial with cheerful tranquillity, and his will-power so great that in three years he learned to walk again. He was then living with his brother in the little town of Camden: by the age of sixty-five he thought himself well enough to settle in a small house of his own. A year later sunstroke brought on another seizure which left him with his arms and legs 'turned into gelatine'. He tried to retain his cheerfulness, but he was now condemned to a shut-in life, and this was a torment to him. He had many friends who loved him dearly; they gave him a trap; he wept with joy and the same day he set off through the streets at a round trot. He thought the horse too old and changed it for a more spirited animal. In this way he was able to move about the countryside for years. He managed to work two or three hours a day, he read the papers and magazines, entertained his friends and dined with some one of them every Sunday evening. He did not talk much, but he was a good listener and people sought him out. From time to time he gave a public reading, to make a little money. His treatment consisted of baths and massage. He did not show it outwardly, but in his poems he admitted his distress:

> As I sit writing here, sick and grown old,
> Not my least burden is that dullness of the years, querulousness,
> Ungracious glooms, aches, lethargy, constipation, whimpering *ennui*
> May filter in my daily songs.

And again:

> . . . An old, dismasted, gray and batter'd ship, disabled, done,
> After free voyages to all the seas of earth, haul'd up at last and
>   hawser'd tight,
> Lies rusting, mouldering.

He celebrated his sixty-ninth birthday in the company of a great many friends, and it was at this time that he wrote,

> . . . Of me myself – the jocund heart yet beating in my breast,
> The body wreck'd, old, poor and paralysed – the strange inertia
>   falling pall-like round me,
> The burning fires down in my sluggish blood not yet extinct,
> The undiminish'd faith – the groups of loving friends.

Poetry, friendship and nature were still enough for his heart to remain cheerful, in spite of his awareness of his decline. But two days later he had another stroke, followed by two more. He trembled all over, wandered in his mind, and called out to absent friends in a stammering voice. For a week, he would not see the doctor. At last he came and helped him to recover. 'The old ship is not in a state to make many voyages. But the flag is still at the mast and I am still at the wheel,' he said. His convalescence was slow; he felt very tired and at times he fell into a state of lethargy. Yet he congratulated himself on having a clear mind and the use of his right arm. 'Now that I am reduced to these two things, what great wealth they are!' He had diabetes and prostate and bladder troubles that made him suffer horribly. He had to sell his horse and trap. In his little room, filled with heaps of papers but with the windows always open, he dragged himself painfully from his bed to his chair. His friends bought him a wheel-chair and the young Traubel took him to the banks of the Delaware, which he loved to gaze at although his sight was now very poor. With Traubel's help he corrected the proofs of his last poems, *November Branches*, and brought out his complete works. Sometimes his old optimism came to life again: he wrote,

. . . But as life wanes, and all the turbulent passions calm . . .
Then for the teeming quietest, happiest days of all! . . .

He also spoke of the '. . . grandeur and exquisiteness of old age'. No doubt he was trying to convince himself; but that did not prevent him, on the verge of seventy, from describing himself with no cheerfulness at all as '. . . Dull, parrot-like and old, with crack'd voice harping, screeching'. His seventieth birthday was celebrated in great style; his seventy-first very quietly. He lingered on for another two years.

Swift and Whitman suffered from serious physical disorders; but even when the aged man remains in very good health the weight of the body makes itself felt. His contemporaries were astonished at Goethe's vitality. He had never been so elegant as he was at sixty. At sixty-four, he could ride for six hours without dismounting. At eighty he had no infirmities of any kind: his faculties, including his memory, were intact. Nevertheless, in 1831 when he was eighty-two, Soret, a close friend, recorded in his diary, 'I have just been to see Goethe – it was very painful. He seemed out of sorts: he gave me something to look at and went into his bedroom. A few moments later he came out in a state of great agitation, which he tried to hide: he was very red, sighing and muttering to himself. Twice I heard him exclaim, "*Oh das Alter! Oh das Alter!*" as though he were blaming his age for some infirmity.' One day as he was making a speech he had

310

a lapse of memory: for more than twenty minutes he stared in silence at his audience while they sat rigid with respect, and then went on speaking as though nothing had happened. From this it would appear that his apparent equilibrium was achieved by overcoming many small weaknesses. In the end he was apt to tire easily, and he worked only in the morning: he had given up travelling. He often dozed during the day.

Tolstoy possessed a legendary vigour; he owed this to his care in maintaining his strength. He learnt to ride a bicycle when he was sixty-seven, and in the following years he went for long excursions by bicycle, on horseback and on foot. He played tennis and bathed in the ice-cold river; in the summer he scythed, sometimes for three hours on end. He worked on *Resurrection*, wrote his diary and a great number of letters; he had visitors, he read and kept himself in touch with the world. When the Czar sent his Cossacks against the old religious sect of the Dukhobors in 1895, Tolstoy wrote an article violently opposing the repression and had it published in London. He also signed a manifesto denouncing the persecution and saw to its distribution. He launched a press campaign abroad, made appeals to public charity and agreed to accept royalties in order to give them to the 'aid committee'. His seventieth birthday was very gay. He was excommunicated by the Holy Synod; there were huge manifestations in his favour. Around 1901, however, his health began to fail and he suffered from rheumatism, heart-burn and headaches. He grew very thin. A fit of malaria obliged him to take to his bed. He reconciled himself with the idea of dying. But he recovered and went to the Crimea for a rest. He went out for drives and began to write an essay called *What is religion?* Chekhov was struck by finding how much he had aged: 'His main illness is the old age which has taken him over entirely,' he wrote to a friend. Tolstoy had pneumonia in 1902 and his life was in danger; but for all this he dictated his thoughts and letters to his daughter Masha as he lay there in his bed. When he recovered he became extremely careful of his health, which irritated Sophia intensely: 'Hour after hour, from morning till night, he thinks of nothing but his body and how to look after it.' In May he had typhoid: once again he got over it. But Sophia noted that he had become 'a little old man, pitiful and thin'. He did not give up the struggle. He took to going for longer and longer walks; he returned to physical exercises and riding. And he started to write again. He compiled an anthology called *Pensées des Sages*, wrote short stories and two plays, and an essay in which he cut his hated Shakespeare to pieces. He took up *Hadji Murat* again, a novel he had begun in 1890 and in which he severely criticized autocracy. In 1905 he wrote open letters both to Nicolas II and to the revolutionaries: he refused to commit himself. He drew up a children's reader, wrote *Christ's teaching explained to children* and organized evening classes for the peasants' children, who rarely attended them. All this time he was racked with guilt because, against his principles, he was in fact living as a landed proprietor, in spite of having made over all his possessions to his family. His quarrels with Sophia became more frequent and they utterly shattered him. During the winter of 1907 he had several short fainting-fits accompanied by loss of memory. He was horrified by the furious repression directed against the terrorists and he sent a protest and a warning to Stolypin, the minister responsible. He made a public appeal: *I can no longer remain silent.* The execution of the rebellious peasants revolted him. 'I cannot go on living like this,' he said, in tears. He had an attack of phlebitis and once again he was thought to be dying, but he got better and noted down seven new ideas for novels. His eightieth birthday was an astonishing spectacle – an apotheosis; he felt it so deeply that it brought tears to his eyes. He was utterly exhausted when he left the party, and as he went to bed he said to his daughter Masha, 'My spirit is weighed down', but he went to sleep calm and pacified. In the next few months scenes with Sophia wore him out. He went to Moscow in September 1909, and when he left there were huge numbers of people to watch him go by and cheer him. Getting out at the Kursk station he was wedged in the crowd and almost crushed – the police were powerless to help and he only just managed to hoist himself into the train. Frightened, tottering, his jaw trembling, he dropped on to the seat and closed his eyes, exhausted and happy. A few hours later he fainted; he spoke meaningless words at random and it was thought that he was going to die. But the very next day the indomitable Tolstoy went out riding and worked on his articles and correspondence. He wrote a tale called *The Khodynka* and a preface to the *Ways of Life.* He kept up a correspondence with Bernard Shaw and Gandhi. The conflicts in his life and the quarrels with Sophia became so unbearable that he fled. For years he had dreamed of abandoning his family and possessions for the ascetic life and poverty his ideals required. At his age the decision to leave assumed the possession of a very young man's fire and strength of will. But Tolstoy had an old man's body;

he could not stand the fatigues of the journey and he died in a station-master's house. He too had kept his health and his ability to work to the end, but only at the cost of an incessant struggle against the diseases and weaknesses of age.

From his sixtieth year onwards, Renoir was half-paralysed. He could no longer walk. His hand was rigid. Yet he went on painting until his death at the age of seventy-eight. His paints were squeezed on to the palette for him: a brush held in a finger-stall was fastened to his wrist and he moved it with his arm. 'You don't need your hand to paint,' he said. He was wheeled about the countryside in a chair, or if the slope was too steep he had himself carried bodily up to the places he liked best. He worked prodigiously, he had retained all his creative power; he felt that he was making continual progress and it filled him with great happiness. His only regret was that although time was making him richer as an artist, it was also carrying him on towards the grave.

At the age of seventy, Giovanni Papini was still in good health. On 9 January 1959 he wrote to a friend, 'I do not yet see any of the decline of age as far as I am concerned. I still have a great eagerness to learn and a great eagerness to work.' For many years he had been working on the two books that he looked upon as the most important he had ever written: the one was *Le Jugement universel*, of which he had already written six thousand pages by 1945, and the other *Le Rapport aux hommes*. He wrote a book on Michelangelo and began *Le Diable*. But then he was struck by amyotrophic lateral sclerosis, a disease that inevitably leads to bulbar paralysis (though no doubt he was unaware of this). As an ardent Christian, he attributed a spiritual value to suffering, and he bowed to the divine will. Yet his mind was preoccupied with his two great unfinished books: 'I should have to be able to read and reread; I should have to have a new pair of eyes, days when I do not go to sleep, half a century before me. Instead of that I am almost blind – I am almost a dying man.' He could scarcely walk and he became very tired. His disease grew worse. 'Always blinder, always more incapable of movement, always more silent. . . . I die a little every day, in small doses, according to the homeopathic recipe.' He had lost the use of his left leg; he now lost that of his fingers. 'The idea that I shall not be able to finish the books I have begun saddens me,' he said. And in fact he never did finish the two most important works. They were too great an undertaking for him to be able to complete them by dictation. He dictated only the end of

313

Le Diable and some pieces that he called *Eclats* and that appeared in the *Corriere della Sera*. One of them was called *Le Bonheur des malheureux*: in it he described his own state and listed the reasons that made it bearable for him. 'I always did prefer martyrdom to imbecility,' he observed. His conversation remained as lively as ever. But gradually his voice became incomprehensible. He invented a code, rapping on a table – the number of raps gave the letter. And so he dictated, letter by letter, with unbelievable patience. He had himself read to aloud until at last his mind gave way.

Renoir's dogged resolution, and Papini's, arose from their consuming passion. Others, less wholly committed to their work, nevertheless stand out firmly against their decline from a feeling of personal dignity. They live through their last years as though those years were a challenge. This is the theme of Hemingway's tale *The Old Man and the Sea*. An old fisherman goes off alone to catch a huge fish; the taking of it exhausts him; he manages to bring it back to land but not to protect it from the sharks, and it is a fleshless skeleton that he leaves on the beach. It does not matter. The adventure was an end in itself: for the old man it was a question of refusing the aimless life lived by most in his condition and to assert the manly values of courage and endurance to the end. 'A man, you can destroy him but you can't beat him,' says the old fisherman. In this not very convincing fable Hemingway tried to exorcize the obsessions that were haunting him: it was becoming difficult for him to write; he could no longer keep up the image of himself that all his life he had wanted to show to the world – the image of overflowing vitality and manliness. He had thoughts of suicide and in the end he shot himself.

The old fisherman's determination is to be found in many other aged men, though in a less epic form. Even at the age of ninety-two some go on with their athletics, tennis, football or bicycling. Usually they have never been very good, but still, without expecting to accomplish anything remarkable, they like to check their times. Many of them are to be seen on the track more often after their retirement than before. For two-thirds of them sport is dangerous after sixty.* Yet they do not experience any functional inconvenience. Sport does not delay the ageing of the organs. But it does help them to work

* Dr Longueville, of the *Groupe d'études du 3e âge sportif*, speaks of a sixty-three-year-old swimmer who dives sixty times from a ten-foot board in spite of his auricular fibrillation and vascular hypertrophy; of a sixty-year-old parachutist with coronary sclerosis; of an eighty-five-year-old cyclist who does nearly twenty miles a day although he suffers from the after-effects of an infarctus; etc.

properly. Psychologically, the old athletes' perseverance has a tonic effect that should be respected by those who are only too apt to discourage them. Too great a reduction of activity brings about a lessening of the whole person. This is thoroughly understood by the old women of Bali, who continue to carry heavy burdens on their heads. The aged man knows that by struggling against this decline he slows it down. He also knows that the unpitying eye of those around him sees in his physical weakening that generalized degradation that is expressed by the words old age. He is determined to show others and himself that he is still a man.

The mind and the body are very closely linked. For a man to carry out the work of re-adapting a deteriorated organism to the outside work, he must have retained his pleasure in living. And it works in the other direction: good health encourages the survival of emotional and intellectual interests. Most of the time the mind and body travel together 'towards their growth or their decline'. But not always. La Fontaine's excellent health did not prevent his mental decay; and a fine intelligence may sometimes live on in a shattered body. Or the two may deteriorate at different rhythms, the mind trying to hold out but being overtaken by the organic degeneration, as it happened with Swift. In these cases the aged man has the tragic experience of being unequal to his own requirements. Alain said that we desire only that which is possible: but this is too simple a rationalism. The old man's tragedy is that often he is no longer capable of what he desires. He forms a project, and then just when it is to be carried out his body fails him; weariness breaks his impulse; he searches in the fog for his memory; his thoughts wander from the object they had set themselves. When this happens, old age is experienced – even when there has been no pathological impairment – as a kind of mental disease in which the sufferer feels the anguish of losing his grasp upon himself.

Those moralists who for political or ideological reasons vindicate old age claim that it sets the individual free from his body. According to them, by a kind of swing of the pendulum what the body loses the mind gains. 'The eyes of the spirit begin to grow sharp only when those of the body begin to fail,' said Plato. I have already quoted Seneca's words, 'The soul, no longer having any great commerce with the body, burgeons and comes into full flower.' Joubert said, 'Those who have a long old age are as it were purified from their bodies.'* When Tolstoy began to lose his strength he comforted himself with untrue statements: 'The progress of mankind is due to the old. Old men grow better and wiser.' When poor Juliette Drouet was seventy-one she wrote Hugo, to persuade him of the strength of her love, 'All that old age takes from my body, my heart wins back in undying youth and radiant love.' But after 1878, when she was ravaged by cancer, she no longer felt old age as anything but a cruel decay. 'I prop myself up with my love, but in vain: I feel everything slipping away and dissolving in me – life, memory, strength, courage, spirit and zest.'

Jouhandeau extols the inner wealth that, according to him, accompanies the body's decline. 'As the body wanes, so the soul rises to its apogee.' How? Towards what? He does not say. He preaches resignation for the sake of some undefined aesthetic. 'Gradually our eyes see less far. Death settles into us, stage by stage, and we remain in this world, living as though we were already cut off from it. Do not let us be so inelegant as to let it vex us.'

This mystical twaddle is indecent when we look at the real condition of the immense majority of old people: hunger, cold and disease certainly bring with them no kind of moral gain. In any case, this nonsense amounts to mere statements devoid of the least foundation. Even among the neo-Taoists, for whom age was a necessary condition for holiness, it was not sufficient. Asceticism and a state of trance were required for detachment from the flesh and the achievement of immortality. Experience is in direct contradiction with the notion that age brings freedom from carnal desire. At the first beginnings of old age the body may retain its former vigour or reach a new state of equilibrium. But in the course of years it deteriorates, grows burdensome and hinders the activities of the mind. In 1671, when he was only sixty-one, Saint-Evremond wrote, 'At present my spirit is coming back into my body and uniting with it more closely. To tell the truth, it is not in order to enjoy an agreeable liaison that they are trying to come together, but rather out of their need for help and mutual support.' On 19 March 1943 Gide complained of 'all the little indispositions of great age that make an old man such a wretched being. My mind almost never succeeds in

* He was a traditionalist, moralist and spiritualist writer; he believed in God, and Madame de Chastenay said of him, 'In him everything is soul.' Not that that prevented him from marrying for money, from becoming the head of the university and from dying the wealthy possessor of many official decorations. He also said, 'The evening of life brings its lamp with it.'

distracting me from my flesh or in making me forget it, and this is more harmful to work than I can say.' In fact, instead of being an instrument the body becomes a hindrance: a 'fine old age' can never, never be taken for granted: it represents perpetual victories and perpetual recoveries from defeat.

The purification of which the moralists speak consists for them essentially in the extinction of sexual desires: they are happy to think that the elderly man escapes from this slavery and thereby achieves serenity. In his well-known poem *John Anderson my Jo*, Burns described the ideal old couple in whom carnal passion has died quite away. The pair have climbed the hill of life side by side and once they tasted blissful hours; now with trembling steps but still hand in hand they must go together along the road that leads to the end of the journey. This stereotype is deeply imprinted upon the hearts of young and middle-aged people because they met it countless times in the books of their childhood and because their respect for their grand-parents persuades them of its truth. The idea of sexual relations or violent scenes between elderly people is deeply shocking. Yet there also exists an entirely different tradition. The expression 'dirty old man' is a commonplace of popular speech. Through literature and even more through painting, the story of Susanna and the elders has taken on the value of a myth. The comic theatre has endlessly repeated the theme of the ancient lover. As we shall see, this satirical tradition is closer to the truth than the edifying speeches of idealists who are concerned with showing old age as it ought to be.

In both sexes the sexual drive lies on the borders of the psychoso-matic realm: we do not know exactly how it is conditioned by the organism. What has been observed, as I have said, is that the degeneration of the sexual glands, which is a consequence of ageing, brings about the reduction or even the disappearance of the genital functions. Reaction to erotic stimulus is less frequent and slower or even non-existent: the subject reaches orgasm with difficulty or fails to achieve it; men find their power of erection becomes less or vanishes.

But Freud has established that sexuality is not confined to the genital aspect; the libido is not an instinct – that is to say a ready-made form of behaviour – with an object and a set goal. As far as its object is concerned, it is the energy that is used to transform the sexual drive; in relation to the source of stimulus, it is its goal. The libido may grow, diminish, shift its locus. In childhood, sexuality is polymorphous: it is not centred upon the genital organs. 'Only at the end of a complex and hazardous evolution does the sexual drive assume a preeminently genital aspect; at this point it takes on the apparent fixity and finality of an instinct.'* From this we may at once draw the conclusion that a person whose genital functions have diminished or become non-existent is not therefore sexless: he is a sexed being – even eunuchs and impotent men remained sexed – and one who must work out his sexuality in spite of a given mutilation. Sartre† says that there is a form of sexuality based upon satisfaction: it disappears only with death. The reason for this is that it is by no means a mere collection of reflexes that beget a pattern of sensations and images. It is an intentionality that the body experiences, lives through, an intentionality that exists in relation to other bodies and that conforms to the general rhythm of life. It takes form in relation to a world which it provides with an erotic dimension. An inquiry into the sexuality of the aged amounts to asking what happens to a man's relationship with himself, with others and with the outside world when the preeminence of the genital aspect of the sexual pattern has vanished. Obviously it would be absurd to imagine that there is a simple return to infantile sexuality. Never, on any plane, does the aged person lapse into 'a second childhood', since childhood is by definition a forward, upward movement. And then again, infantile sexuality is in search of itself, whereas the aged man retains the memory of what it was in his maturity. Lastly, there is a radical difference between the social factors affecting the two ages.

Sexual activities have a plurality of ends. They are directed at the resolving of the tension created by the sexual drive, a tension that has the extreme urgency of a need, above all in youth. Later, the subject – unless he is suffering from serious sexual frustration – looks more for a positive pleasure than a release, and this he obtains by orgasm. It is preceded and accompanied by a train of sensations, images and myths, which provide the subject with 'preliminary pleasures' arising from the relief of 'partial drives' rooted in his childhood; and the subject may rate these pleasures as high as the orgasm itself, or even higher. It is unusual for this quest for pleasure to be reduced to the simple exercise of a function: generally speaking it is an adventure in which each partner realizes his own being and the other's in a unique manner: in the turmoil and desire of sexual activity the consciousness

* *Vocabulaire de la psychanalyse*, J.Laplanche and J.-B.Pontalis.
† *L'Être et le Néant*.

and the body become as one in order to reach the other as a body and in such a way as to enthral and possess him; there is a twofold reciprocal embodiment, a transformation of the world, now a world of desire. The attempt at possession necessarily fails, since the other remains a subject; but before it reaches its end, the drama of reciprocity is experienced in the act of love in one of its most extreme and most revealing forms. If it takes on the character of a struggle then it begets hostility: more often it implies a 'togetherness' that encourages tender affection. In a couple whose love does away with the distance between the 'I' and the other, even failure is overcome.

Since in love-making the subject causes himself to exist as a body, a spell-binding body, he has a certain narcissistic relationship with himself. His manly or womanly qualities are asserted and acknowledged; he feels more valuable as a person. It may happen that the search for this heightened worth may dominate the whole of a love-life, which becomes then a continuous attempt at conquest, a perpetual assertion of masculine vigour or feminine charm – the glorification of the character whose part has been chosen.

As we see, the enjoyment the individual derives from his sexual activities is rich and manifold to a very high degree. It is understandable that a man or woman should be bitterly unwilling to give it up, whether the chief aim is pleasure, or the transfiguration of the world by desire, or the realization of a certain image of oneself, or all this at the same time. Those moralists who condemn old age to chastity say that one cannot long for pleasures one no longer desires. This is a very short-sighted view of the matter. It is true that normally desire does not arise as mere desire – as desire in itself: it is desire for a particular pleasure or a particular body. But when it no longer arises spontaneously, reflection may very well regret its disappearance. The old person often desires to desire because he retains his longing for experiences that can never be replaced and because he is still attached to the erotic world he built up in his youth or maturity – desire will enable him to renew its fading colours. And again it is by means of desire that he will have an awareness of his own integrity. We wish for eternal youth, and this youth implies the survival of the libido. Some try to fight genital degeneration by means of physical remedies.*

* It is primarily men who turn to electuaries, and 'virility pills' and hormone therapy to preserve their powers of erection. Nowadays there are some women who undergo treatment to delay the menopause. But although they may still be anxious about remaining young, after the menopause has happened, they do not have to worry about retaining sexual 'vigour'.

Others resign themselves to it, but do their best to assert themselves as sexed beings in some other way.

This presence is found only among those who have looked upon their sexuality as something of positive value. Those who, because of complexes rooted in their childhood, took part in sexual activities only with aversion eagerly seize upon the excuse of age to withdraw. I knew an old woman who got her doctor to supply her with certificates so that she could avoid her disagreeable 'conjugal duties'; as she grew older, the number of her years provided her with a more convenient alibi. A man, if he is half impotent, or indifferent, or if the sexual act worries him badly, will be relieved when age allows refuge in a continence that will seem normal from that time onwards.

Subjects who have had a happy sexual life may have reasons for not wishing to prolong it. One of these is their narcissistic relationship with themselves. Disgust at one's own body takes various forms among men and women; but in either, age may provoke it, and if this happens they will refuse to make their body exist for another.* Yet there exists a reciprocal influence between the image of oneself and one's sexual activity: the beloved individual feels that he is worthy of love and gives himself to it unreservedly; but very often he is loved only if he makes a conscious effort to be attractive, and an unfavourable image of himself stands in the way of his doing this. In this event a vicious circle is created, preventing him from having sexual relations.

Another obstacle is the pressure of public opinion. The elderly person conforms to the conventional ideal that is offered for his acceptance. He is afraid of scandal or quite simply of ridicule. He becomes the slave of what other people might say. He inwardly accepts the watchwords of propriety and continence imposed by the community. He is ashamed of his own desires, and he denies having them; he refuses to be a lecherous old man in his own eyes, or a shameless old woman. He fights against his sexual drives to the point of thrusting them back into his unconscious mind.†

* As we have seen, Saint-Evremond put forward a contrary view: according to him, the less one loves oneself, the more inclined one is to love another. But he was speaking of platonic love.

† At the twenty-second Congress of the American Medical Association in December 1968, Dr Runciman gave the results of his research upon two hundred persons aged from forty to eighty-nine. He came to the conclusion that it was 'psychological barriers' that halted sexual activity in elderly people. They, and particularly the women, were the victims of the taboos and inhibitions of a Victorian morality.

As we might on the face of it suppose, seeing that there is so great a difference between them in their biological destiny and their social status, the case of men is quite unlike that of women. Biologically men are at the greater disadvantage: socially, it is the women who are worse off, because of their condition as erotic objects.

In neither case is their behaviour thoroughly understood. A certain number of inquiries into it have been carried out, and these have provided the basis for something in the way of statistics. The replies obtained are always of dubious value; and in this field the notion of an average has little meaning. Nevertheless I mention those which I have consulted and that have provided me with some information in Appendix IV, p. 571.

As far as men are concerned, the statistics as it so often happens merely confirm what everybody knows – sexual intercourse diminishes in frequency with age. This fact is connected with the degeneration of the sexual organs, a degeneration that brings about a weakening of the libido. But the physiological is not the only factor that comes into play. There are considerable differences between the behaviour-patterns of individuals, some being impotent at sixty and others sexually very active at over eighty. We must try to see how these differences are to be explained.

The first factor, and one of perfectly obvious importance, is the subjects' marital status. Sexual intercourse is much more frequent among married men* than among bachelors or widowers. Married life encourages erotic stimulus; habit and 'togetherness' favour its appeasement. The 'psychological barriers' are far easier to overcome. The wall of private life protects the elderly husband from public opinion, which in any case looks more favourably upon legitimate love than upon unlawful connexions. He feels that his image is less endangered. The word image in this context must be thoroughly understood. Whereas the woman-object identifies herself with the total image of her body from childhood on, the little boy sees his penis as an *alter ego*; it is in his penis that his whole life as a man finds its image, and it is here that he feels himself in peril. The narcissistic traumatism that he dreads is the failure of his sexual organ – the impossibility of reaching an erection, of maintaining it, and of satisfying his partner. This fear is less haunting in married life. The subject is more or less free to choose the moment for making love. A

---

* Firmly-established liaisons are to be counted as marriages.

failure is easily passed over in silence. His familiarity with his partner makes him dread her opinion less. Since he is less anxious, the married man is less inhibited than another. That is why many very aged couples continue their sexual activities: the experience of social workers and sociologists confirms the results I have quoted.

Nevertheless, a fairly considerable number of married men no longer have anything but a very much reduced activity or even none at all. When sexual degeneration comes before its time it is often explained by causes that have nothing to do with sexuality – mental or physical fatigue, care, infirmity or, in some cases, eating and drinking too much. It is a known fact that sexually a man, even when he is young, feels the need to change his partner: monotony kills his desire. When he is old he grows tired of a companion he knows too well, even more so since she has aged and he no longer finds her desirable. When they can, many elderly men recover their sexual vigour by changing their old partner for a new and generally younger one.

The loss of his wife will often cause a traumatism that shuts a man off from all sexual activities, either for a longer or shorter period or for ever. Widowers and elderly bachelors have much more difficulty in finding an outlet for their libido than married men. Most have lost their charm: if they try to have an affair, their attempts come to nothing. And the danger tends to put them off. Social morality looks upon these elderly capers as shameful or ludicrous. There is nothing to protect them against the very great distress of failure. All that remains is venal love: many men have shrunk from it all their lives, and it would seem to them a kind of giving-in, an acquiescence in the decline of age. Yet some do turn to it: they either go with prostitutes or they have a liaison with a woman they help financially. Their choice, continence or activity, depends on the balance between the urgency of their drive and the strength of their resistance.

Many find an answer in masturbation. A quarter of the subjects questioned by *Sexology* said they had indulged in it either for many years or since the age of sixty: the latter were therefore brought back to it by ageing. Statistical cross-checks show that even among married men, many turn to this practice. Coition is a far more complex and difficult undertaking than masturbation, since it constitutes a relationship with a second person. And no doubt many elderly men prefer their fantasies to their wife's age-worn body. Then it may happen that either because deep-rooted complexes or awareness of age turns her against physical love, the companion refuses. Masturbation is then the most convenient outlet.

It would be interesting to know at what age women seem most desirable to elderly men. Many like them very young: quite apart from any consideration of money, it is possible that their desires may be fulfilled, for some young women are gerontophiles. Other old men are interested only in experienced women: young ones seem to them of no consequence. Still others would feel awkward, indecent or ridiculous with too young a partner; they would be made too disagreeably aware of their own age. Their choice depends upon what they expect from love and the picture they have of themselves.

The subject's sexual activities are influenced by his social condition. They go on far longer among manual than among brain workers, among men with a low standard of living than among those who are well to do. Workers and peasants have more straightforward desires, less dominated by erotic myths, than the middle classes; their wives' bodies wear out early, but they do not stop making love to them. When a working man's wife is old, she seems to him less spoiled than would be the case with a richer husband. Then again he has less idea of himself than the white-collar worker. And he does not take so much notice of public opinion, which has less and less force as one goes down the social scale. Old men and women who live almost entirely outside convention – tramps of both sexes, and inmates of institutions – lie together without any shame, even in front of others.

Finally, the happier and richer sexual life has been, the longer it goes on. If the subject has valued it because of the narcissistic satisfaction it gives him, he will break it off as soon as he can no longer see a flattering reflection of himself in his partner's eyes. If he has intended to assert his virility, his skill or the power of his charm, or if he has meant to triumph over rivals, then he may sometimes be glad of the excuse of age to relax. But if his sexual activities have been spontaneous and happy he will be strongly inclined to carry them on as long as his strength lasts.

Yet the elderly man does not take so vehement a pleasure in intercourse as a youth, and this is because the two stages of ejaculation are reduced to one: he no longer has that piercing sensation of imminence which marks the passage from the first to the second, nor yet the triumphant feeling of a jet, an explosion – this is one of the myths that gives the male sexual act its value. Even when the aged man is still capable of normal sexual activity, he often seeks indirect

323

forms of satisfaction: even more so if he is impotent. He takes pleasure in erotic literature, licentious works of art, dirty stories, the company of young women and furtive contacts; he indulges in fetishism, sado-masochism, various forms of perversion and, particularly after the age of eighty, in voyeurism. These deviations are readily comprehensible. The fact is, Freud has established that there is no such thing as a 'normal' sexuality: it is always 'perverted'* in so far as it does not break away from its origins, which required it to look for satisfaction not in any specific activity but in the 'increase of pleasure' attached to functions dependent upon other drives. Infantile sexuality is polymorphically perverse. The sexual act is considered 'normal' when the partial activities are merely preparatory to the genital act. But the subject has only to attach too much importance to these preliminary pleasures to slip into perversion. Normally, looking at and caressing one's partner plays a great part in sexual intercourse. It is accompanied by fantasy; sado-masochistic elements appear; and often fetishism, clothes and ornaments evoking the presence of the body. When genital pleasure is weak or non-existent, all these elements rise to the first place. And frequently the elderly man prizes them very highly because they are manifestations of that erotic world which is still of the greatest value to him. He continues to live in a certain climate, his body still existing in a world filled with other bodies. Here again it is often timidity, shame or difficulties from the outside that prevent him from indulging in what are called his vices.

Psychoanalysts say that genital disinvolvement often means that the sexuality of the aged moves back to the oral and anal stages. It is true that some old people are given to bulimy; and no doubt they indulge in the pleasure of eating extraordinary amounts of food by way of compensating for their erotic frustration: but can this be considered as coming under the heading of sexuality? The same applies to the 'anality' of the aged, some of whom are in fact very much taken up with their excretory functions. But is it not excessive to label all the individual's relations with his organic functions 'sexual'?

Even if we do not accept this interpretation, senile libido does very often persist: it reveals itself in certain pathological cases. In senile dementia, where the impaired brain is no longer capable of exercising control, we see the development of erotic delirium. Men of

* Here, of course, the word does not imply any kind of moral judgement.

seventy, whose behaviour up until the appearance of a cerebral tumour has been faultless, may attack the women around them, either verbally or by acts. Some pieces of police-court news tell us a great deal. I shall only quote one: it dates from March 1969. A seventy-year-old managing director peremptorily summoned his three secretaries at nine in the evening. They imagined he had some urgent work for them to do and went to his villa. They found him in the garden, naked, with an alarm-pistol in his hand. He rushed at them, shouting, 'I am the god Pan, Pan, Pan',* firing a shot at each 'Pan'. They fled. Later he said that he had taken a drug; it had made him feel amorous but unhappily its effects had faded very soon. The symbolism of the pistol shot is perfectly clear. It is also clear that the reason why he had taken this drug was that he was obsessed by erotic fantasies without being able to carry them into effect. Unfortunately the papers never said what happened to him afterwards.

Do senile perversions often cause crimes or not? It is a controversial point. Kinsey accepts the fairly widespread idea that impotent old men are sometimes guilty of assaults upon children. Dr Destrem is of the same opinion: he says that old men's erotism may assume forms verging upon pathological compulsion. They commit offences against decency – exhibitionism and the fondling of children. These statements have been strongly denied. According to Dr Isidore Rubin,† inquiries have established that as far as indecent behaviour is concerned, the critical periods are adolescence, the years between thirty-five and forty, and those just before fifty. Donald Mullock, an authority on child-welfare, has drawn up statistics covering a certain number of assaults upon children: according to these, the men who attack boys do so between the ages of thirty-nine and fifty, whereas those who attack girls are between thirty-three and forty-four. The girls were never solicited by men of over sixty-three: at this age a very few men were attracted by boys. Yet Dr Ey‡ asserts that most of the sexual crimes against children that are seen in forensic medicine are committed by old men. They are often accused of exhibitionism, and here again opinions vary. Many psychiatrists accept that it begins in adolescence, reaches its height towards the age of twenty-five, and is almost never met with in its pure state after forty. Dr

* *Pan* is not only the French for the god but also for the report of a pistol and for bangs in general (trs.).
† *L'Amour après soixante ans.*
‡ *Manuel de psychiatrie.*

Dénard-Toulet is of the opinion that exhibitionism appears only in youth; it could continue in the elderly man; but seeing that the exhibitionist is profoundly neurotic and poorly equipped for living, he does not make old bones. There are sadistic exhibitionists who take a great pride in insulting women by displaying their erect penis: it is unlikely that there are many old men in their ranks. But the typical exhibitionist is a masochist who, without any aggressive display, shows his penis in its flaccid state. Dr Ey, as well as others, says that there are some old men among these.

In 1944 East examined the English prison records, and he states that for 1929–38 only 8·04 per cent of the sexual crimes punished by imprisonment were committed by men over sixty. Figures drawn up in the United States show the percentage, by age, of the crimes committed in 1946: for every hundred thousand of population the number of aged delinquents is negligible; the figure is a little higher for sexual assaults, but still very low indeed when it is compared with that for younger men.

I personally knew a case which illustrates the persistence of an active sexual life among the aged, and of their children's disgust at it. Monsieur Durand was a former teacher of history; he was married and he had several children and grandchildren. He had been handsome and proud of his looks, much admired by women and particularly by his pupils. Through indifference his wife more or less shut her eyes to his love-affairs. Mademoiselle G., one of his former pupils, a teacher and unmarried, became his mistress when he was sixty-five. It was rumoured in his family that they had been seen going into various hotels together. Then Mademoiselle G. was given a post in Algeria, and Monsieur Durand was eighty-five by the time she came back. His wife had just died and he was somewhat lost because it was she who had always run the household. His daughter was in her fifties: she was very fond of him and came to see him every day. She found him a devoted servant whom she had known for many years and who came to live in his flat. He had all his faculties, and when he invited former pupils to come to see him, which he often did, he talked entertainingly, with zest and intelligence. He was not physically infirm but his legs were weak; someone had to hold him by the arm when he was out in the street because he was afraid of falling. Earlier in life he had been generous and had paid little attention to money. But in growing old he became mean and suspicious. He thought he was being robbed by the publisher who brought out the manuals he had written and that sold rather well. He had a pension but could not grasp the meaning of a regular income: sometimes he complained of having a 'bad' month and sometimes he rejoiced in a 'good' month, although he always received the same amount of money. He suffered from constipation and attached great importance to the functioning of his bowels. He liked talking about it. When he was about eighty-five, in the evening he would say, 'I have had a good day today', or with a sigh, 'A blank day today', depending upon whether he had been to the lavatory or not. Formerly he and his wife had spent the holidays with some member of the family – brothers or cousins; he had been extremely high-handed with them. Now he was taken in for the summer by one of his sons and he felt he was in a dependent position. This humiliated him. He worked up a positive hatred for his eldest son Henri and his wife.

After she came back to France Mademoiselle G. spent most of her time with him except when his daughter was in the house. The servant told the family that Mademoiselle G. often masturbated him but that he did not touch her. When she had put him to bed she gave him a slap on the bottom as she said good-night.

Things went on in this way for some years. The old man's animosity towards his sons grew and grew. One summer when he was staying with the eldest he had an enema and fouled the walls on purpose. Another time he defecated in a cupboard, pretending to have made a mistake. When he was living in Paris at about the age of ninety, he had fits of extreme agitation and two or three times he tried to throw himself out of the window. His family decided that these troubles arose from his sexual excesses. Had not the servant said that Mademoiselle G. masturbated him 'until the blood came'? They held a family council. The servant's evidence led them to believe that Mademoiselle G. wanted to take the old man to live with her. The eldest son undertook to kidnap his father and did so. They installed him in his daughter's house, in a ground-floor room facing the garden. The servant looked after him. After they had uprooted him and cut him off from Mademoiselle G. he survived for no more than a year; he lost his memory and became genuinely senile. He never directly rebelled against what had been done to him. Sometimes he pretended to be in a dream-like state: 'I went on a journey last night. It's strange. . . . I left my flat and found another exactly the same . . .' He said to his daughter, 'Thank you for having set me up in a flat which is so like my own.' (As a matter of fact there was not the least resemblance.) He made timid attempts at seeing Mademoiselle G. again. One day he gave ten francs to the maid's son: 'Last year a kind lady came to see me. You don't know what her name was?' He also took a sly revenge on those around him. He was more and more preoccupied with his bowels, and one day, speaking with obvious malice, he asked a fifty-year-old female cousin, 'Now then, my dear, how do you manage when you go to the lavatory? Do you sit on the seat?' 'Yes,' said the poor cousin, blushing furiously. 'All right. And then? You make an effort. . . . And after that? You wipe yourself. . . . And then you get hold of your stick and give a good stir?' He remained interested in sexual matters. He said his daughter had visits from a lover. One day he pretended not to know her and made advances to her. 'Listen, child. We could have fun, we two.' He used his senility as an instrument for revenge against his family. But in fact he was no longer right in his mind. He no longer knew who he was and as a compensation he made up extraordinary tales. He described journeys he said he had made the day before, or two days before. After a year he broke the head of his femur and died within forty-eight hours.

Mademoiselle G. managed to find out where he was buried. She went to the village grave-yard and for twenty-four hours she lay stretched out on his grave.

We have a fair amount of evidence upon elderly men's sexual life. It depends on their past and also upon their attitude towards their old age as a whole and towards their image in particular. As we have seen, Chateaubriand so loathed his aged face that he refused to sit for his portrait. In the first part of *Amour et vieillesse – chants de tristesse*, which he wrote when he was sixty-one, no doubt for the Occitanienne, he rejects the amorous advances of a young woman: 'If you tell me you love me as a father, you will fill me with horror; if you claim to love me as a lover, I shall not believe you. I shall see a happy rival in every young man. Your deference will make me feel my age, your caresses will give me over to the most furious jealousy. . . . Old age makes a man as ugly as can be wished. If he is unhappy, it is even worse . . .' 'Grown old on this earth, having lost nothing of his dreams, his follies, his undefined sorrows, always seeking what he cannot find, adding to his former woes the disillusionment of experience, the loneliness of his desires, the stagnant tedium of his heart and the insult of the years. Tell me, have I not in my own person provided the fiends with an idea for a torment they have not yet invented in the regions of everlasting pain?' He was cruelly sensitive to the 'insult of the years', and his refusal was dictated by a kind of inverted narcissism.

Goethe at sixty-five, on the other hand, was pleased with his worldly position, and he looked upon himself with satisfaction. As he was travelling towards Wiesbaden, the country of his youth, he saw a rainbow through the mist – and because of the mist the rainbow was white. He wrote:

> So, lively brisk old man
> Do not let sadness come over you;
> For all your white hairs
> You can still be a lover.

Although he was of a cold temperament, with a considerable homosexual element, he had always set a very high value on love; in *Faust*, the hero grows young again partly in order to be able to love once more; and, when reversing this idea, Goethe expected from love a renewal similar to that of the snake's when it sloughs off its old skin. The 'brisk old man' needed a fresh passion to stir his blood again. He met it at Wiesbaden: his friend the banker Willemer introduced him to his wife, Marianne; she was thirty, and he had just married her. She was beautiful and very intellegent; she had a passionate admiration for Goethe, and she made him sign the admirable poems she wrote at his side. At first he joined in the game, but then he was caught fast; and as he had hoped it seemed to him that he recovered his youth. He came back to the Willemers' a year later; but Marianne's passion alarmed him. He left her and never saw her again. They wrote to one another for many years. This adventure was the inspiration for 'Suleïka's book', the essential part of his *West-Östlicher Divan*.

His behaviour was far less prudent when, at the age of seventy-two, he was very much attracted to the enchanting seventeen-year-old Ulrika at Marienbad. The first year, in 1821, he did no more than talk with her and bring her flowers. In the following years he spent almost all his time with her, doing everything he could to anticipate her wishes. 'Dear child, are you happy?' he would ask anxiously. He fell in love with a well-known, elegant and very beautiful Polish pianist, Madame Szymanowska, but he soon came back to Ulrika. 'I see her in a hundred different forms,' he wrote to her mother, 'and every time it is a fresh delight.' Gradually his passion increased; he wanted to marry her, and he consulted a physician to learn whether marriage was inadvisable in view of his age. Acting for him, the Grand-Duke Charles Augustus asked for Ulrika's hand. Goethe received no immediate reply. He accompanied the family to Carlsbad and celebrated his birthday with them. But when he left them a few days later he understood that this was to be a definitive farewell. In the carriage that took him away, he wrote a heart-broken poem. No one could ever console him, he said, neither his friends nor his studies. 'The world is lost for me and I am lost for myself, I who was the favourite of the gods until this moment. They have tried me, sending me Pandora, so rich in treasures but even more in danger; they urged me towards her freely-giving lips. Now they part me from her, leaving me shattered and destroyed.' His son and daughter-in-law made scenes – they feared for their inheritance. Madame Szymanowska came to Weimar to give a concert, and he had the consolation of seeing her again. As her carriage moved off on the day she left he cried, 'Run after her! Bring her back to me!' She returned and, weeping, he clasped her in his arms without a word: he was saying goodbye to love and to youth. He fell ill, or at least he took to his bed, perhaps to escape from the turmoil in the house, for the plan of marriage had not been wholly given up. His friend Zelter came to see him and read him the elegy he had written after Ulrika's refusal – read it aloud three times in succession. Goethe then agreed to get up and he recovered very soon. He included the poem in a larger work that he called *Trilogie der Leidenschaft*. But from that time on, women no longer existed for him: he remained set in his bitterness until the day of his death.

Old men's loves are not always doomed to failure: far from it. Many of them have a sexual life that goes on very late. The Duc de Bouillon was sixty-six when his son Turenne was born. The famous Duc de Richelieu's father married for the third time in 1702, at the age of seventy. When his son was sixty-two and governor of Guienne, he led a life of debauchery. In his old age he seduced a great many young women. At seventy-eight, bewigged, made-up and very thin, he was said to look like a tortoise thrusting its head out of its shell: this did not prevent him from having affairs with the actresses of the *Comédie française*. He had an acknowledged mistress, and he spent his evenings with whores; sometimes he used to bring them home –

he liked listening to their confidences. He married when he was eighty-four and had recourse to aphrodisiacs: he made his wife pregnant. Furthermore, he deceived her too. He continued his sexual activities right up until his death, at the age of ninety-two.

Lakanal married at the age of seventy-seven and had a son. Tolstoy is a well-known example of sexual vitality. Towards the end of his life he preached total continence both for men and for women. Nevertheless, when he was sixty-nine or seventy he would come back from a very long ride and make love to his wife. All the next day he would walk about the house looking pleased with himself.

Sexuality was of great importance in Hugo's youth and during his middle years. He was something of a voyeur. In his verse he was fond of imagining such things as a faun peeping at naked nymphs; a schoolboy at a hole in the wall, watching a shop-girl undressing for bed; a woman bathing, with her bare foot visible; the glimpse of a bosom, a raised skirt. At Guernsey he said he might possibly suffocate in the night, and with his wife's consent he made a servant-girl – usually a young and pretty one – sleep in the room next to his. Sometimes he would make love to her; but according to his notebooks it would also seem that he watched her undress without her knowing it. When he brought out his *Les Chansons des rues et des bois* at the age of sixty-three, the outraged Veuillot likened him to the elders who surprised the bathing Susanna.

These notebooks provide a great deal of information about his erotic life in his later years. Between sixty-three and sixty-eight, his amorous exploits were very few in number – half a dozen a year, on the average. But subsequently this figure rose. He no longer had sexual relations with Juliette, but turned secretly to other women, and often to whores. When he was living on Guernsey, he often went to Fermain Bay, near Hauteville House, for his private amusements. The place is mentioned four times between 14 and 17 June in the notebooks for 1867; it also appears in those for 1868. Guillemin has published those for 1870 and 1871. Hugo used a code to circumvent Juliette's jealousy. *Poêle* meant *poils* – body, and particularly pubic, hair. *Suisses* and *saints* – *seins*, breasts. *N.*, *nue* – naked; *toda*, entirely; *osc.*, a kiss; *genua*, knee; *pros*, prostitute. An examination of the notebooks shows that he rarely carried out the whole of the sexual act; generally he confined himself to looking at the wholly or partially naked woman, to fondling and kissing her. Here are the details of his activities during the summer of 1870:

29 July	Fermain Bay. Night with Young,* Alice Cole.† *Poêle* and coal.
31 July	Hand, *poêle. Suisses.*
2 August	Fermain Bay. Young. *Suisse.* Hand. *Les saints.*
3 August	Fermain Bay.
4 August	Had to leave this morning. L.Y.‡
10 September	Given to Mairat [for Marie] rue Frochet 3. *N.* 5 francs.
13 September	Saw Enjolras§ *n.*
17 September	Given to Berthet [Berthe] pros. 9b Pigalle *n.* 2 francs.
19 September	Saw Mmme Godt. *Poêle.* Given to C. Montauban. Hébé *n.* 10 francs.
22 September	Given to Mairat [Marie], shirtmaker, 2 francs.
23 September	Emile [Emilie] Taffari, rue du Cirque 21, 6th floor no. 1. *Osc.*
27 September	Saw A. Piteau again after twenty years. *Toda.* Given to Zdé [Zoé] Tholozé, 0 fr 50. Given to Louis [Louise] Lallié *n.* 2 francs.
28 September	Elabre Tholozé *n.* Gave 5 francs.
30 September	Eugène, 9bis rue Neuve-des-Martyrs. *n.* Gave 3 francs.
11 October	A. C. Montauban. Gave 10 francs.
5 October	Mmme Olympe Audouard. Nipples. *Osc.*

And the list goes on. Almost every day, and sometimes twice a day, a name, an address and a note – *n*, or *osc*, or *poêle*, or *genua*. The 'gifts' vary, no doubt according to the importance of the favours purchased.

The next summer he took Marie Mercier as his mistress; she was the widow of a Communard who had been shot, and he had asked his daughter-in-law to engage her. When he settled in Luxemburg she went there too: she was eighteen, and he loved watching her bathe naked in the Our. He often went to see her at night. His notebooks are full of triumphant entries. 10 September: 'Misma. Pecho [bosom]. *Toda.*' 11 September: 'Misma; se ha dicho toma y tomo.'¶ 12 September: 'Ahora todos los dias and a toda hora, misma

* Young was a servant: she is mentioned in the notebooks for 1867 and 1868.
† Mentioned 23 and 30 March 1870.
‡ Louise Young.
§ Mentioned 23 and 30 March 1870.
¶ She said, 'Take,' and I took.

Maria.'* He saw her every evening until she left for Paris on the twenty-third. A year later – he was seventy – he told Burty that he now found it difficult to make speeches. 'Talking tires me as much as making love three times.' After a moment's thought he corrected himself: 'Even four.' That year many women admirers offered themselves to him. Sarah Bernhardt, then young, beautiful and much sought-after, flung herself at his head. It may be that she wanted a child by him, since there is this entry in his notebook, 'There will be no child.' It was he who ran after the twenty-two-year-old Judith Gautier, who was famous for her beauty. She yielded. He wrote in his book, '*Toda*.' Theirs was a short-lived affair, because he went off to Guernsey and there fell in love with Blanche, a pretty twenty-two-year-old laundry-maid whom Juliette had unwisely taken into her service. For a little while he struggled against his desires, then began to write poems for her. She too yielded. Juliette became suspicious, interrogated Blanche and expelled her from Guernsey. But he saw her again in Paris: *toda*. He set her up in the quai de la Tournelle and went to see her there almost every day. He loved looking at her with nothing on. In *Océan* he wrote:

> Elle me dit: 'Veux-tu que je reste en chemise?'
> Et je lui dis: 'Jamais la femme n'est mieux mise
> Que toute nue . . . '
> Ce fut superbe. 'Eh bien! dit-elle, me voici.'
> Et devant Adonis, Vénus était ainsi.†

They went for long walks together; Hugo was attached to her both sentimentally and sexually, and she loved him with passion. Sometimes his conscience troubled him. In *Océan* he wrote,

> O triste esprit humain par le corps possédé!‡

Juliette was suspicious; she had him followed by private detectives and on 19 September 1873 she discovered what she called 'his shameful intrigues'. She fled, going far from Paris, and then came back; he promised to break and did not do so. Yet his conscience troubled him more and more. He made a draft of a comedy, *Philémon perverti* (about 1877), in which he accuses himself of going off to his pleasures without troubling about the unhappy Baucis' tears.

* Now, every day and at every hour, the same Maria.

† She said, 'Would you like me to keep my shift on?' And I said, 'A woman is never better dressed than when she is quite naked.' . . . It was magnificent. 'Well,' said she, 'here I am.' And Venus was like this as she stood before Adonis.

‡ Oh wretched human spirit, to be governed by the body.

Prendre une jeune au lieu de la vieille qu'on a! . . .
Je sens que je vais être une horrible canaille.'*

Coming home, he finds Baucis dead from grief. And the young
Eglé turns him to scorn when, between fits of coughing, he pours out
his declarations of love. He ends by stating that Philémon had been
deceived by the Devil, whereas Baucis was the incarnation of an
angel. Nevertheless, Hugo went on frequenting whores. On 28 June
1878, when he was seventy-six, he had a slight stroke, and his doctor
urged him to diminish his sexual activities. 'But, Doctor, you must
admit that nature should give one some warning,' he replied. He did
not lay aside his weapons until the very end. His notebook for 1885
records five more amorous performances, the last on 5 April, a few
weeks before his death. Yet since his stroke his health had declined
a little.

The image of old age that he had always set up for himself allowed
him to accept his sexual desires until he was very old: no doubt he
thought of Booz when a young woman offered herself to him. He
wrote the sonnet *Avé, dea, moriturus te salutat* for Judith Gautier,
and in it he said,

> Nous sommes tous les deux voisins du ciel, Madame,
> Puisque vous êtes belle et puisque je suis vieux.†

In his view, age was by no means a blemish, but rather an honour;
it brought one nearer to God and it was in harmony with everything
that is sublime, with beauty and innocence. The aged Hugo certainly
suffered from no feeling of inferiority whatsoever. Yet he did not
shut his eyes: his comparison of himself and Blanche with Venus and
Adonis was of course ironical. And his old Philémon is ludicrous
when he plays the pretty boy between fits of coughing. But for all
that he was proud of himself. 'I am like a forest that has been cut
again and again; every time the new growth is stronger and more
hardy.' Then again beautiful young women loved him: this was
enough – he granted himself the right to love them. It is not so easy
to see how he reconciled his character as an august old man with the
furtive pursuit of venal delights. Juliette suspected them; and it gave
her great pain, and at times he blamed himself for his actions. Yet
even after his doctor's warning he went on in his old course. He had

---

* To take a girl instead of the old woman one has! . . . I feel that I am going to be a
revolting blackguard.
† We are both of us near to heaven, Madame, since you are beautiful and I am old.

attached so much importance to sex since his marriage that he would have felt himself lowered if he had given up; and his 'shameful intrigues' amounted to a rearguard action. And above all, in his opinion he was answerable to no one but himself: at no time in his life did he ever yield to public opinion – if he had desires, he satisfied them.

There are many other examples to show that an elderly man may be importuned by the most urgent sexual desires. In his *Journal* Edmond de Goncourt wrote, '28 September 88. In the train I was tormented by a need for intercourse, and I thought of everything that has been said, written and published about *dirty old swine*, those poor old swine whom the little spermatic beast still gnaws with all its might. Is it our fault if nature has implanted in us such an imperious, persistent and stubborn desire for coming together with the other sex?' He was sixty-six.

When he was seventy, he wrote on 8 July 1892: 'Just now the napes of women's necks have an aphrodisiac effect upon me, both the rounded and the fluted napes with that wicked little curl of hair against the glow of the skin. For the delight of seeing it, I find myself following a nape, as other men follow a leg.'

5 April 1893: 'How absurd, at my age, still to be the prey of the spermatic beast! For the last fortnight I have been trying to keep my thoughts entirely concentrated on my play, and for the last fortnight, in the dark of my closed eyes, the little brute has been presenting me with erotic pictures warmer than Aretino's.'

Wells was sixty when he fell in love with Dolores after they had corresponded; he fell passionately in love and he found himself possessed of unsuspected sexual powers. 'For the first time in my life it was revealed to me that I was an astonishing fellow, an extra-ordinary chap, an outstanding virtuoso. Casanova certainly could never have held a candle to me,' he wrote with a smile. The affair turned sour; there were ugly scenes; in the end he could no longer bear Dolores and when he was sixty-six he broke with her. Having done so, he met the girl he called Brylhil: this was the most violent passion of his life – mutual passion that lasted many years.

Among our contemporaries there are a very great many examples of elderly men married or attached to young women. Charlie Chaplin was no longer young when he married Oona, by whom he had several children. Picasso was over sixty when he had two children by Françoise Gilot. When she left him, he fell in love with Jacqueline

Roque and married her. (At this period he produced some very fine drawings showing a splendid naked woman opposite a withered, shrunken old man or even a monkey.) The photographs show that he was then full of youth and vitality; he undoubtedly had a favourable image of himself, one that was strengthened by Jacqueline's love. It was a kind of narcissism at one remove that induced him to caricature himself – he was so sure of himself in his uniqueness that he could make game of amorous old men in their generality as an amusement. The revolting or ludicrous side of their pretensions no longer applied to him once he had pointed them out. Pablo Casals is in splendid health at ninety. Henry Miller says, 'He gets up early every morning and goes for a walk on the beach at Porto Rico. He comes home and plays Bach on the piano for half an hour before going on to three hours of 'cello. He travels and gives lectures.' Ten years ago, when he was eighty, he married one of his pupils, a girl of twenty: they have remained a united couple. A journalist describes Miller himself as 'a wrinkled but exuberant young man, exhausting those around him with his vitality; he is sunburnt, happy and relaxed'. When he was seventy-five he married a twenty-nine-year-old Japanese. Sex, health and activity are all connected: it seems almost as though the individual's life were programmed from the very beginning, with both his vital energy and his longevity – apart from outside accidents – being built into his organism.

These examples confirm the notion that if it has been rich, sexual life goes on for a long time. But it may also happen that a man who has been indifferent to women for most of his life discovers the delights of sex in his later years. Berenson, who died at the age of ninety-four, wrote, 'I only really became aware of sex and of women's physical, animal life at the period that might be called my old age.'

Rodin lived with Rose Beuret (who had been very much in love with his pupil Camille Claudel) from his early days, but in his middle years he had little time for women. Yet when he was about seventy he became extremely attentive to them. He said, 'I did not know that I could scorn women at twenty and be charmed by them at seventy.' They grew more and more attractive to him, and he received all his female admirers, letting them in whenever they chose to come. An American woman, married to a duke, dominated him for years on end: according to his friends she was rather old, pretentious, absurd and not at all beautiful. Rilke, his former secretary, deplored it:

336

'Each day turns his old age into something grotesque and ludicrous.' After six years he ended by breaking with the American and going back to Rose.

Trotsky had looked upon himself as old since the age of fifty-five; but at fifty-eight he had an odd outburst of eroticism. Deutscher tells how his vitality flooded into the letters he wrote to his wife at that time, 'as well as his sexual desire for Natalia. He tells her that he has just been rereading the passage in Tolstoy's memoirs which describes the way he, at the age of seventy, would return from his long rides filled with desire for his wife. And how he, Trotsky, came back from his exhausting journeys on horseback with the same kind of feelings at fifty-eight. His desire for her makes him use sexual slang and he feels extremely bashful at putting down such words on paper for the first time in his life and at behaving exactly like a young military cadet.'

One of the most striking pieces of evidence upon the sexuality of elderly men is to be found in Tanizaki's two largely autobiographical novels, *La Confession impudique* and *Journal d'un vieux fou*. Japanese eroticism mingles modesty and shamelessness in the strangest way: they do not undress to make love, yet their prints and books describe the different postures in the crudest way. Tanizaki's novels are in this tradition. The first was written in 1956. The hero is fifty-six (the author was older). He is a teacher. He sleeps with his wife once every ten days: he is exhausted for hours afterwards – so much so that he has not even the strength to think. The female foot is very much of a fetish for him and he is annoyed because his wife allows him only the most usual embraces and refuses to take off her clothes. One evening she drinks too much brandy and passes out: he takes advantage of this to light up her naked body with a torch and examine her minutely. He licks her toes. On the following days he manages to make her drunk again and he photographs the various parts of her body with a polaroid camera, sticking the photographs in his diary. There is a sadistic element in this behaviour, since he leaves his diary about for his wife to read; but he suspects her of connivance and of tricking him as he is tricking her. The curious pleasure this gives him comes under the heading of masochism. It is this masochism that prompts him to ask his pupil Kimura to develop the photographs of his wife – Kimura, who certainly desires her and whom she certainly desires. He has himself given male hormone treatment and he secretly injects himself with hypophisia hormone. He has fits of giddiness, lapses of memory and very high blood-pressure. Insidiously he encourages his wife and Kimura to enter into a very close relationship, highly erotic, if not complete; and his jealousy heightens his pleasure. His wife knows perfectly well that all these sexual activities may kill him and she encourages them; for his part he knows that she does so consciously. Masochism and a taste for danger make this a delightful situation for him. One night he lets his wife bring him up to the very height of pleasure; he makes love to her more violently than ever before and dies of a heart-attack in her arms.

The same pattern is to be found again in the *Journal d'un vieux fou*: eroticism, death, and pleasure heightened by danger. This time the hero is seventy-seven – about the same age as the writer – and he has lived a very active sexual life. He is somewhat attracted by young male actors who play female parts: 'Even if you are impotent, a certain sexual life seems to carry on,' he notes. A few years earlier he has had a slight stroke and he is forced to lean on his nurse or daughter-in-law in order to walk. He delights in imagining that he is dead: the funeral, the tears. 'I wonder what my face will be like when I am dead': this idea haunts him. He is also obsessed by women. 'I have no desire to cling to life, yet as long as I am alive I cannot prevent myself from being attracted by the other sex. I have become completely impotent, but I enjoy all unnatural and indirect forms of sexual excitement.' He is always ill and he loves to describe his ailments, even the most repulsive, as well as the ugliness of his face. His blood-pressure is very high. He eats and drinks a great deal. He undergoes stretching treatment to ease the suffering of his distorted bones; he has sharp pains in his hands, arms and legs which excite him sexually. 'It is odd, but even when it hurts me I feel sexual desires; indeed it would be more exact to say I feel them *when* it hurts. . . . There is a masochistic tendency here. . . . It has developed in my old age.'* He likes women who give him an impression of being cruel. His daughter-in-law – he had once given her a very beautiful and expensive handbag as a present – lets him come into the bathroom while she is having her shower and allows him to kiss her leg under her knee. One day he licks her leg from knee to heel and puts her toes in his mouth. His eyes grow bloodshot and his blood-pressure mounts. 'My face was on fire and the blood flowed into my head as if I were about to have an apoplectic fit and die that moment.

* In all Tanizaki's earlier novels there is evidence of masochism.

I really thought I was going to die.' The more frightened he becomes the more his excitement grows. He does the same things another day but his blood-pressure does not rise and his pleasure is far less. Other people's love affairs also excite him, particularly when his daughter-in-law brings her lover to the house. The erotic games in the shower go on. Once he kisses her neck for twenty minutes on end. He gives her a diamond worth three million yen while at the same time he refuses to lend his daughter the modest sum she asks for. He likes his daughter-in-law Satsuki to see him without his false teeth. He says, 'A chimpanzee would be less hideous.' Then, 'The uglier I look to myself in the mirror, the prettier Satsuki seems.' Here, instead of being a hindrance, the ugliness of the reflection is a help to erotic excitement because of the hero's masochism. One day when his bones are really hurting him he groans and says, 'Satsuki, I have such pains.' He bursts into sobs, dribbling and howling. She is angry with him for making such a scene. He wants to kiss her but she refuses; all she will do is let a drop of her saliva fall into his mouth. He takes more and more sleeping-pills; he is given injections. He decides to go and choose the place for his grave, and leaves for Kyoto with the nurse and Satsuki. He thinks of having Satsuki's body sculptured on his tombstone, Satsuki dressed as the goddess Kannon; he likes the idea of lying under her feet. Another thought strikes him: he will have his daughter-in-law's footprints carved on the tombstone, passing them off for Buddha's. He sets about taking the prints himself, daubing Satsuki's feet with ink and reaching a high state of erotic excitement. His blood-pressure mounts to a dangerous height. Satsuki, who has put up with his fumbling all day long, runs off next morning, her patience exhausted. He has a stroke and then recovers, although it leaves him very much less of a man than he was.

The strangest aspect of these two novels is the relationship between sexuality and death. Literature has often brought them together: the idea of death gives rise to a reflex of life. And there is the classical association of Eros and Thanatos. But I know of no other case in which a man finds it necessary to endanger his life before he can reach the paroxysm of pleasure.

These examples are in agreement with the general remarks that precede them. Impotence does not exclude desire: desire is most often satisfied through deviations in which the fantasies of middle age are accentuated – voyeurism in Hugo, masochism in Tanizaki. Many elderly men look for younger partners. Those subjects for whom sex continues to play an important part are gifted with excellent health and lead an active life.

We have one most remarkable piece of evidence concerning an old man's relationship with his body, his image and his sex: this is Léautaud's *Journal*. He provides us with a living synthesis of the various points of view that we have considered in this chapter.

Léautaud always looked at himself with a certain approval. When he was forty-one he wrote, 'I am not so ugly. My face is out of the ordinary: it is even quite expressive.' He admits that it is the face of a forty-one-year-old man, 'a face already marked by life'. Later, he often says he feels younger than he is. It was from the outside that he learned he was ageing and it made him very angry. He was fifty-three when a railway official referred to him as 'a little old gentleman'. Furious, Léautaud wrote in his *Journal*, 'Little old man! Old gentleman? What the devil – am I as blind as all that? I cannot see that I am either a little or an old gentleman. I see myself as a fifty-year-old, certainly, but an exceedingly well preserved fifty-year-old. I am slim and I move easily. Just let them show me an *old gentleman* in such good shape!' At fifty-nine he looked at himself with a critical eye: 'Mentally and physically I am a man of forty. What a pity my face does not match! Above all my lack of teeth! I really am remarkable for my age: slim, supple, quick, active. It is my lack of teeth that spoils everything; I shall never dare to make love to a woman again.' Yet this did not prevent him from flying into another passion when he was over sixty, because a young man gave up his seat in the underground. 'Oh! Be damned to old age, that hideous thing!' In him we see with remarkable clarity how impossible it is for an old man to realize his age. On his birthday he wrote, 'Today I begin my sixty-fourth year. In no way do I feel an old man.' The old man is Another, and this Other belongs to a certain category which is objectively defined; in his inner experience Léautaud found no such person. There were moments, however, when his age weighed upon him. On 12 April 1936 he wrote, 'I do not feel happy about my health nor about my state of mind; and then there is the sorrow of ageing, too. Ageing above all!' But at sixty-nine he wrote, 'During my seventieth year I am still as lively, active, nimble and alert as a man can be.'

He had every reason to be pleased with himself: he looked after his house and cared for his animals, he did all the shopping on foot, carrying heavy baskets of provisions; wrote his *Journal* and he did not know what it was to be tired. 'It is only my sight that is failing. I am exactly as I was at twenty. My memory is as good as ever and my mind as quick and sharp.'

This made him all the more irritable when other people's reactions brought the truth home to him. He was seventy when a young woman lost her balance as an underground train started off with a jerk; she cried out, 'I'm so sorry, Grandpa, I nearly fell on you.' He wrote angrily, 'Damn it all! My age must show clearly in my face. How impossible it is to see oneself as one really is!'

The paradox lies in the fact that he did not really dislike being old. He was one of those exceptional cases I have mentioned, where old age coincides with childhood fantasy: he had always been interested in old people. On 7 March 1942, when he was seventy-two, he wrote, 'A kind of vanity comes over you when you reach old age – you take a pride in remaining healthy, slim, supple and alert, with an unaltered complexion, your joints in good order, no illness and no diminution in your physical and mental powers.'

But his vanity demanded that his age should be invisible to others: he liked to imagine that he had stayed young in spite of the burden of his years.

Sometimes indeed he did find his age difficult to put up with. On 2 July 1942 he wrote, 'Seventy-two and a half. It is all very well to be in excellent health, but old age does affect me deeply, and so does the thought of death. My sight has become very poor.' He was afraid that one day his false teeth might fall out: 'What a sight I should be! ... If that happened I think I might shut myself up at home for good.' On another day he wrote, 'I should so love to be only fifty, but still retaining all my present maturity and the knowledge I have gained since then.' 'Damned old age! It is summed up in these words: resignation and making the best of things.'

But then his satisfaction returned. 'My face is ageing a great deal. My chin is beginning to be wrinkled with little criss-cross lines. Well, I am no longer young. On 18 January I shall be in my seventy-fourth year. In Paris a little while back I looked at myself in mirrors, and I found that I had turned into what interested me so much as a child; when I was growing up and in fact all my life: a singular old man, with an unusual, expressive face, dressed in a kind of old-fashioned way, someone that people would look at, taking him for an old and unsuccessful actor.' He was justifiably proud of his health. 'When you have reached a certain age, as I have – I shall be in my seventy-fifth year in a few days – and when like me you do not know what it means to be tired, and your state of health remains good except for love-making, alas, you feel a kind of pride. You look upon youth as it were with pity. Youth is not the important thing. What is important is to live a long time.'

He only gave way to discouragement at the very end of his life, when his health failed. On 25 February 1945 he wrote, 'I am very low indeed. My eye-sight. The horrible marks of age I see on my face. My *Journal* behind-hand. The mediocrity of my life. I have lost my energy and all my illusions. Pleasure, even five minutes of pleasure, is over for me.'

He was then seventy-five and his sexual life had come to an end. But except in his very last years one of the reasons for his pride was that he still felt desire and was still capable of satisfying it. We can follow his sexual evolution in his *Journal*.

He only became fully aware of women when he was approaching his fiftieth year. At thirty-five he wrote, 'I am beginning to regret that my temperament allows me to enjoy women so little.' He lacked the 'sacred fire'. 'I always think too much of other things – of myself, for example.' He was afraid of impotence and his love-making was over very quickly: 'I give women no pleasure since I have finished in five minutes and can never start again. . . . Shamelessness is all I really like in love. . . . There are some things not every woman can be asked to do.' He had a lasting affair with a woman called Bl—. He says he loved her very much, but he also says that living with her was hell. When he was about forty, although he was still rather indifferent since he could give his partner no pleasure, he delighted in looking at pictures of naked women. Yet a few years later he speaks sadly of the 'rare love-scenes in my life which I really enjoyed'. He reproaches himself for being 'timid, awkward, brusque, over-sensitive, always hesitant, never able to take advantage of even the best opportunities' with women. All this changed when at fifty he met 'a really passionate woman, wonderfully equipped for pleasure and exactly to my taste in these matters' and he showed himself to be 'almost brilliant', although up until then he had thought that he was very little good – as he had only known women who did not suit him. From this time on sex became an obsession with him; on 1 December 1923 he wrote, 'Perhaps Madame* is right: my perpetual desire to

* One of the names he gave to his mistress.

342

make love may be somewhat pathological. . . . I put it down to a lifetime's moderation – it lasted until I was over forty – and also to my intense feeling for her, which makes me want to make love to her when I see so much as a square inch of her body. . . . I think it is also because I have been deprived of so many things, such as that female nakedness for which I have acquired such a liking. I am quite amazed when I think of what has happened to me in all this. . . . Never have I caressed any other woman as I caress Madame.' In the summer they parted, and abstinence lay heavy upon him: he masturbated, thinking of her. 'Of course I am delighted to be such an ardent lover at my age, but God knows it can be troublesome.' Madame was a little older than he: all his life he had loved only mature women. A twenty-three-year-old virgin threw herself at his head, and he agreed to have an affair with her; but it did not give him the least pleasure and he broke immediately. Except for this one fling he was faithful to Madame for years. He liked watching himself and her in a mirror during their love-making. From 1927 on, he was forced to take care not to make love too often; he found consolation in bawdy talk with the Panther.* He did not get on well with her; 'We are attached to each other only by our senses – by vice – and what remains is so utterly tenuous!' But in 1938 he did recall with great satisfaction the 'seventeen years of pleasure between two creatures, the one as passionate and daring as the other in amorous words and deeds'. When he was fifty-nine his affair with the Scourge, as he now called her, was still going on, though she was already sixty-four. He was shocked by couples where the woman was much younger than the man. 'I myself at fifty-nine would never dare to make any sort of advance to a woman of thirty.' He was still very much attracted to the Scourge and he took great pleasure in his 'sessions' with her. Yet he did complain 'What a feeble ejaculation when I make love: little better than water!' Making love tired him and his doctors advised him to give it up. Once in a while he would masturbate. He and the Scourge wrote each other erotic letters: he found the written words intensely exciting. On 25 September 1933 he wrote, 'Once again amorous desires are tormenting me cruelly – they did last Monday. . . . I watch myself in this state with curiosity and anxiety.' It goes on in the same way throughout 1934 and 1935 – masturbation, erotic correspondence, 'sessions' with the Scourge, and another affair which troubled him very much with a certain C.N. The

* Another name he gave to his mistress.

Journal records erotic thoughts more and more often. 'Beware of amorous play. I am still desperately keen on it; all too keen for my age.' Having been disappointed in C.N. he wrote on 13 August 1938, 'All I think of is making love with a woman like myself, a woman with my tastes: it torments me cruelly.'

On 18 January he wrote, 'I am certainly better when I do not make love at all. Not that it comes hard – far from it – but it is always a great effort, and I do not get over it as quickly as I did a few years ago.' 'What I miss most is female nakedness, licentious attitudes, and playing amorous games.'

On 17 February 1940 he wrote that he dreamed of women: 'The face and the body of an attractive woman. I spend my nights in impossible dreams.'

When he was over sixty-nine he complained of 'fasting'.

Speaking of his youth he says, 'Sexual pleasure meant little to me. The sight of a woman's body and all its details even less, and yet after forty this became such a very great and vivid delight to me.'

'Until I was sixty-six or sixty-seven I could make love two or three times a week.'

Now he complains that his brain is tired for three or four days after making love, but he still goes on, and he corresponds with three of his former mistresses. He is very sad that C.N. will not sleep with him any more. He loves recalling amorous memories and speaking of them in his *Journal*.

When he was seventy he wrote, 'I miss women and love terribly.' He remembers how he used to make passionate love to the Scourge from the age of forty-seven to sixty-three, and then for two years with C.N. 'It was only three years ago that I noticed I was slowing down.'

'I can still make love, and indeed I quite often feel sad at being deprived of it; though at the same time I tell myself that it is certainly much better for me to abstain.'

On 29 September 1942: 'I go on being thoroughly ridiculous. I miss women and love and all that goes with them quite horribly.'

3 November: 'I am in the depths of sorrow at being deprived of all that belongs to women and love.'

At seventy-two he was still planning idylls that never came to anything, and he had erotic dreams which gave him an erection. 'At night I still feel ready for anything.' But that same year he observed that his sexual powers were declining.

'It is no use giving yourself over to love-making when the physical

344

side is dead or nearly so. Even the pleasure of seeing and fondling is soon over, and there is not the least eagerness to begin again. For a real appreciation of all these things, there must be the heat of physical passion.' It is clear that Léautaud's greatest pleasure was visual. He retained it longer than any other form of sensual enjoyment and after the age of forty he prized it very highly indeed. When he lost it he considered that his sexual life was over. It is also clear how a man's image of himself is bound up with sexual activity. He was 'in the depths of sorrow' when he could no longer experience these pleasures. Still, his narcissism did survive his sexual decline at least for some time.

There are also examples of sexually active old age among homosexuals. Should Michelangelo be included? Some people say that his passion for Tommaso Cavalieri was platonic, but the burning sonnets he wrote to him from the day of their first meeting (Michelangelo was fifty-seven) up to his death show feelings unmistakably sexual in origin whether they were sublimated or not. Jouhandeau certainly remained sexually active for a long while, since he was already an old man when he wrote, 'I am burdened with a chastity that I cannot yet like or grow accustomed to; I do not know what use one can make of it, since it is neither virtuous nor voluntary.' When Gide was over seventy-five he recalled passionate nights of love in his *Journal*. On 3 April 1944, 'I cannot bring myself to despise carnal delights, and in any case I make very little effort to do so. An aeroplane breaking down . . . gave me one of the most vivid that can be imagined two nights ago.' And on 24 January 1948, 'No shame at all after the most casual, easy indulgence that can be imagined.'

Proust obviously based his description of Charlus' old age upon flesh-and-blood examples. When young, Charlus gave himself such airs of virility that people who did not know how his tastes lay thought he must be very successful with women. His aristocratic pride stood out against his corruption. His homosexuality appeared only as one of the elements that made up his strong personality. When the narrator returns to Paris in 1914 after a long absence, he walks behind two zouaves and notices 'a tall, stout man in a felt hat, wearing a long overcoat. I hesitated before putting a name to the mauve face I saw: should it be that of an actor or a painter? They were both equally well-known for their innumerable homosexual scandals.' It was Monsieur de Charlus: 'Monsieur de Charlus had come to a point as far as possible from himself; or rather he was himself, but so perfectly disguised by what he had become and by what did not belong to him alone but to many other perverts as well, that for a moment or two I had taken him for another of them.' He had given himself up entirely to his vice; he was attracted by little boys and he saw pederasts everywhere. He often went to Jupien's shady hotel and there he had himself chained and whipped by paid youths who insulted him as they flogged him. He now lived only with his inferiors and he had almost entirely stopped putting on his virile airs. Yet his eager insistence upon the heaviest fetters and the most savage instruments still showed his dream of virility. His case resembles that of heterosexuals whose fantasies become enormously important after the whole or partial loss of their sexual powers. The masochistic dreams that Charlus had earlier kept in check now overcame him, and he tried to bring them into real life. The narrator saw him once again a few years later. He was a very old man but he was still a rake and he managed to evade Jupien's supervision – Jupien had become his nurse. Sometimes he had crises in which he describes his homosexual activities quite baldly: words had become the substitute for deeds, deeds that had after all greatly diminished.

Biologically women's sexuality is less affected by age than men's. Brantôme bears this out in the chapter of his *Vie des dames galantes* that he dedicates to 'Certain old ladies who take as much pleasure in love as the young ones'. Whereas a man of a certain age is no longer capable of erection, a woman 'at no matter what age is endowed with as it were a furnace ... all fire and fuel within'. Popular tradition bears witness to this contrast. In one of the songs in the Merry Muses of Caledonia* an old woman laments her elderly husband's impotence. She longs for 'the wild embraces of their younger days' which are now no more than a ghostly memory, since he no longer thinks of doing anything in bed except sleep, while she is eaten up with desire. Today scientific research confirms the validity of this evidence. According to Kinsey, throughout their lives women are sexually more stable than men; when they are sixty their potentialities for pleasure and desire are the same as they were at thirty. According to Masters and Johnson, the strength of the sexual reaction diminishes with age; yet a woman can still reach orgasm, above all if she is regularly and properly stimulated. Those who do not often have physical relations

* Popular Scottish songs collected in the eighteenth century.

sometimes find coition painful, either during the act or after, and sometimes suffer from dyspareunia or dysuria: it is not known whether these troubles are physical or psychological in origin. I may add that a woman can take great pleasure in making love even though she may not reach orgasm. The 'preliminary pleasures' count even more perhaps for her than they do for a man. She is usually less sensitive to the appearance of her partner and therefore less worried by his growing old. Even though her part in love-making is not as passive as people sometimes make out, she has no fear of a specific failure. There is nothing to prevent her from going on with her sexual activities until the end of her life.

Still, all research shows that women have a less active sexual life than men. Kinsey says that at fifty, ninety-seven per cent of men are still sexually active and only ninety-three per cent of women. At sixty it is ninety-four per cent of men and only eighty per cent of women. This comes from the fact that socially men, whatever their age, are subjects, and women are objects, relative beings. When she marries, a woman's future is determined by her husband's; he is usually about four years older than she, and his desire progressively lessens. Or if it does continue to exist, he takes to younger women. An old woman, on the other hand, finds it extremely difficult to have extramarital relations. She is even less attractive to men than old men are to women. And in her case gerontophily does not exist. A young man may desire a woman old enough to be his mother but not his grand-mother. A woman of seventy is no longer regarded by anyone as an erotic object. Venal love is very difficult for her to find. It would be most exceptional for an old woman to have both the means and the opportunity of getting herself a partner; and then again shame and fear of what people might say would generally prevent her from doing so. This frustration is painful to many old women, for they are still tormented by desire. They usually find their relief in masturba-tion: a gynaecologist told me of the case of one woman of seventy who begged him to cure her of this practice – she was indulging in it night and day.

When Andrée Martinerie was conducting an inquiry she gathered some interesting confidences from elderly women.* Madame F., a rich middle-class sixty-eight-year-old, a militant Catholic, mother of five and grandmother of ten, told her, 'I was already sixty-four. . . . Now just listen: four months after my husband's death I went down

* Quoted in *Elle*, March 1969.

into the street just like someone who is going to commit suicide. I had
made up my mind to give myself to the very first man who would
have me. Nobody wanted me. So I went home again.' When she was
asked whether she had thought of remarrying she answered, 'That is
all I ever do think of. If I dared I would put an advertisement in *Le
Chasseur français*. ... I would rather have a decrepit invalid of a
man than no man at all!' Talking of desire, Madame R., sixty years
old and living with her sick husband, said, 'It is quite true that you
don't get over it.' She sometimes felt like beating her head against the
wall. A woman reader of this inquiry wrote to the magazine, 'I must
tell you that a woman remains a woman for a very long time in spite
of growing older. I know what I am talking about, because I am
seventy-one. I was a widow at sixty; my husband died suddenly and
it took me at least two years to realize fully what had happened. Then
I started to answer advertisements in the matrimonial column. I
admit that I did miss having a man – or rather I should say I do miss
it: this aimless existence is terrifying, without affection or any outlet
for one's own feelings. I even began wondering whether I was quite
normal. Your inquiry was a great relief. ...' This correspondent
speaks modestly of 'affection', an 'outlet for one's own feelings'. But
the context shows that her frustration had a sexual dimension.*

The notion that women's sexual drive continues for a long time is
confirmed by the observation of lesbians. Some continue their erotic
activities well into their eighties. This proves that women go on feeling
desire long after they have stopped being attractive to men.

In other words a woman continues in her state of erotic object
right up to the end. Chastity is not imposed upon her by a physiological destiny but by her position as a relative being. Nevertheless it
may happen that women condemn themselves to chastity because of
the 'psychological barriers' that I have mentioned, which are even
more inhibiting for them than for men. A woman is usually more
narcissistic in love than a man; her narcissism is directed at her body
as a whole. She has a delightful awareness of her body as something
desirable, and this awareness comes to her through her partner's
caresses and his gaze. If he goes on desiring her she easily puts up

* The reaction of a young woman who wrote to *Elle* is typical: 'In our group of
young people we laughed heartily about the passionate widow (the member of the
Action Catholique) who cannot "get over it". I wish you would now hold an inquiry
on love as it appears to the fourth age of women, in other words those between eighty
and a hundred and twenty.' Young people are very shocked if the old, especially old
women, are still sexually active.

with her body's ageing. But at the first sign of coldness she feels her ugliness in all its horror, she is disgusted with her image and cannot bear to expose her poor person to others. This lack of assurance strengthens her fear of other people's opinions: she knows how censorious they are towards old women who do not play their proper role of serene and passion-free grandmothers.

Even if her husband wants to make love with her again later, a deeply-rooted feeling of shame may make her refuse him. Women make less use of diversion than men. Those who enjoy a very active and uninhibited sexual life before, do sometimes compensate for their enforced abstinence by extreme freedom in conversation and the use of obscene words. They become something very like bawds, or at least they spy upon the sexual life of their young women friends with a most unhealthy curiosity, and do all they can to make them confide their secrets. But generally speaking their language is as repressed as their love-making. Elderly women like to appear as restrained in their conversation as they are in their way of life. Their sexuality now shows only in their dress, their jewellery and ornaments; and in the pleasure they take in male society. They like to flirt discreetly with men younger than themselves and they are touched by attentions that show they are still women in men's eyes.

However, it is clear from pathology that in women too the sexual drive is repressed but not extinguished. Alienists have observed that in asylums female patients' eroticism often increases with age. Senile dementia brings with it a state of erotic delirium arising from lack of cerebral control. Repressions are also discarded in some other forms of psychosis. Dr Georges Mahé recorded twenty cases of extreme eroticism out of 110 sixty-year-old female patients in an institution; the symptoms included public masturbation, make-believe coition, obscene talk and exhibitionism. Unfortunately he gives no idea of the meaning of these displays: he puts them into no context and we do not know *who* the patients were who indulged in these practices. Many of the inmates suffer from genital hallucinations such as rape and physical contact. Women of over seventy-one are convinced that they are pregnant. Madame C., seventy and a grandmother, sings barrack-room songs and walks about the hospital half-naked, looking for a man. Eroticism is the most important factor in many delirious states; it also triggers off some cases of melancholia. E. Gehu speaks of an eighty-three-year-old grandmother who was looked after in a convent. She was an exhibitionist, showing both homosexual and heterosexual tendencies. She fell upon the younger nuns who brought her meals; during these crises she was perfectly lucid. Later she became mentally confused. She ended up by regaining her mental health and behaving normally once more. Here again, we should like a more exact, detailed account of her case. All the observations that I have just quoted are most inadequate; but at least they do show that old women are no more 'purified of their bodies' than old men.

Neither history nor literature has left us any worthwhile evidence on the sexuality of old women. It is an even more strictly forbidden subject than the sexuality of old men.

There are many cases of the libido disappearing entirely in old people. Ought they to rejoice in it, as the moralists say? Nothing is less certain. It is a mutilation that brings other mutilations with it: sexuality, vitality and activity are indissolubly linked. When desire is completely dead emotional response itself may grow loose at its edge. At sixty-three Rétif de La Bretonne wrote, 'My heart died at the same time as my senses, and if sometimes a tender impulse stirs me, it is as aberrant as that of a savage or a eunuch: it leaves me with a profound feeling of sorrow.' It seemed to Bernard Shaw that when he lost interest in women he lost interest in living. 'I am ageing very quickly. I have lost all interest in women, and the interest they have in me is greater than ever and it bores me. The time has probably come for me to die.'

Even Schopenhauer admitted that 'it could be said that once the sexual urge is over life's true centre is burnt out, leaving a mere shell'. Or again, 'life is like a play acted at first by live actors and then finished by automata wearing the same costumes'. Yet in the same essay* he says that the sexual instinct produces a 'benign dementia'. The only choice left to men is that between madness and sclerosis. In fact what he calls 'dementia' is the spring of life itself. When it is broken or destroyed a man is no longer truly alive.

The link that exists between sexuality and creativity is very striking: it is obvious in Hugo and Picasso and in many others. In order to create there must be some degree of aggression – 'a certain readiness' says Flaubert – and this aggressivity has its biological source in the libido.† It is also necessary to feel united with the world by an

* On the difference between ages.
† We shall return to this when we discuss creativity among the aged.

emotional warmth; this disappears at the same time as carnal desire, as Gide understood very clearly when on 10 April 1942 he wrote, 'There was a time when I was cruelly tormented, indeed obsessed by desire, and I prayed, "Oh let the moment come when my subjugated flesh will allow me to give myself entirely to. . . . But to what? To art? To pure thought? To God?" How ignorant I was! How mad! It was the same as believing that the flame would burn brighter in a lamp with no oil left. If it were abstract, my thought would go out; even today it is my carnal self that feeds the flame, and now I pray that I may retain carnal desire until I die.'

It would not be truthful to state that sexual indifference necessarily and in all fields bring inertia and impotence. There are many examples to prove the contrary. Let us merely say there is one dimension of life that disappears when there is no more carnal relationship with the world; those who keep this treasure to an advanced age are privileged indeed.

There is one passion that is profoundly rooted in sexuality and that is inflamed by age: this is jealousy. Lagache shows that it is often caused by a transference of emotion; the hairdresser whose business is failing readily persuades himself that his wife is deceiving him and makes terrible scenes. And since old age is a time of generalized frustration it begets a general resentment that may take the form of jealousy. Then again, in many old couples sexual decline often brings with it either one- or two-sided resentment, and this easily turns into jealousy. Sometimes in the papers we read of a seventy-year-old man who has beaten or killed the woman he has lived with for years out of jealousy, or that he has had a fight with a rival. Maybe he was taking his revenge for his partner's frigidity, or for his own impotence. Women of over seventy are brought before the courts because they have fought over an aged lover. In institutions where both sexes live together many violent quarrels break out, with jealousy as their cause. Dr Balier and L.-H. Sébillotte conducted an inquiry in the XIIIth arrondissement in Paris. They concluded that couples find ageing more difficult than solitary individuals, because the emotional relations between husband and wife worsen and grow more complex with age. The decline in their health together with the loneliness resulting from retirement and from their children's leaving home means that each lives almost exclusively through the other. More than ever each demands love and protection; and each becomes less and less able to satisfy this demand. Their permanent state of dissatisfaction makes them insist upon always being together; it excites jealousy and even persecution. Separation may indeed be a mortal blow to those who literally cannot do without each other. But living together brings them more torment than happiness.

Apart from couples where the woman is much younger than the man, it is the woman who has more reason to be jealous. The man retains his sexual appetite when she is no longer a desirable object. I shall describe two cases of female jealousy: those of Juliette Drouet and Sophia Tolstoy.

Juliette suffered from Victor Hugo's infidelities all her life, and they became even more painful to her when physical relations between them had ceased. She felt defenceless, vanquished, humiliated. In 1873 Hugo had an affair with Blanche, and Juliette, who was sixty-nine, reacted with more violence than she had ever done in the past. She borrowed two hundred francs from friends and on 23 September she disappeared without leaving any address. He was terribly upset and had a search made for her: she was found in Brussels. She agreed to come back; he went to meet her at the station and they made it up. Four days later she sent him one of her 'scribbles': 'My dear and best beloved. Today is the first day since that horrible week of black, hellish despair that as I open my eyes, so my mouth, my heart and my soul open to look at God, to smile at you, pray to you and bless you. So that horrible nightmare is over! And it is true that you love me, me alone . . .' But then again on 16 October 1873 she wrote, 'This never-ending conflict between my poor old love and these youthful enticements that tempt you will soon be the end of me . . .'

He must have seen Blanche again after his promise to break: the contrast between the pretty laundry-maid's youth and her own old age was unbearable to Juliette. She expresses the same hopelessness on 18 November 1873: 'I do not want to nag about your affairs, but you know I cannot help feeling that my old love looks very shabby among all these hussies in their fine feathers. From today on I shall leave the lodging of my heart.'

11 March 1874: "He whose heart is younger than his age has age's unhappiness to the full."

'In its laconic, commonplace fashion this quotation explains and excuses the trouble that I involuntarily bring into your life, suffering like one of the damned as I do . . .'

4 April 1874: 'As I see it, unfaithfulness does not begin only with the act; for me it is already certain as soon as desire comes into existence. From now on, my great and dear friend, I beg you not to have any scruples, but to behave as if I were already gone.'

Later, she became more cheerful again.

11 April 1874: 'I feel an upsurge of youth that probably comes from these seventy summers I have swallowed without making a grimace.'

But presently grief seized upon her once more. Not only was she jealous of Hugo's young mistresses but of his family as well. He took a two-storeyed flat at Clichy: the reception-rooms were on the lower floor and the bedrooms above. He lived on the upper floor with his daughter-in-law and grandchildren, and Juliette had settled there too. But the daughter-in-law sent her downstairs, giving lack of space for the children as an excuse.

'My heart is full of sad misgivings,' wrote Juliette on 7 May 1874. 'This floor is like a broken bridge between our two hearts. . . . I am in despair and have to make a great effort not to weep.'

She no doubt attached so much importance to this removal because she knew that Hugo was still being unfaithful to her. She suffered from this as from a want of love; but she was also ashamed for Hugo, whose sexual life, as we have seen, was not very edifying.

21 June 1874: 'What remains of my poor heart seems to be the prey of all these women in search of vicious and shameful adventures: for my part I admit defeat without a struggle . . .' 5 o'clock: 'Every day Sisyphus rolls his love to the summit and every day he feels it fall with all its weight upon his heart: this martyrdom appals me and I should a thousand times rather have instant death than this hideous torture. Have pity on me, let me go . . .'

There were painful scenes between them in which she begged for a separation.

28 July 1874: 'You are not happy, my poor too-well-beloved, and neither am I. What you are suffering from is a woman's open wound, a wound that grows and grows because you lack the courage to cauterize it once and for all. My suffering comes from loving you too much.'

6 July 1875: 'I do assure you that if I could feel you were happy and peaceful I should suffer less away from you than I do here, feeling that my presence is continually keeping you from your work, from your freedom, from calmness and from quietness in your life. . . .

Anything is better, for your heart as well as mine, than the thought of my no longer being enough for you . . .'

1877: 'My heart is down: and I have doubts about heaven and about you . . .'

He behaved no better as time went on and she found it hard to reconcile her high ideas of him with the rakish old man that he really was.

After Hugo had his stroke in June 1878, Juliette, supported by Lockroy,* made him break with Blanche. They terrified the poor girl by telling her that Hugo would die in her arms if she did not leave him. Juliette sent her money and she resigned herself to getting married.† But other young women took her place. During the summer of that year, which they spent in Guernsey, Juliette wrote to Hugo on 20 August:

'Your dawn was pure. Now you must have a venerable, consecrated twilight. I would give the rest of my life to keep you from committing certain faults that are unworthy of your age and your majestic genius.'

It was in vain that Hugo wrote to her, 'I am sure my soul belongs to yours.' She could not bear him to go on having letters from other women. The wife of Hugo's secretary says, 'She took any excuse to pick a quarrel, even in Guernsey. She would have died for the Master, but for all that she delighted in tormenting him with continual pinpricks. . . . One morning a scene broke out over a letter from a former servant. Madame Drouet had opened the letter, hence the tears and gnashing of teeth . . .' When Juliette found a bag containing five thousand francs in gold she wanted to know what pleasures this money was meant to buy. Once she discovered some old notebooks full of women's names: another scene. And yet another when she learnt that he had been strolling about the red-light district; she wanted to go off and live with her nephew at Jena.

They came together again, and she settled in Paris, in the same flat as Hugo. But she went on tormenting herself, and on 10 November 1879 she wrote, 'Dread of remembering what has happened, of fore-seeing what will happen: I no longer dare look forward nor back, either in you or in me. I am afraid.' And on 11 November she

---

* Second husband of Adèle, Charles Hugo's widow.

† She was inconsolable. She went to see Hugo's friends to talk about him. She would find out the times of his leaving the house so that she could see him from a distance. She tried to renew their relationship after Juliette's death, but his friends intercepted her letters.

reproached him for his 'acts of sacrilege and his many attempts at suicide'. His behaviour seemed to her not only 'unworthy' but dangerous.

8 August 1880: 'My too-well-beloved, I spend my life sticking together the pieces of my broken idol as best I can: but I cannot hide the cracks.' The day she saw Blanche looking out for Hugo in the avenue Victor-Hugo she flew into a terrible passion. At times she was too sad and discouraged to go on writing her 'scribbles'. She continued to live with Hugo until she died, but scarcely ever again did she know the meaning of peace.

She sometimes took a grossly unfair advantage of her position as long-established mistress, particularly in Blanche's case; but her disillusionment is understandable. She had imagined they would quietly grow old together, side by side, both of them tired of carnal pleasures. But not at all. He either had affairs in which his heart was engaged so that she suffered because he did not entirely belong to her, or he contented himself with venal loves, which she considered degrading. Her tears and hysterical nagging had the excuse of a sincere and whole-hearted love.

Sophia Tolstoy's jealousy was of quite another kind. She had always hated sleeping with her husband, and very early her resentment turned into jealousy. As far back as 1863 she noted that her jealousy was an 'inborn disease'. All through her diary she keeps repeating that she is 'eaten up with jealousy'. She suffered from her 'relative' position beside a man with such a crushingly strong personality, and from living such an austere and lonely life, a life which even her many pregnancies could not fill. She loathed the country and the peasants. The happiest hours of her married life were those when Tolstoy was writing *War and Peace* and *Anna Karenina*: she copied out his rough drafts and felt that her collaboration united them. When he stopped writing novels she had an impression of being betrayed. But above all, she could not accept her husband's attitude towards money. From 1881 on, Tolstoy's moral and social preoccupations took the first place in his life. He would have liked to give away his land to the peasants and to renounce all his literary earnings. But he did no more than make over the management of his estates to Sophia, so that he should have nothing more to do with it. In 1883 they agreed that she was to see to the publication of all the books he had written before 1881, the year of Tolstoy's 'second birth', and that she should have the royalties. To offset this, Tolstoy and his favourite disciple Chertkov founded a publishing house which they called The Mediator. Its aim was to circulate good books cheaply among the masses. All this was not enough to bring peace to the household. Sophia reproached Tolstoy with sacrificing his own children to the peasants; he hated the life she made him lead: it was too soft and too worldly. 'It is a fight to the death between us two,' he wrote to her. From then on he confided the care of his manuscripts to his eldest daughter Masha. Sophia boiled with rage, and on 20 November 1890 she wrote, 'He is systematically killing me; he excludes me from his personal life, and I suffer terribly.' She hated Tolstoy's followers, and above all Chertkov, the favourite. *The Kreutzer Sonata* increased her resentment: in it Tolstoy condemned marriage and praised chastity. Their scenes became more and more violent. To ease his conscience Tolstoy made over his entire fortune, real and personal, to his wife and children. But he decided that his latest works should fall into the public domain; this so maddened Sophia that she rushed to the station, intending to throw herself under a train;* but she did not actually do so. In January 1895 Tolstoy finished writing *Master and Servant*. Instead of publishing it through The Mediator and giving it to Sophia to include in his collected works he promised it to a magazine run by a woman. Sophia suspected him of wanting to leave her for this 'adventuress'. She was then fifty. She rushed out into the Moscow streets in bedroom-slippers and with her hair down, intending to die of cold in the snow. Tolstoy ran after her and made her come home. The following day she went off again and this time her daughter Masha brought her back. Once again she ran away: she took a cab to the Kursk station to throw herself under a train but her son Serge and Masha caught her. Tolstoy gave in.

However, he never thought of leaving her. One day, when he was sixty-seven, a disciple of his who was mowing next to him suggested a separation. In his extreme fury Tolstoy threatened him with his scythe – he collapsed in tears. When Sophia was fifty-two her romance – her platonic romance – with Taneiev the musician infuriated her husband. 'I have not slept all night; I have a pain in my heart: I was unable to dominate my pride and indignation,' he wrote on 26 July 1896. There were perpetual scenes between them over this relationship: recriminations, explanations by word of mouth, by letter and telephone. She noted 'The morbid jealousy shown by Leo Nikolýevich when he heard of Taneiev's arrival hurt me very much; it also

* She meant to imitate Anna Karenina.

filled me with alarm.' He had indeed written her some very harsh letters: 'It is infinitely painful and humiliating that a stranger – a totally useless stranger of no account whatever – should now rule our life. It is horrible, horrible; it is base and shameful.' 'Your relations with Taneiev disgust me. . . . If you cannot put a stop to this state of affairs then let us separate.' They did not separate. In his seventieth year he was still sleeping with her; he did so on the very day of his seventieth birthday.

For some years they lived together more or less peacefully. But when in 1908, after ten years of exile, Chertkov came back to Russia Sophia lost her head. This tyrannical, sectarian, intriguing disciple had such a strong influence over his master that it might be damaging to the interests of the family. He got hold of Tolstoy's manuscripts; he longed to monopolize his whole work and to be seen as his one, sole representative by posterity. He had been banished from the Tula district where Tolstoy's property lay, but nevertheless he managed to go and live in a cottage near enough for Tolstoy to ride over and see him. Sophia reproached him violently every time he went. She feared that he would make over all his copyrights to Chertkov. There was a dreadful scene in which she insisted on inheriting all her husband's works, whether they had been written before 1881 or not. She was also against his going to a world peace conference in Stockholm. He gave in on the second point, but not on the first.

In June 1910 Tolstoy went to spend a few days with Chertkov whose local banishment was about to be cancelled: this horrified Sophia. She sent a telegram insisting upon her husband's returning home a day early, and he refused. In her nightgown, sobbing and with her hair on end, she confided to her diary, 'What is the matter with me? Hysterics? Attacks of nerves? Heart-attack? Onset of madness? I cannot tell. . . . He is enamoured of Chertkov in the most disgusting, senile way (he often fell in love with men in his younger days) and here he is ready to agree to everything he wants. . . . I am hopelessly jealous of Leo Tolstoy's relationship with Chertkov. I feel he has taken away all that I have lived for these forty-eight years. . . . I think I shall go to Stolbora and lie down under the train.' After Tolstoy's return she sobbed for days on end, reproaching him for his love for Chertkov. One morning she was found on all fours behind a wardrobe, with a vial of opium in her mouth: it was taken from her. She made Tolstoy confess that he had given his intimate diaries of the last two years to Chertkov to read; she rushed out into the park in the rain and when she came back she refused to take off her wet clothes, 'so that I might catch a cold and die'. A few days later Tolstoy, his daughter Sasha and Chertkov shut themselves in a room to talk. She kept watch behind the balcony door, barefoot so as to make less noise. 'Another plot against me!' she cried. It certainly was: they were discussing a will that was to disinherit the family in favour of the peasants and the public in general. She angrily demanded that Chertkov should give the diaries back. Next day she could not bear seeing Tolstoy and Chertkov side by side on a sofa: 'I was utterly overcome by feelings of disgust and jealousy,' she noted on 5 July 1910. At night she imagined 'unnatural' relationships between the old man and his disciple. During the night of 10 July, after yet another scene, she shrieked, 'I shall kill Chertkov,' and rushed out into the park. Later she wrote, 'So I went into the garden and I stayed two hours lying there on the wet ground in nothing but my thin dress. I was frozen, but all I asked and all I still ask is to die. The alarm was given. ... Now it is three o'clock in the morning and neither of us is asleep. We said nothing to each other.'

On 15 July after she had asked Tolstoy for a receipt for the diaries, which was to be taken to the bank: 'He flew into a terrible passion and said, "No, not at any price. Not for anything in the world"; then he fled. I had another frightful attack of nerves and wanted to take opium, but once again I lacked courage, and I most basely deceived L.N. by pretending to have drunk it; but straight away I confessed, and cried and sobbed ...'

A few days later she wrote, 'I should like to kill Chertkov, to burst open his gross body and set Leo Nikolýevich's soul free from his evil influence.' The day after this she decided to leave home: 'I am despised by my daughter and rejected by my husband; I abandon my home because my place is taken by a Chertkov, and I shall never come back unless he goes away.' She wrote an anouncement for the Press and drove off to Tula, with a revolver and a bottle of opium in her handbag. She met her son at the station and he brought her home again. Tolstoy wrote and told Chertkov to keep away for a while, but they had friends who carried letters to and fro. 'Secret love-letters are passing between you and Chertkov,' Sophia shrieked at her husband. The older she grew the less could she control her obsessions. She had lost all sense of judgement and she convinced herself that there was a 'guilty' liaison between Chertkov and Tolstoy. She showed her husband a page of his youthful diary in which he had written, 'I have never been in love with a woman. But I have quite often fallen in love with a man.'

Infuriated, he ran and shut himself up in his room. She repeated her accusations of homosexuality to those around her. When she found out that the two men met in a pine-wood, she secretly followed them and she had them spied on by children from the village. She went through Tolstoy's papers looking for proofs of his homo-sexuality. One day she thought she would make her peace with Chertkov. 'But when I think that I should have to see his face once more, and when I think that on L.N.'s I should see the delight of being with him again, then renewed pain wells up in my heart. I feel like bursting into tears and my whole person shrieks out in protest. The spirit of evil is in Chertkov.'

On 18 August, Chertkov received official authorization to live in the Tula province. 'This is my death warrant! I shall kill Chertkov. I shall have him sent to prison. Either he or I must go!' She searched through all Tolstoy's books for signs of his homosexuality. However, on 22 August she did note, 'My birthday. I am sixty-six and have lost none of my energy. I have the same passionate emotions and people tell me that I still look as young as ever.'

Once when she was alone at Yasnaya Polyana she went into her husband's study, took down the photographs of Chertkov and Sasha and hung her own in their place. Tolstoy put them back as soon as he returned. Sophia wrote on 26 September, 'L.N. has replaced it [Chertkov's portrait] and this has plunged me once more into a deep despair. . . . I took it down again, tore it into tiny pieces and threw it down the lavatory. L.N. was cross, of course. I had another fit of despair and my jealousy of Chertkov came surging back, and once again I cried until I was utterly exhausted and my head ached. I thought about suicide.' She let off two shots with a toy pistol which Tolstoy never even heard.

She found one of the notebooks in which Tolstoy kept a diary 'for myself alone', and saw that a will had been made which left her nothing. She wrote a furious letter to her husband; she wept and kissed his hands, trying to soften his heart so that he would change the will, but in vain. On 16 October, convinced that he was riding off to meet Chertkov, she went and posted herself in a ditch near the cottage, watching it through field-glasses. Tolstoy did not come. She went back to Yasnaya Polyana and a servant found her sitting on a bench and trembling with cold. Once again she begged Tolstoy to give up seeing that 'disgusting' Chertkov. He was at the end of his tether: he made up his mind to go away and left her a letter without giving her any address. She wrote in her diary:

28 October: 'L.N. has run away on the spur of the moment. Horrible! He says in his letter that nobody is to go and look for him – that he has left his peaceful old man's life for ever. As soon as I had read part of it I rushed out in my despair and threw myself into the nearby pond . . .'

After writing a note to his wife, Tolstoy had gone off that morning with Dr Makovitsky. They took the train and stopped at the monastery of Optina. He was thinking of renting a cottage near another monastery at Shamordino when his daughter Sasha arrived – he had given her his address. She described the hysterical scenes that Sophia was making and advised him to flee to an even greater distance. They took the train once more together with Sasha: everybody knows how it ended – Tolstoy dying in the station-master's house at Astapovo and Sophia, warned by the journalists, waiting outside, not allowed to come in. She survived her husband for nine years. She and Sasha were reconciled only a short time before her death in 1919.

All this is far from the ideal couple that Robert Burns dreamed of. Even for couples who have had a happy and contented life, old age is often a disturbing factor: for those who have been torn by indifferently-resolved conflicts, it intensifies their antagonism. Neither Juliette's flight nor her harshness to Blanche have their equivalent in her youth or middle age. And Sophia's violence and paranoiac crises reached their height only during the last years of her married life. This increase is partly explained by the old person's feelings of frustration, which provoke demanding and aggressive forms of behaviour. And no doubt the shrinking of his future leads him to increase his demands on the present: he must have the love, the trust, all that he asks for at once, or he will never have them at all. This feeling of urgency makes him incapable of tolerating anything that thwarts him. We can fully understand senile jealousy only if we examine the old person's experience – the experience as he lives it – in its entirety.

6

Time, activity, history

For human reality, existing means existing in time: in the present we look towards the future by means of plans that go beyond our past, in which our activities fall lifeless, frozen and loaded with passive demands. Age changes our relationship with time: as the years go by our future shortens, while our past grows heavier. The aged man may be defined as an individual with a long existence behind him, and before him a very limited expectation of life. The consequences of these changes influence one another and bring into being a situation that varies according to the individual's earlier history but whose constant factors may be isolated.

And in the first place, what does *having* one's life behind one mean? Sartre has explained this in *L'Etre et le Néant*: one does not possess one's past as one possesses a thing that one can hold and turn in one's hand, inspecting every side of it. My past is the in-itself that I am in so far as I have been outstripped; in order to possess it I must bind it to existence by a project; if this project consists of knowing it then I must make it present to myself by means of bringing it back to my memory. There is a kind of magic in recollection, a magic that one feels at every age. The past was experienced in the *for-itself* mode, and yet it has become *in-itself*; in remembering we seem to attain that impossible synthesis of the in-itself and the for-itself that life yearns for, but always in vain.* But it is above all the old who love to call the past to mind. 'They live more by memory than by hope,' observed Aristotle. In his *Mémoires intérieurs* and *Nouveaux Mémoires intérieurs* Mauriac often looks back longingly at the little boy he was

---

* This is why memory shows us the person we were with a fullness of being that endues it with a kind of poetry. Frozen in the past, a pain that we may have had does not cease to have the meaning of a for-itself, and yet it exists in itself with the silent fixity of a pain experienced by another, a statue's pain. (Sartre, *L'Etre et le Néant*)

and whose world seems to him more real than that of today. In a recent *Bloc-notes* he wrote, 'Even if an old man does not become childish, he secretly returns to childhood – he gives himself the pleasure of calling on Mama under his breath.' This delight in former days is characteristic of most old people, and indeed it is often this that makes their age most evident. How is it to be explained? And to what degree can they 'recover time past'?

'It is the future that decides whether the past is living or not,' says Sartre. A man whose project is to get on, to advance, takes off from his past; he defines his former I as the I that he is no longer and he dissociates himself from it. For some for-itselfs, on the contrary, their project implies the refusal of time and an intimate solidarity with the past. This applies to most old people: they refuse time because they do not wish to decline; they define their former I as that which they still are – they assert their solidarity with their youth. Even if they have overcome the identification-crisis and have accepted a new image of themselves – the dear old grandmother, or the retired person, or the elderly writer – each in his heart preserves the conviction of having remained unalterable: when they summon their memories they justify this assertion. They set up a fixed, unchanging essence against the deteriorations of age, and tirelessly they tell stories of this being that they were, this being that lives on inside them. Sometimes they choose to see themselves in the most flattering character; they are a perpetual ex-serviceman for ever, or an adored, run-after woman, or a wonderful mother. Or else they bring the bloom of their adolescent years to life again, their early youth. More often, like Mauriac, they turn back to the time when the world first took on its face for them, the days when the man they have become was first defined – their childhood. All their life, whether they are thirty or whether they are fifty, they have still continued to be that child though at the same time they were that child no more. Once they have recovered him, once they have merged with him, it does not matter whether they are thirty or fifty or even eighty: they have escaped from age.

But what in fact can they recover? How far does memory allow us to retrieve our lives?

Professor Delay* rightly distinguishes three forms of recovery. The first is the sensor-motor memory, in which recognition is a matter of action and not of thought; it is made up of a series of montages and

* *Les Dissolutions de la mémoire.*

362

automatic forms of behaviour that obey the laws of habit and that normally remain intact in old age. The second is the autistic memory, which is governed by the dynamics of the unconscious and which actualizes the past in dream and delirium in a paralogical and affective mode: the subject is not aware of remembering, but re-lives past impressions in the present. (I may add that up to a certain point it is possible to make use of this memory in order to arrive at a re-knowing, a recognition of the past as such: this is what psychoanalysis attempts to do.) The third form is the social memory, an intellectual operation that reconstructs and localizes past facts, basing itself upon physiological data, images and a certain knowledge, and making use of logical categories. This is the only one that allows us, to some degree, to tell ourselves our own history. If we wish to do so, and to do it well, many conditions are required.

In the first place this history must have been recorded. We know that memory requires forgetfulness – if we were to note down and store everything, we should have nothing at our disposal. Many occurrences are either not retained or are wiped out by others. Let me take my own case, and I can do so here, for what is valid for me is *a fortiori* valid for those older than myself: when I am talking to Sartre or my sister I often discover immense gaps in my past. For example, Sartre told me about the evening when we heard that the U.S.S.R. had entered the war: everywhere there were voices singing the Internationale. That evening mattered to me, and yet I have retained nothing of it.

Then again, the nerve-circuits that allow the renewal of the images must remain intact. There are some diseases – senile dementia and cerebral atherosclerosis, among others – that destroy great numbers of them. Even a man who is still fit may be affected by quite serious lesions. Berenson complains of this: 'Now I am seventy-five, strange things happen to me: so much of what seemed to be part of my intellectual furniture only yesterday has disappeared, fading and gone before I realized it! . . . Great sections of memory crumble and vanish in forgetfulness. Why? How?'

The images that we can call upon are far from possessing the richness of their original object. An image is the seeing of an absent object by means of an organic and affective analogon. As Sartre says, there is 'a kind of essential poverty' in it. And Alain observes that when we evoke an image of the Pantheon we cannot even attempt to count its columns. An image does not necessarily obey the principle of identity, it produces the object in its general and not its specific aspect; and it appears in an unreal space and time. Our images therefore cannot resuscitate the real world from which they emanate, and that is why we so often find images that we cannot place rising up in our minds. When I was writing my *Mémoires* I would sometimes have brilliant visions of scenes that I could not integrate with the rest of my account because I had no fixes, no coordinates, and so I abandoned them.

'A very old man's memories are like ants whose ant-hill has been destroyed,' says Mauriac. 'One's eyes cannot follow any single one of them for long.' And Hermann Broch:* 'Memories rise up, then sink down, often vanishing altogether. How timid they are! . . . Oh, what chasms of forgetfulness underlie our life; from what a great way off we must recall a memory that is scarcely a memory any more.'

With the help of reasoning, comparison and cross-checking, it is possible to set a certain number of hypotheses that cannot always be verified. 'We guess at the past,' as Henri Poincaré used to say. However, some exact images do exist. At a distance of thirty years I saw that the gulf of Porto in Corsica had the same colour and the same shape that it had in my memory: my surprise proves how accustomed I am to being harshly contradicted by reality. Indeed, how very often have I actually laid my finger upon mistakes of this kind. And clearly they represent only a small proportion of those I have committed.

Most of the time, logically reconstructed and situated images remain as foreign to us as those of some event that is part of the general history of mankind. 'We have only a distorted idea of the past, and few moments of that past are linked to us by any living contact,' as Berenson so rightly says. These moments often assume an entirely set character: we bring them to mind without changing them and without enriching them, since it is impossible for us to get more out of them than we put in. I often combine data belonging to different periods, making one single memory out of them – the faces of Louise, my father and my grandfather remain unchanged throughout the whole of my childhood. Even when I evoke some particular scene, it is built up from general patterns: in the class-room of our school the twelve-year-old Zaza thanks me for a bag I have given her – she has the shape and the features of Zaza in her twenties.

These stereotypes persist in the midst of a changing world, with

* *Le Tentateur.*

the result that in spite of their unalterability they take on a curiously exotic aspect. This would not occur in a repetitive society. If I wore the same traditional clothes as my mother did, a picture of her in her youth would show me a young woman of today: but fashions have changed, and in her fine jet-black dress she belongs to a past age. A return to my twenties makes me feel as lost as though I were at the other end of the world. I look at a photograph of the old Trocadéro, a building whose ugliness I used to love: can I really have seen it with my own eyes? Another of the Champs-Elysées in 1929: I had on one of those cloche hats and a roll collar, and the men who passed me in the street wore caps and soft felt hats. It seems to me that this scene can never have been part of my life. As the years go by, it is always the present moment that appears natural to us; and since the past seems natural too, we have the vague impression that it was the same. But in fact the images of the past that we recover are dated. In this way too our life escapes us – it was freshness, novelty and bloom. And now that freshness is out of date.

This is what Emmanuel Berl felt when he wrote in *Sylvia,* 'My past escapes me. I tug at one end, I tug at the other, and all that stays in my hand is a rotten scrap of fraying cloth. Everything turns into a ghost or a lie.

'I can scarcely make myself out at all in the pictures my memory offers. What have I in common with this character arriving at Le Touquet in a blue pseudo-Morand racing-car with a pseudo-Van Dongen young lady? If all these puppets, all these mere imitations make up my memory, then my history is not me.'

A friend said to me, 'I find very old people touching because of the long past they have behind them.' Unfortunately this is just what they do not have. The past is not a peaceful landscape lying there behind me, a country in which I can stroll wherever I please, and which will gradually show me all its secret hills and dales. As I was moving forward, so it was crumbling. Most of the wreckage that can still be seen is colourless, distorted, frozen: its meaning escapes me. Here and there, I see occasional pieces whose melancholy beauty enchants me. They do not suffice to populate this emptiness that Chateaubriand calls 'the desert of the past'.

There are many things that we are powerless to summon up but that we can nevertheless recognize. Yet this recognition does not always give us back the warmth of the past. The past moves us for the very reason that it is past; but this too is why it so often disappoints us – we lived it in the present, a present rich in the future towards which it was hurrying; and all that is left is a skeleton. That is what makes pilgrimages so pointless. Very often we cannot find our own footsteps however hard we try. Space takes over time's betrayal – places change. But even those that seem to have remained unaltered are not the same for me. There are streets in Uzerche, Marseilles and Rouen where I can walk about, recognizing the houses, the stones; but I shall never find my plans again, my hopes and fears – I shall not find myself. And if, when I am there, I call to mind some scene that happened long ago, it is fixed against that background like a butterfly pinned in a glass case: the characters no longer move in any direction. Their relationships are numbed, paralysed. And I myself no longer expect anything at all.

Not only has this past's future ceased to be a future, but in becoming the present it has often disappointed our hopes. More than once I have known the beginnings of what was meant to be an unending friendship: some have fulfilled their promise, others have turned into indifference or even hostility. How are we to interpret an alliance that has been severed by a quarrel? Was it valid at the time, but fated to survive no longer than the situation that gave it birth? Was it based upon an illusion? Might it have lasted for ever, instead of being broken by some misunderstanding? No verdict can possibly be final: the meaning of a past event can always be reversed. Not only does the material aspect of the facts escape us, but we cannot decide upon the weight we are to give them; and we are in a continual state of suspended judgement.

The death of someone we are fond of amounts to a sudden violent break with our past: and an old person is one with many deaths behind him. 'My too-long life is like those Roman roads lined with monuments to the dead,' wrote Chateaubriand. The death of a friend, of one who was close to us, not only deprives us of a presence but of the whole of that part of our lives that was committed to them. When it is our elders who die, then it is our own past that they carry away with them. There are people in their sixties who suffer, when they lose friends or relatives of their own generation, from the loss of a certain image of themselves that the dead possessed: with him there vanishes a part of youth or childhood that he alone remembered. And for the old, it is a never-ending grief to lose those who are younger than themselves and whom they associate with their own future, above all if they are their children, or if they have brought them up: the death of a child, of a small child, is the sudden ruin of a whole undertaking; it means that all the hopes and sacrifices centred upon him are pointless, utterly in vain. The death of friends of our own age does not possess this character of bitter failure; but it does wipe out the relationship we have had with them. When Zaza died, I was too intent upon the future to weep for my own past; I wept only for her. But I remember my distress, much later, at the death of Dullin, although indeed he and I had never been really intimate. It was a whole section of my life that had collapsed: Ferolles, the Atelier, the rehearsals of *Les Mouches* and those wonderfully gay dinners when he used to tell his reminiscences – all these disappeared with him. Later our agreements and disagreements with Camus were wiped out: wiped out too my arguments with Merleau-Ponty in the gardens of the Luxembourg, at his home, at mine, at Saint-Tropez; gone those long talks with Giacometti and my visits to his studio. So long as they were alive memory was not called upon for our shared past to remain alive in them. They have carried it away with them into the grave; and my memory can recover only a frigid imitation of it. In the 'monuments to the dead' that stud my history, it is I who am buried.

Yet may not the past, taken as a whole, sometimes be an object of enjoyment? May not a successful life be enough to make the ageing person happy? That is what one supposes when one is young. When I was twenty a man's life seemed to me something as solid as a physical object and yet imbued with consciousness. If I caught a glimpse of a gap between a man and his biography, I was scandalized. Baudelaire, knowing who he was, should never have been worried because fools misunderstood him, thought I. Much later, when Sartre began thinking what he wrote at the end of *Les Mots*, his disillusioned remarks irritated me. I should have preferred him to rejoice in being Sartre. What an absurd mistake! For himself he *is* not Sartre. Even Victor Hugo only 'took himself for Victor Hugo' (as Cocteau put it) at odd moments. It is a good expression, for it points out that a man may play with an image of himself but that he may not merge into it. There is a vast miscomprehension between the people who from the outside look at a 'successful' man in the apparent fullness of his being-for-others and his own experience of himself. In one of his most recent poems Aragon drew up what might be called a failure-report on his own life: some critics accused him of fishing for compliments. 'You have succeeded and you know it,' they said; whereas in fact he was talking about the failure of all success. Vigny says that a really good life is youth's idea realized in maturity. Very well. But the dream dreamt is infinitely remote from the dream made real. That is what Mallarmé expresses so well when he alludes to

> ... Ce parfum de tristesse
> Que même sans regret et sans déboire laisse
> La cueillaison d'un rêve au coeur qui l'a cueilli.*

Sartre explains this shift, this disjunction, in *L'Etre et le Néant*. 'The future does not allow itself to be overtaken, but slips into the past, a future that is future no more. . . . This is the origin of the ontological disappointment that waits for the for-itself at every outlet into the future. Even if in its content my present is strictly identical with that future towards which I projected myself from the other side, it is not that present towards which I projected myself because I projected myself towards that future as a future, that is to say as a point of junction with my being.' That is why, without falling into self-contradiction, I could say in my *Mémoires d'une jeune fille rangée*, 'No life, not any moment of any life could fulfil the promises which made my credulous heart beat so wildly,' and then, in *La Force des choses*, 'The promises have been kept,' ending, nevertheless, 'I have been swindled.' Even if the present conforms to my expectations, it could not bring me what I expected – that fullness of being at which life so vainly aims. The for-itself *is* not. And no man can say, 'I have had a fine life' because a life is something that one does not *have*, that one does not possess. I am not in the least of the opinion that fame is a 'brilliant mourning for happiness'; fame, in fact, is nothing, except perhaps a fleeting illusion in the eyes of the outside world. Tolstoy's eightieth birthday was celebrated with extraordinary splendour and enthusiasm; yet as he went to bed he said to his daughter, 'My soul is heavy.' Andersen wept when his native town greeted him with cheers: 'How happy my parents would have been,' he said. For them, his fame would have been a reality; he would have seen it reflected in their eyes.

To be sure, it may happen that a man looks back at his past with pride – above all if he finds the present in which he is living and the

---

* This scent of melancholy that the realizing of a dream leaves in the heart of the man who has realized it, even when there is neither failure nor regret.

future that he foresees disappointing. If this is so, he will prop himself up with his memories: he will turn them into a defence or even a weapon. But these intermittent outbursts of pride do not imply a whole-hearted enjoyment of that which was.

In fact, it is the past that maintains its grasp: it is by means of what that past has made of us that we know it. A man who is discontented with his lot will only find food there for his bitterness, still another reason for being sad about the present. Thus we find Swift writing a letter on 5 April 1729, when he was sixty-two: 'I never wake up in the morning without finding life a little more devoid of interest than it was the day before. But what saddens me most is remembering my life as it was twenty years ago and then suddenly coming back into the present.' At the age of fifty-four Flaubert wrote, 'The future holds nothing for me, and I am being devoured by the past. Mark of old age and decay.' Three years later, and still with bitterness, he wrote, 'The older I get, the more and more firmly the past takes hold of me.' As we have seen, the financial insecurity and social humiliation caused by his niece's ruin had given him the premature feeling of being a man whose life was over. For him the past was not an object for pleasant meditation but a sad obsession: he compared it with the present and he felt that he had come down. And his obsession with the past confirmed this idea of degradation.

The contrast between the present and the past may become intolerable. There are few more pitiful stories than that which Brummell's valet told of his master. The sixty-year-old Brummell, wandering in his mind, sick, lonely and penniless, was living in France. One evening he had his rooms set out as though he were about to receive a great many guests – armchairs, whist-tables, wax candles (a luxury, since they were usually tallow). He put on a splendid but moth-eaten blue tail-coat with gilt buttons, a white cravat and primrose-coloured gloves, and gave his valet a list of guests to be ushered in every five minutes from seven o'clock onwards. The valet took up his station at the door, holding a link, and began to announce the ghosts with splendid names, while Brummell welcomed them ceremoniously. All at once he collapsed in his chair, weeping. Then he stood up and said to his valet, 'Call the carriages. You may go to bed when everybody has left.' This way of re-living the past is related to those ecmnesic phenomena I have already spoken of. To what extent was Brummell possessed by that past which he was making present once more? Was his mind still clear, and did he realize that he was playing an ugly game? Judging from the anecdote he seems to have wavered between possession and conscious pretence.*

It is his childhood above all that returns to haunt the aged man: ever since Freud's time we have known the great importance of the first years in the formation of the individual and his world – an importance already sensed by Montaigne. The impressions received at that time are so deeply imprinted that they can never be effaced. The adult scarcely has time to call them to mind because he is taken up with finding a practical immediate balance, but they come to the surface again when this tension dies away. 'The kindest privilege that nature grants the ageing man is that of recovering the impressions of his childhood with an extraordinary ease,' says Nodier. In his diary for 10 March 1906, the seventy-eight-year-old Tolstoy wrote, 'All day long, a feeling of stupidity and sadness. Towards the evening this state of mind changed into a longing for caresses and affection. I should have liked to cuddle against some loving, sympathetic bosom as I did as a child, to have wept with emotion and to have been comforted.... To have become a little boy again, to have clung to my mother, as I imagine her.... Mama, pick me up, baby me.... All this is mad, but it is all true.' He was imagining his mother, who died when he was two, but the beginning of his reverie was based on memory.

Loisy devoted his life to the criticism of the Bible; he was excommunicated for his modernist theories and he lost his faith. Six weeks before his death at eighty-three, when he was racked by pain and his mind was wandering, he began singing hymns and parts of the mass, as he had done when he was a young student in the seminary. He told the story of Job, comparing himself with that patriarch.†

The child serves a hard apprenticeship to life; he is attacked by complexes that he has to overcome; he has feelings of guilt, shame and anxiety. The unpleasant memories of this time that were repressed in adult life revive in old age. The barriers that stood up well enough so long as the individual was active and subject to social pressure give way in the lonely idleness of old age. Then again the narcissistic traumatism brought about by the coming of old age no

* There is an analogy between this story and Ionescu's *Les Chaises*.
† In his last years he did believe in a darkly conceived God, and he sometimes referred to the theme of Job. But he was as far as possible from Catholicism.

doubt weakens his defences; and the conflicts of childhood and adolescence spring to life once more. My mother's whole life was marked by her childhood: her father had preferred her younger sister, and towards the end she spoke of this even more often, and always resentfully. Andersen was neither idle nor abandoned, and yet he too was a striking example of this. His life began to darken towards 1854, during the war with Germany that ended in Denmark's defeat: at this time he was fifty-nine. He struggled against his depression by work and travel. He was very well-known, he had great numbers of friends; and yet he took to dreaming of his old schoolmaster Meisling every night, a man who had persecuted and humiliated him cruelly when he was a boy. Andersen was in the grip of that autistic memory which does not allow a control of the past but brings it to immediate life: he was not telling himself the history of his childhood – he was re-living it, re-living it neurotically. When he was appointed a councillor of state he dreamt that it was Meisling who gave him this title by way of mockery and threw his books at his head. He came to Odense, his native town, in 1867, and there he was seized by a 'mad and eerie dread'. He remembered the scorn with which he had been treated by the eldest member of the confirmation class, the mockery of those who learnt Latin with him, the ill-mannered boys who ran after his grandfather in the street, his father's ravings and death. The next day he wept during the banquet that was given in his honour. In 1869 Copenhagen fêted him: it was a splendid climax. And the critic George Brandes devoted an important and enthusiastic book to him. But Andersen's nervous system was deteriorating, and this made life harder and harder for him. His anxiety had always been there in a latent state even in happy times, but now it came out in all sorts of specific, terrifying forms: he dreaded fire, water, disease, everything. Meisling went on laughing at him in his nightmares. And in dreams Andersen was seized with furious anger against old friends: he would wake up sobbing, full of remorse. His diary is filled with accounts of his nightmares. In one of his last dreams, when he was sleeping under the effects of morphine, he had a quiet, pleasant conversation with Meisling on art and beauty. 'At last we became friends,' he wrote with relief. His seventieth birthday was happy. But later, seriously ill and morbidly drowsy, all he longed for was death. 'If I must die, let death come soon; I cannot wait, I cannot lie here crumbling to pieces like a dead leaf.' Soon after he died.

There is nothing exceptional about Andersen's case: all old people's neuroses have their source in childhood or adolescence.

The reason why they turn back so readily to their childhood is clear – they are possessed by it. Since it has never ceased to dwell in them, they recognize themselves in their childhood, even though for a while they may have chosen to ignore it. And there is still another reason: life bases itself upon self-transcendence. But this transcendence comes up against death, particularly when a very great age has been reached. The old person attempts to give his existence a foundation by taking over his birth or at least his earliest years. The individual inwardly experiences that childhood-old age connexion that we observed on the sociological plane: as he is about to step out of this world he recognizes himself in the baby that stepped out of that other unborn world.

We also see why old people are not discouraged by the poverty of the images that they are capable of summoning up. They are not trying to make a detailed, coherent account of their earliest years, but rather to plunge back into them. Again and again they turn over a few themes of great emotional value to them; and far from growing tired of this perpetual repetition, they return to it with an even greater pleasure. They escape from the present; they dream of former happiness; they exorcize past misfortunes. A woman of eighty-six told me that as soon as she went to bed at night she would tell herself about things that had happened in her early childhood; she would tell them over and over again, and they gave her inexhaustible joy.

The aged man's inward experience of his past takes the form of images, fantasies and emotional attitudes. He is dependent upon it in still another way: it is the past that defines my present situation and its outlet into the future; it is the admitted fact, the base from which I project myself and which I must go beyond in order to exist. This is true at all ages. From the past I derive all the mechanisms of my body, the cultural tools I use, my knowledge and my ignorance, my relationship with the outside world, my activities and my duties. Everything that I have ever done has been taken back by the past, and there, in the past, it has become reified under the form of what Sartre calls the practico-inert. He defines this as the whole formed by those things that are marked by the seal of human activity together with men defined by their relationship to those things: as far as I personally am concerned, the practico-inert is the whole formed by the books I have written, which now outside me constitute my works, and define me as their author. 'I am that which I have done and which escapes from me by at once setting me up as Another.'* By his praxis every man achieves his objectification in the world and becomes possessed by it. He creates himself interests there. Interest is 'the whole being as much outside myself as a thing in so far as it conditions praxis as a categorical imperative'. An owner's interest is his property, and he often attaches more value to it than to life itself.

The older we grow, the more heavily the burden of the practico-inert weighs upon us. Gorz shows this very clearly in his book *Le Vieillissement*. He defines youth as 'less inertia to set in motion'. Becoming a full-grown man means becoming Another for the rest – an individual defined by his calling. From this time on, the future that he has freely chosen for himself appears to him as the necessity that awaits him; and in his past he sees an otherness. His life is 'a life that trails outside, among things, like my outside being, lost to my-self'. Projects are frozen. This description suits old age, though old age is still more weighed down than maturity. At this point the whole of a long life is set and fixed behind us, and it holds us captive. Imperatives have increased in number; and the reverse of these imperatives are impossibilities: the owner *must* keep his property; he *cannot* dispose of it. In order to understand to what an extent the old person, confronted with his future, is bound hand and foot, we must now consider how he sees this future. As we shall see, it seems to him *finished*, doubly finished, in that it is both short and closed. It is the more closed the shorter it is, and seems all the shorter for being the more closed.

Once a certain threshold has been passed – a threshold that varies according to the individual – the elderly man becomes aware of his biological fate: the number of years of life that remain to him is limited. If a year were to seem to a sixty-five-year-old man as long as it was in his childhood, then the lapse of time he could reasonably count upon would still outrun his imagination; but this is not the case. The period seems tragically short to him because time does not flow at the same speed at the different stages of our life: the older one grows the faster it runs.

An hour seems long to a child. The time in which he has his being

* Sartre, *Critique de la raison dialectique*.

is a time imposed upon him from without – it is the grown-ups' time. He can neither measure nor foresee it; he is lost in a continuous happening without beginning or end. I took control of time when I began to give life to my projects, parcelled out according to my curriculum; my weeks took shape around those afternoons when I went to school. Now each day had a past and a future. My coherent, dated memories go back to that time. Then again, minutes drag when we are tense or weary. But because of his weakness, his excitability and the delicacy of his nervous system, a child tires easily. Sixty minutes of reading calls for more sustained effort at five than at ten, and at ten than at twenty. Distances are long, concentration difficult: the child cannot get through his day without fatigue. And above all, the world is then so new, and the impressions it makes upon us so fresh and lively that, since we gauge its extent by the wealth of contents, we think it far greater than it comes to appear when familiarity has impoverished us. As Schopenhauer says, 'During childhood, the novelty of things and events means that everything is impressed upon our consciousness: the days are therefore so long that their end cannot be seen. The same thing happens to us, and for the same reason, when we are travelling, and when one month away seems longer to us than four at home.'*

'I remember the quarter of an hour's break at my primary school,' says Ionesco. 'A quarter of an hour! It was long and it was full, there was time to think of a game, play it right through and begin another. ... But next year was nothing but a word; and even if I did think that this next year might come, it seemed to me so far-off that it was not worth troubling about; it was long as all eternity before next year would come round, which was much the same as not coming round at all.'†

As we leave childhood space draws in, objects grow smaller, the body becomes stronger, concentration increases, we get used to clocks and calendars, and memory takes on breadth and precision. But for all that, the seasons go on revolving with a wonderful or a

* Speaking of this elongation of time in travelling, the ethnologist Georges Condaminas says, 'It must be understood that when a day spent in travelling is transposed to memory it takes up a far greater "space" than a day spent at home. Above all, if the journey takes one into an entirely unknown country. . . . The hours spent in perpetually drinking in and absorbing this new world go beyond the natural and measurable intervals of time. The facts beat so powerfully upon the memory that the images come back in rather the same way as a film in slow motion. The playing-back time is magnification of the real time' (*L'exotique est quotidien*).

† *Journal en miettes.*

terrible slowness. When I was fifteen and I leafed through my new school-books, the journey through the school year seemed to me an immense, passionately interesting voyage. Later, the going back to school plunged me into depression: I felt that I should never reach the end of the ten months that would have to be spent in our dreary flat. But as soon as I recovered from my lowness of spirit the vastness of the future spread out at my feet filled me with enthusiasm – forty years to live – perhaps even sixty! Since a single one seemed so enormous, this was eternity.

There is more than one reason for the change in the evaluation of time that occurs between youth and age. In the first place it must be pointed out that we always have the whole of our life behind us, reduced to the same form and size at all ages: in perspective, twenty years are equal to sixty, and this gives the units a variable dimension. If a single year amounts to a fifth of our total age, then it seems ten times longer to us than if it represents only the fiftieth part. Clearly, I am not speaking here of a precise calculation, but rather of a spontaneous impression. And then young people's memories give them back the past year with a wealth of detail that spreads over an enormous extent: they therefore suppose that the year to come will have the same dimensions. When we are old, on the other hand, few things make much impression on us; the passing moment brings little new, and upon that little we do not dwell for long. As far as I am concerned, 1968 may be summed up in a few dates, a few patterns, a few facts. And for me, 1969 has the same label of poverty. I have scarcely returned to Paris in October before it is already July.

There is still another factor that comes into play: I know that in twelve months I shall, at the best, be the same as I am today; whereas when I was twenty, 'being oneself means coming to one-self', as Sartre puts it. One is in a state of waiting for the world and for oneself. Each year brings us a maelstrom of new things and experiences, intoxicatingly delightful, or hideous, and one emerges transformed, with the feeling that the near future will bring about a similar upheaval. It is a period at which one cannot seize and embrace time either by projects or by memory, since time tears one from oneself. No person is capable of making its unity real if to begin with the *I* is other than that which it is going to become. An incalculable distance separates these two strangers: or at least that is what they suppose.

The reason why the emotional memories that restore childhood

are so treasured is that for a fleeting instant they give us back a
boundless future. A cock crows in a village whose slate roofs I see in
the distance; I am walking in a meadow covered with hoar-frost; all
at once it is Meyrignac and there is a catch at my heart – this day now
just beginning stretches out, a vast expanse, as far as the distant
twilight; tomorrow is no more than an empty word; eternity is my
portion.

And then suddenly it is not: here I am back in my days when the
years go by so fast. I can appropriate Ionesco's words for my own
use: 'I have reached the age . . . when an hour is worth only a few
minutes, when the quarters no longer have any meaning.'

He too thinks that the best way of recapturing the childhood sense
of time's duration is to travel.

Every day since then I have been trying to anchor myself to something
solid; desperately I try to discover a present once more, to fix it and to
make it broader. I travel so as to recover a whole, undamaged world
upon which time has no hold. And indeed, two days of travelling and
the sight of a new city does slow down the racing flow of events. Two
days in a new country are worth thirty lived in familiar surroundings,
thirty days worn and shortened, spoiled and damaged by habit. Habit
polishes time – you slip as you do on an over-waxed floor. A new world,
a world always new, always young, an everlasting world – that is what
Paradise means. This speed is not only hellish, it is hell itself – it is the
acceleration of the fall. There was the present; there was time; now there
is no longer either present or time: the geometric progression of the
fall has launched us into the void.*

The paradox is that this hellish speed does not always protect the
old person from boredom: far from it. Everyone at any age has
had this experience – those days spent in travelling that take so long
to pass through one's mind actually went by like a flash because one
was perpetually in suspense; and weeks that seem short when one
looks back at them because they contain nothing to remember, did
in fact drag on endlessly, hour by hour.

The way in which we experience the day-to-day flow of time
depends upon what it holds. But if the aged man looks forward to
this flow in the future, in its pure form, it seems so rapid that his
head spins.

The essential difference between the point of view of the old
person and that of the child or adolescent is that the first has

* *Journal en miettes.*

discovered his finite nature whereas at the beginning of his life he was unaware of it: in those days he saw such manifold and such un-defined possibilities lying before him that they seemed limitless; in order to receive them the future in which they had their being broadened to infinity. The young people of today early realize that society has prefabricated their future, but many dream of escaping from the system or even of destroying it, and this leaves a wide field open to their imagination. At some given moment, a moment that comes sooner or later according to the class to which he belongs, the individual is under the obligation to reproduce his life: he is the prisoner of his calling, and he sees his world draw in, his projects grow fewer in number. Nevertheless, the grown man still has years enough before him to make up his mind to act, to decide upon undertakings and to take changes in the world or in his personal history for granted; he peoples the future with his hopes – a future whose end he does not yet see. The old person, for his part, knows that his life is accomplished and that he will never re-fashion it. The future is no longer big with promise: both this future and the being who must live it contract together. Human reality, indeed, possesses a twofold finitude: the one is contingent and it results from facticity* – the existence of a term imposed from without. The other is an ontological structure of the for-itself. In a man's last years both the one and the other become apparent at the same time; and the one by means of the other. If I were to have a short expectation of life and if at the same time I had the physical and mental potentialities that I had when I was twenty, then my end, faintly seen through the crowd-ing projects, would still seem to me remote. If I were given health and another hundred years to live, I should be able to launch into fresh undertakings, to set off on the conquest of unknown realms. I should not feel that I was irremediably shut up in my own uniqueness. As it happens, I should be mistaken – the length of my days would not take my finitude from me. Even immortality would not shatter it. 'Human reality would remain finite even if it were immortal,' says Sartre, 'because by electing to be human it has made itself finite. . . . The act of freedom itself both creates and assumes my finitude. If I make myself, I make myself finite, and because of this fact my life is unique.'† Because the beginning of my history must for ever

---

* The for-itself as necessary connexion with the in-itself, hence with the world and its own past (trs.).

† L'Etre et le Néant.

remain unchanged, it is a given, set past that I am for ever required to outstrip: nothing will ever be able to make me quit my own skin. The aged man's years are counted, and he will never escape from himself: this double certainty forces itself upon him.

Thus the very quality of the future changes between middle age and the end of one's life. At sixty-five one is not merely twenty years older than one was at forty-five. One has exchanged an indefinite future – and one had a tendency to look upon it as infinite – for a finite future. In earlier days we could see no boundary-mark upon the horizon: now we do see one. 'When I used to dream in former times,' says Chateaubriand, harking back to his remote past, 'my youth lay before me; I could advance towards the unknown that I was looking for. Now I can no longer take a single step without coming up against the boundary-stone.'*

A limited future and a frozen past: such is the situation that the elderly have to face up to. In many instances it paralyses them. All their plans have either been carried out or abandoned, and their life has closed in about itself; nothing requires their presence; they no longer have anything whatsoever to do. This is what happened to Michel Leiris after the success of *Biffures*. 'It seemed to me that my life had reached a kind of horrible culmination. As I saw it, this ending of life was rather like the last days of my stay in Florence. We had "done" the Tuscan capital from top to bottom, and all we had left to see was a few trifles: in just the same way I had only a few trifles left to do in the time that still remained for me to live,' he says in *Fibrilles*. In the same book he explains why his future had become so depopulated.

When one no longer looks upon being wiped out by death or senility as a fate but expects it as an evil that is about to strike, then – and this was the case with me – one loses even the smallest wish to undertake any new thing: one reckons the very small amount of time that still lies ahead – a throttled time that has no relation with that of the days when it was unthinkable that any undertaking should not have space enough to develop freely; and this puts out one's fire entirely. In the same way, when a man has been accustomed to it for many years, as I have been, it is hard to tell oneself each day that the night, now cluttered with weariness and sleep, will not be that limitlessly open time in which – supposing that nothing has weakened him – he may make love, spending

* Letter to Madame Récamier.

his strength without counting the cost. It may be that I am clearer-minded than others, more vulnerable or more graspingly concerned with my own person, but it seems to me that a man whose life has thus moved from the boundless to the bounded lives in a kind of asphyxia. . . . Art and poetry, those last resources, stand there as a means of breaking the strangle-hold. But surely it is a pity to climb down so far as to treat them as a substitute, something that will allow one to soothe the heartbreaking poverty of old age?

In fact, the project of writing had such deep roots in this case that it stood firm against the crisis; indeed, his very anguish provided Leiris with new themes and he wrote *Fibrilles*. But it may happen, either for reasons of health or because of outside difficulties, that the old person is utterly and finally disheartened: either he sees nothing more to do, or he gives up his undertakings, supposing he has no time to carry them through to the end.

Yet there are also cases where the categorical imperatives arising from the past retain all their strength: this piece of work must be finished, that book written, these interests safeguarded. When this is so, the elderly man starts a race against time that leaves him not a moment's respite. 'My most painful experience, as old age came nearer, was that of losing all sense of leisure,' said Berenson at seventy. It is even more painful to be unable to finish that which one longs to finish: as we have seen, Papini was bitterly distressed at not being able to reach the end of his greatest book, *Le Jugement dernier*.

Our projects may aim at goals that lie beyond our death: it is common knowledge that most people attach great importance to their wills and to the carrying out of their last wishes. In repetitive societies and those in which history moves slowly, a man has not only his own future at his disposal but also that of the world in which he takes it for granted that the results of his labour will continue to exist. When this is so, an eighty-year-old may take pleasure in building or even in planting trees. When the majority of undertakings, whether they were agricultural, commercial, financial, or run by craftsmen, were of a family nature, forming part of an economically stable society, the father could hope that his sons would carry on with his task and hand it down in their turn to their children. He thus avoided 'touching the boundary-stone' – the estate or firm in which he had given himself an objective state would last indefinitely. He would survive himself: his labour was not lost.

At present the aged man can no longer reckon upon an eternity of this kind: the pace of history has increased. Tomorrow it will destroy what was built yesterday. The trees the old man has planted will be cut down. Almost everywhere the family unit has fallen apart. Small firms are either taken over by monopolies or they fail. The son will not re-live his father's life, and the father knows it. Once he has gone, the estate will be abandoned, the shop sold, the business wound up. All that he has achieved and all that gave a meaning to his life lies under the same threat that menaces him. If he has a generous love for his children and if he approves of the course they have chosen he may be happy to think that he lives on in them. But because of the chasm that usually divides the generations, this does not happen very often. Generally speaking, the father does not see himself in his son. The void swallows him entirely.

Modern society, far from providing the aged man with an appeal against his biological fate, tosses him into an outdated past, and it does so while he is still living. The acceleration of history has caused an immense upheaval in the relationship between the aged man and his activities. Formerly it was supposed that with the progress of the years a treasure piled up within him – experience. A certain knowledge of things, a certain knowledge of life that was not to be learned from books gradually accumulated in his mind and body, much as crystals are deposited on twigs plunged into petrifying springs. Hegelian philosophy puts forward a rational justification for this idea, according to which every past instant is enfolded in the present instant, which necessarily prepares a still more perfected future, even failures being put right in the end: old age, the final stage of a continual advance, is life's highest pitch of perfection. But in fact this is not how life progresses at all. Its line of advance is perpetually broken by the falling back of our projects into practico-inert reality. At every given moment it provides its own sum, but this summation is never completed: 'Human action amounts both to the whole and to the destruction of the whole.'* That is why our motion is not a firm advance, but rather that reeling, staggering movement that Montaigne speaks of. Sainte-Beuve observed, 'We harden in some places and rot in others: we never ripen.' Old age is not the *summa* of our life. As time gives us the world so with the same motion it takes it from us. We learn and we forget; we enrich ourselves and we lose our wealth.

* Sartre, *Critique de la raison dialectique*.

The eighty-year-old Mauriac wrote, 'Neither lessened nor fallen nor made richer – but the same: that is how the old man sees himself. Let no one talk to him about life's acquisitions: it is unbelievable how little we retain of all that which has poured in throughout all these years. Facts are forgotten or have grown muddled. And what am I to say about ideas? Fifty years of reading: and what remains of it?'

The notion of experience is sound when it refers to an active apprenticeship. Some arts and callings are so difficult that a whole lifetime is needed to master them. As we have seen, manual workers manage to cloak their physical deficiencies by means of their experience: it allows them to organize the field of their activities. From the intellectual point of view, Herriot used to say that 'culture was what was left when everything else was forgotten'; and indeed, something does remain – a greater skill in re-learning what was known, method in work, resistance to error, safeguards. In many fields, such as philosophy, ideology and politics, the elderly man is capable of a synthetic vision forbidden to the young. In order to be able to appreciate the importance or unimportance of some particular case, to reduce the exception to the rule or allot it its place, to subordinate details to the whole, and to set anecdote aside in order to isolate the general idea, one must have observed an enormous number of facts in all their aspects of likeness and difference. And there is one form of experience that belongs only to those who are old – that of old age itself. The young have only vague and erroneous notions of it. One must have lived a long time to have a true idea of the human condition, and to have a broad view of the way in which things happen: it is only then that one can 'foresee the present' – the task of the statesman. That is why, in the course of history, elderly men have been entrusted with great responsibilities.

Yet it is in scarcely any but repetitive or at least stable societies that age can confer a qualification. If he has taken care to move forward, the elderly man is more advanced in an unchanging world than those who have set off after him. This is not the case in the changing world of today. Individual development or 'becoming' exists in the context of a social development with which it does not coincide: this difference of rhythm is harmful to the elderly man, who necessarily finds himself out of date. To move forward he must perpetually be tearing himself free from a past that holds him with an ever-tighter grasp: his advance is slow. Yet mankind is not all of a piece; when confronted with that past which weighs down the former generations, the new are free; they take up the torch and carry it on until they too are crushed by the weight of the practico-inert, and they in their turn are outstripped by the young. It is not in the power of an individual to keep up in this race, in which the project is perpetually reborn in all its freshness. He is left behind. In the midst of change he remains the same: he condemns himself to supersession.

As far as knowledge is concerned he necessarily falls behind. I see this clearly from my own example. I have learnt a great deal since I was twenty, but year by year I become relatively more ignorant because there are more and more discoveries; the sciences grow richer, and in spite of my efforts to keep abreast at least in some fields, the number of things I do not know increases.

For a more exact understanding of this disqualifying process we must leave generalities and consider the particular aspect of various activities. But let us first observe that it is in so far as he wishes to be a factor in the evolution of society that the old person is behind the times; as a consumer he takes advantage of technical progress without being worried by it at all – indeed, he welcomes it eagerly. In theory Tolstoy loathed novelty, yet he was wonderstruck by the gramophone and the cinema, and he thought of writing film-scripts. He went to watch car-racing and he longed to see aeroplanes. Andersen, at sixty-five, was charmed by the speed of the new forms of transport: the journey across Sweden had taken a week in the old days; now it could be done in twenty-four hours. 'We old people are affected by the unpleasant side of a transitional period straddling two generations; but it is very interesting.' When he was seventy, Wells was extremely enthusiastic about all modern inventions, particularly the cinema.

Morin studied the commune* of Plodemet and published the results of his research in *Commune en France*: here there were some infirm, sick, decrepit and abandoned old people who said of themselves that all they were good for was to guard the house like a dog. Although they were physically fit, a few others shut themselves up in the past: they could not read or write, and they refused running water, gas and electricity. 'What's the use? It's not suitable for people of our age,' said one of them. But most were amazed and delighted by the modern world. 'Now we shall have seen everything, from the

* Roughly the equivalent of a parish (trs.).

bicycle to men on the moon,' said an eighty-year-old joiner. They could remember their astonishment at the sight of the first cars and the first aeroplanes; they were enchanted by oil heating and the television. In their opinion the past was a barbaric age. 'A hundred years ago they were real savages, here in these parts, indeed they were. Now we're civilized: everyone can at least read and write. It was a wretched life in the old days; now it's fine.' They are pleased that the young men use machines and radar for fishing. They are subjectively proud that the world has objectively advanced. In so far as their own interests, their past and their activities are not called into question there is no antagonism cutting them off from mankind as a whole: they see themselves as part of it with delight. Its evolution is a magnificent spectacle, one that they watch from a distance without feeling that their way of life is in dispute.

In Plodemet there is a striking contrast between the attitude of the very old and inactive men and that of the men between fifty and sixty who work. The latter come into conflict with the present age because it endangers their economic and ideological interests. They are against the modernization of farming, which would require an apprenticeship that they are unwilling to undergo. They cling to the routine that has formed their lives; they do not want to give up the advantages of their experience and find themselves on a lower footing than the young, who are cleverer at handling the new machines than they. Many grow pig-headed in their refusal: when this happens the sons go off to work in the town and the fathers feel that they have been betrayed. 'So many old parents are deserted by their children!' said one fifty-five-year-old farmer. 'They have based their whole lives on setting something up, and then there is no one to carry on.'*

The following piece of police-court news comes from an issue of *France-Soir* of October 1968. 'There was an explosion in the yard – my father-in-law had just killed Wolf, our Alsatian. Jean, my husband, opened the door. His father rushed in. He was holding a grenade in his hand. Jean threw himself on him: they fought. The grenade fell to the ground and went off.' This was Dominique's evidence. Albert Rouzet, sixty-five, a farmer at Chinay (Côte d'Or), suffered from neurasthenia, and the day before he made up his mind to do away with the whole family, beginning with his twenty-five-year-old son Jean, whom he blamed for running the farm on

* I refer to this conflict in the chapter on the social question.

modern lines. 'In my days we got up at dawn to get the day's work ready, and there was no need to spend all the money on buying machines to work the land,' he used to say. The explosion killed both father and son.

As far as farmers are concerned, society does allow a choice between traditional methods and progress; but there are other cases where the advance of industry or commerce condemns the elderly craftsman or shopkeeper without appeal. Towards the end of the nineteenth century the rise of the big stores ruined many small traders. It is their story that Zola tells in *Au Bonheur des Dames*. He describes the older generation's struggle against the future that is taking away their living; he describes their despair. Baudu, a yellow-faced, white-haired, authoritarian patriarch, is the owner of Au Vieil Elbeuf, a little hundred-year-old shop with a low ceiling and deep, sombre, dusty windows; on the other side of the street there is the big store in all its splendour, and the gleaming windows of its drapery department seem to defy him. When his niece, just arrived from Paris, sees him, he is standing in the doorway, his mouth twisted, his eyes bloodshot, staring furiously at the display of Au Bonheur des Dames. The old-fashioned little shop with its worn, polished oak counters, its drawers with massive handles, its dark bales of cloth rising to the ceiling, has almost no customers left. Baudu is eaten up with rage and hatred. 'Oh God, oh God,' he groans, glaring at the store where his niece is going to work. He is outraged and he foretells the ruin of the new establishment: a draper's shop ought not to sell goods outside their line of business – it is a 'bazaar'. 'Draper's assistants selling furs – how ridiculous!' He cannot accept the overturning of all the traditions by which he has lived. He eats his heart out. In former days his old shop had more customers than any other in his part of the town, and he was proud of it. And now, like all its small neighbours, it is dying. 'It was a slow death, with no sudden shock – business continually dwindling, customers lost one by one.' The Bonheur des Dames does well, and Baudu is compelled to admit it. 'They are succeeding: so much the worse for them! As for me, I protest. That's all: I protest.' To pay his bills, he sells his house in the country. He is ruined, and endlessly he complains of these modern times – everything is falling to pieces; there is no such thing as the family any more. And at the same time he is humiliated; he feels that he has been beaten. 'The knowledge of his defeat stripped him of his former assurance, the assurance of a respected patriarch.' In the end he is offered a job at the Bonheur des Dames; but he refuses it and shuts himself up in his despair. Here we see the relationship established between biological and social time. If Baudu had been younger he would have wanted to modernize his shop and he would have done so. But this shortness of his future and the weight of his past close all outlets to him. His shop was the reality in which he had his objective being: once it is ruined he no longer exists – he is a dead man under suspended sentence. Blind to the rest of the world, to the end he stubbornly preserves the man he has been by means of his refusals and his memories. Tragedies of this kind happen today when the big stores set up branches in little towns, ruining the local shopkeepers. In capitalist countries the phenomenon is all the more frequent because of concentration.

There are many occupations in which advancing years are no real disqualification – they do not prevent the worker from doing his job: nevertheless, age does affect the individual who is engaged in them. As we have seen, at a given moment workers, office staff, executives and civil servants are retired. Society takes an ambiguous view of ageing in doctors, barristers and professional men in general. This is particularly striking in the case of doctors. For a certain length of time age adds to their value; it is thought to bring experience, and a man with a long career behind him is preferred to a novice. Later the picture changes. The old doctor is looked upon as worn out, in biological decline, and as one who has therefore lost much of his ability. And above all he is thought to be out of date; people imagine that he is not familiar with modern discoveries. Patients leave him: his waiting-room empties. In almost every field, the elderly man, even supposing that he is not compulsorily retired and that he is still up to his job, is condemned to idleness because of this prejudice.

In those callings that require great physical qualifications, old age is decisive. Very early the athlete is debarred from competition. He often carries out a reconversion in his own branch – the ski-ing champion becomes a trainer; the professional boxer a manager: but he may also turn to quite a different area, and this often happens – Carpentier opened a bar, Killy sells sports-cars, Marielle Goitschel has moved to films. There is a break in their lives; they foresaw it, but nevertheless many of them have difficulty in finding other jobs and they grow bitter. There is a similar break for dancers and singers

– the dancers lose their suppleness and the singers' voices fail. Many take to teaching the art they no longer practise, and in this way they may still transcend themselves through the success of their pupils. Others, either from necessity or from choice, retire altogether. Actors have to reckon on change in both their voices and their appearance. Some prefer to deny it altogether: I saw De Max playing the role of the young Nero when he was eighty. When it is a question of 'holy cows' the public love this stubborn perseverance: they applauded the eighty-year-old Sarah Bernhardt when she played Athalie with a wooden leg. Actors usually change their roles; but there are not many parts for elderly people on the stage and still fewer in films. On the stage, if the text is important, there is the danger of a lapse of memory. Here again, actors try to find a new career without moving too far from their past; but the possibilities are few, and most of them are condemned to retirement and poverty. The *chansonniers*, who sing their own songs in cabarets and night-clubs, are more fortunate; no extraordinary technical skill is required of them, and they can adapt their acts to their capacity. Indeed, in their case the very fact of being old may be an asset: when he was eighty Maurice Chevalier gave a show whose immense success was largely due to the fact that he was an octogenarian. Even so, this calls for excellent health and the ability to keep the favour of the novelty-loving public for years and years. It is the executive musicians, the pianists, violinists and 'cellists, who most usually overcome their physical decline, in spite of the body's importance in their careers. They may retain their fame and talent to the age of eighty, always supposing that they are not struck by an illness that would destroy their skill and that they go on practising. If they resist biological ageing, social ageing does not affect them adversely, because all they are asked to do is to maintain their standard. Though there are cases where musicians surpass themselves towards the end of their lives, because of their ever-deepening comprehension of what they play.

Brain-workers are less troubled by their physiological decline than the rest. A certain number enjoy a unique autonomy in their relationship with society: these are the creators. There are not a great many of them, but because of their privileged position they are, as it were, touchstones or detectors – by them we may judge what is practically possible for an elderly man when he is given the maximum of opportunity. They help us to see the nature of the relationship between age and fruitfulness in the various intellectual and artistic fields, and they tell us how we are to understand it.

It is most unusual for a scientist to make discoveries in his old age. Euler did carry out important mathematical work when he was seventy-one and seventy-two. Galileo was seventy-two when he finished his best book, the *Dialogues concerning the New Sciences,* and he was seventy-four when he wrote his *Mathematical Disquisitions and Demonstrations.* Buffon wrote the last seven volumes of his *Histoire naturelle* between the ages of sixty-seven and eighty-one, and they contain the best of his work. Between seventy-eight and eighty Franklin invented bifocal lenses and studied lead-poisoning. Laplace finished his *Mécanique céleste* at the age of seventy-nine. Herschel was reading important papers to the Royal Society when he was eighty and more. Michelson was seventy-seven when he published the results of the experiment on the speed of light that he carried out with Morlay. Gauss and Pavlov continued the work of their youth when they were old men, adding much to it. But all these are exceptions. Lehman* tried to establish a correlation between age and human accomplishment in his book *Age and Achievement*; and basing himself upon Professor Hildich's *Brève histoire de la chimie* he shows that the most important discoveries in chemistry have been made by men between twenty-five and thirty, and the most in number by those between thirty and thirty-five: out of 993 examples of outstanding work, only three are due to men of over seventy. In physics, the most favourable age seems to be between thirty and thirty-four; in astronomy, between forty and forty-four. Lehman observes that Edison was productive all his life, but that his best period was at thirty-five. Chevreul lived to be 103 and he went on working far into old age; but he is chiefly known for the discoveries on animal fat that he made when he was thirty-seven.

It is above all in mathematics that late discoveries are so very rare. There is one brilliant exception. Elie Cardan was sixty-seven when he published an epoch-making paper that was completely new in relation to his earlier work; in this paper he solved problems that he had himself propounded at the age of twenty-eight and that the greatest mathematicians had been unable to answer. Some other cases of this kind may be quoted; but they are very few. The elderly

---

* Lehman's statistical method is utterly erroneous when it is applied to art and literature. In science it is easier to evaluate the number and value of the discoveries.

mathematician's sterility is so notorious that Bourbaki's group would not accept anyone over fifty.

Ageing in the scientist is not of a biological nature. Here there is no question of overwork, nervous wear and tear or mental fatigue; some scientists remain in excellent health to the end of their days. Why is it that once they have passed a certain age they no longer make discoveries?

In order to find the answer, we must first understand the nature of the choice that a man makes when he decides to devote himself to science. The object of his study is the universal as it can be grasped by means of abstract symbols and concepts. This implies that he makes the universal part of himself. He does away with his subjectivity in order to think along the lines of a universally valid rational system. Even if he works by himself, he is not alone: he is taking part in a collective work that tries to reach a common goal, though by different paths. In any case, nowadays he is usually one of a team, all of whose members are on the same footing. The scientist is not a lone wolf; he inherits from those who have gone before him; the path he follows has already been opened to some degree, and he travels in the company of other workers; they meet with the same difficulties, and it may happen that the means of overcoming them is discovered simultaneously in several different places – it is science as a whole that prepares the individual discovery and calls it into being. To be sure, however much the worker may be ruled by the object of his research, he nevertheless remains a unique subject, almost in spite of himself; he has his own vision of the world, his own imagination, his own way of making decisions. It is for this reason that he sometimes emerges from the general body and discovers an original idea. But his option in favour of the universal means that these flashes neither come often nor last long. It is understandable that they should be most frequent in youth or at the beginning of maturity, for that is the time at which the scientist is mastering the body of knowledge that forms his particular study; he sees it with a new eye, and this allows him to perceive its gaps and contradictions. He has the courage to attempt to repair them because he has his whole life before him to correct his errors and to develop the truths whose existence he divines. Later a considerable amount of work has to be done to verify, organize and exploit his discovery. Once more the research becomes collective, and it is not necessarily the discoverer who is best qualified for carrying it through. Most often he remains the man of that moment, of that idea; whereas what the evolution of science requires is a fresh break with the past.*

A great mathematician of fifty-five has told me that he reads mathematical works with greater ease and profit than he did when he was young: his power of comprehension, his experience and ability to synthesize have increased. But his curiosity has grown somewhat dull. When he was twenty-five and the victim of that youthful illusion which stretches the future indefinitely, he formed the plan of knowing everything in all the branches of mathematics. Now he is resigned to reading only those works that have a direct bearing on his speciality, and to leaving many others to one side. He explains that in modern mathematics specialization is so highly developed, and the various branches so shut off from one another, that he would find it easier to follow a biologist maintaining his thesis than a fellow-mathematician lecturing on some foreign area of his own science. In his opinion a worker who is not cut off from research retains the possibility of making discoveries for a considerable period: but he is hampered by epistemological obstacles of which the young know nothing. In our day an Evariste Galois† would be impossible: a man must be twenty-five or thirty to master the whole mathematical edifice in all its complexity, and that is the most favourable period for discovery. Later there is often a sense of inhibition. When a man knows that no one has been able to prove the truth or the falsity of a given proposition, and when he has done all he can without success, he decides that it would be wasting his time to persist and he gives up. This happened to my friend eleven years ago. Then a Russian mathematician told him that he had solved the problem. My friend returned to it; and since he knew that the solution could be found, there was no longer any question of letting go. And he did find it; he found it very quickly, by the simple juxtaposition of two other theorems that were perfectly familiar to him. He told me that this was a very frequent occurrence. Here the young are at a great advantage: they are often unaware that others have struggled in vain with the question that occupies them, and try to tackle it with the utmost confidence. They have time and to spare before them, and they are not tempted to economize their energy.

* Nearly all the exceptions I have mentioned date from a time when scientists worked alone: some of these discoveries made late in life are of an almost craftsmanlike nature.

† Evariste Galois died when he was nineteen (trs.).

Above all, said my informant, it is the past that weighs upon the elderly scientist, the past in the form of habits of mind and ideological interests. All present mathematics is being renewed at a dizzying speed, and the change calls the whole structure in question. With every alteration an entirely new form of language has to be learnt; and clearly the reason that it is preferred to the old form is that it is quicker and more suitable, and that it makes discovery easier. The mathematician who cannot make up his mind to adopt it is obliged to translate the new truths into the terms he is familiar with, and this slows down his work very seriously. It may happen that a forty-year-old professor is unable to comprehend a statement of his own theories explained by a twenty-five-year-old mathematician to his contemporaries in the new language, common to them but unknown to their older colleague. The older man can never hope to outstrip those who are in possession of the more precise instrument. Yet after a certain stage it is both hard and discouraging to learn Hebrew or Chinese, and many ageing scientists recoil. The mathematician has as it were a withdrawal, a shrinking from his line of thought. 'If I have the intuition of a new theorem,' said my friend, 'I realize that it will compel me to revise everything I had hitherto taken as established, and I hesitate.' Then again he said, 'In growing older one becomes both more and less free. Freer in relation to others, since one is not afraid of surprising them, or of ignoring certain prejudices or of challenging established ideas. But less free in relation to one-self.' Last year he wrote a mathematical book that is now going through the press. But since then he has written an article that makes the book out of date; it was painful for him to have to inflict this contradiction upon himself, but he disregarded it. And now this very article itself is called into question by still more recent work that he has just finished. The progress of mathematics is not a placid, smooth advance. It is a series of arguments and disputes that results in a perpetual modification. A great deal of enthusiasm and of time and energy is called for if everything that one has learnt hitherto is to be turned upside down: it is a process more suited to young men than others.

This particular case confirms my general remarks upon the activities of the elderly man: the weight of the past slows him down or even brings him to a halt, whereas the young generations break free from the practico-inert and move forward.

We can come to a more exact definition of what holds the elderly scientist back. In the first place, he has ideological interests: he is 'alienated', transferred to his work, that 'aggregation of inert meanings based on verbal material'* in which he has built up his being outside himself. All this is imperilled in the world, since it exists for others, who transcend it by the light of their own projects. Its author does his utmost to defend it, opposing theories and systems that tend to discredit it. He is quite willing to correct and to enrich, but not to deny it, although at a given point a denial might be necessary for progress. For him it contains inert requirements with which he must comply, and this may lead him into blind alleys. Some research workers are so alienated to their ideological interests that they will falsify the results of experiments that contradict their theories. Darwin was aware of this danger and he made it a rule to make an immediate note of facts and ideas that ran counter to his doctrine, 'for I knew by experience that ideas and facts of this kind vanish more easily from the memory than those which are in our favour.' Yet it is said that in his old age he would not listen to the reading of anything written in opposition to his views: and Auguste Comte did the same. Obstinacy of this sort makes it impossible to review a work in the light of fresh knowledge, so as to detect errors and attempt to correct them. Lévy-Bruhl was an exceptional case: in his notebooks for 1938–9 he renounces all his former ideas on the prelogical mental patterns, participation and non-conceptualization that he thought he had observed among primitive peoples. Yet he made no new discoveries.

Even if he is truly disinterested the scientist still comes up against inner resistances. He has habits of mind that make him obstinately persist in out-of-date methods. That same specialization which made his successes possible prevents him from keeping abreast of work that runs parallel to his; and it might happen that a knowledge of this work would be necessary for fresh discovery on his part. The more clear-sighted among them are aware of these gaps. Shortly after he had been awarded the Nobel prize, Professor Kastler spoke of going back to the students' benches to follow a course of lectures on the quantum theory. And above all the elderly scientist is so familiar with some ideas that he looks upon them as self-evident and therefore never thinks of questioning them: but they have to be discarded for any advance to be possible. When Bachelard spoke of 'epistemological obstacles', old age seemed to him one of the most important.

* Sartre, *Critique de la raison dialectique*.

In order to defend his outdated concepts, the aged scientist will often deliberately block the progress of science; and the standing he enjoys makes it possible for him to do this. As Bachelard says, 'The great scientists are useful to science in the first half of their lives and harmful in the second.' Arthur Clarke has made a survey of a very large number of discoveries that were said to be impossible by scientists, not because they lacked the necessary knowledge, but because they did not possess the necessary imagination and daring: this he puts down to their age, and for him a scientist is old as soon as he has reached his fortieth year. Some eighty years ago, the notion that electric light could be used in homes was hooted down by all the experts; nevertheless, the thirty-one-year-old Edison worked on the incandescent bulb, making it a practical reality. But later in his life he too was just as backward, setting himself against the introduction of alternating current. Newcomb, the American astronomist, wrote a very well-known essay proving that it was impossible for objects heavier than air to fly. When the Wright brothers actually took off, Newcomb stated that their machine would never be capable of carrying more than a single person, and that it therefore had no practical application. Another astronomer, W. H. Bickering, was of the same opinion. By this time the principles of flight were understood; but the two scientists refused to draw the obvious conclusions. In 1926 Professor Bickerlow advanced proofs of his assertion that no projectile could ever be sent to the moon: the only source of energy that he took into consideration was nitro-glycerin, and his calculations assumed that the fuel had to form an integral part of the missile. In 1938 a Canadian astronomer, J. W. Campbell, worked out that it would need a million tons of fuel to remove a weight of one or two pounds from the gravitational pull of the earth; and from this he drew the same conclusions as Bickerlow. His calculations were based on the supposition that the rocket would have to be endowed with a fabulous speed and that the acceleration would be so slow that the fuel would be exhausted at a low altitude. Rutherford was sixty-six when he died in 1937: he stated that it would never be possible to set free the energy contained in matter. Five years later the first chain-reaction began to operate in Chicago. When Pontecorvo said that the highly penetrating particles called neutrinos would allow the observation of the interior of stars, those astrophysicists who were qualified to utter an opinion laughed him to scorn: a little later he carried out his experiments successfully. Clarke's conclusion is that 'the man who knows most facts about any given subject is not necessarily the one who will most clearly foresee the future in this field'. And he condemns old scientists even more harshly than Bachelard: 'Scientists over fifty are no longer good for anything but holding congresses, and they should at all costs be kept far away from laboratories.'

Clarke's account is not very satisfactory. He attacks men of widely differing value. He does not study the reasons for their resistance. He confines himself to saying that it is inevitable that they should have preconceived notions. 'A completely open mind would be an empty mind.' Yet he does emphasize one important fact: instead of being of use for foretelling the future, knowledge can be a hindrance. Thus, when Auguste Comte was thirty-five he asserted that it would never be possible to know the composition of the sun. I might also quote the declaration on the subject of travelling by train, made by the Lyons Academy of Medicine in 1835: this prophesied that the human frame would be unable to bear the dizzy speed. 'The vibration will bring about nervous diseases ... while the rapid succession of images will cause inflammation of the retina. The dust and smoke will give rise to bronchitis and pleural adhesions. And lastly the anxiety caused by the continual danger will keep the travellers in a perpetual state of tension, and it will be the precursor of cerebral disorders. For a pregnant woman, any journey by train must inevitably bring on a miscarriage, together with all its consequences.'

After a certain age even very great minds find it difficult to move with the times. In 1935, when he was fifty-five, Einstein speaking of the suicide of his friend Ehrenfest, the physicist, attributed it to the inner conflicts that attack any deeply honest scientist who has passed the age of fifty. Ehrenfest had a clear understanding of certain problems that he was unable to solve in a constructive manner. 'During these last years,' said Einstein, 'the strangely turbulent development of theoretical physics made the situation worse. It is always hard to learn and to teach things that one cannot fully accept in one's heart. And to this there is added the ever-increasing difficulty of adapting oneself to new ways of thought, a difficulty that always confronts any man who has passed fifty.'

Einstein himself had to deal with this situation, and it is interesting to look into his case. He was not alienated to any ideological interests. He had never sought to have the last word and he was comparatively indifferent to his reputation. His love for the truth was absolutely pure. But he had so firmly anchored a view of science that it never occurred to him to give it up at any price whatsoever: it had to provide a harmonious and rational image of the world. The paradox of his career is that his theory of relativity had a great influence upon the quantum theory, and yet Einstein, when he was over forty-five, looked upon the quantum theory with an unfavourable eye. The Polish physicist Infeld, who had earlier worked with Einstein, says, 'There is something ironic about the role of champion that Einstein assumed in the great revolution, since later he turned his back on that very revolution which he had helped bring about. As time goes by he moves farther and farther from the younger generation of scientists, most of whom are carrying out research on the quantum theory.'

Antonina Vallentin, in whom Einstein confided on the subject of his 'mathematical torments', says that this was not a question 'of the usual divorce between a fresh generation, fully aware of the boldness of its thought, and an old man left over from the past like a rock in the middle of a road that runs on beyond him. His tragedy was rather that of a man who, in spite of his age, stubbornly goes on travelling a more and more forsaken path, while almost all his friends and all the young people around him assert that this path leads nowhere and that he has set out along a blind alley.'

He was not sure that he was right. In March 1949, when he was seventy, he wrote to Solovine, 'You suppose that I contemplate my life's work with calm satisfaction. But seen close to the whole thing has quite a different look. There is not one single notion that I am convinced will hold its ground and broadly speaking I am not certain of being on the right path. Our contemporaries look upon me both as a heretic and as a reactionary who has, as it were, outlived himself. To be sure, this is a question of fashion and of a shortsighted view; but the feeling of inadequacy comes from within.'

Yet he found it impossible to modify his position. As he saw it, a theory was valid only if it possessed an 'inner perfection': an abundance of 'external confirmations' was not enough for him. The theory of unitary fields that he tried to perfect for thirty years did conform with these requirements: that of elementary particles did not. He understood Niels Bohr's quantic theory right away – so much so that he said, 'I should probably have managed to reach something like this myself.' But immediately after he added, 'Yet if all this is true, then it means the end of physics.' He did not choose to admit that physics might take on an unharmonious aspect. Later Bohr's results stopped looking paradoxical; they were included in a new general theory that reconciled a corpuscular and the 'wave' points of view by means of the 'probability wave' idea. It was an idea that Einstein would not admit, although the whole structure was built up on the basis of his own system. He was not a man to be satisfied with old truths; but, seeing that it never occurred to him to give up these criteria, he did not find the new ideas conclusive.

His theory of unitary fields was so difficult to express mathematically that he was never in a position to verify it. And on the other hand, his resistance prevented him from taking part in the advance of quantum physics. Since he was utterly devoid of egocentricity he did not experience his frustration and isolation as a subjective tragedy. But objectively it is almost universally agreed that he wasted the last thirty years of his life in pointless research. Kouznetsov, his biographer, observes that some of Einstein's ideas, dating from the forties and dealing with relativist quantum physics, have now come to fruition. He therefore concluded that Einstein's criticism 'showed the limits of quantum physics, beyond which could be seen the outline of even more revolutionary theories'. As science advances by repudiating the past in order to outstrip itself, in later times the laggards may always be looked upon as forerunners. But the fact is that towards the end of his life Einstein hindered rather than helped scientific progress.

The philosopher's choice is radically different from the scientist's. Whereas the latter describes the world from the outside, the former takes the view that it is man who makes science: he wishes to understand the relationship between the world and man posited as a subject. The philosopher is both for and against science: he accepts it in so far as it is a human product, but refuses to see in it the reflection of a reality existing within itself. The scientist does not call into question him by whom and for whom society exists – man. The philosopher is one for whom man in his being is in question; he is one who interrogates himself upon man's estate taken in its entirety. But he is himself a man, all man: what he has to say is himself in his universality. When Descartes says, 'I think . . .', it is Universal Man who thinks in him. He therefore needs no one as an interlocutor and he is answerable to nobody. There is one science: there are many philosophies. To be sure, no philosophy is built up from nothing – the philosopher is subject to various influences and he meets with problems set by others. But each system can be criticized only from within and not by reference to exterior data. The critic may expose its contradictions, gaps and inadequacies: he cannot object to it on the grounds of facts established by others. For indeed there is at the very beginning what Bergson called a 'philosophical intuition', that may also be defined as an ontological experience upon which a version of the world is built up.

It has an unanswerable inner obviousness. The philosopher, faced with new philosophies, may accept certain aspects of them and he may be led to ask himself new questions; but he will not relinquish his initial position, his starting point. He may add, he may take away and he may correct, but he always does so from a certain point of view, a view that is his own and to which all others are foreign: and therefore no outside person can go beyond him, invalidate him or contradict him.

Generally speaking the philosopher's thought grows richer with age. His primary intuition comes to him in his youth or his early middle age, or even, as in the exceptional case of Kant, at over fifty. He needs time to grasp all its implications, for his aim is nothing less than a comprehension of the relationships of man as a subject with the entirety of the world. It is an inexhaustible field. Once his system has been laid down, the philosopher stands back from it; this allows him to criticize it, to propound fresh problems, and to discover other solutions. There was one instance in which progress was halted by the very nature of the work: this happened to Hegel, whose system closed in upon itself when he was about sixty. He had set himself at the termination of history, persuaded that he had provided an exhaustive account of the world's progress. The finished work allowed of no further evolution, and any challenge could come only from the outside. In all other cases the systems remained open, and although the philosophers' last years may not have been their most fruitful they still added to the edifice. I shall only mention two – Plato and Kant.

Plato wrote the *Laws* when he was eighty, and in spite of some fine and original passages on time and memory, everyone agrees that it shows a falling-off compared with the general body of his work – an 'impoverishment', an 'ebb', a 'relinquishment'. It would seem that experience had made him pessimistic. He granted that 'our kind was not entirely without worth', but he also said that 'the share of evil outweighed that of good', and that the greatest benefits were 'sullied as though by an evil fate'. He carried gloom so far as to declare that man was little more than a puppet in the hands of the gods and the demons. This being so, it was no longer a question of seeking a perfect political system for the city, but only the least bad that could possibly be found. To govern men Plato no longer put his trust in reason, education and the knowledge of truth. Laws had to be imposed upon them, and they had to be induced to obey these laws, no matter what the means. Plato had already accepted the notion of the useful lie in the *Republic*, but he gave it little importance; whereas in the *Laws* this unilitarianism triumphs unopposed. It is a didactic book in which the three speakers are old men – in the earlier dialogues there had always been at least one young man. Its style is heavy. Plato's thought, cautious and involved, had become stiffened with age. He no longer shows that thirst for truth which gave his earlier books their inspiration. This last phase of his old age is intellectually a decline.

Yet it was from about his sixty-second year that he wrote his deepest and most truly personal works. He had needed time to break away from the influence of Socrates and his predecessors and to understand all that was implied in his own conceptions. When Plato was sixty-two there occurred a crisis in his development: he could see his work in perspective and he discovered the objections that could be brought against his theory of ideas. In order to answer them, he took up the problem again from the beginning in the *Theaetetus* and the *Parmenides*; and he clarified his position with regard to the Megarians. His doctrine was renewed and enriched throughout the *Sophist*, the *Politics*, the *Timaeus*, the *Crito* and the *Philebus*. It was in the *Philebus*, which he wrote when he was about seventy-four, that he replied to the question in the *Theaetetus* on knowledge and error. 'Knowledge is the imitation in one's soul of the relationships that exist in the being.' And it is this work that contains the broadest exposition of his dialectic. With the exception of the *Laws*, the works of Plato's old age represent a continual advance.*

Kant published the *Critique of Pure Reason* when he was fifty-seven. He was sixty-six when he wrote the *Critique of Judgement*

---

* Some historians of philosophy think his middle years more powerful and creative (Yvon Brès, for example, in his *La Psychologie de Platon*); but even they acknowledge the importance of the works he wrote when he was old.

and he was still older when he produced *Religion within the Limits of Reason*. These two books treated certain essential points of his system with an entirely new depth; they enriched and renovated his earlier work. He continued to work on his *Opus Posthumum* until the decline of his intellectual powers. According to Lachièze-Rey it is the crown of his whole philosophy. His earliest works raised certain problems that he only managed to solve in the *Ubergang*, written at the end of his life. The chief of these was the following: what is the mode of the mind's presence to itself, considered as a constituting presence? Earlier, he had been troubled by the importance he attributed to psychological realism; he hesitated to apply the transcendental method in all its rigour. Far from stiffening as he grew older, he acquired sufficient self-confidence to overcome his resistance and to set himself free from earlier prejudices. He reduced the psychological pseudo-realities to the rank of simple moments in the constitution of the world and the self. The *Ubergang* harmonized his whole system. Here consciousness at last found its autonomy and caused its reality to be acknowledged. The *thing* vanished in favour of activity. The cogito asserted itself as the determining force.

Of course, although a philosopher may add to his own system even in his old age, he is unable to break free from it and discover a radically new philosophy. Kant fore-shadowed Fichte, but it is un-thinkable that he should have discovered the Hegelian dialectic. Like the scientist, the philosopher is to some degree alienated to ideological interests. Although he goes beyond his earlier ideas, it is in trying to preserve them that he does so: he cannot bear to see them discredited. And he too has his habits of mind – the way of thinking that is so natural to him that it seems necessary, and presuppositions that are so firmly rooted in him that he does not distinguish between them and the truth.

How do writers age? There are so many kinds of writer and they pursue such different ends that it is hard to answer this question. Some remain creative to a very great age: Sophocles produced *Oedipus at Colonus* when he was eighty-nine. Voltaire wrote his finest work in the last twenty years of his life. The last volumes of *Mémoires d'outre-tombe* and of *La Vie de Rancé* were the fruit of Chateaubriand's old age. Goethe composed his best poems during his last twenty-five years – the period of *Dichtung und Wahrheit* and the second *Faust*. The aged Hugo rightly felt in no way inferior to his past: 'It is half a century now that I have been writing my thoughts in prose and verse, but I feel that I have not said the thousandth part of what is in me.' What he wrote after the age of sixty-four amounts to an important body of work. Yeats excelled himself at the end of his life.

These are exceptions. Generally speaking great age is not favourable to literary creation. In Corneille, Tolstoy and so many others we see a shattering contrast between the work of their maturity and that of their last years. Many old men go on writing, either out of habit or because they have to earn their living, or because they do not wish to admit their decline. But most of them justify Berenson's remark – 'What a man writes after he is sixty is worth little more than tea continually remade with the same leaves.' Let us try to see why this should be so. What is a writer looking for? And in what conditions can he obtain it?

Philosophy considers man *qua* notion: it seeks to know his total relationship to the world. The writer too aims at the universal, but from the standpoint of his uniqueness. He does not claim to provide a knowledge, but to communicate that which cannot be *known* – the inwardly-experienced meaning of his being in the world. He conveys it by means of a unique universal, his work. The universal is not made unique nor has the work any literary dimension, unless the author's presence is revealed by a style, a tone and an artistic power that bear his mark. Otherwise we are dealing with a document, something that conveys reality in its impersonal objectivity on the plane of exterior knowledge, and not as the inward experience of a subject. But how can my inward experience become that of another? In one way only – by means of the imagination. The reader of a document gathers information about one of the parts of his world without leaving that world: he remains in his place there – he does not move from the given spot or the given moment in his life. The reader of a literary work enters a world that is *other*; he becomes part of a subject other than himself. This implies that he denies reality in order to plunge into the imaginary. This is possible to him only if the work he reads offers him an imaginary world. The communication of inward experience, of experience that has been lived through, does not consist of setting down words on paper directly designed to express it. That which has been lived does not assume a given form: for the writer it is a question of extracting clear and intelligible statements from the opaque confusion of the unsaid. He thus creates an object that interprets no reality and that exists in the imaginary mode; and for his own part he provides himself with a fictitious composition. Sartre alludes to this process in his essay *Des rats et des hommes*, when he observes that all writers are possessed by 'a vampire'.

Of course, it must not be supposed that a writer first elects to communicate and then turns to the imagination. It is his primary choice of the imaginary that determines his vocation: this choice has different motivations according to different individuals, but it is always to be found at the root of any literary work. A literary work is the materialization by means of marks made on paper of the unreal world that the subject has created in play, dreams and musing – an unreal world that can take on consistence and allow the transmission of experience only because it is the projection of reality in another dimension.

Writing is therefore a complex activity: it means a simultaneous preference for the imaginary and a desire to communicate. And in these two choices there appear very different and at first sight contradictory tendencies. A man who wishes to replace the given by an imaginary universe must violently refuse the given; anyone who is as much at home in the real world as a fish in water will not write. But the project of communicating presupposes an interest in the outside world: even if dislike and contempt enter into the relationship between the writer and mankind – even if, like Flaubert, he writes to lash it or to sap its confidence, to denounce it or to expose its baseness, he wants it to take notice of him: otherwise his very project of denouncing it would be foredoomed to failure and would have no meaning. He grants humanity a greater importance by the act of writing than he does in his verbal statements. Only silence could suit total despair and a fundamental hatred of everything and everybody.

The project of writing therefore implies a tension between a refusal of the world in which men live and a certain appeal to men themselves: the writer is both for and against them. This is a difficult position: it implies very lively passions; and to be maintained for a considerable length of time it calls for strength.

Old age reduces strength; it deadens emotion. As we have seen, with the disappearance of the libido there vanishes a certain biological aggressiveness. Age often sinks into physical weariness, general fatigue and indifference, and these turn the mind from its intense concern with the outside world. The tension born of the reconciliation of two projects that are if not contradictory then at least divergent, slackens. The elderly writer finds himself deprived of that quality which Flaubert called *alacrité*. Overwhelmed by his niece's ruin, he said in one of his letters, 'To write anything worthwhile, a man needs a certain "alacrity".' And in another, 'To write well, a certain "alacrity" is required, and I no longer possess it.' Rousseau at sixty-four felt his creative powers fading, and it saddened him deeply. In his *Rêveries* he speaks of one of his walks and says, 'The countryside was still green and smiling, but many of the leaves had fallen and already there was scarcely a movement in the fields – on every hand the landscape held out the image of loneliness and the coming winter. It breathed out a mixture of sad and gentle feelings too like my age and my fate for me not to apply them to myself. In this landscape I saw myself, in the decline of an innocent and unfortunate life, my heart still full of eager, enduring sensibilities and my spirit still adorned with here and there a flower – but with flowers already faded by unhappiness and withered by troubles. Alone and abandoned, I felt the coming of the first icy blasts; and my failing imagination no longer peopled my solitude with beings shaped after my own heart.' And again, at the same period, he wrote, 'Already my imagination is less vivid, and it no longer glows as once it did at the view of an object that stirs it into life; dreaming is less of an intoxicating rapture and there is more of recollection than of creation in what it gives me now. A lukewarm weariness drains my faculties of all their strength; little by little the spirit of life is going out; and it is only with pain that my soul leaps from its now decrepit frame . . .'

This weariness is all the more harmful to an elderly writer since it is essential for him to feel inspired: when he is young all that is needed is the mere desire to write to be persuaded that he has 'everything' to say. When he is old, there is the dread of having reached the bottom of the barrel, of being capable of nothing but self-repetition. Towards the end of his life Gide observed sadly, 'I fall back on themes I have handled again and again, themes that no longer seem capable of yielding me anything.' And in *Ainsi soit-il.* when he was eighty-one, he wrote, 'I have said, more or less well, all I thought I had to say, and I am afraid of repeating myself.'

The danger of repetition arises partly from the fact that the writer is alienated to certain ideological interests. He has defended some given values, criticized some given ideas, taken up some particular positions: there is no question of repudiating them. It is not impossible that a writer, remaining faithful to his past, may take on fresh life: it is also possible that he may prefer his freedom to his interests. This happened to me. My readers required optimism of me above everything, particularly in so far as the fate of women was concerned: the end of *La Force des choses* and my most recent pieces disappointed this expectation and I was sharply rebuked. But I refuse to be owned by a fixed image of myself.

In any case, as we all know, whether he is Flaubert, Dostoyevsky, Proust or Kafka, no man ever writes merely that which appears in his books. It is inevitable that they should bear his mark, since literature expresses the writer in his uniqueness. It is always he who is there in all his different works, and he is there in his entirety, as life has made him. Things change and we with them, but without losing our identity. Our past, our roots in the world remain unalterable: it is upon this basis that the goals awaiting us in the future are defined, the things to be done and the things to be said. We cannot arbitrarily invent projects for ourselves: they have to be written in our past as requirements. Camus points this out in the preface to *L'Envers et l'endroit*: 'In this way every artist has deep within him a unique spring that flows during his life, feeding what he is and what he says. When the spring dries up, we see his work gradually shrivel and crack. It is the unprofitable soil of Art that is no longer watered by the unseen flow. Once his hair has grown sparse and dry, the balding artist is ripe for silence or the *salons*, which comes to much the same thing.'

To be sure, a man's work as a whole develops neither mechanically nor organically from some seed containing it in posse; throughout its course, growing richer or losing its direction or retreating, it follows the shape and rhythm of life. But it is as it were programmed by our childhood: that is the time when the individual makes himself into what he will basically remain for ever; it is then that he projects himself into those things that are to be done. When Disraeli was quite a small child he elected to be a cabinet-minister one day; the infant Sartre decided to be a writer. Their lives were directed by this intention, and they fulfilled it. Those who take to writing late in life are just as dependent on their earliest years: we see this clearly in Rousseau's works – his childhood is there, still fully alive in the man it formed. The initial strength of the intention to write decides

402

whether it will come to a very early end or whether even a late death will find it unexhausted: at twenty Rimbaud felt he had nothing more to say, whereas the eighty-year-old Voltaire wrote on tirelessly. In any case, finitude has an effect upon a man's work. The elderly writer grows aware of it and, like Gide, he often loses heart – he has not the courage to use the years that are still left to him.

There is still another reason for the silence of some aged writers. As Sartre has shown in the case of Genet and Flaubert, their vocation is brought into existence by the contradictions in their situation; living seems impossible: they are in a blind alley and they struggle to get out of it. The only escape is writing – they choose the imaginary as the one area where they can resolve the conflicts that are tearing them to pieces. By the time they are old, this resolution has been accomplished. And in any case their life has been lived: well or badly, but still lived, thus proving it to be possible.

The least suitable form of literature for the elderly writer is the novel; although in this field too there are exceptions. Defoe wrote all his novels after the age of sixty and Henry James some that are numbered among his best. Cervantes was sixty-eight when he wrote the second part of *Don Quixote*. The work of Hugo's old age includes two novels. In our time, the astonishing John Cowper Powys wrote all his great novels when he was more than sixty. At seventy-three, Albert Cohen has just published his finest book, *Belle du Seigneur*. But generally speaking elderly writers turn rather towards poetry and essays than to novels. Thomas Hardy was a prolific novelist up to the age of sixty, but after that he wrote nothing but poems. When she was old, Colette wrote only recollections of the past. Martin du Gard was never able to compose the novel he had planned after *Les Thibaud* and for which he had gathered notes for years. Why?

Mauriac suggests an answer. In his *Mémoires intérieurs* he says, 'But as the years go by, and as our time to come grows shorter, and when the stakes are down, the book finished and in the printers' hands, and when the human adventure is nearing its end, then the characters of a novel no longer have room to move about in us: they are caught between the hardened, impenetrable mass of our past, into which nothing can now make its way, and that death, near at hand or farther off, which is now present.' And again, 'With youth over and the last turning no great way off, our own inward hum no longer drowns the daily roar of politics; for now everything in us becomes silence and loneliness. And now we admit that the reading of novels bores us; that unimaginable history is to be preferred to the finest imagined tales.'

And still again, in 1962, 'The truth is that once we have reached the last chapter of our own history, all that is merely invented seems insignificant.' 'On that vague boundary between the finite and the void that we call old age, only creatures of flesh and blood still survive in us.'

It is certainly true, I believe, that if our eager spring towards the future is broken, we find it hard to recreate it in an imaginary hero: the human adventure does not concern us passionately enough, either in him or in ourselves. As to the relationship between the novelist and the past, I see it in another light. The book that I write depends both on its remote source and on the present moment. More than any other literary form, the novel requires that the present should be shattered in favour of an unreal world; and that world has life and colour only if it is rooted in very early fantasies. Daily happenings and the immediate world may provide the novelist with support or with a starting-point: but he has to transcend them, and he can only do so well by drawing from his own depths. But if he does so, then what he finds is the same themes, the same obsessions, and he runs the risk of perpetual repetition. Memoirs, autobiography and the essay, on the contrary, reconstruct or reassume experiences whose variety is enriching for the author. It is still the writer who speaks; but he is in less danger of repeating himself when he is speaking of new things than when, on some fresh pretext, he expresses his fundamental and still unchanging attitude towards the world.*

The happiest fate for an aged writer is to have begun with projects so firmly rooted that he retains his originality for ever, and so immense that they remain open until his death. If he has not ceased to maintain a living relationship with the world, then neither will he cease to feel its pull or to hear calls from the outside. Voltaire and Hugo were among these fortunate men. Whereas others either go on pouring hot water on the old tea-leaves or fall mute.

Composers do not tell us much about the way they work; but it is observable that generally speaking their work improves with the years. There are some, like Mozart and Pergolesi, who show their

* By his own example, Mauriac confirms the truth of what I say here. He renewed himself, at least up until a certain time, when he wrote his *Bloc-Notes*. On the other hand, his last novel is like a parody of those he wrote in his prime.

powers early: if they had gone on living would they have developed still further or would they have repeated themselves? One thing that is certain is that the works of the ageing Bach are among the finest he ever composed, and that Beethoven surpassed himself with his last quartets. Sometimes it is at a very advanced age that the composer writes his greatest masterpieces. Monteverdi was seventy-five when he composed *Poppoea*; Verdi seventy-two at the time of *Otello* and seventy-six at that of *Falstaff*, the most adventurous of his operas. The elderly Stravinsky, still remaining himself, has managed to adapt to the new musical forms. The music of his old age is original in relation to that of his prime and it is of no less value. It seems to me that this steady rise is to be explained by the severity of the discipline to which the musician is subjected: he needs a long apprenticeship to acquire the mastery that will allow him to bring his originality into play; and this is all the harder since music is above all others the field in which influence is strongest – the composer is rightly mistrustful of what may lie in his memory. Whereas the writer's task is to give a universal significance to his personal experience, the uniquely personal quality of the musician is at first overlaid by the universality of the technique he uses and of the sonorities upon which his invention is based: to begin with he expresses himself with modest caution. In order not only to do new things within the set rules but also to break free from them to a certain extent he needs a great deal of self confidence, and therefore a considerable body of work behind him. Thus we find the mature Monteverdi allowing himself chords that seemed 'hellish' to the audience of his time, and Beethoven not shrinking from 'discords' that shocked the average listener. For the composer, ageing is a progress towards a freedom that the writer possesses from his earliest days or at least from the time he is fully adult, because the writer's system of rules is less stifling.

Painters are not subjected to rules so strict as those that govern musicians; but they too need time to overcome the difficulties of their calling, and it is often in their last years that they produce their masterpieces. It was when he was old, and after Antonio de Messina had visited Venice, showing Italian painting fresh paths, that Giovanni Bellini really found himself. Between the ages of seventy-five and eighty-six he painted his greatest works, including his Saint Zacharias and the famous portrait of the Doge Loredano. When Dürer met him in Venice he was eighty and the city's most famous painter. Titian painted very fine pictures in his extreme old age.

Rembrandt was scarcely more than sixty when he painted his last picture, his masterpiece; but Franz Hals was eighty-five when he reached his topmost peak with the Regents. At the age of seventy-six Guardi painted *The Grey Lagoon* and *The Burning of Saint Marcuola*, his most inspired and astonishing canvases, splendidly foreshadowing the Impressionists. Corot was about eighty when he painted his most accomplished pictures, particularly the *Intérieur de la Cathédrale de Sens*; and Ingres painted *La Source* at seventy-six. Monet, Renoir, Cézanne and Bonnard all surpassed themselves in their last years.

Painters are less hampered than scientists by the weight of the past and the brevity of the future; their work is made up of a multiplicity of pictures; each time they stand in front of a virgin canvas their work is a series of fresh beginnings. And a painting calls for less time than the working out of a scientific theory: when a painter sets about a picture he is almost certain of finishing it. Compared with writers they are very fortunate, for they do not feed upon their own substance. They live in the present and not in an extension of the past. The world provides them with an inexhaustible source of colours, lights, varying subtleties of tone, and shapes. It is true that they too never confine themselves solely to their painting; but their work remains open to an unlimited extent. Towards the end of his life every creator is less afraid of public opinion and he has more self-assurance. The idea that he will be praised whatever he does may lead him into facility and blunt his critical sense; but if he does not yield to this temptation it is a great advantage for him to be able to work accordingly to his own personal standards, without troubling about whether people like what he does or not. But the writer, on the other hand, gains little from this freedom, since he often has nothing left to say: whereas for the painter there is always something to paint, and he can exercise that mastery without which there is no genius. Like the composer, the youthful painter is deeply influenced by his time: he sees the world through the pictures of the preceding generation, and it is the work of years to learn to see it with his own eyes. Thus Bonnard began by copying Gauguin, and he attributed great importance to the subject. Beginning with the *Café du Petit Poucet*, which he painted when he was sixty-one, the subject tends to disappear in favour of colour. At the age of sixty-six he wrote, 'I believe that when one is young, it is the object, the outside world, that fills one with enthusiasm – one is carried away. Later, it comes from the inside: the need to express his feelings urges the painter to choose some particular starting-point, some particular form.' He took to progressively more daring short-cuts in his drawing; he almost abandoned perspective; he moved resolutely away from the conventional vision of things, for his intention was to express their colour and life. This is the reason for the astonishing youthfulness of his latest pictures.

Goya's old age was not only a continuous rise towards an ever greater perfection, but also a constant renewal. In 1810 he was sixty-six; deeply concerned and distressed by the French occupation and its bloody consequences, he began to work on the eighty-five plates of *The Disasters of War*. He had been present at the rising of 1808 and he eagerly subscribed to equip the guerilleros. Yet he did not refuse to paint the portraits of the chief French dignitaries: with two other painters he presided over the choice of the best pictures that were to be sent to Paris: he accepted the 'red ribbon of the Order of Spain' (nicknamed the aubergine) from the French. When the liberation came in 1814 he was only just acquitted by the Purge Committee. Nevertheless, he painted a big official portrait for Ferdinand VII. And it was in that same year – he was seventy – that he painted his tragic and magnificent pictures *The Charge of the Mamelukes* and *The Fusillades*. He also painted *The Colossus* and a very fine self-portrait in which he gave himself the features of a man of fifty. In 1815 he produced the series of prints collected under the title of *Tauromaquía*. He accepted orders for a certain number of portraits of officials and friends, and painted them exceedingly well. In 1818, after he had painted *The Junta of the Philippines*, he decided that his career as an official and as a fashionable painter was over; henceforward he would no longer accept commissions and he would paint only for himself – he needed complete freedom to carry on with his work. He bought a remote house: the neighbourhood called it 'the deaf man's house', because for years he had been unable to hear. He had lost his wife in 1812, and he sent for Doña Leocadia, a distant relation, to look after the household; she brought Rosarita, her three-year-old daughter with her. He covered the walls with his famous 'black paintings', and in these he let his imagination run, without thinking for a moment about the public.* *Saturn devouring a Child, The Witches of the He-Goat's Meadow, The Dog in the*

* An admirer, Baron Erlanger, bought the house, had the pictures taken off the walls and fixed to canvas, and gave them to the Prado.

Quick-Sand – all works that are astonishing in their entirely fresh approach and handling and in the sombre wealth of their inspiration. At the same time he carried out the series of engravings called *Los Disparates*, including the *Dreams* and the *Proverbs*, in which he savagely portrayed the triumphs of stupidity.

Continually in search of self-renewal, he introduced lithography into Spain in 1819: it had been discovered at Leipzig in 1796. His first plate was of an old woman spinning, and he subsequently made many more.

He was seventy-seven when the White Terror was unloosed in Spain. At first he hid, and then fled to Bordeaux. 'Goya has arrived. He is old, deaf, enfeebled; he speaks no French and he has no servant . . . and yet he is very pleased and very eager to see the world,' wrote his friend Morantin. He made one journey to Paris and then went back to Bordeaux, where he settled down. He could no longer see distinctly, and to work he had to put on several pairs of spectacles, one over the other, and use a magnifying-glass. But for all that he carried out *The Bulls of Bordeaux*, an admirable series of lithographs, and others called *Love, Jealousy,* and *Andalusian Song*. He drew animals, beggars, shops, crowds. The little Rosarita, who was now ten, wanted to paint miniatures; he was very fond of the child, and in spite of his weak eyes he painted some with her. A year before his death, when he was eighty-one, he painted a portrait of a nun and another of a monk whose treatment is reminiscent of Cézanne.

In his last years he often dealt with the theme of old age. In *Until Death* in the *Caprichios* he had already returned to that subject so often exploited in the literature of the sixteenth and seventeenth centuries – the old woman who believes she is still beautiful. His drawing shows a hideous old creature, putting on her hat and looking complacently into the mirror. Behind her there are young men laughing up their sleeves. In 1817 he went back to the same theme in *The Old Women*: two dreadful ancients gaze at themselves in a glass: behind them stands Time, with two great wings, and a broom in his hand. It is in *La Celestina* that Goya's close connexion with the Spanish literary tradition is most clearly to be seen: in this picture a girl with a sensual face and a very low dress is displaying herself on a balcony, and behind her can be made out the well-known character of the duenna go-between; she is a revolting old woman with a hooked nose and a sly, conniving look, and her claw-like hands are telling the beads of her rosary. He also painted many witches in his

Sabbaths. When he was eighty he drew an ancient man propped on two sticks, with a great mass of white hair and beard all over his face, and the inscription 'I am still learning'. Goya was making fun of himself and his eagerness for everything new.

Baudelaire was struck by his astonishing rejuvenation – for rejuvenation was what old age meant for Goya. 'At the end of his career Goya's sight had failed to such a degree that it is said he had to have his pencils sharpened for him. Yet even at that period he carried out very large and important lithographs, splendid plates that are immense pictures in miniature – a fresh piece of evidence in support of that strange law ruling the fate of great artists, a law which lays down that their lives and intelligences should run in opposite directions, that what they lose on the one hand they should gain on the other, and that they should thus go on in a continual youth, gathering fresh strength, new spirit and even greater daring right up until the very edge of the grave.'

Here we have pertinent instances of our general statement about old age – that it makes us aware of our twofold finitude. These examples concern intellectuals and artists: they are conscious of the shortness of their future and of the unique nature of the history which encloses them, a uniqueness that cannot be transcended. Two factors come into play to define their situation: the first is the breadth of their original project, and the second the more or less paralysing weight of the past. As we have seen, for scientists old age almost inevitably brings sclerosis and sterility. Artists, on the other hand, often feel that their work is not yet done and that they might still add to it: but then they lack time to bring it to an end; they overwork themselves, but in vain – in spite of his frenzied toil Michelangelo never saw the dome of St Peter's. Often a state of balance comes into being – much is still to be done but time is not desperately short. It is still possible that there might even be progress. But progress at this stage of life is of a disappointing kind: a man keeps going, certainly, but only by marking time. At the best, the aged artist will not go much further than the point he has reached. There are some who twist and turn in a vain attempt to break out: all they achieve is self-caricature, not self-renewal. The truth is that a man's work can grow richer only in harmony with what it is and always will be.

This idea may dishearten the artist, particularly if physiological decline, illness and liability to fatigue make work arduous. But some aged men continue the struggle with a passionate heroism. What is heroic is not only Renoir's, Papini's or Michelangelo's wrestling with an unwilling, stubborn body; it is also the delighting in a progress that must soon be cut short by death, the carrying on, the attempt to outdo oneself in full knowledge and acceptance of one's finitude. There is here a living assertion of the value of art and thought that arouses our admiration. Even more so since it is not merely the scientist but also the artist and the writer whose worth is disputed by the rising generation. Bonnard suffered from the 'hardness' of the young, who turned from him when he was adding to and improving his work.

What is most painful at the end of a creative life is the intimate knowledge of this inner doubt. Some young men may carry their struggle to the point of despair, and even to suicide – Van Gogh, for example, and Nicolas de Staël. Finitude, and all the impossibilities it implies, may become apparent at any age. Generally speaking, even if he is deeply dissatisfied with himself, a young man sets his hopes on the future that is open before him. For an old man the stakes are down. If he finds something lacking in his work, it is painful for him to know that he cannot fundamentally do anything about it. There were moments when Monet had radical doubts about the value of his painting, and it made him bitterly unhappy. Even when the elderly man is satisfied with his work, he feels that it is in danger in the opinion of the outside world, particularly as far as the verdict of posterity is concerned.

This verdict may be seen as an appeal against death, a promise of survival. The work will exist for the coming generations – it may be fortunate enough to echo on without limit of time. In the days of Ronsard and Corneille this was a comforting idea; they thought the monarchical system would last for ever, that neither men nor civilization would change; their fame, as fresh as when they had won it, would go down the centuries. We no longer have illusions of this sort. We do know that our society is in full development: we do not know what kind of socialism or technology or barbarism it will end in. But we have no doubt that the men of the future will be unlike ourselves. (That is why Franz in the *Séquestrés d'Altona* imagines them looking like crabs.) Even supposing that our message reaches them, we cannot foresee how they will decode it or on what basis; and in any case a picture or a novel cannot have the same meaning for the people of our time and for the future centuries. Reading or seeing in the present is one thing: reading or seeing through the depths of the past is quite another.

Even if we confine ourselves to the immediate future, a man's work runs the risks that cause him the more anxiety the more he believes in its value. In the first place there is that of its being destroyed by outside forces – this was the fate Freud dreaded for psychoanalysis. It is no less distressing to think that it may be distorted. Newton was aware that his theory of gravity would be mishandled and that it would lose its suppleness; again and again he uttered warnings in a vain attempt at preventing these errors. Nietzsche was very much afraid that his philosophy might give rise to false interpretations; and indeed he would certainly have had nothing to do with the Nazis' version of the Superman. The vain man is less concerned with the future of his work than with that of his reputation. If he thinks he is unappreciated he is very apt to appeal to future generations – Edmond de Goncourt assured himself that they would place him above Zola. Bernard Shaw, on the contrary, who was famous during his lifetime, was persuaded that the rising generation, obeying a kind of pendulum-law that had already dealt with Hardy, Meredith and many others, would not acknowledge him. In any event, whether he is forgotten, misunderstood, cried down or admired, no one is there when his posthumous fate is decided: this ignorance alone is certain, and as I see it it makes all hypotheses idle and trifling.

To finish this study of the relationship between the elderly man and his praxis I shall speak of the old age of a few politicians. The politician has chosen neither the scientist's nor philosopher's abstract world nor that of the imaginary. He is anchored in reality, and his intention is to act upon men in order to guide the history of his time towards certain ends. In some cases this project may take the form of a career (it was so with Disraeli, who wanted to be a minister from his childhood), and at first politics has the appearance of a mould in search of something to fill it; the primary goal is the exercise of power, power of any kind, and the standing that arises from that exercise. The two attitudes usually overlap. The careerist will elect certain ends and will then find that it is they who are his master – this again was the case with Disraeli. And the man who is called by a distinct mission will seek power in order to carry it out. In any event, the politician is more immediately dependent on the outside world than the intellectual or the artist. They need recognition, but they call for it by means of work whose raw material is not man himself; whereas man is the essential stuff of the politician. The politician may make himself useful to men, but he does so only by making use of them; his success or failure is in their hands, and to a great extent he is incapable of foreseeing their reactions. Before we ask what the consequences of this may be upon the old age of politicians, we must first look at the general relationship between the ageing individual and history.

History has many different faces. It does not intervene at all in repetitive societies. In the middle ages it seemed to be catastrophic – salvation came from another world. In the century of enlightenment it was filled with hopes of every kind. Today it holds promise but also threat – the total or partial destruction of our planet by the bomb. I have known people look forward to this possibility without any very great distress – once one is dead, what does it matter what happens afterwards? And some even go so far as to say that they would be spared all regrets if they knew that the whole world would vanish with them.

There are others, and I am one of them, who are horrified by this idea. Like everybody else, I am incapable of conceiving infinity; and yet I do not accept finity. I want this adventure that is the context of my life to go on without end. I love young people: I want our species to go on in them and I want them to have a better life. Without this hope, I should find the old age towards which I am moving utterly unbearable.

It may sometimes happen that great social and political changes transform a man's old age. From the moment the Bastille had been taken, Kant gave up his invariable daily walk to meet the mail-coach bringing news from France: he had always believed in a progress that would bring society and the individual into full development and he thought that the Revolution was fulfilling his prophesies. Good fortune of this kind is rare, for seen day by day defeats have an absolute value and successes are uncertain. We are often disappointed in our hopes, and we never know the unmixed happiness of having been right. 'Truth never triumphs in the end: its opponents die,' said Planck, the physicist. For my own part, I went through the Algerian war with utter horror: independence had been won at too great a price for me to be able to welcome it with any joy. 'The road that leads to Good is worse than Evil,' said Mirabeau. When one is young, with an illusory eternity ahead, one makes a single leap to the far end of the path: later one no longer has impetus enough to go beyond what has been called 'the incidental expenses of history', and they seem terribly high. And at this time too, retreats and failures have something final about them. The young cherish the hope of seeing the birth of a different future, and for them a falling-back may mean a fresh leap ahead. Old people, even if they do believe in the future, the long-term future, do not reckon on being present when the change is brought about. Their faith does not protect them against disappointments in the present. Sometimes indeed they may lose it, and then the march of events, submerging them, seems like a denial of their whole existence. One of the things that distressed Casanova was the sight of the French revolution destroying the world in which he had lived. From the depths of the Bohemian castle in which he was imprisoned he called Mirabeau 'that infamous writer'.

Anatole France provides us with a most striking example of this kind of disillusionment. He was a socialist after the style of Jaurès, humanist and optimistic, and he imagined that a better and a juster world was to be born soon and without violence. In 1913, when he was sixty-nine, he thought that 'all the nations of the world were travelling towards peace'. He said that 'the proletariats of the different nations would soon unite'. He was persuaded that in all countries the proletariat was pacifist and ready to rise up against war. He also believed that capitalism did not necessarily lead to war. Coming back from Germany he asserted, 'It is certain that Germany does not want war.' In a speech in April 1914 he announced 'the forthcoming union of a reconciled Europe'. He trusted in human reason: killing and destroying was disastrous for all: mankind had enough common sense to know what was to its own advantage. He was thunderstruck in August 1914; it shook him so that in October he thought of suicide. To a friend he wrote, 'Life is unbearable to me; I am in such a state of prostration that I cannot go out; and I beg you to procure me some poison.' He published a few pieces – he regretted them later – in which, carried along by the current, he condemned German militarism; but after this he remained silent until the armistice. It is clear from his letters that he renounced his idealist and reformist illusions. From that time on it was impossible to believe that the masses were able to prevent war. He was often in a state of total despair. In December 1915 he wrote, 'Life is unbearable and the void is all I hunger and thirst for.' In June 1916, 'I am losing my reason. It is not so much men's wickedness that is killing me as their stupidity.'

413

In December 1916, 'Human stupidity has no bounds.' He was out-raged because the war was not stopped. He ended a long, passionate, ironic letter with the words, 'We are in no hurry. The war is only losing France ten thousand men a day!' In November 1917 he wrote, 'There are no longer any limits to my anguish and sorrow.' He supported the men whom Clemenceau caused to be condemned, discreetly in the case of Callaux, loudly and openly in that of Rappoport. 'I have lived one year too long, indeed seventy years too long,' he wrote in another letter. 'I no longer even want to see the end of the horrors that are devastating Europe. I neither believe in anything nor desire anything; all I hope for is the everlasting void.'

He was very deeply moved by the Russian revolution. 'The first decisive step towards a better future would be the application of Karl Marx's teachings. Pacifism is outdated,' he wrote. The war had shown him the necessity for violence, but he could not easily resign himself to the idea. 'I am very much afraid that this war will not end the age of violence. It would need a rising of the nations to ensure world-wide disarmament . . . this horrible war is pregnant with three or four equally horrible wars. That is the hideous truth.' It tortured him cruelly. On 3 October 1918 he wrote, 'People believe that old men's hearts grow hard, but mine on the contrary has become more tender than it was and for me life has turned into an unending torment.'

When the armistice was signed he cherished the hope that 'the war would bring about world-wide revolution', and he asserted his admiration for the Soviets. In 1919 the strikes and unrest among the workers encouraged him to believe that the coming of socialism was at hand. Once again he publicly took part in the struggle. He launched an appeal to the voters: 'The class-war will only be brought to an end by the disappearance of classes . . . everything is hurrying us towards socialism.' He became a member neither of the Socialist nor of the Communist Party, but he had friends in both. In 1922 he published *Salut aux Soviets* in *l'Humanité* – 'the first trial of a power that governs by the people, for the people'. Together with Barbusse he became a member of the *Clarté* group. Yet in his letters and his conversation he was deeply pessimistic. He had doubts about the fate of his posthumous reputation. He published *La Vie en fleur* in 1921; it shows his deeply sorrowful view of the future. 'We shall have no more posterity than had the last writers of the Roman world.' He thought that Europe and its civilization were about to die. 'The powers of evil rule the world.' 'Europe is sinking into barbarism.' He still wanted to believe in socialism; but this socialism was no longer anything like that of which he had dreamed. In reply to Gorki's appeal he condemned the trial of the Revolutionary Socialists, then beginning in Moscow. He was incapable of renouncing the humanistic values by which he had lived – tolerance and bourgeois freedom. His way of thinking was as out of date as his way of writing. He did his best to follow the movement of history, but he remained a man of another age. His writing no longer had the least effect. In 1923 *l'Humanité* attacked him violently, accusing him of dilettantism, anarchism and scepticism. He was also expelled from *Clarté*. In fact, despite his efforts at adapting himself to the new age, the Great War had entirely wrecked his hopes in a reasonable and happy world.

The overthrow of Wells in 1940 was even more radical. He remained extremely young up to the age of seventy, and to begin with he adapted himself to his times remarkably well. He went to the United States, where he met Roosevelt – Wells dreamt of bringing about closer, more friendly relations between the East and the West. He realized that he had not succeeded: 'I have failed in an undertaking that was far too big for me.' When the Second World War broke out he was so overcome, so distressed that he fell ill. Speaking of the world of 1942 he said, 'This sight has completely broken me.' He said that he was 'at the end of his tether', and stated, 'The author no longer has anything to say and never will have anything to say again.' He lived on until 1946 in a state of horror without any hope at all. His faith in mankind was dead. All his work, all his earlier struggles and even the very meaning of his life had been based on trust in his fellow-men – once this was gone there was nothing left for him at all, no refuge of any kind; all that he could do was to let go, to long for the void, and to die.

Despair of this kind may lead to suicide. Virginia Woolf lived in a small, privileged group, and she was little concerned with politics; but the declaration of war and the bombing of London overwhelmed her: at the age of fifty-eight she was unable to survive the shattering of her world.* How much more, then, will an aged person, threatened by the course of events, feel that for him the game is lost, that the struggle is useless and that the best thing to do is to put an end to it. When France was occupied, it was above all aged Jews who killed themselves.

If an elderly man has helped to bring about events that he deplores

---

* She had already had fits of depression in which she thought of suicide.

it will strike him harder than if he were young. A younger man, instead of wasting time in vain regrets, will try to put things right; whereas the other no longer has enough time ahead of him to feel that he can do so. This was the unhappiness that darkened the last years of Einstein's life. He was very much aware of the scientist's responsibility in the matter of the application of science: he was worried about the possible consequences of the liberation of atomic energy, which had been carried out on the basis of his discoveries. 'Thrusting back this menace has become the most urgent problem of our times,' he said before the war. In 1939 the physicists Wigner and Szilard, who were afraid that Germany would make the uranium bomb, persuaded Einstein to write to Roosevelt, warning him of the danger. He did so, and asked that there should be permanent contact between the administration and the physicists who were studying chain-reaction; the United States should be provided with stocks of uranium and the experimental work should be speeded up. His advice was followed. Very soon Einstein began to dread the results. As early as 1940 he spoke of this letter as the most unfortunate event of his life. As soon as he had a hint of the plans for destroying Japanese cities with the atomic bomb he sent Roosevelt a memorandum: the President died before opening the letter. Einstein did not think that any one individual could seriously affect the course of history by his own unaided strength. And his action in 1939 was justified: a German uranium bomb did at that time seem possible. So he did not allow himself to be eaten up by remorse: but the conflict between the wealth of scientific creation and the destructive use to which it was turned distressed him very deeply.

Had he been younger he would certainly have committed himself entirely to a struggle for peace and he would have tried to neutralize the discovery of the atomic bomb in one way or another: the shortness of his future did not allow him any hope of finding a remedy.

Even when history runs on without any great disaster, there is another reason why the elderly man derives but little pleasure from it: as we have seen in the case of Anatole France, the elderly man finds it very hard to follow the general movement. It is known that he has difficulty in adopting a new 'set'. Furthermore, most of the time he does not want to do so – his ideological interests hold him back. His spoken or written words and the persona that he has created for himself make up an 'outside being' to which he is alienated. An old professor merges with the lectures that he repeats year after year and with the titles and honours they have procured for him; reforms vex him not only because he has grown incapable of making a dialogue take the place of his set course of lectures but also because he thinks that with reform he would lose everything that has constituted his reason for existence. An old man's political activity, like his work, is encumbered by the weight of the past. Often he fails to understand an age too far removed from his own youth. He lacks the necessary intellectual tools. His life has moulded him definitively and when events come upon him unawares, he does not find the right answers. Although he was still young, Guéhenno, speaking of his regret at having plunged into a blind, stubborn pacifism in 1940, wrote, 'Deep in the men of my age there is a host of paralysing memories.' He had not realized that the words 'war' and 'peace' did not have the same meaning in 1914 and in 1940: the lessons to be drawn from some forms of experience become outdated, and there are some abstract principles that must be called into question when circumstances change. Alain, like Guéhenno, was the victim of his own memories in his leanings towards collaboration: but what is more, he did not try to see the situation as it really was because pacifism, the ideological interest that he had defended all his life, held him back. Bertrand Russell fell into the same error and for the same reason: he set the cause he had always served above the present reality, and in the name of pacifism he preached non-resistance to Nazism to the English.

The case of Jeannette Vermeersch is significant. Throughout all that happened between her youth and the autumn of 1968, her political line never wavered. She was unconditionally faithful to the USSR; she was a dogged, immovable Stalinist, and she tried to hold back de-Stalinization in France after Stalin's death: she therefore found herself more and more cut off from a changing world. While the Communist Party was modifying its policy, she clung firmly to her old positions. At the time of the Czechoslovakian crisis she hurried to the support of the Soviet leaders, all men of about her own age whom she knew personally and whom she regarded as the embodiment of Communist truth. She found herself completely alone within her party, not a single member of the central committee supported her and she was forced to resign. Her rigidity of mind meant that she was out of date; and here again it is to be explained by her ideological interests. She had been a Stalinist and she had

417

been very closely associated with Thorez' policy: she refused to call into question either her former self or the policy. This refusal to challenge one's own being is to be seen in almost all old people, and the reasons are understandable. Since, as Hegel puts it, all truth is a 'becoming', something at which one arrives, it would be possible to accept former mistakes as a necessary stage in that approach; but a man will make up his mind to do so only if he can hope to take advantage of this new truth, to follow its evolution and to profit by it. When the future is closed it is usual, though not inevitable, that the aged man will obstinately continue to stake everything on the past and to refuse to change the idea that he has made of this past.

As we have seen in our survey of historical societies, whatever the regime and whatever the party to which they may belong, the old tend to join the ranks of the conservatives. It is hard for them to escape from the past that has formed them: they see the present through the medium of this past, and their understanding of it is poor. They lack the time and the means for adapting themselves to new circumstances, and their interests prevent them from even attempting to do so. They do their utmost to preserve the status quo. Revolutions are made by young men: when they grow old they no longer continue to lead except in the cases where the revolution has become institutionalized, and even then their role is often more that of a figurehead than of an active leader.

Generally speaking, politicians find that their old age is a time of lost power and glory. They did represent one moment in history: but history changes, and in changing it calls for new men. In his book *Louis XIV et vingt millions de Français,* Pierre Goubert observes, 'When he died he left behind him an excellent image of the monarchy; but this image already showed signs of age, if indeed it was not completely out of date. Like many other kings and like almost all men he stiffened as he grew older, losing his intellectual suppleness.' What is more, he felt that the century was no longer his own and that luck had deserted him. Everyone knows the words he addressed to the old Marshal de Villeroy after the defeat of Romilly – 'Luck does not serve men of our age, Monsieur le Maréchal.' Since he was an absolute monarch, he retained his throne; but an 'out-of-date' minister is not so fortunate. History is full of resounding falls from office. And since a politician is usually an ambitious man, he finds his misfortune hard to bear. The gloom of the aged Chateaubriand was essentially caused by the fact that as far as public life was

418

concerned he was finished and done with – out of the running. I think it would be interesting to take a close look at the old age of a few politicians: we see every time that it is a complex adventure in which many factors come into play – the man's past, his biological state, the impact of events, and the counter-closures of history. I shall take three examples in which one or another of these factors predominates.

In Clemenceau we see that a man who follows his youthful political line throughout the course of his life is eventually outstripped by the present, for the very reason of his faithfulness to the past. It is a well-known saying that a man must change if he is to stay the same. Clemenceau, remaining attached to a given form of democracy, found that he had passed from the extreme Left to the side of reaction – a reaction, furthermore, that did not like him, because of his past. His worth, his character, and the fact that the country needed him brought him to the highest pinnacle of glory. But immediately after he was reduced to powerlessness because there was no room for him in the new political life of France.

Churchill was chosen to fight the war because he had foretold it and had called for warlike preparations; but he did not make the effort needed to inspire the English with confidence when the time had come to live in peace once more. In any case he was not capable of doing so: he had not evolved with the times and he had no clear idea of the new problems that were arising. But what saddened his old age above all was his inescapable physiological decay; he fought furiously against it, but little by little it destroyed him entirely.

Gandhi was blessed with excellent health right up until his death, and he successfully carried out his lifetime's aim – the independence of India. But the means he had employed to achieve it, including the excitement of religiosity, had consequences that denied all the principles by which he had lived, and he died in despair.

Clemenceau's father, a ferocious republican who scoffed at the Empire, brought up his son in the worship of the French Revolution; and the young Clemenceau eagerly embraced the father's opinions. When he was studying medicine in Paris he joined a group of young positivists and atheists; he contributed to a subversive paper, and in 1862, when he was twenty-one, he was imprisoned at Mazas for having written an article calling upon the workers to gather in the Place de la Bastille on 14 July to celebrate that glorious anniversary. When he left prison he came under the influence of Blanqui. A stay of four years in the United States strengthened his love of democracy. In 1869 he married an American woman in a registry office, and on coming back to France in 1870 he plunged into political action. He was appointed provisional mayor of the XVIIIth arrondissement in Paris and, on 8 February 1871, deputy for the city. At the Bordeaux Assembly on 1 March 1871 he, together with Victor Hugo and a few others, voted against the treaty that handed over Alsace-Lorraine to Germany: the government's surrender filled him with indignation. Back in Paris, he tried to play the role of peace-maker between the government and the Commune, but in vain. He resigned his seat because, under the influence of Thiers, the Assembly refused to pass a law preparing for municipal elections. 'Let Paris yield first,' said Thiers. Clemenceau thought that to bring a real democracy into being France should base itself upon the people. When the municipal elections did take place in 1874 he was elected and the next year he became president of the municipal council: a little later he was chosen as deputy for the XVIIIth arrondissement.

Now began a great parliamentary career in which Clemenceau appeared as a man of the Left and even of the extreme Left. He called for an amnesty for the Communards: it was not granted until 1879, and even then only partially. After 1881 the party to which he belonged took the name of *radical socialiste*. He was one of its most brilliant members, one of those who commanded most attention. In parliament and in his newspaper articles he fought for secularization of the republic and of education, for freedom of the Press, the right of public meeting, for a plan for national education and for economic reforms. His party had a social programme that was considered very advanced: it called for the protection of work, for granting the trade unions a legal entity, and for the improvement of the worker's living conditions.

His eloquence was the dread of his opponents: he attacked Jules Ferry's colonialism and brought about his fall, as well as that of Freycinet and Gambetta. He was the unchallenged leader of the extreme Left, and his nickname was the 'minister-killer'. He helped to defeat Boulangism, and, by way of revenge, Déroulède tried to implicate him in the Panama scandal. He defended himself brilliantly and was freed from any hint of suspicion. But for all that he lost his seat in parliament.

He was fifty-two. He plunged into journalism. He was not solely concerned with politics: he had friends among the writers and the painters and he passionately supported Rodin and the Impressionists. What is more, Jaurès was of the opinion that in Clemenceau's articles 'socialist thought asserted itself with an ever-increasing clarity.' He played a part of the first importance in the revision of the Dreyfus trial.

He was elected senator in 1893, supporting Combes against the religious congregations and defending the disestablishment of the Church; yet at the same time he called for freedom in education. He was in favour of a 'progressive socialism', and his activity began to run counter to that of the socialists who called for the expropriation of the capitalist class and the total socialization of the means of production and exchange. Clemenceau for his part would have nothing to do with the class-war, and he wanted reforms that should be carried through by constitutional means. Yet he was faithful to the spirit of 1848, and in the miners' strikes of 1882 he defended the right to strike against the opposition of the mine-owning companies. He denounced the killings at Fourmies.

It was twelve years later, when he was appointed minister of the interior, that his political position took on a completely new appearance. Not that he had changed. But the situation had wholly altered. Liberal society had remained the same while the proletariat had become far more numerous and its wretched conditions even worse. The result of this was a social tension that called for the most radical solutions. Clemenceau desired above all to maintain republican order, that is to say bourgeois order. Strikes broke out at Lens and they degenerated into riots: he sent in troops, who fired upon the workers. Wherever he felt that repression was needed, he called upon the army. He said of himself that he was 'France's top policeman'. The socialists attacked him furiously: from now on the break between them and the radicals was total and permanent.

In 1906, when he became prime minister, Clemenceau was sixty-five: he was at this time the leader of the Radical Party, which had a majority in the Chamber, and which was now struggling against the progressives. Trade unionism among the workers had become revolutionary. Serious conflicts were breaking out all over the country. Clemenceau dealt with them by force. The repression was bloody: at Villeneuve-Saint-Georges in 1908 there were, according to official sources, four workers killed and forty wounded. He strongly opposed the setting-up of unions for civil servants. The socialists, particularly Jaurès, burst out in fury against him. He offered still further pledges to reactionary opinion, giving Lyautey full powers to occupy the country behind Casablanca. But although he paid great attention to the defence of the country – he appointed Foch head of the *Ecole de Guerre* – the right wing cried out that he was neglecting it. After the blowing up of the *Iéna*, Delcassé denounced the total inadequacy of the admiralty, and the ministry fell. Briand formed a new government.

At this moment in his history Clemenceau was an illustration of the fact I mentioned earlier – an elderly man who obstinately clings to his former positions finds himself out of step with the present. Clemenceau's 'socialism' had become so out of date that it had turned into a policy of reaction.

He said he was very happy to have recovered his freedom and set off on a lecture tour in South America, speaking on the subject of democracy. 'I am the soldier of democracy,' he declared. In 1913 when he was back in France, he founded a paper, *L'Homme libre*, and wrote articles in it almost every day. He felt that war was coming nearer, and although he hoped it would be avoided, he fought against pacifism. He launched a campaign in support of the law increasing military service to three years.

Once war was declared, he so bitterly criticized the way in which it was run that his paper was suspended. It reappeared under the name of *L'Homme enchaîné*. Viviani offered him a ministry in 1914: he refused. He was convinced that he alone could save France, and he wanted the premiership or nothing. From January 1915 onwards he played an important part as president of the Senate committees for the army and for foreign affairs. Although he was seventy-five he often visited the front and inspected the trenches – he spent a night in the fortress of Douaumont. He violently criticized the miserable organization of the medical service. In his paper he also attacked 'defeatism' with great energy. And he entreated the United States to come to the help of France. After the mutinies of 15 May 1917 he made an extremely violent speech against Malvy, the minister of the interior.

His patriotism and energy won him an immense popularity throughout the country; but in political circles he had aroused hatred in every quarter. Poincaré loathed him, blaming the seventy-seven-year-old Clemenceau for 'his immense vanity, his instability and his levity'. Nevertheless he decided to call upon him. Clemenceau was a little deaf, but he had retained all his intelligence and all his vitality.

He remained in power for twenty-six months, working from six in the morning until ten at night. He had gathered a fresh team around him. The situation was critical, and in order to save it he called up new classes of recruits, made parliament vote fresh supplies and fought mercilessly against defeatism. He was violently attacked by the socialists. He succeeded in forcing a united command upon the Allies and supported Foch, now at the head of all the armies. When the Germans began to fall back he was triumphantly welcomed in the liberated regions. 'It was more than enthusiasm; it was downright madness,' observed Mordacq. 'I found it almost impossible to prevent his being smothered.' Clemenceau had been savagely criticized during his ministry, and this was a very sweet revenge for him. 'A man really has to have a sound heart to withstand emotions of this kind,' he said. 'They make up for a great deal of bitterness.' Poincaré, Pétain and a certain number of other politicians and soldiers wanted the German army to be chased as far as Berlin. Clemenceau supported Foch in his decision to sign the armistice. 'No man has the right to prolong the bloodshed,' said Foch. This was not the only reason for this attitude. Now that the essential war-aims had been achieved, public opinion called for an armistice; it would have been dangerous to 'play with the morale of the troops and the country'.* And then again, if the war had gone on, the part played by the American armies would have become increasingly important and the peace would have depended even more upon the United States. Lastly, Foch, like the Allied leaders, was afraid that a continuation of the war would favour the spread of Bolshevism in Germany.

When he announced the signature of the armistice Clemenceau was cheered by both chambers. A crowd gathered outside the ministry of war and insisted upon his coming out on to the balcony of his office: the ovation moved him to tears. Yet by that evening his joy had already vanished. His children took him to the Grand Hôtel so that he could see the happiness of the crowds in the Place de l'Opéra. He watched them in silence. 'Tell me you are happy,' said his daughter. 'I cannot tell you that because I am not happy. All this will turn out to have been useless.' He was called Père la Victoire; statues of him were set up. But he dreaded the future. 'Now we are going to have to win the peace, and maybe that is going to be harder,' he said. He also said, 'If I cared about my fame, I should die now.'

* Tardieu, *La Paix*.

423

He was very tired; his digestion was ruined; his hands were covered with a rash; he slept badly.

He went to London, where he was enthusiastically welcomed. Strasbourg greeted him with such an ovation that he wept. After a short rest in the Vendée, his native country, he opened the Peace Conference and returned to very hard, steady work. On 9 April 1919 a twenty-three-year-old anarchist named Cottin shot ten revolver-bullets at him.* One hit him, but he was not seriously wounded.

The negotiations with Wilson were extremely difficult. Clemenceau stood out for the interests of France: he won acceptance for the principle that Germany should pay France reparations; it was also agreed that the French army should occupy the left bank of the Rhine for fifteen years and that the country should have a certain number of other advantages. Yet Foch blamed him for making too many concessions and the Right began calling him Perd la Victoire. Strikes broke out all over the country: there were claims and demands on every hand. He ordered a pitiless repression. The police violently dispersed a manifestation of war-widows: on 1 May the parading workers were set upon by the forces of order with bared swords – some were killed and others wounded. The police even charged a parade of badly disabled servicemen with unbelievable savagery. Clemenceau granted the workers the eight-hour law, but he had lost all popularity with them. On 28 June the Treaty of Versailles was signed: when he came out with Wilson they were very nearly smothered by the enthusiastic crowd. But he was not satisfied with the peace: in his opinion France had not obtained the guarantees she needed. The treaty was severely criticized by many French politicians. Cambon called it 'a powder-magazine'.

Against him he had the whole of the left wing, which blamed him for his 'narrow patriotism, filled with the spirit of revenge'.† The intellectuals were angered by his nationalism. The ordinary French people accused him of having made a poor defence of French interests. He had lost a great deal of his prestige, and he longed for retirement. Nevertheless, he did make a few speeches. Some parliamentarians wanted to reform the constitution, and Clemenceau defended it against their attacks. Again and again he called for national unity; he also attacked Bolshevism with fanatical violence,

---

* The inside story of this affair was never known. Cottin was condemned to death, but he was reprieved and later he was set free. It appears that he was a visionary.

† *Revanchard* – revenge for the defeat of 1870 (trs.).

thus provoking the fury of the extreme Left and, five days before the elections, a total strike among the printing workers of the Paris newspapers.

The *Bloc national*, that is to say the Right, triumphed at the elections: this was the *Chambre bleu horizon*,* in which the majority was made up of declared opponents of the left-wing parties. Clemenceau was not at all pleased with the results of the election. 'Clemenceau has missed the right moment for retiring from the stage,' observed Pierre Miquel.† 'The *Chambre bleu horizon* is beginning with the rout of the left-wing Clemencistes.'

On 8 November, at the first sitting of the new chamber he welcomed the members for Alsace and Lorraine with deep feeling. He was cheered. However, he did not seek re-election to the Senate. He was eighty, and he was tired. His friends would have liked him to stand in the presidential election. 'They want to kill me!' he protested. On his return from a journey to London he agreed to stand, perhaps under the influence of Lloyd George; but he showed so little eagerness that his enemies accused him of contempt for parliament. He was a notorious anticlerical, and he opposed the renewal of relations between France and the Vatican: all the Catholics were against him, and they allied themselves with the socialists. Foch, Briand and Poincaré all conducted campaigns against him. The preliminary meeting, held immediately before the elections, showed a majority for Deschanel. Clemenceau refused to offer himself the next day and he declared that if this was ignored and if he were elected, he would not accept the mandate. That evening he said to Barrès, 'I could still be useful. But for me this is the better way. I am eighty. Nobody knows it. But I know it, and sometimes I know it cruelly.' The next day Deschanel was elected.

Clemenceau did not accept being 'pensioned off' without bitterness. It wounded his pride very deeply. He retired to a small, lonely house on the coast of the Vendée, and from that time on he refused to read anything that was written about him, whether it was praise or criticism. His health was astonishing. He visited Egypt and then made an extremely tiring journey to India, observing when he came back, 'I feel younger than ever.' 'It looked as though in growing older he amassed life rather than spent it,' said Alfred Capus. But the political situation caused him great distress. He made a speech at Sartène, in

* The French soldiers wore 'horizon blue' uniform (trs.).
† Poincaré's biographer.

425

Corsica, deploring the fact that the Treaty of Versailles was not being applied in its entirety. The withdrawal of America, the problem of reparations, the concessions made to Germany, Briand's return to power – he hated Briand – and what he called France's moral decadence – all these things gave him great pain and uneasiness. He fought on by means of others. He founded a paper, *L'Echo national*, and made Tardieu the editor: it was a failure.

The *New York World* asked him for his views on America's role in war and peace, and he decided to go over as a private person and tell the United States what he was and what he stood for. He left on 11 November. He was welcomed in triumph. Although he was eighty-one he spoke thirty times in three weeks, doing his utmost to 'wake the Americans up'. He had huge and enthusiastic audiences; but his journey had not the least political effect. A little later the occupation of the Ruhr increased the antagonism between America and France.

When he was home again he refused to return to parliament in spite of the advances that were made to him; but he followed the course of events with very great distress. On 26 April 1922 he wrote, 'Every day the situation is getting worse and worse at Genoa, where they let themselves be cruelly bullied by Lloyd George. Whether they break or whether they yield, it still means falling to the bottom of the abyss. . . . I suffer from all this beyond my power of expression.' And again, 'Betrayed by its governments and betrayed by its press – that is our nation's fate.' He attacked Briand for the concessions he made. When Poincaré succeeded Briand in 1922 and carried out the occupation of the Ruhr, Clemenceau was of the opinion that the measure was too late and that it no longer had the least value. It seemed to him pointlessly dangerous. 'Your Poincaré looks to me like a child sitting among powder-barrels and playing with fire,' he wrote to a friend.

He took comfort in driving or walking along the shore, growing roses and seeing visitors. He worked on his *Démosthène*. In a letter to a friend he said, 'I am eighty-two, and that explains everything. Physically I am not bad. Mentally reasonably fit. And the same applies to my heart.' And again, 'I ask nothing; and I cannot be accused of selfishness when I say that I shall die more or less happy in the midst of the bitter struggle of conflicting fates.' He also wrote *Au soir de la pensée*: 'Thanks to this,'* he said to Wurmser in October

* To the fact of writing.

1925, 'four years that would otherwise have been sorrowful have passed very well. . . . It is odd, is it not, that the end of my life should be in such contradiction with what I have been and with my character. It is to my work that I owe all this. It has turned my mind from my cares – it has raised me above them. All this ant-hill no longer touches me at all.'

In fact he had fits of weariness and depression. His melancholy showed through his letters and speeches. A left-wing coalition succeeded Poincaré and sought closer relations with Germany. Clemenceau burst out in fury. He saw the rehabilitated Caillaux and Malvy become ministers once more. Briand signed the Treaty of Locarno and was hailed as the new apostle of peace. For Clemenceau all this was one unbearable slap in the face after another. In 1926 a *Union nationale* government was formed, the cabinet including his two greatest enemies, Briand and Poincaré: his anger reached its highest point, and when Tardieu agreed to join this ministry Clemenceau broke with him. He wrote an indignant letter to Coolidge when the American president called upon France to repay her debts. He foretold disaster: 'In five years, ten years, whenever they like, the Boches will walk into the country.' Which was true, by the way. He also said, 'What utterly abject times we live in.' René Benjamin came to see him in the country, and Clemenceau said, 'This poor fleeting thing, twentieth-century France, is finished and done for; I stand aside. . . . Any man worthy of the name would die of disgust among the dwarfs that rule us. I am very well where I am.' He uttered dark prophecies. 'You will have a general deliquescence; and it will not last very long, either. Briand and Germany between them will see to that for you. You will live in the high-flavoured, half-rotting peace of all decadent civilizations.' He had lost all passion, all conviction. 'Hope? It is impossible! I can no longer hope, I who no longer believe in anything, I who no longer believe in what filled my life – in democracy.'

He had a great friendship for Claude Monet. He admired *Les Nymphéas* and he asked the painter to give the pictures to the nation: the Beaux-Arts authorities put the Orangerie at Monet's disposal. But Monet, whom Clemenceau called 'the king of cross-grained grumblers', found one difficulty after another and in the end he cancelled the gift. Later he agreed to it again, but he died in December 1926, before the pictures were finally hung. Six months earlier Clemenceau had lost Geoffroy, to whom he had been deeply attached.

He also lost his brother Albert and his faithful servant Clotilde. Loneliness weighed upon him. 'Oh, how sad it is to reach the end of one's life! There is no one round you any more,' he said. His health began to fail somewhat. 'It is my sorrow to be almost well, the only thing wrong with me being that I can no longer walk.' Yet he said that work gave him 'a young man's happiness'. He wrote a book on Monet. Foch's *Mémorial* appeared three weeks after the soldier's death in April 1929; it criticized Clemenceau harshly, and this wounded him. He hit back with his *Grandeur et misère d'une victoire*. These attacks saddened him: 'What I chiefly resent is that he [Foch] should not have allowed me to end my days in the modest pride of a silence upon which I based my best, my deepest happiness.' But he looked back over his past with pleasure. 'I have had everything ... everything a man can have. ... I have lived through the finest hours a man can live through in this world. We who experienced the armistice, my young friends ... ' He kept his astonishing vitality right up to the very end. It was only just before his death that he murmured, 'I grow old. I am clinging to life with softened claws.'

Clemenceau's vigorous, green old age makes an astonishing contrast with Churchill's, although there were striking likenesses between the two men. Churchill, called to power in 1940, when he was sixty-six, was also looked upon as his country's saviour in the hour of victory, and he too enjoyed immense popularity. And yet he too was expelled from office immediately after the war. But his biological fate was quite unlike Clemenceau's.

In 1940 Churchill was hailed as the Heaven-sent leader: the whole country called for him to be placed at the head of affairs. Behind him he had a long career as a member of parliament and as a minister. It was very largely because of his presence at the admiralty in 1911 that the British fleet had become so strong. When the defeat of the Conservatives brought about the fall of Baldwin's government in 1930, Churchill, then Chancellor of the Exchequer, lost his place. He was kept out of power for ten years. But during this time his speeches attracted great attention. He had early understood the gravity of the Nazi threat, and in 1936, speaking before the Conservative Party's foreign affairs committee, he appealed to the League of Nations against Germany. The papers gave his views wide publicity. He launched a campaign in favour of rearmament and subsequently he denounced all concessions made to Hitler. He was accused of war-mongering: but when war was declared he was seen to have been a true prophet – it had been criminal not to believe him. The walls of London were covered with posters that said *Winston to power!* Chamberlain placed him at the head of the admiralty. After the Germans entered Belgium on 10 May 1940 Chamberlain resigned and Churchill became prime minister in a coalition government. It was then that he made his famous speech, 'I have nothing to offer but blood, sweat, and tears.' He was sixty-six.

During the war years he took on the work of three men. He got up at eight, worked until lunch, slept for an hour and then worked again until two or three in the morning. After December 1943 his body betrayed him: he fell ill at Carthage and he was never quite the same man again. His physician, Dr Charles Moran, made daily notes of his pathetic struggle against bodily and mental decay. On 22 September 1944, when he was seventy, he said, 'As far as my mind goes, every-thing is all right. But I feel very tired. I have a very clear impression of having finished my task. I did have a message to bring: I have one no longer. From now on I confine myself to saying "Down with these damned socialists." ' The past had marked him. He wrote to General Scobie, 'We must hold Athens. It will be a splendid feat if you can do so without bloodshed, if possible: but shed blood if it is necessary.' Speaking of these instructions in 1953, he said that he had been thinking of Balfour's words to the English authorities in Ireland: 'Do not hesitate to fire.' He added, 'This memory of a remote era haunted my thoughts.' It may be that he brought forward this recollection by way of excuse, but the fact is that he was no longer adapting himself to changing circumstances as well as once he did. At Yalta it was not his fault that he had to make great concessions to Stalin: he defended his views firmly and skilfully. But his health went on declining. His power of work diminished. He grew so garrulous and prolix that he exasperated the members of his cabinet. He had always been so taken up with his own ideas that other men's did not interest him. But now his isolation grew even more pronounced. He could no longer manage to follow an unfamiliar line of thought. And to some degree he had lost his sense of reality. Deceived by the triumphant ovations that greeted him in the London streets and the House of Commons, he believed that a Conservative success in the elections was certain. He plunged eagerly into the 1945 campaign; but he had not troubled to work out a solid programme. He did no more than cry out against the disasters that would be caused by a Labour government – it would lead to a police-state, a state that controlled everything, he said. These attacks upon the men with whom he had worked throughout the whole war were disturbing. People wondered whether his pugnacity, although it had been valuable in time of war, would not be disastrous for peace. The party's central office had been asleep since 1940, and it had lost touch with the people. The Labour Party, on the other hand, had a most attractive programme – social services, full employment, cheap living, the nationalization of certain industries. Their propaganda was very good indeed. People said, 'Labour has a programme: the Conservatives have a photo – Churchill's.'

The Labour Party's victory was overwhelming and Churchill had to resign. The defeat was very bitter to him: 'I was dismissed by the British electorate and deprived of all subsequent share in the conduct of affairs,' he wrote later. He could not bear feeling 'unemployed' and he sunk deep into melancholy. When someone suggested that he should make a lecture tour he replied, 'I refuse to be exhibited like a former prize bull whose standing depends only on his past feats.' He kept his seat in parliament, but for a while he was politically inactive. He retired to the country, where he painted and began writing his memoirs (very much inferior to his account of the 1914–18 war: his helpers' share is far more considerable). Then he took charge of the opposition, once more sitting regularly in the Commons; he attacked the government's economic measures and above all its policy of decolonization. His vehemence disturbed and worried his followers, they would have liked him to retire. In 1949 he had a slight stroke and became deaf. His memory weakened. He walked with difficulty. 'I am at the end of my tether,' he said. The disappearance of old customs such as the king's eight white horses saddened him. After the devaluation of the pound parliament was dissolved, and at the elections Labour lost ninety-five seats. Attlee remained prime minister, but Churchill could see revenge ahead and he made some brilliant speeches in the House. In 1951 the troubles in Iran and the strikes caused a fresh dissolution: the Tories won the election and Churchill again became prime minister. But his power of work had gone: five or six hours was his limit, and he left the greater part of the task to his ministers. He was always tired; he knew that his blood-pressure was too high; he often dropped asleep; and he was afraid of becoming senile. Touchingly he complained, 'Mentally I am not what I was.

Nowadays a speech to be made is a burden and a worry. Charles, tell me the truth: am I gradually going to lose all my faculties?' Yet in spite of his doctor's advice, and in spite of his poor health and his strokes, he would not give up power. The Queen made him a knight of the Garter. But on 25 June 1953 he collapsed at the end of an official dinner: as it had been in 1949, the stroke was caused by an arterial spasm. With his indistinct speech and his mouth awry, he felt that he had become 'a bundle of old rags'. He recovered, and in October he made a fifty-two-minute speech at the annual Conservative Party congress that was very much applauded. But his intervention in the House on 5 April 1954 was disastrous: during the debate on the hydrogen bomb he reduced the whole problem to a party quarrel. There were cries of 'Resign' and 'Retire'. The next day he said regretfully, 'When you are old you live far too much in the past.' But he did not loosen his grip. However, with all his ups and downs he did come to realize his state: 'Alas, I have grown so stupid! Is there nothing you can do for me?' And on another occasion he said with astonishment, 'It is an extraordinary business, Charles, growing old.' Moran asked him what signs struck him most. 'All,' he replied. He did everything possible to remain in power, but he was less and less fitted for it. He took tranquillizers in order to sleep. He often had tears in his eyes. His eightieth birthday was an immense triumph. In the evening, gazing at the portrait that had been given him as a present, he said to Eden, 'It is the picture of a man who has retired. That is not like me, you must admit.' Yet the young Conservatives wanted him to go. He was making the most shocking blunders.* The crumbling of his mind was almost complete. He often dozed during cabinet meetings. In 1955 he at last made up his mind to resign. He ate and drank a good deal, but he smoked less than he had before. His sight was often disturbed; he had long periods of silence and torpor. 'Am I losing my mind?' he asked. In 1956 he had an apoplectic fit. He became completely deaf, apathetic and taciturn. He often went to the South of France, where he still read and painted a little. He was re-elected in 1959, and in the same year he went to Paris, where de Gaulle decorated him with the Cross of the Liberation. He looked very old and very tired. After this he

---

* He was thoughtless enough to say, 'In 1945, when the Germans were surrendering by the thousand, I sent Field-Marshal Montgomery a telegram asking him to store their weapons: it might become necessary to give them back to the soldiers of the Wehrmacht in the event of the Russians continuing their advance.' Called upon to explain, he offered only a feeble defence.

sank completely. He dragged on for five more years, decrepit, his faculties quite gone.

Gandhi's body never betrayed him. His vigour was even more astonishing than Clemenceau's. He had committed his entire life to a single undertaking – the liberation of India from the English – and this undertaking he carried out successfully: but his victory turned against him in the cruellest manner.

In 1919, having made up his mind to expel the English, he instituted the Satyagrana, that is to say disobedience to the harsh Rowlatt laws that they were trying to impose. He called for non-cooperation. In 1920 he became president of the All-India Independence League, and he travelled all over the country, spreading the doctrine of passive resistance. He also called for a revival of handicrafts, thus making a boycott of English goods possible. He succeeded in paralysing economic life. At the same time he was active within the body of Indian society, working to do away with prejudice against the Untouchables. He also wished to keep up the friendship between Hindus and Muslims. They had lived together on good terms for a very long while, but in the twentieth century serious tensions appeared between the middle classes of the two communities in the towns, where they competed for influence and position. In 1924 Gandhi undertook a prolonged fast in order to bring them together: it lasted for three weeks, and during this time Gandhi lived with a Muslim. Yet since he was himself very pious, he gave his movement a deeply religious character. 'Sometimes I was worried by the way religion was taking an increasing hold over our policy, whether it was a question of Hindus or of Muslims. I did not like it at all,' writes Nehru. He adds that at least on some points it was exceedingly difficult to induce Gandhi to change his mind. 'He was so set, so anchored in certain ideas that everything else seemed unimportant. ... Once the means were good, the end must necessarily be good too.'

When he was seventy, Gandhi was more persuaded of this than ever. His splendid health had resisted the many very severe fasts he had undergone; he could endure long walks, heat and discomfort; he was venerated by one and all, and he wanted to live to be a hundred and twenty-five. But whereas Gandhi believed in a unifying nationalism, Jinnah, the Muslim leader, wanted the partition of India – the creation of a Muslim state. After the Second World War the English agreed to withdraw, and they encouraged the formation of a provisional government: but the Muslims refused to take part in it – they claimed the provinces in which the majority of the inhabitants were of their religion. The most horrible massacres broke out: in Calcutta there were thousands of deaths on either side, and in Bihar ten thousand Muslims were killed. By this time Gandhi was seventy-seven; he travelled to the region of Noaklabi, where Hindus had taken refuge, and he visited forty-nine villages, preaching non-violence and often staying with Muslims. Fresh massacres followed one another in the Punjab and at Delhi. On his seventy-eighth birthday Gandhi said, 'There is nothing in my heart but anguish. I have lost all desire to live long.' He also said, 'I am not in agreement with what my dearest friends are doing.' And again, 'In India as we see it today, there is no place for me. . . . I have not the least wish to live if India is to be overwhelmed by a flood of violence.' All the letters he received now were full of hatred: hatred from the Hindus because he blamed their violence, from the Muslims because he was against their splitting of the country. The members of Congress were convinced that partition was the only way of avoiding a civil war, and finally they voted for it on 14 June 1947. Gandhi was 'reduced to despair'. For him partition was a 'spiritual tragedy'. On the day he had been waiting for all his life, the day of the proclamation of independence – 15 August 1947 – he refused to take part in the ceremonies. The Indians had betrayed those principles of non-violence which, in his eyes, counted for more than independence itself. 'If God loves me, He will not leave me on earth for more than a moment longer,' he said. He visited refugee-camps, he made public speeches, he did everything to reconcile the two communities: in vain. In Pakistan the Hindus were massacred; in India the Muslims; and in both countries the Sikhs. 'Has something gone wrong inside me?' Gandhi asked himself. He had always tried to live in harmony, but now he observed that he was 'far from being in possession of his equilibrium'. The longed-for independence brought him nothing but despair. And he died a violent death, murdered by a Hindu who looked upon him as a traitor.

He was the victim of that counter-closure which Sartre has described and which is an inescapable moment in the course of history – praxis is frozen into the practico-inert, and in this form it is taken up again by the world as a whole, which distorts and falsifies its meaning. A man who dies young cannot be present at this reversal: but it inevitably happens in the course of time. Einstein was an innocent victim of this. Gandhi's responsibility, on the other hand, is perfectly clear. Nehru had had a terrible foreboding of the catastrophe that was about to unleash the religious fanaticism that Gandhi was stirring up: whereas Gandhi, utterly set in the idea of non-violence, could not see the degree of violence that was smouldering within the two communities. He put principle before reality, the means before the end: and the result was a contradiction of his whole lifetime's purpose. There are not many fates more tragic for a man than that of seeing his course of action fundamentally perverted in the very moment of accomplishment.

It is not by mere chance that these three old ages ended in failure. The politician is created to make history and to be killed by history. He is the embodiment of a certain moment in it, and whatever he does he can no longer free himself from that moment. Even if he were to adapt himself to the new state of events, for the public he would still be the man of some given strategy, method or decree. Clemenceau was the man of the war: the post-war period at once set him aside. In the same way Churchill, who led England to victory, found that his country looked upon him as out of date once the victory was won. Gandhi led India to independence; but independence created a situation that required the renouncement of all his principles. There are some old people who manage to close their eyes to the harsh contradiction of events: the only result is that they look even more antiquated.

Old politicians who have fallen from office, being thrust out so that a policy, a line that is not theirs may be followed, are full of reproach for the present and they foresee no good in the near future; at all events, action is not the same as a body of work – it can only survive in memory, never in a material shape; and all the man of action can hope to leave the future generations, further along the unpredictable course of history, is the memory of what he accomplished and of what he was like. Most of them attach the utmost importance to this. When they have been set aside from power, and sometimes even when they are still exercising it, they write memoirs that are always vindications of themselves and attacks upon their opponents – memoirs whose historical value is usually dubious. Before posterity they plead their cause against the present age which, as they see it, has not done them full justice.

We see that in almost every field, apart from a few rare exceptions, the elderly man's relationship to the time in which he lives is profoundly altered. And the curious phrase 'in my time' is an expression of this alteration: in *Blanche ou l'oubli* Aragon remarks upon its strangeness. The time that a man looks upon as his own is that at which he conceives and carries out his projects: then there comes a period when they close behind him. Now, as far as he is concerned, the time belongs to the younger men; it is the time in which they fulfil themselves by their activities and which they bring to life with their projects. The elderly man, unproductive and powerless, sees himself as a left-over from a former age. That is why he so readily turns towards the past: that was the time that belonged to him, the time when he looked upon himself as a first-class individual, a living being.

His time was also the period which was inhabited by people of his own age. Loss by death is less usual now than it used to be. Formerly, the average man of fifty had mourned his parents, his aunts and uncles, several of his brothers and sisters, no doubt his wife, and some of his children. Life was a series of funerals, and living to be old was a condemnation to loneliness. Nowadays, as far as their families are concerned, many people of fifty have lost only their grandparents. But if a man reaches seventy or eighty, he will have seen most of his contemporaries die, and he will drift alone in a century peopled by those younger than himself. Even at my age, my relationship with the various generations has quite changed: there is only one left that is older than mine; it is exceedingly sparse, and death lies in wait for it. My own, once so busily teeming, has been severely thinned. What I used to look upon as the young generation is now made up of mature men, fathers and even grandfathers, thoroughly settled in life. If I want to know the really youthful point of view on some subject I have to ask the generation below. In a few years I shall reach what Madame de Sévigné called 'the position of oldest member in our family'. From that stage onwards there is the threat of loneliness and the unhappiness that comes with it. In 1702 the eighty-two-year-old Ninon de Lenclos sadly observed that those who live long 'have that melancholy privilege of remaining alone in a new world'.* From the dreary castle in which he was shut up, Casanova wrote, 'The greatest misfortune a man can have is to

---

* It will be remembered that Swift foresaw this banishment in his description of the Struldbrugs.

outlive all his friends.' In *La Vie de mon père* Rétif speaks of a very old man with the utmost respect; but this ancient says to a youth, 'Boy, do not envy either my fate or my old age. It is forty years now since I lost the last of my childhood friends; it is forty years since I have been as it were a stranger in the midst of my own country and my own family. There is no one left who looks upon me as his equal, his friend and his companion. Too long a life is a curse.' He says that he has not the least feeling for his great-grandchildren, and they for their part take no notice of him. 'That is the truth, my good friend, and not the comfortable words of our town talkers.'

An aged man has not only seen the people of his particular generation die: very often a completely different world has taken the place of his own. As we have seen, some old people welcome this change with pleasure and even with pride – but only in so far as it does not challenge their past. If it calls all that they have done, believed and loved into question, they feel themselves exiled.

This is one of the sides of old age that struck Balzac and that he described with particular success – the aged man survives both his time and himself. Thus we have Colonel Chabert, who was thought to have been killed at Eylau and who comes back to Paris after years of wandering to make himself known and to recover his wife and his fortune once more. His physical appearance itself shows his condition: 'The old soldier was lean and gaunt. He purposely drew the hair of his wig over his forehead and this lent him a certain mystery. His eyes seemed to be covered by a transparent film. . . . His pale, livid, hatchet-face . . . looked dead. The hat-brim that covered the old man's forehead threw a black furrow across the top of his face, and although it was natural, the sharp contrast of this odd effect emphasized the white wrinkles, the frigid curves and the blanched impression of this cadaverous visage. And lastly the absence of all movement in his person and of all warmth in his eye matched his curious look of melancholy decorum.' His wife, remarried and wealthy, refuses to give Chabert the money that belongs to him but that is in her possession. He has not the strength for litigation: 'He was bordering upon one of those illnesses for which medicine has no name . . . a disease that should be called depression's own depression.' Out of generosity he decided to remain legally dead. But his wife's behaviour fills him with such disgust that he thinks of suicide. He disappears, becoming a tramp by the name of Hyacinthe, and eventually he ends up in the Bicêtre asylum.

436

Another of these survivors is Facino Cane. The narrator catches sight of him playing a clarinet at a wedding-feast.

Imagine the plaster mask of Dante lit by the red light of an oil-lamp and crowned by a forest of silvery-white hair. His blindness increased the harsh, bitter and painful impression of this splendid head, for thought had brought the dead eyes to life once more. A kind of burning gleam came from them, a fire produced by the single, incessant desire engraved on that domed forehead, marked by furrows that ran across from side to side like the lines of masonry in an ancient wall. There was something magnificent and despotic in this aged Homer who had within himself an Odyssey doomed to oblivion. It was so true a nobility of mind that it still triumphed over his extreme degradation, so undying a despotism that it overcame even poverty. Not one of those violent passions that lead a man either to good or evil, turning him either into a galley-slave or a hero, was lacking in that nobly-carved, lividly Italian face with its greying eyebrows throwing their shadow into its cavernous hollows. There was a lion in that iron cage, a lion that had exhausted its vain fury against the iron of its bars. The fire of despair had died away, leaving only ashes; the lava had cooled; but the ridges, the shattered landscape and a little smoke still bore witness to the fury of the eruption, the ravages of the blaze.

The man was in fact the descendant of a Venetian noble; after a life of wild adventures he found himself penniless and blind. With him as with Chabert, survival goes hand in hand with a degradation through which nobility of mind is clearly to be seen.

The strange and disturbing old man whom Balzac describes at the beginning of *Sarrasine* should also be mentioned.

A creature for whom the human language has no name, a form without substance, a being without life or a life without motion. . . . He wore black silk breeches that flapped about his fleshless thighs in folds like those of a windless sail. An anatomist, seeing the frail legs that propped up this strange body, would at once have detected the signs of a terrible wasting disease. You would have said two bones set crosswise on a grave. When the inevitable attentive glance revealed the marks that decrepitude had set upon this fortuitous mechanism, one's heart was seized with a feeling of deep horror for mankind. The unknown was wearing a white gold-embroidered waistcoat in the fashion of former times and his linen was brilliantly laundered. A brownish jabot of English lace, rich enough to make a queen envious, hung in yellow ruffles on his chest; but on him this lace was more of a rag than an ornament. In the middle of the jabot a diamond of inestimable worth blazed like the sun. This antiquated luxury, this tasteless, solid wealth threw the face of that strange being into even stronger relief. The frame was worthy of the portrait. The blackish, angular face was full of hollows. The chin was hollow; the temples were hollow; the eyes were lost in their yellow-ish sockets. The jawbones, protruding because of this indescribable thinness, outlined hollows in the middle of either cheek. . . . The years had stuck the fine, yellow skin of this face so firmly to the bones that it was criss-crossed in every direction with innumerable wrinkles . . . as deep and close-packed as the leaves at the cut edge of a book. . . . But what helped most to give this apparition before us the look of an artificial creation was the rouge and the powder with which he was adorned. . . . His cadaverous skull was hidden by a blond wig whose innumerable curls betrayed an extraordinary pretentiousness.

Balzac describes the jewels that he wore all over his person. 'And lastly, this sort of Japanese idol kept his blueish lips in a set, de-termined smile. When the old man turned his eyes towards the company, it looked as though these wholly lustreless globes were moved by some invisible coupling device.' This man had once been the famous castrato Zambinella, who, dressed as a woman, had sung in the theatres of Rome. He had been overwhelmingly beautiful, a heart-breaker, and men had killed themselves for him. One, the sculptor Sarrasine, had foretold his appalling fate. 'Surely letting you live means condemning you to something worse than death.'

Tolstoy drew an excellent picture of a man of the eighteenth century stranded in the nineteenth: this was the old Prince Bolkonski, Prince André's father. His description was based upon what he had been told about his own maternal grandfather, Nikolai Volkonski, who had tyrannized over his daughter, Tolstoy's mother; and this daughter too had had a French governess, Mademoiselle Henissienne. The portrait there has a documentary value. The old prince wears a laced coat and he powders his hair: when he appears one feels trans-ported to another century. He has good teeth and excellent general health. He no longer has any real influence in society, but he is re-spected. He is regular and orderly beyond reason; he surrounds him-self with unchanging ceremony and his exacting severity is the terror of his household. He still has some occupations and even gives up a good deal of his time to them; but there is something old-fashioned, out of date about them – he builds, he plants, and above all he shuts himself up in his laboratory to devote himself to experiments, in the manner of the scientific amateurs of the eighteenth century. Faithful to the old customs and a prisoner of the prejudices of his own day, he jeers at the soldiers of the new school and he does not take Bonaparte seriously. One morning as he is dressing he asks his son to explain the plans for the next campaign, but he does not listen. He is fully informed about the military and political situation, but he looks upon the modern world with irony and scorn. He has 'a cold, harsh and disagreeable laugh'. The old prince is a domestic tyrant, terrorizing his daughter Marie, crushing her and refusing to be parted from her. Because of him she never marries. He is furious when his son wants to remarry with Natasha and receives her with so poor a welcome, wearing a dressing-gown and a nightcap and making unpleasant remarks, that she leaves the house, deeply wounded. As he grows older he keeps his health, losing only one tooth; but he becomes more and more easily vexed and more and more sceptical about what happens in the world. Then his health declines a little and he accuses his daughter of irritating him on purpose. André takes his sister's side: at first this embarrasses the old prince and he looks awkward, but then he bursts out, 'Get out! Never set foot in here again.' His mind weakens. He lets Mademoiselle Bourienne, the French governess, get round him. He has sudden strange whims, shutting himself up in his study for a week, and then returning to his building and his plantations. He will not talk to Mademoiselle Bourienne, nor to his daughter. He pretends to take no notice of the war. He is always busy; he sleeps little and he changes bedrooms every night. At a time when the enemy is already on the Dnieper he asserts that they will never cross the Niemen. He takes less and less account of reality. His son sends him a disturbing letter and he says that it is news of a French defeat. Then he reads it again and all at once he understands the danger; he orders his daughter to leave and makes a violent scene when she refuses to abandon him, although at heart he is really very pleased. When the French come he puts on his full-dress uniform with all his decorations in order to go to see the commanding general. But on the way he has a stroke and for three weeks he lies with his right side paralysed. He has much pain, and he tries in vain to speak. Now his daughter's devoted self-sacrifice moves him: he strokes her hair. He manages to whisper, 'Thank you for everything.' He asks to see his son and then remembers that he is with the army. 'Russia is lost; *they* are the cause of its loss,' he says in an undertone, the *they* stressing his hostility to an age that he does not acknowledge as his own. And he bursts into tears. Then he grows calmer and a little later he dies, leaving his small, wizened body there on the bed.

A survivor: for the outside world he is a dead man under suspended sentence. But is that his own view of himself? How does he feel the approach of his end? The social context has an influence upon the aged person's relationship with death. In some societies the whole population lets itself perish with indifference – an indifference caused either by extreme physical decay or by circumstances that take away all desire to live – and in this case death is no problem for anyone. Others surround it in old age with a ritual that enhances it to such a degree that it seems desirable; although indeed there are some individuals who would prefer to elude it. Death does not wear the same face in traditional societies, where the father reckons upon his life's work being carried on by his children, and in the industrial societies of our time. Yet death has one element that runs throughout all history: by destroying our organism it wholly does away with our being in the world.* From the most ancient times to our own, there are constant factors in all the evidence that describes the attitude of the aged confronted with death.

This attitude varies according to age. A child is utterly overwhelmed by the revelation of death. The young man loathes the idea of it, although he is more capable of facing it freely than others. He revolts at the forcible taking of his life; but often enough he hesitates neither to risk it nor to give it. The reason is that he values it so highly only because he intends it for something other than itself; his love for life is made up of a generosity that may lead him to sacrifice it. The fully-grown man is more prudent. He is possessed by his interests, and it is because of them that he refuses to disappear – what would become of his family, his property, his undertakings? He does not often think of his end because he is taken up by his occupations, but he avoids incurring risk and he pays attention to his health.

For the aged person death is no longer a general, abstract fate: it is a personal event, an event that is near at hand. 'The notion of life as a grant in perpetuity – the illusion in which most men live – is one that I possess no more,' wrote Edmond de Goncourt in his *Journal* on 17 August 1889. Every old man knows that he will die soon. But

---

* Even if one hopes to live again in another world, death means being torn from this one.

what does *knowing* mean in this case? Take the negative turn of Goncourt's remark: he no longer believes that he is immortal. But just how does a man look upon himself as mortal?

Death belongs to that category in which we have placed old age and which Sartre calls the 'unrealizables'; the for-itself can neither reach death nor project itself towards it; death is the external limit of my possibilities and not a possibility of my own. I shall be dead for others, not for myself: it is the Other who is mortal in my being. I know that I am mortal, just as I know that I am old, by adopting the outsider's view of me. This knowledge is therefore abstract, general, and assumed from without. My 'mortality' is in no way the object of any close, inward experience. I am not unaware of it; in practical life I take it into account in my plans and my decisions, in so far as I treat myself as an Other: but I do not *feel* it. I may try to come closer to it by fantasies, by imagining my corpse and the funeral ceremonies. I may meditate upon my absence: but it is still I who meditate. In the very heart of my projects my death obsesses me as their inescapable reverse, their negative aspect: but I shall never realize it; I do not realize my mortal state.

Just as old age, that unrealizable, may be assumed in different manners, so its relationship with that other unrealizable death is not determined in advance. Every individual elects it in accordance with his situation as a whole and with his former choices. An elderly man who still feels young will revolt at the near approach of death as violently as a forty-year-old with an incurable disease. He has not changed; his vitality and his interest in the world are undiminished; and now a sentence from the outside tells him that his expectation of life is reduced to ten years or so! Casanova, who could not bear being called old, remained intensely curious about the future in spite of his sadness, loneliness and decline. 'Death, Oh cruel death!' he wrote at the age of seventy, 'Death is a monster that expels the intent spectator from the great theatre before the end of a play that interests him beyond measure. This alone is reason enough to make it hated.' Before the 1940 war, when he too was seventy, Wells likened himself to a child who is sent to bed just after having been given some wonderful toys. 'I have not the least wish to put my toys away. I hate the idea of going.' Even if he is fully aware of his age, so long as a man is involved in some undertaking he will hate the death that annihilates it – there was Renoir, for example, who never wanted to stop painting and painting better.

It may happen that as the years go by, this repugnance may diminish. Swift, mentally and physically broken, wrote to Bolingbroke, 'When I was your age I thought often about death; but now, after these last ten years or so the thought never leaves me, yet it terrifies me less. From this I conclude that Providence reduces our fear at the same time that it reduces our strength.' Here the pessimistic Swift displays a singular optimism in supposing the existence of a providential balance between our physiological state and our dread. We must seek another explanation for the apparently paradoxical fact that very often the nearer it is, the less death terrifies. Freud supposed* that as the years piled up, so the 'death-wish' prevailed over the desire to live. But most psychoanalysts have given up this idea: Freud does not explain the relationship between age and the death-wish. How does it come about then that indifference to death should increase with time?

The truth of the matter is that the idea of death's coming closer is mistaken. Death is neither near nor far: it *is* not. Over all living beings, whatever their age, there hangs an inescapable exterior fate: in no case is there a set moment at which this fate will strike. The old man knows that he will die 'soon': the fatality is as present at seventy as it is at eighty, and the word 'soon' remains as vague at eighty as it was at seventy. It is not correct to speak of a relationship with death: the fact is that the old man, like all other men, has a relationship with life and with nothing else. What is in question is his will to survive. The phrase 'putting an end to it all' or 'finishing with life' expresses its meaning very well. The positive significance of accepting or wishing for death is accepting or wishing for 'an end to it all', a 'finishing with life'. It is natural that as the decline of old age grows worse and worse, so life should seem less and less bearable.

To realize the truth of this, one has but to remember the evils and the mutilations that this decline brings with it. In the first place there is physical suffering. Freud admitted this: it was suffering and not the death-wish that made him desire to leave the world† – a desire common to all whose bodies torture them. Then again, too long a life means outliving all those one loves. Some old men who are basically

* In 1920, when he wrote *Beyond the Pleasure-Principle*. At that time he thought that every living being had a fundamental tendency to return to the inorganic state. He repeated this assertion up to the end of his life. Yet some of his letters show that at times he doubted the truth of the proposition.

† Cf. p. 524.

selfish or who are wholly taken up by their projects, like Tolstoy, cultivate their insensitivity and resign themselves to these losses with ease. Others, whose affections are more committed, find that bereavement takes away all wish to remain alive. After Juliette's death, Victor Hugo began to long for the end. And death was all that Verdi looked forward to, once he had lost his wife.

When the world alters entirely or displays itself in such a way that remaining in it becomes unbearable, a young man can hope for a change: an old man cannot, and all that is left for him is to wish for death, as did Anatole France, Wells and Gandhi. Or else it is his own situation that the elderly man finds painful and that he can no longer hope to transcend. In his *Journal* for 3 April 1894 Goncourt wrote, 'What with my state of continual suffering, with this series of crises, coming one after the other every week, with the unsuccess of my latest literary efforts, with the overwhelming new popularity of people in whom I see no kind of talent whatsoever, and God help me, with a certain uncertainty about the real depth of my closest friendships, death seems less black to me than it did a few years ago.'

Above all, even if the old person is struck by no particular misfortune, he has usually either lost his reasons for living or he has discovered their absence. The reason why death fills us with anxiety is that it is the inescapable reverse of our projects: when a man is no longer active in any way, when he has ceased all undertakings, all plans, then there remains nothing that death can destroy. It is usual to put forward wearing-out and fatigue as an explanation for the way some old people resign themselves to death; but if all a man needed was to vegetate he could put up with this life in slow motion. But for man living means self-transcendence. A consequence of biological decay is the impossibility of surpassing oneself and of becoming passionately concerned with anything; it kills all projects, and it is by this expedient that it renders death acceptable.

Even if the elderly man does retain some health and strength and if society does not suddenly tear him from his occupation, his desires and his projects, as we have seen, wither away because of his finitude. The programme laid down in our childhood allows us to do, know, and love only a limited number of things; when this programme is fulfilled and when we have come to the end of our possibilities, then death is accepted with indifference or even as a merciful release – it delivers us from that extreme boredom that the ancients called *satietas vitae.* Gide found it hard to bear the end of his life, which was condemned to repetition, to treating the same subject again and again. He knew that he no longer had anything to say or to discover. On 7 September 1946 he wrote, 'I believe I am sincere when I say that death does not frighten me very much.' And when he was eighty, in *Ainsi soit-il,* 'My want of physical and intellectual appetite has increased to such a degree that I can hardly tell what keeps me alive, unless it is the mere habit of living. Wholly resigned to death.' At the age of eighty, Churchill said, 'I don't mind dying. I've seen everything there was to see.' Taken literally, the remark is stupid – he had not seen the world of tomorrow. It is easier to understand Casanova's complaint at being thrust out before the end of the show. But in fact it is Churchill who was right: he would have seen this new world with an old man's eyes; he would have understood it according to the views that he had always held; he would have comprehended only that part which resembled what had gone before, what had already been seen. The rest would have escaped him.

It is for a somewhat different reason that the idea of death saddens less than it did in former times: death is absence from the world, and it was that absence that I could not resign myself to. But by now so many absences have torn their gaps in me! My past is absent; absent are my friends who have died and those I have lost; absent too so many places in the world to which I shall never return again. When total absence has swallowed everything, it will not make so very great a difference.

There are some old people who are eaten up by fear of death. I have been told of a rich, active, well-known man of ninety-one, married to a very young wife; every night when he goes to bed he is devoured by the most terrible anxiety of mind. Its expression takes the form of worrying about what will happen to his wife after he dies. He knows perfectly well that she will mourn for him, but that since she is young, beautiful and wealthy her future is assured. It is really for himself that he is terrified. Yet psychiatrists state that an old person is haunted by death only if he has had a morbid dread of it in the past. Clinical experience shows that obsession with death, like the other neuroses, has its roots in childhood and adolescence.*

* According to the American psychoanalyst Martin Grotjhan, old men's castration-anxieties should be analysed before their death-anxieties: the latter often conceal a castration-anxiety which revives that of childhood to such an extent that it causes a longing for death.

It is often bound up with notions of culpability: if the subject is a believer, he is terrified by the idea of being thrown into hell.

According to the evidence that I have collected, fear of death is usually not the reverse of a passionate love for living: far from it. 'The idea of death haunted me, because I did not love life,' writes Sartre, speaking of his childhood. Just as solicitous parents and married couples are not those who love most but those who are conscious of something lacking at the core of their feelings, so the people who most persistently brood upon their death are those who are ill-adapted and uneasy in their minds. And we should not believe that those who, like Lamartine, perpetually clamour for it, really desire their death: all their incessant talking shows is that they are obsessed by it.

In my opinion, the idea that it is unusual for the old to be seriously worried by the prospect of death is confirmed by the way they neglect their health. As we have seen, they take advantage of the ambiguity between old age and illness: but this ambiguity would not be maintained if the elderly man were in fact gripped by the fear of death.

Research-workers questioned the inmates of a CNRO home: did they think about death? And what was the nature of their thoughts? Here are their replies. 'You have to come to it one day.' 'You think about it: you often think about it.' 'When I can't get my breath it would be a release.' 'When I'm low-spirited, I think about it.' 'It's better to die than to suffer.' 'It's the natural end.' 'Some people think about it: but it doesn't worry me.' 'For my part I don't think about it at all. We're here so as to make room for others.' 'I've already bought myself a grave.' 'Everyone knows you have to die.' 'I often think about it. For me it would be a happy release.' 'I don't think about it. People are always dying.' 'That's life. Death is the continuation of life. You think about it when you're low.' 'It's not right to know just when you're going to die.' 'We must all come to it one day.' 'I do think about it since I've been here. I thought about it less when I lived in the town. I shouldn't like to drag on, suffering.' 'I think about it pretty often.' 'Rich or poor, we all come to it. That's the way life is.' 'It's sad. In the Home some people younger than me have died.' 'One must come to it.' How far are these answers sincere? The subject may cheat out of a feeling of shame, or to hide his anxiety from himself, or to put a good face upon it. But their similarities are significant. Death seems preferable to suffering. Death comes to mind when one is low-spirited: it does not appear that it is death which causes the lowness of spirit but rather that it reveals itself in its threatening absurdity when the present has a harsh, ill-omened aspect. Death is not an object of anxiety. People worry about clearly-defined realities that are outside their control, such as health, money and the immediate future. Death belongs to another species. Because it is an unrealizable, it appears as a vague and indefinite future event. Its inevitability is grasped from without. 'Rich or poor, we all come to it.' One thinks about it, but without reaching a true comprehension.

'It's not right to know just when you're going to die.' This reply is full of meaning. If the moment were fixed and near at hand, instead of being lost in the misty future, there is no doubt that the old person's attitude would be different. In the *Alcestes* Euripides observes that old men complain of their state and say that they long for death: when they are brought to the point they change their minds. Admetes' father stubbornly refuses to take his son's place and go down to Hades. The aged Tolstoy said that he did not care one way or the other about dying, but he irritated Sonia by the care he took of his health. 'All old people cling to life more than children and they leave it with less good will, a poorer grace,' says Rousseau in the *Rêveries*. 'The reason is that all their labour has been directed towards this same life of theirs, and at its end they see that theirs was labour lost.' There is some bias in these words; Rousseau felt that one should enjoy the present rather than sacrifice it to a future that would be swallowed by the void. In fact it is not resentment at having worked in vain that makes death hated. And this refusal of death is not invariable. But it is quite true that a fair number of old people do hold on to life even when they have lost all reasons for living: in *Une Mort très douce* I described the way my mother, at seventy-eight, clung to it to the very end. So it is the subject's biological state or what is vaguely termed his vitality that determines his refusal or his acceptance. My mother was as religious as my grandmother, for whom leaving the world was restful; yet she had an animal fear of death. Many old people are afraid, and being afraid is the realization in one's own body of the refusal to die. What often makes death easier for old people is the fact that illness wears them out in the end, and that they do not fully understand what is happening to them.

Yet there are also clear-minded and peaceful deaths: when all desire to live is physically and spiritually gone, the old person prefers an everlasting sleep to the daily struggle or boredom. The proof that in old age death does not appear as the greatest of evils is the number of old people who decide 'to put an end to it all'. In the conditions that society provides for them today, living on is a pointless trial, and it is understandable that many should choose to shorten it.

7

Old age and everyday life

Lessened, impoverished, in exile in the present day, the aged man still remains the man he was. How does he manage to deal with a situation of this kind in his daily life? What opportunities does it leave him? What defences can he put up? Can he adapt himself to it, and if so at what price?

Since every qualification is at the same time a limitation, might it not be supposed that in losing his qualifications the individual finds the world more open to him? He is not required to work; he is no longer intent upon the future: does he not therefore enjoy a freedom that allows him to take his ease in the present? When he was eighty Claudel wrote in his *Journal*, 'Some sigh for yesterday! Some for tomorrow! But you must reach old age before you can understand the meaning – the splendid, absolute, unchallengeable, irreplaceable meaning of the word today!' Some say that when they are old they find happiness in the very act of living. 'Never,' says Jouhandeau, 'have I felt myself attached to life by so slender a thread, so slender that it might snap at any moment. It is this that crowns my joy in still being.' And again, 'Survival is extraordinary. You are no longer attached to anything and yet you are more sensitive to all.' Mauriac* says more or less the same thing: 'I do not feel detached from anyone or any thing. But from now on living will be enough to keep me occupied. This blood which still flows in the hand I lay upon my knee, this sea I feel beating within me, this transitory, not eternal ebb and flow, this world so close to its end – all these insist upon being watched every moment, all these last moments before the very last: that is what old age is.' 'I should like to think of nothing at all except that I exist and that I am here.'

It is old age far more than youth, therefore, which would appear to be the time of *carpe diem* – the moment when 'you reap what you

* *Nouveaux Mémoires intérieurs.*

448

have sown' as Fontenelle says, and 'The time of enjoyment, no longer that of toil,' according to d'Aubigné. This is untrue. The society of today, as we have seen, allows old people leisure only when it has removed the material means for them to enjoy it. Those who escape utter poverty or pinching want are forced to take care of a body that has grown frail, easily fatigued, often infirm or racked with pain. Immediate pleasures are either forbidden or parsimoniously measured out: love, eating, drinking, smoking, sport, walking. Only the privileged can do something to avoid these frustrations; for example, they can go out for a drive in a car instead of walking.

But even for these it is doubtful whether the enjoyment of the present moment is very great. Many aged writers complain of the aridity of their days. 'Time has taken my hands in his. There is nothing left to pluck in these barren, flowerless days,' says Chateaubriand. According to him it is the weight of the past that darkens the present. 'When you have seen Niagara there are no more waterfalls. My memory never stops setting one journey of mine against another; one range of mountains against the next; and my life is destroying my life. The same thing happens to me with regard to men and to society.' Stendhal, although he was not really old, complained in *Promenades dans Rome*, 'Alas! In one aspect all knowledge is like old age, whose worst symptom is that *knowledge of life* which prevents one from becoming passionately concerned, from behaving madly over nothing. Having seen Italy, I should have liked to find the waters of Lethe at Naples, to have forgotten everything, then to have started travelling all over again and so to have spent my days.' Schopenhauer expresses a similar point of view. 'Old age is only half aware of life. . . . Inperceptibly the mind so loses its edge from long habit of the same perceptions that to an ever increasing extent things glide over it without leaving any impression.' In *La Mise à mort* Aragon speaks nostalgically of 'that vanished freshness of the world', and in *Le Roman inachevé* he writes:

> Je me sens étranger toujours parmi les gens
> J'entends mal, je perds intérêt à tant de choses,
> Le jour n'a plus pour moi ses doux reflets changeants;
> Le printemps qui revient est sans métamorphose,
> Il ne m'apporte plus la lourdeur des lilas;
> Je crois me souvenir lorsque je sens les roses.*

* Among people I always feel a stranger: I hear badly, I lose interest in so many things; for me the day no longer has its gentle shifting lights; returning spring is not

Jouhandeau was also conscious of this swallowing up of the present by a too-strongly experienced past. 'As one grows older, everything, even the present, takes on the appearance of something recalled. One looks upon oneself as already belonging to the past.' No one has better expressed this attrition of the world and the sadness it causes than Andersen in a letter he wrote when he was sixty-nine. 'If I go into the garden and walk among the roses, what have they (and even the snails on their stalks) to say to me that they have not already said? If I look at the broad leaves of the water-lilies, I remember that Thornbeline's journey is already ended. If I listen to the wind it has already told me the story of Valdemar Daae, and it has no better tale to tell. Under the old oak-tree in the woods I remember that long ago it told me the last of all its dreams. So no new impression comes to me; and it is sad.'

How are we to explain this silence on the part of things? Chateau-briand, having spoken of the very real 'desert of the past', contradicts himself when he claims that our memories may wipe out our present perceptions. They have in fact a greater clarity and intensity. In one way, Stendhal's wish is granted – we do drink the waters of Lethe. Every year I see Rome with the same delight; the Rome of the present moment prevails over all the pictures of it I had retained; and indeed the confused recollection of former impressions rising through the present enriches and adorns the city. It was thanks to this intensity of the present that Aragon was able to end the poem whose beginning I have just quoted,

> Quand je croyais le seuil de l'ombre outrepassé
> Le frisson d'autrefois revient dans mon absence
> Et comme d'une main mon front est caressé.
> Le jour, au plus profond de moi, reprend naissance.*

Our memories cannot take away the value of our present experience; it is rather the consciousness of having forgotten so much that diminishes it – we shall forget this too. When one is young one does not suppose that one is going to remember everything, and for ever; but one does escape from time because there is an infinite future at one's disposal. The passing moment took my breath away when I

* When I thought the threshold of darkness had been crossed, in my absence the thrill of former times comes back and my forehead is stroked as though by a caressing hand. In my deepest heart day is reborn.

a time of metamorphosis, it no longer brings me the lilac's heavy scent; and when I smell a rose it seems to me that this is only memory.

thought I saw eternity within it – it could never, never be wiped out. Since I have come to see that my future has an end, moments are no longer eternal; they no longer give me the absolute: they will wholly vanish, or else they will fall into ashes that my grave will swallow together with my person. During his long, aimless walks, Rousseau used to delight in the free wandering of his dreaming mind; returning to Madame de Warens' house at a time when he was no longer in love with her he found the precision of his goal oppressive to his imagination – the charm had vanished. 'I was where I was; I was going where I was going, never farther.' This barrenness is the fate of many of us after the age of sixty – we are too well aware of where we are going. On 10 May 1925 Freud wrote to Lou, 'The change is not perhaps very obvious; everything is still as interesting as it was and qualities have not undergone important modifications either; but something in the nature of a resonance is lacking. I am no musician, yet here I feel the same difference that there is when one presses on the pedal or when one does not.' Vailland's seventy-year-old Don Cesare leads the same life that he led before, but 'his words sounded in an unechoing world.' There is a striking analogy between the two comparisons. For the young, the world has a boundless wealth of meanings and promises; the slightest incident awakens innumerable harmonics: later, when it has shrunk to the standard of our brief future, the vibrations die away.

The values and the goals we meet with outside ourselves are the fruit of our own investments. It is our want of passion, our inertia that creates emptiness around us. Andersen's roses and water-lilies fell silent because the desire to write had abandoned him. All moral doctrines confined to the moment are false because they disregard the truth of time: the three temporal 'ek-stases' can only be applied together; the present *is* not; the for-itself exists only by basing itself on the past and transcending itself towards the future, and it is by the light of our projects that the world reveals itself; if they diminish so it grows poorer. Giving up our occupations does not mean reaching idle pleasures that they have deprived us of; it means depopulating the world by sterilizing the future. If habit has made our perceptions 'lose their edge', and if things seem already to have been swallowed by the past and to have no freshness any more, it is not because we drag too great a wealth of memories with us: it is because our vision is no longer given life by fresh projects.

The aged man is no more capable than the young of being satisfied with that immobility of which Mauriac dreams when he says that 'living' would be enough to occupy him: he is himself a proof to the contrary – he never wrote so much as during these last years. To desire nothing, to do nothing means condemning oneself to the dark, evil apathy into which so many retired people sink. The unfortunate part of it is that reasons for activity are hard to find again, once former occupations are forbidden. Few indeed are those for whom leisure can mean the flowering of some hitherto frustrated vocation or the discovery of some unexpected possibilities. Two examples of this kind are very well known in America. Lilian P. Martin left the University of Stanford to become 'chief counsellor' to the aged. At sixty-five she learnt to use a typewriter, at seventy-seven to drive a car; at eighty-eight she went up the Amazon in a boat; at ninety-nine she undertook the running of a fifty-acre farm, with four sixty-year-old women to help her. The old woman they called Grandma Moses was past manual labour when she was seventy-five, so she took to painting. When she was a hundred she produced her most famous work, *Christmas Eve*. She died in New York at the age of a hundred and one.

These cases are exceptional. As we have seen, it is often impossible to open new paths even within our own praxis. How much vainer, therefore, is the claim to make an arbitrary discovery of new interests and pleasures. 'Only those pleasures in which one delighted before the age of thirty can please for ever,' observed Stendhal. Churchill devoted much of his time to painting; yet he complained, 'It is hard to find new interests at the end of one's life.'

This is why age takes the wish to learn away from us. It is very rare for a man to be like Socrates: to want to know for the sake of knowing, knowing immediately; one learns for a given end. Otherwise what is the point? The absence of project kills the desire to know: 'To tell the truth,' says the aged Saint-Evremond, 'I look for what pleases me in books more than for what teaches me. As I have less time to make use of things, so I have less curiosity to learn them.' In the *Rêveries* Rousseau makes a similar observation: 'Confined in this way within the narrow sphere of my former knowledge, I do not have the happiness that Solon knew, the happiness of learning something every day as I grow older; and indeed I have to guard against the dangerous vanity of wishing to learn what I am now no longer capable of understanding thoroughly.' One of the most striking characteristics of the old is their want of intellectual appetite, so much so that at eighty-two André Siegfried said, 'Old age is no more than the fading of curiosity.' Speaking of his father, John Stuart Mill said, 'He thought human life a poor thing, once the freshness of youth and of curiosity had withered.' For him it was perfectly natural to associate the two.

In the *Mémoires intérieurs*, and particularly in the second volume, Mauriac often remarks upon his lack of curiosity about new books and new records. He is astonished by 'the extreme preoccupation with culture and information' that Gide had retained to an advanced age. And yet even in Gide we see indifference gradually settling in. In his *Journal* for 30 July 1941 he wrote, 'The end of life. The last act rather slow: reminders of the past, repetitions. One would like some fresh unexpected turn and one does not know what to invent.' When he was eighty, in *Ainsi soit-il* he wrote, 'I do not yet feel any weakening of my intellectual powers; but what can I turn them to?'

The old man's want of curiosity and his lack of interest are aggravated by his biological condition. Paying attention to the world tires him. Often he no longer has the strength to assert even those values which gave his life a meaning. Thus when Proust saw Monsieur de Charlus for the last time, that once haughty and arrogant man had lost his aristocratic pride. Earlier he had despised Madame de Sainte-Euverte, but now, meeting her in the street he greets her as though she were a queen. 'In one stroke he utterly abolished all his former attention to rank by the sedulous timidity, the anxious zeal with which he took off his hat.' The reason for his gesture was, no doubt, says Proust, 'a kind of physical gentleness, of detachment from the realities of life that is so striking among those whom death has already taken into its shadow'.

The old man's intellectual and emotional indifference may reduce him to complete inertia. The aged Swift no longer felt concern about anything whatsoever. 'I wake in such a state of indifference to everything that may happen in the world and in my own narrow circle that . . . I should certainly stay in bed all day if decency and the fear of illness did not rouse me out of it.'

The people whose old age is most favoured are those whose interests are many-sided. It is easier for them to reconvert than for others. Clemenceau, removed from power, took to writing. A scientist who finds his scientific activity diminishing may, if he is politically committed, still find scope for his energies. Yet even in this case it is hard for a man to give up what has been the centre of his dearest interests. With most of us a vicious circle comes into being: inactivity discourages both curiosity and enthusiasm, and our indifference depopulates the world in which we no longer see any good cause for action. Death settles into us and into the things around us.

There is one passion to which the aged man is very liable – ambition. Since he no longer has any grasp on the world and since he therefore no longer knows who he is, he wishes to have the appearance of someone considerable. He has lost his image: he does his utmost to find it again outside himself. He yearns for decorations, honours, titles, an Academician's sword. Now that his vitality has died quite away, he knows nothing of the fullness of real desires or of passions that are directed at a real object: he seeks imitations. The most striking example of this was Pétain. De Gaulle, speaking of him as early as 1925, referred to 'two equally strong yet contradictory phenomena – a senile want of interest in everything and a senile ambition for everything'. These characteristics are not in fact contradictory: far from it, since each is the explanation of the other – it is because he has no concrete hold on anything that the old man desires the abstract possession of everything, that is to say of no matter what. Wanting everything in this hollow, meaningless fashion, is the same as wanting nothing at all. The same ambiguity is to be found among the very young. 'I want everything and at once,' says Anouilh's Antigone, and she says it because she possesses nothing. I remember when I was eighteen how earnestly I wrote in my diary, 'I shall say everything. I mean to tell all', whereas it so happened that I had nothing whatsoever to tell. When a man no longer really possesses either interest or curiosity or affection, then he is ripe for empty ambition and for vanity, its necessary associate.

In his younger days Pétain had an outstandingly independent mind: in his lectures he supported the theory of the counter-offensive, opposing the fashionable doctrine of offensive at any price; and he called for heavy artillery for France, a demand that made him very unpopular with the war ministry. His promotion suffered. 'I was an old lieutenant, an old captain, an old colonel: I was old in all my ranks,' he said bitterly. Those around him were struck by his coldness, his harshness and his conceit. In November 1914 Fayolle, who was his friend, wrote that Pétain 'did not hesitate to break commonplace men and to have the unreliable shot. "During the first clashes, I played a butcher's part," he said.' And in January 1915, when Pétain had twenty-five soldiers who had purposely shot themselves in the hand, bound and driven towards the enemy trenches, Fayolle wrote, 'Character, energy! Where does character stop and where does ferocity and savagery begin?' Colonel Bouvard observed that when Pétain visited the wounded 'he always remains unmoved, closed, as though he did not care.' Galliéni said of him, 'This man is a block of ice.' The bloody repressions that he ordered during the war are proof of this. Nevertheless, he did refuse to waste human material. He was looked upon as the victor of Verdun. He won the highest military distinction, the title of Marshal of France.

Earlier Fayolle had remarked, 'He thinks a very great deal of himself', and one of Pétain's officers wrote, 'He loves boasting.' As he grew older his vanity increased. Pétain, president of the *Conseil supérieur de la guerre* and Inspector-General of the army, could not forgive Foch for the glory he had won: in his speech to the *Académie français* in 1930 he blamed Foch for having signed the armistice. And he never forgave de Gaulle for having put his name alone to *La France et son armée* in 1938, a book for which he had had the idea fifteen years earlier but of which he had never written a line.

As early as 1914 he was haunted by the fear of losing his memory. And indeed it began to fail early. General Laure observed, 'His memory is weakening. For things that happened long ago, the Marshal is perfect. For recent events, he either does not take them in at all or he takes them in badly.' The reason that he no longer saw the present clearly was no doubt 'senile want of interest'. His health was splendid; Colonel Bouvard put it down to 'that indifference which makes a fine old age possible'. For his selfishness struck all who came into contact with him: 'The Marshal is now a man with a withered heart. He no longer has either generosity or resolution,' wrote de Gaulle. He had periods of abstraction, of 'not being there' that grew longer and longer. Loustanau-Lacau said that there were days when 'Closed on account of old age' should have been written across his forehead, adding, 'The arrival of the car he is waiting for interests him as much or as little as the fall of a government or the death of someone he knew.' Pétain attached an immense importance to anything that had to do with him personally; great events with no direct personal bearing left him unmoved.

He had no idea of taking power in 1938. Gustave Hervé's campaign 'We need Pétain' irritated him. Jacquinot said to him, 'You will become prime minister': he replied, 'I can only work three or four hours a day.' Yet according to de Gaulle there was no lessening of his ambition. 'Nothing and nobody will now stop the Marshal on the path of senile ambition. And his vanity is casting off all restraints. He no longer keeps his inner demons under control.' He agreed to go to Spain as ambassador to Franco. De Gaulle continued, 'He accepts the embassy. He is so overcome by senile ambition that he will accept anything at all. It is terrible and lamentable. He is no longer in a condition to take responsibilities upon himself.' In Spain the losses of memory became more frequent. 'There are two or three hours of Pétain a day,' said one of his subordinates.

His indifference to the present and his fixation on the past explain certain facts for which the words senile decay are inadequate. When he returned to Paris and was appointed minister of state in June 1940 he rarely uttered a word. Yet one day, says Laurent-Eynac, when he was asked how he explained the French collapse, he replied, 'It may be that we gave up pigeon-fanciers and their homing-pigeons too early.' He was obviously remembering the important part that these birds played during the defence of the Fort de Vaux. Senile ambition explains why he agreed to sign the armistice. But he was also convinced that the armistice signed by Foch on 11 November 1918 was a very serious mistake, one that really lost the war for France – he had wept when Foch granted it to the Germans. He supposed that the 1940 armistice would bring about a similar disaster for Germany. 'He is haunted by precedent,' said one of his intimates.

He talked incessantly about 'our country', the salvation of France and the welfare of the French; but Weygand noticed that when he signed the armistice (and its crushing terms are notorious), his face displayed a sly satisfaction – it was *he* who had been sent for to save the country. He thought he was taking a brilliant revenge upon those who had hampered his career in former days and upon those who had later claimed to share his fame. During the years that followed he let the adulation, the cheers and the outward show of power go to his head to such a degree that he could happily declare, 'I have more power than Louis XIV' at a time when he was in the hands of the Germans and when half the country was under their immediate rule. A little later he said to the Comte de Paris, 'I am renewing the royal tradition. I tour the provinces. They give me presents. It is just as it was under the kings.' Two years after the armistice Madame Pétain made this appalling remark to Monsieur and Madame Massis, 'If only you knew how happy he has been, these last two years!'

Bonhomme, who acted as his aide de camp and who was very close to him, said, 'His very old man's insensitivity is growing. With the passing of the years, disasters make less and less impression on him.' And Darlan observed, 'This man manufactures carbonic acid snow.' Nothing moved him; he was rooted in his vanity; no communication with him was possible. No event, no person could reach him. When he allowed the first measures against the Jews, General Mordacq said to him, 'Monsieur le Maréchal, you are dishonouring your uniform.' 'I don't give a damn,' he replied, he who never opened his mouth without talking about honour.

Like many very old men, he sometimes gave the appearance of feeling strong emotion; but this had no effect upon his behaviour. One of his chief assistants, Du Moulin de La Barthète, says, 'I saw this gloomy, cynical and cruel old man cry like a child when the news of the shooting of the Châteaubriand martyrs came through.' For a moment he understood that he was dishonouring himself and he spoke of surrendering himself as a prisoner. But the next day he easily let himself be dissuaded. He shed a few tears over the fate of the men from Alsace-Lorraine; but when Robert Schumann came to discuss them with with him he cut him short: 'All this business would have a bad effect on the country's position and the food-supply.' A report on the raid at the Vel' d'Hiv' seemed to touch him, but he soon recovered. 'It is true that these Jews did not always have a good influence upon France.'

His withdrawals and his deafness were often feigned – he preferred to evade dialogue. He was capable of understanding what was said to him, at least for several hours every day. But there was no longer any connexion between intelligence and will. 'The driving-belt is broken,' said Bonhomme, who also observed, 'He has become a monster of selfishness: it is his age.' When the Germans insisted upon his putting Weygand on the retired list, Bonhomme asked François Valentin, one of the chief men of the Vichy Légion, to persuade Pétain not to yield. In the presence of a dozen horrified witnesses there was a shocking scene, and Valentin went so far as to say, 'Take care, or one day the French nation will spit on your stars.' Pétain looked round the room as though for help, but he made no reply. Valentin reported, 'He is completely lucid. But age has ruined his will-power.' From time to time he said, 'I am dishonoured. I must go . . .' But he stayed.

He attached very great importance to food. When Michel Clemenceau came to beg him not to allow Reynaud and Mandel, who were imprisoned in the Fort du Portalet, to fall into the hands of the Germans, he said he was sorry but 'I can do nothing'. Then he added, 'Stay with us. Today I have some prime crayfish from Corsica.' When Colonel Solberg, speaking for the White House, asked him whether he would agree to leave for Algiers without the Germans' knowledge, Pétain would only talk about the past – the Great War, Pershing, the American expeditionary force. Then he brought a menu out of his pocket; 'Ah! We are going to have something very good today.'

He had always been much given to running after women and his sexuality had not entirely died away. 'Some evenings,' says Leroy Ladurie* who was then minister of agriculture, 'after Madame Pétain had gone to bed, we and two or three old friends would go out with the Marshal. In a bedroom in the Hôtel du Parc the wife of a well-known explorer would dance lewd, suggestive dances, naked to the waist. The old soldier delighted in the performance.'

When Hitler escaped from an attempt on his life, Pétain said he should send him a congratulatory telegram. Dr Ménétrel, his physician, who had a good deal of influence over him, urged him not to do so. In vain. He signed the telegram. Gabriel Jeantet, coming into the office, saw him. 'Monsieur le Maréchal, you are dishonouring yourself.' 'What ought I to do?' asked Pétain. 'This.' Jeantet tore the telegram to pieces. Pétain did not react. A little later, when General von Neubron was present, Pétain noticed a fly on a map of the front and crying, 'Look! A Boche! I'll kill him', he squashed it. With a civil look he added, 'One tends to generalize too much.'

When he was carried off to Sigmaringen, he stated that he looked upon himself as a prisoner. But it was in vain that Ménétrel begged him to confine himself to that role. He did not break with Brinon, whom the Germans had chosen as head of an 'imitation government'. He maintained cordial relations with Bentler-Fink, who had deceived him and had taken him to Germany by force. The heart-broken Ménétrel observed that Pétain 'always ran away from clear-cut situations', and that he did not even have 'the courage to defend his name'. Yet when he learnt that his trial was about to begin, he

---

* Quoted by Tournoux in *Pétain et de Gaulle*. Jules Roy also mentions the fact. 'If only the French knew!' said Bonhomme.

458

recovered sufficient dignity to return to France voluntarily. During the trial, once he had read out a declaration written by his counsel, he feigned deafness and replied to no questions. When it was over, he said to his lawyers, 'That was an interesting business. I learnt a great deal.'

In prison he read a little, and tried to learn English. From 1949 onwards his mind went completely. He confused the two wars. On 11 November he thumped the table, crying, 'These Germans, good God! But I beat them!'

His very last years teach us nothing: after a certain degree of mental decay, there is no point in speaking of indifference; and as for ambition, the circumstances were no longer favourable. But during the Vichy years we see as through a magnifying-glass the horror and wretchedness of that empty ambition to which many old men are a prey. They do not attempt to do anything; all that matters to them is the character which they assume and with which they merge – a character to which they are ready to sacrifice anything and everything, including the very qualities they pretend to glorify. The contradiction is glaringly obvious in the case of Pétain, the servile tool of the Germans who at the same time believed himself to be a sovereign: the words 'honour' and 'our country' were continually in his mouth, and yet he was dishonouring himself and betraying France. The pretentions and the selfishness of an ambitious man, obstinately rooted in himself and deaf to outside voices, make him dangerous if circumstances give him some degree of power.

Ambition is within the scope of only a handful of privileged men, and many are aware of its vanity. Generally speaking the old have no refuge from the emptiness of their lives. Except when rest is all their exhausted bodies long for, their lack of appetite in a dreary, faded world condemns them to boredom. Schopenhauer asserts that they are unconscious of this because for them time moves by too fast. Yet he does remember Aristotle's dictum, 'Life resides in movement.' And he himself states that 'activity is necessary to happiness'. Elsewhere he says, 'Total inactivity very soon becomes unbearable, for it begets the most horrible boredom.'

It does indeed. If life does not transcend itself, moving towards given ends, and if it falls back, dull and motionless, upon itself, then it brings about that 'nausea' which Sartre has described. Young people often feel it: they have not yet acquired any hold upon the world;

they are reduced to their mere presence; and for them, as for the aged man, the world is silent. And this silence, making a kind of ring from which they can see no escape, freezes all their hopes. I passed two or three of my youthful years in cruel boredom because I had left the world of childhood but had not yet entered that of the adults; I had no outlet of any kind and I did not suppose that anything would ever, at any time, call me out of this state. However, from this point of view there is a great difference between the young man and the old: the first is not indifferent to the world; he is stirred by vague plans and by precise desires, and he is bored only because society, his parents and his situation prevent him from launching out. As soon as this oppressive control slackens, as soon as there is some opening or favourable event or meeting, then the circle is broken and curiosity and delight in life return. Whereas the old man is bored because either circumstances or his own indifference have detached him from his projects and because his curiosity* has entirely died away. We have seen how in institutions and even outside them a horrifying gulf can open, and how boredom can become so deep that it does away with all possibility and even all desire to escape from it.

If an old man turns his back on the world in which he lives, he will find nothing in it capable of extricating him from his gloom. But even if he remains attentive to his surroundings, his life is darkened by its lack of aim. On 19 September 1941 Gide wrote, 'The spirit falls into boredom when it has no goal left, when it is a prey to leisure.' Later, in *Ainsi soit-il*, he described the extinction of all desire in himself, using the term anorexia. 'I no longer have any great curiosity about what life may still bring me. . . . I am surfeited with days and I can scarcely tell how to make use of the time that is still left to me on earth. Anorexia, boredom's hideously inexpressive face.' Sometimes he had the feeling that he was no longer numbered among the living. On 10 November 1942 he wrote, 'In a new setting, it is the same act of the same play that goes on. It is a long time now since I ceased to exist. I merely fill the place of someone they take for me.'

* When Baudelaire was still young he was subject to extreme lowness of spirits; he clearly saw the connexion between want of curiosity and boredom.

'Rien n'égale en longueur les boiteuses journées Quand sous les lourds flocons des neigeuses années

L'ennui, fruit de la morne incuriosité, Prend les proportions de l'immortalité.'

Nothing equals the length of those limping days when, beneath the heavy flakes of the snowy years, boredom, the fruit of dull incuriosity, takes on proportions of everlasting life.

The words setting and play express a feeling of becoming unreal that is even more marked in this passage from *Ainsi soit-il*: 'Yesterday in the train I suddenly found myself quite sincerely wondering whether I were really still alive. The whole world was there and I could see it perfectly well: but was it indeed myself that was seeing it?... Everything was existing and continuing to be without my help. The world had not the least need of me. And for quite a long period I withdrew myself.' Here he is describing an experience of depersonalization similar to that observed among some neurasthenics: there is nothing left that interests or stirs them; they have no projects any more; they see the world as so much pasteboard scenery and themselves as living corpses.

As to those elderly people who go on working, they often do so against a background of disillusionment because they have become aware of their limits. As we have seen, some artists excel themselves towards the end of their life: Michelangelo's last Pietà is his finest. But even then they know that they will never accomplish anything but *their* work. This wearisome monotony calls up a disconsolate 'what is the point?' This is the question that we read in Rembrandt's last self-portrait. Although he went on with his sculpture, the aged Michelangelo cast a cold eye upon his work: he called his statues his 'puppets'.

In one of his poems Yeats imagines a dialogue between a mocking spirit and an old writer. The writer begins by congratulating himself:

> 'The work is finished,' he reflected, grown old,
> 'Just as I conceived it when I was a child;
> Let fools cry out, but I have failed in nothing.
> I have brought something to perfection.'
> But louder still this spirit sang, 'What then?'

Verdi wrote his last operas, his finest, with no pleasure or delight. Old creative artists are particularly sensitive to that 'scent of sadness' which all accomplishment, all realization leaves in one's heart. They have not 'overtaken their being' and from now on they know they never will overtake it, whatever they may accomplish.

The old person is condemned to boredom because he is no longer directed to any aims nor faced with any requirements; but there is a compensation, one to which some attach great value – they no longer have to make any effort, and they are allowed to be idle. It will be remembered that what Emerson and Fontenelle admired in old age

461

was that it allowed a man to sink below himself. 'Sloth is not without its charm,' said the ageing Saint-Evremond. According to Jouhandeau the last years stand for 'the real long vacation after the strain of life, the overworking of the senses, the heart and the mind that was life'. 'The approach of old age brings a kind of absolute leisure. There is no longer the least need to exert oneself for success of any kind. . . . What a relief!' 'The privilege of old age: it has nothing either to win or to lose.' It is unusual for old people to have guilt-complexes: their age serves them as an excuse and as an alibi; and it does away with competition in their calling. It also does away with sexual competition – impotence and frigidity are justified. All shortcomings such as thoughtlessness and incompetence become normal. Some defects are eliminated: ugliness is as one might say reabsorbed by the general degrading effect of the years: indeed, there are some women who seem retrospectively beautiful, whereas their youth could make no claims at all. People who found the status of adult disagreeable and who adapted themselves poorly to it find advantage in growing old.

But they pay a high price for the indulgence they enjoy – their individual inferiorities are forgiven because they are looked upon as definitively inferior beings; they no longer have anything to lose because they have already lost everything. They are freed from their guilt-complexes: for most of them the price is a bitter feeling of decay. Middle-aged people treat them as children, as objects. The fact is that biologically, economically and socially their status has declined. All the tests to which they are submitted show a self-disgust: this is the more marked the lower their economic level has fallen, and it may bring about lasting states of depression.

'It is not death that is so grieving; it is decay,' wrote Ballanche. 'I am strongly aware of it in Madame Récamier and in Monsieur de Chateaubriand; that is to say, I am aware how strongly this sad impression exists for them.' A man who has exercised some degree of authority cannot resign himself to having lost it. Churchill clung desperately to power; Pétain preferred an ugly imitation of it to honour. Even if they keep their standing, once managing directors, industrial leaders and the heads of firms are removed from office, they are mere souls in Purgatory. Even in what seem to be unusually favourable cases, the aged person suffers from having to come down. Ninon de Lenclos, gay, agreeable, surrounded by friends, but elderly, wrote to Saint-Evremond, 'Everybody says I have less reason to complain of time than others; but however that may be, if anyone had suggested such a life to me, I should have hanged myself.' When Virginia Woolf was fifty-eight she wrote in her diary for 29 December 1940, 'I loathe the hardness of old age. I feel it coming. I creak. I am embittered.

> The foot less quick to tread the dew
> The heart less feeling to emotions new
> Crushed hope less quick to rise again

I have just opened Matthew Arnold and I have copied out these lines.'

Discontent may flare up into rebellion, as we see in Ionesco. 'How can I tolerate this situation? How can one accept living, with time bearing down on us so unbearably, like the load on an ass? Unbearable. One ought to rebel' (*Mémoires en miettes*).

And in Leiris. 'Deep in me there is something that has been destroyed and that I can never hope to see built up again: this old age that always frightened me so has at last fixed upon me, and every day I am surer that the crisis, which was as quick in passing as it was fierce in its attack, was my rear-guard fight against it, my volley in honour of the colours' (*Fibrilles*).

Rebellion is pointless; in the end a man resigns himself, but not without regret. Most old people sink into gloom. Long ago Aristotle observed, 'They can no longer laugh.' Dr Baumgartner writes, 'On the mental plane one of the clearest and most constant characteristics of the ageing man is undoubtedly the loss of gaiety.' When he was over sixty Casanova said in one of his letters, 'As far as my memoirs are concerned, I do not think I shall go on with them, for since I was fifty I have not been able to produce anything but what is sad, and that saddens me.' Ballanche wrote, 'Madame Récamier continues to take the situation sadly; Monsieur de Chateaubriand takes himself sadly; Ampère takes the world sadly. .... Sadness is creeping over me.'

Although Edmond de Goncourt speaks little of himself in his *Journal*, an underlying sadness shows through. On 17 June 1890 he wrote, 'Friends out of touch, acquaintances leaving Paris, and together with all this the weight of old age, the feeling of infirmities that show through – it fills my heart with darkness.'

During his last years Gide tried to put a good face on things, both in his *Journal* and even more in his letters. But writing from Saint-Paul-de-Vence to Martin du Gard on 1 July 1949 he said, 'Have just

463

gone through some *appalling* days of impenetrable depression, caused by a something or other in my failing heart, by the un-breathable atmosphere of this place – unbreathable for me – by my loneliness (Pierre and Claude gone off in their car for three days), by idleness. . . . *Appalling*.'

On 15 June 1950 he wrote from Sorrento, 'In spite of Catherine and Jean Lambert's being here, in spite of magnificent weather, an enchanting journey and almost satisfactory health, I have just passed through a sequence of the most distressing days of my long existence. I am not out of the tunnel yet, but at least I catch a glimpse of freedom.'

11 July 1950: 'Alas! Appetite fails, together with . . . all the rest and with curiosity. What quarter can I reasonably look to for some true, deep and lasting happiness? I can scarcely tell.'

A young woman wrote to me on the subject of her father: 'He is seventy and his only illnesses are trifling or most of the time imaginary. He is sad; more and more often he is sad. He reads sadly, as it were on the surface; he listens to us sadly; he laughs sadly. The other day he was whistling softly in his room and then suddenly he stopped. He must have said to himself, "What's the point?"'

The sadness of old people is not caused by any particular event or set of circumstances: it merges with their consuming boredom, with their bitter and humiliating sense of uselessness, and with their loneliness in the midst of a world that has nothing but indifference for them.

The decline of old age is not only distressing in itself; it also means that the elderly man is endangered in the outside world. As we have seen, he leads a very much reduced life very close to illness and on the verge of extreme poverty. He has an extremely painful feeling of insecurity, a feeling that is made all the worse by his powerlessness.

People condemned to inactivity are the prey of care. The less busy a woman is, the more she is eaten up by it. The same applies to the aged: they perpetually brood upon dangers that they have no means of averting. Even if no particular threat hangs over them, it is enough for them to know that they are defenceless to be filled with anxiety: the peace they enjoy seems to them precarious; and since they are no longer masters of it, the future is heavy with frightening possibilities. The disaster that has broken over their heads consists of their having suddenly passed from the status of a responsible adult to that of a dependent object. The dependence places them at the mercy of others, and they are most unpleasantly aware of this, even when it does not make itself apparent. This emerges from an inquiry conducted in a CNOR institution. The inmates who were questioned were in fact to stay there until their death. But they could not bring themselves to believe it. Many were afraid of being sent away and of finding themselves in the street, without any resources whatsoever. The very comfort in which they lived worried them. They said, 'It's hard to believe that this place can go on. . . . I'm afraid this can't continue. . . . I see there aren't very many of us here yet. So one wonders why. Is it that it costs too much? Yes: so then I wonder whether it can go on with so few people. . . . It's wonderful here: but can it last? . . . They must know what they're doing. But after all, it does make you think a little . . .'

When my maternal grandmother agreed to come and live with my parents, because she was worn out and somewhat infirm, she grew suspicious, even rather sly. She suspected that my father found her presence irksome. She lacked for nothing, yet she hid biscuits and pieces of gingerbread in her wardrobe and various places, and she nibbled them in secret.

The old person remains on the alert even when his security is guaranteed because he does not trust the middle-aged: this distrust is the figurative expression of the dependence in which he lives. He knows that the children, friends, nephews who help him live, either by giving him money or by looking after him or by housing him, may refuse their assistance or diminish it; they can abandon him or dispose of him against his will – for instance, they can force him to move house, and that is one of his terrors. He is acquainted with the double-dealing of the adult world. He is afraid that the motive for the help he is given may be a conventional morality that implies neither respect nor affection for him personally; he feels that he is being treated according to the demands of public opinion, and public opinion can be circumvented: or it may count for less than certain advantages. The misfortunes dreaded by the old – illness, infirmity, a rise in the cost of living – are all the more to be feared since they may also bring about disastrous alterations in the behaviour of others. The aged man, far from hoping that his natural irreversible decline will be slowed down or counterbalanced by those near to him, suspects that they will hasten it – for instance, if he becomes infirm, they will put him in an institution.

Married couples are no less anxious than others: far from it. The anxieties of each merge with and reinforce those of the other: each feels a double burden of care, both for himself and the other.

The old person tries to defend himself against the objective precariousness of his situation and against his inward anxiety; and the majority of his attitudes must be interpreted, at least to a great extent, as forms of defence. One attribute is common to almost all old people – they take refuge in habit. 'There is one characteristic of age that strikes me more than all the physical signs, and that is the formation of habits,' says O.W. Holmes. The fact is certain. But the word habit has more than one meaning, and we must distinguish between them.

Habit is the past in so far as we do not re-present it but live it in the shape of attitudes and forms of behaviour; it is the mass of acquired reactions and automatic reflexes that allow us to walk, speak, write, etc. In a normal old age they do not deteriorate; indeed, their role increases, since they are made to help in the establishment of a routine. Routine is present when the action I perform today has as its model that which I performed yesterday, which in its turn reproduced that of the day before, and so on indefinitely. In order to walk I make use of long-established sets of reflexes: but I can invent a new route. Routine is setting out on the same walk every day. It is habit in this sense whose role generally increases with the years. A principle of economy is operative in routine, and active people of all ages take it into account. Being obliged to ponder over unimportant matters is a waste of time. A given timetable, a given arrangement of one's living space, a given store and restaurant are chosen once and for all. But when one is young the rules are vague and they leave room for improvisation, whim and fresh choice. The old person looks upon new things with uneasiness; making a choice frightens him; his inferiority complex expresses itself in doubt and hesitation. It is more comfortable for him to fall back on set, tried formulas. His reflexes and automatic reactions are put to the service of repetitive forms of conduct: he uses the mechanism of walking to take the same path every day without deviating from it. Habit spares him the effort of difficult adaptations; it provides the answer before he has had to ask himself the question. As they grow old, people follow habit more than they did in the past. Kant had always obliged himself to comply with a strict

466

discipline, but in his old age he made a religion of it. The aged Tolstoy organized his day with the utmost precision. Paradoxically, habit is even more necessary to idle people than to those who work: if they do not want to bog down in the ooze of stagnant days they must counteract it with the rigour of a clearly-defined timetable. When this is done, their life takes on something very like necessity. The old person escapes from the sickening quality of excessive leisure by filling it with tasks and duties that for him take on the form of obligations; and in this way he avoids having to ask himself the dreadful question, 'What shall I do?' There is something to be done every moment of the day. I remember the strictness of my grandfather's programme: the reading of the papers, the inspection of his rose-beds, lunch, nap and walk followed one another in an unchanging order.

The more an old person's mental life has diminished, the more essential to him is the part played by habit, in its double form of automatic reaction and routine. Among other things it can alleviate the shortcomings of a failing memory. We have a detailed account of a woman who had almost entirely lost her memory and yet who adapted her behaviour to her surroundings.* She did not recognize people, but she was aware of the social category to which they belonged, and she treated the nurses, doctors, ward-maids and other patients in different ways. She knew she had lost her memory and it vexed her if there was any attempt to make her recall past events; but her judgement was sound, she was capable of discrimination, and she joked readily. She lived with neither past nor future, in a perpetual present.

Set reactions and routine can operate only if the outside world is running smoothly and if it presents no problems of any kind: everything must be in its place, every event must happen at the right moment. It is partly because of this that the least upset vexes the aged person to a degree that might seem morbid. It is also because the screen of customs and ceremonies behind which he shelters ensures him a minimum of security: if an outsider breaks one of these rules, there is no telling how far the riotous course of his tyranny may take him. These set habits are defensive; but they also possess a more or less aggressive character: the only way in which an old man, reduced to powerlessness, can impose his will is to oblige others to respect them. Thus the old Prince Bolkonski in *War and Peace* surrounds

* Paul Courbon, *Journal de psychologie*, 1921.

himself with a rigid set of habits in order to make his authority evident. And the eighty-one-year-old Goethe: after his son's death he took over the running of the house, which up until then had been very badly looked after, and he established a most scrupulous regularity. He slept with the cupboard keys under his pillow, and every morning with his own hands he weighed out the bread that was to be eaten during the day.

It is clear that the old person has more than one reason to cling to his habits; but he also acquires the habit of having habits, and this leads him to persist in fads that are quite devoid of significance. Playing cards every afternoon in a certain café with certain friends is a habit that in the first place was freely elected and its daily repetition has a meaning. But if the card-player is angry or upset because *his* table is occupied, it means that a lifeless requirement has come into existence, one that prevents him from adapting himself to the situation. Inveterate habits of this kind create impossibilities – there will be no travelling abroad because the customary food is not to be found there. If he lets himself be overcome by them, an old person's mind will grow crippled, hardened, sclerotic.

On the other hand, when a habit is thoroughly integrated into a man's life, it makes it richer, for habit has a kind of poetry. If some ritual – the ceremony of tea among the English, for example – is an exact repetition of that which I observed yesterday and that I shall observe tomorrow, then the present moment is the past brought to life again, the future anticipated; I experience both together in the for-itself mode – I reach (or I *seem* to reach, for the synthesis is not in fact accomplished) that dimension of being which the existent seeks. Habit brings about a crystallization like that which Stendhal describes when he is speaking of love: some given object, possession or activity acquires the power of revealing the whole world to us. In *L'Etre et le Néant* Sartre tells how distressing he found it, at a certain period of his life, to make up his mind to give up smoking. 'Being-susceptible-of-being-met-by-me-smoking – such was the concrete quality that had spread over all things without exception. It seemed to me that I was about to tear this quality from them, and that in the midst of this universal impoverishment, life would be a little less worth while.' More than anyone, the old person values the poetry of habit: by merging past, present and future it removes him from his enemy, time, and it provides him with that eternity which he no longer finds in the present moment.

Because habit confers a certain quality upon the world and a certain charm to the passage of time, at any age we lose something when we give one up. But in youth it is not ourselves that we lose, since it is in the future and in the accomplishment of our projects that our being lies. The old person dreads change because he is afraid that he will not be able to adapt himself to it, and he therefore does not see it as an opening but only as a break with the past. As he does nothing, he identifies himself with the rhythm and the framework of his former life: tearing him from it means removing him from his very being. 'When one grows old,' wrote Flaubert to Caroline, 'habits are more tyrannous than you can possibly imagine, my poor child. Everything that vanishes, everything that leaves us has the character of that which can never be undone, and you feel the tread of death upon you.'

Habit thus provides the old person with a kind of ontological security. Because of habit he knows who he is. It protects him from his generalized anxieties by assuring him that tomorrow will be a repetition of today. But this defence that he erects against the arbitrariness of others and against the perils that fill the world by reason of this arbitrariness is itself in danger, since it depends upon the will of the outside world. Because it is his shield against anxiety, habit becomes the focus of all his anxieties: confronted with the idea of having to give it up, the old person 'feels the tread of death upon him'.

And indeed, if this misfortune does occur, it is often unbearable. My grandmother was equal to moving into my parents' house because the decision had slowly ripened in her mind. But an old person who is suddenly transplanted, even if it is only to his children's home, loses his bearings; he is bewildered and often reduced to despair: when they are uprooted like this, one out of two die within the year. Nor is it unusual to see both members of an old couple die within a few hours or days of one another: the frontier between habit and the bond of affection is hard to trace.

Clinging to one's habits implies an attachment to one's possessions: the things that belong to us are as it were solidified habits – the mark of certain repetitive forms of appropriate behaviour. The possession of a garden means being able to take one's walk in it every afternoon: this armchair is waiting for me to sit in it every evening. Ownership too is a guarantee of ontological security: the possessor is his possessions' reason for existence. My objects are myself. 'The totality of my possessions reflects the totality of my being.'* The proprietor maintains a magic relationship with his property. Since it is no longer the old person's role to cause himself to exist by doing, he wishes to *have* in order to be. That is the reason for the avarice† which is so often observed in him. It is concerned with concrete objects: the old person very much dislikes having his things used or even touched by others. It also focuses upon money, their abstract equivalent. Money represents an insurance against the future and it protects the old person from the precariousness of his position: but this rationalist explanation is inadequate – its inadequacy becomes staringly obvious when we see a man of ninety dying in extreme poverty with a small fortune under his mattress. Money is synonymous with power; it is a creative force and the old person identifies himself with it on the magical plane. He feels a narcissistic pleasure in gazing at and handling this wealth in which he recognizes himself and in which he also sees the protection he needs so badly. 'Possession is a defence against the Other.'‡ By means of what I possess I recover an object that the outside world may assimilate to my being, so that it is therefore not for the outside world to decide who I am. Thanks to his possessions the old person assures himself of his identity against those who claim to see him as nothing but an object.

But here again his system of defence is imperilled in the world. Others may take away his money; they may extort it from him. Avarice becomes a mania; it takes on neurotic forms because the property in which the old person seeks refuge against anxiety becomes the object of his anxiety. While on the one hand it is a defence, avarice is also often a form of aggression against others. The old person revenges himself upon his children by refusing to help them financially, or, if they are dependent on him, by obliging them to live at a wretchedly low level: it is the only kind of power left to him, and he takes an ill-natured pleasure making them feel it.

Because of his anxiety, the aged person takes important, far-reaching measures against the attacks of the outside world. He cannot do away with them: but he can reduce his contact with the exterior. With many

* Sartre, *L'Etre et le Néant*.

† Freudian teaching explains it by a return to the anal stage. But this notion of a return seems to me very obscure, and I find the explanation of avarice by anal eroticism inadequate.

‡ Sartre, *L'Etre et le Néant*.

of the aged, distrust causes communications to be cut off. Intellectually it is difficult for the old to be open to new ideas; but they also close themselves deliberately – every intervention from outside amounts to a threat. Words are so many traps. They feel that there is some attempt at manipulating them. They refuse to listen. This is the explanation for the deafness that so many of them affect; words make no impression on them; it is not in their interest to hear, although if it is they understand wonderfully well.* They are deaf: they are also more or less dumb, at least on certain subjects. With regard to their financial resources in particular, they are sly and secretive. The less is known about them, the less anyone can interfere in their affairs.

They often withdraw even more radically, defending themselves not only by their conduct but also by carrying out an operation upon their feelings. As the American gerontologist Cummings puts it, they 'un-commit' themselves, that is to say, they cut off their emotional relationships with others. They feel the need for this all the more since they are emotionally vulnerable. It is not known exactly why, for the way in which ageing affects the nervous system is unstable; and in this they resemble children. They have sudden fits of ill-temper; they express their feelings violently; they cry easily. After the age of seventy-three Goethe had tears in his eyes for a mere trifle. The elderly Tolstoy wept prodigiously – he wept when he listened to music, when people cheered him, when Sonia was ill or when she looked after him with particular care. When he was old, Churchill too wept very often. Dostoyevsky gives Prince Sokolski this infantile emotiveness: his expressive face 'changed from extreme seriousness to a wild gaiety' and he sobs for nothing. When he meets the Adolescent again after a separation he bursts into tears. In *The Possessed* the fifty-three-year-old Stephan Trophimovitch is already an old man in all respects; he is susceptible and ridden by anxiety, and when out of principle he leaves the rich widow who maintains him, he does so in floods of tears. In the midst of a meeting in which he defends his views, he bursts into convulsive sobs.

These are exhausting reactions, and there is the danger that they may have wearing or harmful consequences: if one takes pity on another one is obliged to help him, give him time and money. In order to husband his strength and guard himself against dangers, the old man walls himself in. It is a striking fact that Tolstoy should have

* We saw an example of this in Pétain.

471

shown so great an insensibility at the death of his children. He began growing hard at about the age of fifty-eight. On losing a four-year-old son he stated that at one time it would have saddened him, but that now the death of a child seemed to him 'reasonable and just' because it was God's will and because it brought one closer to Him. He was sixty-seven at the time of the death of the seven-year-old Vanichka, whom he seemed to love dearly. He was quite overcome. But the day after the funeral he declared that the loss was a 'merciful' event, since it brought him nearer to God. He at once returned to his work, and in his letters he asserted 'There is no death; he is not dead, because we love him.' His favourite daughter Masha died in 1906, at the age of thirty-five. He held her hand during her last moments. But he wrote in his diary, 'It is an event of a carnal nature and therefore immaterial.' He did not go into the graveyard. He went back to his study and wrote, 'They have just taken her, carrying her away to bury her. Thanks be to God, my morale remains high.' The exaggeratedly expressed feelings were accompanied by failure in sensitivity. This is a characteristic that is also to be found in the aged Goethe and a very great number of old people.

Tolstoy and Goethe had always been self-centred. Old age is less barren in those who were capable of warm-hearted feelings in their middle years. They remain accessible to others: but to what extent, and in what conditions? It is hard to give a general reply to this question; all that we can do is to make a few observations.

The mutual relationships of old people are ambiguous. They like being together in so far as they share common memories and the same turn of mind. Some, like Clemenceau, delight in keeping up their earliest friendships. But old people are also mirrors for one another, mirrors in which they do not care to see themselves – the marks of old age they behold vex them. During the last years of their long friendship Gide blamed 'the little lady' for being deaf and for frequently contradicting him. Sometimes a foolish competition grows up between very old men: each is irritated by the other's having lived as long as himself. I knew one who could scarcely wait for the death of his last rivals: he wanted to be the only one still to have certain memories and to be able to tell them. But the most widely-spread attitude among the old is indifference, particularly among men. Old women have more shared interests and therefore more subjects for agreement and disagreement.

In many old couples, the two live under the same roof, but completely apart. In others, as we have seen, the relationship is anxious, demanding and jealous: each is wholly necessary to the other, but they do not help one another to live. A small number live in real harmony.

The emotional balance of the aged depends primarily upon their relationships with their children. These are often difficult. The son has not entirely overcome his youthful resentment of his father; and in so far as he has succeeded in doing so, it is by symbolically killing him – the son either detaches himself from his father or even supplants him. The father, on suddenly finding that his son is a grown man, goes through a phase of 'reversed Oedipean feeling': he is obliged to rebuild his relationship with his son, and in proportion to his success in doing so – a success that depends both on his son and himself – so will the feelings he has for him in his old age be affectionate, ambivalent, or hostile. The old man's demanding and distrustful attitude is above all focused upon his sons; he realizes that they find it hard to bear the authority he retains or the burden that he has become. Normally a daughter loves and admires her father; she does not have to kill him to fulfil herself; her affection for him remains pure and unmixed, and he returns it – Cordelia and Antigone are instances of this relationship. But sometimes he is jealous when she marries; he feels abandoned and he displays resentment. On her side, she often adopts the usual adult attitude of superiority and impatience. A mother's love for her son is one of the least ambivalent of all relationships; and if he remains a bachelor he is a source of happiness to her in her old age. If he marries, she too feels herself abandoned; she grows bitter and she is jealous of her daughter-in-law. A mother seeks to identify herself with her daughter. But the daughter does not always grow out of the classical hostility of adolescence; she retains her desire to break free from her mother and shows it by keeping her at a distance;* the older woman suffers from this and resents it. And on her side, the mother also goes through a phase of 'reversed Oedipean feeling' when her daughter grows up and threatens her mother's youth: their later relationship is deeply influenced by the way in which this crisis is resolved. As for the relationships between parents and their children's spouses, they vary a great deal. The rivalry between mother-in-law and daughter-in-law is classic; yet a young woman who has been deprived of maternal

---

* As in the case of Madame de Grignan and Madame de Sévigné.

love may transfer her daughterly feelings to her husband's mother and the older woman may receive an affection from her that she was unable to arouse in her own daughters; when this happens their relationship is very warm and positive. This happens quite often, because failure in the mother-daughter relationship is so usual. Similar transferences may occur in the relationship between the young wife and her father-in-law and the husband and his mother-in-law; but they are much rarer. It is rarer still to see son-in-law and father-in-law united by a genuine affection. But these are only rough generalities: the relationships between the two generations depend very largely upon the affinities that exist or do not exist between the individuals.

The warmest and happiest feelings that old people experience are those which have to do with their grandchildren. These are not always plain and uncomplicated to begin with. It may happen that both for men and women the existence of grandchildren makes the 'reversed Oedipus' phase more difficult: it appears from the inquiry into the awareness of age of a group of fifty-five-year-old teachers that I have already mentioned that those who were grandparents felt older for that very reason. The grandmother's attitude often begins by being markedly ambivalent. If she is hostile to her daughter she is also hostile to the children through whom her daughter asserts herself and escapes from her: if she loves her daughter and identifies herself with her then she loves her grandchildren, but nevertheless she is vexed at playing no more than a secondary role with regard to them. She loves her son in his offspring, but they are also the children of the daughter-in-law, the object of her jealousy. Because it is as mothers that women prize themselves, the rivalry with the daughter or daughter-in-law in this field may be very bitter. Women put up with the disagreeable feeling of being set back a generation when grandchildren are born less easily than men. A man does not enter into competition with his sons nor with his sons-in-law in the area of paternity. Then again he is less often called upon for his help. For these reasons he is generally more unconcerned than the grandmother. But if it so happens that he is involved in his grandchildren's life, then his feelings are as warm as hers and less ambiguous. Both Hugo and Sartre's grandfather consciously played the part of grandparent; but also they had the liveliest and most sincere affection for their grandchildren. Freud mourned and lost all pleasure in life when his grandson died.

Generally speaking, when the grandchildren have reached the age of about ten and when the old people have accepted their age, the grandparental state brings great comfort. The grandparents are spared all those factors – desire for self-identification and compensation, feelings of guilt and frustration – that cause the ambivalence of the parental state. They can love the children in a completely disinterested, wholly generous manner because they have neither rights nor responsibilities; it is not the grandparents who are required to assume the thankless task of bringing them up, of saying no, and of sacrificing the present to the future. So the children often show a great deal of affection for them, looking upon them as a refuge against their parents' severity. For his grandparents the child feels none of the jealousy, desire for identification, resentment and revolt that make his relationship with his father and mother so dramatic. When the grandchildren become young people and then adults, there is nothing in their earlier history to cloud their relationship with their grandparents. For the old people the affection of the grandchildren is a revenge upon the generation in between, and the contact with their youth makes them feel younger. The friendship of the young is very valuable to old people, quite apart from any family tie: it gives them the feeling that these times in which they are living are still their times; it revives their own youth; it carries them along the infinity of the future: and it is the best defence against the gloom that threatens old age. Unhappily, relationships of this kind are rare, for the young and the old belong to two worlds between which there is little communication.

The relationship with children and with grandchildren is usually more important in a woman's life than in a man's. Age does not bring women down from such a height; there are more things they can still do; and not being so embittered, so demanding, they 'uncommit' themselves less. They are also more used to living for and by means of others. When they are old, women, for the better or the worse, remain accessible.

Even if he retains affection for his family and his friends, it is usual for an old person to become somewhat detached from them. His egocentricity is made easier by the indifference which gradually overtakes him but which he also cultivates. It is both a defence and a form of revenge: since he is not treated as he ought to be treated and since he can rely only upon himself, the old person devotes all his thoughts and energies to his own person. Replying to a friend who had blamed him for his silence, the seventy-year-old Roger Martin du Gard wrote,

The fact is that I am growing old, that my activities are diminishing, and that I withdraw a little farther from the world every day. Since my bereavement, I find it hard to be interested in anything but my own fate (and not very much in that), and the circle of my attention has shrunk to a few private cares, among which my work* has the most important place. This does not mean that I am false to my friendships: but the vitality of these friendships dwindles, as does vitality itself. . . . I soon grow tired; every evening I reach the limit of my powers; I need a great deal of sleep and quietness; my days are short and even spring does not seem to lengthen them. I am obliged to conserve my strength, to draw myself in, and to concentrate upon these two strangely incommunicable worlds that I now bear within me – the immense, deserted world of my past, in which I wander some of the time, and the shrunken limited world of the present, cut to my measurements. . . . I am building myself a little cottage in the roaring forest of the world.

Sometimes this withdrawal leads to peace. It did so for Rousseau. To begin with he found it very hard to bear the weight of the years. In his explanation of why he still wished to believe in God in the *Rêveries* he drew a dark picture of his state: 'Now that my heart is wrung by grief, my soul oppressed by troubles, my imagination shocked, my mind bewildered by all the appalling afflictions that surround me, now that all my powers, weakened by age, care and distress, have lost their spring, am I wantonly to deprive myself of all the resources that I had laid up?' A little later he began to grow resigned. 'It is true that now I am reduced to myself alone I feed upon my own substance, but it does not fail and I am sufficient to myself although my mind has nothing to work on, although my imagination has dried up and my lifeless ideas no longer produce anything for my heart to feed upon. My soul, clogged and darkened by my body, sinks every day a little more; and under the weight of these heavy masses it no longer has the strength to launch itself from its worn envelope as once it did.' But in his last two years his sky cleared. 'I have recovered serenity, peace and even happiness, since every day of my life I recall that of yesterday with pleasure and wish it to be none otherwise for tomorrow.' And farther on, 'Harassed on all sides, I still retain my

---

* He was working without much conviction on a long novel which he had begun years before and which he never finished.

balance; for since I am no longer attached to anything, I rely solely upon myself.'

Rousseau suffered from persecution-mania, but he got tired of it; he stopped worrying about plots directed against him. This he achieved by an exaltation of his ego; it was another form of paranoia, but it brought him peace.

Withdrawal into himself is not usually enough to protect the old person against the outside world: his emotivity is concentrated within the limits of his narrow world, but it is not abolished. He remains vulnerable in his person, in his habits and in his possessions. Threats persist and anxiety remains.

Decline and distrust beget not only insensitivity with regard to others in the old person, but also hostility. Just as the woman's state arouses resentment, so that of the old person arouses a demanding attitude. Age takes us by surprise, and its sudden coming gives us an ill-defined feeling of injustice, a feeling that finds its expression in countless examples of resistance, defiance and refusal. The aged person looks upon himself as the victim of fate, of society and of those around him. He has been unfairly treated, and this continual injustice goes on all the time. It may happen that his resentment arouses and maintains a fury that brings him to the verge of madness. A woman writing to me about her eighty-year-old aunt says,

She has gradually been driven mad by the unhappiness and distress of the idea that she is old. Her suffering is so unbearable that I shall not go to see her again. In any case, she does not care in the least whether one goes or not. We are not there ten minutes before she sends us away, pretending she wants to go to bed. She refuses to go shopping any more because people compliment her on her briskness and her wonderful health (which is true). 'They exasperate me. I can't bear them any longer.' Her unhappiness is so great that everything else seems a grotesque, insulting mockery. She no longer does anything at all. She neither dresses nor undresses. She wanders about all day long like a hunted beast, groaning and carrying with her a pain that has no physical existence. 'Oh, if only I were really ill, then at least I could be looked after!' And she is beginning not to recognize us any more nor to remember her past: it is not because her brain is softening but because she does not want to. Everything that is not her unhappiness is an intolerable irony. She was a very intelligent woman, not particularly cultivated, very active, always gay and amusing.'

477

The old person's resentment does not usually display itself so openly or so violently: but it smoulders deep inside him. He feels that he is excluded from his times: he survives rather than lives. He sees everything that he has desired, believed in and loved called into question or even denied; he revolts against this fundamental dispossession.

The fall is the more distressing the higher the position the subject held, the greater his power or standing. If he still retains a little authority – within his family, for example – the old man abuses it: this is both a compensation and a revenge. Thus the old Prince Bolkonski becomes a domestic tyrant, and Tanizaki's hero feels a malignant pleasure in refusing his daughter money: reduced to a state of physical dependence, the old man takes his revenge by proving that those close to him are economically dependent upon his whims. In his last years a man who was always of a sour-tempered and gloomy cast of mind will of set purpose behave odiously. Chateaubriand deliberately did so with Madame Récamier.

Wagner could not resign himself to being old; for him it was a humiliation. He revenged himself upon Cosima, blaming her for her affectionate treatment of Liszt, her old father, and breaking out into fits of anger that reduced her to tears.

But it is chiefly the rising generations that arouse the old person's fury or hatred, for he feels that they are dispossessing him. He delights in foretelling a disastrous future for them: thus Goethe, talking to Echermann about humanity in 1828, said, 'I see the time coming when God will no longer take any pleasure in mankind and when He will have to wipe everything out once more and make a fresh creation.' He looked upon contemporary French writing as a 'literature of despair'. 'Outdoing one another in the horrible, the vile, the hideous and the base, exaggerating their odious farrago to the point of madness – that is their hellish task.' After 1830 he foretold the coming of an age of barbarism, and in 1831 he went so far as to say, 'We are right in the middle of it now.' A little before his death he wrote, 'A muddled doctrine based upon a muddled turmoil of the mind now rules the world.'

Saint-Evremond had earlier spoken of this tendency of the old to shut their minds to the age in which they live and to derive a feeling of superiority from their ignorance: 'It seems that long practice of life has made them forget how to live among men. . . . All they do appears to them virtuous; all they cannot do they rank as vice. . . .

478

Hence comes the peremptory authority they take upon themselves to censure everything.' Alain observes, 'It is a well-known fact that the aged man praises his youth and blames all that surrounds him now.'

It was thus that Edmond de Goncourt, shut away in the past, held aloof from his times. 'There is nothing in the papers any more,' he said. In his *Journal* for 7 April 1895 he wrote, 'Oh, these modern days! A madness in enthusiasm – Mallarmé and Villiers de L'Isle-Adam the great men of the younger generation!' And on 31 March 1896, 'The antiquated, school-masterish, dogmatic side of the young magazines, and their unreasoned, fanatical enthusiasm for foreign literature!'

At the beginning of the First World War, Rodin, whose health had recently been impaired by a slight stroke, said to Judith Cladel, 'We are living in a completely decadent age; the war shows the present state of mind; it is the age of barbarism; ignorance reigns and the restorers are killing sculpture. . . . Europe is done for. . . . It will become another Asia.' From the depths of his retirement Clemenceau, as we have seen, despised his times and played the Cassandra.

These set attitudes may be irritating. But they must be understood. The elderly man, forgotten and treated with disrespect by the new generations, is challenging his judges both now and in the future.

Tyrannizing over others, persecuting them, foretelling disaster: this can be done only by those few who have retained some degree of standing. Most have none. It is they who are the victims of tyranny, persecution and mockery. Even if they are treated properly they are still looked upon as objects, not as subjects. Their opinion is not asked; nobody takes notice of what they have to say. They sense danger in the looks that rest upon them: they suspect an underlying ill-will. Dr Johnson said to Boswell, 'There is a wicked inclination in most people to suppose an old man decayed in his intellects. If a young man or middle-aged man, when leaving a company, does not recollect where he laid his hat, it is nothing; but if the same inattention is discovered in an old man, people will shrug up their shoulders and say, "His memory is going." '

In his *Nouveaux Mémoires intérieurs* Mauriac says, 'In this last state of growing old, it is not the least of sorrows that people expect the worst for us. If your hand trembles as you put down your coffee-cup, the trembling is noticed. Even the way they say how well we look saddens us profoundly. People exclaim at an old man's youthful appearance; whereas it would never enter their minds to try to persuade a hunchback that his spine is straighter than it seems.'

Old people know that they cannot measure their own deficiencies: they might be senile or at any rate very much reduced without realizing it. They find meanings, right or wrong, for the looks, smiles or words of those around them. And it is on the basis of these interpretations that they retaliate with fits of ill-temper, wilfulness, deliberate blunders, complaints and scenes that often seem unjustified. The old person cries out before he is hurt: he flies into a rage over trifles. And indeed, in some given cases he may not have had the least cause to be angry: but he is in a permanent state of vexation, a permanent state of extreme sensitivity. Everything wounds him, including the attempts that are made to humour him.

Wronged and oppressed, he retaliates by refusing to take part in the game. The adult world is no longer his: he challenges its watchwords and even its ethics. He no longer imposes any discipline upon himself. He feels that 'everything is allowed'. He quite openly seeks his own pleasure or advantage. He says anything that comes into his head, including ill-natured and disagreeable remarks. He no longer governs his impulses, not that he is incapable of control, but because he sees no reason why he should. In 1930 Paul Courbon published a detailed study of a case of this kind. The subject was a woman of seventy-two who had always been fashionable and well-to-do. At the age of sixty she was left a widow with one daughter; the daughter had to be shut up with dementia praecox. Now that she was alone and at a loss, her character deteriorated. She took to speaking and behaving thoughtlessly, even if she sometimes had to regret it afterwards. She became so mean, fussy and interfering with her servants that they left her; she engaged others who only stayed a few months and then still others who lasted no more than a few weeks. After this, whenever a prospective maid came to the flat she at once declared that she was not suitable: she thought the girl was in league with the concierges, whom she loathed. She accused them of being disrespectful, of doing their work badly and of losing her letters on purpose. She went so far as to have her letters and parcels sent to the concierge of the neighbouring block. She quarrelled with all the shops – their prices were too high, their quality too low. With her friends and relations her behaviour was both beseeching and aggressive. She would appear at all hours and either talk a very great deal or go to sleep, leave abruptly or stay for ever. She fell out with most of them because of the unpleasant remarks she continually made. She also quarrelled with the manager of her block of flats, whom she pursued in the street, badgering him with her complaints. She was perpetually making charges against people at the police-station. She was exceedingly unpleasant with both her own doctors and her daughter's. She was dreaded at the asylum where her daughter was shut up: she quarrelled with the nurses, and to avoid going to the lavatory she would urinate in the stove and then blame the cat. She had unending feuds with her neighbours. Yet one of her friends had influence over her, and in this woman's presence she behaved properly. For three years she took her meals with her in the same restaurant, and there she conducted herself in a perfectly normal manner. In time her memory began to fail and a paranoiac element appeared in her behaviour. But for seven years on end she had made herself unbearable by her 'senile mental incontinence'. She was capable of reflection, however, and she proved it not only by the way she behaved with her friend, but also by managing her fortune very cleverly.

There are cases where the old person's unadapted forms of conduct contain no element of intention. They are to be explained by his physical decline: the rambling and continual repetition so characteristic of old age are examples of this. The old person is turned towards the past; he has no hold on the future and he is harassed by care. He perpetually revives the same memories; he talks to himself about the same anxieties; the weakening of his memory and his inability to make new acquisitions condemn him to stagnation. But generally his apparent aberrations of mind are more or less overlooked. A San Francisco gerontologist, Dr Louis Kuplan, has hit upon the notion of 'senile delinquency': it is said that this, like juvenile delinquency, is caused by the feeling of exclusion, and it expresses itself not by violence but by 'antisocial behaviour'. Dr Kuplan gives way to the tendency to look upon the aged as a species to be described from the outside, in the manner of the entomologists. He forgets that these are men who base their conduct on their situation. Many of their attitudes are attitudes of protest: but their state is one that calls for protest. One striking characteristic of asylum inmates, particularly the men, is their dirtiness. Dirtiness? But they have been tossed on to the rubbish-heap, so why should they obey the laws of health or decency? With regard to their family, their resentment expresses itself in forms of behaviour that may seem

481

neurotic but that are in fact prompted by aggression or self-defence. One old man will go to bed and never get up again, pretending that he has rheumatism – it is the consequence of a quarrel with his children. Another, whose son has taken the management of his affairs out of his hands, will walk about the garden naked – he, like Lear tearing off his clothes, is using this nakedness as a symbol of the stripping that has been inflicted on him. Incontinence of urine or faeces is often a revenge. Refusing to eat, go out, wash, and behaving strangely are usually ways of making a claim. The same applies to the wandering away from home which is often seen in the aged. Since he has no satisfactory role at home, the old man spends whole days roaming about, without telling his family: he does not know what it is he seeks, but he gives himself an impression of seeking. He thus shows his people that he can do without them, and he takes pleasure in thinking that he is worrying them.

There is a striking account of female old age in Saltykov-Shchedrin's *The Golovlevs*: Arina Petrovna's tragedy is that of dispossession, a man's tragedy in general, that of Lear and of the old Fouan in *La Terre*. The Russian novelist, basing himself upon one or more examples he knew in his own family, gives an astonishingly subtle and vivid description of his heroine's reactions.

Ever since her youth Arina Petrovna, a landowner, hard to herself and to others and cruelly grasping, has lived only to increase her estate. By the sweat of her brow and at the cost of extreme labour and privation she has succeeded in doing so. But the emancipation of the serfs throws her into confusion; she no longer knows how to direct her life, and although age has not yet destroyed her physical strength she is weak enough to share out her possessions among her descendants – two sons and two grand-daughters, the children of her daughter who is dead. Judas, the smooth, cunning elder son manages to strip her almost entirely. He is now the master of Golovlevo: she leaves the house, going to live with Paul, the younger brother, a drunkard. They settle down in a kind of dark, ill-omened coexistence; but Paul falls seriously ill – he is on his death-bed. Until this point there was nothing that could daunt Arina Petrovna, but now she cannot tell what to do with herself, since she hates her eldest son; and she sinks into dazed, bewildered distress. 'At last she sat down and began to weep. . . . It was a bitter, total despair, combined with an impotent stubbornness. And everything, her old age, her infirmities, her abandoned state, everything seemed to call for death as the only way to peace: but at the same time . . . memories of the past goaded her, binding her to this world. . . . Agony, mortal agony, seized upon her being. . . . For the sake of her family she had spent all her days in hardship, she had tortured herself, she had crippled her whole existence; and now all at once she realized that she had no family!' As we have seen, this heart-broken clarity of mind is often the lot of the aged; and often, although it makes them long for death, it also attaches them to life, because, as Rousseau says, they cannot bear the idea that it has all been in vain. 'That it was labour lost.'

Once Paul is dead, Arina Petrovna, wishing to have nothing to do with Judas, uses what little capital she has left to restore Pogorielka, her grand-daughters' estate, and she settles there with the orphan girls. But now that she no longer has any aim in life the weight of the years suddenly crushes her. 'Arina Petrovna had never dreamt that a day might come when she would be a useless burden; yet this day came stealing upon her at the very moment when for the first time she realized that her physical and spiritual strength was undermined.' These moments always come unexpectedly: although a man may have been affected much earlier, he holds out, he is still in control; and then suddenly this last side-blow strikes him – the blow that instantly, irrevocably turns a still hearty man into a wreck. She does not meet with any great difficulties in the management of the estate; but she no longer has the least pleasure in looking after it, and her strength has diminished. 'She suffered from the infirmities of age, which prevented her from going out. . . . The old woman fought and struggled, but she was reduced to helplessness.'

Her grand-daughters long to go away. To their great surprise, their grandmother listens calmly to their request. She is not angry, in the first place because with the loss of her physical energy, her authoritarian character has grown gentler; but also because as it sometimes happens her disillusioned old age has broadened her outlook. 'It was not only senile weakness that brought this change about but also an understanding of something better and more just. These last blows of fate had not brought humiliation alone, they had also thrown light on some corners of her intellectual horizon that her thoughts seemed never to have reached before.' Now that the harsh and ill-omened present has shown her that certain hopes and wishes are allowable, she no longer has the strength to set herself against them and she lets her grand-daughters leave Pogorielka.

But now she is surrounded by an unbearable emptiness. She feels as though 'she had suddenly been given a boundless freedom, so boundless that stretching out before her she saw nothing but an unending void'. She has a great many of the rooms shut up, keeping only two; she dismisses all the servants apart from two old women. 'Very soon the feeling of emptiness made its way into the two rooms where she had thought she would be safe from it. Incurable loneliness and a dark, sorrowful lack of occupation – those were the two enemies that confronted her. . . . Close behind them came physical and moral destruction, a destruction all the crueller the less her listless, idle life offered any resistance. . . . Once she had bored and wearied all around her: now it was she who was tired of everyone and everything.' She who had been so busy and stirring in former days, now falls into a drowsy idleness that 'gradually sapped her will-power and brought wishes and desires that Arina Petrovna would never even have dreamt of a few months before. Nobody would ever have thought of calling this strong, reserved woman old; but from now on she was a ruin, one for whom neither the past nor the future existed, but only the present moment that she had to live through.' She spends most of the day drowsing. 'Then she would start and wake up, and for a long pause, without thinking of any one particular thing, she would gaze into the distance. . . . The best part of her being still lived among those bare fields.' She stares at them, thinking of nothing, and falls back into her senile doze. Sometimes memories come back to her, but 'with no sequence, in disconnected flashes'. Some wring her heart and she sobs; then, surprised, she wonders why she was crying. 'She lived as though she took no personal share in existence.' The nights are a torment to her. In this remote old house she is afraid of everything – of the silence, the darkness, the noises, the lights and the shadows. At six in the morning she is up, worn out and exhausted. She eats poor food, and little of it. She suffers from the cold. 'The weaker she grew, the louder was the voice of her desire to live. Or rather . . . the desire to indulge in pleasant things, combined with a complete absence of the notion of death. Earlier she had been afraid of death; now she seemed to have forgotten it entirely. She longed for all those things she had deprived herself of. . . . Greed, gossip and a self-seeking pliability developed in her with astonishing speed.' She dreamt of the good food she had once eaten at Golovlevo and of the comfort of the house: it had been 'the good life' in those days. Gradually she loses the strength to keep up her resentment against her son. 'The transition from cantankerous despotism to

484

submissive flattery was no more than a question of time. . . . All at once Judas . . . was no longer hateful.' The former offences drop into forgetfulness of themselves and Arina Petrovna takes the first steps towards a reconciliation. She asks her son to send her things from Golovlevo – mushrooms, fish, poultry – and he invites her to come and eat them at his house. Arina Petrovna accepts: she goes there often in order to eat well and to spend the night in safety. She is very friendly to the woman Judas lives with and they all three play cards together. In the end she goes to live with this once hated son and she dies in his house.

Clearly, there is one preconceived notion that must be totally set aside – the idea that old age brings serenity. From classical times the adult world has done its best to see mankind's condition in a hopeful light; it has attributed to ages that are not its own, virtues that they do not possess: innocence to childhood, serenity to old age. It has deliberately chosen to look upon the end of life as a time when all the conflicts that tear it apart are resolved. What is more, this is a convenient illusion: it allows one to suppose, in spite of all the ills and misfortunes that are known to overwhelm them, that the old are happy and that they can be left to their fate. In fact they are hagridden by anxiety: the Rorschach test detects this state in all old people, even in those who claim to know nothing of it and to be content with their lot. A standard portrait of the old person was drawn up in America in 1956, using the Rorschach formula: 'Elderly people are distrustful, anxious and evasive in their approach to the Rorschach test . . . they display an introverted inner life, devoid of maturity and with fantastic and unreal colours . . . they show difficulties in their relations with others: little in the way of emotional needs . . . rigidity of mind, persistence of stereotyped ideas, intellectual impotence.' We have seen all these characteristics among old people and they appear to us to be the answer to their difficulties.

Dr Reverzy, who has treated many old people, says in his preface to Jacoba Van Velde's *La Grande Salle*, 'It is only the novelists, good or bad, who believe in a happy old age. There is only one old age: the fate of the bedridden hospital patient and that of the dowager lying upon her sofa converge and meet. . . . Yet these half-petrified beings have a strange resemblance to the adults and the children they once were. And often enough they are not much better. The will to live has not died out in them. Desire, passion and sudden impulse still live on. In none that I have ever met with has the experience of years provided that wisdom or that serenity which we find in the worthy old grandparents in books.'

In fact the dowager's lot is more favoured than that of the inmates of an institution: what Reverzy means is that she too is a prey to anxiety and care. He is right: but what I challenge is the harshness of his description. Why should an old person be better than the adult or child he was? It is quite hard enough to remain a human being when everything, health, memory, possessions, standing and authority has been taken from you. The old person's struggle to do so has pitiable or ludicrous sides to it, and his fads, his meanness, and his deceitful ways may irritate one or make one smile; but in reality it is a very moving struggle. It is the refusal to sink below the human level, a refusal to become the insect, the inert object to which the adult world wishes to reduce the aged. There is something heroic in desiring to preserve a minimum of dignity in the midst of such total deprivation.

There are some old people who refuse to be defined as 'a reduced, diminished individual struggling to remain a human being'. Jouhandeau says, 'The aged man may no longer be touched by the same sights and the same music as a youth; for all that the skies he gazes at are no less astonishing, the melodies he hears no less wonderful.' According to him the old person is not a mutilated adult any more than the child is an uncompleted man, but a whole individual, living an experience entirely his own.* Maybe. But whereas the child's world with its unique quality has often been described, that of the old, as we see it in their books, is distinguished from the adult world only by its gaps. The wisdom of age leaves me equally sceptical. Gide echoes Montaigne – and I agree with him – when he wrote in his *Journal* for 25 January 1931, 'I wholeheartedly despise that kind of wisdom that is reached only by weariness or by the loss of all warmth.'

Yet the hypothesis that I mentioned at the beginning of this chapter is not wholly to be rejected: it may happen that age and its disqualifications may be accompanied by enrichment and liberation. Bernard Shaw was very much afraid of death and senility when he was between fifty and sixty; but later he stated that after the age of sixty he began 'his second childhood', and that it gave him an enchanting feeling of freedom, adventure and irresponsibility. In an

* This was what Jacob Grimm maintained in the well-known 1860 lecture that I have already quoted.

interview he gave when he was seventy, Giono said much the same. Paulhan, a little before his death, observed, 'It is a very interesting time, old age: you experience a whole mass of feelings that you thought never existed outside books.'*

In his little book *On Old Age*, John Cowper Powys sings its praises. According to him it is then permissible for a man to practise 'that passive activity by which our human organism merges with the Inanimate'. One becomes more and more solitary; and the Inanimate is solitary. 'There is an inexpressible relationship between an old man warming himself in the sun and a piece of flint being warmed by the sun.' At last set free from his tasks, a man can give himself up to the pleasures of contemplation. Powys tells how as a child he suddenly came upon his grandfather sitting motionless on a sofa, gazing at the evening lights and shadows. 'Remember, Johnny,' said he, 'that at my age I can't do anything else.' Powys thinks that he was wrong to apologize. The old person has a right to inactivity. At last no more duties! Peace at last! The rules no longer apply. One is amoral as a child is amoral, and this amorality brings with it 'a magic equilibrium, an inner light'.

The fact is that for Powys old age was a coming into flower. He had never been well adapted to life in his middle years; he had been obliged to teach and lecture – work that he found burdensome and that kept him from contemplation and dreaming, the only pleasures that counted for him. His behaviour often seemed very strange, even to his friends. When he became old, his eccentricities appeared normal. He was able to devote himself to the delights of 'inaction'. In fact his leisure produced a large number of admirable books that called for a great deal of work. He was one of those rare people for whom retirement means the possibility of fulfilling a hitherto suppressed vocation.

His was an exceptional case. But it is true that broadly speaking old age does have certain advantages. Being relegated to the fringe of humanity means escaping from the obligations and the alienations that are its portion; most old people do not take advantage of this opportunity, but it is held out to a certain number and some do grasp it.

The individual who loses his social status together with his occupation has a most distressing feeling of being reduced to nothing.

---

* Churchill also said that old age was an astonishing experience: but he said this when he was very much reduced.

He sinks into depression, or, if he is in a privileged position, he tries to make a show by way of consolation for no longer being – he is greedy for functions, titles, honorary roles, decorations. Yet nevertheless it is possible for him to derive truth and strength from his nakedness: when Lear has lost everything he strips off his finery and denounces the shams and pretences that had deceived him up until then. Many old people, rejected by society, find that the rejection works in their favour, since they no longer have to trouble about pleasing. In them we see that indifference to public opinion which Aristotle called 'shamelessness' and which is the beginning of freedom. It means that they no longer have to practise hypocrisy. Research-workers asked a group of old people of various ages what counted most for them in life: those between sixty and seventy spoke of the affection of those near them and their own activities; those of eighty bluntly replied 'Eating', which was in fact true for most of the others as well. The inhabitants of the Victoria Plaza, who were pleased with their new conditions of life, said, 'At last I can be myself! I am not so-and-so's wife, not so-and-so's employee, I am myself.' They no longer defined themselves by their social function: they felt themselves to be individuals, with the power to decide upon their conduct not according to accepted ideas but according to their own wishes. They also said, 'At last I can do whatever I like.' The people in that Sunset City of which I have already spoken have no cultural activity whatever nor any of those occupations that are termed 'constructive': an observer who has looked after them since the foundation of the community states that this is because they no longer feel compelled to have any. Earlier, social pressure required them to follow these pursuits and they pretended to be interested in them; now they are really themselves.

It is for women in particular that the last age is a liberation: all their lives they were subjected to their husbands and given over to the care of their children; now at last they can look after themselves. Japanese women of the middle class are strictly disciplined: they often have a very lively old age – I have been told of some who have divorced at the age of seventy so as to make the most of their last years and who have never stopped being thankful. Brecht's play *The Unworthy Old Lady*, which was made into a film, has as its theme the heroine's revolt against the obligations and prohibitions that had oppressed her until then. She is left a widow at seventy-two, and to the great indignation of her family she mortgages her house, indulging herself in all the amusements she yearns for – driving about in a brake, drinking red wine, seeing films, going to bed late, lying long in the morning. She no longer respects social taboos: she sees a great deal of a cobbler who belongs to a lower class than her own. Up until this time she has been obliged to bow to an ideal of proper behaviour, and now she tramples it under foot, preferring to follow her own impulses. To be sure, many cling stubbornly to the values by which they have lived and try to force them upon the younger genera-tions. But their situation does offer them the possibility of breaking free.

Liberty is frightening, and that is why the elderly man will some-times refuse it. When Gide had been given the Nobel prize, Sartre said to him, 'Well, now you have nothing left to win and nothing to lose: you are free to do and say whatever you like.' 'Oh, free, free . . .' said Gide, in a dubious tone. And it was not in his last years that he wrote his most stimulating books. But there are others who feel, as they grow older, that they no longer have to worry about public opinion. Thus in his *Bloc-notes* for 28 July 1953, Mauriac wrote, 'This is the advantage of the waning years: one is too well-known, too much and for too long in the public eye for any words, good or bad, to make any difference.' In his younger days he did not commit himself politically to any great extent. As he says himself, the Fascist aggression in Abyssinia and the Spanish civil war provoked no more than a 'feeble outcry'. Under the Occupation he did write the *Cahier noir*. But then he 'went to sleep again'. After the Nobel prize, which he received on the very day of the Casablanca massacres, 'I was woken out of my torpor, determined to be committed again: after the butchery of Casablanca the Moroccan tragedy made me renew my contacts with the young Catholics – I was once more the Mauriac of the *Sillon* of 1904, the Mauriac of the Basques and the Spanish war: *France-Maghreb* came into being.' Elsewhere, referring to this period again, he wrote, 'From that time onwards I was committed.' He wrote articles protesting against the torture in Algeria and he took part in manifestations. In 1958, out of admiration for de Gaulle and perhaps out of weariness too, he withdrew from the struggle.

Voltaire, bold and free in his writing, managed his actual living with a caution that often bordered upon double-dealing. It was only in his old age that he actively declared himself against intolerance and injustice. He was sixty-six when he heard of the Calas trial. He used every possible means to gather information. He travelled to see people who might be able to tell him something; he questioned members of the family. Once he had made up his mind he began to use his influence with his friends and acquaintances. In 1762, when he was sixty-eight, he published a pamphlet that stirred public opinion, and in the end he brought about a reversal of the sentence. He had taken all the experiences of the case upon himself. Three years later he came to the support of the Sirvens, a couple accused of having thrown their daughter down a well because she wanted to change her religion: she was mad and in fact she had killed herself. They managed to escape, leaving all their possessions behind, and they were executed in effigy. Voltaire fought for their rehabilitation until 1771. After the execution of the Chevalier de La Barre in 1766 he went through some days of extreme alarm and fled to Cleves. But he rallied. He intervened in several other cases. In the Montbailli affair, where a couple were accused of parricide, the husband was put to death; the pregnant wife was given a respite, and during her imprisonment Voltaire succeeded in proving their innocence.

There are some old men who possess something indomitable and even heroic: they will coolly risk a life to which they no longer attach much importance. Malesherbes was seventy-two when he defended Louis XVI at his trial in 1792. 'During the case nothing could stop him saying "the King" and, on addressing him, "Sire". A member of the Convention said to Malesherbes, "What makes you so bold?" "Contempt for life," he replied.'* He was arrested in 1793: he refused to defend himself and walked calmly to the guillotine, first taking care to wind his watch. Without going so far as to risk their heads, others are ready to stake their reputation or their career. Thus Dr Spock, the well-known American paediatrician, who was indicted in 1968, when he was eighty, for his struggle against the war in Vietnam, said, 'At my age, why should I be afraid to make public protests along with Stokely Carmichael?'

With men who have taken risks all their lives, it often happens that their boldness shines out with particular brilliance in their last years. Russell was always brave and determined, but he never showed it in so striking a manner as in 1961, when he was eighty-nine. At this time he was a member of the Committee of a Hundred against nuclear weapons: he called upon the public to join in a non-violent manifestation, and in spite of the police prohibition he sat down on the ground among the others. His age and his name gave his act such

* Michelet, *Histoire de la Révolution française*.

importance that there was no possibility of its being overlooked, and in fact he spent a week in prison. The Conclave had a mistaken idea of old age when it elected Cardinal Roncalli pope, supposing him to be harmless. He had always done what he considered his duty, without allowing himself to be intimidated by anyone. The papacy opened vast possibilities, and he made the most of them. Under the name of John XXIII, without asking any outside opinion and crushing all opposition, he set about a reform of the Church three months after his election and summoned a Council whose work was largely inspired by him. It was interrupted, but nevertheless it began a great change whose scope is increasing every day. A blazing, fearless passion in an old man's frail body is a moving sight. Emile Kahn, the president of the *Ligue des droits de l'homme*, was in his eighties and scarcely able to stand when he testified in the Ben Saddok trial. He read out a letter from his son describing the way FLN fighters were tortured in Algeria, and he indicted the government and the army with a vehemence that many younger witnesses might have envied.

On the intellectual plane, old age may also bring liberation: it sets one free from false notions. The clarity of mind that comes with it is accompanied by an often bitter disillusionment. In childhood and youth, life is experienced as a continual rise; and in favourable cases – either because of professional advancement or because bringing up one's children is a source of happiness, or because one's standard of living rises, or because of a greater wealth of knowledge – the notion of upward progress may persist in middle age. Then all at once a man discovers that he is no longer going anywhere, that his path leads him only to the grave. He has climbed to a peak; and from a peak there can be a fall. 'Life is a long preparation for something that never happens,' said Yeats. There comes a moment when one knows that one is no longer getting ready for anything and one understands that the idea of advancing towards a goal was a delusion. Our personal history had assumed that it possessed an end, and now it finds, beyond any sort of doubt, that this finality has been taken from it. At the same time its character of a 'useless passion' becomes evident. A discovery of this kind, says Schopenhauer, strips us of our will to live. 'Nothing left of those illusions that gave life its charm and that spurred on our activity. It is only at the age of sixty that one thoroughly understands the first verse of Ecclesiastes.' In his old age Tolstoy wrote more harshly, 'One can only live when one is drunk with life; as soon as the drunkenness fades one sees that it is nothing more than a fraud, a stupid fraud.'

If *all* were vanity or deceit there would indeed be nothing left but to wait for death. But admitting that life does not contain its own end does not mean that it is incapable of devoting itself to ends of some kind. There are pursuits that are useful to mankind, and between men there are relationships in which they reach one another in full truthfulness. Once illusions have been swept away, these relationships, in which neither alienation nor myth form any part, and these pursuits remain. We may go on hoping to communicate with others by writing even when childish images of fame have vanished. By a curious paradox it is often at the very moment that the aged man, having become old, has doubts about the value of his entire work that he carries it to its highest point of perfection. This was so with Rembrandt, Michelangelo, Verdi and Monet. It may be that these doubts themselves help to enrich it. And then again it is often a question of coincidence: age brings technical mastery and freedom while at the same time it also brings a questioning, challenging state of mind. Doing, while at the same time 'placing one's activity into a parenthesis', means achieving authenticity; it is harder to adopt than falsehood, but, once reached, it cannot but bring happiness. This sweeping away of fetishes and illusions is the truest, most worth-while of all the contributions brought by age.

It may be said that one could have got rid of them earlier. For example, I long ago accepted the idea that for the existent the search for the being was pointless – the for-itself will never be realized as an in-itself. I should have taken this inevitable failure into account and never have dreamt of that absolute whose absence I lamented at the end of *La Force des choses*. But just as foreseeing is not knowing, so knowing is not feeling. All truth is 'that which has become'. The truth of the human state is accomplished only at the end of our own becoming.

Freedom and clarity of mind are not of much use if no goal beckons us any more: but they are of great value if one is still full of projects. The greatest good fortune, even greater than health, for the old person is to have his world still inhabited by projects: then, busy and useful, he escapes both from boredom and from decay. The times in which he lives remain his own, and he is not compelled to adopt the defensive or aggressive forms of behaviour that are so often characteristic of the final years. His oldness passes, as it were, unnoticed. For this to be the case he must in his middle age have committed himself to undertakings that set time at defiance: in our society of exploitation this possibility is refused to the immense majority of human beings.

As I have said, mental illnesses are more frequent among the old than among any other age-group.* Yet they were very poorly understood until the end of the nineteenth century: they were all grouped under the single heading of senile dementia. The Swiss Dr Wille began a new epoch in 1873, and his studies were followed by many others. In 1895 there was a congress on the psychoses of the aged at Bordeaux. Since then a great deal of work has been done on the neuroses and psychoses of degeneration. Yet since old age is a 'normal abnormality' it is still often difficult to draw the line between the mental disturbances that ordinarily accompany ageing and those which are of a pathological nature. Some changes of temper and behaviour which seem to be justified by the situation are in fact the forerunners of a disease; while others which appear to be neurotic find their real explanation in the circumstances in which the old person lives. But in any event, there are a great many distinctly pathological cases. Old people are physically fragile; socially they are outcasts; and this has serious effects upon their mental state, either directly or by means of the physical deterioration that is its consequence; and both their existential situation and their sexual state are favourable to the development of neuroses and psychoses.

A person becomes neurotic when 'in the identification of his own character he is unable to find good relationships with others and a satisfactory internal equilibrium.'† When this is the case, he presents a cluster of symptoms that are in fact so many defences against an intolerable situation. Many psychiatrists emphasize this 'weakness of identification' which is the most marked characteristic of the neurotic personality. Now one of the elderly man's greatest difficulties is the retention of his feeling of identity. The very fact of knowing that he is old turns him into another being whose existence he cannot manage to realize; what is more, he has lost both his 'label' and his role in society – there is no longer anything by which he can identify himself,

---

* I will give the US figures again: out of 100,000 subjects all of the same age-group, the number of mentally sick is 2·3 below 15 years of age, 76·3 between 25 and 34, 93 between 35 and 54, and 236·1 among the aged.

† Ey, *Manuel de psychiatrie.*

and he no longer knows who he is. When, as it often happens, the 'identification crisis' is not overcome, the old person remains in a state of confusion and distress.

Then again, the psychoanalysts – and many psychiatrists agree with them – hold that neuroses are the expression of a sexual conflict rooted either in the subject's childhood past or in his present difficulties. The old person is more subjected to the influence of his childhood than the adult, for the censors and the defences of middle age crumble: and as far as the present is concerned, his sexual life is difficult, since his libido persists, whereas quite frequently its genital concentration is no longer possible for him. And these situations have to be dealt with by a weakened or failing organism. It is understandable that often enough what is called a 'normal adaptation' to the circumstances is impossible.

The neuroses most frequently met with among the aged are:

1 *Characterial neuroses of a paranoid nature.* Here the reactions that are normally seen in the majority of old people are carried to extremes. The subjects protect themselves by a positive 'characterial armour': their distrustfulness and aggression become far more pronounced; and they develop hypochondriac forms of behaviour, complaining of various physical troubles, pains, diseases, headaches and digestive disturbances, and blaming their families for not being concerned about their health and not taking care of them. They are demanding and often the victims of a morbid jealousy. Their temper is very uncertain: they have sudden fits of extreme agitation. Dr Dolto distinguishes two kinds of characterial neurotics among elderly women: some are passive, closed in upon themselves; they hate life, movement and emotion and they have a pathological dread of death: others exhibit a hypertrophied ego and paranoiac tendencies.

2 *Anxiety neuroses.* According to Freud they are evidence of a gap between the somatic sexual libido and its psychic elaboration: and a gap of this kind exists in most old people. As we have seen, they are normally eaten up by anxiety for other reasons too. Many sink into a neurotic depression, and in this state they carry the boredom, sadness and anxiety that are usual in most of their fellows to an extreme point of acuity.

3 *The hystero-hypochondriac neuroses.* Their origin lies in a latent neurosis that ageing has brought to violent life: in this case the source of the conflict is in the subject's childhood, and the symptoms

amount to a symbolic compromise between desire and defence. The subject exercises an emotional tyranny over his family, takes refuge in illness, insists on being looked after, plays on the feelings of others; he pretends to feel pain that he does not feel and sometimes he brings about a somatic conversion of his repressed anxiety. He suffers from various forms of pruritus, pains and digestive or urinary disturbances.
4 *Obsessional or phobic neuroses.* These are much more rarely seen among the aged.

Some gerontologists, including Dr Blajan-Marcus and Dr Pequignot, are of the opinion that the neuroses of the aged always have their roots in childhood or youth, and this is admitted in the case of the hystero-hypochondriac neuroses. Yet Freud acknowledges the existence of 'present' neuroses, in which the subject is defending himself against immediate conflicts. And this notion suits many of the anxieties of the aged: their situation, not only on the sexual plane but also on all the others, justifies the setting up of that defensive system we call a neurosis.

A neurosis does not mobilize the whole of the subject's personality. When the entire personality is changed for the worse, taking on a fresh structure, we speak of a psychosis. The most widely-spread psychosis among the aged is involuntary melancholia. It was isolated and described by Krapelin in 1896. Women are most affected. The disease is particularly characteristic of ageing, since there is no pathological event in the mental history of those who suffer from it. If we reflect upon the general nature of melancholia, we shall see that old age is conducive to this psychosis.

Melancholia is 'a state of intense depression, experienced as a feeling of mental suffering and distinguished by the slowing down and the inhibition of the mental and psychomotor functions'. Freud compares it to mourning. Although the sufferer from melancholy has not lost anyone, he behaves as though he had been bereaved: it is for his lost ego that he is grieving – 'I am nothing; I get nowhere,' he is saying. Minkowski, among others, observes that this loss brings with it a distressing impression of diminished value, and this leads the subject to fall back upon his past. Minkowski also says that melancholia is a 'disease of time'. The future is blocked: the subject no longer has any impulse towards it, for he sees it only in the context of death. As far as the present is concerned, he is a mere embodiment of powerlessness: he feels that he is living in a vacuum and he suffers from an appalling boredom – 'A vast steppe with neither beginning nor end, in which nothing ever comes to break the monotony' as the Infanta Eulalie said. It is 'filled with nothingness'. He turns to stone in the midst of a devastated world where nothing either concerns or moves him any more. He stops living. The void of the present makes him the slave of his own past being; and he suffers its inevitable consequences. He is anxious because he bears the weight of the past: he dreads the future because of what he has been and of what he has done in former times. He is incapable of doing anything to avert the consequences. He is condemned to inaction.

This description of the sufferer from melancholia applies to the majority of old people – loss of ego, loss of value, boredom, blocked future, powerlessness. It is therefore not surprising that the reverse should obtain, and that the sufferer from old age should often suffer from melancholia too.

Yet not all do so, and for any given person to be attacked, particular circumstances are called for. Involuntary melancholia often makes its first appearance at the time of some emotional crisis such as bereavement, separation or transplantation; or it may be provoked by the fact that ageing makes the subject's pattern of living difficult. The premonitory signs are boredom, disgust, asthenia, hypochondria, remorse and a feeling of sexual guilt.

The patient shows the same symptoms as the younger melancholics. His psychosis may take different forms – simple, stuporous, anxious, or violent. In all these cases there is one characteristic in addition to those I have mentioned – a feeling of guilt. Freud says that the patient recovers his aggressiveness against the escaping ego. As I have said, normally this feeling is rare among the aged; but we must pay particular attention to the form that it assumes in these cases: the subject does not accuse himself in the present of any fault or omission imputable to him. His guilt is something that is undergone; it is inflicted upon him, an inevitable consequence of his past, against which he can do nothing. It is an attack upon him by fate.

In the stuporous form the patient remains motionless, frozen, mute. He literally stops living. His paralysis may reach the point of catatonia. It is of frequent occurrence among the aged, for they suffer from a disturbance of the general physical pattern* – when they have taken up an attitude they retain it because they do not know how to change it; after a muscular contraction they are

* This is evident in their Rorschach interpretations, as we have seen.

unable to impose a relaxation, and indeed the muscles concerned often refuse their office.

If he escapes this petrification then at least he imprisons himself in rigid habits; he refuses anything in the least degree new; all his movements are stereotyped, and he repeats them endlessly. Sometimes he retires into a total silence; sometimes he bursts out into words that are apparently devoid of meaning. He meets the requests and commands of others, the requirements of the outside world, with a stubborn negation. He no longer has any kind of activity whatsoever. According to the psychoanalysts this regression is intentional; it fulfils an unconscious wish; and the patient, having lost the possibility of concentrating his libido on any object other than himself, returns to auto-eroticism. But most psychiatrists think that the regression is undergone rather than 'realized', and that it depends upon organically determined psychopathological structures. The inadequacies and deficiencies of ageing bring about self-depreciation, and the subject's reaction is to stop living.

Instead of passive withdrawal, the defence of some melancholics is anxious perturbation. The patient is mentally excited, agitated; he develops pessimistic ideas; he endlessly repeats negative themes – the world does not exist; he himself no longer exists either. This anxiety often assumes a hypochondriac form: more than half the hypochondriacs treated in the hospitals are over sixty and most of them are women. They worry about their body or some part of their body which they believe to be diseased. Some of them live in a permanent state of panic about their health; this results in respiratory troubles and nausea or diarrhoea – all the bodily symptoms of very great fear. Sometimes the agitation reaches paroxysm: the patient writhes screaming on the ground in a violent hysteroid fit. The anxious melancholia of the aged sometimes takes acute forms: they have high temperatures; they either stop eating or no longer digest their food, and this lack of nourishment may cause death.

In violent melancholia, which is often accompanied by illusions, hallucinations and oneiric delirium, the subject organizes his feeling of guilt and defends himself by projecting it on to others: he believes that he is persecuted. He will sometimes go over and over his self-accusations and ideas of persecution in a set, rigid form for years on end; but sometimes he also enriches them with interpretations. There are patients who enter into a delirium of negation.

The death-wish is strong in all melancholics. They cannot feel that they are alive any more and they would like to vanish entirely. Since death is all the future holds out to them, they want it to strike as soon as possible. There are many who yield to the temptation of suicide.

The patient with melancholia exhibits physical disorders, such as digestive cardio-vascular troubles and disturbances of the sympathetic nervous system. No marked intellectual deficiency is detected in those whom it is possible to test; but because of their agitated state and their negativism it is very difficult to measure their mental capacities.

Many melancholics are to be found in old people's institutions: the inmates are treated as objects and virtually cut off from the world: their feeling of nothingness becomes very intense.

Sometimes the crisis only lasts six or seven months, but usually the subsidence is only temporary – in most cases the patient relapses. And sometimes these disorders 'take a bad turn': the anxiety-state or the violence or the catatonia becomes permanent, or the cessation of mental life brings about an intellectual degradation.

Maniacal states as a defence against melancholic depression are rare among the aged; but on the other hand we do find a fairly considerable number of chronic violent psychoses. Paranoia makes its appearance when the ego's reality-relationships with the world are disturbed. Sometimes the ego takes on such dimensions that it engulfs all reality, the world becoming pliable and no longer offering any sort of resistance. Sometimes on the contrary the ego shrinks; the world crushes it, and the patient suffers from an 'unworthiness mania' – he feels guilty and undeserving of life. Sometimes the disorder is poised between these two extremes: the ego remains the centre of the world, as in the first case, but only in so far as the world accuses it of faults that it may have committed and punishes it excessively – this is persecution-mania. The relationships of the old person's ego – which he has more or less lost – with a world upon which he no longer has any hold, are deeply disturbed. He is predisposed to paranoia.

Krapelin isolated and described a 'senile injury-mania' which, in his view, was chiefly seen among women. He described it as a persecution-mania, provoked by the state of distrust and exacerbation usual in many old people. The patients complain of injuries inflicted upon their health: they feel unwell because of their food; they accuse the suppliers or they think they are being poisoned by their family. Like some hysterics, they complain of the 'drying-up of their brains' or of the 'dislocation of their bones'. They also think they are being injured in their possessions: their things are stolen; the locks have been picked and the furniture moved; they find footprints or fingerprints in their room. They suspect their spouse of deceiving them. Their disturbed ideas are not successfully organized into a system; they are fleeting and unsettled, and they do not therefore end in dementia. But the condition implies a weakening of the judgement and a high degree of emotional irritability.

At present it is no longer admitted that this 'injury-mania' amounts to a nosological entity. But in Kleist's 'involuntary paranoia', which he described in 1912 and which is still accepted, we see more than one of the characteristics mentioned by Krapelin. Against a background of hypoparanoiac characteristics – touchiness, obstinacy, distrust, jealousy, vanity, irritability – the old person develops wildly aberrant ideas; they do not succeed in forming a system and they do not end in dementia, but they cut him off from reality. They are often accompanied by serious hallucinatory disturbances. They chiefly affect women and they are encouraged by defects of sight and hearing. Sometimes the subject falls into megalomania: he imagines that he is prodigiously gifted and that the young are conspiring to prevent him from showing his powers. But generally he is the victim of a persecution-mania that he feeds with interpretations. The main themes are those mentioned by Krapelin: he believes himself to be attacked in his health and his property; he is tormented by jealousy. Often, between the ages of seventy and eighty, the subject's mood and character change. His memory, power of concentration and judgement weaken. He becomes misanthropic, querulous, suspicious. He accuses his wife of deceiving him. One seventy-year-old alleged that his wife 'had a booth for prostitution at the Le Trône fair'. Another heard a voice calling him cuckold in the middle of the night and got up to look for his wife's lovers. Another heard the boasting of imaginary rivals and saw a dark form lying by his door at night. Sometimes the jealous man suspects his wife of wanting to poison him, and it may happen that he shuts her up. There was one old man of this kind who imprisoned his wife for six years, reducing her to an appalling state of general debility.

The mental illness of the aged that has been longest known – so much so that all others were grouped under its name – is senile dementia. It has become more frequent in recent years because the number of old people has increased. Women are more affected than men. It has assumed a considerable social importance, and because of the destruction of the family-unit and the consequent need to look after the patients in hospital, it arouses difficult problems. Living conditions have great influence upon the appearance and evolution of the disease, since they can either retard or encourage physical degeneration. Physiologically, the brain of the sufferer from senile dementia is atrophied: its weight shows a considerable loss. Atrophy of the neurons is also observed, together with intercellular lesions and senile plaques. Mentally, the disease may make its first appearance in many different ways. The beginning is often insidious: there is a progressive deterioration of the memory and an increasingly evident rigidity of the mental processes. In other cases it begins with sharply-defined crisis-perturbation, a state of confusion, aberrant ideas of the kind we have just described. Or the subject may present a depression syndrome.

Subsequently social behaviour becomes disorganized; the subject has odd, muddle-headed activities, he does absurd things that may also be dangerous, such as leaving the gas on or throwing lighted matches about. Yet in some areas his automatic reactions may help him to seem less affected than he is. There are some who doze all day long. Others have a morbidly voracious appetite. Nocturnal restlessness is seen in most cases: they sleep badly and toss about.

One characteristic shared by all is the progressive loss of memory. There is a retrograde amnesia very like that described by Ribot: the subject no longer sees the present clearly and his memories disappear, the unsettled going before the settled, the unorganized before the organized and the recent before the long-established. The subject's lack of focus and his forgetfulness bring about a temporo-spatial disorientation: he no longer knows the time or the place in which he is living. This want of knowledge often leads to amnesic wandering,* the patient being incapable of telling where he is and therefore of finding his way again. His sense of former life deteriorates, a point particularly emphasized by Minkowski. Since he has no past he lives solely in the present, but in a present that he apprehends in a general timelessness: nothing ever appears new to him. 'I have known you for years; I recognized you straight away,' said one woman to a doctor whom she was seeing for the second time. The patient is

---

* Not to be confused with old persons leaving home on purpose and wandering about without losing their sense of space or time.

instantly prepared to systematize the present on the model of a past that never existed. Another woman, addressing a doctor who had come to examine her in her institution, said in a well-bred voice, 'I am so sorry. If I had been told you were coming I should have had lunch ready for you,' as though she usually invited him to share her meals. As the patient has no true memories he will invent an immediate antecedent, devoid of all reality, for this present: it is as though, on being confronted with the blankness of his memory, he feels a need to assert the continuity of duration: he 'has just' done this or that; his son 'has just' been to see him; the doctor 'has just' told him . . . etc.

His amnesia affects his speech: the patient first forgets proper names, then abstract and then concrete words. As we see in many cases of aphasia, his practical activities are disturbed. Concentration is weakened and perception becomes vague, which leads to mistaken recognition. The subject lacks judgement in his personal life; he has inappropriate or uncontrolled reactions. But he may make apposite remarks about others and about the world in general.

The character undergoes serious alterations; the patient becomes irascible and querulous. He is fiercely attached to his property. He talks nonsense and harps on the same grievance for hours on end. Generally speaking, he does not realize his own condition. Yet some do have moments when they are conscious of it; they become extremely unhappy and they weep.

As his condition deteriorates so the subject's reaction becomes more and more unadapted. He yields to all his impulses, particularly those on the sexual plane – and there are a great many of these. His desires are no longer censured; he makes them evident and goes through the motions of fulfilling them. This leads him to acts that come within the scope of forensic medicine. From the physiological point of view, however, his health may remain fairly good.

The evolution of the disease takes a few months or a few years: it may be interrupted by outbursts similar to those that marked its beginning – agitation, confusion, violent excitement. It ends in dementia and the cachexy that causes death.

One striking form of senile dementia is presbyophrenia, which was first described in 1906. It has the same anatomical characteristics as senile dementia, and it is mostly seen in women. It is marked by a fixation-amnesia, a temporo-spatial disorientation and compensatory fabulation. The subject preserves some acquired knowledge and attainments. The women, in particular, may be deceptive: they appear properly and even well dressed, they speak pleasantly, and at first glance they seem normal. But the amnesic disturbances are serious among all presbyophrenes. By way of compensation, the patient invents memories for himself; he dreams; he recognizes people and things, but mistakenly. It is an imaginative 'delusion of memory' that is almost always a delusion of grandeur as well. The subject has a broad, optimistic view of his life; he claims to have known the great men of this world, to be immensely rich: it may happen that he will deny these tales himself and laugh at them.

Another form met with among the aged is arteriopathic dementia. It has become far more frequent both because the aged population has increased and because their living conditions have grown more difficult. It is connected with the lesions caused by cerebral arteriosis. It appears after the age of sixty, particularly in men, no doubt because they make greater use of alcohol and tobacco and because they more often suffer from overwork. In many cases it assumes minor and widely varying forms.

1 Physically the subject suffers from peripheral arteriosis and high blood-pressure. Mentally he displays asthenia, proneness to fatigue, headaches; he is sad, he can no longer concentrate, he is extremely emotive and it may happen that some emotion, especially the shock of retirement, may cause him to sink into hypochondria.
2 The subject is affected by anxious or stuporous melancholia.
3 On rare occasions it may happen that there is manic excitement.
4 Often, on the contrary, he falls into states of confusion.
5 He wanders in his mind.

The dementia properly so called often follows an apoplectic stroke that causes serious losses. It may also begin with states of depression or confusion. Sometimes it takes the form of lacunary dementia, the patient being conscious of his intellectual and emotional disorders. Usually the mental deterioration is similar to that seen in senile dementia, with which this disease was confused for many years. The memory is gravely disturbed, showing amnesia, dysmnesia and obvious mistakes of which the subject may sometimes be conscious. The possibilities of concentration diminish. The association of ideas is poor, the imagination barren, mental life very much reduced and exceedingly monotonous. A striking feature is the patient's emotional incontinence: he laughs and weeps spastically. If we may rely upon the tests, his intellectual decline is not so marked as might be supposed: his intelligence is clouded and unavailable rather than destroyed.

When bilateral sub-bulbar lesions occur we speak of a pseudo-bulbar syndrome: it is characterized by high blood-pressure and disorders in phonation and swallowing; the subject laughs and cries spastically; he utters strange noises that resemble barking or whinnying rather than laughter. He walks with very small steps, and in those cases of astasia where sitting is impossible, he is obliged to mark time with his feet. He loses the control of his sphincters.

The pre-senile atrophic dementias, or Pick's and Alzheimer's diseases, are kinds of precocious senile dementia arising from bulbar disorders.

It must be added that some organic troubles which are to be seen outside old age also occur among the aged. There are cases of general syphilitic paralysis which appear after sixty: the patients, like those of other ages, often have delusions of grandeur. Some cerebral poisonings, oedemas and tumours of the brain may cause delirium and hallucination: cure is sometimes possible. Certain mental illnesses depend not on the brain but on other organs, especially the nervous system and the endocrine glands.

Neuroses are often successfully dealt with by treatment based upon psychoanalysis. Elderly people readily accept it, because they are very fond of going back into their past. They set up less resistance to recollection than younger patients. They will admit even distressing facts more easily – the reality that they had fled hitherto they now accept. But they take longer to benefit from this awareness because of the very fact that it is acquired without conflict. Many disorders are efficaciously treated by chemical medication.

Today it is thought that most disorders might be avoided if the social condition of the aged were less wretched. Bastide* writes, 'It may be asked whether senility is a consequence of ageing or whether on the contrary it is not rather an artificial product of a society that rejects the aged.' He quotes Dr Repond: 'Indeed, it is reasonable to wonder whether the old concept of senile dementia, the alleged result of cerebral disorders, should not be entirely overhauled, and whether these pseudo-dementias are not the result of psychosociological factors – whether they are not rapidly made worse by removal to inadequately equipped and managed institutions and by confinement

* *Sociologie des maladies mentales.*

in psychiatric hospitals where these patients are abandoned to themselves, deprived of the necessary psychological stimuli and cut off
from all vital interests, and where they have nothing to look forward
to but an end that everybody hopes will come soon. We even go so
far as to claim that the clinical picture of senile dementia may be an
artifact, due in the majority of cases to shortcomings in the treatment
and in the attempts at prevention and rehabilitation.'

8

Some examples of old age

When the old person is not the victim of economic and physiological conditions that reduce him to a subhuman state, he remains the individual he has been throughout the change and impairment of the ageing process: to a great extent his last years depend upon those of his middle life. Voltaire's open-minded approach earned him a fine old age, in spite of his cruel infirmities; whereas Chateaubriand prepared a most dismal end for himself. Swift the misanthrope and Whitman, the lover of life, were both tormented in the flesh, but they reacted very differently: the rage of the one made his distress far worse, while the other's optimism helped him to overcome his trials. Yet there is no inherent justice: far from it. Illness and the social context may wreck the end of an active and open-hearted life. Earlier choice and present chance step in to give each old age its particular aspect. We shall see the truth of this when we look into some individual cases.

It is very rare for old age to be looked upon as the crown of a life; but it does happen. As we have seen, this was so with Cornaro and Fontenelle, who had made ready for it throughout the course of their prudent, temperate lives. It was more strikingly so with Victor Hugo, who, even when he was young, had given old men a place of honour in his books. His example leads one to suppose that knowingly or not, we prepare a given old age for ourselves at the beginning of our life: chance, and particularly biological chance, may distort it; but in so far as it depends upon the individual, he has defined his old age by his way of life. As we have seen, that hatred of mankind which led Swift to imagine his ill-omened Struldbrugs led him to become a kind of Struldbrug himself in his last years. In Booz, Eviradnus and Jean Valjean, Hugo drew the patriarchal figure that he dreamt of becoming – the figure that he did in fact become.

As we know, when he was fourteen he wrote, 'I want to be Chateaubriand or nothing.' What he dreamt about was in fact a Napoleonic glory. This is confirmed by his words in the preface to *Marion Delorme*: 'Now, in our day, why should there not come a poet who would be to Shakespeare what Napoleon is to Charlemagne?' Hugo, the poet, seer and prophet, wished to be the pope of the creative world, and he expected age to confer this power upon him: he led his life in such a way that his hope should not be disappointed. In 1848 Lamartine condemned himself to an appalling old age: in 1852 Hugo saved his by going into exile. He became the glorious symbol that he had dreamt of becoming.

In his old age his sexual life remained active, as we know; and until 1878 his health was excellent. In 1873 Goncourt felt uneasy at seeing him, bare-headed, over-flowing with life, at the side of his son François-Victor, deathly pale and stretched on a chaise-longue. He was proud of still being able to run upstairs four steps at a time and he seemed to think that he was invulnerable. 'The old fellow is younger and more delightful than ever,' noted Flaubert in 1877. He remained cheerful and full of spirits. His 'little slit eyes darted a firework display of gaiety all round him' said a man who knew him well in his last years. His power of work did not fall off. But there were times when he felt that his inspiration was false and that his skill was all that was left to him. In 1869 he wrote in his secret poetry:

> On passe en vieillissant du trépied au pupitre . . .
> Adieu l'élan superbe et l'essor factieux . . .
> C'est fini, l'on devient bourgeois de l'Hélicon
> On loue au bord du gouffre un cottage à balcon.*

Yet, in a letter of 7 January of that same year he said, 'Oh, I know very well that I am not ageing but that on the contrary I am growing bigger: and it is that which tells me of the coming of death. What a proof of the soul! My body wanes, my mind waxes: in my old age there is a coming into flower.' In 1866 he had published *Les Travailleurs de la mer*, which had been enormously successful. He was working on *L'Homme qui rit*. Age had not dried up his romantic

---

* Growing old, one moves from the tripod to the desk. . . . Farewell to the splendid glow and the seditious flight. . . . It is over; one turns into a Heliconian bourgeois, and takes a cottage with a balcony on the edge of the abyss.

imagination – a most exceptional fact. He returned to the writing of plays with *Torquemada*. The war broke out. He went to Brussels and asked for a passport to Paris, saying that he wanted to enlist as a National Guard. His secret papers show that he had loftier ambitions: in his exile he had been the heart and soul of the opposition, so he expected the Republic to offer him full powers. He had made up his mind to accept and then to retire as soon as France was saved. By the time he reached Paris the provisional government had already been formed without his having been called upon. Nevertheless, a huge crowd was waiting for him at the station and they welcomed him in triumph. From a balcony and from his carriage he had to address them four times. 'In one hour you have repaid me for twenty years of exile,' he said. He had countless visitors. He was disappointed at having been set aside by the republicans, but for all that he did his best to influence the situation; he wrote an *Appel aux Allemands*, which was ignored, and an *Appel aux Parisiens* – 'Citizens! Every man to the front!' *Les Châtiments* was read in the theatres, and the takings were used to buy three pieces of artillery. Elected a deputy for Paris, he refused to help the supporters of the Commune to overthrow the provisional government: with the enemy at hand, it seemed to him too wild an adventure. But he felt nothing but disgust for the National Assembly: he wrote, 'I shall go to Bordeaux with the thought of earning banishment there.' In the Assembly he presided over the left wing. He refused to sign the 'odious treaty' put forward by Thiers. He defended Garibaldi against the attempt at cancelling his election: he was prevented from speaking – he resigned.

In 1868 he had lost his wife. At Bordeaux his son Charles died of apoplexy, and Hugo brought his coffin back to Paris, going on to Brussels to deal with his estate. He was shocked by the violence of the Commune; but in his poem *Pas de représailles* he begged the Versailles government not to act harshly. The executions outraged him – six thousand prisoners were shot for sixty-four hostages. He announced that he would give shelter to those who had been proscribed. The Belgian government expelled him. He went to Luxemburg, and there he continued to protest against the reprisals. He wrote *L'Année terrible, Quatre-vingt-treize* and some poems for a new *Légende des siècles*. He returned to Paris, where he met with a cold reception. He persuaded Thiers not to proscribe Rochefort. He was beaten in the January 1872 elections – people resented his defence of the communards. He left for Guernsey. He went on with the books he had roughed out and began *Théâtre en liberté*. He also wrote some poems which appeared in *Les Quatre Vents de l'esprit*, *Toute la lyre* and *Dernière gerbe*. He returned to Paris in 1873; and in December of that year he lost his son François-Victor. He wrote some poems that are numbered among his finest. What sets these late works apart is their combination of daring invention and mellifluous run. He plays with words and images with a greater freedom than ever before, recoiling at no wild flight or audacity – he is a soldier of fortune. But there is something a little mechanical about the virtuosity of these rhythms, this soaring, these dying falls. It is a surprisingly young poetry, and yet it is one that is marked by age.

Hugo liked reading his latest works to his friends. 'Gentlemen,' he said to them one evening, 'I am seventy-four and I am beginning my career.' He read *Le Soufflet du père* aloud. Many political friends who wanted him to return to public life came to see him. He was elected senator. He called for a law to amnesty the communards: only ten others voted with him. He made a speech against Mac-Mahon's proposal to dissolve the Chamber, and the left wing cheered him. The dissolution was passed by 149 votes to 130, but at the elections the republicans won 326 seats against 250, and Mac-Mahon resigned. It was an undeniable victory for Hugo.

In 1877 he published *L'Art d'être grand-père*, a monument to childhood and also to himself. He had been a tyrannical father to his sons and his daughter Adèle, who, incidentally, had just been put into an asylum. But he loved his grandchildren sincerely: he paid a great deal of attention to them; he was very unhappy when they were not with him, and he wrote them long letters. He was fond of antitheses, and he delighted in making the most of the spectacular contrast between his two aspects – that of the terrible giant who makes great men tremble and that of the kindly grandfather.

> Je suis dans notre temps de chocs et de fureurs Belluaire,
> et j'ai fair la guerre aux empereurs . . . [j'ai]
> Eté quarante ans fier, indompté, triomphant
> Et me voilà vaincu par un petit-enfant.*

and again

> Le tonnerre chez lui doit être bon enfant.†

---

* In our times of clash and fury, I am a belluarius, and I have made war on emperors. . . . For forty years I have been proud, untamed, triumphant; and see me now, conquered by a grandchild.

† At home even the thunder must be good-natured.

At other moments he claims deliberately to forget both fame and grandeur:

> . . . Triste, infini dans la paternité
> Je ne suis rien qu'un bon vieux sourire entêté
> Ces chers petits! Je suis le grand-père sans mesure . . .*

Just so much kindness ready to smile: but the fact is that he had a right to be proud of his life. It is also possible that he was helping himself to realize his old age (which for him as for everyone else remained an unrealizable) by means of fantasies – and he had a whole arsenal of them. There had already been Eviradnus, the old warrior before whom emperors trembled. Hugo invented new ones: 'I have the massive, haughty immobility of the rock.' He was turning the physical decay that makes the old man even more a slave of his body than ever into a mineralization, setting him free from the merely organic.

But above all he saw himself as a sacred character, a 'priest by right'. In *L'Epée* he wrote:

> Etant l'Ancien du peuple, il est prêtre de droit.
> C'est l'usage en nos monts. Nul front qui ne se baisse
> Devant ce sacerdoce auguste, la vieillesse.†

We have already seen this theme – like beauty, old age brings one closer to the divine. But the basis of his thought is even more radical: the aged man is God himself. When the little Jeanne speaks, 'God, the good old grandfather, listens, filled with wonder.'

If God is the good old grandfather, then the grandfather is like God. The world that God has created is extraordinarily like that which Hugo created in his books; and Hugo is speaking of both together when he writes,

> Moi je n'exige pas que Dieu toujours s'observe
> Il faut bien tolérer quelques excès de verve
> Chez un si grand poète . . .‡

In his poetry Hugo identifies the antitheses of nature with his own.

---

* Sad, infinite in paternity, a kindly obstinate old smile is all I am. Dear little souls! I am the boundless grandfather.

† Being the Elder of the people, he is priest by right. That is the custom of our hills. No forehead but that bows before this august priesthood that is old age.

‡ For my part I do not insist that God should always be circumspect. We must put up with some extravagance of spirits in so great a poet.

God is a great poet; the old poet is God. In another poem dated
1870 he writes:

> Mon vers sanglant, fumant, amer,
> . . . Est le vomissement de Dieu sur votre honte.*

In 1877 he could still write *L'Histoire d'un crime*; but in 1878,
after his stroke, he had to stop: the collections his followers published
contained poems written long before. From that year on, 'the handsome old man's health and then his mind seemed to move down a
step,' wrote Madame Alphonse Daudet.

Immediately after 28 June his family had taken him to Guernsey,
and a witness says, 'In the red drawing-room he had moments of
terrible depression during the evening: he leant his hands on the
chimney-piece, rested his forehead on them, and stood bowed there,
motionless for a long while.' Juliette, tormented by jealousy, tormented him – so much so that one August evening it made him
weep. He had always been economical, though at the same time very
open-handed. Gradually he became miserly. He was fascinated by
the enormous amount of money that he was then earning, and
Juliette had to beg for the modest sums she needed. Yet he still
experienced great happiness: his seventy-ninth birthday was celebrated as though it were a national holiday – a triumphal arch was
set up, and six hundred thousand people paraded under his windows.
A little later the name of the avenue d'Eylau was changed to avenue
Victor-Hugo and there was another parade in his honour on 14
July. Even the middle classes had come over, and in the end the
communards were amnestied. When he came into the Senate a few
days after his birthday, the whole Assembly rose and cheered him.
He received these tributes with tears of happiness. He was not
tortured by childhood resentments, as Andersen was, nor torn
apart by insoluble conflicts like Tolstoy; he was in complete harmony with himself. He had desired this apotheosis, this meeting
between a powerful old man and fame, from the very beginning;
his whole life had been directed towards it; and when it came it
filled his cup of happiness to overflowing.

He lost Juliette: her death moved him very deeply, and he began to
long for his own. 'What am I to do until the time comes for me to
die?' And again, 'There is so much mourning in my life that there
are no feast-days in it any more.'

* My bleeding, smoking, bitter verse . . . is God's vomit on your shame.

His strength, his hearing and his fitness all declined; he grew taciturn, and there was a frightened look in his eye; he no longer did any work at all. He got up at noon and his life was dull, uneventful, monotonous. Camille Saint-Saens wrote, 'Alas! Nothing can hold back time, and this fine intelligence is beginning to show signs of straying.' Yet Hugo looked forward to his death with an easy mind. His grandson says, 'He saw his end coming, and he spoke to us about it with such untroubled serenity that he never gave us the appalling vision of death.'

He had his fill of glory. 'It is time for me to disencumber the world,' he said one day. He believed in immortality. As early as 1860 he had written, 'I believe in God; I believe in the soul.' Dying meant meeting God, that is to say, another Hugo, and he looked forward to this tête-à-tête with a delighted curiosity. To a friend he said, 'I am old; I am going to die. I shall see God. See God! Talk to him! What a tremendous event! What shall I say to him? I often think about it. I am getting ready.' He never wondered what God would say to him. He died at eighty-three without agreeing to see a priest.

An elderly man is very fortunate indeed if it is possible for him to be actively occupied until his death. But it may happen that with age he values his activities less and therefore derives less pleasure from them. I shall quote two cases of men who retained their creative powers to the end and who yet died disillusioned – Michelangelo and Verdi.

It might almost be said that Michelangelo was born ill: age and worry finally ruined what was left of his health. His old age was an incessant battle against men and against a body worn out by vexations of every kind. When Paul III was made Pope, Michelangelo had been working for the last thirty years on the tomb of Julius II: the plans were on the grandest scale – a vast mausoleum for which he had already finished or roughed-out ten statues; but ill-will on the part of Julius himself and then of his descendants had not allowed him to finish it. Paul III insisted upon his spending all his time on the Last Judgement on the wall in the Sistine Chapel. He was forced to yield. He slept badly and ate little; he had fits of dizziness; in 1540 or 1541 he fell from the scaffolding and hurt his leg badly. At this time he was sixty-five. When the Last Judgement was unveiled on 25 December 1541 it earned him enormous fame, but he was also bitterly reproached for its obscenity. Paul III then insisted upon his painting

511

the frescoes of the Pauline Chapel; he complained of the extreme fatigue that this would cause him – fresco was not suitable for old age, he said. He had serious money-troubles: Julius ɪɪ's heirs accused him of having spent a fortune on the mausoleum, and they claimed repayment. The Pope told him not to worry about it but to devote himself entirely to his painting. 'But an artist paints with his head and not with his hands,' replied Michelangelo. 'A man whose mind is not free disgraces himself, and I can do nothing of value with all these troubles upon me.' He felt old and sick; he was afraid of death. But there were firmly-based friendships that helped him to support this arduous life. There was, for example, Cavalieri, whom he met when he was fifty-seven and with whom he was in love – platonic love or no, we cannot tell – while Cavalieri remained passionately devoted to him to the very end. He had great affection for his pupil Urbino, who worked with him on the Pauline frescoes and who was a steady support, a prop to his old age. He had many other followers and friends. But above all he was intellectually very closely attached to Vittoria Colonna, whose acquaintance he had made when he was sixty-three and she forty-six. She was ugly, and he looked upon her as a great friend – a man friend. He respected her opinions on art. In their conversation and their letters they spoke of a subject that mattered a great deal to both of them – the reform of the Church. He was deeply grieved when she died. 'She was very fond of me, and I was no less fond of her.'

In 1544 he fell so seriously ill that he thought he was in danger of death: he thanked Riccio his physician for having 'snatched him back from the grave'. In 1545 he was obliged to give up all idea of carrying out Julius' tomb as he had conceived it; it was pushed away into a corner of Saint Peter ad Vincula, where only the statue of Moses bears the mark of his genius. He went on painting the frescoes ordered by the Pope, and at the same time he busied himself with the fortification of Rome, worked on the building of the Farnese palace, and planned the palaces and the square of the Capitol. In 1548 he carved the bust of Brutus. When the Pauline Chapel was finished in 1549 he stopped painting and gave himself over entirely to architecture and sculpture.

In 1547 he was made chief architect of Saint Peter's; he was extremely unwilling to accept the appointment, and he was exposed to the persecutions of the Sangallo faction who loathed him – on various occasions the Pope had preferred Michelangelo's plans to Sangallo's.

Sangallo had died in 1546, but his friends were faithful to his memory. They had spoilt the work left unfinished by Bramante; Michelangelo insisted upon being given full authority and he began by destroying everything that was false to the original plan. He was accused of tyranny and of megalomania. In order to enforce his ideas, he spent his days on the site. His health was still causing him grave anxiety. 'As to the disorder that stops me urinating, I have been very ill with it; I have roared day and night without a moment's rest, and it is the opinion of the physicians that I have the stone.' Once again he was in danger of death.

In 1555, after twenty-five years of working together and of the closest friendship, he lost Urbino. Now all he wished for was to die. He had been obsessed by the idea of death all his life: when he was still quite young he spoke in his letters and poems of his 'coming death'; and he complained of being 'not only old but already numbered among the dead'. In his poems he described the way he felt his skin drying and growing leathery. As he grew old he tried to overcome his anxious distress and to look upon death as a deliverance that would open the gates of Paradise to the soul. When Urbino was taken from him, he began to long for it with all his heart. He had been deprived not only of a friend he loved but also of a support that was essential to him because of his age. He wrote to a friend, 'Living, he was my life; and dying he has taught me to die, not with regret but with a longing for death.' And in a sonnet:

> . . . His death
> Draws me on and makes me hasten towards another road
> To go where he is waiting for me and to live with him.

At the same period he wrote to Vasari, 'I no longer have any desire for anything, except death.' He described himself,

> Poor, old, compelled to serve others,
> If I do not die soon I am a man destroyed.

He lived on for eight years, and the end of his life was very dark and sad. He felt old, weak, sick, and he hated it. 'I am betrayed: my mirror is the traitor, and my fleeting days,' he wrote. He told Vasari that age prevented him from overseeing the work on Saint Peter's as closely as he should. The workmen perpetually found new excuses for not finishing: 'If shame and distress were mortal, I should no longer be alive,' he wrote. Writing to Ammannati in 1558 he complained of his age and his poor sight: 'I am old, blind and deaf, out of harmony with my hands and with my whole body.' His hearing was bad, and there was a buzzing in his ears.

But what saddened his last years more than anything was the change in his attitude towards his art. He had always been extremely pious and he thought that art's sole justification was the service of God; but he also thought that by painting and sculpting with love he was in fact serving Him. In his opinion, it was God Himself who guided the hand of the sincere artist – and imitating the beauties of creation by statues or paintings was a way of praising Him. This conviction had sustained him all his life, but towards the end it wavered. As early as 1538, when he heard that the Portuguese nobility attached no value to painting, he replied, 'They are right.' One of his sonnets shows that by 1554 he looked upon art as nothing more than a trifling occupation, one that had turned his mind from attending to his soul's salvation:

> So now, from this mad passion
> Which made me take art for an idol and a king
> I have learnt the burden of error that it bore
> And what misfortune springs from man's desire.

In another he wrote,

> The world's frivolities have robbed me of the time
> That I was given for reflecting upon God.

Sending these sonnets to Vasari, he said, 'When you are eighty, you will understand what I feel.'

He called his statues 'my puppets'. He thought he had been wrong to give himself up to art rather than to devote himself entirely to God. The idea that he was fulfilling a divine mission was mistaken: all he had done was to endanger his salvation. His disillusionment is explained by the greater intensity of his religious feeling, by the imminence of death – death, for which he was preparing himself with dread – and by all the troubles and vexations inflicted upon him and by his great weariness.

Yet he went on working. He drew up admirable plans for the Porta Pia. The building of Saint Peter's advanced: but he did not succeed in imposing either his conception of the whole or his plan for the façade. Only the dome corresponded to his dreams. He was racked by gout, and he could not sleep at night. He wandered about his studio and took up his chisel, cutting into the marble with

514

youthful vigour. He carved his loveliest Pietà. Sometimes at night, to turn his thoughts from his pain, he would ride about the deserted streets of Rome. It seemed to him that his mind had weakened. He wrote to Vasari, 'My memory and my brains have gone to wait for me somewhere else.' In his poems the idea of death recurred again and again. In 1561, when he was eighty-six, he had a heart-attack: for a long time he was much reduced and rather strange. Yet his energy was still undaunted. In 1563 his chief associate, a man he had appointed to control the work on Saint Peter's, was stabbed by his enemies, who also threw one of his best assistants, Gaeta, into prison on an accusation of theft. Michelangelo went to see the Pope, who had Gaeta set free. Michelangelo put him in charge of the building. The managing council appointed a man called Nanni in his place, and this Nanni tried to take over. Michelangelo stood up to him and secured the position for Gaeta. By this time he was eighty-eight. A little later, having caught cold during one of his nocturnal rambles, he died, crippled with pain, without having seen the completion of the dome of Saint Peter's.

The paradox of his old age is that although he was convinced that 'art and dying do not go together' (an idea he often expressed in his sonnets), and although he longed to devote himself to prayer, to his salvation, and to God, and although he continually complained of weariness, of vexations, and of the spiritual errors that were the price of the 'divine objects' he created, yet nevertheless to the very end he went on working and fighting for the undertakings to which he was committed. His letters and poems are dark, saturnine, disillusioned; yet it was at this very moment that, with the dome of Saint Peter's and the Rondanini Pietà, he reached his highest peak.

In spite of his splendid health, Verdi did not willingly accept old age. He was sixty-eight when his statue was unveiled with great pomp at the Scala in Milan. He was intensely annoyed: 'It means that I am old (which is true, alas!), that I am an old soldier fit for honourable retirement.... I did deplore this ceremony and I do deplore it now.' A little before he had worked over and much improved one of his earlier works, *Simon Boccanegra*, which had been played with great success. He set about recasting *Don Carlos*, and at seventy-one he conducted the rehearsals himself: the opera was warmly applauded, but this gave him no sort of pleasure. 'Poor artists, whom many people have ... shall we say the kindness ... to envy, slaves to a public that is most of the time ignorant (a lesser evil), capricious and unfair.' Throughout the world he was famous, and in Italy he was a kind of national monument – whenever he appeared at a play or a concert or even in the street he was cheered and applauded. But he was very strongly affected by that disillusionment which comes over many creative artists towards the end of their lives. When his friend Boito had given him the libretto of *Otello*, Faccio, the director of the Scala, urged him to write the music for it. Verdi replied, 'So you feel that I really have to finish this *Otello*? But who for? Who for? As far as I am concerned, I do not care one way or the other. And the public cares even less.' He lived mostly in the country, together with his wife, whom he loved, looking after his estate and his farms – he built a hospital on his land. He travelled; he went to see exhibitions; he led what seemed to be a pleasant life. But he was filled with a deep unhappiness: 'Life is born and then it vanishes: most of the time pointlessly. You reach the age of illness and infirmities, and then ... Amen.' He often said with great indignation, 'To work so hard and then to have to die!' He lost Carcano, one of his best friends, and in a letter he said, 'When we reach our age, fresh gaps appear around us every day.' And in another, on his seventy-second birthday: 'Today is the horrible date – I am seventy-two years old. How quickly they have passed, in spite of all the sad or happy things that have happened, in spite of all this overwork, all this weary labour. At our age we feel a need to lean on someone else. A few years ago I thought that I could stand on my own feet, that I had no need of anyone. Presumptuous creature! I am beginning to understand that I am ... very old.' More and more often he complained of being physically and mentally tired, and he was furious with nature for taking away his strength. He lost another of his dearest friends – a woman.

Yet during the years 1884–5, when he was seventy-two and seventy-three, he worked on *Otello*. When he handed over the music to Faccio he was exhausted, but he was satisfied with his work. He conducted the rehearsals himself. Well-known people from all over the world came for the first performance. Verdi was cheered, and the opera was immensely successful all over Italy: but people were disconcerted by the novelty of the work.

In 1888, the fiftieth anniversary of his first production, his jubilee was celebrated: the ceremonies, the flood of telegrams bearing the most illustrious names, all these tokens of his immense fame left him sullen and unmoved. In his opinion it was no more than a pointless fuss and excitement. He wanted to offset it by doing something he thought really useful, and he founded a rest-home for musicians and gave up a great deal of his time to it.

He had always wanted to write a comic opera. In 1889 he began *Falstaff*: but he did little work on it. He lost Prioli and Muzio, the best friends who were left to him. Faccio became senile. During the winter of 1890 he said that these deaths 'had quite thrown him off his balance'. He was so prostrated that he was unable to work. Yet by 1893 the opera was finished and in January he conducted the rehearsals, working six to eight hours a day. He was then eighty, and the doctors were astonished by his physical and mental equilibrium. Lombroso wrote, 'The anomaly is so great, so extraordinary, that it may well throw the ideas of those who have done research upon the subject into confusion.' The admiring Corrado Ricci described him: 'A cloud of white hair merges with his beard, forming a halo. Tall, slim, upright – people turn round when he goes by: lively in his way of talking and remembering names and dates: clear-minded when he explains his ideas on art.'

Falstaff was a triumph, with ovations for the author in Milan and Rome. In Paris too it was immensely successful. But Verdi's health was failing; from time to time he had a slight stroke. He composed religious music, but he found his state hard to bear. 'I am old, very old; I soon grow tired.' 'I am not very ill, but there are innumerable little things that go wrong. My legs will scarcely carry me and now I hardly walk at all. My sight is going: I cannot read for long. In short countless infirmities.' His wife's death was a terrible blow to him: 'I am alone. Sad, sad, sad.'

He had his *Pezzi sacri* performed in Paris and then at Turin; and they were very well received. But this did not take away his sadness. In 1901 he wrote, 'Although the doctors tell me I am not ill, everything tires me. I can no longer read, I can no longer write. I see little, feel still less, and above all my legs no longer hold me up. I am not living, I am merely existing. . . . There is no longer anything for me to do in this world.' A little later he left it, struck down by hemiplegia.

It may happen that old age, carrying on the life of the middle years without a break, may as it were pass unnoticed. For this to happen, it must develop in favourable circumstances. And the old person's earlier life must have provided him with a constellation of intellectual and emotional interests that will stand up to the weight of the years. A good example is Lou Andreas-Salomé, that remarkable woman who was beloved by Nietzsche, Rilke and many others, and who became Freud's friend and follower at the age of fifty. She had won her independence early in life; she had worked very hard, writing rather indifferent novels – she had no exaggerated opinion of them, but they brought her a great deal of success. She was inquisitive, strong-willed, active, passionately in love with life, and when she discovered sexuality – which she did only at the age of thirty-five – it became an enormously important part of her existence and of her conception of the world. In her book *Die Erotik* she explored the relationship between sex and art. In 1911 she discovered Freud, who provided her with scientific confirmation of her intuitions: she devoted herself to psychoanalysis. When she was over sixty she became a professional psychotherapist, obtaining excellent results that filled her with joy. She wrote a little, mostly on psychoanalytical subjects. Her husband, who meant little to her, died in 1920 and for some years she was in serious financial difficulties. She lived in Germany, in a big country house looked after by one old servant. Her work, her friendship with Freud (they exchanged many letters) and with Anna Freud filled her life. She was in disagreement with Freud on one important point: physical love had meant so much to her that she could not but look upon sexuality as the splendid and ennobling fulfilment of the individual, whereas Freud had a determinedly pessimistic view of man and of his sexual life. Yet this difference did not damage their understanding. When she was seventy she wrote *My Gratitude to Freud*, in which she paid public tribute to the scientist and the man; nevertheless, she was critical of his ideas on the creative process, the subject that had interested her most throughout her life. Freud praised the book warmly. 'It is a positive synthesis, one that allows us to hope that the bundle of nerves, muscles and sinews resulting from the analytical scalpel's transformation of the body may be reconstituted as a living organism.' She was proud of this praise: 'My psychoanalytical work makes me so happy that I should not give it up even if I were a millionaire,' she wrote.

At the very end of her life this happiness was seriously threatened. Nazism was triumphant: she was a Jewess, and Nietzsche's terrible sister hated her. However, she led so quiet and inconspicuous a life that she was not disturbed. Her body began to fail her. She suffered from diabetes and she had cancer of the breast. The breast had to be removed, but she did not tell her friends until she came back from hospital; then, having stuffed the top of her dress, she said with a smile, 'Nietzsche was right after all. Now I really do have a false bosom.' Her interest in life, ideas and people remained unaltered. She said she felt united to everything in existence, 'in one vast sharing of a common fate'. Her generosity and her intelligence earned her many friends. People who had liked her books often came to see her – there were girls among them. What is more she, who had always attached such importance to her masculine relationships, still had very close and valuable, though platonic, friendships with two young men. König, a professor of philosophy, and she had long intellectual conversations. Her relationship with Pfeiffer was closer and deeper. He told her all about his life and asked her advice: she became absolutely necessary to him. She had great confidence in him and gave him all her literary property as a gift. She decided to write her autobiography because it seemed to her that her story had a comforting, strengthening significance and because it was therefore useful to make it public. During the last months of her life she suffered from uremic poisoning; Pfeiffer came every day; they talked and he read her pages of her memoirs – she liked going back into her past. A few days before her death she said, in a surprised whisper, 'All my life I have done nothing but work. And really, when you come to think of it, why?' Her new friends cannot have managed to replace those she had lost, since she also said, 'If I let my thoughts wander, I find nobody. Death is best, after all.' She died in her sleep, on 5 June 1937. It is clear from her letters to Freud that sometimes she found physical pain 'enough to drive one to despair'. But she did not despair. She had given the world too much for the world not to give her back a great deal.

Yet it should not be supposed that by some kind of inherent justice a rich and courageous life is always rewarded with 'a fine old age'. Physical misfortunes and political and social circumstances may make the end very dark. This was so for Freud. His life displays a remarkable continuity – in transcending his past so he preserved it. He was a dashing innovator and a great worker; and although he frightened the age he lived in he succeeded in imposing his ideas upon it; he was a man of a fearless and unbending character, a loved and loving husband and father; and he should have had a fruitful and serene old age. Although it did not succeed in breaking him (in 1938 he terrorized the Nazis who had come to search his house, merely by appearing and looking at them), it was in fact an overwhelming trial for him because of his state of health, the rise of Nazism, his fears for the future of psychoanalysis, and the loss of his creative powers.

In 1922, when he was sixty-six and suffering from heart trouble, he wrote, 'On 13 March of this year I suddenly entered real old age. Since then the thought of death has never left me.' It was in the following year that he underwent the first operation on his palate: he suspected that the trouble was cancer, since he asked his doctor to provide him with the means of dying decently if he were condemned to long-drawn-out sufferings. He found those he did have to endure very hard to bear: and at this period he wrote to Lou Andreas-Salomé, 'I entirely share your views on the extreme distress we feel when we are confronted with exceptionally painful physical disorders; like you, I think them heart-breaking and, if someone were personally to blame for them, I should call them unspeakably base.' A month later he lost a four-year-old grandson whom he loved very dearly.* This was the only time in his life that he was ever seen to weep. 'I do not think I have ever felt such grief . . .' he wrote to a friend. 'My work is now forced and strained; fundamentally, I no longer care about anything at all.' He told others that he had entirely lost all pleasure in life. 'That is the secret of my indifference – of my courage, as people call it – with regard to the danger that threatens my own life.' That same year the committee which directed psychoanalytical work in Austria and to which he attached great importance threatened to fall apart. 'I have outlived the committee that was supposed to be my successor,' he wrote. 'Maybe I shall outlive the International Association. Let us hope that psychoanalysis will outlive me. But all this does darken the end of one's life.' He lamented the barrenness of his mind. 'I no longer have a single new idea. I have not written a single line.'

He was painfully conscious of the threat that hung over him. Writing to Abraham on 4 May 1924, he said, 'I am supposed to be on the road to recovery, but I have a deeply-rooted conviction that my end is near, a conviction that derives its nourishment from the unpleasant feelings and unending wretched little troubles caused by my scar, a kind of senile depression that centres about the conflict between the irrational desire to live and the resignation dictated by

* Three years earlier he had lost his daughter Sophie, the child's mother.

common sense. And in addition to this I feel a need for rest and an aversion for human intercourse.' On 13 May 1924 he wrote to Lou, 'I have indeed accepted all the terrible realities; it is the possibilities that I find hard to bear: I cannot resign myself to the idea of living under a perpetual threat. . . . Six hours of psychoanalysis – that is all that is left to me of my power of work. . . . How very many things have to be given up! And in return I am overwhelmed with honours for which I should never have raised my little finger.'

He who had brought so much passion into living now became less sensitive both to things and to people: when he was sixty-eight he wrote to Rank, assuring him of his friendship, and he said, 'Although I now look upon things *sub specie aeternitatis* and although I can no longer concern myself with them as passionately as once I did, no change that might alter our relations could leave me unmoved.' To Lou, on 10 May 1925: 'An armour of insensitivity is slowly forming around me: I observe it; I do not complain of it. It is a natural evolution, a way of beginning to become inorganic. It is what I believe they call "the detachment proper to old age". It must be connected with some decisive turning-point in the relationship between the two drives whose existence I have assumed. . . . Apart from that my life still remains bearable. Indeed, I believe I have discovered something of fundamental importance to our work; but I shall keep it to myself for some time yet.' It was very largely out of consideration for his family that he compelled himself to go on living; but on 11 October 1925 he wrote to Pfister, 'I am as weary as it is natural to be after a hard-working life, and I think I have fairly earned my rest. The organic elements that have held out together for so long are tending to fall apart. Who would wish them to remain forcibly connected any longer?'

Of all his followers, the one whose work he valued most highly and upon whom he relied for the advance of psychoanalysis was Abraham: and Abraham died in December 1925. Freud wrote to Jones, 'He filled me with a total confidence – it was the same with all of us – and this gave me a feeling of security. We must go on working and giving one another mutual support. . . . The work must continue: compared with that, we are scarcely of any importance at all.' He was worried by the opposition that psychoanalysis encountered: 'The world has come to have a certain respect for my work, but up until the present psychoanalysis has been accepted only by the analysts.'

He wrote essays and he began his autobiography. But he was obliged to undergo another extremely serious operation: part of his palate and his jaw were removed, and they were replaced by a very large apparatus which hurt him so much that he was sometimes compelled to take it out. It made him half deaf and it hindered both his eating and speaking. The only person he would allow to look after him was his daughter Anna. In addition to all this, his heart gave him trouble. 'I have so many physical disorders that I wonder how much longer I shall be able to go on with my professional work, particularly since the giving up of my beloved tobacco has dulled my intellectual interests. All this throws a threatening shadow over the near future.'

In 1926, speaking to the American Viereck, he said, 'It may be that the gods are merciful when they make our lives more unpleasant as we grow old. In the end, death seems less intolerable than the many burdens we have to bear.' He could no longer work, Writing to Jones on 20 March 1926 he said, 'My condition may prevent me from working any more at all – that is what I am coming to believe . . .' But he preserved an unshaken confidence in the value of his ideas: 'Both contradiction and recognition are utterly without importance once one possesses a certainty,' he wrote to Lou.

The committee (which did survive in the end) met to celebrate his seventieth birthday. But Ferenczi, his best disciple and his friend, began to move farther away from him. There were quarrels and disagreements at the Innsbruck congress. He still had great pain, and his apparatus had to be changed. 'I hate my mechanical jaw because the mechanism eats up so much of my precious strength.' He began writing *The Future of Civilization*, but pain made work difficult. And then again, as he wrote to Jones on 1 January 1929, 'Ideas used to come easily, but with advancing years this power I had, this facility of conception, has left me.' He no longer attached much value to what he wrote. Writing to Lou on 28 July 1929 and speaking of his last book, he said, 'This book . . . seems to me – and rightly, I am sure – completely superfluous, in comparison with my earlier works, which always corresponded to some inner necessity. But what else could I do? Smoking and playing cards all day is impossible. I cannot go for long walks any more and most of the things one reads no longer interest me.' When he exchanged letters with Einstein on the subject of peace three years later, he criticized his side of the correspondence harshly: he said he lowered his claims for his work, just as he had for his apparatus. That year he had to undergo five operations. To his grief Ferenczi was shut up in a lunatic asylum. And the psychoanalytical review, the *Verlag*,* which was kept going by his royalties, was threatened with extinction, since his books hardly sold at all.

Yet he had lost nothing of his fierceness and his attack. When Hitler came to power in 1933, Viereck publicly endorsed a letter in which his cousin, the Crown Prince, denied the existence of racial persecution. Freud wrote indignantly, 'I shall therefore tell you plainly that I am sorry you should have lowered yourself so far as to support such deplorable lies as those contained in your imperial cousin's letter. . . . With my deep regret.' The outlook was agonizing: 'I no longer feel anxious about the future of psychoanalysis. It is assured and I know it is in good hands. But the future of my children and my grandchildren is in peril. And my own powerlessness is heart-breaking!' In spite of his anxiety and his torments, he began his book on *Moses and Monotheism* in 1934. But he had doubts of himself. On 2 May 1935 he wrote to Zweig, 'Ever since I have not been allowed to smoke when I want, I have had no wish to write . . . or perhaps this excuse is useful to me to mask the barrenness of old age.' And to Lou on 16 May, 'I do not know whether I can still create anything: I do not think so, but in any case I have to pay such attention to my health that I do not have the time." And to Wittkowski on 6 January 1936, 'My power of production is exhausted. Most probably it is too late for it to come back.'

His want of intellectual power, his sickness, and his struggle with his failing body all became more and more hateful to him: the only reason that he forbade himself suicide was his reluctance to hurt his family. 'If I were alone,' he said to Jones, 'I should have done with life long ago.' He wanted to die: 'I believe I have discovered that the desire for everlasting rest is not something primordial or elementary: it expresses the need for getting rid of the feeling of inadequacy that comes upon the old, especially in the smaller details of life.'

In June 1935 he wrote to Thomas Mann, and speaking of his sixtieth birthday he said that he did not wish him to live to be too old. 'From my own experience, I think it is good if a merciful fate sets a reasonable limit to the length of time we live.' On 18 May 1936 he wrote to Stefan Zweig, 'Although I have been exceptionally happy in my family life . . . I still cannot get used to the grief and

* *Internationaler Psychoanalytscher Verlag.*

afflictions of old age and I look forward with longing to the journey into the void.' On 6 December 1936 he wrote to Marie Bonaparte that he was most painfully torn 'between the desire for rest and the fear of fresh sufferings if I live longer on the one hand, and on the other the anticipated pain of being cut off from everything that is still dear'. At the beginning of 1937 he was allowed to smoke a little and he suffered less; but his practice was falling off. 'It is understandable that patients should not rush to an analyst whose age offers so little in the way of security,' he wrote. He took to doing a little work once more and he finished *Moses II*. What gave him most distress was that he now doubted whether psychoanalysis would outlive him. On 17 October 1937 he wrote to Zweig, 'My work *is* behind me, as you say yourself. No one can tell in advance how posterity will judge it. I am not so sure myself. . . . The immediate future seems dark for my psychoanalysis too. At all events, nothing very pleasant can happen to me in the weeks or months I still have to live.' In 1933 he had believed in the future of psychoanalysis, but since then Nazism had triumphed: in 1933 Freud's books were publicly burnt in Berlin and in 1934 psychoanalysis was totally abolished in Germany. In 1936 the Gestapo seized everything belonging to the *Verlag* (which was finally confiscated in 1938). Freud was of the opinion that he personally could make no fresh contribution. His *Moses*, a continuation of the *Totem and Taboo* that he had written twenty-five years earlier, seemed to him more or less a going over of the same ground. 'An old man no longer discovers new ideas,' he wrote, speaking of this book. 'All that is left to him is self-repetition.' And again, 'I do not agree with my contemporary, Bernard Shaw, when he claims that men would become capable of doing something of value only if they were allowed to live three hundred years. Making life longer would be of no use whatsoever unless the conditions in which it was lived were wholly transformed.' Elsewhere he spoke of the 'decay of the creative faculties caused by old age'.

From all this it appears that in his opinion it was above all the weight of the past that brought about barrenness. Yet it seems to me that this hardening of his mind was largely due to the shrinking of his future. When in 1897 he found that his theories on hysteria were mistaken, he wrote to Fliess, 'I will tell you confidentially that I feel victorious rather than beaten.' The hysterical patients who came to see him had not been raped by their fathers as they claimed: they had dreamed of being so raped, and that was far more interesting.

He had what seemed an eternity before him to work out this discovery and to make the most of it: he could happily draw a line under the past. But now the near approach of his end deprived him of all spring. He had no new thoughts because he dared have none.

After the Anschluss he left for England. London gave him a warm welcome, and he discovered how widely famous he was. But still another operation, the most painful of them all, caused him atrocious suffering. He was full of anxiety for his sisters, who had stayed in Austria.* He feared for the future of his work. His last year was very dark and melancholy. He retained all his intellectual powers, his character remained unconquered – refusing the solution of suicide out of love for his wife and even more for his daughter Anna was a great proof of courage and altruism. He died in 1939. He had undergone thirty-three operations since 1923.

Chateaubriand loathed his old age. 'Old age is a shipwreck,' he used to say. He had dreaded it from the time he was thirty. When he was still young he cried out in distress, 'Unhappy man, I who cannot age and who am growing older every day.' During his last years he was not much unlike the man he had been before. He had always swung from passionate ambition to a contempt for the riches of this world. He had desired fame, and he had denounced its emptiness. He complained that he turned everything he touched into ashes: the moment his desires were satisfied disgust overwhelmed him. Whether he was eager or whether he was disillusioned, he was perpetually in search of the magnification of his own ego. His old age matched this pattern, but in darker colours.

He bitterly resented the Bourbons' ingratitude. He was a minister in 1816 and he was dismissed for having attacked the ordinance of 5 September in *La Monarchie selon la Charte*. He carried on a ferocious campaign against Decazes in his articles in *Le Conservateur* and succeeded in bringing about his fall. The government gave him, as the acknowledged leader of the ultra-monarchists, a mission to Berlin. In 1821 he was restored to the list of ministers and sent to London as ambassador. Then, to his delight, he was appointed plenipotentiary to the Congress of Verona: on his return he was made foreign minister. But Louis XVIII and Villèle hated him. Instead of supporting Villèle's bill for the reconversion of government stock in the Chamber of Peers he remained silent, and the motion was

* They all three died in the gas-chamber.

525

rejected. It was thought that he had wanted to bring Villèle down and Louis XVIII dismissed him. To get rid of him, he was sent as ambassador to Rome. He resented this bitterly, and he thought the monarchy was going to ruin for want of attending to his advice. In 1830 he was a minister once more: he refused to take the oath to Louis-Philippe – 'Unhappily I am not a creature of the present moment; I will not compound with fortune.' He gave up his office, he renounced his pension as a peer and he resigned as a minister. He was proud of this spectacular withdrawal. 'I was a loyal supporter of the *possible* Restoration, of the Restoration with liberties of all kinds. That Restoration came to look upon me as an enemy; it fell, and I must share its fate,' he wrote. Nevertheless he held himself out as a victim. 'He is perfectly absurd,' said the Duchesse de Broglie on this occasion. 'He always wants people to pity him for the misfortunes he inflicts upon himself.'

He was sixty-two. He had long been of the opinion that an elderly man ought to say farewell to the passions and to pleasure. As early as 1822, when he was fifty-four, he had written, 'Do not let us linger here below: let us go before we have seen the disappearance of our friends and of those only years that the poet thinks worthy of being lived. ... What is delightful at the age of love-affairs becomes an object of pain and regret in the forsaken years. One no longer yearns for the return of the smiling months; indeed, one dreads it ... all those things which make one need happiness and long for it are mortal now. You still feel the force of these charms, but they are for you no more: and the young people who enjoy them there beside you and who look at you with scorn fill you with jealousy.... You can love, but no one can love you any more.... The sight of renewal, of happiness everywhere, reduces you to a painful remembrance of your own pleasures of long ago.'

In 1823 he wrote *Délie*, a poem for a woman he loved and who loved him:

> Je sens l'amour mais ne puis l'inspirer
> La gloire hélas! ne rajeunit qu'un nom.*

He thought he was too old for any woman to be able to love him for himself. When he was sixty-two and a sixteen-year-old girl fell in love with him, he repulsed her. 'I have never been so ashamed – arousing a kind of fondness at my age seemed to me a downright

---

* I feel love but I cannot inspire it. A name alas is all that is made young by fame.

mockery; the more this eccentricity might have flattered me, the more I found it humiliating, rightly looking upon it as a piece of ridicule.' He explained this refusal in *Amour et vieillesse*.*

He did not retire from political life. He thought he had an important part to play: he put his pen at the service of the Legitimists and he hoped to cause the fall of Louis-Philippe. He wrote 'memoirs' and 'open letters'. He came to the support of the Duchesse de Berry, which earned him arrest and imprisonment: after a little while the charge was dismissed and he was let out. In his *Mémoire sur la captivité de la duchesse* he declared, 'Madame, your son is my king.' The day after the duchess had publicly stated that she had been secretly married in Italy he was brought before the courts. He was acquitted. The duchess begged him to go to Prague to plead her cause with the exiled royal family: she wanted to retain her title of Princess of France and her name. Chateaubriand agreed to go. He obtained permission for her to keep her title. Then he went to Venice to see the duchess, who sent him back to Prague again: she wanted Charles x to make an official declaration of her son's majority. Chateaubriand obeyed. His feelings for the former king were ambiguous: the man touched his heart, the ruler wounded it.

Chateaubriand now displayed an ostentatious contempt for the age he was living in. 'The meanness and triviality of men and things during the years 1831–2,' he noted. More than ever he spoke of himself as being disillusioned. Writing to his friend Hortense Allart he said, 'Power and love – everything is indifferent, everything is a weariness to me. . . . I have known a greater age, and the dwarfs who dabble in writing and politics today do not move me in the least.' In June 1834 he wrote to a friend, 'I am still just as you saw me last, devoid of faith, devoid of hope, and as things are now I find it very hard to preserve even a little *charity*. Society is vanishing, and it will not come to life again.' That year he published an essay called 'L'Avenir du Monde' in which he foretold the ruin of civilization.

By this time the Legitimists had been completely and finally defeated, but he went on writing against Louis-Philippe. This attitude earned him friends in all the parties of the opposition – the Legitimists, republicans and Bonapartists. He was particularly intimate with Armand Carrel; he went to see him at Sainte-Pélagie, and it was he who saw to his funeral. But many of these friendships were broken almost as soon as they were formed. In 1835 he defended

* Cf. p. 329.

the freedom of the press in a letter he sent to *La Quotidienne*: never-theless, the law forbidding attacks on royalty was passed. In this same year he suffered a literary setback: his tragedy *Moïse* was received with shouts of laughter. There were only five performances.

He already showed a very marked physical decline. In 1834 Lammenais wrote, 'I had not seen him for ten years. It seemed to me that he had changed and aged astonishingly – hollow mouth, nose pinched and wrinkled like the nose on a dead man's face, eyes sunk in their sockets.' He felt lost in a world that was no longer his. He wrote bitterly, 'The old men of former days were less unfortunate; they were strangers to youth but not to society. Nowadays one who lingers on in the world has seen not only men die all round him – he has also seen the death of ideas. Nothing resembles what he knew, neither principles nor customs nor deeds nor pleasures nor pains nor feelings. He belongs to a race unlike the human species in the midst of which he ends his days.' No elderly man has so frankly confessed the hatred he felt for the young. In the second part of *Amour et vieillesse* he makes the ageing René say, 'The sight of the happiness of the new generations rising all round me filled me with transports of the blackest jealousy; if I could have wiped them out I should have done so in an outburst of revenge and despair.' Resentment blinded him, and in a letter of 1834 he declared that literature was wholly dead in France.

He had refused the peer's pension that Charles X offered him and he was painfully short of money. In 1836 he decided to sell his *Mémoires d'outre-tombe* in advance to a partnership. He was then comfortably settled not far from Madame Récamier in a house in the rue du Bac. It was long since he had been in love with her: she had been passionately in love with him, though probably without being his mistress.* Now their relationship was one of very great, very close friendship. He led an extremely regular life, getting up at six, break-fasting with his wife, and working all the morning with his secretaries. In the afternoon he went to see Madame Récamier. His emotional life was not very cheerful; the misunderstandings between him and Madame de Chateaubriand sometimes reached the point of hatred. From 1835 onwards Madame Récamier was often unwell: she suff-ered from a neuralgia that made it almost impossible for her to speak. He had no social life. Sometimes Juliette invited friends, and from 1834 onwards he read them pieces of the *Mémoires d'outre-tombe*.

* It seems that for physiological reasons she never went to bed with any man.

528

But he almost never accepted any invitations, saying, 'I no longer belong to this world.' The feeling of banishment was very strong in him: 'And I, a spectator in a deserted theatre, its boxes empty, its lights put out, I sit there, the only man of my time left, alone before the lowered curtain, in the silence and the night.' He had always been easily bored: now it was even worse. 'Whoever lives long sees his life grow cold,' he wrote in 1836. 'The next morning he can no longer recover the interest that he had in the day before.' He did not even dream any more: 'Since I no longer have a future, I no longer have any dreams.' 'Lip-service is all I pay to life now; I have the spleen, a real disease.' Loménie said of him, 'This unfortunate great man is hideously bored; nothing moves him any more, nothing amuses him; he no longer has the least pleasure in anything; and the world is becoming more and more foreign to him.' In his 'Préface testamentaire' to the *Mémoires* Chateaubriand spoke of 'the boredom of those last forsaken hours that no one wants and that no one knows what to do with. At the end of life there comes a bitter age: nothing gives pleasure because one is worthy of nothing; of use to no one, a burden to all, one has but to take a single step to reach one's last resting-place. What is the point of dreaming on a deserted shore? What charming shapes could the future possibly have to show?'

It was not without regret that he had brought himself to sell his *Mémoires*; they would now appear immediately after his death, whereas he had intended them to be published only after fifty years had passed. 'I have mortgaged my grave,' he said, sadly. Nevertheless, he worked on the book with the greatest application. In 1830 he had made up his mind to *enlarge* and to *complete* it. He wanted to make it the 'epic' of his times. He rewrote the first part and placed it between a 'préface testamentaire' dated 1 December 1833 and a conclusion dealing with the future of the world. He began the writing of the second part in 1836. In 1837 he settled at Chantilly to write *Le Congrès de Vérone*, which he published in 1838. It was a defence of the Restoration, but one that was blended with severe criticism: the book also contained his own apologia – it was he who had started the war with Spain in 1823, and he boasted of it; he blamed France for sinking into the sleep of peace and he exhorted the country to make war on England; it would be an easy war he said, 'if we are not frightened of making a few necessary sacrifices'. He had lost none of his talent; he had never told a story better. But the book annoyed everyone, both the republicans and even more the Legitimists; and his criticisms irritated the royal family, who from that time onwards looked upon him as an enemy.

Chateaubriand's cantankerous indifference to his century grew worse with the years. He wrote to Vinet, 'I no longer believe in anything in politics, literature, fame or human affections. It all seems to me the emptiest as well as the most lamentable of vain imaginings.' He was the victim of a narcissistic melancholia and he complained without pause; he groaned over his agonies in the past and he made continual allusions to his coming death – to his grave. He was misfortune's special prey, the man who was to perish very soon, his heart quite broken. Tirelessly he returned to the disgust he felt for the present and the future. In 1839 he wrote, 'I have so great a disgust for everything, so great a contempt for the present and for the immediate future, so firm a persuasion that from now on men, taken in the mass, will be despicable creatures (and that for many hundreds of years), that I blush to employ my last hours in telling of things past, in drawing the portrait of a vanished world whose language and whose name they will no longer understand.'

'After Napoleon, an utter blank: we see the coming neither of an empire nor of a religion nor of the barbarians; civilization has risen to its highest point, but a material, unfruitful civilization, one that can produce nothing because life can be given only by the spirit; the paths of heaven are the only road to the birth of a nation. All these railways will do is lead us to the abyss with greater speed.'

'Old age,' says Vitrolles, 'had made the coldness of his heart and the sourness of his temper even worse. Although he was still wholly taken up with his fame, he could not forgive the world for outliving him. His prophecies were all dark and gloomy, but as vague and undefined as an evil dream.'

In 1841 Chateaubriand returned to the future, to its void, its nothingness: 'As it decomposes, the present civilization is not falling into barbarism; it is merely being lost; the vase that holds it has not poured its contents into another vase – the vase is broken and its liquid spilt abroad.'

He could not resign himself to old age. 'The years are like the Alps: the first are barely crossed before one sees others raise their heads. Alas, these last and highest mountains are sterile, uninhabited and white.'

Like many old men, he cried easily. He said that he had made 'a

530

wild expenditure of tears' when he wrote to the Duchesse de Berry; and when he was with Charles x his eyes were wet with emotion. 'A trifle would make him weep,' said his barber. He defended himself against this emotiveness by drawing an armour of insensitivity about him: he had always had a cold heart; he became a monster of selfishness. He behaved odiously to Madame Récamier. In 1841 she said to Loménie, 'Monsieur de Chateaubriand has a very noble mind, a vast degree of proper pride, and he possesses the utmost delicacy: he is ready to make any sacrifice at all for those he loves. But as for true sensitivity, he has not the slightest trace of it. More than once he has hurt me very much.'

'Monsieur de Chateaubriand,' said Alphonse de Custine, 'is not yet quite seventy-five, yet everything is failing him and above all he fails himself. Every evening he pays this poor woman his last farewells. . . . You find her weeping like a girl. . . . She is withering, breaking her heart; and neither she nor their friends can do anything with this spoilt old child.' In 1842 the Duchesse de Dino wrote, '[Barrante] also told me that Monseiur de Chateaubriand, whom he sees at l'Abbaye-aux-Bois at Madame Récamier's, has grown querulous, taciturn, discontented with everyone and everything. Madame Récamier's is a hard task, for she has to soothe the chafing of a morbid vanity and to compensate for his lost feelings of success.'

He finished his *Mémoires* in 1841, although he went on revising them until his death. In 1843, prompted by his confessor, he began a *Vie de Rancé*. He lived more and more closed in upon himself. He did write letters, particularly to women; but he no longer read anything at all. 'It is not his sight that has failed him for reading,' said Ballanche, 'it is the desire itself.' In company he was silent and ill-tempered. His health was very poor: from 1840 onwards he was tormented by rheumatism and fits of coughing. After this date all the descriptions left us by his contemporaries are dark and gloomy. There is one exception: in 1840 Custine wrote, 'Monsieur de Chateaubriand is livelier than ever, and he is more sincere than he was in his youth. . . . He has gained in truthfulness since he has given up hoping to accomplish anything. . . . I prefer him as he is now.' But three years later Custine found this 'sincerity' misplaced and unseemly. 'Old age makes the great writer envious and shameless. He now says all that he used to keep to himself.' In the same year Ballanche was concerned about his friend's health. 'Monsieur de

Chateaubriand is sinking in the cruellest way. . . . Real old age has come.'

Yet he was capable of going to London to see the Duc de Bordeaux. This was one of the greatest happinesses of his old age. The prince treated him with the utmost kindness: he sat on the side of his bed and drove about with him alone in his carriage. Chateaubriand felt 'enchanted and filled with hope', but his happiness showed itself only in tears: 'There I was, weeping like a fool,' he noted. Cuvillier-Fleury wrote to some friends of his, 'Chateaubriand was pitiful – all he could do was cry. . . . He looked more like one of those hired mourners who follow a coffin than the determined forerunner of a Legitimist renaissance, and his tears reduced his friends to despair.'

In 1844 he had a shock that quite shattered him: Emile Girardin bought the right to publish the *Mémoires d'outre-tombe* in instalments in *La Presse* before they appeared in book-form. The 1836 contract had not foreseen this possibility and there was no clause forbidding it. In a preface that remained unpublished Chateaubriand uttered a cry of indignation: 'With no respect for my unqualified, directly-stated wishes, with no regard for my memory, my ideas are to be sold by retail.' He was wounded in his pride as a writer and in his dignity as a man. He took up his manuscript again, suppressing passages that now, with this kind of publication in view, seemed to him indiscreet. The book did not reach its final form until 1847.

In 1845 Chateaubriand still had strength enough to go to Venice to see the Duc de Bordeaux for the second time. But he was more and more silent, gloomy, motionless. In 1846 Manuel was struck by his appearance: 'He was old, very old, and as it were ashamed of being so; he was so broken that the man was quite lost in the ancient.' He exaggerated his deafness, shut himself up in silence for hours, and sat unmoving in his armchair, as though he were paralysed.

There were moments when he came back to life. 'Why,' said Sainte-Beuve, 'that man whom we saw reduced to sitting there dumb, gloomy, and saying no to everything – he has delightful returns to himself, flashes of life.' But gradually he became completely ossified. In 1847 Hugo wrote, 'This morning [Alexis de Saint-Priest] saw Monsieur de Chateaubriand, in other words a ghost. Monsieur de Chateaubriand is completely paralysed; he no longer walks, he no longer moves. Only his head is alive. He was very red, and his eye dull and lifeless. He rose, and uttered a few indistinct sounds.'

His wife died in 1847. Madame de Récamier became blind: Chateaubriand was carried to her bedside, and they held hands in silence. He was only half aware of outside events. In February 1848 the Comte d'Estourmel observed, 'Nothing can equal the profound indifference with which Monsieur de Chateaubriand, once so passionate in politics, accepts the revolutions. . . . When he was told of the fall of the July government he said no more than "Very well. It had to come." ' He died immediately after the insurrection of June 1848.

There is something both exemplary and extreme about the case of Lamartine. As I have said, and as we have seen, good and bad fortune make the notion of an inherent justice illusory. Yet it was the faults of his youth and his middle age that Lamartine paid for so dearly in his last years.

As a young man he loved money, luxury, social success and fame. The reputation that he had won as a poet was not enough for him: his ambition was to become a politician of the first rank. He was narcissistic, overweening and vain, squandering several inheritances to support his role of the great man. After one failure, he was elected to the *Académie*. At this time he was enormously popular as a writer. He was a most zealous Legitimist, and as soon as he had reached the necessary age he began to campaign for election as a deputy: he was defeated the first time, but the second he was elected. Being reluctant to sit either on the Right or the Centre, he said he would prefer to be 'on the ceiling' – above the parties. He was a friend of Lammenais (who, by the way, dissociated himself from his opportunist, shifting policy) and he called for a 'reduction' of social injustice. He had discovered the existence of the proletariat. But the discovery frightened him and his advice was that they should not be stirred up – 'All that you will find there is everlasting blindness, want of meaning, cruel jealousy of all social superiority, cowardice and cruelty.' As a landed proprietor, very strongly attached to his possessions, he wanted order to be maintained above all; but he disliked the growth of capitalism and the business world. He attacked the bankers, industrial concentrations and the rule of money; and this earned him many enemies among the wealthy. He was very widely blamed for his inconstancy. Elected by the Legitimists, he nevertheless came out in favour of liberty in 1834, and then he supported the reactionary laws.

In 1843, furious with the conservatives, who had inflicted several defeats upon him (he had been refused the presidency of the Chamber), he broke with the bourgeois monarchy and joined the opposition. Being filled with admiration for himself and persuaded that he knew everything, he became more and more convinced that a great political destiny was awaiting him. He decided to be the champion of democracy. 'Remember that you were too fond of luxury, horses and gambling: take care you do not grow too fond of popularity,' said a friend. And popularity was in fact his ultimate passion. In 1848 he thought his hour had come. The opposition triumphed. The people were shouting for the republic. He stood forward as its great supporter. But in his heart he dreaded any far-reaching social upheaval: he defended the republic only because he saw it as the most conservative form of society; and indeed the universal suffrage that it implied provided the 'volcano of the masses' with a 'safety-valve', and an 'outlet for the steam'. Since in 1848 the peasants far outweighed the proletariat, and since they would obviously vote for the conservatives, then it would be the people themselves that would resist the 'reds'. Lamartine's aim in setting up the republic was to preserve order. And it was this double game that earned him his triumph in February. The republicans saw him as the man who had installed the republic; the others, as the man who had managed to keep it within bounds. It was thus that at the age of fifty-eight he appeared as *l'homme du salut commun*, his country's saviour.

On 27 February he wrote to his niece, 'The Legitimists, Catholics and republicans are all rallying to me as to a single party.' On 23 April he was elected in ten departments, ten million people voting for him. He wrote, 'I see myself as a positive miracle. I cannot appear anywhere without a riot of love breaking out.' But the misunderstanding upon which this unanimity rested was bound to vanish; and then it became apparent that far from being the point of meeting of the Left and Right, he represented neither the one nor the other, and he was reduced to a nullity.

It was the Right that first felt itself betrayed. The right wing would have liked him to assume power alone, and to have taken their men under his orders: they would have swept the republicans aside and unleashed a civil war immediately. He did not wish to put so early an end to the work that was his pride. He refused to play the part of liquidator and he successfully pressed for the appointment of an executive committee of five. From that moment on he was hated: he was only elected the fourth member of the committee, one place above his candidate Ledru-Rollin, who was looked upon as an extremist. The right-wing press and the salons burst out in furious attacks upon him. He was accused of having provoked the events of 15 May, when 150,000 Parisians, summoned by the Clubs, invaded the Assembly. On 21 May, on the champ-de-Mars, the National Guard did not cheer him. Yet his entire policy was making ready for the massacre that made him so hated by the people. He had Cavaignac appointed minister of war and allowed him to take over important powers. At the beginning of June he agreed to the closing of the National Workshops. When he saw that blood was about to flow, he called for a huge display of military force to prevent the uprising: he did not get it. Together with the whole committee he resigned on 24 June. Cavaignac had the workers shot down and for some months he exercised a positive dictatorship: the National Guard took part in the massacre. Lamartine wrote to his niece Valentine, 'I no longer have a single blond hair left: it is all wintry white.' And again, 'I am finished as a statesman and as a tribune: that sinew is broken for ever.' It had been very presumptuous and irresponsible of him not to have foreseen that his double-dealing would inevitably end in this disaster: the proletariat could not possibly endure being used to set up a regime that would wipe out their claims; and the owners of property could only drown the workers' revolt in blood.

Lamartine made one more well-received speech on the election of the president, demanding that he should be chosen by universal suffrage: but at the election, in which although he did not put himself forward he was in fact a candidate, he received no more than 17,910 votes as against a million and a half for Cavaignac and five and a half for Bonaparte. 'He lay down that night, believing that he had France at his bedside; he went to sleep drunk with self-esteem; he dreamt of Lamartine the dictator; he awoke – he was alone,' wrote Louis Blanc. The entirety of his old age was tragically marked by these events: he never recovered. He had squandered two or three million francs of inherited money, his wife's dowry, and the five or six millions his writing had brought him. By the end of 1843 he already owed one million two hundred thousand francs; and his unfortunate speculations increased his debt. He set himself to writing with furious energy in order to satisfy his creditors: his wife could not copy as fast as he poured out his work. The coup d'état of 2 December swept away the newspapers he had founded and he lost still more money. He left his handsome flat in the rue de l'Université for a humbler dwelling; but he still kept four houses, an army of servants and a great many horses; he bought waist-coats and shoes by the dozen. Duns and process-servers harassed and badgered him. He imagined that he had a genius for business and he would listen to no advice: bad harvests and bankruptcies came one after another, and at the age of sixty-five he wrote, 'I am deeper in the mire than ever, tired of the struggle and of life: hoping and losing hope is worse than plain despair. And that is how things are with me.' He ransacked history-books for his lives of great men. He was called a public writer, a street-corner scribe; people spoke of 'his disreputable old age'; he was insulted in the papers, treated as a figure of fun. For all that he retained a childish vanity bordering upon paraphrenia: he thought that success was owing to him, that his setbacks were the revenge of fate, and that God and the world were concerned only with him. He started a *Cours familier de littérature*, which began to appear in 1856. He begged for subscriptions in a preface: 'Like the ghost in Macbeth my years thrust their hands over my shoulder, showing me not crowns but a tomb; and would to God I lay there now.' He was haunted by the events of 1848: 'Happy are those who die at their task, struck down by the revolutions of which they were a part! Death is their punishment, that is true; but it is also their refuge. And what of the punishment of living? Do you reckon that a nothing?'

His name still meant something, for in 1857 Flaubert's friends wanted him to join in the defence of *Madame Bovary*: he shilly-shallied. More and more he felt overwhelmed by life. 'When life is not a scaffold it is a pillory. Which is better, a twenty years' agony of mind or the blow of an axe that lasts a second?' He had stopped writing verse, but he did produce one well-known poem, *La Vigne et la maison*, in which an old man, lost in the midst of a forgetful world, calls his memories to mind:

> Quel fardeau te pèse, ô mon âme,
> Sur ce vieux lit des jours par l'ennui retourné . . .*

Once he had been a dandy: now he walked about in a threadbare coat, all sprinkled with tobacco. He wanted a national subscription to be opened for him. But he was so ashamed of it that he said, 'I

* What a burden weighs on you, oh my soul, upon this bed of many days tumbled by care and trouble.

wish I were dead.' And again 'I am so humiliated by my misfortunes that I no longer dare to go to see a friend for fear of meeting an enemy.' As for friends, he had practically none left at all. At the Académie his fellow-members avoided speaking to him; he stayed in his corner. 'My crime is that by preventing them from killing one another as they chose during the days of anarchy I was of service to all the parties, and I displeased them,' he wrote bitterly in one of the many manifestoes that he produced to defend his cause. He wrote numbers of them, but in vain: the subscription did not answer. He indulged in so shameless a publicity that an American suggested that he should show himself in the States, delivering his speech on the red flag in one town after another for two years. He was forced to cut the timber on one of his estates to live, but he refused to sell his land. The municipality of Paris granted him a pretty house just outside the city, but he was still hard pressed, quite desperate. 'He has fits of despair that drive me to distraction,' said his wife.

He perpetually went over his political past, lamenting it with bitter grief. He maintained that the statesman was superior to the poet, and he went so far as to regret that he had ever written. Apart from these reflections, he never spoke of anything but money, which he did until his listeners were worn out. In 1860 he at last agreed to sell Milly. Instantly his creditors flocked about him, four hundred appearing in seventeen days. On the day of the sale he came into his niece Valentine's room, carrying a sprig of ivy. 'This is all that is left to me of Milly,' he said, bursting into tears. A little later he said to a friend, 'Would you like to see the unhappiest man in the world? Then look at me.'

His wife died in 1863 and he secretly married Valentine. In 1867 his mind began to fail. And he had the humiliation of being granted a pension by the Empire. On 1 May he had a stroke. Ever more shut up in himself, he became almost dumb. One evening, as he was going to bed, he sat down on the stairs. 'What is the point? What is the point of sleeping and beginning the task all over again? Leave me here.' When he was in the country in 1868 he often escaped after dinner, and they would find him wandering in the fields. That same year he died.

Lamartine owed this appalling old age partly to the faults that were obvious in his youth and middle years – childish levity, capriciousness, vanity, love of making a display, presumption, want of critical sense and of foresight. But above all it was the price of his conduct in

1848. Here he fully showed himself for what he was. Out of love for popularity he acted the conciliator; he took himself in with his own pretence, whereas in fact he had only been playing a hypocritical part. His love for money and dissolute living, his respect for aristocratic values and his desire to maintain order all made him a man of the Right; yet he made a show of liberalism in his defence of the republic, which in fact suited his reactionary schemes. He earned himself hatred on every side. The owners of property, who had already distrusted him, cast him out with loathing because he would not agree to be a mere tool in their hands. Yet he did serve them against the people, whose cause he had pretended to make his own; and in the end he 'slipped in the workers' blood and so fell'.

Conclusion

Old age is not a necessary end to human life. It does not even represent what Sartre has called the 'necessity of our contingency', as the body does. A great many creatures – the may-flies, for example – die after having reproduced their kind, without going through any phase of degeneration. However, it is an empiric and universal truth that after a certain number of years the human organism undergoes a decline. The process is inescapable. At the end of a certain time it results in a reduction in the individual's activities: very often it also brings about a diminution in his mental faculties and an alteration in his attitude towards the world.

A particular value has sometimes been given to old age for social or political reasons. For some individuals – women in ancient China, for instance – it has been a refuge against the harshness of life in the adult years. Others, from a pessimistic general outlook on life, settle comfortably into it: for if the will to live is regarded as a source of unhappiness, then it is reasonable to prefer a semi-death to life. But the vast majority of mankind look upon the coming of old age with sorrow or rebellion. It fills them with more aversion than death itself.

And indeed, it is old age, rather than death, that is to be contrasted with life. Old age is life's parody, whereas death transforms life into a destiny: in a way it preserves it by giving it the absolute dimension – 'As into himself eternity changes him at last.' Death does away with time. Let us take a man who has just been buried: his last days had no greater truth than the rest; his life has become a whole, all of whose parts are equally present in so far as they have all been engulfed by the void. Victor Hugo is at the same time both thirty and eighty; and he is both thirty and eighty for ever. But when he *was* eighty, the present he was living through overlaid the past. This dominance of the present is saddening when it is a degradation or even a denial of what has been; and almost always this is so. Former happenings and acquired knowledge retain their place, but in a life whose fire has died: they *have been*. When memory decays, they sink and vanish in a mocking darkness; life unravels stitch by stitch like a frayed piece of knitting, leaving nothing but meaningless strands of wool in the old person's hands. Worse still, his acquired indifference challenges his passions, convictions and activities: thus we see Monsieur de Charlus wrecking the aristocratic pride that was his reason for existence by a single greeting, or Arina Petrovna making her peace with a hated son. What is the point of having worked so hard if one finds that all is labour lost, as Rousseau puts it, and if one no longer sets the least value upon what has been accomplished? Michelangelo's contempt for his 'puppets' is heart-breaking; and if we go along with him into his last years we too are oppressed with sadness by the emptiness of his endeavours. But these moments of depression can in no way affect the splendours of his work as a whole. Not all old people give up the struggle: far from it – many are remarkable for their stubborn perseverance. But in this case they often become caricatures of themselves. Their will goes on, by its own impetus, with no reason or even against all reason. They began by forming their desire, their will, with a given end in view. Now they desire because they have desired. Broadly speaking habit, automatic reactions and hardened, set ways take the place of invention among the old. There is some truth in Faguet's* observation: 'Old age is a perpetual play that a man acts in order to deceive others and himself, and whose chief drollery lies in the fact that he acts badly.'

Morality teaches a serene acceptance of those ills which science and technology are powerless to abolish – pain, disease, old age. It claims that the courageous endurance of that very condition which lessens us is a way of increasing our stature. If he lacks other projects, the elderly man may commit himself to this. But here we are playing with words. Projects have to do only with our activities. Undergoing age is not an activity. Growing, ripening, ageing, dying – the passing of time is predestined, inevitable.

There is only one solution if old age is not to be an absurd parody of our former life, and that is to go on pursuing ends that give our existence a meaning – devotion to individuals, to groups or to causes, social, political, intellectual or creative work. In spite of the moralists' opinion to the contrary, in old age we should wish still to have passions strong enough to prevent us turning in upon ourselves.

* He wrote a furious little essay against old age called *Les dix commandements de la vieillesse*.

One's life has value so long as one attributes value to the life of others, by means of love, friendship, indignation, compassion. When this is so, then there are still valid reasons for activity or speech. People are often advised to 'prepare' for old age. But if this merely applies to setting aside money, choosing the place for retirement and laying on hobbies, we shall not be much the better for it when the day comes. It is far better not to think about it too much, but to live a fairly committed, fairly justified life so that one may go on in the same path even when all illusions have vanished and one's zeal for life has died away.

But these possibilities are granted only to a handful of privileged people: it is in the last years of life that the gap between them and the vast majority of mankind becomes deepest and most obvious. When we set these two old ages side by side we can answer the question we asked at the beginning of this book: what are the inescapable factors in the individual's decline? And to what degree is society responsible for them?

As we have seen, the age at which this decline begins has always depended upon the class to which a man belongs. Today a miner is finished, done for, at the age of fifty, whereas many of the privileged carry their eighty years lightly. The worker's decline begins earlier; its course is also far more rapid. During his years of 'survival' his shattered body is the victim of disease and infirmity; whereas an elderly man who has had the good fortune of being able to look after his health may keep it more or less undamaged until his death.

When they are old the exploited classes are condemned if not to utter destitution then at least to extreme poverty, to uncomfortable, inconvenient dwellings, and to loneliness, all of which results in a feeling of failure and a generalized anxiety. They sink into a torpid bewilderment that has physical repercussions: even the mental diseases from which they suffer are to a great extent the product of the system. Even if he keeps his health and his clarity of mind, the retired man is nevertheless the victim of that terrible curse, boredom. Deprived of his hold upon the world, he is incapable of finding another because apart from his work his free time was alienated, rendered sterile. The manual worker does not even manage to kill time. His gloomy idleness leads to an apathy that endangers what physical and intellectual balance he may still possess.

The injury he has suffered during the course of his life is still more radical. The reason that the retired man is rendered hopeless by the want of meaning in his present life is that the meaning of his existence has been stolen from him from the very beginning. A law, as merciless as Lassalle's 'brazen law' of wages, allows him no more than the right to reproduce his life: it refuses him the possibility of discovering any justification for it. When he escapes from the fetters of his trade or calling, all he sees around him is an arid waste: he has not been granted the possibility of committing himself to projects that might have peopled the world with goals, values and reasons for existence.

That is the crime of our society. Its 'old-age policy' is scandalous. But even more scandalous still is the treatment that it inflicts upon the majority of men during their youth and their maturity. It prefabricates the maimed and wretched state that is theirs when they are old. It is the fault of society that the decline of old age begins too early, that it is rapid, physically painful and, because they enter in upon it with empty hands, morally atrocious. Some exploited, alienated individuals inevitably become 'throw-outs', 'rejects', once their strength has failed them.

That is why all the remedies that have been put forward to lessen the distress of the aged are such a mockery: not one of them can possibly repair the systematic destruction that has been inflicted upon some men throughout their lives. Even if they are treated and taken care of, their health cannot be given back. Even if decent houses are built for them, they cannot be provided with the culture, the interests and the responsibilities that would give their life a meaning. I do not say that it would be entirely pointless to improve their condition here and now; but doing so would provide no solution whatsoever to the real problem of old age. What should a society be, so that in his last years a man might still be a man?

The answer is simple: he would always have to have been treated as a man. By the fate it allots to its members who can no longer work, society gives itself away – it has always looked upon them as so much material. Society confesses that as far as it is concerned, profit is the only thing that counts, and that its 'humanism' is mere window-dressing. In the nineteenth century the ruling classes explicitly equated the proletariat with barbarism. The struggles of the workers succeeded in making the proletariat part of mankind once more. But only in so far as it is productive. Society turns away from the aged worker as though he belonged to another species.

That is why the whole question is buried in a conspiracy of silence.

Old age exposes the failure of our entire civilization. It is the whole man that must be re-made, it is the whole relationship between man and man that must be recast if we wish the old person's state to be acceptable. A man should not start his last years alone and empty-handed. If culture were not a mere inactive mass of information, acquired once and for all and then forgotten, if it were effectual and living, and if it meant that the individual had a grasp upon his environment that would fulfil and renew itself as the years go by, then he would be an active, useful citizen at every age. If he were not atomized from his childhood, shut away and isolated among other atoms, and if he shared in a collective life, as necessary and as much a matter of course as his own, then he would never experience banishment. Nowhere, and in no century, have these conditions obtained. Although the socialist countries may have come a little closer to them than the capitalist, they still have a very long way to go.

We may dream that in the ideal society that I have just spoken of old age would be virtually non-existent. As it does happen in certain privileged cases, the individual, though privately weakened by age but not obviously lessened by it, would one day be attacked by some disease from which he would not recover: he would die without having suffered any degradation. The last age would really comply with the definition given by certain bourgeois ideologists – a period of life different from youth and maturity, but possessing its own balance and leaving a wide range of possibilities open to the individual.

We are far from this state of affairs. Society cares about the individual only in so far as he is profitable. The young know this. Their anxiety as they enter in upon social life matches the anguish of the old as they are excluded from it. Between these two ages, the problem is hidden by routine. The young man dreads this machine that is about to seize hold of him, and sometimes he tries to defend himself by throwing half-bricks; the old man, rejected by it, exhausted and naked, has nothing left but his eyes to weep with. Between youth and age there turns the machine, the crusher of men – of men who let themselves be crushed because it never even occurs to them that they can escape it. Once we have understood what the state of the aged really is, we cannot satisfy ourselves with calling for a more generous 'old-age policy', higher pensions, decent housing and organized leisure. It is the whole system that is at issue and our claim cannot be otherwise than radical – change life itself.

APPENDIX I

The hundred-year-olds

I must say a few words about one very particular category of old people: the centenarians. There were between six and seven hundred in France in 1959 and the majority of these were to be found in Brittany. Most were under a hundred and two, and between 1920 and 1942 none was over a hundred and four at the time of death. There are many more women than men: Dr Delore, who directed the 1959 inquiry, estimates that the proportion is more than four out of five. He counted twenty-four women out of a total of twenty-seven individuals. These women had had a great variety of jobs. They had been retired for thirty or forty years; and they were then living in the country with their children or grandchildren, or in some cases in institutions or rest-homes. They had lost their husbands twenty to forty years earlier. They had very little money; they were all thin, not one of them weighing more than 9st 7lb. They loved their food but ate little. Many of them were strong and well, and this also applied to the men – there was one who played billiards at over ninety-nine. Some of the women were slightly shaky, they were a little hard of hearing and their sight was dim, but they were neither blind nor deaf. They slept well. They passed their time reading, knitting or taking short walks. Their minds were clear and their memories excellent. They were independent, even-tempered and sometimes gay; they had a lively sense of humour and they were very sociable. They were high-handed towards their seventy-year-old children and treated them as young people. Sometimes they complained of the present-day generation, but they were interested in modern times and kept in touch with what was going on. Heredity appeared to be one of the factors in their longevity: they none of them had any pathological history and had never suffered from any chronic illness. They did not seem to be afraid of death. In the main, they behaved very differently from old people junior to them. Had they survived because of their exceptional physical and mental health? Or did their satisfaction in having lived so long give them their serenity? The inquiry has no answer to this question.

Dr Grave E. Bird gave the Society of Oriental Psychology the results of his twenty years' research on four hundred people of more than a hundred years old. His conclusions are in agreement with those of Dr Delore: 'Most of the people in this group make careful plans for the future; they are interested in public affairs and are capable of youthful enthusiasm. They have their little fads and a sharp sense of humour; their appetites are good and they have great powers of resistance. They usually enjoy perfect mental health; they are optimistic and they show no sign of being afraid of death.'

Those centenarians who have been under observation in the United States gave the same impression: they were active and happy. Visher studied two men of over a hundred who were active, happy and seemingly in good health, although later their post-mortems showed that several of their organs were diseased.

In 1963 the Cuban newspapers devoted a whole page to some people of over a hundred. Among them was the particularly interesting case of a former black slave; an ethnologist recorded his recollections on tape. Historical evidence showed that he really was a hundred and four years old, as he claimed to be. He had an excellent memory which, although it was a trifle confused over certain periods, allowed him to recapitulate his entire life. His hair was white, his health good. He was a little suspicious at the beginning of the series of interviews, but later he listened willingly to his interviewer's questions and replied at great length. He was in full possession of his intellectual faculties.*

In remote parts of the world many of those who claim to be a hundred obviously are not; as there are no birth certificates they can claim an extraordinary longevity in all good faith. But those who really are more than a hundred years old are almost always quite exceptional beings.

* *Esclave à Cuba*, by Miguel Barnet, published by Gallimard.

APPENDIX II

Robert E. Burger:
Who cares for the aged?*

Approximately one of every ten Americans is over sixty-five, and the proportion is increasing every year. Two-thirds of these Americans suffer from some chronic condition – high blood pressure, arthritis, diabetes, or other afflictions. Yet there are only about thirty thousand institutions of all kinds designed to take care of them – with enough beds to handle only one out of fifty. The majority of the aged, in addition, do not qualify for either Medicare or Medicaid. The *median* annual income for the single person over sixty-five is $1,055, and thirty per cent – single or married – live in poverty. Their families, therefore, must be able to pay what amounts to half of a normal take-home wage per month for even the most limited care.

The financial dilemma posed by nursing homes reflects a more fundamental question. What is the place of the aged in America? Most Americans have accepted the assumption that the aged are better off by themselves. We seem to believe that their medical needs are different, and that they can be treated more efficiently as a group; that their interests and their sensibilities are protected when they are among others of their own age; and that they live longer, happier lives away from the pressures of the competitive, youthful world. All of these assumptions are fundamentally incorrect, but the pressures leading to them are easy to understand. We have not been able to face the basic medical need of the aged – rehabilitation. A definitive study in 1966 of two thousand public-welfare patients of New York nursing homes concluded that, 'extensive rehabilitation of aged

* An article in the *Saturday Review* of 25 January 1969. Robert E. Burger is co-author with Richard Garvin of *Where they go to die.*

546

residents in nursing homes is neither practical nor socially productive. . . . Maximum rehabilitation efforts should be applied earlier,
and in other sites than nursing homes.' We have habitually viewed
the nursing home not as a place for rehabilitation at all, but as 'the
last resort' for a 'difficult' older person. Thus, the basic technique
of rehabilitation – keeping the patient active – has been systematically precluded by the way such homes are filled and financed.
Bedridden patients receive a higher welfare payment, require less
attention, and seldom leave.

The rapid industrialization of America has also stripped our aged
of the responsibilities and functions they possessed in an agrarian
society. Unproductive, they soon feel unwanted. And so the pressures for separation from society grow on both sides, a tendency that
seems to have psychological validity among younger and younger
age groups. The executive 'retires early' because his fifty-ish age level
has put him out of contention for a promotion. The blue-collar
worker buys a condominium in a 'retirement village' (minimum
age, once fifty-three, is now down to forty-five), because his grown
children have no real contact with him.

These psychological pressures, working to widen the gap between
the old and young, have received unexpected impetus from another
source. The miracle that has made old age possible for many more
Americans has also made it more frustrating. Modern medicine has
increased the life expectancy for American men from forty-nine
years in 1900 to almost seventy years today. Yet the life expectancy
for men at the age of sixty-five is fourteen additional years, compared to thirteen in 1900. We have prolonged life in general, thereby
creating a larger group of the aged; but we have not prolonged the
life of the aged. Worse, we have not made the life of the aged meaningful or in any sense self-sufficient. Instead, we have placed most of
the burdens of health care on the shoulders of the aged and their
families.

The American 'solution' – nursing homes, homes for the aged, rest
homes, retirement villages – begs the question of whether the aged
are better off away from society. We have been able to hide the problem of the impossible demands of medical attention for the aged
only by putting the aged who are ill out of public sight.

The latest fad in the stock market, according to financial colum-
nist Sylvia Porter, is the nursing home business. Even before Medicare was voted in, such firms as Holiday Inn and Sheraton Hotels

were planning nursing home chains. At least seven chains are now publicly owned and, according to *Business Week*, 'most have become high fliers'. Federally financed programmes are obviously behind this boomlet, as they are responsible for the construction of housing for the aged in low-income redevelopment projects. Tax laws have also made church-sponsored old-age apartment complexes financially feasible. It would seem that, although the cost to the individual family may still be high, care for the aged is catching up with the medical and environmental problem.

A basic misconception, however, clouds the issue. Medicare covers only a small minority of the aged – those who require post-hospital care for a maximum of a hundred days. In the language of the bill, Title XVIII of the Social Security Act of 1967, a Medicare patient is one who needs 'extended care' in a 'medically orientated' facility. 'Extended' means extended from a hospital, not extended in time or extensive in nature. The idea of Medicare was to take old people out of hospitals when they could be treated adequately in a nursing home near a hospital before going home. Medicare pays sixteen dollars a day for room, board, and medical care to the nursing home, for each qualified patient. It is not intended to provide a solution for old people who wish to retire from society.

The nursing home chains touted in financial circles have been developed merely for the specialized need of providing hospital-related, short-term care. It is a sad commentary on the standards of nursing homes prior to Medicare that such a wide-open market exists for facilities that meet even the nominal requirements of Title XVIII. To qualify under Medicare, a home must have a physician and a registered nurse 'on call' around the clock – and, since the home must be affiliated with a hospital in the first place, this presents no problem. The physical-therapy specialists required by Medicare would also be only a matter of cost, not availability.

In the strictest sense of the phrase, these Medicare facilities are nursing homes. Yet the expression has been used so loosely in the past that a new nomenclature has been felt necessary. Such homes are officially referred to as 'medically oriented nursing homes'.

Non-medically oriented nursing homes, a contradiction in terms, make up the market for long-term or terminal care of the aged. Such facilities, as well as the more aptly described rest homes and homes for the aged, benefit from another provision of the 1967 Social

Security Act, Title XIX. Dubbed 'Medicaid' but usually confused with Medicare, this legislation is far broader in application and depends on matching programmes established state by state. The Medicaid programme is really nothing new as far as the aged are concerned, nor, in many cases, does it increase the level of care for the aged offered in state welfare programmes. Institutions are paid about the same amounts under Medicaid as they were under previous programmes (a basic rate of about $300 a month per patient), but more of the money now comes from Washington. Medicaid simply provides a financial base for medical assistance to citizens of all ages who fall in certain income categories. Residents of New York State are familiar with the comprehensive programme initiated by Governor Rockefeller under the Medicaid programme, which directly affects about one out of ten people in New York City. Besides dramatizing the skyrocketing costs of providing adequate medical care for the general public, Medicaid initially gave promise of establishing some kind of uniformity and enforceable standards among participating doctors and institutions.

Yet Medicaid has proved to be toothless in regulating the institutions that are subsidized by this law to care for the aged. 'Welfare' or 'MAA' (Medical Assistance to the Aged) patients and the homes that will take them are still the responsibility of *state* licensing agencies. This was assured by powerful lobbying by nursing home associations in writing key provisions of Medicaid. For years, state authorities have grappled with the problem of how to regulate substandard homes for the aged when strict enforcement would bring only further hardship on their patients. When threatened with being closed up for persistent violations, operators of ragtag homes shrug, 'What do you want us to do – throw them out in the street?'

Of the roughly thirty thousand institutions offering long-term care for the aged, more than half make no pretence of offering adequate nursing care. The law in most states requires a registered nurse or a licensed practical nurse to be in attendance eight hours a day at homes that care for MAA patients. But the standards for a 'practical nurse' hardly measure up to the demands of aged patients with both psychological and medical problems. The shortage of registered nurses for good paying jobs in hospitals suggests the quality of care offered by registered nurses in nursing homes – whose average salary breaks down to $2.40 an hour. Practical nurses average $1·65, and the national average for all employees in nursing homes is less than $1·25. 'Nurse's Aide' has become almost a meaningless designation in the trade, yet it is constantly used by nursing home operators to rationalize their fees. If a licensing agency finds that a home is ignoring the requirement of having a professional nurse on duty, a 'grace period' is extended until the situation can be remedied. Some homes have been in 'grace periods' for a year at a time. The Oregon Board of Health only expressed the common dilemma when it stated, 'It is a hoax on the public to call these institutions for old people "nursing homes" when there is no nursing service.'

The hoax is perpetuated by individual states, however, in refusing to reorganize their agencies which regulate the field. And the three hundred dollars or more per month paid by the state for each welfare patient subsidizes substandard homes and spawns new ones.

At the other end of the medical profession, an equally destructive masquerade goes on. This is the practice of doctors setting up or sponsoring a nursing home to which they refer patients without disclosing their interest. Several years ago, Consumers Union termed this a 'festering scandal that warrants prompt attention by the American Medical Association'. The AMA, however, lobbies side by side with the American Nursing Home Association. Far from being attended to, this problem of conflict of interest has been openly dismissed by the new nursing home promoters. (Four Seasons Nursing Centers of America, Inc., is one of many developers who finance their homes by selling interests to physicians. Four Seasons reports that fifty per cent of its beds are often filled by referrals from their doctor-owners.)

Potentially more dangerous than conflict of interest is the moral and financial weight that the medical profession is throwing behind nursing homes as *the* solution to the problems of the aged. Rehabilitation is simply not a profitable field for investment.

It can be argued that at least these new physician-sponsored homes are correcting the abuses that have plagued the industry for the last thirty years. Yet, for every new home with private rooms, a beauty parlour, a cocktail hour, and physiotherapists (at $600–$900 a month), there are a dozen that exist by cutting all possible corners to make a $300 a month subsidy from the state profitable.

According to the National Fire Prevention Association, the most dangerous place to be in America, with respect to fire, is in a nursing home. Nursing-home fires are especially terrifying because of the helplessness of their victims. The N.F.P.A. has stated that deaths resulting from these fires could be greatly reduced or eliminated if sprinkler systems were universally required. But in many states, such a regulation has been systematically opposed by nursing-home or homes-for-the-aged groups on the grounds that it would put many homes out of business. In the most disastrous fire in Ohio's history, a modern, concrete-block structure became a funeral pyre for sixty-three aged patients in 1963 – yet the state association successfully blocked a sprinkler ordinance that might have made such a fire impossible.

A second abuse is the threat to health in general. Gerontologists tell us that one of the most dangerous treatments for non-psychotic seniles is enforced inactivity. Under the pressure of Medicaid payments (and other 'welfare' payments before Medicaid), patients are confined to bed more often than necessary, to earn a $3 to $5 additional subsidy. They are also easier to deal with, pose less of an insurance hazard from falls, and are more permanent guests.

Mere confinement to a bed, moreover, is only the beginning of the health hazard to the patient. In the typically understaffed home, the patient is not turned in his bed often enough to prevent the dreaded decubitus ulcer (euphemistically, a bedsore), an open wound which is as painful as it is difficult to arrest. The misuse of drugs, either to control patients or to cut expenses, is widespread and leads to irreversible medical problems that untrained help cannot be expected to handle. A less publicized abuse is the deprivation of those small conveniences and human activities that make up the stuff of life and, in many cases, are all that make life worth living. Food, for example, is a constant problem in the substandard home. In the states with admittedly the best nursing homes, the average spent per patient per day for food is ninety-four cents – and this is according to the homes' own figures supplied to justify the highest possible welfare rate. The patient's sense of purpose, or even the mere feeling of accomplishing something is absent – and this void is exploited by unscrupulous nursing home operators to cow the patients, to prevent exposure of other abuses, or to magnify their own importance. One of the most common complaints from visitors to nursing homes is the disregard for the privacy of patients. Operators often conduct an inspection tour for the benefit of prospective customers without the faintest apology to the dumbfounded patients on exhibition.

Perhaps the basic abuse is the insult to the patient as a person.

Sometimes this occurs by intention. The notorious 'life-care contract', for instance, amounts to an insurance policy, paid in advance by the patient or his family in a lump sum, and guarantees a bed as long as the patient lives. Whether he lives or dies, however, the money is in the hands of the person who stands to benefit from the patient's early demise. By stripping the patient of his will to live – through daily sniping, snubs, and slurs – a nursing home can kill a man. Even where life-care contracts are simply a reasonable bet by both parties, the unconscious resentment of a guest who is 'overdue' cannot fail to have its effect.

In spite of numerous newspaper exposés, voluminous testimony at Congressional hearings, and an endless recitation of personal experiences by nurses, patients, and their relatives, the official stance of the industry is first to deny the existence of a problem, and second to blame any documented abuses on government red tape. When the Attorney General of California recently issued a report charging an $8-million 'bilking' of Medical by doctors, pharmacies, hospitals, and nursing homes, spokesmen for these groups called the accusation 'unfounded'. 'Only a small minority' always seems to be the culprit. Yet the state, which pays an average of $140,000 a year to each home under Medical, claims that *most* of these homes are guilty of double billing, over-servicing, padding, or all three.

The Department of Health, Education, and Welfare has promised a nation-wide review of Medicare and Medicaid as a result of the California scandal. This review could well be the opportunity for a look into the social and medical aspects of our old-age institutions as well as their financial meanderings.

Hopefully legislators and government agencies will examine the obvious alternatives to institutional care of the aged. In the parallel field of the mentally handicapped, 'de-institutionalization' has already begun. Three-fourths of the population of the village of Botton, England, consist of mentally handicapped adults who have achieved a degree of isolation consistent with their malady but have, at the same time, avoided the hospital atmosphere and psychological imprisonment of an institution. At recent conferences in the United States, specialists in this field have called for an end to the 'bounty' that government agencies confer on institutions for each handicapped inmate, thereby frustrating any other form of care.

Among the alternatives to institutional care of the aged are two

552

general courses of action: greater stress on rehabilitation, socially and psychologically as well as physically, will have to be made as profitable as 'terminal care' for any chance of success on a large scale. Medicare, with its higher medical standards and limitation to short-term care, is a step in this direction. Unfortunately, its impetus has been all but smothered in the far broader and less selective provisions of Medicaid.

Perhaps the most direct method of encouraging rehabilitation is simply to offer Medicare and Medicaid benefits to the person rather than to the institution that claims him as a patient. Payments could be made to the family for medical treatments under the supervision of their doctor and for nursing care when no adult relatives are at home. If this seems a less efficient method than mass-care in an institution, consider the success of Homemakers, Inc. This profit-minded operation now has franchises in some fifteen major cities, offering in-home nursing or attendant care at well under the cost of a nursing or rest home. Similar services are offered in some metropolitan areas by non-profit groups.

The point is that Medicare provides only for emergency in-home care, and Medicaid offers a maximum of four hours a day. Far too many old people who desperately require some sort of personal care therefore find themselves caught in a trap between the regulations of federal and state programmes – simply because these programmes are built on institutional requirements rather than the variety of personal needs. H.E.W. officials are now exploring an 'intermediate' form of Medicare that would recognize more general medical needs of old people other than post-hospital recuperation. Given our commitment to institutions, this at least offers a measure of relief for the present.

Amendments to Medicaid, to become effective in 1969, indicate that Congress is not unaware of the drawbacks of the present system. Although state agencies must still police the programme, benefits are to be broadened beyond institutional care, and higher standards will be required – such as disclosure of ownership of nursing homes, accounting for drugs, and a level of health services similar to that of Medicare. By 31 December 1969, national fire safety regulations will go into effect for Medicaid facilities.

Strict enforcement of Medicaid provisions at the state level will have to come before the stranglehold of substandard institutions can be broken. Nursing-home associations must realize that such enforcement and such exposés as the Attorney General's report in California can only help them, not hurt them. The need for good nursing homes will remain for a long time to come in a competitive, profit-motivated society. At the same time, the more basic need for a just, human, and respectful treatment of twenty million aged Americans cannot remain unfulfilled.

Charles Boucher, senior medical officer in the British Ministry of Health, says: 'Our philosophy is that old people want to remain at home, in their own houses, surrounded by their own possessions, their own memories. We don't mind whether it is a good home, a bad home, a tiny home. That's where we believe they should be ... where they feel secure, where they've got confidence. It's tempting to think that it's a matter of institutions and that sort of thing. I think it is rather like condemning old cars to the scrap heap.'

The condition of aged workers in the socialist countries

In France, Greece, Italy, Portugal and Iceland the employee pays a contribution, it is less than the employer's except in Iceland where it is twice as much. In the USSR and the popular democracies, on the other hand, social security is financed entirely by public and social organizations: Hungary, where workers have to contribute, is an exception. These countries' economy is run according to an overall plan of which their old-age policy is a part, and it is not subject to interference from private interests. Old people's lives should be better looked after in these states than they are in the capitalist countries. But unhappily it seems that this is not always the case.

My sources of information are varied. Sometimes they are official reports and sometimes they come from private individuals. In both cases it is difficult to know their exact value. I give them for what they are worth, as some sort of general indication.

According to official sources this is how matters stand in the USSR. There are twenty million people over sixty, which is about ten per cent of the population. The right to social security was laid down in the 1836 constitution; it had been acknowledged ever since the Soviet regime came into existence. Its application has progressively spread and taken shape. Up until 1964 members of the kolkhoz did not benefit from it: they were insured through mutual assistance funds. In 1964 a special social legislation was worked out for them. Co-operative workers, artists and household workers also benefit from a special system. All wage-earners benefit from the general plan. Men draw their pensions at sixty so long as they have twenty-five years of paid work behind them; women draw theirs at fifty-five if they have worked for twenty years. For particularly exacting work the pension-age is fifty with twenty years' work for men, and for women forty-five with fifteen years' work. Higher pensions are provided for those who have worked at least ten years longer than the necessary minimum. The state budget for pensions was 2·9 thousand million roubles in 1955: in 1956 a law was passed raising it, and by 1965 it had become 10·5 thousand million roubles.

The lower the salary the higher the coefficient by which the pension is calculated. For a monthly salary of thirty-five roubles the pensioner receives a hundred per cent; those earning more than a hundred roubles get only half their pay. The highest possible pension is fixed at a hundred and twenty roubles. Pensioners have the right to go on working for a monthly salary of up to a hundred roubles; their work is supervised by social security commissions. About two per cent of pensioners work; this includes kolkhoz members.

Traditionally, even in the towns old parents live with their children. This solution is encouraged in all socialist countries be-cause of the housing problem. A very great many of the women work in the home. They are retired earlier than the men so that grand-mothers with pensions can take the mother's place. I have spoken of the disadvantages of this system. A grandmother who takes on the mother's duties gets little satisfaction from doing so; she is only a substitute and her authority is uncertain. The children may be taken from her if, for instance, the young couple goes away to live in a remote place where she cannot accompany them. But at least old people do not end their days in loneliness.

On the other hand, in the USSR they can also live by themselves, in either traditional dwellings or in centres. These last years many old people have been housed in special buildings where they live on the lower floors. There are a great many old people's homes, most of which are in the suburbs. The equipment of the majority is modest, but it is made possible for their inmates to partake in various cultural activities and amusements. They are much less abandoned by their families and by society than they are with us.

As people are much more closely linked with political and social life, the old do not feel excluded from the community; they continue their activities either within the Party in their district or the building where they live, etc.

The country as a whole has a lower standard of living than France. But there is far less difference between a pensioner's income and what he used to earn than there is here; he has a far more decent life than our very poor people.

Perhaps this picture is a little too optimistic. One must remember that in the USSR and most other socialist countries the official salary represents only about sixty per cent of the worker's real resources. And his pension is calculated upon that sixty per cent. To know what the real conditions of pensioners are, one would have to know whether the old can still find the 'black-market jobs' and the 'arrangements' that allow workers to make ends meet. If not they would experience a considerable drop in their standard of living.

I have the following report from Hungary.

In Hungary, as in all other countries, old age is accompanied by problems which touch each individual concerned but at the same time society as a whole. These problems are composed on the one hand of those general factors necessarily connected with the effects of ageing and on the other of those which are specifically connected with the form of society. The latter therefore vary according to the country. Hungary's particularities account for the following picture.

During these last twenty-five years statistics show a general ageing of the population. This arises from two factors – the growth in population and the lengthening of the average life.

It is widely known that after the extraordinary increase in the number of births of the early fifties the following ten years saw a very considerable decrease; in 1954 the number of births reached the record figure of 23 per mille, but in 1962 it went down to 12·9 per mille. And although during the last three years this tendency has been replaced by an ascending curve – the birth-rate reached 15 per mille in 1968 – the long earlier period of increase has nevertheless caused a relative ageing of the population.

At the same time the Hungarian population has aged in the absolute sense. This phenomenon arises largely from the social, economic, sanitary and cultural measures that have been taken over the last twenty-five years and that have had the effect of lengthening the average duration of life. In 1941, the average expectation of life at birth in Hungary was 54·9 years for men and 58·2 for women; now it is 67 for men and 71·8 for women. Since the end of the Second World War, therefore, the number and proportion of people aged sixty and over has considerably increased. In 1941 there were reckoned to be 997,400 people of over sixty, that is to say 10·7 per cent of the population; in 1949 these figures increased to 1,073,000 and 11·6 per cent; in 1960 they went up to 1,372,700 and 13·8 per cent; the most recent figures, for 1968, show 1,685,000 people over sixty, amounting to 16·4 per cent of the population.

The population research department of the Central Statistics Office foresees that, in conformity with this ageing process, by 1975 the percentage of over-sixty-year-olds in Hungary will be 18·5 per cent. And even if there should be another huge increase in births, this process will not slow down, since the average expectation of life will certainly go on increasing with each generation. The present average expectation of life for aged men and women is as follows:

PRESENT AGE	EXPECTATION FOR MEN (IN YEARS)	EXPECTATION FOR WOMEN (IN YEARS)
60	+ 15·88	+ 18·33
70	+ 9·75	+ 10·99
80	+ 5·27	+ 5·76

In Hungary too the three main problems of the old are means of subsistence, illness and loneliness. The socialist state makes a considerable contribution towards lessening these problems, on the one hand by a system of grants and on the other by means of its social policy as a whole. In this respect, we should compare the present situation with that of twenty-five years ago and note the magnitude of the progress and the changes that have been brought about. Broadly speaking, it may be said that there has been a radical change of principle; for whereas the former social insurance discriminated between the various categories of worker, both in the quantity and the quality of its grants, the new legislation, developing progressively with the adoption of socialism, has created a homogeneous system of social security.

In practice, this change and progress is shown by the fact that on one hand the number of beneficiaries from social grants has continually increased, eventually including the peasants who, before the 1945 Liberation were automatically excluded from any social security benefits, and on the other, that these grants have shown steady and important increases in amount, keeping pace with the economic consolidation of the State.

At the present time 97 per cent of Hungary's population, or in other words very nearly everybody, benefits from the social services.

From two points of view, however, this figure of 97 per cent calls for some explanations. First from that of evolution: the number of beneficiaries has continually grown, rising from 31 per cent in 1938 to 47 per cent in 1950, and then to 85 per cent in 1960. Secondly there are the 3 per cent who do not benefit: these are mostly old people who were formerly in the liberal professions and who had therefore not troubled about retirement pensions. Although they are still not pensioned at present, in the case of illness they do get certain grants if they need them – free medical treatment, free medicines and free hospitalization. In Hungary, therefore, old age is seen in the general context of a socialist society's concept of assistance.

As far as the means of subsistence is concerned, this is assured for the great majority (three-quarters) of the aged by what is termed the homogeneous law of retirement and other pensions. A little less than a quarter of those old people who do not benefit from these grants because they had not earned them by paying insurance, do nevertheless receive regular help from the State, except in cases where their families are so prosperous that they should be able to keep them. Speaking of this category of the old, we should observe that the number of regular recipients of State aid reaches 150,000, and that even those who are kept by their families have the right to various medical and hospital benefits from the social services.

The 'homogeneous law' is so called because it guarantees equal and identical rights to all workers. Before the Liberation the pension scheme was worked out in such a way that there was discrimination according to class and social level, some being treated as privileged; and this necessarily caused discontent. The first homogeneous law on pensions in socialist Hungary dates from 1 January 1952, and the second (an extension of the first) was promulgated on 1 October 1954. The third, which is now in force and which modifies the earlier laws in many places, adding to the benefits, has been in operation since 1 January 1959.

The essential characteristics of this pension scheme are as follows: workers benefit from it just as much as office staff and the like; intellectual workers, members of agricultural and artisanal co-operatives just as much as independent craftsmen; in other words it affects all levels of society. The scheme also benefits the families of those who are insured and of rightful claimants; it covers old age and incapacity from work; it is primarily concerned with the aged but in the case of the death of a person with a right to a pension it guarantees his benefits to his widow and to the parents or grand-parents he supported.

At present wage-earners must be fifty-five (women) and sixty (men) to receive a pension. In agricultural cooperatives women must be sixty, and men sixty-five. Those who have been employed in work that is dangerous to health (men for twenty-five years and women for twenty) receive their pensions five years earlier. The law governing pensions gives detailed lists of what constitutes dangerous work, distinguishing between the various categories: for example, it provides special advantages for those who have worked for fifteen years in an atmospheric pressure exceeding the normal.

The amount of the pension is calculated according to the number of years worked and the average wages received. In 1969 it was necessary to have worked twenty-four years to have a full pension; from 1970 onwards twenty-five years will be required. Those who can show at least ten years of work (less than the necessary time for the whole pension) receive a reduced pension. Two factors govern the total amount of these full or partial payments: the basic and the complementary pension. The basic comes to fifty per cent of the average wages received and the complementary (which also applies to the partial pensions) provides one per cent of the basic for every year worked since 1 January 1929.

The following table, which shows the increase in the number of the beneficiaries and in the cost to the State, is a valuable illustration of the increasing scope of the pension scheme in Hungary in the last ten years:

YEARS	NUMBER OF PENSIONERS (PER MILLE)	STATE EXPENDITURE (IN MILLIONS OF FORINTS)
1959	623	3,722
1960	636	4,427
1961	796	5,080
1962	912	5,737
1963	983	6,421
1964	1,046	6,992
1965	1,101	7,712
1966	1,156	8,711
1967	1,213	9,514
1968	1,269	10,339
1969	1,319	—

Although the Hungarian system of pensions ranks among the world's most highly developed systems, it has problems which have not yet been solved. One example of this is the striking difference between the pensions laid down in the past and those established more recently: a difference that persists in spite of the fact that earlier pensions have been increased several times. Again, there are differences between pensions based upon the same system but at different periods. Because of the regular rise in nominal salaries the present pensions are worth more than those established earlier.

The authorities are paying a great deal of attention to these and many other questions. For example, in recent talks between the government and the central committee of the unions there was discussion of the reduction of the real value of pensions on account of the rise in prices in 1969 and earlier years, although this reduction is not yet very great. The secretary-general of the central committee of the unions therefore called upon the government to take all proper measures to safeguard the purchasing power of the pensioners. The new laws, the measures taken by the authorities and more recently those taken on their own initiative by industrial and other concerns, all pay particular attention to the needs of the aged. Thus, the recently-made law on the running of agricultural cooperatives stipulates that no one should lose his membership of a cooperative because of illness or incapacity for work; furthermore, quite apart from the work theoretically due from them to the cooperative, the old and infirm may not be deprived of the tenure of their own domestic holdings.

Recently the Minister of Public Health passed decrees increasing the benefits in kind and the regular social assistance available to those disabled in the war. Elderly manual workers and others, including teachers, can go on working even after they have retired, either in their former place of work or in social employment centres set up by local councils. They are given easy jobs and of course they work fewer hours; they usually earn about five hundred forints a month (in some jobs up to eight hundred), which rounds out their low pensions. This year the Medicor works at Debrecen in eastern Hungary, a concern that sends highly-esteemed medical and surgical apparatus all over the world, allotted shares to its now-retired old workers. In Kocs, a village of western Hungary, the farming co-operative sends its machines to work its old members' personal holdings for nothing and it also sees to the free carriage of their crops.

The other great problem for old people is illness. Preventive medicine and the care of the sick is assured by the Hungarian Public Health organization, whose medical staff has an international scientific reputation. All Hungarians may benefit from the social security's medical service, either by right or by being a member of an insured person's family; and if they belong to neither of these categories, then in case of needy old age. These services include free medical care, hospitalization and surgical operations. The patient makes a very small contribution for medicines, bandages, medicinal waters, false teeth, invalid carriages and hearing aids. Although there are no detailed statistics to show medical expenditure by age-group, we may presume that the needs of the aged are also satisfied.

At present, or to be more exact, according to the findings at the end of the year 1969, there are 21,865 doctors in Hungary, or 21·3 for every 10,000 inhabitants; and there are 3,549 medical districts, so that every 2,895 inhabitants have a district physician who gives all but specialist care. The number of beds in hospitals, sanatoria and hydropathic establishments is 82,465, or 80·3 for every 10,000 people. For each hundred hospital beds there are nearly ten doctors, and thirty-six nurses and other auxiliaries. It should also be mentioned that since 1952, the diagnosis of cancer, particularly as regards the aged, has been organized throughout the country; and by means of a network set up in 1968, sixty cancer centres have carried out 510,000 preventive examinations. At the same time, the aged have had a considerable share in the consumption of pharmaceutical products, whose value increased to 3,488 million forints in 1968.

While we are speaking of medical care, we must also mention gerontological treatment; it would indeed be very wrong to overlook the work of those geriatricians whose researches into the state of the aged, on the particular diseases that affect them, and the best means of treating them have produced striking results in a short time. The group of young physicians who specialize in gerontology work under the general guidance of the gerontological commission of the Hungarian Academy of Science: their activities come under the heading of the 'biological basis of ageing and its social incidence' in the national plan for long-term research. A Research Institute for Gerontology has recently begun to function in Budapest. Gerovit, a medicine made in Hungary, is already highly appreciated in other countries: it stimulates the basic metabolism and accelerates the circulation of the blood, and it is rich in vitamins.

The following statistics throw some light upon the third problem – loneliness in old age. A little more than three-quarters of old people live in a family environment. 33·9 of these at home, 7·9 per cent with their spouse and child or children, 5·5 per cent with their spouse and child or children as well as grandchild or grandchildren, 7·5 per cent with only their child, 11·8 per cent with their child and his or her family, 1 per cent with a grandchild, 6 per cent with other relations and 2 per cent with friends. On the other hand one out of four people of over sixty lives alone and cannot rely upon any family help. Most of them live in this way because they never had children, and some (but they are in the minority) because of the ingratitude or selfishness of their children. Some pensioners are condemned to live by themselves because their children have emigrated. The number of old people who remain absolutely alone can therefore be reckoned at about 400,000; and the duty of doing something to help their solitude thus becomes the responsibility of society.

Society is indeed making an effort to remedy this situation. At present 242 old people's homes exist in Hungary, and these provide 25,520 beds. These homes are run by the State, local councils and the Church. The inmates contribute only a third of the real expense of lodging, food and so on; however, the authorities foresee a rise in this contribution, but only in the case of relatively well-off old people of course; for whereas in the past the usual reason for going into a home was insufficient means, now it is more the old people's loneliness and the impossibility of looking after their own household.

Most of these establishments provide housing, food and care of a quality that does them credit. As examples we may mention the Old People's Home at Szeged (a town in southern Hungary), the Home for Veterans of the Workers' Movement, and the Home for Old Actors (both in Budapest), and the centre run by the Reformed Church at Leanyfalu, a watering-place on the Danube. Each of them has a library, television, radio, a sitting-room and a games-room. But the fact remains that there is still not enough accommodation in these homes to meet all demands. Today nearly six thousand old people are waiting for vacancies.

The existence of what are called 'life-contracts' also helps to solve a few problems of loneliness and of living. They are usually entered into by old people who have plenty of living space and by young couples suffering from the housing shortage. According to the terms of these contracts, the young couple agree to look after the occupier or occupiers of the place, while in exchange they will have part of it to live in and a promise that after the death of the occupier or occupiers they will enter into full possession. To safeguard the old people's interests and to prevent abuses, the Hungarian government recently gave the local councils power to investigate the actual situation before a contract is signed, and then to see that it is scrupulously respected.

However, even in a socialist country it is not easy to solve the problem of old people's loneliness. There are some who live alone because they wish to do so, either for sentimental or material reasons. After a marriage that leaves only happy memories, many cannot bring themselves to marry again; what is more they are often attached to their home and physical comforts. Thus forty per cent of Hungarian pensioners live in the country in their own houses, and it has been observed that in 68·9 per cent of these the housing coefficients are higher than the average for the country; these advantages lead the old people to prefer a solitary life.

This being the general pattern, State and society do their best to help the aged. In many places the local centres of the Popular Patriotic Front and the National Council of Hungarian Women have organized meeting-houses and clubs where old people can spend their day; there are now two hundred and fifty in operation, and seven thousand old men and women enjoy the free advantages which they provide. And at present a network of social workers is also being formed: they regularly visit the old in their own homes and attend to their needs. Finally, let us add that the aged are given special passes for cinemas and stadiums where they can see programmes of their own choosing and that they also have special tickets for trams and buses in country towns and in Budapest.

In Rumania there was no system of social security whatsoever before the last war. The following account of the services established since then was sent to me by a Bucharest doctor, and I pass it on to my readers without guaranteeing its accuracy.

The problem has two diametrically opposed aspects:

1. That of the 'social' pensioners, or those who have no real right to a pension because they have not worked in a State concern for the necessary number of years.

2. That of the State pensioners.

a) *First category*. The material means of subsistence are reduced to a minimum. The pensioners receive a monthly 'old-age indemnity' of about 300 lei (just under £7). This is an absurd amount, of course; it would buy one pair of shoes. However, those who are physically capable of it are allowed to take certain jobs – lowly and very poorly-paid jobs, of course. As soon as they are employed they no longer receive the 'old-age indemnity'. But this work may allow them to reach the twenty-five years required before they can ask for the pension due to everybody as soon as he has worked this length of time for a State concern. But this can only apply in exceptional cases, as an old man can rarely hope to go on working another twenty-five years after he has reached the legal retirement age. If this pension is granted it is calculated upon the last pay to be received.

This category of 'social pensioner' is made up of those who cannot prove that they were employed before 23 August 1944. That is to say, shopkeepers large and small, doctors with private practices who did not work in a State hospital, small artisans who had their own work-shops, and so on. All these are considered to have been 'exploiters' and they are condemned to an extremely precarious existence, both materially and socially.

b) *Second category: Pensions in rural districts*. Three years ago the State, having realized the success of its policy of collectivization, decided to give the peasants a pension once they had become in-capable of earning their living either because of illness, incapacity for work or old age. In all these cases the peasants now receive a monthly pension of forty lei (90p); but a loaf of bread costs two or three lei according to the quality of the flour, and a litre of cooking-oil twelve lei.

These pensioners have no right to free medical care nor even to free hospitalization. (The other categories are allowed free medicines on condition that their pension does not exceed 550 lei a month.)

Since the young have priority where employment is concerned, the old are by no means sure of being able to keep the jobs they may have managed to find after reaching retiring age. The same applies to people who are employed when they reach that age. Even if their physical and mental state allows them to continue their activities, they are at once thrust aside whenever a young man is judged equally capable of carrying out the same duties. This rule applies without discrimination to manual and intellectual workers and even to scientists.

On the other hand, old people's active participation in social life is a widespread phenomenon. Members of the Party continue their activities within the Party organizations that they belong to, and may be used for certain propaganda missions as well as some supervisory posts, such as the inspection of hospitals, public food services, etc.

People who do not belong to the Party are also used in certain social activities. Some categories of the aged may be admitted into old people's homes where they are housed and fed and where their health is cared for. Conditions of admission are based upon the candidates' situation as regards their family, and upon their physical state: priority is given to the disabled. The extremely rigorous selection reflects the inadequate number of beds: and it is often of a political nature. Favouritism is very general. Then again, the old people who are admitted to the Geriatric Institute run by the very well-known Dr Aslan – a woman – also form a kind of privileged category.

The problem of the aged is even more difficult when it is considered from the ethical point of view. The lessons of the social revolution and the slogans of a society in a period of active creation ('What is old must vanish; what is new must take its place') have a serious effect upon the relationship between the generations. Because of this, the old are looked upon with suspicion and they are generally considered irremediably lost for the revolution that the country is carrying through.

State pensioners: These have worked twenty-five years in a State concern, and they are in a much better position when they retire: their pension is very nearly the same as their last wages.

However, by far the most favoured category is that of people who belonged to political bodies such as the security organization; though this also applies to soldiers and others. These reach retirement age much earlier than the rest (the set age for all categories is sixty for men and fifty-five for women). But they are also allowed to go on receiving their very good pension and to take new jobs, thus receiving the twofold income of pension and salary at the same time.

In Czechoslovakia the average age of the population has increased. Thirty years ago only 10 per cent were over sixty, whereas today the figure is 17 per cent. Yet, the working population has decreased because schooling goes on longer. Men receive a pension at sixty that they have worked for for at least twenty-five years; if they have worked longer their pension is larger. It represents 50 per cent of their earnings over the last five or ten years and 75 per cent if a man has worked thirty-five years. For women the retiring age is fifty-seven if they are childless and fifty-five if they have brought up one child; fifty-three if they have brought up two children and fifty-two if they have brought up three or more. Miners, pilots and men with dangerous callings can claim their pension at fifty-five. In all callings workers may go on as long as they are able, but in such cases they only receive half the pension (which is added to what they earn). As there are not enough specialized workers, the State encourages some of them to stay at their jobs after they reach retiring age. Many intellectual workers and executives are not fully qualified until they are fifty, as they continue their studies during their middle life; and after this age they can be of great service for a long time. These old people's good fortune lies in the fact that society needs them.

The situation of unqualified manual workers is very different: their physical powers diminish after fifty and if they retire late their basic rate of pay lessens. And as their work is tiring and not particularly interesting they long to rest. The women above all: at fifty-five they are happy to stay at home, helping their children and looking after their grandchildren. Once they are retired, many men who belonged to the liberal professions take to occupations which they enjoy and which can be really interesting. They go into the public services, putting forward plans and acting as consultants.

Pensions were increased by 8 per cent by the law of 1964; this was a modification of the 1956 law, which in its turn had modified the law of 1948. This rise is insufficient because of the increase in prices. Five years ago* there were discussions in the newspapers upon the living conditions of old people; they complained that they had no rights although they had earned them by all their years of working life. Their reactions to retirement are much the same as in France: they find inactivity hard to bear and they feel useless; they roam about the places where they used to work and they watch others working. Often, and above all if they have personal difficulties, they fall ill and die. Or they do away with themselves: the suicide rate grows with increasing age.

* Written in November 1968.

In hospitals 70 per cent of the aged inmates have no one to care for them. When they are well again nobody from their family comes to fetch them home. Although Czechoslovakia has more hospital beds than anywhere else in Europe there are still not nearly enough.

The housing shortage has an acute effect upon everybody: young couples live with their parents and sometimes with both sets of parents. It is usual for three generations to live under the same roof and the results of this are not happy.

The services dealing with nursing, health and household assistance are absurdly inadequate. When old people are sick, helpless, and neglected because their children have jobs, there is no one to take care of them.

The adults used to accept this situation and it was the young who found it scandalous. Since January 1968 and the beginning of 'the new way', they have been making protests all over the country and have awakened a great deal of interest in the aged. Local organizations which had been neglected are now being developed. More care is being taken of old people. There are now canteens where they can have their meals. Various clubs organize amusements for them. Theatres and cinemas give them seats at a reduced rate. Thanks to the agitation of the young people society has become aware of the serious nature of the problem and is trying to find a solution.

Yugoslavia's case is interesting because the country has passed from a socialist form of economy to one which, since 1960, gives an increasing importance to profit. This has its effect upon the condition of the aged.

The Yugoslavian community is keenly aware of the problems of old age. It has discussed them thoroughly and has taken protective measures. Up until 1 January 1965, in order to receive a full pension men had to be fifty-five with thirty-five years of work behind them, and a woman had to be fifty with thirty years' work to her credit. In principle the law gave them 72 per cent of their average salary (but in Slovenia they only received 62 per cent). For the partisans, time spent during the war counted double. Those who had fought as early as 1941 had the right to a pension of the same amount as their last pay. There was very little difference between pensions because the pay-differential – at least that of officially declared earnings – was so small: the highest was only $3\frac{1}{2}$ times the lowest. The State's idea was to assure a decent standard of living for the old, even though the

568

amount of money required might seem impossible to find. The burden on the State was very heavy because the health of so many men had suffered so much in the war: in Yugoslavia there were one million pensioners for four million wage-earners. Workers contributed at the same time as the State. This money was not put into special funds, but invested in factories, building projects and so on.

Ever since 1960, Yugoslavian economy, linked to world economy, has been adjusting its prices according to those of the capitalist countries; it is trying to bring its productivity up to the level of the world market. It therefore tends to reduce 'useless' costs, particularly those arising from the maintenance of non-workers. Retirement age has been increased: for men it is sixty (with forty working years) and for women fifty-five (with thirty-five working years). In theory pensions have been raised to 85 per cent of the salary. But in fact they have been reduced to 59 per cent in Slovenia.

On this point there is a struggle between the generations. The old say that they used all their strength in order to create the prosperity the country enjoys today: they demand a share in it. It is a debt that must be repaid. They think it unfair that life should have become better for everyone except them. They claim that they should be integrated politically as well as materially. They are represented in the administration that applies the laws, but they also want to be represented in the political assemblies that make the laws. They wish to belong to the local parliaments which among other things look after the local budget and social problems. They have their own organization: the Management Committee for the disabled and pensioners, which belongs to the Social Insurance Parliament. They are all collectively members of unions. Their newspapers must be counted among their means of defence: in Slovenia their monthly *Upokojence* sells 110,000 copies more than any other paper.

The old-age problem differs very much from republic to republic. In the rural republics a patriarchal civilization still exists: the men rule over the women and the old over the middle-aged. There is a positive cult of old age. The generations all live under the same roof. In Slovenia and Croatia – the parts which I have been discussing hitherto – there is a housing problem. Slovenia has forty-two old people's homes, with room for three thousand. There are also thirty-three recreation-centres. Belgrade is deplorable from this point of view. An article written on 14 April 1968 emphasizes the fact that there is room for no more than six hundred in the old people's homes.

'It is hard, being old in Belgrade. Many one- and two-roomed flats are being built, but it is not easy for the old to get them. As a general rule there is no room for them . . . '

By and large, however, the state of the aged is thought to be satisfactory materially, but not psychologically or spiritually. Many suffer from ill-health because of what they went through during the war, in prison or in concentration-camps. Few of them are an integral part of the community: it rejects them. The most imperfectly solved problem is that of the old partisans.

Among them there are fifty thousand former officers. Eighty per cent of them were villagers and their joining the resistance prevented them from being educated or serving an apprenticeship: they came out with no qualifications whatever. They were employed in the civil service, but now a very much better qualified generation has grown up and they are no longer needed. They are embittered and unsatisfied. I was told of a former officer who was pensioned off at forty-two: his wife works in a book-shop and he looks after the house. And of a forty-eight-year-old colonel who became a partisan in 1941 (nine out of ten partisans of that date were killed); he has four children, and he is now the gate-keeper in a factory where the head man is a former royalist – the colonel is obliged to salute him humbly. People of this kind become the enemies of socialism. Even in less extreme cases there is a strong feeling of frustration: the Party is everything and the individual nothing. Many have refused to bow to Party discipline; they no longer amount to anything at all. They have lost all reason for living.

APPENDIX IV

Some statistical data upon sexuality of old people

According to the Kinsey report male sexual power is greatest at about the age of sixteen. In youth, the average weekly number of copulations for unmarried men appears to be two or three and for married men between four and eight. The average is said to go down to 1·8 at fifty for both groups, to 1·3 at sixty and 0·9 at seventy. Kinsey studied the cases of eighty-seven white and thirty-nine black males over sixty. The average number of ejaculations went from once a week at sixty-five, 0·3 at seventy-five and less than 0·1 at eighty. At sixty, 6 per cent were totally inactive; at seventy, 30 per cent, and the curve went on falling. But there are exceptions. One white subject of seventy had on the average seven ejaculations a week. One black of eighty-eight had intercourse with his ninety-year-old wife from one to four times a week. A quarter of the white men were impotent at seventy and more than half at seventy-five. A certain number of subjects between seventy-one and eighty-six masturbated, and between the ages of seventy-six and eighty nocturnal pollutions were observed.

Other inquiries, more modest in scope, followed Kinsey's. In 1959 the magazine *Sexology* questioned six thousand people listed in *Who's Who*. Eight hundred men replied; they were all over sixty-five. Seventy per cent of the married men had a regular sexual life and averaged four coitions a month. Even in the group of one hundred and four subjects aged between seventy-five and ninety-two half said they had normal ejaculations and six of them said they had sexual relations more than eight times a month. A quarter masturbated: they had either done so all along or they had started after the age of sixty. A great many had morning erections even after they had reached seventy-five.

571

In North Carolina in 1960 two doctors, G. Newman and C. E. Nichols, questioned 250 white and black people of both sexes aged between sixty and ninety-three. Their survey lasted for seven years. One hundred and forty-nine subjects were married and lived with their spouse. The number of sexual relations varied between once every two months and three times a week. The figures sharply fell after the age of seventy-five. The blacks were more active sexually than the whites, the men more than the women, and people of a moderate or inferior standard of living more than the well-to-do. (This perhaps explains the difference in behaviour between the whites and the blacks: the blacks belonged to the poorest class.) Those who had had a very full sexual life continued to be active: the others did not. As to the hundred and one unmarried or widowed subjects, only seven of them were sexually active. The comparative lack of activity in the women was presumably explained by the fact that their husbands were older than they.

In Philadelphia in 1961 Dr Freeman examined seventy-four men whose average age was seventy-one. Seventy-five per cent still had erotic desires but only fifty-five per cent satisfied them. The number of their ejaculations varied from three times a week to once every two months; at least forty-two per cent of them said their desires had diminished since they were sixty, and twenty-five per cent had become impotent at that age. At eighty, twenty-two per cent admitted that they still felt sexual desires but only seventeen per cent had sexual relations. Thirty-six per cent had erotic dreams and twenty-five per cent reacted to visual stimuli.

Dr Destrem, writing in France in 1963, produced some complementary observations. According to him, between sixty and seventy an old man's behaviour resembles that of a middle-aged person. It depends very much on his former capacities. The married worker remains more sexually active than the intellectual. The unmarried man and the man who has long been a widower do not behave in the same way as an old married man for whom habit and the existence of erotic stimuli maintain his sexual life. Again, the recent death of a partner often leads to impotence. Coition takes place about once a week at sixty, and at seventy once a fortnight. Masturbation is quite frequent and it follows the same rhythm as normal coition. Between seventy and eighty married men retain an active but reduced sexual life. Widowers suffer from unsatisfied desires and some of them take to masturbation.

Index

friends; ageing of, 288–90; death of, 366–7
friendship, 366; of old people, 472
Fukasawa, *Narayama*, 54–5
future, the; change in evaluation of, 368–9, 377–8; prospect of ageing, 4–5; attempts to survive into, 379–80, 410–11

Galen, Claudius, 18, 20, 285
Gandhi, Mahatma, 7, 419, 432–4
Gautier, Judith, 333, 334
generations: succession of, 435–6; conflict between the, 89, 123; in mythology, 95–7; resolved, in *19C.*, 199
geriatrics, origins of, 21, 22–3
Germany, introduction of social insurance in, 223–4
gerontocracy; primitive, 61–4; in *19C.* France, 198–9
gerontology, development of, 23–4; in Hungary, 562; psychological, 32–4
gerontophilia, 220, 347
ghosts, 82; *see also* spirits of the dead
Gide, André, 486, 489; writings on own old age, 294, 295–6, 299, 316–17, 401, 453, 472; anorexia, 460–1; depression, 463–4; prospect of death, 444; sexuality in age, 345, 351; *Les Faux-monnayeurs,* 210
God: Christian, paintings of, 134 and *; heathen, incarnate in chiefs, 40–1; *see also* religion
Goethe, Johaan Wolfgang von, 283, 310–11, 398, 468, 471, 472, 478; sexual life in old age, 329–30; *Faust,* 191
Goldoni, Carlo, 187–8
Goncourt, Edmond de, 302, 411, 440–1, 443, 463, 479; sexuality of, 335
Gorz, *Le Vieillissement,* 373
Goya, 407–9; self-portrait by, 301

Graffigny, Mme. de, *Cénie,* 185
grandparents, 474–5; in primitive societies, 53, 65, 70, 72, 84–5; in France, 196, 197; *19C.,* 200; in literature, 206–7; *20C.,* 220; grandmothers, 556
Greek: early civilization, 98–9; 7C., 99–103; *1–5C. AD,* 112; drama, 103–7; mythcine, 17; mythology, 96–8, 138; philosophy, 108–12; pictures and sculpture, 112–13; views on time, 138
Grenoble, clubs of, 272
gribouillisme, 303–4
Grimm, Jacob; lecture on old age, 204; tales collected by, 5–6, 131, 135–6
guardians, of community experience, 41, 43
guilt: in melancholia, 496; release from, 461–2

habits, 466–9, 497
Hals, Frans, 162
Harrington, M., *The Other America,* 245, 246
health: of workers, 273–4; of old people, 28–30, 285–6; their attitude towards, 288, 301–5, 445; mental, 35, 493–504; effect of retirement on, 268–9; and age of retirement, 263
Hegel, 396; philosophy of, 380, 418
Hemingway, Ernest, 262; *The Old Man & The Sea,* 314
Hesiod, 96
Hippocrates, 13*, 17
hobbies, 270
Holmes, Oliver Wendell, 288, 466
Homer, 97, 98–9
homosexuality, 345–6
Hopi, the, 45
Horace, 121, 122
hospitals, 25–54